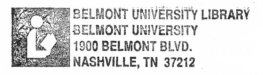

The History of the Book
A Series Edited by Bill Katz

1. *A History of Book Illustrations: 29 Points of View,* edited by Bill Katz. 1994
2. *Dahl's History of the Book, Third English Edition,* by Bill Katz. 1995
3. *A Bibliographic History of the Book: An Annotated Guide to the Literature,* by Joseph Rosenblum. (Magill Bibliographies.) 1995
4. *Cuneiform to Computer: A History of Reference Sources,* by Bill Katz. 1998

Cuneiform to Computer

A History of Reference Sources

Bill Katz

History of the Book Series, No. 4

The Scarecrow Press, Inc.
Lanham, Md., & London
1998

SCARECROW PRESS, INC.

Published in the United States of America
by Scarecrow Press, Inc.
4720 Boston Way
Lanham, Maryland 20706

4 Pleydell Gardens, Folkestone
Kent CT20 2DN, England

British Library Cataloguing-in-Publication Information Available

Library of Congress Cataloging-in-Publication Data

Katz, Bill, 1930–
    Cuneiform to computer : a history of reference sources / Bill Katz.
        p.   cm. — (History of the book : no. 4)
    Includes index.
    ISBN 0–8108–3290–9
    1. Reference books—History.   I. Title.   II. Series.
    Z1035.1.K35   1998   97-7094
    028.7′09—dc21   CIP

ISBN 0–8108–3290–9 (cloth : alk. paper)

♾ ™ The paper used in this publication meets the minimum requirements of
American National Standard for Information Sciences—Permanence of
Paper for Printed Library Materials, ANSI Z39.48–1984.
Manufactured in the United States of America.

For Sam Rothstein whose scholarship and imagination inspired this history

Contents

Preface

There is a lovely moment in Muriel Spark's 1962 play *Doctors of Philosophy* in which a lorry driver who has given the professor's postgraduate daughter a ride home gapes at the books in the house and asks the housekeeper for the family whether they have actually read them all. She replies: "They don't use them for reading, they are educated people, they refer to them."[1]

The humble reference book, often quickly dated and discarded, is familiar to almost everyone. It may be a telephone directory or a definitive guide to the secrets of a full, lively life. Reference sources have existed since the first people left informational marks on a dark cave wall, and probably will remain after the last individual has signed off the World Wide Web.

The reference book is a universal sign of civilization, of culture, of collective curiosity. Defined in numerous ways, generally a reference work is one filled with specific facts and is not normally read cover to cover. There have been reference sources since the beginning of history, or more properly since the earliest Egyptian or Mesopotamian. Some five thousand years ago someone inscribed data on clay tablets or papyrus. The first formal reference work was born.

The history of reference books parallels both intellectual and technological developments from those first cuneiform tablets and papyrus rolls to the present-day digital database.[2] It is a complex, fascinating story that is arranged here by type (i.e., encyclopedia, dictionary, almanac, and the like) and chronologically within each of the divisions. Various bridges are constructed between sections and chapters to attempt to show the reference work as a major tool or, at best, a reflection of social developments in general and publishing growth in particular. The net is cast wide rather than in narrow, although important, circles of bibliographical interest.

Granted electronic delivery of data has shattered, and may soon completely ruin the centuries-old concepts of reference book form and order, but this does not deny the place of reference titles in the development and recording of history. Technical changes of format are not likely to change the broad pattern of use.

Today reference books are found everywhere: fifteen thousand or more in a library and one or two in a home and among the latest best-sellers in the bookstore. Paper and print remains the usual format, but these days the reference material may be reduced to a database on a CD-ROM, online, or on the ubiquitous World Wide Web. No matter what their appearance, reference books are as basic as any information source. What has changed, and drastically, is the type and size of the audience for the typical reference compilation.

For the sake of time, it is satisfactory to accept the historical landmarks of Robert Heilbronner,[3] the economic historian who labels events from the foundation of civilization in the Middle East to the middle of the eighteenth century as belonging to the first large division, or the "distant past."

Reference books developed simultaneously with writing and the keeping of records. The Egyptian or Mesopotamian scribe of five thousand years ago conscientiously employed indexes to find material inscribed on clay or papyrus. Also in the early libraries one found basic reference titles from government publications to annuals. Before the miraculous rise of Greece, reference titles, such as they were, rarely left the official library or archive. Certainly they were not used by more than a few privileged scribes, priests, or bureaucrats.

Around 500 B.C. the Greeks not only changed the way people were governed and their notions of state and self, but also instigated the notion of education for free men. (Women and slaves, generally, were excluded.) The educational program varied, of course, from city to city, century to century, but in the broadest terms followed what we now consider the liberal arts. Modified, the liberal arts dominated education until well into the nineteenth century and produced reference works to be used both in education and by well-educated individuals in need of information. The pattern is familiar to this day. The primary difference is in the audience. The Greeks widened the educated reading public but generally, only scholars and bureaucrats relied on reference books. Until the Industrial Revolution, the vast number of reference titles were for a limited public with a better-than-average education.

After the Egyptians, Greeks, and Romans, religion dominated learning until the Renaissance. It is no surprise that the majority of manuscripts produced during the Middle Ages were religious—from Bibles to commentaries. Broadly speaking, the scriptoriums of the monastic communities concentrated on copying Bibles, commentaries, and related work. Later, lay copying and lay publishers grew up around the European universities and, while they turned to other works, often reference in nature, they too tended to concentrate on theological titles. Gradually the secular, commercial publishing venture issued books in the vernacular, and particularly romances and chronicles for the better-educated laypersons. Production of books changed dramatically with the advent of printing in the mid-fifteenth century, and with it came a new focus on nontheological material in basic reference forms as well.

While today the best known book of the Middle Ages is the illuminated manuscript, there were thousands of other less rich works, less pretentious publications of the basic religious forms. These forms included first and foremost the Bible and then the Gospels, usually the latter as a separate title. Then followed the basic titles for any monastic community: liturgical books and the works of the church fathers. Most were copied from exemplars that were carried from religious community to religious community. The amount of manuscript production is hard to determine as only eighteen hundred manuscripts (and many only fragments) survive prior to A.D. 800. By the ninth century A.D. both the production and the distribution of manuscripts improved and for that century alone there are fifty-seven hundred surviving manuscripts. The number of extant works doubles with almost every century up to the time of printing. By the thirteenth century the religious titles had expanded in number and type. Textbooks for university use as well as handbooks of sermons dominated much of publishing.

With the Renaissance the average individual began to take an interest in reference works. This was the natural consequence of a developing middle class, of the vast production of the printing press, and of the public moving to the threshold of the Industrial Revolution.

The real change came in the period Heilbronner terms "yesterday" (i.e., from about 1750 to 1850) when education, literacy, and the urbanization of the population drastically broadened the audience for books in general, and for reference works in particular. In the nineteenth century, the mass magazine and newspaper, the truly public library, the increase in expendable income and much more brought reference works into the average home for the first time. With the close of the nineteenth century these important social changes moved reference books from the province of the scholarly few to laypersons' living rooms, coffee tables, and fireside bookshelves. The history of the reference work employed by scholars, well-educated bureaucrats, and theologists is as old as recorded history itself, but the real impetus, for the widespread development of reference books begins with the founding of the democratic educational system that the employed the liberal arts in schools.

Publishers were not far behind these developments. By the end of the First World War, encyclopedias, almanacs, atlases, and dictionaries became part of the output of most publishers. Some specialized in reference titles (particularly more esoteric indexes), but almost all publishers produced one or more types of reference books.

Heilbronner's "today," which is little more than yesterday and tomorrow in the history of things, has seen vast technological changes as dramatic as the social and economic developments of the eighteenth and nineteenth centuries. Reference books are now on a chip, and the computer promises to change not only the traditional format of reference sources, but also how and by whom they are used. This book is concerned primarily with the period before today—an overview of the "distant past" and the "yesterday" of reference works. Most of the focus is on the period before the Second World War. The future can be left to others.

The purpose is to give the lay reader and librarians a brief history of how reference works developed and how they reflect attitudes of their particular period of publication. In each chapter a basic reference form is discussed. Most forms are familiar in libraries today, although several, such as commonplace books, are no longer particularly well know. Major titles in the evolution of the reference work are highlighted and the primary signposts along the historical road are indicated, but, unlike in specialized histories and bibliographies, no effort has been made to be inclusive. The stress is on the interrelationship of reference sources and social change and development.

Notes

1. Andrew Field, "A Footnote about Footnotes in Biography" in *Reading Life Histories,* ed. James Walter (Canberra: Australian National University Press, 1981), 20.

2. There are numerous histories of particular forms of reference works, such as encyclopedias and dictionaries, and these are referred to throughout this exploration. Here, however, the effort is to look at the development of not one, but all major forms of reference works.

3. Robert Heilbronner, *Visions of the Future* (New York: Oxford University Press, 1995).

1

Reference Books from Cuneiform
to Computer

Patrick and his men were seen . . . "with written tablets in their hands"; the
people mistook the wooden tablets for some kind of sinister weapon, and the
Christian party was nearly lynched.[1]

The much-quoted anecdote about St. Patrick's early adventures in Ireland (c. A.D. 600) is indicative of the potential threat of reference works.
They can be sinister weapons, if not against the person, at least against ignorance. Beyond St. Patrick there is no record of a reference compiler being nearly lynched, [the ultimate book review] but many did meet peculiar
fates. Pliny, for example, gained fame as much from his encyclopedia as insisting he be taken to Pompeii hours before it (and Pliny) was destroyed.
The history of reference sources is more than the laborious compilation, organization, and publication of data. Reference books reflect the will of the
compiler who, in turn, mirrored the place and period in which he lived.

In the beginning reference books had little impact on the mass of people.
Most individuals, lost in the dust of history, gained information in a fashion
still favored by the majority—word of mouth. Before the height of the Middle Ages (c. A.D. 1000–1200), there existed distinct written and an oral cultures. Most of the emphasis was on the latter, primarily because there was
both a lack of mass literacy and written materials. By about 1000 A.D., "a
new type of interdependence . . . arose between [oral and written traditions]
. . . . Oral discourse effectively began to function within a universe of communications governed by texts."[2] This development was only noticeable
among the educated, it had a filter-down effect for all people. Assumptions
about life, politics, and almost anything governing a person's life were now
based upon texts and ephemeral written publications, usually of a governmental nature. "Texts thereby emerged as a reference system both for every-
day activities and for giving shape to many larger vehicles of explanation."[3]

Again, though, this situation was applicable only for the educated. It
would remain so until well into the nineteenth century. Meanwhile, at least
a minority recognized the importance of supporting oral communication in
reference works that would bridge not only their present experience, but the
experience of generations before and possibly after.

In today's age, when one may trace 25 to 50 million books at a computer terminal, when most are available in the immediate library or on interlibrary loan, it is sometimes difficult to imagine a medieval library where the average number of titles hardly numbered more than fifty to one hundred. And, of course, that twelfth century library had no periodicals, reports, research studies, or other familiar reference forms. In times past, the problem for the general reader or the highly specialized scholar was to find the handful of books useful for particular interests. Inevitably the reference book—usually an encyclopedia, dictionary, or almanac—would be only one or two of the dozen or more books available to consult.[4] The lack of material had numerous consequences, the more comforting being that, when one had explored the titles in a given subject area, one was relatively certain to have read everything available and to know everything there was to know about X or Y.

The Age of Difference

The current sharp separation between specialized reference works can be misleading when one considers their history. Prior to the nineteenth century, all types of compendia—from dictionaries and manuals to encyclopedias and almanacs—were available. Distinctions between forms were not clear. For example, a dictionary might be in part an encyclopedia and vice versa. McArthur makes a point concerning the "text book" and the "reference book" in Medieval universities and culture. Teachers and students may use reference books, but unlike textbooks, reference books "are seldom mediated by teachers and hardly ever seen as needing mediation by teachers . . . the reference books is half outside the educational systems we use. Schools and colleges do not normally give their students courses in how to use dictionaries, encyclopedias, gazetteers, directories, etc. Even the use of language is different for them: you 'read' or study a textbook, but you 'consult,' look things up . . . in a work of reference."[5]

During the Medieval period, commentaries were written into almost every book. The assiduous interlinear explanations, the glosses (i.e., for unusual or foreign words needing an explanation or definition), and interpretations were common and created a new type of reference work, known generally as a postil (*postila verba,* after those words). What began generally as notes in the Gospels spread to other books; the marginal note or comment (i.e., postil or gloss) became a common feature of all titles employed by scholars. The majority of titles in an average thirteenth century library, therefore might be called reference works.

The gloss explains why separate reference titles were not needed. Why consult a tertiary source when an original work was at hand, and probably the one from which the encyclopedia compiler, for example, garnered most of his data. Reference books in any great number developed only after the press of original material was such that summaries and explanations were needed as things apart.

Order, Order

Little wonder a literate individual might pick up one or two books and consider he had all of the world's knowledge in his hand. There were not enough books or reference works in existence to challenge his assumption, which also explains why so many early reference sources seem to lack order.

Taxonomy, or the law of classification, is an essential part of today's reference work. The concept comes from the ancient Greeks who, from the first philosopher, were vastly interested in the way things were systematically categorized and named. (Today the term is associated with particularly the classification of plants and animals, but it had a much broader base in earlier centuries.) Philosophically it seemed interesting enough and was applied in the ordering of the Alexandria Library, for one, but little attention was given such matters when it came to assembling a reference book. Alphabetization, for example, is a relatively new notion.

Alphabetization, so necessary for printed reference works, but no longer for electronic databases, was a latecomer. Some three to four hundred years passed from the time alphabetization was considered in the Middle Ages to the first alphabetically arranged printed book. "Even so . . . it took more than 100 years after the advent of printing [1455] for alphabetization to establish itself as a series and regular took in the world of reference . . . [Prior to 1600] you went for a set of themes as Pliny . . . or you contemplated the newly interesting possibility of ABC order."[6]

Alphabetical arrangement originated with the Greeks. In the margins of their papyrus rolls they used the aforementioned "glossa" to describe and define difficult words. Over time the glossa became a glossary or word list and, more generally, a dictionary. Alphabetization, though, was haphazard and slow, used for a group of words, but not for others, used by one compiler, but not by another. The primary reason alphabetical order was so slow in developing is that scholars looked to thematic order as the traditional way of doing things, and particularly in reference works where sections might be committed to memory.

With printing, with the relative mass production of books, it became necessary to superimpose some order, i.e. alphabetization. Still, even this took time and it was not until the seventeenth century that alphabetical order became common (rather than by subject or by the mood of compiler).

Trivium/Quadrivium

If alphabetization seemed less than necessary because of the limited number of sources and how they were read, another factor was the educational method employed from the time of the Greeks. As education was limited to the few, so were the various divisions, the various parts of knowledge to be studied.

Over the ages, reference history runs parallel with at least the various divisions and subdivisions of education. Conveniently, by the Middle Ages, knowledge (and educational practices) was neatly divided into the seven liberal arts,[7] which, in turn, were subdivided between the humanities and the sciences. The trivium, or three lower division arts, were grammar, rhetoric, and the dialectic. Sciences were placed under the quadrivium and included mathematics, geometry, astronomy, and, because it was considered more of a craft than an art, music.

The Greeks, although they had different titles for the divisions, stressed the trivium with the quadrivium coming up as a poor second. The latter was considered the material of tradespeople, and while of interest, such subjects were of little real concern to would-be scholars or well-educated men. This point of view held through the Roman Empire and most of the Middle Ages with the quadrivium coming into its own only with the Renaissance.

The quadrivium, translated roughly as the discipline of science, had its beginnings around 2500 B.C. In Egypt and Mesopotamia a combination of religion, astronomy, and mathematics developed to assist in planning public works and irrigation systems. Practical arithmetic, with degrees, minutes, and seconds evolved out of these same needs. Gradually the mathematics went far beyond daily business activities and was turned to an understanding of the heavens and chronologies. Sophisticated mathematical relationships and theorems were understood by Babylonian and Egyptian scientists who had one major flaw—they saw themselves as describing the laws of the Gods, not explaining them, as did the Greeks. Unlike the Middle East, where theologies flourished, Greece lacked an overall theology. By the sixth century B.C., the Greeks struck out for more intellectual explanations of nature. Thales of Mletus, who achieved success about this time, was the first Greek philosopher who relied on astronomy and mathematics to explain, for example, a solar eclipses. Nothing of his work is extant, although his work influenced later scholars and is quoted in part by them in their writings. The second major figure was Pythagoras (580–500 B.C.) who about the same time established basic geometric theorems including the basic one named after him.

Greek science reached its zenith with Aristotle in the third century B.C., Archimedes in the second century B.C., and Ptolemy in second century

A.D. with his *Mathematike syntaxis* (*Mathematical Collection*). Unfortunately the more pragmatic Romans found scientific investigations foreign to their nature and except for what was borrowed from the Greeks, science ground to a halt. It might be argued that Pliny's first century A.D. *Natural History* was a scientific work, but by today's standards it is more a general reference encyclopedia with a nod to science and several nods to myth, history, and conjecture.

By the seventh century A.D. the Arabs, to whom science and knowledge was sacred, had translated much of the Hellentic scientific work, including the philosophers. They did not just assimilate the Greek findings, but were highly innovative: they saved Greek science for rediscovery in the European Renaissance, added much mathematical knowledge, and practically founded the theory of algebra. The Christians conquered much of Spain in the eleventh century, and, by 1085, the vast Islamic library at Toledo fell into the hands of intellectual monks who began translating the Greek and Arabic works into Latin. By the thirteenth century the way was cleared for the findings of the Renaissance. During the two-hundred-or-more year search for antiquity, the integration of science, philosophy, and religion first worked in the service of science, but later against it, as witness Nicolaus Copernicus whose *Revolution of the Celestial Spheres* (1543) was the beginning of the real scientific revolution in the West. Once it was understood that the Sun, not the Earth, was the center of the cosmos, the complex relationship of religions and science was shattered. Without religion the scientists were free of often irrational shackles, which in turn opened the way for publication of scientific reference works, as well as those in the more nebulous social sciences.

The Social Sciences

Human behavior in the context of society and a particular culture always interested philosophers, but not until St. Thomas Aquinas's *Summa theologiae* (1266–1273) was particular attention given to what became known as the social sciences. Outside of both the quadrivium and the trivium, the universities took up the subject. Dealing as they do with basic aspects of human behavior, from the political and the historical to the social and the economic, the social sciences, technically speaking, did not come under close observation until the nineteenth century. Still, Aquinas and others, such as Roger Bacon (1214–1292) in the same century, were interested in the broader aspects of today's disciplines.

The eighteenth century enlightenment, coupled with a fervid interest in the deductive process advocated by René Descartes (1596–1650) and a renewed interest in the classics, contributed significantly to the social sciences, or at least part of the group. The nineteenth century industrial revolution and the changes in government throughout Europe transformed thought and set the stage for the study of social geography and social statistics, which were employed by most of the disciplines within the social sciences. By the end of the nineteenth century, the social sciences had become a separate study as differentiated from philosophy. Among the disciplines formed and put under the social sciences umbrella were economics, sociology, cultural anthropology, and political science.

The Renaissance

Hailing as it did the advance in the understanding and appreciation of the individual, the Renaissance saw a rapid pace of change in attitudes toward knowledge. Fifteenth century chronicles, for example, stressed the notion that Europe had been in almost steady decline between the collapse of Rome and the end of the fourteenth century. Leonardo Bruni (1370–1444), a leading Italian humanist established the millennium break and the notion of the Middle Ages. Others followed his lead and the sense of evolution in knowledge took hold. This became a central feature of the new Humanism along with, paradoxically, the recovery and correction of hitherto forgotten Greek and Latin texts. The aim to recover original texts was accompanied by translations into the vernacular as well as extensive emendation. Erasmus (1466–1536), working as an editor for Aldus Manutius (1449–1515), proved a leader in the move to bring the classics back to mainstream education.

Careful textual criticism of Greek and Latin authors, such as demonstrated by Erasmus and his "Annotations" of the *New Testament* (1505) was typical. Unfortunately, too many humanistic scholars between about 1400 and 1550 were more anxious to publish a Greek classic than, as Erasmus, to correct and check its contents. The result was chaos, and many of the early works simply disappeared through careless handling. By the seventeenth century more attention was given to reconstructing ancient texts. Wherever possible editors considered the original works rather than the inaccurate translations of the fifteenth and sixteenth centuries.

Another major outcome of the Renaissance, which gained momentum through the fifteenth to eighteenth centuries, was the secularization of knowledge. What had been almost the sole concern of the clergy was now shifted to laypeople. The result was new ideas and a permanent escape from the chains of theological dogma and thinking that had controlled the flow of information for more than twelve hundred years.

With the exception of theology, the most popular nonfiction works of the Renaissance can be described as types of reference books: how-to approaches to trades and professions. Practical mathematics could be found in Richard Grafton's *Little Treatise, Containing Many Tables and Rules.* Those seeking to improve their conversation might turn to Nicholas Ling's *Politeuphia,* filled with appropriate aphorisms. Most were addressed to "the better understanding of the unlearned" and offered health and medical advice as well. The anonymous *Rich Storehouse or Treasury for the Diseased* (1596) "advertised that it was written for the great benefit and comfort of the poorest sort of people that are not of ability to go to the Physician." Most of these and scores of other similar titles were reprinted ten to twenty times in the sixteenth and seventeenth centuries.[9]

Along with an emphasis on the practical reference book came a sense of national identity. From Spain and Germany to England, nationalism played havoc with facts. Scholars deliberately hunted for manuscripts of the Middle Ages that would celebrate a given people and their borders. *The Germania* of Tacitus (55–120), printed in Germany in 1473, not only gave the territory its name but was used as proof that Germany was an old nation and should be freed of all outside influence. Sebastian Munster in *Cosmographia* (1544) described the whole of the known world, but more than half of the 800+ pages was devoted to Germany. Patriotic preoccupation's shaded almost all reference titles during the sixteenth to twentieth century, and some would say well toward the twenty-first century. Patriotic reference books that play ping pong with facts became more subtle with the passing of time, but the basic fibs remained.[10]

From the Renaissance to the Twentieth Century

The masses did not consider reference works or any other type of books, as they were illiterate. Also, few could afford most reading, even cheap broadsides. The emergence of printing in the mid-fifteenth century radically speeded the wide distribution of reading materials. Yet, even if books were a thousand times more plentiful and much less expensive than handwritten manuscripts, they were still relatively costly and well beyond the average individual. It would take nineteenth-century mass production, among other things, to bring books within the reach of all would-be purchasers.[11]

The eighteenth century Age of Enlightenment belief that continuous progress was not only possible but highly probable was an optimistic idea whose beginnings went back to the work of Francis Bacon (1561–1626) and René Descartes. A byproduct of the belief in progress was the notion that the past could be forgotten and jettisoned. Many who were involved with eighteenth century encyclopedias, particularly the French *Encyclopedie,* were encouraged to ignore history. Much of the development in eighteenth century historiography, while bound to chronological facts, did formulate general rules to explain human progress. The supreme example of this rational approach is Edward Gibbon's *History of the Decline and Fall of the Roman Empire* (1776–1788). He attempted to prove that, no matter what the setbacks, continuous progress was possible for mankind. Furthermore, Gibbon was determined to show that England was not in decline, but rather had attained a superior stage of development that made it immune to the follies and destructive forces that destroyed Rome.

Valid or not, the major philosophical ideas of the Enlightenment fired the rise of democratic societies and an ongoing interest in mass education that radically changed the course of reference books. From the mid-1750s, there was a dynamic sense of new hope and optimism. Material progress, as well as intellectual gains, were possible through the application of reason and the Industrial Revolution. The rise of capitalism, the increase in wealth for the developing middle classes, the extension of suffrage, and a score of other progressive elements in society heightened interest in reference works as well as all reading matter, which contributed to what many believed would be human perfectibility.

From the late eighteenth and through most of the nineteenth century, reference publishing began to develop differently than in previous centuries. As universal education spread throughout Europe, so did bookstores, libraries, and newspapers.

Another major change was the growth of intellectual freedom. If free expression was not possible everywhere, it at least was an accepted aspect of reference publishing in English-speaking countries. Not all information has been universally available. Every company, government, and individual had and has secrets. Experts and professionals guard their skills, whether they are surgeons or nightclub entertainers. Until the advent of printing and for several centuries later, most knowledge was treated as sacred and the special province of scribes, priests, and rulers. With the growth of nationalism the keepers of secrets moved into the political arena and the battleground. If no longer sacred, much knowledge became carefully guarded by the state.[12]

Mystery religions with guarded scientific discoveries, remain to this day. All societies condemn certain forms of knowledge as perversions or a danger to whatever the state sees as a potential threat. Even the most open society keeps the secret of the bans on knowledge a secret. Most twentieth-century Westerners, for example, believe all information is available to them in an encyclopedia, index, or any other type of reference work, whether in print or online. Actually, such mundane items as the words to a popular song or a lengthy quotation from a treatise on earth worms may be generally unavailable because of copyright. And if someone who has discovered a new mouse trap patents the idea, it is not available until such time as the inventor releases it to the public. At a more controversial level, while the French pill for birth control could be purchased in most of Europe, in the mid-1990s it was not available in the United States although the formula is well enough known. The paradox of free flow of information is that it flows freely only when those who control the feeding streams and rivers wish it to flow.

One of the fascinations of the Internet/World Wide Web is that in their anarchy of information they offer a free flow, generally unchecked by traditional market or state forces. The problem is that in the great mass of data it is sometimes impossible to find the necessary fact, particularly for reference purposes. And when the "fact" is found there is the question of authority. Is the person or persons who put the fact online qualified? Is this a fact, or propaganda—a question which often cannot be answered as there is no authority given.

More Reference Books

Publishers are quick to meet the demand of laypersons and librarians. This is evident in a rough count of reference titles available from the period after printing to this day. A cursory check of the number of books published between 1400 and 1700 (and recorded in the Online Computer Library Center (OCLC) files) with "reference" in the title shows about 230 separate works. The number increases slightly in the next centuries: 1700–1800, 330 titles; 1800–1900, 13,402 titles; and from 1900 to 1996, 100,974 titles. Even with countless variables (from total number of titles published in a century and the percentage of reference titles; to the growth of libraries and number of readers) reference works have increased in number . . . and probable importance.[13]

After the first World War, specialization took hold in Western countries—a grip that it never relinquished. At the end of the 1940s, there were more and more distinct subject fields as well as countless splits and divisions of standard areas of knowledge. Add to this, the astonishing number of Americans graduating from college and universities (about 25 percent of all high school graduates) and the consequent rise in the size and use of academic libraries is understandable. The college and university reference section became more popular and even more necessary as the curriculum divided and subdivided. Reference served both as a synthesis of knowledge as well as a magnet that could pick the particular fact from masses to specialized materials.

Today new technologies, as represented by the computer, have revolutionized the collection, storage, and retrieval of reference data. Although one once turned to a book, today it is more efficient, at least for current material, to turn to a computer terminal. Useful as computer developments may be for reference publishers and readers, they poses numerous problems that, again, parallel the cultural, economic and social developments of society as a whole. For example, increasing levels of unemployment and lower wages continue to widen the gap between the rich, the middle classes, and the poor (a phenomenon not seen since the eighteenth century). This, in turn, has meant narrowing, rather than widening the audience for reference works, no matter what their format. For every library with a sophisticated staff and technologies, there are hundreds of libraries with insufficient funding for even daily activities.

Most people touchingly believe all data may be located in a reference work, but these same optimists may be more pessimistic about the data's reliability. The doubt is an interesting outcome of educational, social, and economic divisions. The growing skepticism about the authority of reference works particularly is evident among the better educated. The belief in the ubiquitous authoritative reference source is hard dying. The concept of certainty about facts, and the proper attitude toward culture, was reflected in reference books from the mid-seventeenth century until almost the middle of the twentieth century. The published Merriam Webster dictionary torpedoed the concept of reference equaling correct judgment when the descriptive, rather than prescriptive, unabridged dictionary was issued in 1961, symbolizing a turn in reference works which, again, reflected the age. As author Julian Barnes puts it, thus began "the age of uncertainty."

The question about the authority of reference books has many facets. Even a cursory observer realizes that the editing of reference books is now a careless affair and what once might be considered a fact, may now be a proofreader's oversight. No longer is a reference work entirely unimpeachable. Sought-after facts may or may not be accurate. More often the entry is not expansive enough to offer a full response to a query. One may argue, and with some justification, that this situation is pretty much as it always has been, although in the past the "bad" facts or interpretation were more likely to be deliberate on part of the compiler, rather than a comma overlooked by a proofreader.

The sometimes sloppy regard for accurate data seems to support a late 1960s prognostication by an American scholar who made the point that today's rush down the information highway has neither encouraged accurate reference works nor increased real knowledge. Bad editing, for example, "gives us a foretaste of the scholarship of the future, when ingenious but ignorant computer programmers will cast their secondhand data in a metalanguage designed to yield new knowledge without leg- or brain-work. . . . Fortunately, for the comfort of those future scholars and their readers, everybody by then will be as happy as if the results squared with direct experience. For that experience will be deemed primitive, superseded, irrelevant, the consumers of books having long since forgotten that knowledge grows only out of knowledge and not out of information."[14] Unfortunately, new technologies from the World Wide Web to the CD-ROM have done little to change the grim situation. In fact, many would claim they have made it much worse.

Libraries

A brief overview of the development of libraries[15] in general and reference services in particular is advisable for anyone who would understand the development of reference sources. The library, from the first collection of cuneiform tablets in Mesopotamia to today's computer databases, has been a potential source to answer reference queries. The library hardly exists by itself, and has been from the first a byproduct of civilization. Three elements worked against general reference services until well into the nineteenth century. The Egyptians, Greeks, monastic communities, and Renaissance centers of learning—all—had a limited number of books. Finding a particular subject among several thousand, or more likely under a hundred, titles was relatively easy. And in that sense, the whole library truly was a reference section. Second, only specialized groups of people employed the library and these tended to be scholars, bureaucrats, and theologians who by training and inclination had little or no reason to ask others for assistance in finding material. Third, for the most part libraries were seen as storehouses of information, not as sources that might spark research or inquiry. It is no accident that well into the Renaissance, libraries—no matter their size or purpose—were places to preserve material, whether papyrus rolls of laws or tax records and textbooks. Reference service might be employed to find a particular law, text, record that the user knew existed, but did not know precisely where it was located in the library.

Before 1500, before the impact of printing, the average college collection of books, for example, at Oxford, was about one hundred to five hundred volumes.[16] There was a preponderance of titles in theology and related philosophy. The sciences were lightly represented as were Latin and Greek classics. Here and there one might find a title not found in most of the other universities, but throughout Europe collections were similar in both quantity and quality. Printing was to bring drastic change in number and content, but at the time of the Renaissance the vast majority of libraries were small, consisted primarily of manuscripts, and focused on religious interests.

Reference works, few as they were, followed the typical path of eternal preservation, i.e., they were chained to reading desks. This solution to possible theft or overenthusiasm on part of the reader probably dates back to the eleventh or twelfth century. By the time of printing, the decision to chain or not to chain was based on two suppositions. First, if the book was a manuscript and probably valuable, it was designated to be chained. Second, and more important, if it was a much-used title, and in this sense a reference work, it was chained. By about 1500 a new system developed. Much-used titles for reference were put on a wheel (something like a water wheel) and the user turned the wooden system in order to find the necessary book. Thus the time-worn cliché that a reference book may be defined as one that cannot be checked out of the library dates back to the Middle Ages. Databases have changed the definition somewhat but the majority of librarians remain satisfied with the traditional meaning.

With the growth of the number of titles, as well as readers, a much simpler organizational system was employed. In the fifteenth and sixteenth century, the circulated books were housed in one section of the library (*bibliotheca publica*). The reference titles, and valuable books, were in the other section (*bibliotheca secreta*) where they continued to be chained to a desk-bookcase. Each desk would hold from fifteen to twenty titles. The number of desks averaged around ten to fifteen per library, with a high of fifty.

Private libraries, an important consideration from Plato (428–347 B.C.) and Aristotle through the Roman Empire, virtually disappeared after the fifth century A.D., only to reappear again in the tenth century, although at a much reduced scale. In one sense the monastic libraries, often the work of one or two devoted monks, were small private collections. Normally in the monastic libraries, as in the few individual collections, the emphasis was on theology with support from the standard Latin works from Cicero to Plutarch. An average private collection usually was no larger than found in a monastery—from fifty to one hundred titles. Accounts of private libraries are found in *Biblionomia* by Richard de Fournival (b. 1201), a description of his library, which eventually went to the Sorbonne; and the more famous *Philobiblion* (*Love of books,* 1344; printed 1473) by Richard deBury (1287–1345). Neither speaks of reference works as such, although many of the titles would qualify.

Italian libraries of the Renaissance reflect the interests of the key figures in that period. Petrarch (1304–1374), the father of the Renaissance who reinstated classical literature, boasted a private library of about 200 volumes, primarily Greek and Latin classics, although the former were translated into Latin. The Medicis (1434+) whose books passed on to the Biblioteca Laurentiana, had several thousand titles, among which were found the basic reference works of the day, i.e., medieval encyclopedias and grammars.

Reference books remained much the same in content, if not always in quantity or quality, until the early twentieth century. Then two revolutionary developments changed the reference book dramatically. The wide availability of relatively inexpensive books brought—for better or worse—reference works, heretofore a scholarly enterprise, into the popular mainstream of publishing. The encyclopedia became as common in a living room as today's television set. Second, the development of public libraries resulted in the introduction of reference services. People of every walk of life could ask a librarian for answers to questions that the librarian could answer with an ever-growing number of reference titles. Reference books became as common as a biography or novel. No longer was the reference work primarily the tool of the scholar. It was for everyone.

Reference Services

Libraries began (c. 2500 B.C.) as storehouses, archives, treasure troves of materials. Only a select group of people had access to libraries. There was no suggestion of a reference librarian, although by the Middle Ages there was the concept of certain sections in the library (or, on a more modest scale, certain desks with chained books) being designated as a place where a few reference titles could be examined. At the end of the eighteenth century, the Royal Library in France was impressive in scope, yet more of national treasury than a library. The British Museum opened in 1759, but the era of public service for which it became world famous did not begin before the reforms of the middle of the nineteenth century.

The public library as known today did not become general until the late nineteenth and early twentieth century.[17] Public reference sections, on the other hand, were a fixture in most European libraries from about 1500. Anyone who was literate—a student, bureaucrat or otherwise accepted by the establishment—had free use of cathedral, private, national, and, to a lesser extent, university libraries. Confusion arises as many of these were called town or public libraries, whereas in truth they were connected with colleges or churches. The designation "public" has more to do with the community in which the library appeared than its finance base or its attitude toward service in general and reference service in particular. A more acceptable, descriptive term for such libraries is the "subscription" library which began in England in the eighteenth century.[18] Commercial circulating libraries (rental libraries) were popular from the eighteenth century. The "social library" or subscription library in the nineteenth century took root in America and were found in every part of the country by the close of the Civil War. The majority, complete with a reading room, usually had no more than a few hundred volumes and a handful of reference works. In larger cities the mercantile library gained a position of importance from the 1820s through the first part of the twentieth century. Modeled after the "mechanics'" libraries in England, they were organized to improve the education of working men and women, and often financed by the businesses in which the workers were employed. By the close of the nineteenth century the largest such library in New York had close to two hundred thousand volumes, but the majority were in the two- to three-thousand-title category.

Several American towns claim the distinction of having the first public library with public financial support, from Lexington, Massachusetts (1827) to Peterborough, New Hampshire (1833), but little happened nationally until a large urban public library was opened in Boston in 1854. By the 1880s, the Boston collection was well over four hundred thousand volumes, and there were several branches. Boston, for the time, was the best run and largest public library in the world, in terms of both circulation of books and professional reference services. [It would be surpassed by the

New York Public Library, which was not founded until 1895.] By 1913 the U.S. Office of Education reported there were just over three thousand public libraries in the United States. Unfortunately, the majority had only a few thousand volumes and certainly only informal reference services.

The concept of reference services, i.e., professional assistance to an individual in quest of information, developed in late nineteenth-century America. Samuel Rothstein, the leading expert on the subject, believes reference services happened in the United States first because American research libraries developed as institutions serving general readers as well as scholars. The flood of inexperienced laypeople demanded the librarian to serve puzzled individuals. The traditional laissez-faire attitude had to go. No longer was it enough just to gather and catalog books. Many people needed help in finding not just books, but specific passages in those books as well as material in a growing number of periodicals.

Samuel Green, in a lugubriously titled paper "The desirableness of establishing personal intercourse and relations between librarians and readers in popular libraries," hinted in the late nineteenth century that reference service might be desirable.[19] The head of the Worchester (Massachusetts) Public Library hardly set a fire, but gradually the notion of public service, including help with reference questions, developed in parallel with the idea that the library should encourage self-education. By 1887 the prestigious and influential Boston Public Library had gone so far as to recommend a single individual staff person be charged with assisting users. In 1891 the *Library Journal* first used the term "reference work" rather than the more ambiguous, more common "aid to readers." With the twentieth century "there was no longer any disposition on the part of librarians to dispute the fact that reference service was an integral part of American library practice."[20]

Much the same happened in college and university libraries. The democratic idea of higher education for anyone with talent, coupled with increased emphasis on research and many more new materials to search, resulted in a demand for an easier path to information. Late-nineteenth-century American scholars were ambiguous about how much help should be available to them. They were primarily interested in the library gathering books, not in teaching or showing anyone where to find data. Reference services, such as they were, seemed considerably less important than the library concentrating on purchasing books. "While most academic and reference libraries were still hesitating over the value of individual assistance . . . at least . . . Columbia College Library had already recognized that such assistance was more than just another aid or subsidiary activity."[21] Under the direction of Melvil Dewey, a reference department at Columbia was operative by the mid-1880s. By the 1890s, libraries at major eastern (private) universities and more than a few state universities had specialized reference workers, although often only part time. Gradually, reference services became an accepted part of the academic library's function, and, by the end of the first World War, the services had begun to move from the general to the specialized. Many libraries "had gone well beyond the stage of specialization by function to the more fruitful assistance implicit in subspecialization by subject."[22]

Well into the twentieth century, reference services continued much in the same fashion. Then, in 1940s came "documentation"— a word that became the base of a revolution in reference services and the publication of reference books. The so-called documentalist turned the focus away from books and periodicals to reports, semi-published material, and any form of information including the much-heralded microfiche. Closely associated with science, documentation appealed to many librarians, particularly in special libraries, as it divorced the specialist from the traditional, stereotypical librarian. Flourishing from the early 1940s, documentation soon gave way to another even more modern descriptor: information science, which emerged from the inability of the documentalists to keep up with the flood of reports and nonprint materials; more important, information scientists captured the high ground of technology.[23] Where before the mid-1960s the microfilm reader had been the symbol of documentation, by the late 1960s the computer pushed the reader aside. To this day, in the mid-1990s, the descriptor had held and most library schools, for example, are now schools of information science.

Technology, whether it be fired mud or a digital database, is neutral. The confusion is equating the technology with the skills, perceptions, and intelligence of the individual. As centuries have proven, the individual and technology do not always match. It is just as easy to be stupid today, computer or no, as five thousand years ago in the streets of Ur.

Notes for Chapter 1

1. Rosamond McKitterick, ed., *The Uses of Literacy in Early Medieval Europe* (Cambridge: Cambridge University Press, 1990). Actually, Patrick had six wax tablets inscribed with a text from the Psalms, which hardly posed a threat. Even if the story is in question, it remains a good one.

2. Brian Stock, *The Implications of Literacy* (Princeton, N.J.: Princeton University Press, 1983), 3.

3. Ibid. After the invention of printing, in the mid-fifteenth century, the focus shifted to book production and reading.

4. Throughout history, there were exceptions to the lack of reading material and, when the exception occurred, as in a private library or a phenomenon like the library at Alexandria, then numerous reference works were available.

5. Tom McArthur, *Worlds of Reference* (Cambridge: Cambridge University Press, 1986), 62.

6. Ibid, p. 77. Prior to 1600 there were some reference books in alphabetical order, but this was the exception. The preferred method was arrangement by theme.

7. Martianus Capella (fl. A.D. 430) composed from 410 to 439 a series of didactic treatises for his son. Combining prose and poetry, the lessons were consolidated in *De Nuptiis Mercurii et Philologiae* (*Marriage of Philology and Mercury*). In this fantasy Philologia is accompanied by her seven Liberal Arts handmaids on her ascent to heaven. Here she is married to the god of Eloquentia, Mercury. Despite the much copied fantasy, the basic foundation of the work is to introduce and explain the Seven Arts. Actually, Martianus simply compiled existing information, but his work was the subject of countless commentaries of the Middle Ages.

8. The institute of the university was a Middle Ages concept. It had no classical counterpart. The "think tanks" at Alexandria and Pergamum, and later at Constantinople, were quite different in that none had a corporation of students and teachers. The oldest university is at Bologna, although it concentrated on law. It was established in c. 1158. Close behind were the University of Paris (c. 1208) and Oxford (c. 1200). Other European universities, from Prague to Leipzig, were founded in the fourteenth century.

9. Laura Stevenson, *Praise and Paradox; Merchants and Craftsmen in Elizabethan Popular Literature* (Cambridge: Cambridge University Press, 1984).

10. Impartiality, since the first person took up writing, is barely possible, much less always possible. Rewriting and forming history to suit a country or a ruler is as old as the written word and hardly limited to nationalism. Martin Luther, for example, during the Reformation had to rewrite Christian history, much as early Christians had to rewrite Jewish history. Luther's arguments may or may not be persuasive, but they are based as much on emotion and shaded reasoning as on chronological events. An examination of almost any edition of the *Britannica* before the mid-twentieth century will show masses of embarrassing data about everything (from warfare and housekeeping) to everybody (from women to non-English speaking people). Yet, in keeping with the culture of the times, the data, the biases were thought to be the last word in objective, honest presentation suitable for an outstanding encyclopedia.

11. Little of this takes into account libraries, private, public, and academic, [maintained by the Arabs, the Chinese, and others from c. A.D. 400 to the Renaissance] that did make otherwise costly books available to scholars and the better-off literate laymen. The Arabs, in particular, were better supplied with books during that time than most Europeans. But this is another study. In the early twelfth century the level of scientific and philosophical education was much higher in Spain than in Europe. The major

difference was that Latin learning was based on second- to fourth- or fifth-hand versions of Greek writers while the Arabs had available—in Arabic—almost all major authors in the original translated texts. The Arab writer Said al Andalust is praising Abul Fadl Iban Hasdai (1046–1100). A late-eleventh-century Muslim writer described the program of study for an educated Arab, as well as Jew, living in Spain. The passage is interesting for its focus on Aristotelian scientific works that would not be available in the Latin West for another two hundred years. A gentleman, a courier not only understood science but considered poetry as part of his necessary training. The wise man, the Muslim explains, "has a proficiency in Arabic language and a good knowledge of Arabic rhetoric and poetry. He is remarkable in arithmetic, geometry and in astronomy. He understands the theory of music." The Latin West, from the Carolingian period (beginning in the seventh century) until the early twelfth century, had little or no notion of the superior learning of the Arabs. John Tolan, *Petrus Alfonsi* (Gainsville, Fla.: University Press of Florida, 1993), 5.

12. William Eamon, *Science and the Secrets of Nature: Books of Secrets in Medieval and Early Modern Culture* (Princeton, N.J.: Princeton University Press, 1994). Eamon, an American historian, shows how secrets were maintained, even in the early stages of printing.

13. OCLC/Online Computer Library Center is the acronym referring to the recorded holdings of more than 15,000 libraries in some 52 countries. In 1996, the online OCLC union catalog contained records of more than 30 million items. Of course reference books often do not have "reference" in the title or go by another name, e.g., the Romans called reference works "thesauros" and Livy (59 B.C.–A.D. 17) reports in his *History of Rome* that he had to go through about two thousand such titles in order to gather twenty thousand noteworthy facts.

14. Jacques Barzun, "The Book, the Bibliographer and the Absence of Mind," *American Scholar* (Winter 1969): 12+.

15. For a broader view, and by far the best current history of libraries see Michael Harris, *History of Libraries in the Western World,* 4th ed. (Metuchen, N. J.: Scarecrow, 1995). Useful lists of readings help the well-considered text.

16. The New College Library, which opened at Oxford about 1380, is typical of some 70 college libraries of the time. There were 62 volumes for the chapel library and 312 for use and circulation. Of the latter, about one-half were devoted to theology, and the remainder split about evenly between philosophy, medicine, and canon and civil law. Fellows of the College could borrow two books and keep them up to a year.

17. Until the mid-nineteenth century, "public" did not mean the same as today, but rather signified a special group of people, e.g., the Oxford Bodleian library, founded in 1597, was open to a "publick" that consisted of scholars familiar with Latin or Greek, as well as members of the House of Lords (and their sons), those who donated books to the library and

certain groups of graduate, but not undergraduate, Oxford students. In the seventeenth and eighteenth centuries the definition of public was broadened for other libraries, though not for the Bodley, to include laypeople willing to pay subscription fees or otherwise support the library.

18. Carl M. White, *Bases of Modern Librarianship* (New York: Pergamon, 1969), 10. The increased reading public in America and the lack of readily available books or shillings to buy them inspired Benjamin Franklin to open a subscription library in Philadelphia. By 1731 he had fifty subscribers, and the plan was carried throughout the colonies.

19. Samuel Rothstein, "The Development of the Concept of Reference Service in American Libraries, 1850–1900," *The Reference Librarian,* nos. 25–26 (1989): 23.

20. Ibid.

21. Ibid, 70.

22. Ibid, 95.

23. Dorothy B. Lilley and Ronald Trice, *A History of Information Science 1945–1985* (New York: Academic Press, 1989). The authors place the beginning of information science after the Second World War, but it really gained power in the mid-1970s. The book is an excellent history of the development that did so much to change reference formats and services.

2

Encyclopedias

All strands of learning [would be brought] together into an enormous Text, an encyclopedia or summa, that would mirror the historical and transcendental orders just as the Book of God's Word (the Bible) was a speculum of the Book of His Works (nature).[1]

The fascinating general concept of the early encyclopedias was that the compiler knew all that was worth knowing. From the Greeks to the Renaissance, the notion was that all knowledge could be included in a handful of reference works.

The idea that one person could know all took a long time to fade and disappear. As late as the early eighteenth century, for example, friends (and foes) of the philosopher and one-time librarian Gottfried von Leibniz (1646–1716) believed he had mastered the total sum of recorded knowledge. He was the last of a long line of scholars to be considered a living encyclopedia, but notice how long the concept lasted. The idea probably began with the first cuneiform tablet library (c. 2500 B.C.) and lasted for well over three thousand years. One could, with the proper reference sources, the proper small library, be in command of everything worth knowing. Only since the eighteenth century have people recognized that it is no longer possible to hold the whole world in one's mind. Imagine the comfort an encyclopedia compiler must have felt when he set out to record all the world's knowledge and knew he could do it in a small number of volumes.

The age of the specialist, a phenomenon of the twentieth century, has its benefits. The drawbacks are frightening as well. If, for example, all that was to be known about physics could have been found in a single encyclopedia one hundred years ago, then today a complete library of thousands of volumes and millions of articles would be far from complete for even a small part, a chapter, in that hundred-year-old physics source. Today even the expert who has mapped out a small area of knowledge lives in fear that the area will expand to a point where it must be divided and subdivided.

The history of the encyclopedia stretches over two thousand years from a Roman's observations about the nature of his world [written on papyrus rolls] to the modern compilation [in print or on CD-ROMs or online] covering the universe. Today the purpose of a general encyclopedia is to offer authoritative, usually relatively easy-to-understand answers to questions about every conceivable topic from Aachen in Western Germany to Wojciech Zywny, a nineteenth-century Polish musician. Depending upon both the size of the encyclopedia and the age-needs-sophistication of the user, the entries may be short or detailed. And there are encyclopedias for all age groups as well as specific subject sets for experts in everything from agriculture to wind power.

Even more than the dictionary and phone book, the encyclopedia is the best-known, most-used general reference work. From century to century and generation to generation, it has reflected the interest of its readers. In the early centuries the readers were academics and theologians, and the focus was on narrow educational and or religious subjects in lengthy, monographic articles. There were few if any illustrations; Latin dominated, and alphabetical arrangement and indexes were unusual. With the advent of printing and the possibilities of wide dissemination of encyclopedias, publishers looked beyond the scholars to professional laypersons. The sets began to reflect practical matters of interest to lawyers, teachers, doctors, and businesspeople. The nineteenth-century revolution in technology and education broadened the market to include the middle classes and those aspiring to that status. By then the vernacular dominated, indexes and alphabetical arrangement prevailed, and, as now, the focus was on the short informative entry rather than the detailed monograph.

The dozen or so CD-ROM/online or printed multiple volume English-language sets today—from the *Britannica* and *Americana* to *Encarta*—are sources of data on facts and theories likely to be considered by a well-educated individual. The goal is to assemble summaries of all the world's knowledge in more or less alphabetical order, complete with illustrations and an exhaustive index. The editorial material is generally from experts and from a trained staff rather than, as in earlier centuries, from an individual.

The traditional *enkyklios paideia,* or "rounded education," began in Greece as a description of an educational process. The phrase became popular after Alexander the Great (356–323 B.C.) and the spread of Hellenism through the Mediterranean and Near East. It was an umbrella term that embraced the primary academic interests from the trivium (grammar, rhetoric, and dialectic) to the quadrivium (mathematics, geometry, astronomy, and music). The pedagogical program, or *enkyklios paideia,* was a major, long-lived innovation and in its late Latin form, "encyclopaedia" or "encyclopedia" was used to describe a general course of instruction, termed "encyclical" by the Romans.[2] Rational thought, according to Plato (428–348 B.C.), depended on knowing as much as possible, hence the value of an encyclopedia.[3] The Romans expanded this into public life where one should have a command of facts in order to function practically. Medieval thinkers modified, even censored the universe of knowledge in order to point to the moral way to worship and live. The Renaissance and beyond saw an encyclopedia as a tool to broaden the mind. The word did not appear in Europe until the sixteenth or seventeenth century.[4] It became a fixed part of a title of Diderot's *Encyclopedie* (1751–1765) and the first edition (1768) of the *Encyclopaedia Britannica.*

In outlining the history of the encyclopedia, the normal chronological framework is from the time of Pliny the Elder (c. A.D. 50) to the seventeenth century. The second period is from c. 1600 to 1800 when the modern encyclopedia was shaped and a beginning effort was made to reach a wider group of readers. The third period is from 1800 to present, during which the modern encyclopedia evolved. Characteristically, before 1600 there were numerous subdivisions. The most noticeable was between the secular efforts of the Greeks and Romans and the religious emphasis of the Medieval period. By the middle of the thirteenth century the growth of universities, urban centers, and international trade called for an emphasis on humanism and the pragmatic. Printing (c. 1455) made possible the wider circulation of encyclopedias for an audience who demanded more practical, less spiritual assistance. During the second period the arts and sciences dominated, culminating in Chambers *Cyclopaedia* (1728) and the ultimate contribution to the objective organization of knowledge: Diderot's *Encyclopedie.* The *Encyclopaedia Britannica* dominated the English-language process through most of the nineteenth and twentieth centuries.

Until the seventeenth century, the majority of encyclopedias were compiled by an individual[5] and were arranged by broad topics rather than alphabetically.[6] In length, few exceeded today's one-volume encyclopedias, and none came even close to the millions of words found in, say, the *Britannica.* The majority of encyclopedias were employed as textbooks or as guides to be read cover to cover, not simply consulted for facts. Finally, and particularly during the Medieval period, moral messages were stressed. Actually, the compilation of moral ideas was hard dying and carried through into the nineteenth and early twentieth century.

Roman Contributions

The Greeks did not compile an encyclopedia in the sense of the descriptor as employed today. One might argue that the collected writings of, say, Aristotle, (384–322 B.C.) or Plato (427–347 B.C.), and the Sophists were encyclopedic in character. One may claim both Aristotle and Plato were interested in encyclopedias as a teaching aid because their respective works follow the *enkyklios paideia* pattern.

Several Romans compiled less ambitious works. Unfortunately, most of what they wrote has disappeared. The earliest was Cato (234–149 B.C.). One of Rome's most outstanding orators and statesmen, he is famous for his *On Agriculture* (c. 160 B.C.), the earliest extant Roman literary work. Earlier, c. 184 B.C., he wrote an encylopedia, in large letters, for his son's education. It has disappeared. Celsus who served under Tiberius (reign A.D. 14–37) wrote an encyclopedia on agriculture, medicine, military science, rhetoric, and probably law and philosophy. Apart from fragments, only the medical section is extant.

Quintilian (c. A.D. 30–100), who was known for his *Institutio Oratorie* on rhetoric, strongly influenced encyclopedia compilers. His published work, written after a lifetime of teaching rhetoric, was quoted time and time again, e.g., by Isidore in *Etymologies.*

Two Romans, Marcus Terentius Varro (116–27 B.C.) and Pliny the Elder (A.D. 23–79) may be said to be the major compilers of the Roman encyclopedie. Varro was a true scholar and concentrated upon academic interests, with particular emphasis on the traditional seven arts. Pliny, through observation and attention to Greek scientific findings focused on scientific topics. In one sense, he was the first to develop a subject, i.e., a scientific encyclopedia, while Varro was concerned with the more diverse approach of today's multiple-volume general sets. The pull between the specific and the all-inclusive is found throughout the history of the encyclopedia.

M.T. Varro, who consistently chose the wrong side in eternal Roman politics and wars, managed to survive to be appointed librarian of the giant public library Caesar envisioned.[7] Nothing came of the library and after Caesar's assassination (44 B.C.) the 72-year-old Varro narrowly escaped death to continue writing until he died of natural causes at age 89. During his life he wrote more than 620 books. Only one of his works, *Treatise on Agriculture,* has survived in its entirety, while only two of the original twenty-five books of *On the Latin Language,* (*De Linqua Latina*) survives now. Scraps and fragments are all we have of his other works. Taken as a group Varro's writing is encyclopedic in range. He compiled only a single encyclopedia *Disciplinae* (c. 50 B.C.), in which he attempted to bring together some of his various works; except for fragments, it is lost. Enough remains to know he followed the pattern of the seven liberal arts—plus two (architecture and medicine)—in the nine books. The later Christian compilers of encyclopedias, at least as far as can be known, owed much to Varro's *Disciplinae,* for as an account of existing knowledge, it was a guide to those who came after him.

Curious about everything, from baking to plows and omens, Pliny set out to explore the world in his *Historia Naturalis* (*Natural History*).[8] The work makes excellent reading today because it covers such a wide variety of material and ideas from painters to Roman medicine. As Edward Gibbon put it, the *Natural History* was "an immense register of the discoveries, the arts, and the errors of mankind." The thirty-seven books served throughout the Middle Ages and into the Renaissance as a type of textbook for a well-rounded, general education. As one of the primary authorities on scientific matters, Pliny probably did much harm, particularly as his marvelous descriptions often were ahead of reality. At the same time he is blessed for preserving in his pages the highlights of Greek science, correct or incorrect. He was so honored that it was not until the close of the fifteenth century that any of his theories or descriptions were challenged, and it was not until the end of the seventeenth century that he was abandoned by most scientists.[9] The fascination with Pliny was due in part to the simple facts that little or nothing was available covering the same material and his approach was plain, but enthusiastic and apparently reliable. His words in part or in whole, governed the early development of science and the way many viewed the Greek and Roman worlds.

Soldier, lawyer, public official, and scholar, Pliny the Elder was in a good position to study "the nature of things, that is, life" as he states in the preface to his *Natural History* (c. 77). Pliny served as an administrator and saw military service in Germany under Claudius and then Nero. He retired to a more quiet life. Most of his later life was spent in research, reading, and writing, but almost everything, including his history of Rome, is lost. Pliny claimed, and probably rightfully so, that he was the first to attempt to bring together all the material that composed the *enkyklios paideia*. "It is an encyclopedia of astronomy, meteorology, geography, mineralogy, zoology, and botany, i.e., a systematic account of all the material objects that are not the product of man."[10] He includes digressions on man's inventions and institutions. In his preface he claims he "deals with 20,000 matters of importance, drawn from 100 selected authors."[11]

Pliny was one of the few early writers to accurately cite sources. As a result many of the more than 100 books and writings from which he drew material are known today because of his citations. "I have prefaced these volumes with the names of my authorities. I have done so because it is, in my opinion, a pleasant thing and one that shows an honorable modesty, to own up to those who were the means of one's achievements . . . I have found that the most professedly reliable and modern writers have copied the old authors word for word, without acknowledgement."[12]

Pliny the Younger (62–113) when describing the working habits of his uncle, may well have been writing about any one-person encyclopedia compiler:

'He had a keen intelligence, incredible devotion to study, and a remarkable capacity for dispensing with sleep. His method was to start during the last week of August rising by candlelight and long before daybreak, not in order to take auspices but to study; and in winter he got to work at one or at latest two a.m., and frequently at 12 p.m. . . . In the summer, if he had no engagements, he use to lie in the sun and have a book read to him, from which he made notes and extracts; he read nothing without making extracts from it— indeed he used to say that no book is so bad but that some part of it has value.[13]

Suitably enough, in his fifty-sixth year his curiosity and scientific diligence cost him his life. He was near Naples on the twenty-fourth of August, A.D.

79 when he observed a cloud of very unusual size and appearance comes from Vesuvius. His adopted nephew, Pliny the Younger, writes: "My uncle, true savant that he was, considered the phenomenon to be important and worth a nearer view. He ordered a light vessel to be got ready, and gave me the opportunity, if I thought proper, to accompany him. I replied I would rather study." The wiser young man watched his uncle set off for Vesuvius and, drawing upon "either an eye-witness or what was heard at the time—when reports speaks most truly," explains how Pliny died studying the volcano.[14] Pliny's motto might have been what he said about a government regulation passed many years before his birth: "Every single thing mattered to our ancestors."

Suetonius (c. A.D. 69–122) and Nonius Marcellus (fl. A.D. 450) are two compilers, influenced by Pliny, but with only a brief impression left in the history of encyclopedias. Suetonius compiled a work—an encyclopaedia called *Prata* (*Meadows*)—that followed the pattern of Pliny. Although bits of it are quoted in early Medieval and late antiquity works, the *Prata* sections of it may be incorporated into his *The Lives of the Caesars*. Nonius Marcellus, the African Latin grammarian and lexicographer, compiled a lexicon in which he preserved work from numerous earlier writers. Of its twenty chapters, the sixteenth is lost; the first twelve deal with language and the latter chapters are more general. He was drawn upon by Medieval encyclopedists, including Isidore.

Not all would agree these Roman encyclopedias were intellectually challenging. In fact, critics—arguing that creative people extend knowledge, while the Romans of the empire were content to simply codify what was then known—suggest that they mark the decline of Roman literature.

The Medieval Christian Encyclopedia

Christianity began as the lightning rod of protest in the Roman empire and evolved to a social-educational point of stability during the Dark Ages. Order was synonymous with the Church. All of this is reflected in the development of the encyclopedia as a guide to religion and education. It evolved as a place to turn to for the organized presentation of facts, usually of ancient writers.

Scholasticism—the effort to intellectualize and analyze knowledge from the ninth century to the Renaissance—supported and fostered the encyclopedia movement. The beginnings of scholasticism can be traced to the encyclopedia from Isidore of Seville and Hugh of St. Victor to Vincent of Beauvais. By the time of Petrarch (1304–1374) and the fourteenth century, scholasticism gave way to the Renaissance, humanism and a new approach to knowledge, and, of course, encyclopedias.

The ignorance about ancient writers in the Dark and Middle Ages was due, ironically, in no small part to encyclopedias. The direct reading of classical authors, checked in part by a poor or total ignorance in Western Europe of Greek, was superseded by the encyclopedia, which gave the reader the "approved" authors and sections to read. Classical learning was largely secondhand, as much from the extensive use of encyclopedias as florilegia, that is, books of extracts. "Their summaries of the various branches of knowledge erred on the side of a jejune brevity; and it has been said that wishing to cover too much, they rank the risk of omitting everything of genuine interest. Certainly, as guides to knowledge they leave much to be desired. To their major fault of condensing too much, they added the further sin of not always following the best authorities."[15] Conversely, the encyclopedia had the virtue of attempting to be comprehensive and, possibly more important, of establishing a practical curriculum for education. "There in lay their originality and their proper claim to fame."[16]

As the Roman encyclopedias developed out of earlier Greek thought, so did the Christian notions of organization and scope come from the Church Fathers, particularly St. Augustine (354–430) and St. Jerome (327–420). Both provided the framework for early encyclopedias. Augustine's *City of God* (426), particularly, was influential in establishing principles of content and emphasis. Ancient writers were used to support Christian ideas. In his *On Christian Doctrine* (*De Doctrina Christiana*), St. Augustine called for an encyclopedia that would embrace the primary tenets of Christianity and explain various aspects of Scriptures. He indicated that a chart of organization would include material necessary to support Christianity, i.e. ancient rhetoric and natural history, for example. At the same time, Augustine was highly critical of Varro's early efforts because they put too much emphasis on the secular. A fine balance was required. In the Middle Ages, such balance usually was achieved by opening with Scripture and Christian history and later turning to matters secular.

Often the individual encyclopedia compiler lifted passages and sections from other works, with or without citations.[17] In this sense one might say many of the Medieval encyclopedias were more compilations than one-person efforts. This is not to detract from the single-authored encyclopedias. They did share one common trait—an ability to take a mass of unrelated data and organize and present it in such a way that it was equally easy to read and to understand.

Cassiodorus and Isidore

Cassiodorus (c. A.D. 480–575), as Varro three centuries earlier, outlived most of his contemporaries and, as Varro and Pliny, had an abiding curiosity about the world. After an active political life, he retired, at age 71, to a monastery of his own creation at his southern Italian summer home in Vivarium. Along with St. Benedict (d. c. 547), Cassiodorus established the principles of the monastic communities that were intellectual outposts during the Dark Ages and well into the early Medieval period.[18] His training in the Ostrogothic civil service insured an interest in practical matters. He supported Greek texts, which he considered beneficial to a study of Christianity, and had many translated into the more accessible Latin. "The pagan authors found a place in both his library and his educational program, but they were reduced to the rank of teaching books and manuals. The only classical work that to our certain knowledge he put on his shelves were Cicero's *De inventione.* . . ."[19] At Vivarium Cassiodorus completed his *Institutes of Divine* and *Secular Literature* (c. 560). The two books cover the "encyclical" or the requirements for a rounded education—in this case for both divines and laypersons. While he broadly followed Pliny's design, his particular gift to the monastic tradition was a logical presentation of how to distinguish between sacred and profane literature as well as how to employ classical literature to support Christian education.

In the beginning of the *Institutes,* Cassiodorus describes briefly the contents of the nine codices that make up the Old and New Testaments and lists names of primary commentators, after which he urges his monks to pursue learning—including the seven liberal arts—so as to better understand the Scriptures. And those unwilling or unable to follow the secular literature should devote themselves to other matters. In addition, there are suggestions from rules to spelling to methods of binding, copying, and lighting. In the second book, Cassiodorus gives a brief account of the trivium and the quadrivium with examples. Little is known of the sources of many of the chapters, and particularly those dealing with geometry, astronomy, and arithmetic.[20] "An impressive feature is the tone of deep religious emotion which keeps breaking out in Cassiodorus—quite in contrast to Isidore."

Cassiodorus's *Institutes* is not a full encyclopedia, or, for that matter, an introduction to the seven liberal arts, as much as it is a reading list for the Benedictine monks at his Vivarium monastery. As such, modern readers find it less than satisfactory as a source of information about the period. The great merit of Cassiodorus's monastic work lay in his determination to utilize the vast leisure of the convent for the preservation of divine and human learning and for its transmission to posterity. Cassiodorus was not the first man to have introduced into monasteries either the copying of manuscripts or the study of the Scriptures. The tradition dates back to 346. What Cassiodorus did originate was the "mass production" of manuscripts rather than the few his predecessors copied. Also, he is to be credited with careful selection of what was copied and, in particular, manuscripts that were the foundation of the liberal arts and rejected earlier by Gregory the Great.

The *Institutiones* served in many centers as a bibliographical guide and an inspiration to the librarians to look around for good old copies of the works recommended. The second book became a basic text or encyclopedia for monastic communities throughout Europe. And most important "Cassiodorus preserved in sound form for generations to come both the Fathers of the Church and the ancient Latin authors.[21] In evaluating the *Institutiones,* Jones observes that the emphasis is on utility, but the "style is still wordy and elaborate, often to the point of obscurity. Superlatives . . . are common. Despite these shortcomings, Cassiodorus has a genuine feeling for style . . . The archaic and artificial quality of his rich vocabulary is impressive."[22]

Isidore of Seville

An early, brief Renaissance blossomed in Spain in the early seventh century primarily because of Isidore of Seville (c. 570–636). Isidore, with a strong interest in Latin classical literature, composed one of the most famous Encyclopedias of the Middle Ages, his *Etymologiae.* The twenty books (incomplete when he died, but finished by his secretary soon after) covered all then known areas of human knowledge.

"God raised him up," a cleric explained, "to revive the works of the ancients that we might not always grow duller from boorish rusticity. . . . You have discussed . . . all things human and divine."[23] In a preface to one of his other books Isidore explains: "I . . . have run over the works of earlier writers, and . . . (describe) . . . all things as they are written by the ancients, and especially in the works of catholic writers."[24]

While written by Isidore, the set drew heavily upon Varro, Pliny, and other early Roman writers as well as Cassiodorus. (Isidore did not always name his sources). No other work, other than Pliny's proved so popular. The Bishop was one of the most "influential agents in the transmission and elucidation of ancient learning. His *Etymologiae* was at the same time the last product of the Roman encyclopedic tradition and the starting point for most medieval compilations."[25] There are more than one thousand manuscripts extant of his encyclopedia in Latin and the vernacular.

Isidore's *Etymologiae* was the first extant effort to genuinely outline all that was known about the world. Isidore stressed four basic areas with subdivisions: history, biography, lexicography, and the arts. Moving from a description of furniture and tools to various public games and the character of cities, Isidore signaled a shift from the narrow, scientific view of Pliny and the essential theological focus of Cassiodorus. Isidore goes beyond Cassiodorus, making the seven liberal arts, especially the trivium (grammar, rhetoric, dialectic) preparatory to professional studies or graduate work. Employing the origin of words as a springboard, Isidore moved to related matters, such as the early history of marriage as well as the characteristics of love. More often than not his imagination outran modern philologists' findings, but his style and inventive approach made the work eminently readable.

Isidore was among the first to offer a chronology for a Christian theory of literature that could incorporate pagan writers. For example, he establishes six periods of history, the last being to the end of the world and the first from Adam to Noah. Homer does not appear until the third period and the Greek dramatists and philosophers in the fifth age. All are preceded by the imaginative writing of Moses, David, Solomon, and similar Biblical figures who invented poetry, philosophy, science, etc. Given a subsidiary position in the history of things, the pagan writers could be accepted and used by Christians. "Isidore . . . integrates the doctrines of pagan late Antiquity into the systematized didascalium of the western church. . . He is usually regarded as a compiler, his work as a mosaic. If one's concern with him is that of a student of sources, no other conclusion can be reached."[26]

The vital point, here and for the majority of medieval encyclopedias, as well as Diderot and major eighteenth century efforts, is that the encyclopedia was much more than a source of bibliographical citations, fact and background reading. Isidore offers a whole, a complete and systematic approach to knowledge that must be read not simply consulted. "Above all, we must read the *Etymologiae* as the medieval reader did—as a book which is all of a piece and of binding authority."[27]

Why was Isidore's work so popular? There are numerous explanations from the paucity of manuscripts at the time to the need for educational materials. Isidore "provided access to works and authors barely identified in the eight century, though occasionally preserved in monastic libraries. He also introduced new ideas and knowledge of ecclesiastical customs quite unknown in the West."[28] As a conglomerate of ten centuries, the encyclopedia reinforced the period's complacent and authoritative world-philosophy. Isidore, as the leading intellect of the Dark Ages had a world view that readjusted the past to explain the ways of God to man, i.e., a pagan past that he completely desecularized.[29] And yet, "Although Isidore is not surpassed in comprehensiveness by any one of the line of Roman encyclopedists who preceded him, in the quality of his thought and the extent of his information he is inferior to them all."[30] Isidore's influence proved pervasive. Between his death in the mid-seventh century and the thirteenth century there were no significant contributions to the art. A possible exception was Hrabanus Maurus (776–856) who compiled *On The Nature of Things* (*De rerum naturis*) in 842. The prize student of Alcuin revised much of Isidore's initial encyclopedia.[31] Intellectually Hrabanus was in a direct line from Isidore, but with a more zealous mission. In keeping with the lesson of his master Alcuin, he sought to elevate the education of what heretofore often had been illiterate clerics. At the same time, the educational path was narrowed to preserve what he saw was the true faith of the church. Piety dominated his thoughts as did his *De Instituione Clericorum* (*The Education of Clerics*) of c. 820. He borrowed liberally from the ideas and methods in this early work for his encyclopedia. The Archbishop of Mainz, put more stress on theology than Isidore. In twenty-two books, the work opened every chapter with a quote from Isidore's work.

Scholasticism and the Medieval Encyclopedia

Bonaventure (c. 1217–1274) described scholastics as one might describe masters of the Medieval encyclopedias,[32] i.e., "compilers and weavers of approved opinions." The object was to reach concordia through textual study and subtle discussion of details. A hierarchy of texts was established: Scriptures came first, followed by opinions of the Fathers and the work of ancients. Drawing upon the literature of Christianity, a system was established to insure an orderly method of learning for all who sought to be educated. Many of the didactic methods are found in the encyclopedias, which served as both reference resources and text books.

The firm base for the scholastic encyclopedia was established by the monk, Hugh of St. Victor (c. 1096–1141),[33] a century before Bonaventure's efforts. A brilliant scholar, Hugh was "merely a precursor. He talked of organizing knowledge but as yet there was none that urgently needed organization."[34] Be that as it may, Hugh's *Didascalicon* (c. 1120) was a major encyclopedia.[35] Compiled in Paris, the work accomplished two primary purposes. First, it established or reconfirmed the classification of knowledge into the seven liberal arts. He also considered seven mechanical arts (weaving, weaponry, navigation, agriculture, hunting, medicine, and drama). He added magic and philosophy. Second, his books stressed the importance of a conservative education, particularly mastering Latin rather than the vernacular. Also, of the encyclopedia as a whole, more than half was given over to a study of Scriptures. This emphasis acted as a counterweight against the prevailing and renewed interest in Latin and, to a lesser extent, Greek authors. "This then is what the arts are concerned with, this is what they intend, namely, to restore within us the divine likeness."[36]

Book two, "concerning the distinguishing of the arts," is typical of Victor's organization approach and comments. After the introduction, he offers brief sections on theology, mathematics, arithmetic, music, astronomy, physics, and concludes with "what the proper business of each art is. Primarily concerned with education, Hugh observes that "the things by which every man advances in knowledge are principally two—namely, reading and meditation . . . It is of reading that this book treats, setting forth rules for it . . . There are three things particularly necessary to learn for reading: first, each man should know what he ought to read; second, in what order he ought to read. . .; and third, in what manner he ought to read."[37]

Hugh died almost a century before his organizational framework and emphasis was to be applied, but, by 1215, "science with its array of facts had arrived, even though the facts in question left much to be desired."[38]

Summa and Albertus Magnus

Medieval encyclopedias sometimes are confused with a similar reference aid, the "summa," which developed out of a need for a systematic exposition and a general introduction to a single, or related, group of subjects. Students and laypersons used summa to gain background material, but in a much more narrow area than visualized by the average encyclopedia. The first genuine summa probably was Hugh of St. Victor's *De sacramentis Christianae fidei* (*On the Sacraments of the Christian Faith*). In his introduction Hugh uses the term "summa" as a comprehensive view of all that exists. What made this exceptional was that Hugh took the term literally and urged readers to "learn everything."[39]

Albertus Magnus (c. 1200–1280) was a scholar who gave summa a popular and lasting importance. After teaching at the University of Paris he set out to see Europe. His observations of nature and daily life joined with his interest in Aristotle to form two voluminous books on plants and animals. While he did not compile a single encyclopedia, his various writings and summa constitute a broad base of knowledge and interpretation that, taken as a whole, might be called the most impressive work of its type to come out of the scholastic movement.[40] He exerted a strong influence and he is remembered best today as being the teacher of Thomas Aquinas (1225–1274), whose *Summa Theologica* (1266–1273) is the most famous of the summa.

In three parts, the *Summa* of St. Thomas is the definitive Catholic Summa. In the sections (the last of which was not completed) Aquinas managed to synthesize the Christian dogma with classical traditions, including Aristotle and the then-known Arab scholars. Reason and philosophy were to be wed to faith and theology. The unfortunate result was the rationalization of the Scholastic—a type of scholar blessed by God and moral excellence without too much attention to the classical heritage.

The Great Medieval Encyclopedias

The climax of the development of the Medieval encyclopedia came in the thirteenth century. Employing the extensive work of Aristotle (translated from Greek into Latin) as well as scientific data from the Arabs, scholars dedicated to Scholasticism sought more objective information. Also, they came to appreciate consistency in presentation and organization, which meant indexes, tables of contents, chapter headings, etc. The intellectuals, who primarily taught in the universities, had a need for material to assist illiterate and often less than well-educated students who later became preachers. From this need arose special encyclopedias, today more closely associated with handbooks and how-to titles. An outstanding example was Bartholomew Glanville, *On the Characteristics (or Properties) of Things* (*De Proprietatibus Perum*, c. 1240), which was turned to for everything from ideas for sermons to facts about nature. Glanville's popular overview was of great help to students, as well as clerics, involved with administration. One suspects the growing merchant classes used it as well. The guide of twenty books depended, as others before it, heavily upon Isidore and Pliny. The first two books dispensed with theology. The author then moved on to matters of particular interest to students and administrators. Among the topic covered were geography, geology, weight and measure, trees and herbs, and even scents and flavors. Glanville, an English friar, had a good sense of organization, and his books are much easier to consult than those of early times. He quoted extensively from the Arabs and Aristotle and had a particular appreciation for medicine, geography, and history. Although the Oxford Franciscan borrowed liberally from his predecessors, and particularly Isidore, he was quick to cite many, if not all his sources. By 1398, Glanville's work was translated into all European languages, and various editions were consulted until the seventeenth century.

Bartholomew suggested a soon-to-become overwhelming problem—too much information for a single encyclopedia. The Dominican, Vincent of Beauvais (c. 1190–1264) recognized the difficulty in his *The Great Mirror* (*Speculum Majus*) of c. 1244–1260.[41] His response was one of the largest works of its type to date, with more than three million words in three major parts. (Comparatively, the one-volume modern *Columbia Encyclopedia* has six million words and the *Encyclopaedia Britannica* claims over 44 million.) More than four hundred sources were employed for Vincent's original three books of *The Great Mirror,* or *Speculum Majus,* a mixture of fact and fancy in over more than three million words divided into close to ten thousand chapters in eighty books. Not until Diderot in the eighteenth century did anyone come close to rivaling the size of Vincent's effort. One may argue that this is really a commonplace book filled with long quotes and passages rather than original work; but, be as that may, it was treated as an encyclopedia from its inception. As a source of background information for poets and writers, it enjoyed centuries of popularity. From it was drawn such classics as the *Roman de la rose,* among the earliest printed works (1472); the Alexander romances; Giovanni da Colonna's *Book Concerning Illustrious Men;* and the recorded lives of the saints.[42]

Vincent wrote just at the moment when the Scholastic organization of knowledge was complete, so that he forms the watershed between discoverers and organizers, on the one hand, and the popularizers on the other. As "the most monumental encyclopedist of the Middle Ages,"[43] the Vincent created what was considered the great achievement of the age. "Louis IX hearing of Vencent's growing compilation . . . wanted a copy for himself and offered the financial assistance needed to finish the project."[44]

"A veritable human encyclopedia,"[45] Roger Bacon (c. 1213–1292), the English Franciscan and teacher at the University of Paris, was the leading thirteenth century advocate of a return to the ancients and particularly to the works of Aristotle. Many of his works (c. 1265 to his death) are wildly varied and, while they cannot be considered an encyclopedia per se, their total is of encyclopedic character. Much of his writing is practical, and there is an emphasis on reformation of education. More important was Bacon's continual stress on the unity of knowledge.

His *Opus majus* (*Great Work*) was a major synthesis of the learning of the time on education and society. In the entry on Bacon in the *Dictionary of National Biography,* his *Opus majus* is termed "the Encyclopedia and Organon of the thirteenth century."[46] The four parts move from classical sources to the support of Aristotle to the study of language and mathematics. In the latter he stressed the importance of science and challenged the questionable notions then prevalent about magic. A summary of topics is found in Part V, and Part VI establishes the early groundwork for scientific discovery and experiment. In the concluding section he took up moral philosophy, not as an end in itself but as a way of leading the good life.[47]

Bacon's influence on the encyclopedia form was negligible, but he did affect the scientific way of thought. He prepared the way for future teachers and compilers of encyclopedias by his methodology and objectivity. Although his *Opus majus* was known to most contemporary scholars, it was not until the fifteenth century that he was rediscovered by the Elizabethans.

Both the first medieval encyclopedia by a layperson and the first work in the vernacular, rather than in Latin, can be claimed by Bruno Latini (1220–1294) a Florentine government official. He compiled three *Treasure Books* (*Le Livres dou Tresor*; c. 1265), which covered primarily the seven liberal arts. As he wished to reach the widest possible audience he used the common secular language, French. The precision of prose and the accuracy of presentation won the work a wide audience. In the first book he summarized what was then known about the secular topics of the time, i.e. science, history, and philosophy. He drew extensively from Isidore. The second book emphasis Aristotle's *Nicomachean Ethics* as well as practical business considerations. Rhetoric and the daily activity of politics was the target of the third and most important book. Here he drew upon Cicero as well as his own experience. The rediscovery of Cicero by Latini, at least in this context, gave his work a pragmatic twist that made it extremely popular.[48]

At an extreme in the history of the encyclopedias is *The Image of The World* (1245), which was written entirely in verse—probably, although not for certain, by a French priest and poet, Gautier de Metz. Four hundred years later another French work in heroic verse appeared as the *La science universelle* (1663). The verse indicated neither skill nor knowledge, so it was hardly a loss, possibly a fitting literary judgment, when the compiler was killed. Another odd contender was a German work, *Apparatus eruditionis* (1676), which carried its message in a series of conversations.

Renaissance Encyclopedias

In the early years of the Renaissance, various new combinations of knowledge were attempted. There was a movement away from the purely pedagogical or theological to highly specialized works. An early example was Gregor Reisch (d. 1525), who published his *Pearls of Philosophy* (*Margarita Philosophica*; 1496) with an almost complete focus on moral issues. His encyclopedia served as a syllabus for the university courses of the day. Dedicated to "ingenuous youth," the twelve books, which today one would describe as textbooks rather than an encyclopedia, offered a brief, easy-to-read survey of knowledge. In 200 pages a student could learn the highlights of just about everything that was known at the opening of the sixteenth century. The work gained in popularity and was reprinted and updated several times. Editions were published as late as 1600.

The seventeenth century and subsequent history of the encyclopedia is dominated by one figure—Francis Bacon (1561–1626), who flourished some 250 years after the death of his famous counterpart, Roger Bacon.[49] Francis, a lawyer, philosopher, and master of English prose dreamed the same dream of encyclopedia compilers from the time of Pliny—he wished to claim that all knowledge could be captured, organized and presented in his compilation. His stress on the scientific method gave him first place in the new age to follow. His goal to clarify and organize all human knowledge was to be realized in his encyclopedia, *Great Renewal* (*Magna Instauratio;* begun in 1620). This established the pattern by which knowledge might be classified. Before he could begin he was locked in the Tower of London on a trumped-up bribery charge. Cut off from libraries, Bacon still wrote two out of six separate books on natural history: *History of the Winds* (1622) and *History of Life and Death* (1623). His *Advancement of Learning* also came out 1623. Three years later he was dead after an attack of bronchitis brought on by an experiment with snow.[50] If Petrarch (1304–1374) was the first Renaissance figure, Francis Bacon was the last.

The Medieval argument as to the organization of an encyclopedia, particularly as to what topics should come first, was settled by Bacon. In his incomplete *Magna* of 1620 he divided the encyclopedia into three main parts: (1) External nature, which dealt with the sciences; (2) Man, which covered the physical person as well as ideas and history; and (3) Man's action on nature, which took in the liberal arts as well as miscellaneous skills from printing to navigation. The arrangement covered every known topic and worked as a type of checklist for future compilers to determine if anything was overlooked. Even Diderot who favored alphabetical arrangement admitted his debt to Bacon.

From Bacon to Chambers

During the remainder of the seventeenth and early eighteenth century, encyclopedias lost much of their popularity.[51] Only a meager few followed Bacon. Encyclopedias for the church continued to be published, although with little of the verve or intellectual quality of the Medieval works. For example, Father Leon (1600–1671) compiled his *Encyclopaedia* in 1635 for clerics. It failed as much for its limited scope as for it being printed in Latin.[52]

An exception to the dismal clerical works and the novelties, best forgotten, was a 1674 set that was in the best tradition of Bacon: *Le grand dictionnaire historique,* compiled by Louis Moreri (1643–1680). Sensing the need for a work in the vernacular, he published it in French. So popular and useful did the encyclopedia become that it grew from one to ten folio volumes. The twentieth edition, almost eighty years after the original compiler's death, represented work of numerous contributors and editors. Along the way it was translated into English (1694), and numerous European works were based, at least in part, on the French set. Why was Moreri so successful? There are two or three explanations: First, the set was one of the first works to be arranged alphabetically, which made it easy to consult for this or that fact. Second, there was a heavy concentration on interests of the day, particularly biography and history. Third, thanks to constant updating and expansion it was, unlike its predecessors, relatively current. Finally, it was in the vernacular and could be read by almost any literate individual. The day of the current popular encyclopedia was near.[53]

Taking the hint from the Moreri success, Antoine Furetiere (1619–1688) turned from books of comic and satirical verse to the novel. Earlier, his *Scarron's City Romance* (1671) dealt realistically with the Parisian middle classes. While popular, it was considered offensive to the Academie Française, of which Furetiere was a member. Late in 1684 he took an unexpected turn and announced his intention to publish a combination French dictionary and encyclopedia. In open competition with the Academie, which had its own dictionary, Furetiere died before his *Dictionnaire Universel* was published in three volumes at the Hague in 1690.

Furetiere claimed to have worked much of his life on what is an early example of the encyclopaedic dictionary. It set the ground rules for what should be included or excluded in such a combination. Alphabetically arranged, the dictionary-encyclopedia not only was a handy source for etymology and current usage, but stressed the arts and the sciences.[54] The well-balanced approach won immediate success for its publisher. It had a strong influence on similar works throughout the coming centuries. The work was expanded to four volumes in its numerous editions from 1690 to 1727.

The 1704 *Lexicon Technicum* was underwritten by the forty-four year old Royal Society and compiled by John Harris (1666–1719). It heralded the triumph of the general encyclopedia in the eighteenth century and the beginning of the set was made up of the original work of experts rather than the opinions and knowledge of a single compiler. Although the focus was on interests of the scientific-oriented Society, Harris wisely published practical articles to attract a wider audience. He took another major step when he invited scholars of the Society (such as Newton) to contribute both articles and advice. Illustrations were a major addition that established a pattern for sets to come. Harris sought excellent, detailed plates for major articles as well as line drawings throughout the text, which vastly improved the quality and size of what preceded his work. With the addition of selective bibliographies, Harris established the primary attributes of the popular encyclopedia.[55]

If Bacon and Harris were scouts for the general encyclopedia, Ephraim Chambers (1680–1740) was the first to realize how it could be sold to a large, literate population. Building on both Harris's success and his methods, Chambers issued his *Cyclopaedia* in 1728.[56] He stressed relatively easy-to-read articles, a change from Harris, and put more emphasis on the arts and summaries of philosophical systems. His arrangement, illustrations, and general presentation followed Harris, but Chambers added numerous cross-references. The two folio volumes were so well received that the next year Chambers, who began as a map maker, was elected to the Royal Society. In evaluating the editing of the encyclopedia, Collison believes that Chambers was "clearly the father of the modern encyclopaedia throughout the world. . . The influence of Chambers' encyclopaedia has been incalculable."[57]

Diderot's *Encyclopedie*

In an effort to repudiate much of the heritage of the encyclopedia in favor of scientific and advanced thought, Denis Diderot (1713–1784) compiled the most famous encyclopedia of the eighteenth, or any, century[58]: *L'Encyclopedie,* published from 1751 to 1772. Diderot faced such opposition that many of the volumes had to be printed in secret and the last ten were issued under a false imprint. As a symbol as well as a leading achievement of the French Enlightenment, *L'Encyclopedie* had many supporters as it had detractors. The latter normally were found among the nobility and the Catholic church where there was strong opposition to the new humanism. The work had wide appeal for intellectuals and, more important, for the rising middle classes in France as well as Europe, England, and the English colonies.

Each volume of the *Encyclopedie* was testimony to what the Enlightenment considered inevitable—the ultimate perfectibility of people through reason rather than through rigid political and religious systems. The *Prospectus* (1750) established it as a voice of the basic principles and applications of the Enlightenment. *L'Encyclopedie* was more an extended argument for the Enlightenment than a traditional work. Rather than cover numerous topics, Diderot chose to concentrate on those subjects that furthered the cause. The polemics and the approximately one hundred and sixty well-known contributors, from Rousseau, Voltaire, Montesquieu, and Necker to nearly every intellectual of the time,[59] won a wide readership and support. Yet, in retrospect *L'Encyclopedie* served as a platform for a necessary debate rather than entirely as a source of information about the world.

Diderot gathered a group of distinguished contributors and editors. Seventeen volumes of text and eleven volumes of plates were planned. The latter were of exceptional quality, and the three to four thousand illustrations are highly prized for their meticulous attention to people and their activities as well as the technology of the period. The first volume appeared in 1751. The printed set was complete in 1765[60] although the set was not totally finished until 1772, when the volumes of plates appeared. Trouble plagued Diderot all of the way. With the seventh volume in 1758, his coeditor resigned. The government expressed its displeasure and Voltaire volunteered to finance publication of the set outside of France. Diderot declined and carried on with the successful completion of the work. At the end, Diderot was an inch from financial ruin. In order to save him, Catherine the great of Russia bought his library. Between 1774 and his death ten years later, he began withdrawing from public life. His last words might be considered by anyone evaluating an encyclopedia or any reference work: "The first step toward philosophy is incredulity."

Beyond its lofty goals, the set represented a new approach to the form. Influenced by the scientific emphasis on experiment and experience, Diderot became a major publicist for the emerging middle classes. He justified their philosophy of commerce and the good life. To this day the general set reflects middle-class values, differing as much from the personal notes of the Romans as from the cosmos-centered involvement of the Medieval compilers. The encyclopedic movement was an attempt by what has been called French capitalism of the second half of the eighteenth century to legitimize the gains of the technological and intellectual revolutions, for free thought and free trade were not unrelated.[61] Nor are the interests of the primary users of today's encyclopedia that far removed from the interests of the encyclopedia publishers. Each reinforces the other, and, when the encyclopedia fails by not keeping abreast of social, political, and scientific changes, it self destructs.

From Larousse to Brockhaus

What Diderot began, the French and German firms of Larousse and Brockhaus carried to a commercial conclusion. Both houses strongly influenced the development of encyclopedias in the remainder of the nineteenth and throughout the whole of the twentieth century. Specifically, first, they established the "team" of experts to be the primary contributors to popular, general sets. Second, the popular European works favored, as they still do today, the alphabetical, short, specific entry. With exceptions for some countries, important events and ideas, as well as a few individuals, the majority of articles are brief, sometimes no more than one or two hundred words, written so anyone can understand them. Examples of this kind of entry are found in the modern *Britannica's* first part, i.e., the *Micropedia,* and in almost any edition of Larousse or Brockhaus. And third, advertising and salespeople stressed the importance of the sets for the average individual as the ideal reference work.

After Diderot, the major name in French encyclopedias was Pierre Larousse (1817–1875), who established the publishing firm that continues today. His first encyclopedia was a young people's work in 1853, and by 1876 he had completed the fifteen-volume *Grand Dictionnaire Universel du XIX Siecle.* The set employed the specific entry system with short informative articles about topics rather than long monographs, with color illustrations. Subsequent variations (from one volume to sets) usually bear the name of the firm: *Larousse,* which is synonymous in France and throughout the world as a combination dictionary-encyclopedia. Today the publishing house *Larousse* is as familiar in Europe and most of the world as is *Britannica.* At the turn of the century Larousse developed an emphasis on art, so Larousse sets often are the first place to turn for data on artists and specific works of art.

Between 1796 to 1811, after several false starts, the first general, German encyclopedia—David Friederich Brockhaus's (1772–1823) *Koversations-Lexikon*—was published. It began a series of encyclopedias that continues to this day. And also, the Brockhaus effort reached beyond Germany. Its approach was used throughout not only much of Europe but also the United States. The early *Americana,* for example, was based on the 1829–1833 English-language version of the *Brockhaus.*

The German publisher struck on the new idea of updating the set frequently. Editions and supplements were part of the regular planning of the small-to-large sets. The text was developed almost entirely by subject experts, and particularly well-known individuals whose names would help sales. Also, Brockhaus claimed the work covered historical and current events thoroughly. So successful was the set that by 1824, slightly more than a decade after the first edition, a sixth edition was published. By the fifteenth edition (1928–1935), the name of the publisher became part of the title, so today most people simply refer to it by the name *Brockhaus*.[62]

The nineteenth edition of the set is typical of activities of the 1990s. Composed of twenty-four lavishly illustrated volumes, it is updated with supplementary volumes. Besides this large version, Brockhaus has a twelve-volume as well as a single-volume set. And there are other variations. The present set is known for its nationalistic overtones, and for its illustrations, accuracy, and detail. Found in most large American libraries, it is a standard work in the united Germany.

The *Britannica* and the Modern Encyclopedia

Today the best-known general encyclopedia, particularly to laypersons, is the *Encyclopaedia Britannica* whose prestige is matched only by its long and sometimes dramatic history. Its story is the story of all general sets from the eighteenth century to the present: essentially the story of the slow movement from a set for a narrow well-educated public to a growing and dominant middle-class in the nineteenth and early twentieth centuries. After World War I, the needs of the middle classes—and their children—shaped the scope, writing style, and certainly sales practices. What had begun as a scholar's whimsy, a work for a narrow group of intellectuals, became the best-selling reference work of its type for the mass public. So while the history of the *Britannica* is unique in detail, in general it is the story of all encyclopedias, from the late eighteenth century to the present.

First published between 1768 and 1771 in one hundred separate paperbound parts, the *Britannica* is now in its much-revised fifteenth edition, with sales in almost every part of the world. The general encyclopedia had been established in 1728 by Ephraim Chambers, and by 1751 Diderot had begun his great set, completing the text in 1765, or three years before the *Britannica* began publication. Under the editorship of William Smellie, a Scotsman with a love of drink, the first three-volume edition was an odd mixture of myth, fact, and speculation. It was a far cry from the scholarly editions of the nineteenth century, yet it had enough appeal to warrant another edition, this time under the supervision of a hack writer and sometimes theologian James Tytler (1746–1805). The only contributors Smellie had encouraged were those long dead, whom he simply reprinted. For example, John Locke's (1632–1704) short piece on organization of commonplace books was printed in full.

Tytler wrote most of the second edition himself or revised first-edition articles when time ran out. The result was an impressive ten-quarto volumes with 340 plates. Issued from 1778 to 1784, its primary contribution was a focus on biographies historical and current, as well as casting a wider net to include an equally wider world. Tytler was wise enough, as would be later compilers, to avoid controversial topics. In this case he simply ignored the American revolution.[63]

Editors and owners changed, but essentially the set remained much the same until the later nineteenth century. The revolution came with the now-famous ninth edition published in Edinburgh from 1875 to 1888. The set of twenty-five volumes is still referred to today by researchers who see it, along with the eleventh edition, as a landmark in accessible scholarship. Notable, in addition to the text, were the outstanding illustrations, some even in color. The lengthy articles, complete with current bibliographies, were written by experts, with a nice balance between articles with a philosophical, theoretical base and those giving clear explanations of how things work. The set was an immediate success. Despite the long delay between volumes, close to ten thousand sets were sold in England. More remarkable, Americans purchased five times that number, due in no small part to the huckstering ability of Horace Everett Hooper (1859–1922).[64] Hooper was the key person in the popularization of the set. What heretofore had sold well enough to a limited group of better-than-average-educated English people now became international, a part of many public and personal libraries wherever English was read.

Recognizing what the press had understood for many years, Hooper capitalized on the population's higher levels of education, increased literacy, and, equally important, increased money and leisure time. Hooper, a Middle Western salesman, put the encyclopedia within the financial and educational reach of the average person.

The wizardry of taking what was essentially a set for scholars and selling it as fast and furiously as a penny dreadful encouraged a tenth edition, first issued in 1899, in thirty-five volumes. Actually, it was no more than the ninth had been (twenty-four volumes) with an added supplement of eleven new volumes. The triumph of the tenth was not the supplement as much as the index, which had some six hundred thousand entries. Despite the tenth's sales success, there was grumbling about buying essentially an older edition. With that, the publishers set out to develop an entirely new work in the eleventh edition, by and large the most famous and most highly regarded edition yet published.[65]

Unlike previous sets, the eleventh was published entirely at one time, in 1911. The twenty-nine volumes were the last that were prepared in Great Britain. After the eleventh, the publication shifted to the United States. The set gained an international reputation, which it maintains to this day. The emphasis was on long monographs. At the same time, the editors, now able to issue a set as a whole, did afford the reader more subject headings, which made the work easier to use for layperson and scholar alike, despite the gigantic chunks of information. The first attempt at an annual update of an encyclopedia was the *Britannica* yearbook, which covering from 1910 to 1912 was issued in 1913. The outbreak of the First World War delayed any other yearbooks.

In 1922, a three-volume supplement was published for the eleventh edition, which constituted, according to the preface, "in combination with the 29 volumes of the eleventh edition, the twelfth edition." The thirteenth edition was published in 1926, but was little more than the original eleventh with some basic, timely revisions to cover current affairs.

To trace the history of the *Britannica* to the mid 1990s one should begin with the fourteenth edition, published in 1929, for the first time, the shift of the publication to America was evident in the content, which reflected American rather than British interests. Through "continuous revision" the fourteenth was updated until it was replaced by the present fifteenth edition of 1974.

The *Britannica* did particularly well both in England and later in the United States. But it had some competitors, the most noteworthy in England being *Chamber's Encyclopaedia* (1860–1868) that was more grounded in the experience of the average person than the *Britannica* was. The set, which continues to the present day, was subtitled "a dictionary of universal knowledge" and the London publishers, who began in Scotland, attempted to cover material that would be of interest to then-growing middle classes. The encyclopedia was a success and further editions followed regularly.

One of the stranger failures in the history of encyclopedias deserves a note: the twenty-eight volume *Encyclopaedia Metropolitana,* published between 1817 and 1845. As a scholarly work it was to rival the *Britannica,* but it failed to gain an audience because of the long time it took to produce and the lack of consistency in editing. Also, the *Britannica* had gained wide success and popularity, and there was simply no room for another similar work. Today its numerous engraved plates are of prime interest, and the fact that Samuel Taylor Coleridge, in 1817, set out a plan for an "ideal" encyclopedia that guided the *Metropolitana* away from alphabetical order to a classified (and disastrous) arrangement. Within months the poet and the publisher had a falling out, and Coleridge cut his ties with the project.[66]

The first American encyclopedia was combined with a dictionary: Noah Webster's (1758–1843) monumental *American Dictionary of the English Language* (1828). Not only was it the largest English dictionary of the time (70,000 words), but it included encyclopedic information. The short entries not only defined words but gave basic data about subjects, and in this sense followed the lead of the French predecessor Pierre Larousse. If one discounts the early *Britannica* as originating in England and counts *Webster's* dictionary as more than an encyclopedia, then *Encyclopedia Americana,* published in Philadelphia in thirteen volumes between 1829 and 1833, is the first genuine (well, almost genuine) American set. The editor was a German who borrowed liberally from the seventh edition of Brockhaus. By the end of the century, the *Americana* was a well-established set. The second edition (1911) was twenty volumes, edited by the editor of *The Scientific American,* and, understandably, strong in science and technology. A reviewed edition (1918–1920) was issued in thirty volumes. After the third edition, the set was under continuous revision with annuals (1923 to date).

The *Americana* and the *Britannica* are the two major "adult" sets of today; but there are at least another dozen equally good, if not as exhaustive, encyclopedias for other age groups.[67] Interestingly, the great change in these and other twentieth century sets was established in the century. All publishers, then as now, were concerned with reaching the widest, general audience to insure necessary profits and growth. Focusing on broadening the audience, publishers developed more attractive layouts, easy-to-understand articles, numerous and current illustrations, and accurate indexes. Beyond their common understanding of the audience, the modern sets differ in many ways from the late nineteenth and early twentieth century encyclopedias. Two examples are continuous revision of existing editions, usually of about 10 percent of the basic contents and a complete updating of easy-to-spot current affairs and annual supplements that give the owner some confidence that the set is being kept current.

Another development is the growth of the subject-specialized sets with in-depth coverage of items that might be of only limited interest in general works. A cursory glance at a library shelf will reveal that there are encyclopedias for every discipline from science and art to sociology and the humanities. In between one finds work devoted to such things as gambling, trivia, and particular historical periods. As important economically to publishers as it is pedagogically to teachers and parents, the children's encyclopedias are primarily a twentieth-century invention. The first children's set was compiled by Johann Wagenseil in the seventeenth century; but for all practical purposes children's encyclopedias did not become popular (and extremely lucrative) until the *World Book* began publishing shortly before the end of the First World War. Arthur Mee (1875–1943) was the pioneer in children's sets, which gained wide popularity by stressing themes common to study in most schools. Arranged thematically, the sets were easy to read, follow, and, more important, fit into the curriculum.[68]

What is more likely to upset the emphasis of the nineteenth century founders of the modern encyclopedia is the new technology. Between CD-ROMs and online hypertext, a user may search the whole set simultaneously and then print out, or hear, or read bits and parts that may make up a quite lengthy entry . . . created by the user, not by the editors of the set. As for the next century, let a well-known author speculate. In the twentieth century, "the traditional encyclopedias in general use for the previous two centuries began experiencing a Serious Crisis, in that their information was out of date the moment it left the printers . . . This led to the compilation of . . . an encyclopedia that was a collection of entries consisting of Predictions of the Future."[69] The *Extelopedia* for example, "contains information about history as it is going to happen."

Notes for Chapter 2

1. Jesse Gellrich, *The Idea of the Book in the Middle Ages* (Ithaca, N.Y.: Cornell University Press, 1985), 18. The focus of this chapter is on Western encyclopedias, which is not to discount the contributions of other cultures. Non-Western encyclopedias are not included because of our lack of space not their lack of importance. See, Robert Collison, *Encyclopaedias: Their History through the Ages* (Kingston: Hafner, 1964). Throughout his history, he traces the development of non-Western encyclopedias, and particularly those from China. He notes that the first Chinese encyclopedia was prepared about 220, "but no part of this work, nor of several of its successors, has survived." (p. 26) The first recorded Arabic encyclopedia was in the ninth century (p. 37–38).

2. *The Oxford English Dictionary (OED),* vol. 3 (Oxford: Clarendon Press, 1933), explores the historical aspect of the "encyclopaedia," or "encyclopedia" in English and explains the form as an erroneous reading of the Greek phrase "occurring MSS of Quintilian, Pliny, and Galen for 'encyclical education,' the circle of arts and sciences" (p. 153).

3. Plato often is given credit as the first encyclopedist, although he never systematically compiled such a work. The title was conferred on him because of his effort to synthesize all Greek knowledge up to his time or to create a type of encyclopedia out of various treatises that discussed what was then known about all areas of knowledge.

4. In the preface to his *Natural History,* Pliny explains the scope of his work, and in so doing he uses the term "encyclic," e.g., "Deserving of treatment before all things are the subjects included by the Greeks under the name of Encyclic Culture." (Preface, 15). Vitruvius sometimes known as Mamurra (c. 61 B.C.), in his *De architectura* mentions "encyclios paideia," (pp. 1, 7) and Quintilian (c. A.D. 30–100) employed the term in the sense of a course of study. Encyclopaedia was used in English in 1531 as "the circle of doctrine" and in 1533 by Rabelais, e.g., *Pantagruel* is visited by an English scholar who in satire points out that Pantagruel opens to him the true power of an encyclopedie (p. 20). Furthermore, a Flemish scholar, Joachim Ringelbergh was the first to use "cyclopaedia" in a title of the form (Basle, 1541). See Collison, *Encyclopaedias: Their History through the Ages,* 80. See his fine summary of encyclopedias in the *Encyclopaedia Britannica.*

5. Actually, in the thirteenth century Roger Bacon sought without success to compile an encyclopedia using experts. While all individual compilers

quoted authors at length, encyclopedias remained the work of an individual. Only with John Harris in the eighteenth century was an effort made to recruit experts to compile a work, i.e., his *Lexicon Technicum* of 1704. A few one-volume encyclopedias continued to be the work of individuals up to the late twentieth century, e.g., Stephen Vincent Benét's *Reader's Encyclopedia* (3rd ed., 1987).

6. There were exceptions, and one of the earliest works was actually in alphabetical arrangement, i.e., Marcus Verrius Flaccus (fl. 20 B.C.) composed a alphabetically arranged encyclopedia that is completely lost, although it was plagiarized by others, such as second-century compiler Sextus Festus. Even Festus's work has disappeared except for minor sections. Another more esoteric problem that follows the historic encyclopedia stream concerns the difference between a "dictionary" and an "encyclopedia," at least when both are arranged alphabetically. See, for example, Tom McArthur, *Worlds of Reference* (Cambridge: Cambridge University Press, 1988), 102–105. For practical purposes scholars and laypersons alike appreciate the difference between the two forms, as does the *Britannica* (vol. 18, 277): "A dictionary explains words, whereas an encyclopaedia explains things . . . While a modern encyclopaedia may still be called a dictionary, no good dictionary has ever been called an encyclopaedia." A linguistic professor and novelists put it another way: "Roughly speaking . . . one can say that a dictionarylike representation should concern a merely linguistic competence while an encyclopedialike representation should take into account, as is commonly said, the whole of our world knowledge." Umberto Eco, "Metaphor, Dictionary, and Encyclopedia," *New Literary History* (Winter 1984): 255. See his complete article (pp. 255–271) for a refined explanation of the ongoing argument. (For further discussion, see the section on Antoine Furetiere and note 63 below).

7. Varro is a good illustration of early Roman-Sabine education. "He tells how, as a lad, he had but a single toga and tunic, sandals, but no legcoverings, no saddle for his horse, and rarely the pleasure of a proper bath." (Stanley Bonner, *Education in Ancient Rome* (Berkeley, Calif.: University of California Press, 1977), 4). This eccentric life was much admired and served him well as an officer with Pompey in 67 B.C. He was on Pompey's side against Caesar, but pardoned by the latter. After Caesar's assassination, Anthony sought Varro's death, but Varro escaped and later secured the patronage of Augustus. He lived the remainder of his life in peace and quiet.

8. McArthur points out that the work just as well might have been called "General Knowledge," although most of the emphasis reflects Pliny's interest in science. "Equally . . . it could be argued that Pliny was the father of the scientific treatises, the monographs, and even the textbook." In addition to content, Pliny's major gift to the word was his striking on a logical arrangement of data—a taxonomy used by encyclopedia compilers for centuries to come. After a preface and a chapter on the universe (including,

ironically, volcanoes and fire), he moves to geography, the human race, animal, birds and insects, trees and agriculture, medicine and drugs, metals, painting and finally minerals. McArthur, *Worlds of Reference,* 44.

9. The concept "it must be right because it is written (printed)" held true for Pliny for almost fourteen hundred years. Although he had, quite naturally, numerous mistakes of fact and judgment, not until the end of the fifteenth century did anyone point out—at least in a published work—the errors in a set that had been followed, plagiralized, and copied for centuries. In his *Institutio oratorie,* Quintilian gives an example of an earlier fabricator, in this case, the Greek playwright Sophocles (496–406 B.C.), whom he accuses of telling people "how amber is formed in the lands beyond India from the tears shed for Meleager by the birds known as Meleager's Daughters." The document is not extant and some believe Sophocles never made the statement, particularly as he was unlikely to have ever seen amber. Still, it illustrates a point about accuracy. Quintilian, *Institutio oratorie,* Book 37/41.

10. H. Rackman in "Preface" to Pliny *Natural History.* Vol. 1, Loeb Classics (Cambridge: Harvard University Press, 1932), viii.

11. Ibid, 21–23. Pliny identifies sometimes authors and sometimes titles of books.

12. Ibid.

13. Ibid., p. xii. In effect, Pliny had been keeping commonplace books from his reading. He later revised and organized his notes for his encyclopedia. But at his death "he bequeathed 160 sets of notes on selected books, written on both sides of the paper in an extremely small hand."

14. Michael Grant, ed., *Roman Readings* (New York: Penguin Books, 1958), 352–54. (This is the young man's letter to Tacitus.)

15. John Boardman, et al., ed., *The Oxford History of the Classical World* (Oxford University Press, 1986), 576–77.

16. R.R. Bolgar, *The Classical Heritage* (New York: Cambridge University Press, 1954), 43. See the chapter on ready reference for a discussion on florilegium.

17. Plagiarism was a common enough aspect of early encyclopedias, and Pliny summarized it all with: "In comparing various authors with one another, I have discovered that some of the greatest and latest writers have transcribed, word for word, from former works, without making acknowledgement." Pliny, *Natural History,* Bk.1, Sect. 22, Dedication.

18. An edict of the Christian emperor, Justinian, in A.D. 541 closed the nine-hundred-year-old Academy at Athens at about the same time Benedict's monastery at Monte Cassino began to influence all of Europe. "The golden chain" as it was fondly styled, "of the Platonic succession" was broken, but taken up by the European monastic communities. Edward Gibbon, *The Decline and Fall of the Roman Empire,* vol. 4, (London: Everyman's Library, 1981), 206.

19. L.D. Reynolds and N.G. Wilson, *Scribes & Scholars,* 2d ed. (Oxford: Clarendon Press, 1968), 73.

20. Leslie Jones, ed., *An Introduction to Divine and Human Readings* (New York: Columbia University Press, 1946), 25. In addition to his introduction, the author has translated the whole of the *Institutes.* See, too, James J. O'Connell, *Cassiodorus* (Berkeley, Calif.: University of California Press, 1979). St. Benedict's Rule included a preface and seventy-three brief chapters or sections that outline the daily life of the monks. There are instructions to set apart of each day for reading as well as the appointment of a lector to read aloud at meal times. "The purpose of the Rule is not to lay down ordinances for a new foundation or even for a new monastic order, but to amend laxity . . ." M.L.W. Laistner, *Thought and Letters in Western Europe,* Ithaca, N.Y.: Cornell University Press, 1957, p. 94. The first book is divided into thirty-three chapters. "The number 33 was sanctified by the year of Christ's life. Augustine's treatise " 'Contra Faustum. . .' has 33 books, Cassiodorus's *Institutiones* 33 chapters." The idea of medieval number symbolism is found in many encyclopaedias of the period. See Ernst Curtius, *European Literature and the Latin Middle Ages* (New York: Pantheon, 1953), 504–6. During the Dark Ages there was no consensus on what specifically constituted the seven liberal arts, e.g., Cassiodorus had one notion, Augustine another, although the basics remained much the same. There was a strong emphasis on practical matters, like arithmetic and geometry while oratory (although not rhetoric) was played down as monks were unlikely to be addressing large assemblies. Cassiodorus had another argument for the study of the seven liberal arts, and, in this particular case, the sciences. "With reason do our holy Fathers persuade us that the sciences ought to be pursued by those who are fond of learning, for these studies are in large measure instrumental in drawing our desire away from carnal matters and in making us desire things which . . . we can see with the mind alone." Jones, *Introduction to Divine and Human,* chap. 111, 2d bk., 180.

21. *Curtius, European Literature and Latin Middle Ages,* 450.

22. Jones, *Introduction to Divine and Human Readings,* 480. "Above all Cassiodorus stresses the need for acquaintance with the liberal arts." M.L.W. Laistner, *Thought and Letters* 99. The physical Vivarium monastic community seems to have died with Cassiodorus. His library, in part, eventually found its way to Rome.

23. "Presumably Isidore from the first was destined for the Church . . . He succeeded his brother as bishop of Seville (in c. A.D. 600), occupying that see until his death in 636 . . . No other trustworthy facts are recorded of his life which was mainly given over to scholarship . . . Isidore was a polymath whose literary pursuits touched every branch of human knowledge." M.L.W. Laistner, *Thought and Letters,* 119–20.

24. Reynolds and Wilson, Scribes and Scholars, 74.

25. Ernest Brehaut, *An Encyclopedist of the Dark Ages* (reissued by Burt

Franklin, e.d., New York: Columbia University Press, 1912, 1951), 23. See, too Marina Smyth, "Isidore of Seville and Early Irish Cosmography," *Cambridge Medieval Celtic Studies* 14 (Winter 1987): 69–102, a fascinating study on how Isidore's work came to Ireland and Europe.

26. Ibid., 28. The "ancients" were almost all Roman, and where Greek authors are cited, they are cited in Latin translation. The almost total reliance on reading rather than observation, as with the Romans before him, resulted in an encyclopedia with repeated references to centuries before, but almost nothing about the time in which Isidore lived.

27. Ibid., 24. As usual, Isidore's contribution is a point of disagreement among historians and literary critics. Reynolds and Wilson (*Scribes and Scholars,* 75), for example, claim it "descends so often into false etymologizing and the uncritical parade of absurd bric-a-brac that it cannot be read without a smile." Laistner fires back (*Thought and Letters,* 123) "It is easy to sneer at the *Etymologiae* and to point to single items in the book that strike a modern reader as puerile. But it was assuredly no small achievement to put together a compendious encyclopedia of the arts and sciences from many sources, at a time when the larger works of earlier authors on different branches of human knowledge were accessible in very few places, and when few men, in any event, would have been capable of studying them."

28. Curtius, *European Literature and Latin Middle Ages,* 451–52. Here Curtius gives in detail the chronology for history and literature as explained by Isidore.

29. Ibid., 453.

30. Judith Herrin, *The Formations of Christendom* (Oxford: Blackwell, 1987), 246. Isidore exercised strong influence for centuries to come, and there are innumerable references to his work by later writers. His contribution is primarily an indication to readers that there had been and might be again such a thing as secular writing. His influence can be traced in writings as late as Sir John Mandeville's travels (published in French between 1357 and 1371) and the English poet John Gower's fourteenth century *Confessio amantis* (*A Lover's confession*).

31. As several modern scholars have demonstrated, the source material is more complex than it had been thought to be. It was not simply a revision of Isidore. Much of the material came from other works. At any rate, he increased the usefulness of his encyclopedia for medieval readers by introducing allegorical and mystical interpretations not contained in Isidore. See *Dictionary of the Middle Ages,* vol. 6 (New York: Charles Scribner's Sons, 1985), 307. The author notes that Hrabanus's reforming zeal resulted in harsh treatment of a monk who had "the greatest lyric talent of the ninth century." Gottschalk of Orbais was imprisoned for life through the efforts of Hrabanus.

32. The sometimes pejorative scholasticism is no more than a descriptor of Christian school philosophy and methods. Out of scholasticism

developed an intellectual autonomy, reflected in the encyclopedias, particularly in the sets that flourished in the golden age of scholasticism in the thirteenth century. By the end of the fourteenth century, the drive toward new knowledge, rather than compilations of the old, took the encyclopedia and its compiler in another direction—a direction that spelled the death of the long-lived scholastic method.

33. After entering the Abbey of St. Victor in Paris, Hugh demonstrated an unusual command of contemplation, Biblical study, and theology. Known as the second Augustine, Hugh mastered all three areas, which made him able to convince others of the necessity of organizing materials in a systematic way for scholars and for students.

34. Bolgar, *The Classical Heritage* 232.

35. "The very title of the word, places it squarely in a long antecedent tradition of 'didascalic,' or 'didactic,' literature concerned in various ways with what arts of disciplines a man should study and why he should acquire them." (Jerome, p. 3). It is a familiar tradition going back to Cassiodorus and Isidore, as well as to the Roman compilers such as Varro and his lost work.

Hugh had limited competition for the time, although several works at least suggested encyclopedia-like scope. An outstanding example is *The Mirror of the World* of about 1100. Probably compiled by Honorius Augustodunensis (c. 1075–1156), the much-revised set was composed of three books covering geography, chronology, and an abbreviated history. Most of the content was drawn from Church Fathers and particularly Bede (c. 673–735) and his *Ecclesiastical History of the English Nation,* which covers the period from the conquest of Caesar of England to about 731. Thanks to a good style and numerous entertaining as well as thought-to-be-informative facts, the combination of secular and theological tradition and legend proved a great success and was often translated into the vernacular. There were perhaps a half dozen or so similar titles in the twelfth century, filled more with anecdotes and eccentric ideas than specific facts.

36. *The Didascalicon of Hugh of St. Victor* (New York: Columbia University Press, 1961). See below, Taylor, translator of the *Didascalicon,* for the relevant points that set it apart from earlier encyclopedias. Jerome Taylor, *The Origin and Early Life of Hugh of St. Victor* (Notre Dame, Ind.: University of Notre Dame, 1957), 28–36.

37. Ibid, 6, 82, 44.

38. Bolgar, *The Classical Heritage,* 232–33. The importance of Hugh's work can be seen in its survival in close to a hundred manuscripts from the twelfth through fifteenth centuries found in libraries from Ireland to Poland. The *Didascalicon,* as Isidore's encyclopedia, must be considered as a whole, a work to read cover to cover, and not simply a place to turn for facts.

39. Hugh's summa failed to capture the imagination. Peter Lombard's (c. 1100–1160) summa, *Four Books of Sentences,* which stressed Augustine, gained real importance. Its success lay in the commentaries by other scholars.

40. A critical edition from Cologne numbers forty volumes, and some are in several parts. For a bibliography, see *Dictionary of the Middle Ages,* vol. 1, 129–130.

41. Before the general use of "encyclopedia" as a descriptor and particularly in ancient and medieval times, numerous metaphors were employed, the most frequent of which were (1) Book of Treasures or gifts, which indicated accumulating information or treasures, such as the work of Brunetto Latini; (2) The Mirror or Image of the World (*imago mundi*) usually transmitted by a mirror (*speculum*); (3) A related expression involved the knowledge of the world's nature, such as Raban Maur's *De naturis rerum;* or properties (*de propriatibus rerum*); and (4) Tree of Knowledge, particularly after Bacon constructed the hierarhtical classification of knowledge. The Arabs and Chinese used similar metaphors.

42. Here, as in numerous works of this type, there are definite roots for the growth of anti-Semitism, and, for that matter, anti-anything that was not Catholic. In bk 25 and the following twenty-eight chapters (about twelve printed pages) is a rewritten version of Petrus Alfonsi's *Dialogi contra Judaeos,* the most influential and widely ready of all medieval anti-Jewish tracts. For a detailed description of the original work, see Tolan, *Petrus Alfonsi,* particularly chap. 5. Vincent's *Speculum* played an important role in the diffusion of Alfonsi's anti-Jewish polemic. Unfortunately Vincent "expunged the voice and the arguments of Moses, a rational Jew who could argue intelligently against Christianity in the name of Judaism and Islam," Tolan, Petrus Alfonsi, 126.

43. Reynolds and Wilson, *Scribes and Scholars,* 102.

44. *Dictionary of the Middle Ages,* 454.

45. Edward Lutz, *Roger Bacon's Contribution to Knowledge,* (New York: Wagner, 1936. (*Franciscan Studies* 17 (June 1936) p. 76. Gives a somewhat popular history of his life, times, and works.

46. *Dictionary of National Biography,* vol. 2, 377.

47. *Dictionary of the Middle Ages,* vol. 2, 41. Other studies and writings are treaties on optics, alchemy, languages, astronomy, and flying machines as well as ships and carriages. Francis described, for the first time in Europe, the process of making gunpowder.

48. Latini was a prominent teacher, as well as an official and he put great stress on culture and proper speech for the officials and merchants of Florence. His fame rests mainly on the central role assigned to him in canto XV of Dante's *Inferno,* on the basis of which a "master pupil" relationship has been generally assumed between Latini and Dante. *Dictionary of the Middle Ages,* vol. 7, 382.

49. People sometimes confuse the two Bacons with each other, particularly as both worked in similar areas and both compiled encyclopedias. John Dee was the famous English alchemist and mathematician.

50. For a lively sketch of Bacon's life, see *Aubrey's Brief Lives,* (New York: Penguin Books, 1987). For example, Bacon would often "drink a good

draught of strong Beer, to lay his working fancy asleep, which otherwise would keep him from sleeping great part of the night" (p. 321). Bacon's many notes and materials for his not-to-be-completed encyclopedia were published later (*Sylva sylvarum*) and are found in his collected works.

51. For detailed histories of encyclopedias for the seventeenth and eighteenth centuries, see Frank Kafker, *Notable Encyclopedias of the Seventeenth and Eighteenth Centuries* (1981); and his *Notable Encyclopedias of the Late Eighteenth Century* (1994). Both published by Oxford University Press. See, too, Clorinda Donato and Robert Maniques, eds., *The Encyclopedie and the Age of Revolution.* Boston: G.K. Hall, 1992.

52. Christofle de Savigny (1530–1608) was among the earliest modern compilers to attempt to systematize all knowledge by demonstrating the interrelationship of the various branches of knowledge. His *Tableaux accomplis de tous les arts liberaux . . .* was published in Paris in 1587. Today it is noteworthy for its complicated and highly imaginative diagrams. It is virtually impossible to understand.

53. What would be called today a "spin-off" was published three years after Louis Moreri's encyclopedia (in 1697) and was edited by Protestant philosopher Peter Bayle (1647–1706). Moreri's basic text was summarized, and Bayle added quotations, anecdotes, annotations, and commentaries. He cleverly had left in place the primary text, but had radically changed the message by his original notes and additions. This "edition" of the *Dictionnaire Historique et Critique* was condemned by the Catholics as well as the Calvinists who claimed Bayle was an atheist in disguise. Bayle's contribution to the history of encyclopedias was not so much his message as his method. Subversive criticism in this oblique method was employed by others in eighteenth century works. Bayle's unusual claim to fame today is that he was a pioneer, if not the founder of the footnote. In an effort to discredit Descartes's (*Discourse on Method,* Bayle filled his encyclopedia with footnotes and footnotes of footnotes. While no one knows who penned the first footnote, the French philosopher (Bayle) began the process in a systematic fashion. See Anthony Grafton, *The Tragic Origins of the German Footnote* (Cambridge: Harvard University Press, 1997).

54. Alain Rey, *Encyclopedies et Dictionnaires,* Paris: Presses Universitaires, 1982. In his first two chapters Rey points out the similarities and differences between dictionaries and encyclopedias. The dictionary has all the words related to the art of say, beekeeping, in alphabetical order; the encyclopedia draws those same words together into a single article on beekeeping. In a dictionary, words and their definitions are important in themselves. In an encyclopedia, they join to support the discourse. In a sense the two forms join in the dictionary-encyclopedia (particular to Europe) where the word may be defined and a short article follows. But even here, one would not go essentially for definitions, but for information about what the word(s) indicate. This is known as "specific entry."

55. The ultimate tribute to Harris came from the French, who heretofore had sent translated versions of their encyclopedias to England and now copied his work. The original 1704 work was reprinted in England in 1708 and a fifth edition of two volumes in 1736. A supplement was added in 1744.

56. Although they have the same name, the modern *Chamber's Encyclopaedia* and the original *Cyclopaedia* by Ephraim Chambers have no connection. The former, which began publishing in the mid-nineteenth century, was from the Scottish publishers, William and Robert Chambers, who were in no way related to Ephraim.

57. Collison, *Encyclopedias: Their History through the Ages,* New York; Knopt, 1992, p. 103–4. The organization, scope, intended audience, etc. had a strong influence on the French and English, and particularly Diderot.

58. See P.N. Furbank, *Diderot: A Critical Biography* 1992. As one of the outstanding men of letters of the eighteenth century, Diderot was involved in almost as many areas as his encyclopedia was—making contributions to philosophy, drama, scientific theories, and fiction. He became interested in translation as a method of earning a living, and the publisher Andre Le Breton suggested the Chambers *Cyclopaedia* be turned over to him for a French edition. This proved less than satisfactory, and Diderot launched an original set with the backing of more than two thousand subscribers. The first volume (1751) was attacked by the Jesuits and suppressed. Diderot overcame that problem and was up to volume 7 (1757) when an article on Geneva managed to antagonize everyone, Catholics and Protestants. And so it went until the complete set was issued. There are countless articles and books on Diderot's encyclopedia. Among the best are Robert Darnton, *The Business of Enlightenment* (Cambridge: Harvard University Press, 1979); John Louch, ed., *Essays on the Encyclopedie of Diderot* (Oxford: Oxford University Press, 1968); and Robert Maniquis, ed., *The Encyclopedie and the Age of Revolution,* Boston: G.K. Hall, 1992.

59. Actually, according to Voltaire, about three-quarters of the articles were the work of Chevalier Louis de Jaucourt (1704–1779) who, among other things, challenged the ideology of Bourbon absolutism. Diderot, "threw the last volumes together haphazardly, leaning more and more on the faithful Jaucourt, who copied and compiled tirelessly and saw the book through to the end." Darnton agrees with Voltaire, saying that Jaucourt, "the nobleman who could trace his lineage well back into the Middle Ages, wrote about one fourth of the entire text," but points out that many of these were short entries. Darnton, *The Business of Enlightenment,* 13, 15. Diderot, who made other numerous contributions, did not find out until 1764 that his coeditor had for years been censoring his articles, rewriting them before publication. (The approved galleys by Diderot were secretly changed by his coeditor and as Diderot did not check the final printed version that carefully, the deletions and additions were not noticed for many years.) C.J.

Panckoucke (1736–1798) published a supplement and index and decided to issue a new, enlarged edition. He received permission and began issuing his *Encyclopedie,* which went on after his death and was not completed until 1832 in 166 volumes.

60. Diderot's encyclopedia is an outstanding example of the subscription reference work that normally was issued over a period of years. The individual literally subscribed to the promised set, agreeing to pay so much per volume, usually as issued. If the publisher did not get enough subscribers or if the first volume proved a failure, the project usually was abandoned—often leaving the advance-payment subscribers with nothing for their money.

61. Stephen Gendzier, ed., *Denis Diderot's The Encyclopedia Selections* (New York: J&J Harper Editions, 1967). This volume offers excellent selections from the set, well translated and usually easy enough to understand.

62. See Collison, *Encyclopedias: Their History through the Ages,* chap. 6 for a chronology of the various editions through 1960. In the Second World War the Leipzig headquarters, occupied by the publisher for 125 years, was destroyed. When the city was taken over by the Russians, the firm moved to Wiesbaden.

63. A Philadelphia publisher, Thomas Dobson, managed to publish the first American pirated edition of the *Britannica* in 1798 in eighteen volumes, based on the eighteen-volume third edition of 1788 to 1797. He deleted the dedication to George III and substituted new articles for those he thought had a British bias. It appeared almost as rapidly as its prototype, at one third the price. Considerably enlarged and with 542 plates, the third edition was notable for attention to individual countries.

The fourth edition (1801–1810) was increased by two volumes and some forty plates to about 16,000 pages, as compared to about 2,670 pages in the first edition. A twenty-volume fifth edition, approximately the same size as the third, was completed in 1814. A six-volume supplement, which for the first time included initials of contributors at the end of the longer articles, was published in 1824. The sixth edition, pretty much a reprint of the previous one with some supplemental material, came out in 1820–1823 in the by-now-standard twenty volumes. The seventh edition (1827–1842) is noteworthy for being the first to include a separate index volume. The eighth edition (1853–1861) was now twenty-one volumes, including the index. There were 402 plates.

64. For the fascinating story of Hooper and the *Britannica,* see Herman Kogan, *The Great EB* (Chicago: University of Chicago Press, 1958).

65. A frequent version of the eleventh edition, found in many American second hand bookstores, was issued in 1915, four years after the main set, and was in a format photographically reduced from 9 × 12 in. to 6 × 8 in., and sold at half the price of the larger work. More than two hundred thousand sets were sold before it was withdrawn in 1923–1924. The contents of the two versions were identical.

66. Collison, *Encyclopedias: Their History through the Ages,* devotes two appendices to information on the role played by Coleridge, including Appendix II, Coleridge's general introduction, or "preliminary treatise on method."

67. The history of the modern encyclopedia since the Second World War deserves a book in itself and is more concerned with business tactics than with scholarly concerns. The period is particularly noteworthy for the development of national sets from the Japanese *Kodansha Encylopedia* to similar sets from Canada to Australia. National works, of course, existed from the beginning, but they became increasingly popular after the Second World War. Another notable development was the growth of the subject encyclopedia. Some suggestion of what makes up the major sets today will be found in William Katz, *Introduction to Reference Work,* 7th ed. (New York: McGraw Hill, 1996). For a detailed report on current sets, nothing is superior to Ken Kister, *Best Encyclopedias,* 2d ed., Oryx Press, 1994. See, too, the biweekly and annual reports on current sets in the "Reference Books Bulletin" section of the American Library Association's *Booklist* magazine.

68. See Collison, *Encyclopedias: Their History through the Ages,* and Kister, *Best Encyclopedias,* for information on the history and the state of current children's sets.

69. Stanislaw Lem, "Offering Vestrand's Extelopedia in 44 Magnetombes," *New Yorker,* 2 April 1984, 38.

3

Commonplace Books to Books of Quotations

> Of all the kinds of book the one that entices you least is surely the common-place book: the book you read, or possibly write, in the lavatory. Yet it hooks you and engages you intimately with the essential qualities of the writer . . . The reader must dig about for truffles, yet when that process is over, it is the atmosphere, the essential attitude that will thrill the most unlikely people.[1]

The commonplace book and the encyclopedia, in earlier centuries some-times difficult to differentiate, are among the oldest forms of reference works. Today the encyclopedia is a fixture in library and home. Its cousin—the commonplace (or common-place) book, the basic reference source for students, scholars, and laypersons from classical Greece through the nine-teenth century—is all but forgotten. In a blank book the reader jotted down memorable quotations, anecdotes, passages, and the like from reading or from listening.[2] Most educated persons kept such a book and used it as ref-erence source for sharpening, embellishing, or improving a speech, letter, conversation, or any type of discourse. Today the same might be accom-plished by drawing from a book of quotations or an encyclopedia.

Normally, when one speaks of "commonplace," it is an umbrella term for a collection of quotations, aphorisms, maxims, anecdotes, proverbs, adages, and, in some cases, long passages taken from favored books. Less usual is the inclusion of music, poetry in full, and conversation. (The latter tends to be put under "table talk.") Some published and personal commonplace books might include only one of these forms.[3] With the advent of printing and the wide distribution of books, publishers took the commonplace books of major public figures and sold them to a wider public. By the eigh-teenth century, the printed commonplace was a basic reference source in countless homes.

Throughout the centuries there were two approaches to the common-place. The most usual was for an individual to maintain his or her own record of what was to be preserved from reading. The principle is familiar to anyone who takes notes from text, novel, lecture, or conversation. The notes, usually arranged in some type of order, are used by the compiler for everything from ideas for speeches and letters to a source for inspiration and, yes, help to pass an exam.

Aristotle (384–322 B.C.) and Cicero (106–143 B.C.) established and refined the commonplace book, which reached a zenith of popularity with Erasmus (1466–1536) and Joseph Lang (1570–1615). Ben Jonson (1572–1637) published a best seller of sorts in his *Timer, or Discoveries* based on his daily reading and views of the human race. The commonplace swerved toward the essay with Samuel Butler (1612–1680) and, by the eighteenth and nineteenth centuries, took on the distinctive format of a highly personalized notebook. Hester Thrale (1741–1821), for example, jotted down her impressions of Dr. Johnson and his circle in her commonplace books. Thomas Jefferson (1743–1826) recorded his thoughts as did Henry David Thoreau (1817–1862). Modern authors from E.M. Forster (1879–1970), and W.H. Auden (1907–1973) to Wallace Stevens (1879–1955) noted their views of the world, although by their time the true commonplace book was moribund. In his *Interplay* (Oxford: Oxford University Press, 1995) even the English poet and critic, D. J. Enright qualified his Collection as "a kind of commonplace book." It is more general and free-ranging than the traditional genre. It depends, too, on acute reading—a skill rapidly disappearing with the commonplace book.

Francis Bacon (1561–1626) claimed "the entry of commonplaces to be a matter of great use and essence in studying . . . A man would do well to carry a pencil in his pocket, and write down the thoughts of the moment." Benjamin Franklin (1706–1790) echoed the claim, "Read with a pen in your hand, and enter in a book hints of what from reading you find that is curious or may be useful."[4] Accumulated material served as rhetorical ammunition. "Thus, to praise or vituperate an individual, one could proceed regularly through a sequence praising or vituperating his family, sex, age, education, physical constitution, state of life, character and occupation."[5] One simply turned to the right topic (i.e., subject) or the specific entry for any need. The ideal book, which grew in dimensions over the centuries, contained something about almost everything.[6] Usually, too, the material was presented in terms of vice and virtue so one could ransack the pages to support or attack.

Thomas Dekker (1572–1632) gives a contemporary hint as to the use of the commonplace book in company in his times: "After a turn or two in the room . . . have some epigrams . . . or sonnets . . . and though it be none of your own, swear you made it."[7] Some years later Thomas Fuller (1608–1661), employing the metaphor of the intellectual at war, wrote, "Divide (learning) between the memory and the notebooks . . . A commonplace book contains many notions in garrison, whence the owner may draw out an army into the field on competent warning."[8] While one might turn to commonplace book as a type of prompter, the ideal was to have memorized its contents. As Max Thomas puts it, "Commonplace books are about memory . . . The commonplace book is like a record of what that memory might look like.[9]

By the late nineteenth century, and the virtual demise of the form, a still enthusiastic professor pointed out that commonplace books assisted in self-educating individuals, "I hope to show this habit to be of use to every man, somewhat as the post office is." He listed the benefits—it helps one to retain the contents of books; it is a method of increasing mental activity by compelling the compiler to think what should and should not be included from the reading; and it is a "fault book for correction," i.e., it demonstrates how little one really knows. The professor, James D. Butler, claimed a man in his mid-sixties found "in the practice a new birth—a higher birth."[10] Due as much to changes in education and mass distribution of reading materials as to developments of new reference forms, the commonplace book did not, as Butler hoped, become as familiar as the post office in the twentieth century. It virtually disappeared.

Early Commonplace Books

In *Topica*, and *Rhetorica* (c. 361 B.C.), Aristotle set the ground rules for the first commonplace books—rules that were applicable to rhetoric. "We should select," he wrote, "from the written handbooks of arguments, and should draw up sketch-lists of them upon each several kinds of subject, putting them down under separate headings, e.g., 'On Good,' or 'On Life.'[11] The result would be a storehouse of images, similes, metaphors, precepts, and ideas that could assist in developing and winning arguments and/or developing speeches of praise or persuasion. There were standard loci (topics) for military and political praise.[12]

Individual Greeks and Romans kept their own commonplace books and developed methods of instruction that used the reference work. Students might turn to the collections of materials that were both a type of commonplace book and aids in the classic Greek notions of *enkyklios paideia,* or "the rounded education." The reference texts later developed into the familiar encyclopedia, but not until Pliny's *Historia Naturalis,* well after the fall of the Roman republic in A.D. 23–79.

The published commonplace book, despite some outstanding examples, was not evident in antiquity. One might argue that Plutarch's collection of biographies (A.D. 46–120) was a type of commonplace, as was Pliny's history; but this is to stretch a definition. Extant examples of widely distributed commonplaces are fewer than a dozen. Many more simply disappeared.

Later, from Cicero to the fall of Rome and to the early Christian period, rules for rhetoric inevitably included advice on the commonplace book. At least a few teachers went much further and would include not only excerpts to illustrate a point, but also whole sections and even whole books from other writers. Despite metaphysical and philosophical considerations the driving force was similar to the one for compilers of encyclopedias. Essentially people believed, or wanted to believe, that human knowledge could be adequately reduced to brief essentials, that it could all be epitomized almost by a mechanical, and even a ritualistic, process of distillation.[13]

Chrysippus (c. 280–206 B.C.), the Greek logician and Stoic philosopher, is credited with about 750 books, although few are extant. According to Montaigne (1533–1592), Chrysippus was familiar with commonplace books. He "scattered through his books not passages simply, but whole works of other authors, and in one, the "Medea" of Euripides. Apollodorus said that, if there were cut out of his work what was foreign to it, the paper would be blank."[14]

Cicero, always at the center of political and personal storms in Rome, composed his *De oratore* at about age fifty. The dialogue, among other things, considers the value of rhetorical rules and addresses the commonplace book. Cicero, who was to be assassinated some thirteen years later (43 B.C.), established the use of *loci* for interpretation of facts in argumentation. His guide, which can be read today as a practical manual for speakers and orators, suggested there was much more to good speaking than memory. There are three principles of rhetoric, one of which depends on the commonplace. "The three principles . . . are the winning of men's favour, secondly their enlightenment, thirdly their excitement."[15] For the second principle one should "have in readiness sundry commonplaces which will instantly present themselves for setting forth the case." Elsewhere, Cicero points out that "the highest distinction of eloquence consists in amplification by means of ornament."[16] The "ornament," from proverbs to metaphors, was the heart of the commonplace book. Julius Caesar (100–44 B.C.), as reported by Cicero in his letters, made a collection of witticisms, which was equivalent to keeping a commonplace book of a kind. Dionysius of Halicarnassus, who was a well-known Roman historian and teacher (c. 30–8 B.C.), suggested, in his *On Composition,* the correct words and phrases to increase the power of a speaker to move an audience to the good. In his well-known work *On the Sublime,* Longinus (early first century A.D.) used quotations and illustrations to make his arguments. Works of great authors have been saved via quotations and excerpts in commonplaces. (Longinus includes, among others, an otherwise lost Sappho ode.)

A close adherent to the ideas of Cicero, Quintilian (A.D. 30–100), carried on Cicero's views in his *Institutio Oratoria,* (*On the Education of the Orator,* c. 95). Among his compendium of theories on rhetoric the well-known Roman teacher and rhetorician stressed the pragmatic value of the commonplace. But in his *Institutio* he established rules of education that would make the student not only a fine orator, but an upright and moral person. One may accomplish both by, in part, learning to write well and to imitate great writers. "Even though to invent was first in order of time and holds the first place in merit, it is nevertheless advantageous to copy what has been invented with success . . . (although) imitation is not sufficient of itself."[17]

The argument for imitation, for copying out passages in a commonplace book were heard throughout the centuries, but rarely with more power than in the words of Quintilian. The influence of the teacher lasted for hundreds of years. He was quoted in encyclopedias, such as compiled by Isidor of Seville (570–636), as well as in poetry. Alexander Pope in the eighteenth century showed evidence of the continuing influence of the *Institutio:* "In grave Quintilian's copious works we find/The Justest rules and clearest methods join'd."[18]

Valerius Maximum (c. 26–70) distributed and sold handwritten copies of his *Facta et Dicta Memorabilia* in about A.D. 30. A type of encyclopedia and commonplace in one format, the nine books cover every interest from marriage and military regulations to quotes from various sources on chastity, good fortune and wise sayings or acts. In addition to his original comments and thoughts, most of the excerpts are from Roman writers, although "in the absence of systematic acknowledgments of his borrowings, it is impossible to give an exact account of the sources . . . Livy has been largely drawn upon, even though he is mentioned but once."[19] Lack of sources and often downright failure to copy excerpts correctly did not prevent *Facta* from becoming popular. There were scores of abridgments and variations on the basic work throughout the Medieval period. Some used it as a source of Roman history, others for what it was originally intended, i.e., as a rhetorical reference work. The excerpts, and many of Maximum's comments, were printed as "memorabilia" during the sixteenth century. Down to the end of the nineteenth century bits of his collection appeared in commonplace books—again, usually without reference to their source.

The parallel between long entries in commonplace books and the traditional essay is evident in *Attic Nights,* a compilation (sometimes with comments) by Aulus Gellius (A.D. 123–170). Several of the short, three- to four-page entries remind one of a later Montaigne. Conversely, Gellius was more intent on copying than on original observations. Some consider his work the first "miscellany." One may dip into the volumes for almost any topic. Unlike earlier compilers he had a deference to learned authorities and habitually names his sources, often with exact references. "We are indebted to Gellius for the preservation of many fragments of early Latin literature, not all of them meager . . . His work is indeed a veritable monument of the second century's enthusiasms for all things archaic."[20] Much used, much quoted, much plagiarized by compilers in centuries to come, *Attic Nights* was the foundation for Greek and Roman quotes in dozens of published commonplace books. Gellius "transmits some very good stories, amongst which 'Androclus and the lion' (5.14) is justly celebrated . . . His opinions are always worth hearing. He compels our attention, not only as a source of information, but in his own right."[21]

By the late third or early fourth century A.D., the so-called Dionysius Cato drew upon the work of M. Porcius Cato (234–149 B.C.) to make available his commonplace book, *Disticha de Moribus.* These were precepts on mortality and rules for leading a good life were ascribed to the earlier Roman orator. Chaucer quotes the Cato of this commonplace several times, and William Caxton claimed it to be "the best book for to be taught to young children in school, and also to people of every age." At least half a dozen Latin editions were published in England before 1640, and Benjamin Franklin issued "an English version in couplets by an anonymous gentleman in 1735."[22]

Books on rhetoric, and especially the exercises (*progymnasmata*) usually had examples from literature that later might be extracted to make up a commonplace book. The earliest exact example of this is the exercise text *On Type of Style* by Hermogenes. At fifteen years of age Hermogenes of Tarsus (A.D. 155–225) so impressed Marcus Aurelius with his oratorical skills "that he was showered with gifts and endowed with an imperial sinecure . . . At the age of 24 he 'took leave of his senses' . . . and "as an old man became like a child."[23] Despite his brief working life, Hermogenes dominated much of the shape and content of commonplace books through the Medieval and Renaissance periods, particularly as his ideas on rhetoric lasted well into the seventeenth century. In his *On Types of Style,* he uses numerous excerpts and quotations to illustrate his treatise, although, once again, this is a manual on rhetoric not a commonplace book per se.[24]

The rhetorical exercises (*progymnasmata*), devised by Aphthonius (fl. c. A.D. 400), were translated from the Greek into Latin and numerous editions surfaced throughout the Medieval and Renaissance periods. Aphthonius belongs to the commonplace tradition because he offered for each of his exercises illustrated excerpts, quotes, metaphors, and other devices drawn from classical literature. The exercises, augmented by other editors, soon contained hundreds more examples adopted for the use of, say, the French or English. "The vice of padding" (Aphthonius) is particularly noticeable in . . . expansion of the fable of the shepherds and the wolves . . . (for) the amplified oration upon a fable . . . Readiness to seek copiousness at the cost of strict relevancy" was found in numerous Elizabethan and later commonplace books.[25]

The Medieval Period

Early Christians embraced the commonplace book concept as an aid for teaching and, more important, for preachers in need of rhetorical assistance. Training in rhetoric was a major part of Christian education and while many might be suspected of pagan ideas—as found in commonplace books, they nevertheless appropriated them for their own particular use. These tended to be rigorously governed both in content and classification by a systematic methods of compilation. They drew upon texts to be used for study and offered ideas for sermons. The books were a type of information retrieval systems which abstracted in whole or in part the canon of the time, e.g. from the Fathers and Doctors of the Church to Cicero and Aulus Gellius. As Curtius points out, Medieval reverence for the authors—both Christian and pagan—went so far that every source was held to be good. The sources or "curriculum authors" were limited to no more than 30 to 40 writers, but "the historical and critical sense were both lacking."[26] The notorious lack of consistency in copying material, from one monastery to another or, later, from one university center to another, explains the lack of accuracy in many of the commonplace books. A Greek or Roman excerpt might be basically the same from copy to copy, although with numerous small—sometimes important—differences.

In a sense, much of the average Medieval library was a commonplace book in that most of the books, except for the Bible and related theological works, were collections of material (from proverbs and fables to select quotations) from the Greek and Latin classics. The books tended to use commonplace headings (fear to honesty), and students drew from those to amplify and embellish paper about similar subjects. Most emphasized the delights of moral philosophy and were copied in part or in whole by students and discourse.

One of the earliest commonplace books, and the leading reminder of Byzantine civilization in the ninth century, was compiled by the Patriarch of Constantinople, Photius (c. 810–891). His *Bibliotheca* is a massive account, with extracts, of his private reading up to about 845. He describes more than four hundred Greek titles from the fifth century B.C. to his time. Today it is an invaluable source of material now lost, as well as an indication of the importance of certain writers and ideas to ninth century scholars.

Wisdom Literature

Similar to commonplace books, and sometimes it is difficult to neatly separate the two, the florilegia proved popular during the Middle Ages as a book of quotations. By the time of printing (c. 1450), however, florilegia had fairly well disappeared as form.[27]

Another second cousin of the commonplace book—wisdom literature had its beginnings five thousand years ago in the Near East. The name is self-explanatory of the scope. Wisdom literature consisted of quotations, aphorisms, maxims, extracts, etc. from professional wise men and philosophers. It differed from both the commonplace and florilegia in that the purpose was specific and considerably more narrow. Here a reader would find inspiration, even rules and regulations, on how to lead a good, happy life. Unlike today's how-to books and books of etiquette, each title in the wisdom literature library was based on strong religious beliefs, or, by the time of the Greeks and Romans, equally strong philosophical ideas.

Beginning with Egyptian scribes and pharaohs, the literature stressed the practical. For example, in 2500 B.C. one pharaoh explained to his son (and, by inference, all government workers) that discipline, hard work, and good manners assured material success. The compilers usually included sections answering such questions as why the wicked, the slothful, and the traitor might succeed. The books of *Job* and *Ecclesiastes* are perfect examples of this trend, as, of course, is *Proverbs.* The latter was probably based on part on the 1000 to 600 B.C. Egyptian text, "Instructions of Amenemope."[28] In a broad sense, wisdom literature was absorbed into both the Bible and the Koran, as well as becoming a major part of Greek philosophy. Still, separate works were published, particularly after the fall of Rome. Two examples will suffice.

Between 570 and 579, Martin of Braga (515–579) wrote his *Formula Vitae Honestae* (*Formula for a Virtuous Life*). Most scholars today believe this text is little more than another version of Seneca (4 B.C.–A.D. 65). His purpose was to list aphorisms for the four virtues: prudentia, magnanimitas, continentia and justitia in order to remind readers "of those things which are worthy of being fulfilled by lay people who live correctly and honestly, without referring to the precepts of Holy Scripture, but only to the natural law of human intelligence."[29]

Petrus Alfonsi (1062–c. 1110) added to the wisdom literature of the Middle Ages with his widely circulated *Disciplina Clericalis* (*Clerical Discipline*), a book of moral tales based upon various proverbs and fables he had read or heard in Arabic. *The Disciplina* "is the only work of its genre in twelfth-century Latin latureautee. Thirty-four stories are recounted in a series of aphoristic conversations between teachers and student."[30] The result, a wealth of fables unmatched in the Latin tradition, is a manual of moral education based not on Christian, but Oriental sources.

The *Disciplina Clericalis* enjoyed widespread popularity. Used by countless Medieval writers, it was available in seventy-six different manuscripts—both in Latin and in vernacular translations. Bits of the work were used in sermons in the fourteenth and fifteenth centuries; later, the moral overtones were dropped in favor of simple tales, as adopted by Boccaccio (1313–1375) and others. What began as a reference work of philosophy, ended as a source for storytellers and dramatists.

There were many other works of wisdom literature, of course, but these two samples suffice to explain their importance, particularly during the Middle Ages.

The Legacy of the Commonplace Book

Returning to the commonplace book, there are a handful that made an impression on Medieval thought and, as such, were widely copied from one place to another, from one century to another. Some belong to the history of both encyclopedias and commonplaces, as for example, the work of Vincent of Beauvais (c. 1190–1264). The Dominican's *Speculum majus* (*The Great Mirror*) (c. 1244–1260) was among the major encyclopedias of the Middle Ages. As noted in the discussion of encyclopedias, the four major books contain little that the compiler did not copy from other sources— hence the *Speculum's* more rigorous classification as a commonplace book.[31] No matter what it might be called, Vincent's work proved a marvelous source of material for preachers and teachers.

After Vincent, there were scores of similar titles, although none half as ambitious. None could claim to be encyclopedias. Among the favored was John Grimestone, who at the end of the table of contents of his commonplace gives the date as 1372. He judiciously copied down religious lyrics, both in Latin and English, as a storehouse of pulpit material. "To what extent these verses were composed by Grimestone and to what extent they were merely copied by him we cannot say,"[32] but most seem to be transcribed from other works. Albrecht von Eyb (1420–1475), a German lawyer and theologian, is credited with several masterpieces of early literary German prose. His *Margarita Poetica,* published in numerous versions between 1472 and 1503, is a collection of extracts from authors arranged under their names rather than by subject, although there is a subject index. The prose and verse were to be used to enliven letters, specifically the user can find key words, "which can make the letters we write richer and more elegant in language, especially when we have seen our way to appropriating to our new kind of letter writing, by a process of imitation, the passages from the poets here set out in order."[33] Petrarch (1304–1374) also urged jotting down phrases and ideas that could be used as models for writing. Imitation, not slavish copying, he stressed, made effective writing possible. Unfortunately as the Renaissance unfolded after the death of Petrarch, the role of the commonplace book was seen as a verbal crutch.

Commonplace books had a strong influence on the development of English written and spoken wit during the sixteenth century. Collections were used from grammar schools through Oxford and Cambridge. William Caxton's translation of *The Dictes and Sayengis of the Philosophres* (1477), a collection of moral philosophy first compiled in c. 1350, was a source of more than a thousand proverbs, sayings, apophthegms, etc. From the time of Caxton and the first printing in England, there was a bias for the use of English rather than Latin. This pattern was followed in the commonplace books, and by the mid-sixteenth century there were several published compilations available in the vernacular.

With the Renaissance the commonplace book became a basic reference work for the majority of educated people. "The presence of collections of commonplaces for use in school, in the court, the pulpit, or in social gatherings testifies to the practical value with which the Renaissance invested them. They were multipurpose means for invention, disposition, and elocution . . . These collections were not a merely perfunctory exercise, but they were functional."[34] The commonplace book of Robert Reynes (c. 1445–1505) is typical for the period. He jotted down such items as charms for bloodletting, geographical notes, theological comments, and a listing of miracles of the Blessed Virgin. The Brome MS (c. 1470–80) differs in that it probably was written by a professional scribe for the eventual owner, rather than prepared by the reader himself. Here one finds "the middle class interests: poems of moral advice, doctrinal poems, gnomic saws, a few carols, some romances and a passage from a play."[35] Blank table books often were presented as gifts to encourage the reader to use them for commonplace books. Renaissance laypersons and scholars alike tended to transcribe bits of their reading, often, unfortunately for later generations, without benefit of attribution, and rarely in any kind of well-defined order.

Printing made it possible to mass produce and distribute commonplace books. The compiler now had numerous printed books from which the draw material. Also, paper and writing materials became cheaper. Given what gradually became a massive amount of reading from which to make excerpts, it became necessary to achieve better methods of selection and organization of commonplaces. There were almost as many solutions as publishers. A scholar of the period explains:

> Make a book of blank leaves of a proper size. Divide it into certain topics . . .
> In one, jot down the names of subjects of daily converse: the mind, body, our occupations, games, clothes, divisions of time, dwellings, foods; in another, idioms or *formulae docendi;* in another, *sententiae;* in another, proverbs; in another, difficult passages from authors; in another, matters which seem worthy of note to thy teacher or thyself.[36]

Erasmus (1466–1536) published three widely reprinted and much used commonplace books. The three works were *Adagia* (1500), *Parabolae* (1513), and *Apopthegmatum* (1531). The quotations, adages, proverbs, brief narratives, excerpts, anecdotes, compiler comments, etc. broke down the whole of classical antiquity into bite-size snippets of sayings that could be introduced into discourse either in whole or paraphrased. In his *De Copia* (1512) he established a logical method of organization and arrangement to make it easier for the compiler to memorize what he had extracted from his reading. It became the guide for most of the sixteenth and seventeenth century for, as Bolgar puts it, "The Renaissance was the age of memorizing" and Erasmus's organizational patterns were found to be among the best.[37] Furthermore, the humanist took the next logical step and provided both an alphabetical and topical index to his "best-seller" of commonplaces, the *Adagia*. The *Adagia* had the widest circulation of any of the three titles. Erasmus continued to add to it until almost his death in the mid-sixteenth century. Everything he read, heard, and saw seems to have been recorded. A final version, published in 1536, was reprinted hundreds of times, and by 1600 there were at least eighty different impression of the *Adagia*. Some claim that in the sixteenth century one volume in every nine published in England was a work of Erasmus. Be that as it may, it is certain that among reference works, it was as popular as a modern almanac or one-volume encyclopedia.[38] The last edition consisted of 4,251 proverbs. Each had a commentary of a few lines or half a column. The purpose, among other things, was to support humanism with a suitable collection drawn from the Greeks and Romans. It served, too, as an advance guard to the restoration of antiquity. The commentaries are directed both to the scholar and the educated layperson. "It spoke in fact to a cultured public, much smaller than the modern one, but very like it; not to the erudite but to the general reader, interested in the classics for what light they could thrown on his own life and on the choices and struggles of his own society."[39]

In terms of practical use, the reference work now became, as the poet Pierre de Ronsard (1524–1585) poetically put it, a painter's palette enabling the writer to select "all the finest materials to paint a picture in a hundred colours, of which he alone is master."[40] The reference works, which were published in every country, served writers for everything from apt quotations and phrases to ideas for further elaboration. Montaigne (1533–1592) and J.C. Scaliger, (1484–1558), among others, brought together essays (or as Montaigne called them, "emblems")[41] amplifying ideas with quotations taken often from commonplace books rather than the original sources. In arguing for the worth of such books, Montaigne echoes de Ronsard: "I do not quote others, save the more fully to express myself."[42] In his 1540 *An Introduction to Wisdome*, Rycharde Morysine recommends the keeping of a commonplace book so one may, from example, learn to speak "quyckely, gravely, lernedlye, wyttilye, comely." The book should "always be at hand . . . wherein thou shalte write such notable thynges, as thou redest thyself, or herest of other men."[43]

A successful reference book could be plagiarized or simply copied and reprinted under the name of a different author. This was the fate of sections of the *Adagia* that underwent several unauthorized editions. For example, "In 1573 James Sanforde published *The Garden of Pleasure,* an English version."[44] What began as modest plagiarism developed into a cottage industry in Europe, and later in America. Before countries introduced copyright and before that copyright was recognized internationally in the twentieth century, it was more usual than not for a publisher to simply lift commonplaces from one or more works, add a new title and sometimes a short preface, and publish it as his own. Everything from almanacs and dictionaries to encyclopedias were stolen.

Printed or private, all too often the accuracy of the sources was in doubt, both in terms of accurate transcription and bibliographic details. Some invented the source, others the quote, and still others both. In his 1553 *Miscellane,* Poliziano charges a scholar "invents many vain and ridiculous things . . . and by doing so he proves . . . he has completely lost his mind."[45] With printing and the ability to compare various editions and sources, the opportunities drawn from consulting unique manuscripts for invention and simple misunderstanding and faulty copying diminished. The selection and interpretation of sources remained an independent decision, but with somewhat closer attention given to the accuracy of citation.

To add confusion, one can never be sure of the compiler, particularly of private fifteenth to seventeenth centuries titles. For example, the Folger Shakespeare Library owns a commonplace book that is inscribed as "Mr. John Oldham's Booke" although the second section opens with the signatures of three of the poet's contemporaries who probably actually put the collection of poems together. It is unlikely to be choices by Oldham or is there "any obvious links between this collection and Oldham's own work, because his connection with the (compilers) was probably only established in the last year or so of his life."[46]

Joannes Ravisius Textor's (c. 1480–1524) *Officina* (1520) is an excellent example of the published sixteenth century commonplace book, and "in many ways one of the most intriguing collection of commonplace material that was ever assembled."[47] In Latin, the collection of excerpts are primarily from the Greek and Roman classics. Enough, though, is taken from the compiler's contemporaries to add up to a marvelous collection of odd facts and curio. Under some three hundred and fifty topics or subject headings, the work is auspiciously for young boys, but because of cost and content it probably was used more by the youngsters' teachers. The book opens with a list of famous suicides, "then parricides, drowned persons . . . people swallowed up by the earth, individuals done away with by poison"[48] and the like. Under each of these subjects Textor lists individual cases—from 185 suicides to 11 people killed by dogs. Each includes an explanation, usually a quote, and references to the source. Additional sections cover biography (from trainers of monsters and wild beasts to geometricians and astrologers), cornucopia (one norm of plenty includes data on countries and the lack, or presence, of such things as bears, moles, ants, iron, cheese, etc.) and related sections. This work was followed by a similar collection, *Epithetorum* (1528), which runs to 622 pages and in alphabetical order gives a listing of words and epithets for use by Latin poetry imitators.

By 1565 Theodor Zwinger, the elder (1533–1588) had published the largest compilation of commonplaces to his time. His *Theatrum Humanae Vitae* went through five editions, and by 1604 was more than five thousand double-column folio pages with tens of thousands of excerpts. The Basel scholar took his quotations from slightly more than five hundred authors. (While the Middle Ages drew almost exclusively on the classical ancient writers, by the time of the Renaissance the authority figure could be a recent contemporary, usually dead, one.) The focal point was history, but the compiler took history to mean just about anything and everything that had happened past and present from religion and science to philosophy and money. A section on warfare, for example, includes material on "conscription of strong men; . . . military haircuts and beards . . . avoidance of wild animals and snakes . . . the hope of happiness, glory, victory, freedom, etc."[49]

The Seventeenth Century

The misguided use of either the personal or printed commonplace book is a common criticism throughout the history of the form. Specific criticism varied from century to century, although the dismissals tended to follow two or three patterns. Commonplace books, as a crutch, destroyed memory (writing down a maxim, for example, drove it from one's memory) a familiar argument from Plato; the overuse of quotations, excerpts, etc. resulted in thoughtless, wordy, and essentially weak discourse; and constant searching of literature for commonplaces destroyed the overall message(s) of the original work. By the seventeenth century, these arguments were heard more often, particularly as the widely distributed printed versions became best-sellers. In quoting a remark by Francis Lockier (1667–1740), who was "brimful of anecdote," Joseph Spence echoes these fears: "Large commonplace teaches one to forget and spoils one for conversation, or even for writing." After this Spence writes, "Query: remember instance of forgetting upon writing down a thing."[50] There is no example.

Seventeenth century intellectuals claimed the headings were useless in printed works for wide circulation. Others, such as Francis Bacon, (1561–1626) deplored published commonplace books as they were not compiled and organized by the individual. One man's notes will rarely profit another, he believed. The commonplace book was attacked by Jonathan Swift (1667–1745) in his *A Tale of a Tub.* "What though his head be empty, provided his commonplace book be full."[51] A censorious aspect of numerous earlier publications is summarized by the editor of John Selden's (1584–1654) table talk: "In a learned person's diary, kept when Selden was a young student, serious notes of sermons are found in company with passages which the modern editor (i.e., *nineteenth century*) thought unfit for publication."[52] And Selden may have had much to hide. According to Aubrey, the English barrister Selden "had got more by his Prick then he had done by his practice." But John Aubrey (1626–1697) was wrong about many things, including "Mr. J. Selden write a book called *Tabletalke;* which will not endure the test of the press."[53]

Francis Bacon was the English equivalent to Erasmus and his numerous works, including *The Advancement of Learning* (1605) are witness to how he employed his own commonplace books, some of which were published to construct and fill out his ideas. "Bacon himself was immeasurably assisted in his work by his common-place book, which still exists and gives us a curious insight into his methods of working. It was his *salina,* his salt-pit, that you may extract salt out of and sprinkle it where you will. He has left us also a collection of "Apophthegms" which makes very amusing reading."[54] By 1624 he had published his favorite apophthegms and his published commonplaces after his death became part of the English tradition.[55] Bacon in *The Advancement of Learning* recommends the collection of them as "a matter of great use and essence in studying. . . ."[56]

The popularity of the commonplace book increased in seventeenth century England. Proverbs, similes, and examples, which had been the favorite means of amplifying a subject in the time of Elizabeth, were abundantly employed by seventeenth century writers. The practice of keeping commonplace books encourages the use of these devices. Charles Hoole's *A New Discovery of the Old Art of Teaching Schoole* (1660) gives copious instructions on the books to turn to find themes, witty sentences, proverbs, etc. The author took a dim view of reliance on other collections, particularly for what today would be equivalent to high school students. Matter should be gathered from "their own authors."

Personalized commonplace books, particularly in the seventeenth century, often included music and, in fact, might be made up entirely of copies of scores. An example is John Baldwin (c. 1615) who gathered some 206 items in his commonplace books (c. 1586–1606) including the keyboard source *My Ladye Nevells' Booke* and Italian Madrigals, English musical puzzles, and proportion exercises.[57] An Anglican clergyman followed the usual pattern by including not only songs with music and poetry, but also fifty-six pages of printed text that he dutifully annotated.[58]

The English in the American colonies followed the trend of gradually turning what had been a rhetorical-educational aid into a catchall for items to remember. A 1667 North Carolina commonplace book features "finely written lines from Horace and Virgil," but most of the book is "filled with a jumble of domestica and medicinal recipes."[59]

Almost all writers maintained personalized commonplace books. Ben Jonson (1572–1637) maintained notes and reflections "on men and matters," drawn from conversation and reading. His commonplace book, *Timber of Discoveries,* was published after his death, in 1640. Another outstanding example is John Milton (1608–1674).[60] And Samuel Butler (1612–1680), the author of *Hudibras,* which satirized the puritans, drew upon his own compilations for this and other works. Thomas Browne's

(1605–1682) book of reflections, *Religio Medici,* shows use of his commonplaces as well.

As Bacon and others had pointed out, by the seventeenth century English publishers had learned there was profit in ready-made, mass-distributed commonplace books. William Winstanley (c. 1628–1690) was one of the more successful, representative authors of such works. The nearly 350 printed pages (published in London in a third edition in 1684 and much reprinted through the seventeenth and eighteenth century) had a marvelous descriptive title of content: "The new help to discourse, or, Wit, mirth, and jollity intermixt with more serious matters consisting of pleasant astrological, astronomical, philosophical, grammatical, physical, chyrurgical, historical, moral, and poetical questions and answers: as also histories, proverbs, songs, epitaphs, epigrams, anagrams . . . & c. . . .: together with the countrymans guide, containing directions for the true knowledge of several matters concerning astronomy and husbandry. . . ."

In 1665, probably about the time of Winstanley's first edition, one John Stafford had printed in London, "The Academy of pleasure furnished with all kindes of complemental letters, discourses, and dialogues: with variety of new songs, sonnets, and witty inventions, teaching all sorts of men, maids, widows & c. to speak and write wittily, and to bear themselves gracefully, for the attaining of their desired ends. . . .: also, a dictionary of all the hard English works. . . . with a poetical dictionary. . . ." Again, this 128-page published work enjoyed wide sales because, as with Winstanley, the commonplace had been expended to include virtually a single reference shelf, from textbook to encyclopedia and dictionary. (A comparison could be made here with present-day CD-ROMs, which offer a dictionary, encyclopedia, almanac, etc. on a single disc).

The continued expansion of the form into a general reference work culminated in the eighteenth century encyclopedia and nineteenth century "fact book." At the same time, it was normal to include, even in the most robust reference work, a section on commonplaces. For example, Thomas Blount's *The Academy of Eloquence* (1654) has short entries or common places for "vanity," "love," "women commended," and the like, although the main purpose of the volume concerns other aspects of rhetoric.[61]

The Eighteenth and Nineteenth Centuries

With the eighteenth century, the suspicion of published commonplace book as a bad crutch for those who could not think or write properly became more and more prevalent. What had begun in classical Greece as a legitimate, much heralded aid to rhetoric had by now lost favor, at least as a reference work offered for sale.[62] And, in fact, by the mid-century the commonplace book was no longer the sure success to publishing profit it had been in earlier decades.

Conversely, the personal commonplace book became even more a part of the resource for good conversation, rhetoric and as a mnemonic device. Intellectuals from John Locke (1632–1704) to Hester Thrale (1741–1821) measured the personalized commonplace as important, particularly as notes and background material for books. Hester Thrale regretted she had not kept a commonplace book to "mark down all passages from different books . . . for one forgets again in the hurry and tumult of life's cares or pleasures almost everything that one does not commit to paper."[63]

Even though by the latter part of the eighteenth century the published commonplace books were considered somewhat lowbrow and not to be found on the coffee tables of the "best" people, they enjoyed wide sales. The blatant focus was on instruction, or how to be a better conversationalist, writer, orator, minister, etc. Given enough quotations and anecdotes, from whatever source, an individual could graduate from mumbling to Ciceronian heights of glory. Titles were self explanatory. John Lockman's *The Entertaining Instructor,* published in London in 1765, gave details on how to better oneself and become a member of the growing, yet-to-be-described middle classes. A best-seller, *The Lounger's Common-Place Book, or Alphabetical Anecdotes* (London, 1792–1793) was reprinted several times, often with "a considerable number of new articles" (1796–1799 ed.) In themselves collections of anecdotes became popular. They included any group of miscellaneous material, from letters to conversations. A typical example is John Nicols's nine volumes of *Literary Anecdotes of the Eighteenth Century* (1812+).

Criticism of the commonplace book, and particularly the widely distributed self-help reference works, continued into the nineteenth century. A critic pointed out that some people could not describe snow as white "without a long quotation from Aristotle in the margin."[64] Conversely, the ambivalent feeling about such matters continued, e.g., still, "there are works in which it is absolutely necessary to show one's learning by quotations."[65]

John Locke, who inspired Thomas Jefferson's (1743–1826) concepts of government, equally contributed to Jefferson's commonplace book. Locke encouraged the keeping of such a work, "Nothing can contribute more to obviate the inconvenience and difficulties attending a vacant or wandering mind, than the arrangement and regular dispersal of our thoughts in a well ordered and copious commonplace book."[66] Furthermore, an essay published after his death offered "a method of making commonplaces . . . I take a white paper book of what size I think fit, I divide the two first pages which face one another, by parallel lines. . ."[67] In meticulous detail he explained how to organize and index the work, which "meant you could enter notes . . . under a very extensive number of headings, arranged not alphabetically but simply as they occurred, and which could be located very quickly by reference to an index no more than two pages in length."[68]

Jefferson, as numerous Americans, partially copied the Locke method in his literary commonplace books from the 1750s through the 1770s. "While Jefferson does not literally follow Locke's advice (about) . . . subject headings . . . he does name his sources and quotes them accurately and sometimes at length."[69] He assembled large parts of Lord Bolingbroke's writings about government, and put them together with parallel passages from Homer, Horace, and Alexander Pope, among others. (His commonplace book is another example of why Jefferson is considered the most literate president this country ever had.)

William Byrd II, a Virginia planter, slaveholder, and politician active in the first decades of the eighteenth century, kept a commonplace book in London from around 1721 to 1726. Primarily concerned with matters political, Byrd turned, also, to "his library and formidable library for related quotations on sex and woman."[70]

In a personal commonplace book (1799–1800), Francis Jeffrey, editor of *The Edinburgh Review,* offered as varied a content as was found in his famous literary journal. The book includes several essays and notes on religion and similar material, but little on poetry, fiction, or current politics. The 151-page quarto has 29 entries of varying length, "an alphabetical index in Jeffrey's hand."[71] Archives today hold scores of such manuscripts, few of which were published although often have been used as resource material for modern critics.[72]

A new use of commonplace book was suggested by a professor of medicine in the mid-nineteenth century. He claimed the assembling of facts would lead to new branches of science. By separating out facts and data, forensic medicine and hygiene would become independent branches of study. "The materials for the construction of both these sciences originally lay wrapped up in works on the several branches of medical knowledge. . . . Almost every science abounds in subjects of this kind."[73] These were among the last articles on the benefits of the commonplace. By the early twentieth century the form, except for literary purposes, disappeared or more precisely underwent a metamorphis and became the "fact" or "table book."

The Fact and Table Books

"Table book" was not a new descriptor, for in the seventeenth century one Richard West complained, "Their brains lye all in notes; Lord, how they'd looke if they should chance to loose their table-book."[74] Here West probably was speaking of commonplace as a blank notebook that one might carry to jot down items to remember, particularly in conversation.[75]

The term, "table book" became useful for "fact" publishers. For example, *The Table Book:* "a daily recreation and information: concerning remarkable men, manners, times, reasons, solemnities, merry makings, antiquities and novelties, forming a complete history of the year with one hundred and sixteen engravings," was published in 1866. The anonymous compiler gives the history of the form and explains: "The old table books were for private use—mine is for the public . . . My object is to blend information with amusement." The sources are from books, gossip, old friends, and "whatever."

It is difficult and probably unnecessary to distinguish between the fact and table book, although the latter was more decorative than useful. The typical nineteenth and early twentieth century fact book was a collection of data on everything from mountains and valleys to the population of China and the depth of the Pacific Ocean, with jokes, anecdotes, and colorful quotations. In many ways, it was a less disciplined, more popular form of printed commonplace than ones from earlier centuries.

The purpose of the fact books expressed by the compilers often was vague. The reader took it as self evident that the work could be used for numerous purposes from entertainment to reference research. William Keddie, in his *Anecdotes, Literary and Scientific,* explains that his work "embraces a great diversity of subjects." His audience is "a general class of readers," but "the interests of the young have been constantly kept in view in the selection, which, it is hoped, contains nothing, either in sentiment or expression, adverse to their moral and intellectual improvement." He then demonstrates the bridge between the nineteenth century fact book and the one-volume encyclopedia that became so popular in the next century, e.g., "the subject of art and artists is deferred for . . . an cyclopaedia projected by the publisher."[76] While few of such works had detailed indexes, leaving the reader to wander about via broad subject headings, Keddie was an exception. He had a sixteen-page "contents" that was really an index by subject, which opened with "Abernathy, Dr." and ended with "Zimmerman's retort to Frederick the Great." Actually, it proves to be more detailed than indexes found in many reference works today.

Keddie's was only one among scores of such titles, many of which became best-sellers. Perhaps the most famous was *Proverbial Maxims* by Martin Farquhar Tupper, an English writer who published his works. It was estimated to have been read by all educated people of the time. Other major works included John Brady, *Varieties of Literature* (London: Whitaker, 1826); John Perry, *The Magazine of Choice Pieces, or Literary Museum* (London: J. Cundee, 1810); John Joynder, *Literary Extracts from English and Other Words, 2nd Series* (London: Painter, 1847); and Frederick Locker-Lampson, *Patchwork* (London: Smith, Elder & Co., 1879). American publishers, too, brought out numerous fact and table books, such as George Cheever, *The American Common-place Book of Prose* (Boston: American Stationers' Co., 1837) and Milcah Martha Moore, *Miscellanies, Moral and Instructive in Prose and Verse* (Philadelphia: E. Morris, 1829).

With a better educated general public, a wider economic base for the middle class, and the ready availability of newspapers, books, and magazines, the emphasis shifted from the personal commonplace to developing a home library for ready reference purposes. Why take notes, laboriously copy out poems, recall quotations when all of these were easily available on the shelf at home—or, later in the nineteenth century, from almost any public library. One may argue, too, that the shift from rhetoric and discourse to pragmatic technology and specialized business interests in education undermined the basic reason for the personal commonplace compilation.

Nevertheless, as in previous centuries, prominent literary and political figures maintained private commonplace books that often were published after their death.[77] When published, many of the private works were identified by "notebook" rather than "commonplace," represents both a continuity (for commonplace books are a form of notebook) and a change, in that by the nineteenth century the average commonplace book was likely to include almost exclusively the thoughts and ideas of the compiler rather than quotations, maxims, proverbs, etc. from reading. Sometimes a quotation might be entered, but it was usually followed by an expansion of content by the compiler, which was done by the dominant literary and public figures as well as lesser known citizens. For example, a Louisiana lawyer, Henry Duffel, recorded thoughts of society and life, family events, politics, etc. from about 1843 to 1855.[78] May Lou Blair put down her thoughts and feelings from c. 1856 to 1858.[79] At the same time, many of the lesser known compilations continued, if only in part, the traditional recording of poetry, quotations, etc. More and more, one is likely to find simple lists, particularly of books read. From 1869 to 1872, a Courtland, Alabama family maintained lists of books and poetry read, and, not unusual by the mid-nineteenth century, recipes.[80]

The End of the Commonplace

With the early twentieth century, the encyclopedia, manual, handbook, book of quotations, and similar reference works replaced the commonplace book. What had begun in classical Greece as a rhetorical aid sank into oblivion. Today shades of the personal commonplace book remain, but are rapidly fading. If one turns to the online catalog services, from OCLC (Online Computer Library Center) to *Books in Print* and the equivalent *British Books in Print,* there are few 1990s titles.[81] No matter what the reason, "the commonplace tradition now seems . . . counterproductive."[82] The one pragmatic exception is the employment of the concept in teaching. Studies conducted at Northeastern University suggest students should maintain commonplace books, jotting down what they enjoy reading. This, it is claimed, will improve their writing and comprehension skills.[83]

There are a few modern examples of commonplace books, two representing the author notebooks and a third, the gatherings of a writer. From

1932 to about 1953, Wallace Stevens (1879–1955) kept a commonplace book that consists of excerpts from his readings, personal reflections, and aphorisms of his own invention.[84] This is in the best tradition, as is the *Commonplace Book* of E.M. Forster (1879–1970).[85] The single true commonplace book of the late twentieth century to enjoy wide sales and popularity was W.H. Auden's original "sort of autobiography . . . a map of my planet." A combination of the published and unpublished commonplaces from Auden's *A Certain World* lets "others, more learned, intelligent, imaginative, and witty than I, speak for me."[86] In fact, the poet has returned to the original Greek and Renaissance form, although its use is more for entertainment and reflection than necessarily to furbish a discourse. Publication in late 1995 of critic D.J. Enright's *Interplay: A kind of commonplace book.* (Oxford University Press) received favorable criticism, although all its reviewers felt it necessary to define "commonplace."

"Commonplace" appears from time to time in titles published by small private presses. Usually these books are no more than thirty of forty pages in length, and the work of dedicated advocates of the handpress. Their contents tend to be antiquarian, such as early examples of printing, verse, etc. For example, Sherwood Grover, Katharine Grover, and James Hammond compiled a number of pamphlets in San Francisco from 1956 to 1983 and called them simply *A Commonplace Book.*[87] In 1988, the Pentagram Press in Minneapolis issued a similar work, as did a New Jersey press in 1985.[88] These are peripheral and hardly in the commonplace main stream, which has dwindled to a dry bed.

Conversely, when one turns to Joseph Bryan's *Hodgepodge Two: Another Commonplace Book,* this is more in the style of the nineteenth century table book. The dust jacket proclaims it is "a storehouse of hilarious literary and historical anecdotes and facts, ear-catching quotations, brazen, blunt observations and arcane trivia. . . ."[89] *Hodgepodge* and scores of similar harmless titles generally are dismissed by libraries. What one critic said in the nineteenth century seems equally true today: "Large commonplacing could be frightfully dull and repetitive."[90] *Hodgepodge* is a commonplace book in subtitle only. In reality, it is simply another title in a massive group given over to trivia.[91]

In the late 1980s, a scholar of the seventeenth century commonplace book asked the rhetorical question, "Has the commonplace any legacy today?"[92] The response is "yes." The traditional commonplace book is stone-dead, but its ghost remains in the ubiquitous quotation book, as well as in countless guides to etiquette and how-to manuals. If the form itself has passed, the primary mission of sparking and maintaining good conversation lingers on—over the dinner table or on the internet.

Conversation continues with the wit and half-wit who may or may not "force the conversation towards his points." A nineteenth century manual on conversation suggests that "every man who goes into society . . . ought to keep some record of the happy talk he hears upon various occasions."

It is assumed that as surely as a man has such a store, which he looks up beforehand, so surely will he force the conversation towards his points, or bring them in when irrelevant; and an irrelevant joke is hardly a real joke. I have known, indeed, of a college Don having a note-book of wit in his pocket, and peeping at it under the table to refresh his memory. This was regarded as far the best joke about him, and the laughter before he spoke was always greater than when he had sped his shaft. In actual society it has never occurred to me to meet any one who has sustained a reputation for wit in his way. We think that if the suggestion of the current conversation is not strong enough to bring up a small point naturally, and without effort, it is better than it should be forgotten or unsaid. Let me add the significant fact, that in spite of endless attempts, no printed collection of jokes has ever attained even a decent position in literature.[93]

With or without a knowledge of the commonplace, it is evident that good advice, and even better stories, continue to enlighten and entertain. And from time to time they find their way into even the most current reference section.

Other Commonplace Forms

The commonplace book naturally led to the book of quotations, but along the way there were several other forms. The most prominent were the "ana," the "florilegia," and the "anthology." Only the latter continued as a popular reference work to the present time. Generally made up of excerpts of conversation, quotations, table-talk, wise sayings, and anecdotes, these forms shared several things, despite their different names. Later refined, many turned into quotation books. No matter their historical development or their name, these books had a major use. They helped the reader to improve conversation and writing by giving suggestions of useful and witty comments. Confined first to the clergy and the upper classes, by the late eighteenth and nineteenth centuries the ready reference aids were employed to improve the social status of the rising middle classes. Today the value of these ancestors of the modern ready reference book lies in the various anecdotes and contemporary remarks about authors, books, social life, personalities, music, and the like. There is much curious history to be found between their pages.

The Florilegia

Florilegia were volumes of a combination handbook and the earliest type of quotation collection. The Latin "florilegium" is derived from the phrase "plucking of flowers," and came to mean selections from a "garden" or ideas.[94] One of the earliest extant florilegium is Philippus of Thessalonica's *Garland of Greek Epigrams* (c. A.D. 40). This was to supplement the *Greek*

Anthology.[95] Seneca's (c. A.D. 1–65) wise sayings were drawn upon, as were those he quoted, for numerous florilegia that remained popular through the Middle Ages. By c. A.D. 124, a collection of epigrams about love was published by Starton or Sardis. Some four hundred years later a Byzantine scholar, Agathias, compiled a book of epigrams from his own circle of friends. He established the approach to quotations by subject. Similar collections were made throughout the Middle Ages from works of such Latin Fathers as Augustine and Jerome. These in turn quoted ancient authors. Sometimes the only quotations from Greek or Roman writers are drawn from the florilegia of the Latin Fathers. "Many classical poets, such as Tibullus and Propertius, were known to the Middle Ages mainly through florilegia rather than from complete texts."[96]

Particularly popular in medieval times, the florilegia took on many forms in content, scope, organization and purpose. One might be extracts from Scriptures and the classics; another, the work of a single author (such as the *Flores Bernardi*); or a third, a mixture of sources. In the twelfth century, and particularly in the second half, medievalists became increasingly conscious of the wealth of information to be garnered from a study of florilega. The collections, along with the individualized commonplace books, became important for rhetorical education. The florilegia were the treasures of wit and wisdom from which the teacher could draw examples for use in eloquent speech and writing. The quotations and verse varied in length, but their numbers were vast. Consulted by laypersons, preachers, students, dramatists, lawyers, moralists, lawmakers and just about any literate individual, florilegia were extremely popular. There are more extant examples of the form (from one hundred fifty to more than three hundred manuscript copies for individual titles) than almost any other type of reference book before the age of printing.

Surviving florilegia, confined primarily to the Middle Ages, vary in length and scope. For example, one collection may be made up of Latin and Greek quotations, another the words, writings and sayings of a single author. Most cited the sources of the extracts, and for that reason are of great help to present scholars.

While the majority were for private use, numerous florilegia were copied and recopied and became widely known throughout Europe. Here the compiler often explains his purpose in an introduction, and that purpose is almost identical to today's book of quotations or manual that assists someone in public speaking.

Anthologies

Anthology is the Greek work to which the Latin florilegium is a cousin. Both mean "flower picking or collecting." The anthology goes back to classical antiquity, regardless of what it may have been labeled over the centuries. Sometimes the contents of a collection were not planned in advance, and in the majority of these situations with entries made over a period of time into a book of blank pages, the result was a commonplace book. When there seemed to be a plan of organization, a specific focus, and a plan to publish, the result was an anthology, e.g., the high organized Bohemian anthology known as the *Summa Recreatorum.* This fifteenth century book of verse and prose was designed specifically for fun and drew its material from earlier anthologies.

Both Greeks and Romans used the word "anthology." For example, Stobaeus (early sixth century A.D.) called his collection of miscellaneous selections, *Anthology of Extracts, Sayings and Precepts.* He saved passages and fragments of early Greek authors. His four books make up a type of encyclopedia. Many passages are represented nowhere else. The comic writers owe most of their extant relics to Stobaeus. He quoted 200 passages from Menander, among others. We are also indebted to this collector not only for many excerpts from lost works in prose, but summaries of the opinions of ancient philosophers, which are not to be found elsewhere.Most anthologies, particularly those clearly associated with medieval monastic houses were compiled for teaching rhetoric and metrical composition. Compilers seem to have drawn on what was, rather than going out of their way looking for books and sources not close at hand. Other anthologies of the Middle Ages were closer to what we understand to be handbooks or manuals, e.g., collections of examples of good writing for the teaching of grammar. Magic formulas and military techniques as well as suggestions about etiquette often were published as anthologies, although today they would be classed as handbooks. Be that as it may, most lacked any indication of an author, a practice particularly noteworthy in famous anthologies of verse, such as the thirteenth century *Carmina Burana.*

By the time of printing and of the rise of the professional bookseller, the anthology and its numerous cousins became relatively common. The Elizabethan anthology was typically presented to its reader as a collection of materials to be used. This is the ideology in play in the titles of such anthologies as John Bodenham's *Belvedere, or the Garden of The Muses* (1600), John Proctor's *A Gorgeous Gallery of Gallant Inventions* (1578), and Clement Robinson's *A Handful of Pleasant Delights* (1584). Many of these are extant and, while limited for reference use today, are invaluable for scholars. "An anthology can serve as a kind of index to the taste of an age, and the selection and organization of its contents can sometimes also give a glimpse into the imagination and literary value of the compilers."[97]

Anthologies, which were really little more than miscellaneous collections of odd and unrelated quotations, anecdotes, and brief stories, were popular during most of the nineteenth century. A typical example is the two-volume set published in London in 1820. The title, which at great length explains the scope of the contents, is *The Parlour Portfolio; or post-chaise companion: being a selection of the most amusing and interesting articles and anecdotes that have appeared in the magazines, newspapers, and other daily and periodical journals, from the year 1700, to the present time.* The publisher of another volume, William Keddie, "secretary to the Philosophical Society of Glasgow," was widely known for his collection of anecdotes. In 1859 in London he published *Cyclopaedia of Literary and Scientific Anecdote; illustrative of the characters, habits and conversation of men of letters and science.* The volume was reprinted many times, including several editions in the United States, such as the 1859 book "from the London edition" published in 1859 in Columbus, Ohio.

In his introduction, Keddie explained the purpose of his anthology which, in fact, summarizes the popularity of this and similar collections. "It has been the purpose of this compiler to combine useful information with innocent entertainment." A problem that was to bother all quotation collectors appears in his explanation of sources. "The contents . . . have been culled from many sources, and embrace a great diversity of subjects. . . The paucity of anecdotes, in the annals of science. . . will account for the meagerness of this department."[98] Keddie followed the usual method of arrangement, which was more or less alphabetical. There was no index, but there was a detailed table of contents. Here, as in numerous works of this type, the focus was more on names (from Abernethy, Dr., and Curran to Yearsley, Ann, the poetic milkwoman) than subjects.

The Facetia

Anthologies suggested other forms for enterprising publishers. Collections of anecdotes, for example, became popular during the late seventeenth and eighteenth century. "From 1769 until the end of the century the genre became a literary rage, and more than a hundred titles containing "Anecdote" reached the public, several of them extending to five volumes or more."[99]

Another form of the anecdote collection was the "facetia." The English adjective "facetious" comes from this Latin word, which describes a collection of witty and often licentious anecdotes. The Florentine Renaissance humanist Poggio Bracciolini gave the title *Liber Facetiarum* (*Book of Pleasantries*) to his collection of anecdotes compiled in the middle of the fifteen century. In explaining "facetia" in his 1964 anthology *Wit and Wisdom of the Italian Renaissance,* Charles Speroni says it is "in general, a brief narrative that varies in length from a few lines to one or even two pages. Its main purpose is to entertain . . . by relating humorous occurrence that often finds it conclusion in a pungent, well timed repartee."[100] The taste for facetiae, or pleasantries, increased throughout the Renaissance, particularly as a useful source of wit and wisdom in conversation. The appreciation for the skills of good talk, the rise of the courtiers were celebrated in Baldassare Castigione's *Civil Conversation.*

The English took over facetiae in the seventeenth and nineteenth centuries, and a number of titles were published that drew on translations of the Latin classics, e.g., Thomas Brown (1663–1704) *The Works of Thomas Brown, Serious and Comical, in Prose and Verse* (London: Various publishers, editions 1703–to date). Actually most of the pages were filled with material from Horace, Cicero, and Martial. Some of the more "erotic" passages were given in Latin.

The descriptor facetia seems to have been rarely used in the subsequent century, although from time to time it surfaced. For example, in 1836 one Richard Gooch edited the third edition of *Facetia Cantabrigienses* (London: C. Mason), which offers "anecdotes, smart sayings, satirics, retorts, etc. by or relating to celebrated Cantabs." (Cantabs is a shortening of Cantabrigian, i.e., a graduate of Cambridge University.) There were similar titles in European countries, but by the twentieth century facetiae seem to have pretty well disappeared.

The -ana

A close cousin to the florilegium and anthology, the "-ana" is often used as a noun suffix to indicate a collection of materials about a given subject or person. Two examples: *Americana* or *Scaligerana.* Today, although rarely used, it retains its original Latin meaning of a collection of information, usually around a person, place, or thing, although numerous early -anas were scattered books of facts, epigrams, quotes, etc. In the best single article on the history and development of the -ana, F.P. Wilson points out that Samuel Johnson believed the term came from the "last syllables of . . . titles; as Scaliger*ana,* Thuani*ana;* they are loose thoughts, or casual hints, dropped by eminent men, and collected by their friends."[101] The -ana tends to be associated with conversation and things unpublished, but the suffix -ana was extended to include a writer's miscellaneous papers, like the *Baconiana* of 1679, or anecdotes about somebody, like the *Addisoniana* (1803), most of which were collected from printed sources.

Some believe the earliest examples of -ana may be found in the Old Testament's *Book of Proverbs.* At any rate, the *Proverbs* served as a model for the collections of the Middle Ages. Francis Bacon (1561–1626) held that while the description "-ana" was late to the language, its roots could be traced back to the Greeks. Aristotle (384–322 B.C.) in his *Topica* (i.e., 14. 105) alludes to -ana when he says, "We should select also from the written handbooks of arguments . . . In the margin too (of the handbook or commonplace book) one should indicate the opinions of individual thinkers." Early versions of -ana could be found in the collected conversations of Epictetus (50–138) set down by his disciple Arrian in the *Encheiridion* and *Discourses;* as well as Pythagoras six centuries before (c. 582–507 B.C.). Although nothing is known of the pre-Socratic Greek philosopher's writings, knowledge of him and his ideas comes from followers. The short, instructive sayings of Cicero (106–43 B.C.) are the subject of a book by Julius Caesar. In Plutarch's *Parallel Lives* (first translated into English by Sir Thomas North (1579), Plutarch (c. 46–120) appears to have depended upon now lost -ana.

The first successful published book of -ana probably was the 1666 issue of *Scaligeriana,* which highlighted the conversation of Joseph Scaliger (1540–1609), the Dutch historian.[102] Here, as in -ana to follow, the reader found conversation and table-talk between Scaliger and his friends, witticisms, anecdotes, and almost anything else that brought out the personality of the scholar. The best French collection of -ana is the collected conversations and witticisms of Giles Ménage (1613–1692). *The Ménagiana* (1693) is a typical apparently uncoordinated collection of philosophical speculation, classical quotes, verse, and epigrams that was reprinted in 1789–1791 and represented several times thereafter, often in part in other works.[102]

By the early eighteenth century the French -ana fell out of favor and, as F.P. Wilson points out, "they were so discredited that collectors of them preferred to disguise their wares under such titles as "Recueils" or "Mélanges."[104] Much was due to the habit of compilers of making up conversations and anecdotes; or, at best, badly copying and transcribing thoughts and words; or, at worse, putting into the person's mouth the sayings and writings of others conveniently copied from earlier -ana. Plagiarism became common. The English looked more favorably than the French upon the -ana, and by 1750 the form was widely represented.

A fine example of the -ana is to be found in the collection of writing of Robert Southey and Samuel Taylor Coleridge. First published in 1812, these short pieces were simply titled *Omniana.* The pieces, closer to essays than short comments and bits of conversation, covered everything from "Welsh names" to "A librarian" Coleridge knew. Actually, the book was more a collection of essays than -ana, but the authors were wed to the old term.[105]

Gradually the various types of collections of wit and wisdom joined to become several well-known and continuous forms. Out of the florilegium, from the -ana, came the essay. The tradition begins with Montaigne (1580) and Francis Bacon (1597), both of whom were familiar with and used the traditional forms to build essays. A related literary work, the anthology, might be said to be an umbrella heading for all of the earlier and later collections.

Today, the essay and the anthology are drawn upon for reference answers, but nineteenth century developments and changes in the earlier forms—

from the -ana to collections of anecdotes—are of more immediate importance because from them came the familiar ready reference book: the book
of quotations.

The Book of Quotations

A natural outgrowth of the commonplace book [as well as the -ana, the
Facetia, Anthologies and Florilegia] was the book of quotations, which is
today as familiar as the encyclopedia or dictionary. In the early years of the
quotation book, it was almost impossible to separate it from the other
forms. Still, the specific form gradually assumed its own shape and by the
late nineteenth century had to some degree pushed aside the other related
books as a reference source.

The popularity of quotations books, and, for that matter, of the ready reference titles from the nineteenth century to this day is summarized by Win-
ston Churchill, "It is a good thing for an uneducated man to read books of
quotations. Bartlett's *Familiar Quotations* is an admirable work, and I studied it intently. The quotations, when engrave upon the memory, give you
good thoughts. They also make you anxious to read the authors and look
for more."[106]

Lively, imaginative conversation could be mastered if one had the proper
number of quotations, anecdotes, epigrams, etc. to employ. These were
freely suggested in many nineteenth century ready reference books. A
Boston publisher offered 165 pages, or about 600 short anecdotes and stories that one might bring up "casually" in conversation and that ranged from
the Greeks to modern politicians and covered everything from the death of
Terence to "The poet no librarian." Carefully screened, all of the comments
were free of any "indelicacy." And the choices were "from the unpublished
treasures of the past, the richest and rarest gems of chaste wit and pure mortality."[107]

Major ammunition for rhetorical purposes, quotations are found scattered through the earliest manuals of Greek rhetoric; but it was not until
the Renaissance that books of quotations as such were published. Until then
quotations were chosen to be parts of the individual (or published) commonplace book, floilegia, -ana, and facetia as well as anthologies. In a sense
all of these were early quotation books, although almost all had other purposes as well.

Lacking few separate books of quotations, most readers and speakers
turned to commonplace books and their cousins. Records of some eighty
sources of quotations published in England between 1550 and 1600 tend
to use "commonplace" as a synonym for quotation. In 1581, for example,
John Marbeck's *A Booke of Notes and Common Places* was published in London. It was an alphabetical collection of quotes "gathered out of the workes

of diverse singular writers." In 1609 Robert Cawdry's *A Treasure or Store-house of Similes* was published with "commonplace" found in the subtitle. Gradually this changed. By the mid-seventeenth century the quotation book had come into its own with such titles as *Wits Labyrinth . . .*" ingenious, wise, and learned sentences and phrases together with some hundred of most pithy, facetious and pathetical complemental expressions."

No matter what the books of quotations might be called, they all drew upon common written sources. These included first and foremost the Church Fathers as well as Latin and, later, Greek classics.

An example of a Christian work from which numerous quotations were taken is Nonius Marcellus's *De Compendiosa Doctrina*. This fourth century compilation of grammar, lexicography, and antiquities was a constant source from then until well into the eighteenth century. Augustine, Acquianas, and other better known Fathers were sources of the quote. In addition, alphabetically arranged sayings of the Desert Fathers (i.e., the apophthegmata) were common from the fourth or fifth century. Collections of Christian proverbs, often borrowed from classical authors, were equally well known.

The earliest quotation books drew on Greek and Latin writers. Sometimes handbooks were given over exclusively to the quotations of an individual. Understandably the only audience for these works were clerics and writers who had a firm command of Latin. It was not until the sixteenth century that the early works were translated into English. With that the Latin and English equivalents usually were given so a non-Latin writer or speaker might appear to know more by dropping in an appropriate quote.

Terence (c. 190 B.C.–159 B.C.), the Roman dramatist, was favored for quotations. He was used extensively by numerous editions of grammars. The importance and influence of Terence was great, as can be seen in the quotations of Cicero, in imitations in Horace, and in the Church Fathers. In 1495, a book of quotations from Terence was published as *Vulgaria therentii*. By 1533, there was an English language edition, *Flowers for Latin Speaking*, which in various forms, was reprinted into the seventeenth century.

Drawn from the classics and the best minds of the Medieval period, Erasmus's commonplace book *Adagia* was shaped and edited to make numerous quotes over: for example, Erasmus modified Horace's "The people are a many-headed beast" to read, "The multitude of gross people, being a beast of many heads." And he modified Menander's "The man who runs may fight again" to "That same man that runneth away/May again fight another day." (This from a similar collection, the *Apothegms* of 1542). Many of the changes, of course, are due to translation and most of the wise sayings are from Erasmus himself. Still, this is an example of an early book of quotations being filled with a startling number of quotes that turned out to be of doubtful provenance. A relatively modern example of such doubtfulness is

General Pershing coming ashore in France in 1917 and saying, "Lafayette, we are here." Actually, someone else made that statement.[108]

Single books devoted to sayings of individuals, which began with the work of Terence and was taken up by Erasmus, appeared in the seventeenth century. The works of John Jewel (1522–1571) were published in 1609 and included "some amendment of divers quotations." Certainly one of the most famous single works was by Sir Walter Raleigh (1552–1618), whose *Maxims of State* (London, 1642) was filled with quotations and maxims.

Rhetorical experts and compilers of commonplace books liberally borrowed quotations from the emblem books (discussed in chapter 5 on Ready Reference Books). The first book of quotations to gain wide circulation in the Renaissance was Dominicus Mirabellius's *Polyanthea,* published in 1503. It consisted of an alphabetically arranged dictionary of Latin quotations.

Montaigne (1533–1592) took up the classical quotations, as well as those from the Medieval and Renaissance periods, and wove them into his *Essays* (1571–1586), which became the model for not only the digressive essay, but also the clever use of quotations to make and support points. Translated into English, an edition appeared in London in 1693 with the subtitle: "With . . . quotations of the cited authors." Then, and until today, readers turn to Montaigne for the delight of his ideas as well as his quotations.

The Latin and/or Greek book of quotations continued well into the twentieth century. For example, in 1798, a London publisher issued *A Dictionary of Quotations in Most Frequent Use Taken from the Greek, Latin, French, Spanish and Italian Languages.* In 1836, another London publisher brought out *Dictionary of Latin Quotations,* "from the most celebrated authors, with an English translation of each quotation." In this case, he increased the value of the book by adding "the Latin mottos of the nobility and gentry of Great Britain and Ireland, with translations."

Paralleling the emphasis on quotes was an equal concern with memory. The ability to learn and casually drop a quote was seen as important for both writing and conversation from the early Greeks through much of the nineteenth century. Mnemonics had been of particular interest in the eighteenth century when Richard Grey, a memory expert, developed a method of mastering dates, weights, coins, measures and other tidbits of information. Numerous handbooks and manuals were published. A.E. Middleton's *Memory Systems: New and Old* (1888) promised to train the layperson to recall the facts found in the printed fact books. The general public's interest in mnemonics, among other things, kept the earlier reason for the quotation book alive. By the early twentieth century the interest waned.[109]

With the nineteenth century the separate book of quotations, covering more than an individual or a single subject, became increasingly popular. In America, a best seller was the *Quotations from the British Poets,* published first in 1702. The "pocket dictionary of their most admired passages" went through numerous editions, and was drawn upon for quotes for still other books of the same type.[110] Compilations of this species . . . (are) supposed to consist of such heterogeneous and miscellaneous articles as casually dropped from the mouths of great men. . . ."[111]

Among the nineteenth century books of quotations, one finds scores of titles. Typical are Edward Day's *Day's Collection: An Encyclopedia of Prose Quotations* (1884), arranged by subject, and Charles Douglas's *Forty Thousand Sumbline and Beautiful Thoughts*. The most famous of the group and the most often republished was Sarah Hale's *Complete Dictionary of Poetical Quotations* (1849). Samuel Allibone's *Prose Quotations from Socrates to Macaulay* as well as his *Poetical Quotations from Chaucer to Tennyson* were also well known and often republished.

Although there are several hundred English-language quotations books in print,[112] both general and for specific subjects, by and large the most used and most famous in the English-speaking world is John Bartlett's *Familiar Quotations*. "Bartlett" has become a synonym for collections of quotations. Bartlett (1820–1905) was a bookstore clerk who kept a commonplace book for answering questions about who said what. In 1855, he published the first edition of his book based upon his commonplace. "The first Bartlett, issued in an edition of one thousand copies, was a relatively small volume of 258 pages of prose and verse quotations, chiefly from the Bible, Shakespeare, and British writers . . . By the end of his life Bartlett had brought out, in all, nine editions."[113] The sixteenth edition, still published by the first publisher of the work, has more than fourteen hundred pages with 340 authors new to the edition. This edition "continues to reaffirm the culture we're told is so gravely at risk but at the same time casts a wider net than its predecessors."[114]

Bartlett established the pattern for the modern quotations book—a pattern followed to this day by numerous competitors.[115] Compilations now tend to be the work of teams, ably aided by computers, and no longer depend solely on the memory and commonplace books of an individual such as Bartlett. And, if today's quotations books are better organized than earlier titles, essentially they are no different. At the same time there are now scores, if not hundreds, of individual books of quotations that are limited to a single topic or individual. Whereas Bartlett and today's general book of quotations considers the universe, a book of quotations, say of bartenders or lawyers (both now in print) is less ambitious. Then, too, there is another variation, known even to Bartlett, which is the concordance, an alphabetical index of the principal words (quotes) in a single book or the entire works of a single author. Concordances are discussed in more detail later in this work.

The one promise of the digital data base is that eventually all quotations will be available online. Today (1996) they are at least available on CD-ROMs, e.g., *Gale's Quotations: Who Said What* (1994), which contains some 117 thousand quotations, often with added information about the author or speaker. Also, there is the *Columbia World of Quotations* (1995), and other publishers are planning similar titles on CD-ROMs and later online. The problems are numerous, from copyright clearance to authentication of quotations, but it is possible, even probable that in a short time it will no longer be necessary to go from quotation book to quotation book in quest of the lost words of a great or near great. A few key words at a computer keyboard will bring the ubiquitous needle in the quotation haystack to the monitor. Obviously more efficient; yet something will be lost. Gone will be the days of the delights of wending through quote after quote, the thoughtful pause, the joy of discovery. This may or may not be a comfortable conclusion. To quote the most quoted writer of all time, perhaps, this is "to put an antic disposition on" the future.[116]

Notes for Chapter 3

1. Peter Levi, "From the Ordinary Commonplace," review of *Interplay: A Kind of Commonplace Book,* by D.J. Enright, *The Spectator,* 7 October 1995, 44.

2. *The Oxford English Dictionary,* vol. 2, 694, defines a commonplace book as one in which passages important for "reference were collected . . . hence a book in which one recorded passages or matters to be especially remembered or referred to, with or without arrangement." Commonplace, in the sense of being ordinary or unremarkable is a much later meaning. The adjective and the noun should not be confused. Classical Greek texts on rhetoric urged students to maintain commonplace books, which were personal and not widely distributed. By the second century, published commonplace books became relatively common. Aulus Gellius's *The Attic Nights* (c. A.D. 160), cites some thirty published previously titles that might quality as commonplace books, although authors can be assigned to only about half.

3. See Mary Thomas Crane, *Framing Authority* (Princeton, N.J.: Princeton University Press, 1993), 7–11, for a discussion of what was and was not included.

4. Quoted in James D. Butler, "Commonplace Books: A Lecture," *Bibliotheca Sacra* 61, no. 163 (July 1884): 482.

5. Walter J. Ong, *The Presence of the Word* (New Haven: Yale University Press, 1967), 84.

6. The Greeks and Romans concentrated on material useful in rhetoric. Compilations of the Middle Ages were concerned with rhetoric, but also with examples of human weaknesses and excellence drawn from both contemporary and classical literature, taking the form of *exempla,* i.e., anecdotes or stories that illustrated a theological doctrine or an example of exemplary behavior. From the Renaissance to the early nineteenth century,

content was broadened to include anecdotes, quotes, maxims, proverbs, proverbial phrases, or medical advice, or recipes and maxims—depending on the use. In England from c. 1620 to c. 1660 the emphasis was on collections of poetry. The variety of content serves to make it difficult to specifically define a commonplace book. Some argue the clue is to the miscellaneous material assembled by a compiler for personal use. Here the narrow definition concentrates on "miscellaneous" but few accept this.

7. *Hugh Library,* Vol. 2, 1992, p. 240.

8. Quoted in Peter Beal, *Notions in Garrison,* Renaissance English Text Society (Chicago: Newberry Library, 1987), 1. Fuller's *History of the Worthies of England,* 1662, was the earliest attempt at a dictionary of national biography; and he drew many of his facts and stories from a vast collection of his own commonplace books.

9. Max W. Thomas, "Reading and Writing the Renaissance Commonplace Book," *Cardozo Arts and Entertainment Law Journal,* Vol. 10, No. 2, 1992, p. 674. The commonplace began in the oral tradition where data had tended to be fragmented. Oral narrators and orators brought together the commonplace bits out of which thought and discourse were made. The commonplace kept the store of passed information alive and accessible largely through oral performance. With the advent of writing little changed. Writing was employed to implement the oral. Primarily one mastered commonplaces (i.e., known knowledge) by listening. There are numerous books on the history of memory. See particularly Frances Yates, *The Art of Memory* (Chicago: University of Chicago Press, 1966).

10. James D. Butler. "Commonplace Books: A Lecture," *Bibliotheca Sacra,* 61, no. 163 (July 1884), 479. Butler gave three familiar reasons for such a compilation. First, "I should be disposed to draw up such a book simply because such has been the custom of so many an eminent scholar" (p. 481). Second, he thought the exercise would improve the memory (p. 484). Finally, it offers "a galaxy of illustrations useful for conversation. . ." (p. 486).

11. Aristotle, *Topica* 14, 105b, in *Renaissance Concepts of the Commonplaces,* Sister Joan Marie Lechner (New York: Pageant Press, 1962); reprint, Westport, CT: Greenwood Press, 1974), 164. This is one of the best sources for a summary of the Graeco-Roman contribution to the commonplace form. Although Aristotle generally is credited with the idea of the commonplace, one might argue it is much older, e.g., *The Book of Proverbs, Old Testament* is a collection of wisdom and sayings that can be defined as commonplaces, at least of sorts. For a discussion of the commonplace during the Renaissance, see Ann Moss, *Printed Commonplace-Books and the Structuring of Renaissance Thought* (Oxford: Clarendon Press, 1996).

12. The material was filed in a memory room or nest to be called up when needed. The place (Greek: *topos/topoi;* Latin: *locus/loci*) would be considered subject headings today. In Aristotle's system there were both

commonplace and special places, but by the time Cicero two hundred years later commonplace was used for both situations. Aristotle lists some 360 commonplaces. The classical "places" are discussed in detail by Curtius, *European Literature and Latin Middle Ages.* In chapters and sections, he considers the "historical topics," "rejuvenation," "Panegyric," etc. They are the departing point for numerous historical works on Medieval and sixteenth and seventeenth century education. Their use in conversation and speech is considered for the eighteenth through the nineteenth centuries. Even among experts there is controversy as to the exact meaning of *topos.* Aristotle considered it ready-made arguments or commonplaces but suggested they were only forms that could be applied as needed. Others later considered them simply as subject headings for organization of the commonplace book.

13. Beal, *Notions in Garrison,* 3. But this is in reference to published, i.e., widely distributed commonplace books. The personal works, which were numerous, often were compiled as much for amusement as for use, e.g., "The Greeks, after wide and varied reading . . . swept together whatever they had found, aiming at mere quantity. . . . Every moment of . . . time I shall devote to collecting similar brief and entertaining memorandum." Aulus Gellius, *The Attic Nights,* vol. 1, Loeb Classical Library (Cambridge: Harvard University Press, 1927), xxxi; xxxvii.

14. *The Essays of Montaigne* vol. 1, (New York: Heritage Press, 1945), 195. Montaigne was too hard on the philosopher, e.g., in his time Chrysippus was considered a major figure and even today is the subject of numerous studies. See, for example, Josiah Gould, *The Philosophy of Chrysippus* (Albany, N.Y.: State University of New York at Albany, 1970).

15. Cicero, *De Oratore,* vol. II, Loeb Classical Library, (Cambridge: Harvard University Press, 1942), xxix, 129–130.

16. Ibid. vol. III, xxvi, 104.

17. Quintilian, *Institutio Oratoria,* trans. and ed. James J. Murphy, Quintilian on the Teaching of Speaking and Writing. (Carbondale: Southern Illinois University Press, 1987), 132, (x, 2).

18. Ibid., xiii (From Pope's "Essay on Criticism," 669–70).

19. J. Wight Duff, *A Literary History of Rome* (London: Ernest Benn, 1964), 56. Duff devotes a complete chapter to Valerius. The lack of sources is more usual than unusual throughout the history of commonplace books. Literary scholars have spent years trying to trace the precise sources and are often perplexed by lack of conformity from one manuscript copy to another.

20. E.J. Kenney, ed., *The Cambridge History of Classical Literature,* vol. 2, Latin literature (New York: Cambridge University Press, 1982), 678. *Noctes Atticae* (*The Attic Nights*) is so called because it was compiled while Gellius was in Attica, i.e., Greece.

21. Ibid., 679–80. The three-volume Loeb classics make excellent bed-

side reading even today. One example from Book 1, xxvi: "I once asked Taurus in his lecture room whether a wise man got angry?" Two pages later comes a suitable answer that draws upon Plutarch and Taurus.

22. William G. Crane, *Wit and Rhetoric in the Renaissance* (New York: Columbia University Press, 1937), 24–25. "Like the early essays, the discourses were often merely jottings from a commonplace book strung loosely together. . . . The writers of discourse pillaged the volumes of selected proverbs, dicata, similes, and examples; and in turn the compilers of commonplace books culled the more striking passages from the moral discourses. Moral discourses in England during the sixteenth century, which reveal any attempt at original thought are exceedingly rare."

23. Thomas Conley, *Rhetoric in the European Tradition* (New York: Longman, 1990), 24.

24. See Hermogenes *On Types of Style,* trans. Cecil W. Wooten (Chapel Hill: The University of North Carolina Press, 1987); and Annabel Patterson, *Hermogenes and the Renaissance* (Princeton, N.J.: Princeton University Press, 1970).

25. Aphthonius, *The Foundation of Rhetorike,* trans. and much expanded by Richard Rainolde (1563; reprint New York: Scholars' Facsimiles, 1945), xvi–xvii.

26. Curtius, *European Literature and Latin Middle Ages* 52.

27. See the chapter on "Ready Reference Books" for a discussion of florilegia.

28. "Early works of wisdom take different forms: collections of fables or proverbs, collections of sayings of one or more famous sages, mirrors for princes, and so on. This tradition was absorbed and modified by Judaism (and passed onto Christianity) to form the Wisdom literature of the Old Testament. It was similarly absorbed and modified by Islam." Tolan, *Petrus Alfonsi,* 78.

29. Ibid, 73.

30. Ibid.

31. In all fairness, Vincent "made no claim to originality and took pride in being the master organizer who collected, classified and arranged his summary . . . into a single unified entity." *Dictionary of the Middle Ages,* vol. 12, 1989, 454.

32. Carleton Brown, ed. *Religious Lyrics of the XIVth Century* (Oxford: Clarendon Press, 1957), xvi–xix.

33. *Margarita.* 1472 ed., Vol. xxix. Quoted by Ann Moss, "Printed Commonplace Books" in Alexander Dalzell, ed. *Acta Conventus Neo-Latin Torontonensis, Medieval & Renaissance Texts & Studies,* vol. 86, (Binghamton, N.Y.: 1991), 513.

34. Ibid., 509. More than one critic believes that sixteenth century commonplace books created for English humanists a central mode of transaction with classical antiquity and provided an influential model for authorial

practice. Mary Thomas Crane's *Framing Authority* is one of the best of its kind on the value of commonplaces and argues the major importance of the form.

35. Russell Robbins, *Secular Lyrics* (Oxford: Clarendon Press, 1961), 237–39. In his introduction, Robbins describes several dozen commonplace books, of which these are examples. Locations are cited.

36. R.R. Bolgar, *The Classical Heritage,* (Cambridge: Cambridge University Press, 1954), 273.

37. *De copia* or *De Duplici Copia Verborum* underwent many editions and reprints. Froban issued a revision in 1517 and again in 1540, but the total number of printings during the sixteenth century was well above one hundred and fifty. (Donald King, *On Copia* (Milwaukee, Wis.: Marquette University Press, 1963), 2). Organization continues to be a major consideration. W.H. Auden, *A Certain World: A Commonplace Book* (1970) has passages under 173 topics from accidie to writing, but lacks an index or a listing of the headings, which considerably limits its use for reference purpose.

38. Erasmus is among the first authors to explain the need for added editions of a reference book. In a letter to a friend who complained about the cost of buying revisions, "Why not produce the work finished once and for all?" Erasmus responded, "No one is so good that he cannot be made better, so no book is so complete that is cannot be improved." Erasmus to John Botzheim, 1623, *The Adages of Erasmus* edited by Margaret Mann Phillips (Cambridge: University Press, 1964), iv.

39. Phillips, *The Adages of Erasmus,* 5.

40. Hylas, lines 417–26, in Pierre de Ronsard, *Oeuvres complete,* ed. P. Laumonier, 20 vols. (Paris: 1914; 975) 15:252. Quotes by Moss, *Printed Commonplace Books* 515.

41. In this sense "emblem" is defined as a visible sign of an idea(s) to support and illustrate, usually by quotations.

42. *The Essay of Montaigne,* vol. 1, (New York: Heritage Press, 1946), 197.

43. William Crane. *Wit and Rhetoric in the Renaissance.* (Gloucester, Mass.: Peter Smith, 1964), 32.

44. Ibid., 37.

45. Anthony Grafton, *Joseph Scaliger* (Oxford: Clarendon Press, 1983), 23. Poliziano notes the scholar in question begins his work by saying he wrote matter drawn from Apollodorus, Lycophron, Pausania, Stabo, Apollonius, and other Greeks and Latins as well. But the scholar actually invented much of what he claimed these writers wrote.

46. P.F. Hammond, "A Commonplace book owned by John Oldham," *Notes and Queries,* December, 1979, 518. The second part consists entirely of poems and in that respect is an anthology rather than a commonplace book. The first part is more a directory and listing of nobility, counties, and parishes than, again, a commonplace book.

47. Walter J. Ong, *Interfaces of the World* (Ithaca, N.Y.: Cornell University Press, 1977), 155.

48. Ibid. Ong points out that Textor "remains a neglected figure today and indeed promises to be neglected even more effectively in the future, for he published in Latin" (p. 152). He was a student and teacher of the University of Paris. The material on the author and his commonplace books is taken from Ong and his superior discussion of the form in chapter 6.

49. Ibid., 173.

50. James M. Osborn, ed., *Joseph Spence* (Oxford: Clarendon Press, 1966), 273, 302.

51. Beal, *Notions in Garrison,* 6.

52. Frederick Pollock, ed., *Table Talk of John Selden* (London: Quaritch, 1927), 1x. The book came about because a vicar "was Selden's secretary for many years and took notes of his talk for twenty years together down to some time near the end of Selden's life in 1654. . . . The book was first printed in 1689 . . . (It was) a bad edition . . . No material improvement was made on it for two centuries" (p. xi–x).

53. Oliver Dick, ed., *Aubrey's Brief Lives* (London: Penguin Books, 1949), 331–32.

54. Crane *Wit and Rhetoric in the Renaissance,* 140–41.

55. Ibid., 152.

56. Ibid., 47. Crane's chapter on the English commonplace books gives numerous examples of sources for the student building his or her own commonplace book. See Stuart Clark, *op. cit.,* for a discussion and detailed bibliography of commonplace books (published and in manuscript form) by Francis Bacon. See, too, Alan Keen, *The Private Manuscript Library of Francis Bacon.* (London: Chiswick Press, 1943), a fourteen-page essay that includes the manuscripts of Bacon's "law clerk and servant William Tottel." Also, Edwin Wolf, *The Textual Importance of Manuscripts Commonplace Books of 1620–1660,* (Charlottesville, Va, Bibliographical Society of the University of Virginia, 1949). (Twenty-four offset typed pages).

57. Hilary Gaskin, "Baldwin's Commonplace Book. . ." *Soundings,* No. 10, 1983, pp. 18–23. This is known as the London British Library Royal 24.d.2, and is discussed in terms of copying scores by the author.

58. Thomas, "Reading and Writing Renaissance Commonplace," 665–79. The printed poem is a work by Thomas Watson, " *The Hekatompathia, or Passionate Centurie of Love*" (1582). Commonplace books of songs and music are normal in the seventeenth century, e.g., the Library of Congress, *National Union Catalog, Pre 1956 Imprints* lists such manuscripts as *A Commonplace of English Madrigals* (1610) and a *Commonplace Book of Songs and Dances for the Lute* (1600), to name only two of a dozen or more.

59. Alice Law, "A New Caroline Commonplace Book," *Fortnightly,* 1 September 1899, 396.

60. John Milton, *A Commonplace Book* (London: Chiswick Press, 1876).

61. Reproduced by the Scolar Press, Menston, England, 1971. As the editor points out, Blount plagiarized much of his material—not extraordinary for most commonplace books before copyright became universal.

62. This opinion is hardly a consensus, however. Some maintained the worth of the reference book, e.g., Crane, 135, quotes Lord Shaftesbury (the third): "The most confus'd head, if fraught with a little invention, and provided with common-place-book learning, might exert itself to as much advantage, as the most orderly and well-settled judgment."

63. Katharine Baldeston, ed., vol. 1 (1776–1784), *Thraliana: the Diary of Mrs. Hester Lynch Thrale (Later Mrs. Piozzi) 1776–1809* (Oxford: Clarendon Press, 1951).

64. Robert Heron, *Letters of Literature* (1785; reprint, Garland, 1970), 396–7.

65. Ibid.

66. John Locke, *A New Method of Making Commonplace Books* (London: J. Greenwood, 1706), 2A.

67. Ibid., 4.

68. Ibid., 3. Locke's method, copied and used extensively throughout Europe and America during the eighteenth and well into the nineteenth century, is complicated, although explained clearly enough by Beal. The original edition of the *Encyclopaedia Britannica* (1771) uses Locke's organizational plan, observing: "There are various methods of arranging commonplace books; that of Mr. Locke is as good as any that have hitherto been contrived" (vol. 2, 241).

69. Kenneth Lockridge, *On the Sources of Patriarchal Rage* (New York: New York University Press, 1992). Lockridge studies the Jefferson and William Byrd commonplace books to conclude "private patriarchal misogyny . . . played a role in limiting the spheres of the republican wife and republican mother at their very inception" (p. 113–114). Here is one of many cases where researchers use commonplace books to reveal facts about an individual, as well as society in general. Jefferson has many quotes from Milton from his earliest entries in 1756 as well as Shakespeare and numerous English plays.

70. Ibid., 9.

71. David W. Pitre, *Francis Jeffrey and Religion: Excerpts from his 1799–1800 Commonplace Book.* Eighteenth Century Life, Vol. 8, No. 1, 1982, 95–107.

72. After World War II, and an explosion of Ph.D. candidates as well as established literary and political critics, numerous commonplace books, compiled privately for private use, were published. For example, George Berkeley (1685–1753) and his development as a philosopher is of enough interest to warrant frequent publication of his commonplace books, e.g., by Faber & Faber as early as 1930 and a facsimile edition in 1984. The commonplace book of Robert Burns (1759–1796) is an example of a work often

reprinted. Robert Southey (1774–1843) is another, although his books are primarily in the next century.

73. William Guy, "On the Method of Collecting and Arranging Facts, with a Proposed New Plan of Common-place Books," *Journal of the Statistical Society of London* (January 1841): 361. Guy, a professor of King College London explained the value of the commonplace book as a ready source for facts: Knowledge can be extended by "original observations and experiments, or by searching and rigorous analysis of facts collected by those who have preceded us" (p. 353).

74. Quoted Beal, *Notions in Garrison,* 12. According to the *Oxford English Dictionary,* vol. 11, the term "table book" was a descriptor used by Thomas Nashe (1596) and Shakespeare (1602) to describe a pocket note book or memorandum book (i.e., a form of the commonplace book). Related, synonymous terms included "memorandum book," "pocket book" and "vade mecum," i.e., any kind of notebooks carried about on one's person. By the nineteenth century it became "an ornamental book for drawing room table," hence it might mean what today would be called a "coffee table book," primarily for decoration; or, as employed here, a selection of material for memory and reference.

75. Confusion over the terminology, purpose, and scope of the commonplace book is recurrent, e.g., Richard Oram, "Thackeray's translation of German poetry and his Weimar commonplace book," *Notes and Queries* (August 1978) 301. Oram believes the Morgan Library (holders of the manuscript) are at fault labeling it a commonplace because the seventy unnumbered leaves really are "a large sketch book into which Thackeray copied his own translations . . . of German poetry, sketches and several original poems and short dramatic scenes." Oram is wrong in that Thackeray's 1830–1831 work is precisely the stuff of a nineteenth century commonplace book. "Common-place" was a normal descriptor for the first half of the nineteenth century, but disappeared for the most part by the turn of the century. For example, between 1820 and 1840, one finds such titles as *Common-place Book of Ancient and Modern Ballads* (Edinburgh, 1824), and the *Common-place Book of Romantic Tales* (New York, 1831). The term had come to mean a collection of songs, ballads, stories, etc., rather than a compilation of material for speeches, and conversation.

76. William Keddie, *Anecdotes Literary and Scientifics* (London: Routledge, n.d.), 1.

77. A few outstanding examples of nineteenth century personalized, compiled commonplace books include those of Thomas Jefferson (1743–1826) (Princeton, N.J.: Princeton University Press, 1989); Henry David Thoreau (1817–1862), published as *Thoreau's Literary Notebook in the Library of Congress* (Hartford, Conn.: Transcendental Books, 1964); Thomas Hardy (1840–1928), published as *The Literary Notes of Thomas Hardy* (Göteborg, Sweden: Cta Universitatis, 1974); and Robert Southey (1774–1843) New York: Harper & Brothers, 1849–1850.

78. Henry Duffel commonplace book, c. 1843–1855, manuscript, University of North Carolina at Chapel Hill.

79. Mary Lou Blair, commonplace book, manuscript, College of William and Mary, Williamsburg, Va.

80. Saunders family commonplace book, manuscript, College of William and Mary, Williamsburg, Va.

81. Although online services pick "commonplace" from titles, abstracts, and subject headings, *Books in Print* and related works do not recognize the heading. The Library of Congress, *National Union Catalog* keeps up the tradition, as much to pinpoint books about the commonplace as to list actual commonplace works. But even it has difficulty in classification, e.g., under Commonplace-books (see also Handbooks, vade-mecums, etc.) one finds C.F. Kleinknechts's *The Kleinknechts's Gems of Thought Encyclopedia* (Washington: 1952), which is more a catchall encyclopedia than a commonplace book, although, again, it is difficult to make a firm division.

82. Walter J. Ong, p. 148.

83. Gayle B. Price, "A Case for a Modern Commonplace Book," *College Composition and Communication* (May 1980): 177–80. Students are asked to make entries under appropriate headings. The entries are of particularly importance and/or interesting ideas and quotations which they encounter during all their reading and learning . . . The key to the effectiveness of this important aspect of the commonplace book is that students learn to tune into what they read and hear to the extent that they will notice things worth writing down." See, too Judith Boyce, "Visions of Communication: The Use of Commonplace Books in the English Class," in *Seeing for Ourselves,* ed. Richard Bullock (Portsmouth, N.H.: Heinemann Educational Books, 1987) and Richard E. Drdek, "Commonplace Book, Venerable Teaching Took," *The English Record* (winter 1974): 62–65, which gives a history of the book as a teaching device. The nickel composition books of the 1930s, for example, were used by students for collections of ideas. "Into them each of us copied those verses, sayings and prose paragraphs we wished to preserve" (p. 62).

84. Wallace Stevens, *Sur Plusieurs Beaux Subjects—Wallace Stevens's Commonplace Book* (Stanford, Calif.: Stanford University Press, 1989).

85. E. M. Forster, *Commonplace Book* (London: Scholar Press, 1978. Forster used the topical/subject approach and would, for example, briefly discuss a play or novel and then make comments about the work.

86. W.H. Auden, *A Certain World* (New York: Viking, 1970), vii–viii. His commonplaces add up to over more than two hundred comments, poems, extracts from biography, and the like on topics from "anagrams" and "anesthesia" to two of his longest alphabetically arranged sections "world, end of the" and "writing." The excerpts indicate the English poet's wide range of readings as well as vast interests.

87. *A Commonplace Book* (San Francisco: Grace Hoper Press, 1956);

Another Commonplace Book (San Francisco: Grace Hoper Press, 1956); *Commonplace Book Three,* p. 37, 1960); *Sherwood Grover and James D. Hammond Compile and Edit a Commonplace Book with Something for Everybody* (Aptos, Calif.: Grace Hoper Press, 1969); *Commonplace Book Six* (Aptos, Calif.: Grace Hoper Press, 1983.)

88. *The Pentagram Press Commonplace Book* (Minneapolis, Minn.: Pentagram Press, 1988). *A Commonplace Book* (Maple Shade, N.J.: Pickering Press, 1985).

89. Joseph Bryan, *Hodgepodge Two* (New York: Atheneum, 1989). The first edition of *Hodgepodge* appeared in 1986, and Bryan had another, similar title, *Gallimaufry To Go* (New York Dell, 1991).

90. Osborn, *Joseph Spence* 302.

91. *Trivia* is defined dismissively by *Webster's Ninth New Collegiate Dictionary* (1983) as "unimportant matters: trivial facts or details."

92. Peter Beal, *Notions in Garrison* 11.

93. Sir John Mahaffy, *The Art of Conversation* (Philadelphia: Penn Publishing, 1896, 89–90. As is often the case, this appears to be a reprint of an unidentified publishers work, this an 1888 English publisher.

94. The term has the added meaning "of the best part of something." By the twelfth century "flores" was one of the commonest terms for selected extracts as the titles of many popular collections suggest: *Liber florum, Florarium, Floretum, Flores paradysi.* A much earlier type of florilegium was the "Sententiae" i.e., Latin for "sentential" is a collection of sentences and maxims on life which can be inserted into papers and speeches. Manuals of sentential were popular during the Sophists period (i.e., fifth century B.C.).

95. *The Greek Anthology* available in translation in five volumes in The Loeb Classical Library (Cambridge: Harvard University Press), includes close to four thousand short poems, epigrams, songs, etc. The collection was made early in the first century A.D. and was added to throughout Medieval times. Some of the material goes back to the seventh century B.C. Epigrams began as inscriptions suitable for carving on monuments. But by the time of *The Greek Anthology* (c. 80 B.C.), an epigram came to mean any brief, often astringent verse or striking quotation. Catullus (c. 84–54 B.C.) originated the epigram in Latin, and Martial (c. A.D. 40–103) gained lasting fame for his verses which served as models to this day.

96. *Dictionary of the Middle Ages,* vol. 1, 318.

97. Ibid., 320.

98. *Cyclopedia of Literary and Scientific Anecdote; illustrative of the characters, habits, and conversations of men of letters and science* (London: William Keddie, 1859), ix.

99. Osborn, *Joseph Spence,* xxi.

100. Charles Speroni, *Wit and Wisdom of the Italian Renaissance* (Berkeley, CA: University of California Press, 1964), 3. In this anthology of work from twelve facetia experts, the editor offers massive, often amusing, sup-

port for his explanation of the form. He believes that of the twelve Ludovico Domenichi (1515–1564) with his *Pleasantries and Witticisms of Certain Most Excellent Wits and Most Noble Gentleman,* had the largest collection of the time and "also the most entertaining and the wittiest of the whole sixteenth century" (p. 9).

101. F.P. Wilson, "Table Talk," *Huntington Library Quarterly* 4 (1940): 27, 28.

102. The *Scaligerana* was compiled during the 1570s and 1580s by one of Scaliger's close friends . . . (These) deal more with problems that with personalities. The *Secunda Scaligerna,* compiled between 1603 and 1607 by two young Leiden students, contains more French than Latin and more spice than scholarship. Aside from his views of the Renaissance and the vigorous language, Scaliger "forecasts the great collaborative enterprises of nineteenth and twentieth century classical scholarship" in advising young men to mine "splendid ancient wills and documents" for material. See Anthony Grafton's, *Joseph Scaliger,* Oxford: Oxford University Press, 1983 and a second volume by the same name, Oxford: Oxford University Press, 1993.

103. Ménage became the leading Parisian intellectual and conversationalist of the seventeenth century. At his Wednesday night soirees, carried on for some thirty years, he is said to have commented more than once that he knew ten things, but had learned nine in conversation. A lawyer, he later abandoned the law for the church. The literary meetings, or "mercuriales" began in 1656. Here one would find Mmme de La Fayette, Mme de Sévigne, (1626–1696) and all the leading French thinkers. Among his books was a history of woman philosophers (1690), but today he is remembered for his -ana, i.e., *Menagiana* where his friends collected his best anecdotes, stories, jokes, etc.

104. Wilson, "Table Talk," 32. It was much the same in England and the United States, where the -ana lost out as a descriptor to synonyms such as "collection" or "compilation"; or a "prose miscellinary."

105. This -ana was reprinted: *Omniana.* Carbondale, Il.: Southern Illinois University Press, 1969. This, in addition to the regular edition, includes additions made from 1809 to 1816 by Coleridge as well as items added in 1836. Coleridge made only about fifty contributions to the 250 pieces.

106. *Bartlett's Familiar Quotations,* 16th ed. (Boston: Little, Brown, 1922), 619. The quotation is from Churchill's *Roving Commission: My Early Life* 1930. For other uses of quotations, see Patricia Mayes, "Quotations in Spoken English," *Studies in Language* 14, no. 2 (1990).

107. *The Sociable Story Teller* (Boston: James French, 1846) 2.

108. Any scholarly quotation book is filled with notes and comments about the startling number of sayings that turn out to be of dubious provenance. For an amusing article on misquotes, see Richard Hanser, "Of Deathless Remarks," *American Heritage* (June 1970) 54–59. See, too, Laurence Urdang, "Accuracy in Quotation," *Verbatim* (spring 1991), 17–18.

109. Linda Calendrillo, "The Art of Memory and Rhetoric" (Ph.D. diss., Purdue University, 1988).

110. Edward Bysshe's *Art of English Poetry* (1702), a subject approach to primarily seventeenth century dramatic and poetical quotations. A similar title was *A Poetical Dictionary: or, The Beauties of the English Poets.* London: J. Newbery, 1761. These and other books are "characterized by a subject arrangement . . . by the absence of a keyword index, and by incomplete and abbreviated source citations. Even if you succeed in finding what you seek in one of these works, you still have far to go." Anthony Shipps, *The Quote Sleuth* (Urbana: University of Illinois Press, 1990), 26.

111. *Anonymiana: or, Ten Centuries of Observations on Various Authors and Subjects* (London: John Nichols and Son, 1809), iv.

112. These are dutifully reviewed in standard library review sources, such as *Library Journal* and *Booklist,* as well as in the popular press. For an example of the latter, by a master of such things, see William Safire, "On Language" *New York Times Magazine,* 12 December 1993, 32. Safire recommends a dozen quotations books and dictionaries.

113. *Bartlett's Familiar Quotations,* vii.

114. Ibid., xi. The Bartlett's editor, Justin Kaplan, a Pulitzer Prize winner, has written an excellent short introduction to the work that should be read by anyone who wishes to understand the place of quotations books in our modern society. For an historical sketch of the work, see the equally excellent essay by Kerry L. Cochrane, "The Most Famous Book of Its Kind" in *Distinguished Classics of Reference Publishing,* ed. James Rettig, (Phoenix, Ariz.: Oryx Press, 1992). There are countless articles on each edition of Bartlett, although most are not historical. For the latter, and another history of the famous book, see Emily Beck, "The Long Happy Life of Bartlett's Quotations," *American Heritage* (August–September 1984): 102–107.

115. See Katz, *Introduction to Reference Work,* for a discussion of major current works including, of course, Bartlett and various CD-ROM/online compilations.

116. Bartlett, 195. The quote is from Shakespeare's *Hamlet.*

4

The Reference of Time: Almanacs, Calenders, Chronologies, and Chronicles

If any reference book deserves the name of irrepressible it is the almanac. "Though we grow old, it renews its youth every year, and greets us regularly with a kind of good natured, 'Here I am Again!' "[1]

Almanacs

An "almanac" is defined as an annual containing statistical, tabular, and general information. This definition has been much the same since its inception, although before the twentieth century the term was usually narrower and synonymous with "astronomical and meteorological data arranged according to the days, weeks, and months of a year."[2]

Today's almanac is best described as a chronology of the year's past events, along with a massive number of facts and information on everything from abbreviations to zoological parks. The 1996 *World Almanac* resembles nothing so much as a one-volume encyclopedia arranged by broad subject areas. In fact, until 1922 the *World Almanac's* full title was *The World Almanac and Encyclopaedia.* More in keeping with the historical tradition of the reference form, today's *The Old Farmer's Almanac* is constructed around a calendar of months and days with astronomical and weather data. Other useful information is included, although the primary focus is on meteorological forecasts. The structure and contents of earlier titles was much the same. Each publisher had his peculiar notion of what would win readers, but essentially the basic scope (from weather forecasts to liturgical calendars) was standard. Furthermore, many almanacs had blank pages for diary entries and a handy hole in the upper left hand corner so the booklet could be strung together with previous titles.[3]

Directed primarily to the common person, the almanac often was looked upon as vulgar. The typical almanac acted the role of the present-day popular press, offering violence and sensational events followed up—whether or not they happened—with lurid broadsides and ballads often by the same publisher. One almanac compiler, for example, promised battles in the sky between ships and armies, while another spoke of dragons in the air over Sussex. Yet, most critics admitted the almanacs did succeed in making current

95

political and social ideas, if only in simplified reference form available to a community. "Young Nathaniel Ames's almanacs of 1766 pictured the colonists happy under as good a King as ever reign'd, but six years later he was extolling . . . the patriotic American farmer for defending the colonists' natural rights . . . In the decade prior to the outbreak of hostility at Concord, almanacs were readying farmers for rebellion."[4] The first American almanacs published current public documents, political tracts, patriotic poetry, and, yes, instructions on how to make gunpowder at home.

Primarily because it was inexpensive and covered a wide variety of popular information, the almanac was a best-selling reference book for centuries after printing. Almanacs were sold wherever a group of people might gather. In addition to booksellers, everyone from haberdashers to grocers and physicians might sell or pass out free almanacs. The traveling peddlers who appeared at fairs and markets and even door-to-door were a major source of almanac supply. English publishers in the 1660s sold an average of four hundred thousand copies annually, "a figure which suggests that roughly one family in three bought an almanac each year.[5] In America an eighteenth century publisher boasted that his almanacs were read by multitudes who read nothing else. In both numbers of individual titles and sales, the almanac continued to be popular until the latter part of the nineteenth century, when it gave way to the cheap newspaper and magazine.

Almanacs were suited for the illiterate and near-illiterate because the information was standard from year to year and, more important, symbols—like drawing the phases of the moon as well as crosses to indicate holidays—were widely used. These symbols were part of the common culture or could be memorized. There were numerous, usually crude illustrations and diagrams. Woodcuts might range from random pictures to detailed renderings of animals and places. Standard typographical decorations often were scattered through as were small caricatures and cartoons.[6]

The curious aspect of the almanac was the combination of scientific data and sometimes ridiculous prognosis with easy-to-understand information mixed with Latin quotations. "We notice in almanacs a non-symmetrical attitude towards academic culture. Popular culture admired erudite culture. It tried, affirming its own field, to reproduce what it admired . . . While erudite culture tried . . . to put away mystery . . . in popular culture and in almanacs particularly, mystery is a fundamental element."[7] The almanac tried to give the uneducated some explanation of the mystery of nature.

Still, astrology was the heart of most almanacs. The illustrations and calendars charted terrestrial movements that, in turn, offered general predictions. The charts showed the most propitious times for actions from marriage to planting a crop. "The circulation of almanacs helped—and in turn was helped by—the activities of astrological practitioners. Their roles were complementary. The almanac spoke in general terms of the harvest, disease and wars, while the consultant found solutions to individual problems."[8]

With inevitable modifications by various publishers and in different periods, a sixteenth century almanac opened with a calendar. This was tied to astrologically planetary movements. Here appeared the familiar "zodiacal man," which showed parts of the body controlled by zodiac signs. While all almanacs were constructed around calendars, differences came in inclusion of added materials. These varied from short sayings and paragraphs on events of interest to lectures on morality and patriotism. Household hints, recipes for improving everything from skin to crops, descriptions of customs, and even short stories and essays were added. The pointing out proper days for bleeding, taking physic, and other odd matters seems to have been one of the important parts of the task of the almanac compilers. Many would not willingly adopt a remedy for disease without consulting the mystical column in the almanac devoted to knees, arms, legs, ankles, feet, etc. It was considered unlucky to take medicine of the sign that influenced that part of the body.[9]

The value of a current almanac is obvious, if as much for entertainment as an accurate source of facts. Older almanacs, too, serve much the same purpose and are of considerable help to historians. Their contents reflect interests of the average person, particularly during the seventeenth to early twentieth century. More important, the data, while not always reliable, is at least indicative of trends. For example, one historian points out the value of nineteenth century almanacs in Minnesota. They may be used as "source material about the immigrant inhabitants, missionary history, and cultural developments."[10]

In the Beginning

The familiar almanac developed by combining earlier calendars, astronomical and astrological data as well as prognostications and chronologies. Originally all were separate reference works, although gradually they combined. With printing the combination was complete, and the almanac emerged.

The basic purpose of the early almanac was to serve as a calendar, charting the year's divisions and linking days and months with major events, past and predicted. The almanac maker became an authority on time. Almanacs or, more precisely, astronomically based calendars date back to the earliest extant periods of writing in Western history. Movements of the stars dictated everything from when to plant to religious ceremonies. One of the earliest almanacs is from the period of Rameses II (1304–1168 BC). It is a compilation of data with good and evil days clearly marked. Injunctions with regard to fire and precautions for guarding against the evil eye are noted.[11]

There is a close relationship between the typical almanac and today's calendar.[12] But there was an even closer relationship between the almanac and astrology. The art of determining the influences of the stars and planets on earth can be traced to the early Mesopotamians who passed astrology on to the the the Greeks and Romans. Although the casters of horoscopes were the target of satire from the Romans through the Renaissance, astrology as a science commanded the ardent allegiance of the best minds of the ancient world. Despite early Christian condemnation, between tradition and a strong Muslim influence, astrology gained dominance. In the end, most theologians adhered to the traditional position, admitting an influence of the stars.[13]

More equivalent to the modern almanac was the Babylonian diary (c. 652–660 B.C.) written in cuneiform on clay tablets. The primary focus of the diary was on astronomical observations, but other material was included. About 450 B.C., the Babylonians divided the zodiac belt into twelve signs.[14] Each of the Babylonian months provided information on imported commodities, the level of the Euphrates River at Babylon, and major local and national events. In one month the death of Alexander the Great, who died at Babylon on June 12, 323 B.C., is recorded. Ptolemy's star charts in his *Almagest* (c. A.D. 140) appear to have translated the Babylonian names into Greek, from which the modern names were translated.[15]

The majority of almanacs used before the eighteenth century might be termed "ephemeris," i.e., a work that contained astrological as well as meteorological forecasts for each day.[16] A saint's calendar was a usual addition. It might be used by the average person as a source of information, too, on medical treatment of a fairly primitive nature.

The medieval almanac—built primarily around calendars indicating Christian holidays, Saints' birthdays, etc.—was relatively common among scholars. Compilers and authors spanned the twelfth and fourteenth centuries, i.e., Solomon Jarchus (1150), Roger Bacon (1292), Walter de Elvedene (1327), and Nicolas deLynner (1386).

Printing and Almanacs

Printing made possible the widespread use of the almanac. It became the first truly popular publication. Its low cost and, in most cases, relatively easy-to-understand content guaranteed success. More important, it gave information of great or suspected great value to the reader. Books were scarce, newspapers and magazines nonexistent, and travel only for a few. The almanac was the major, if not the only, source of easy-to-understand information about that which was outside the immediate community.

The first printed almanac, suitably enough, was pulled from the press by Gutenberg in 1457.[17] A broadsheet to be hung on the wall, it contained the festivals and notable days of the year. Gutenberg also may have printed another almanac in 1460, a quarto of six leaves. From the fifteenth century, the broadside with limited text and numerous illustrations (usually woodcuts) offered the "reference" works for the poor and illiterate. Primarily these ranged from news of crimes and personalities to ballads, proclamations, news sheets, and other ephemera. The majority offered such items as "The true description of a monstrous chyle borne in the isle of Wight, 1564" or "Mamentation & confession of J.R. Jeffery, who now lies under sentence of death (1866)." By the nineteenth century, cheap newspapers, books, and magazines drove out the broadsheet—no matter what its contents. As part of this tradition, the popular almanac paralleled the broadsides and, unlike them, have continued until this day. In the fifteenth through the eighteenth century, many were in broadsheet format, although there was a more ambitious flood of pamphlet-sized titles. Almanacs, particularly from the eighteenth century on, proved to be very profitable pamphlets.

A German mathematician, Johann Müller (1436–1476), a native of Königsberg (for which he received the name of "*Regiomontanus,*" (Königsberg's Latin equivalent) compiled an almanac around 1470. A prototype for other works of the fifteenth and sixteenth century, it was published in Nuremberg in 1472 as the *Kalendarium Novum.* No copy is extant, but a copy of it was published four years later by Erhardus Ratdolt. The twelve leaves are a tribute to Ratdolt's typographical skills. The almanac is among the first books to contain a complete ornamental title page.[18]

By the sixteenth century, bits and pieces were borrowed from *The Books of Hours,* revisions and additions made, and the popular single-page broadsheet to twenty-four-page almanac developed. The early almanacs shared common features with the *Book of Hours,* such as the ubiquitous calendar, but the majority developed their own particular content. One hangover from ancient times was the emphasis on good and bad days. There was little pattern to the selection, particularly between countries where the good or bad luck days differed radically. Many added remarks, such as "Those who fall ill on unlucky days will be in danger . . . If a man married either he or his wife will not live long, or they will not love, or will be always poor." Crude to rather refined astronomical tables, usually illustrated, were also common. Normally these were used in parallel with weather predictions along with such well-worn saws as "Evening red and morning gray is the sign of a fine day." Medical and dietetic advice was usual. The information was often copied from one almanac to another. "The absolute necessity of frequent bleeding and continual physickings is insisted upon in all."[19] In a French manuscript one finds such instructions as "In January it is not good to bleed, but you should take ginger as medicine . . . In October we ought to eat grapes, and drink sweet wine . . . It is good to bleed this month."[20]

Everyone seems to have purchased or been given an almanac in sixteenth and seventeenth century England. Capp points out there are records of almanacs in the libraries of such diverse social groups as the future Charles I, the Bishop of Norwich, Oxford dons, tradespeople, soldiers, artisans and husbandmen. At the lower levels of society . . . "the almanac faced competition from cheap perpetual prognostications . . . which combined crude astrology with elementary magic . . . At the very bottom, the illiterate were forced to rely on educated neighbors."[21]

Books continued to be out of the reach of the average person until well into the nineteenth century. Either they were too expensive or the person was unable to read. One critic puts it: "Although the invention or printed books extended the scope and subject matter of written and recited literature, books only emphasized a division between two cultures—the popular culture of the ordinary folk, and the culture of the privileged classes."[22]

Almanac chapbooks served equally well as escapist literature.[23] The inexpensive, sometimes free, works celebrated what today one finds on the front page of the *National Enquirer* or in the pages of, say, The *Star.* "Monstrous births, the fall of kings and seas red with blood were an important element."[24]

In 1497, Richard Pynson published the first almanac in England, *The Shepheard's Kalendar,* a translation of a French work.[25] The *Kalendar* was a large perpetual calendar that contained religious, moral, and astrological advice, as well as health tips. The *Kalendar* held its own in England (and throughout Europe) until the early seventeenth century. William Parron, published the second series of almanacs in England between 1498 and 1503, in both Latin and English. But then Parron suddenly disappeared from history "as a result of the embarrassing death of the queen at the age of thirty-seven after he had predicted that she would live to be eighty."[26]

A dynasty of Flemish astrologers, physicians and publishers dominated the European almanac scene between 1469 and 1550. The Laet family printed their works in Antwerp and then shipped them throughout Europe in the languages of the various countries.

> The general contents of these early almanacs present a singular mixture of usefulness and superstition, but of the latter only a few years have passed (i.e. from the mid nineteenth century) since our almanacs were effectually purged. Even in our own times . . . if a man found it necessary to take medicine or to be bled, if he had some agricultural operation to perform, even if he wanted to set out on a journey, his first impulse was to consult his almanac.[27]

By and large weather predictions were the most popular feature of almanacs. Ben Jonson's *Sordido* turned to the almanac for help as did country gentlemen of the early eighteenth century, who, according to Jonathan Swift, looked to the almanac for information on whether to hunt or not. The 1636 *Winter's* almanac published at Cambridge immortalizes the famous lines: "April, June and September,/ Thirty days have, as November;/ Each month else doth never vary/ From thirty-one, save February;/ Which twenty-eight doth still confine./ Save on leap-year, then twenty nine."

Publishers saw the benefit of issuing specialized almanacs directed at particular interests, professions, and trades. In time the name of the almanacs became synonymous with given subject area, e.g., "Perkins provided a very full chronology. . . Woodhouse and Dade contained detailed lists of fairs and agricultural advice, Swan's *Ephemeris* supplied data on herbal medicine, and Rose and Fly provided specimen forms of bonds . . . and even wills . . . The Constables Calendar summarized the duties of that office; and the Farriers Almanack listed the diseases of cattle and horses, and prescribed remedies.[28] Also, there were almanacs for political groups as well as regional publications.

A monopoly on almanacs, and the legalization of astrology by implication, was given the Stationer's Company by James I in the early seventeenth century. Licensing various publishers, the Company maintained control until 1775. A typical example of last seventeenth and early eighteenth century almanacs was the one published by William Lilly from 1647 until he died in 1682. His *Merlinus Anglicus Junior* was an odd mixture of calendar, almanac, and prognostication. Both his politics and astrological predictions were extremely popular, although the brunt of jokes among the educated. He managed to word his political forecasts in such a way as to maintain publication throughout the Civil War and the restoration of the monarchy. All of this, to be sure, was in keeping with the ever-watchful Stationer's Company regulations.

English and continental almanacs shared many basic features, but there were important differences. Political, religious, and social ideas were a major consideration in most English works. Not so in European countries where pages were filled with tributes to the rulers. Each country's almanacs made predictions of good and bad periods of the year. As one wag pointed out, "as the English list differed from the French, and the French from the Italian, a man by having the whole three could cheat fate and defy misfortune."[29]

By 1700, many of the publishers were drawing upon Nostradamus (1503–1566), the French physician and astrologer whose book of predictions was published in 1555. John Partridge's *Merlinus Liberatus* for 1700 observed "This will be a remarkable year . . . strange accidents and Disorders in some, in many parts of the World." His dire prediction as those of others was drawn upon a broad interpretation of Nostradamus.[30] Thanks as much to false prognostications as to reliance on astrology, the seventeenth to mid-eighteenth century almanac makers were generally, if not always, considered less than reliable. In 1614, a critic observed that "as for his [i.e., an almanac] judging at the uncertainty of the weather, any old shepherd shall make a dunce of him."[31] The compilers hardly apologized for their work, and more often boasted. Identified by name and "student" or "well willers," they might preface a work, such as one by a seventeenth century English "philosopher." Thomas Bretnor informs his "courteous reader" that he teaches in "Englishe, Latine, French, or Spanish," the arts of arithmetic, geometry, navigation, astronomy and astrology. He defies his detractors to say as much.[32] The most famous author and astrologer of the seventeenth century was one William Lilly who published not only almanacs but textbooks, such as his Christian Astrology (1647). "His autobiography suggests a man of ingenuity but questionable ethics."[33]

As filler in numerous seventeenth century almanacs was the work often of young college graduates, much of it sparking and satiric, although most consisted of short, dull essays on such matters as agriculture or home remedies. Thomas Shepard II is an example of a young American poet who contributed to an American almanac in the mid-seventeenth century. His "entwining of imagery from astrology, mythology and the literal" in his short poems often has "strong sexual connotations," unusual for the time.[34]

Most publishers and compilers tried to make selling points by listing the errors or downright fraudulent statements in their competitors' works. Denouncing "frauds" and "lies" was "a very common situation in the seventeenth and eighteenth centuries." Humorous almanacs usually targeted other almanacs for criticism as well.[35]

By the middle of the eighteenth century, the redirection of the publishers to educate and enlighten a public otherwise deprived of books and certainly of reference works, resulted in a reappraisal. Now treated as one would a newspaper or magazine, the almanac became more respectable.

Today the consensus is that the early almanacs served a valuable educational function. "The better almanacs also provided esthetics satisfaction through quotations and selections from some of the great Continental writers as well as from such eighteenth-century English essayists and poets as Addison, Steele, Thomson and Pope."[36]

The eighteenth century had two major figures involved with almanacs, Jonathan Swift (1667–1745) and Benjamin Franklin (1706–1790). Swift's 1708 almanac (issued in late 1707) was published under the name of Isaac Bickerstaff, Esq. In his preface Swift explains that Patridge's almanack, a primary competitor, was the object of Swift's astrological competence. "I have consulted the star of his nativity by my own rules, and find he will infallibly die upon the 29th of March next, about 11 at night, of a raging fever; therefore I advise him to consider of it, and settle his affairs in time." Swift made other fascinating predictions such as "On the 15th news will arrive of a very surprising event, than which nothing can be more unexpected."[37] Quite alive and angry, Patridge made the mistake of trying to respond to Swift. The only result was that Patridge became the object of laughter and Swift's almanac sold extremely well.

Almanacs were given away as a method of advertising. In advertisements "William Davis informed his readers that he attended at the Red Lion in Broomham, Wilts, each Monday, Wednesday and Saturday to resolve astrological queries and dispense pills."[38] One John Keene offered to teach mathematics and science in Greek and Latin, while Edward Pond offered courses in arithmetic and navigation. The advertisements were a success, and by the eighteenth century the almanac became a primary vehicle for advertising of all types. No longer limited to astrology and "education," the ads broadcast information about everything from books to rooms.

In the mid-eighteenth century, almanacs under various names were bestsellers. The most famous was *Old Moore's* of which the modern *Whitaker's* is a descendant. Of the sixteen to twenty publishers, *Moore's* sold the most copies, some eighty-two thousand in 1761.[39] The English "diary" was a pocketbook substitute for the almanac. The diary contained the requisite number of blank pages, but included much almanac information as well. "It is not always easy . . . to distinguish today between an Almanac and a Diary."[40]

Early American Almanacs

English residents in the American colonies imported numerous almanacs, and between 1639 and 1700 close to 9 percent of everything published in the colonies was an almanac. Other than the Bible it was the most popular publication in America. The second item printed, in what was to be the United States, was an almanac. Writing on March 25, 1639, Governor Winthrop noted in his journal: "A printing house was begun at Cambridge (Mass.) by one (Stephen) Daye, at the charge of Mr. Glover who died on sea hitherward. The first thing which was printed was the freeman's oath (a broadside), the second was an almanack made for New England by Mr. William Peirce, mariner; the next was (The whole Booke of) Psalmes newly turned into metre."[41] Peirce's almanac followed the style of English works and later American publications. Advertisements were found on the back and sometimes front pages as well as lists of events of the past and/or coming years with miscellaneous facts.

The almanac reached its zenith of popularity in America during the eighteenth century, gradually giving ground in the nineteenth to newspapers and, by mid-century, magazines. Hundreds of different almanacs, in thousands of copies each, were published. Many were sixteen pages, but the majority were between thirty-two and forty-eight pages in length. The traditional price was six pence. "Hundreds of almanacs were published in our largest cities and in many of our smaller towns. Peddlers carried them into parts of the country that were not served by booksellers. Farmers, shippers and fishermen often felt they needed an almanac in order to regulate their yearly activities."[42]

Compilers and authors of early American almanacs tended to be well educated, particularly in mathematics, general science, religion, and, more often than not, astrology. "It was no wonder, then, that these well informed men should find their almanacs media for other than tabular information. Occasionally . . . they invaded the realm of pure literature . . . sometimes giving scientific information, sometimes indulging in moral or philosophical comment." There was a strong leaning toward religious instruction. Cotton Mather declared the advancement of Christian piety was "no unsuitable service for an almanack."[43]

Two publishers (Ames and Franklin) dominated American almanacs in the eighteenth century. They owed their success to expanding the contents of the sixteen- to twenty-four-page pamphlet, and by adding bits of humor, quotations, current events, and just about anything guaranteed to win an audience.

The *Astronomical Diary,* published first in 1725 by the junior Nathaniel Ames, was by and large the best-known and greatest of eighteenth century American almanacs. Published until 1775, its only competition was Benjamin Franklin's *Poor Richard.* The format remained standard. One page was given to each month. "In the left hand column would be numbers from one to twenty eight . . . or thirty-one; the next few columns would contain information on the tides, the rising and setting of the sun and moon, and the quarter or sign of the moon. The last column . . . contained such information as saint's days and birthdays of rulers, as well as weather forecasts and sometimes predictions of non meteorological events . . ."[44] Using this blank space, Ames was the first to hit on the idea of adding in a few words of poetry, humor, and sayings on religion, politics, and gossip.

Benjamin Franklin, by and large the most famous American, if not world, publisher of almanacs, put out the first issue of the twenty-four page *Poor Richard* in 1732.[45] It would continue to 1758. According to Franklin, its purpose was to be "both entertaining and useful . . . I consider'd it as a proper vehicle for conveying instruction among the common people, who bought scarcely any other books; I therefore filled all the little spaces . . . with proverbial sentences, chiefly such as inculcated industry and frugality, as the means of procuring wealth."[46]

Picking up on Jonathan Swift's old joke, Franklin confidently predicted the death of his business rival, Titan Leeds of *The American Almanac.* Leeds, fortunately for Franklin, took the bait and gave Franklin much free publicity by insisting he, Leeds, was still very much alive.

Franklin made few original contributions, although he did introduce a pictorial calendar page that still is in use. Conversely his sayings, aphorisms, and encyclopedic coverage of useful data (usually introduced by "Poor Richard say") made him and the almanac famous. By 1748 the almanac had increased to thirty-six pages, added woodcut decorations, and become more sophisticated. In his last issue, Franklin published a collection of sayings from twenty-five issues as "Father Abraham's Speech."[47]

The greatest Monarch on the proudest Throne, is oblig'd to sit upon his own Arse," Poor Richard reminds us in his Almanack for 1737. Such a truism might pass unnoticed except as a bit of humor. However, it serves as a sign of Benjamin Franklin's political and ideological agenda in preparing his annual collection of proverbs, anecdotes, astrological charts, and miscellaneous information.[48]

In the run-up to the American Revolution, it is possible to conclude that almanacs helped readers to become well prepared to take an intelligent part in the great events that lay just ahead. As Sidwell and others have pointed out, the American almanac from its inception was a significant educational instrument. "Writers and printers of these almanacs were well aware of the educational role of their works, and consciously oriented them to this end."[49] The diligent reader had gained a "fairly adequate record of the recent great public events," supported by texts of documents found in the almanacs. Particularly near the beginning of the American Revolution, some met the challenge head on, e.g., Ames *Almanack* for 1765 "sprinkled his work with brief comments, such as "New England luxury cannot be supported, unless more of her Commodities are exported," and "Some brave spirits grow with patriotic Ardor."[50] Poetry in praise of liberty was found throughout the almanacs as were hints on how to become more self-sufficient and less reliant on England. The reader "had even been introduced to the idea of armed resistance and told how he could make his own little store of gunpowder."[51]

Almanacs, Nineteenth Century to Modern

The nineteenth century industrial revolution, and its byproduct of cheap reading materials, removed the almanac as basic reading matter in most homes. It remained important, but it no longer was the primary source of information and entertainment. Still, despite publication of close to two thousand new reference works in America each year, the *World Almanac* is among the top ten best-sellers . . . and with an average of two million copies sold, it often is at the head of the list.

Although the early nineteenth century almanac looked much the same as its predecessors, the content changed. "At the root of the decline lay the reduced intellectual and thence social standing of astrology . . . Most almanacs henceforth offered only a cursory and stereotyped justification of astrology."[52] Prophesises were dropped in many titles and predictions that were offered seemed vague and repetitive. In place of astrology publishers offered wisdom from classical mythology and essays on virtue as well as riddles and recipes. Politics, too, played an important role with satirical, often slanderous attacks on party and individuals. In England, popular hatred of the Pope and the French was reflected in almanac cartoons.

Seeking to maintain and build an audience, almanac publishers fought the flood of cheap publications by offering more for the money. Most titles expanded from thirty or fifty pages to close to two hundred pages and, in fact, became one-volume encyclopedias. By the end of the nineteenth century, it was not unusual to find a two-hundred-and-fifty or three-hundred-page almanac with much the same type of data as offered in today's work. Charles Knight, the gallant, who fought for universal literacy in England and supported his battle with numerous easy-to-read publications, said this in his newly two-hundred-page almanac for 1828: "This is not a mere temporary work." No, it was to be preserved as part of a systematic collection of data that every educated person should have at his or her command—and this included everything from information on medicine and saving banks to lightning rods and "abstracts of parliamentary documents" as well as "notice of the progress of public improvements."[53]

The final great age for the nineteenth century English almanac was in 1839 when Francis Moore's wildly popular *Vox Stellarum,* (which had been begun by Moore in 1699 and was carried into the twentieth century as *Old Moore*) reached sales of over 560 thousand. The success was well deserved as it offered materials from the *Transactions* of the Royal Society, and the calendars and standard data were based on scientific findings, not superstition or astrology. "Much of Moore's appeal came . . . from the section (which gave) an annual review of English and foreign affairs . . . its comments must have been an important formative influence in the growth of English radicalism in the early 1790s."[54] The vigor and bluntness of the almanac won readers, but by the end of the century competition with the popular press, magazines, and inexpensive books proved too much, even for Moore's. In 1895 its sales were down fifty thousand and in the 1920s to a mere fifteen thousand or so. Later revived as *Old Moore's Almanac,* its 1975 "print order ran to one and three quarter million."[55]

Despite the decline of *Moore's,* regional and more elaborate almanacs emerged in the late nineteenth and early twentieth centuries. "There was virtually no house . . . without an almanac. . . The country people believed implicitly in the dramatic and numerous predictions."[56] A typical mid-nineteenth century almanac was filled with facts, statistics on annual temperatures, crop information, famous people, holidays, officials and, well much the same type of material found in a modern almanac.[57]

By the close of the nineteenth century, versions of the almanac could be found everywhere, "and it is hard to say where this pushing, progressive, irresistible little book will not go." There were almanacs for every trade and profession, and "we cannot buy a box of notepaper but we find one in it; perfumer sends it to us scented; our newspaper gives us one illustrated."[58] Advertising almanacs, given free, usually were nineteenth century methods of spreading the word about patent medicines. Religious and political groups used the same approach, e.g., the *American Christian Almanac* by 1850 claimed a circulation of more than 300 thousand.

One particular type of subject—the comic almanac—enjoyed immense popularity well into modern times. "The comic almanac is a purely modern feature of the little book—the pleasant wrinkle added by the nineteenth century. Cruikshank, and those witty clever souls who were the original staff of *Punch,* began the laugh, which America in several publications of this kind had re-echoed."[59] The comic almanacs were little more than variations on Cruikshank's Comic Almanac series. In a sense, these almanacs were closer to magazines than reference books. The content was built primarily around easy-to-understand stories, advice of all sorts, and numerous illustrations. Everything was supposed to be amusing. "The biggest space filler was humorous sketches about the past year's major events, such as Mally Mufindorf's Letter to Queen . . . after the birth of the Crown Prince."[60]

The subject almanac, from humor to agriculture to medicine, dominated the publishing scene. A French critic observed that "there have appeared almanacs upon so many different subjects that it would seem to be impossible to find a subject which would be sufficiently interesting upon which to compile one."[61] There were almanacs of the Gods, the Muses, the Graces, goblins, kings, and eve of the devil. (A 1733–1735 French work, entitled "*L'enfer*".)

Summarizing the role of the almanac, until it was forced into competition with other reference works and inexpensive reading matter, a critic observes that:

> No book or publication has ever been the subject of more ridicule and contempt than the Almanac, yet no book has been more universally read, or more highly valued. . . The almanac constituted the only reading matter in many families and copies were preserved from year to year for the useful information and maxims which they contained, as well as the practical astronomy they taught. When we are aware that the almanac in early days constituted the only method of reaching the people generally, we appreciate the full importance of these publications and gain a clearer knowledge of the tastes and inclinations of the readers.[62]

Today's Almanac

The almanac today is less revered, but remains a basic reference work for most Americans, as well as West Europeans. The *Subject Guide to Books in Print* (1993–1994) dutifully lists some fifty to sixty titles under "Almanacs" with a reminder to see also "Calendars; Chronology; Music-Yearbooks; Nautical Almanacs; Yearbooks." The almanacs listed range from *The Medical Almanac* to *Facts on File Yearbook* with such standard items as *The Old Farmer's Almanac* and the *World Almanac.*[63] In today's library and home the last are dominant and as familiar to both laypersons and librarians as the encyclopedia or general index.

The World Almanac and *The Old Farmer's Almanac,* among the scores of legitimate almanacs now in print, are representative of today's titles. The first, with close to a thousand pages, is a one-volume encyclopedia. The second, much more modest at two-hundred-odd pages, follows the traditional almanac with the emphasis on weather, prognostications, and general advice and opinion. Claiming to be the "Number 1 national best-seller" and "the authority since 1868," *The World Almanac and Book of Facts* has an annual circulation of two million copies. In comparison, one magazine, the *Reader's Digest,* boasts more than sixteen million subscribers, as the top best-selling magazine. But the *Almanac* would be among the most popular twenty-five. As the editor explains, the first edition was "a one-hundred-twenty-page volume with twelve pages of advertising." It was published by the *New York World* from 1868 until 1876 and was revived by the *World* in 1886 and has been published annually since then.[64]

Robert Thomas founded *The Farmer's Almanack* in Sterling, Massachusetts in 1792. It continues today as *The Old Farmer's Almanac,* from Dublin, New Hampshire. Determined to produce a new type of almanac, particularly one that would help in the self-education of its readers, Thomas "gradually replaced astrological signs and weather predictions with advice about imbuing children with book knowledge and school learning. . . Thomas fostered the connection of commerce with culture in the countryside."[65] Editor for fifty-five years, the venerable Thomas struck early on a magic formula for success—accurate weather predictions. The secret has been passed on from editor to editor, but by the 1950s an atmospheric scientist joined the establishment to give scientific credence to the reports.[66] Yes, but how accurate are the weather forecasts for the geographical regions of the United States? Using the monthly temperature and precipitation forecasts, "which are the only elements of the Almanac forecasts amenable to objective verification,[67] two scientists determined that about 50.7 percent of the time the forecasts are correct. This is "to be compared with the 50 percent rate of success to be expected by chance."[68] Much the same can be said about all almanacs and weather predictions from the Sumerians to the present. A 50–50 percent rate of success was and is the norm.

Today, almanacs can be useful tools for the gardener. "Although their weather forecasts might not always hit the mark, at least they offer you an opinion when you are planning your garden and trying to guess whether spring will be early, cold, dry, or all three."[69] Also, every almanac has its moon sign table, which is used by those who plant by phases of the moon. Other bits of information, from lists of perennials for shade to data on trees, are scattered through most almanacs.

The modern almanac is an indispensable reference aid—both in and outside the library. More than that, it is a beloved reference work. Let an "almanacophiliac" summarize:

> I like everything about the almanac. I like its tiny type, which seems somehow more authoritative. . . Some sections (in *The World Almanac*) like "Entertainment personalities—where and when born," I find irresistible. . . The animal section offers an entry on speed . . . Someone at almanac headquarters must be a word nut because we get not only the odd names for animal young . . . but also a round-up of the collective nouns of specific animals in groups. . . It's the discovery of artless little gems of nonjudgmental fact that makes almanacs satisfying reading . . . The only thing that bothers me about the almanac is that my name isn't in it.[70]

Calendars, Chronologies, and Chronicles

... human sciences that preserved memories had to become involved ... [major, historical] days fixed important points in time that helped posterity to date events. .. In short, [chronologies] constituted historical time.[71]

Chronologies and calendars were important parts of the early almanacs, and, in fact, before the Renaissance, chronologies or calendars were found primarily in almanacs. With the Renaissance and the development of astronomy, the possibility of scientific chronologies became possible, and for the most part they became separate publications.

The measurement of time is a study in itself. But here the focus is on two or three aspects of the reference of time: calendars, chronologies, and chronicles. Aside from the familiar calendar, the forms may be defined as (1) **Chronologies,** which compute time by divisions, periods, or other means and then assign events or transactions to each of the divisions. Chronologies might be divided by centuries, by the rise and fall of a country, by professional achievements, by the dynasty of kings, etc. Today the typical chronology is similar to Bernard Grun's *Timetables of History,* which offers a cross tabulation of political, economic, cultural, and social events from the beginning of recorded history to the early 1990s.[72] (2) **Annals** are closely related to chronologies. sometimes the two are used as synonyms. Essentially, though an annual records annual events, arranged for a country or topic: The *Annals of Opera, 1597–1940* traces the development of opera in chronological order with composer, city of first production, etc. for each entry. Mortinmer Adler and Charles Van Doren's *The Annals of America* is a twenty-three-volume arrangement of original source materials from specific periods of American history, word for history, particularly before the nineteenth century. A well-known example is the work of Tacitus (c. A.D. 56–112), *The Annals of Imperial Rome.* (3) **Chronicles,** although in little use today, were, during the Middle Ages popular narratives of a period in a country's history. *The Anglo-Saxon Chronicle* is the earliest vernacular English example of the form, tracing events from the ninth century to 1134. Many chronicles were written by a series of individuals over a long period of time. Today the descriptor primarily is used in fiction as a synonym for a narrative. A well-known example is Anthony Trollope's *The Chronicles of Barsetshire* (1855–1867).

Calendars

The three forms—chronologies, annals, and chronicles—are dependent on a calendar. The daily calendar is not considered a reference work by many laypersons or librarians, but it is glanced at as a point of reference more often than any other work. The calendar appears first in Mesopotamia about 3000 B.C. and shortly thereafter in Egypt. Near the invention of writing, the Middle Eastern calendar divided the year into summer and winter, with each month beginning roughly with the appearance of the New Moon. The Egyptians were more subtle and exact, working out a calendar of 365 days divided into three seasons, each of four months. The ancient Greeks settled for twelve months and about 354 days, which was changed slightly over the centuries. The first Roman calendars reduced the number of days in the year to 304 then raised it to 355, and finally lowered it to 366.

The calendar, no matter how it was presented, is a feature of all civilizations. Each—from the Mayan to the early Greek—has its own peculiar features and additions, but, remarkably, all compute days, months, and years within much the same framework.

Egyptians established the year's length, divided it into twelve months, and established days of birth for individuals. The Greeks used astronomy and mathematics as the basic tools for measuring time, and Aristotle discussed the philosophical implications of "before" and "after" in human perception. The Jews adopted a time measuring system to suit the needs of a wandering people and shepherds. There emerged a calendar that allowed laypersons an overview of time in general and a seven day week in particular.

All of these calendars, with variations for more than three thousand years, failed ultimately because they relied on the month and the phases of the Moon to mark the month. The Egyptians offered exceptions, but it would take Sosigenes, an Alexandrian astronomer, in the first century B.C. to establish the Julian Calendar (named after Julius Caesar who invited the astronomer to make the necessary calculations). Names of the various months changed, although basically they were dependent upon earlier Roman calendars. In 44 B.C., for example, the month previously called Quintilis was changed to Julius (July) in honor of Caesar. Shortly thereafter Augustus had his name fixed to the eighth.

Early Roman calendars are called "*fasti.*" The *fasti* also covered lists of magistrates, priests and rulers, as well as notes on festival days. The earliest extant *fasti* in book form is the *Fasti Idaciani* from A.D. 350. Earlier examples are mentioned in connection with the library at Alexandria, but none is extant.

The Christians took over the Roman *fasti,* or calendars, changing the Roman holidays to Christian landmarks. Out of this developed the ecclesiastical perpetual calendar that could be adjusted to meet the needs of a particular year. The earliest extant Christian calendars was compiled about A.D. 354 and is typical probably of the genre for numerous centuries. The fifty parchment leaves were both an almanac and a calendar. Data about Christian holidays and the like was given. Today, the so-called *Liberiusa Almanac* is best known as one of the earliest sources of December 25 as Christmas day.

The Julian calendar failed to settle the ancient Christian problem of the proper date for Easter. The technical reasons are complex, but essentially the difference arose over whether the figurations were based on a lunar or a solar year. The Julian was, as its Egyptian predecessors, constructed on the solar year. In the sixth century, the Roman abbot Dionysius Exiguus established the Christian chronology and the all-important date of Easter. Prior to that, numerous controversies arose over the date. "The resulting differences in the celebration of Easter caused concern for the church; various councils stressed the need for celebrating Easter on the same day in all Christian communities . . . The discrepancies between the computed dates of the Easter moon and the actual full moon were recognized throughout the Middle Ages."[74]

More often than not, through most of the Middle Ages and into the early Renaissance the term "almanac" was employed for a calendar. This becomes confusing as there were almanacs in the traditional sense of the descriptor being prepared at the same time, and these, to be sure, contained calendars.

Clog almanacs (really calendars) were common from the fifth century until the sixteenth century.[75] These were mnemonic devices, usually composed of symbols and signs carved into a straight piece of wood, a horn, or even into brass. The symbols, lines, and notches acted as a calendar. Some fitted into a pocket, while others were large and found over fireplaces.

As the name of the almanac made upon a square stick, "clog" apparently was in use in England into the early seventeenth century. Some were called "public because they were of a large size, and commonly hung at one end of the mantel tree of the chimney; others (were called) private because they were smaller, and carried in the pocket."[76] Three months were contained on each of the four sides with notches for the number of days and symbols indicating cycles of the Moon as well as officers of the saints and notes on festivals. For January 13, in one clog, St. Hilary is indicated by a cross. With the spread of printing and the cheap almanac, the clog versions disappeared, although according to Moskowitz, clog almanacs were in "use in England as late as the seventeenth century."[77]

More precise celestial observations—for this was the period of Copernicus (1473–1543) and Galileo (1564–1642)—prompted the by-then-urgent need to reform the calendar. The major problem with the Julian calendar was that it lost eleven minutes, fourteen seconds each year, or about seven days in one thousand years. Due to religious holidays, it was difficult to rectify the error, but finally in 1582 Pope Gregory XIII established the improved, more accurate Gregorian calendar, which is employed to this day.[78]

Fixing the dates of the year was one thing, but before printing or even the widespread use of block prints, there were a few calendars to consult. During the Middle Ages, Easter tables, designed to indicate movable feasts, were the favorite place to turn. To use them, one needed a "*computus*" to determine the Easter date. (A "computist" was an individual skilled in using the tables to establish the dates.) This medieval set of tables helped calculate not only Easter, but other astronomical events and movable dates in the calendar. The *computus* was a reference book that used coordination of lunar and solar cycles to establish the days of the week—and, of course, Easter. People became experts and prepared books, which often were chronologies and annals. Noteworthy examples of these experts would include the Venerable Bede (c. 673–735) who used his knowledge in his *History of the English Nation;* as well as Roger Bacon (c. 1214–1294) who urged that the skills associated with the compilation of a *computus* become part of the university curriculum.

Calendar markings indicating days of the saints were a common feature of medieval religious manuscripts, particularly the *Psalter.* This was the most commonly employed book by individuals until the advent of the Books of Hours.[79] The majority of *Psalters* were illuminated. By the fourteenth century the *Book of Hours,* even more elaborately decorated, had replaced the *Psalter* among the rich. Few reference books can claim to be esthetic delights, but a few calendars—at least in the late Middle Ages—were the exception and are delightful. Often the calendar was a part of a splendidly illuminated *Book of Hours.* On the Continent, particularly in the fifteenth and the beginning of the sixteenth century, the private prayer book became a visible sign of wealth for rich individuals. Decorated by some of Europe's outstanding artists, the *Book of Hours* often was the sole book found in many households. And, at a more modest level of decoration, it was often used by parents and teachers to teach children how to read. The calendar, while only a small part of most books of hours, was nevertheless important. Usually one page of the book was devoted to each month, for which feats and commemoration days of saints wee noted. "From the early moment in the Middle Ages it became the custom to decorate calendars with the Signs of the Zodiac and the Labors of the Month . . . This tradition reached its fullest expression in the Calendars of Books of Hours, and in particular in the full-page illustrations to the *Tres Riches Heures . . .* in 1416."[80] The famous pages by the Limbourg brothers have the astrological signs in a lunette at the top of the page and landscapes and labors in miniature.

It is significant that Gutenberg's forty-two-line Bible may be the first major book printed (1455), but possibly most of his money, and the money of those who foreclosed on him and took over his printing shop came not from printed books but from printed calendars. With the advent of printing the most popular, certainly the most widely read, books of the Middle Ages (the *Bible* aside) were turned over to the engraver. The average middle-class person could now afford a relatively inexpensive book of hours, calendar and all. These were printed throughout the sixteenth century and, as in earlier centuries, might be the only book in an average household.

The single-sheet calendar was a common type of printing from the earliest years until this very day. Unfortunately, the importance of issuing such matter has been overlooked. "Many . . . aspects of job printing and the changes it entailed clearly need further study. The printed calendars and indulgences that were first issued from the Mainz workshops of Gutenberg and Fust . . . warrant at least as much attention as the more celebrated Bibles."[81] By the seventeenth century, the familiar wall calendar was a fixed part of most households, or at least those able to afford the item. "A calendar with some miscellaneous information and a few pious thoughts, began to make its way annually into the houses of people whose literary needs were easily satisfied. . . The educationalists of the Enlightenment transformed these . . . into vehicles of popular instruction for the lower classes."[82] The notion of incorporating the calendar into an almanac was popular, and by the early eighteenth century, as in the Middle Ages, the calendar and the inexpensive almanac were often one and the same.

Chronologies

Dealing in scores, if not hundreds, of years rather than in days, chronologies predated both the calendar and the almanac.[83] The chronology probably dates from the dawn of writing about 3000 B.C. However, the earliest extant example is from about one thousand years later—a fragment of one of the earliest chronicles that was discovered in an Assyrian diplomatic archive of 1800 B.C.[84] The most common chronology is a list of kings. The king lists are found throughout the Middle East from c. 2000 B.C. to the dawn of Christianity. The chronicles listed kings from the beginning of time to the present rule; and were supplemented by material on the activities of the current king. A method of destroying an enemy was simply to erase his position in the king list and eliminate any records of activities. For example, the lack of records in Babylonian history before 747 B.C. is due to the obliteration of earlier chronologies by less than historically impressed rulers with whopping egos. In one swipe they managed to clear the country of more than 2,000 years of kings—and history.

"Ptolemy's Canon," is a king list that covers the chronology of Mesopotamia in general and Babylonia and Assyria in particular from about 747 to 540 B.C. Every document before then is lost or not trustworthy. Written by a Greek astronomer during the early Roman Empire, the chronology has proven to be generally correct. Cuneiform tablets recovered throughout the area support the dates. Before 747 B.C. there are documents that have large gaps, but at least indicate the direction of history from the late Sumerian dynasty in about 2000 B.C. to 747 B.C.

Much of today's knowledge is derived from second-, third-, and fourth-hand sources who quoted earlier chronologies. For example, Ptolemy II (285–246 B.C.) commissioned Manetho, an Egyptian priest, to write a history of Egypt. This was done, but Manetho's manuscript was lost and known today only from third-hand accounts and quotations. The chronologies Manetho employed have long since ceased to exist.

The two books of Chronicles in the Old Testament offer a history of the world from its beginning to the destruction of the First Temple by the Babylonians in 586 B.C. Unlike other chronicles, there are narrative sections of varying length. Like earlier works of the same type, though, there are the familiar lists, prophetic stories, and bits of oration. The Chronicles fall into the tradition of the earlier Mesopotamian works.[85]

The early Greeks followed the lead of the other Mediterranean countries and tied recorded history to king lists of heroes. Athenians chronologies went back to 683 B.C., although they stopped at the end of the Greek Dark Ages and did not take into account the much earlier annals of Mycenae, founded in about 2900 B.C. The Greek writer Hellanicus (c. 400 B.C.) was one of the earliest compilers of a chronological table in Greece. His *Atthis,* the first history of Athens, includes an inaccurate chronology, followed by other chronological tables. With Herodotus and the development of the historical analysis of time, there was a recognition of the need for accurate chronology. This culminated in the work of Eratosthenes of Cyrene (275–194 B.C.) called the father of chronology and at one time head of the Alexandria Library. His first scientific attempt to fix dates was based on a list of Olympic game winners. Eratosthenes's tables produced dates that went back to the fall of Troy (c. 1184–83 B.C.), but are only chronologically accurate from about 500 B.C. His methodology was employed later by others, however, and has been supported by literary and archaeological evidence as well as coordinated with astronomical findings.

Early Romans, at least until about the first century B.C. depended upon "yearbooks" compiled by authors who simply listed major events, rulers, and the like year by year. This type of "documentation" was used by the Roman historians as acceptable primarily because the historians seem to have had little direct concern with facts vs. the dramatic effect of events that might or might not be true. Not until Cicero (106–43 B.C.) was the notion of historical scholarship developed in Rome. Cicero's friend, to whom he wrote numerous letters, drew up chronological tables. Atticus's *Liber Annalis,* now lost, was a chronological table of the world particularly Roman history.

Christian Chronologies

Early Christian chronicles faced a multiple problem of fitting pagan Greek and Roman history as well as Jewish writing into historiography suitable to the faith of Christians. The Old Testament was nicely modified into the Christian pattern with the addition of the New Testament. Both, however, are highly selective of early recorded and oral archives. By adopting the Old Testament, the Christians linked their faith with universal history, although with peculiar overtones. By melding Jewish-pagan-and Christian dates into a synchronized chronology, the Christians included some early pagan archives. Sextus Julius Africanus (fl. 3rd century A.D.) was the first chronicler to attempt the feat of picking and choosing dates to give an authentic record of God's revelations and patterns. The result was a confident chronology that gave six thousand years to human history. St. Jerome took over the work and gave it a Latin adaptation, which was the rule of Christian history for at least a thousand years. The chronicle was modified, but essentially accepted by Christian historians. Eusebius recorded as much fact as imagination in his *Ecclesiastical History* (c. 312–324).

The Christian chronology was fixed by Dionysisus Exiguus (c. 500–550), an Italian monk, whose chronology was a byproduct of the lengthy debate over the date of Easter. While hardly without critics, it established major dates of the Christian Era including the date for Christmas.

The Venerable Bede made chronology a relatively popular form in the eighth century. His *Ecclesiastical History of the English People* covers the years from about 600 to 730, and he conscientiously listed his sources, including numerous archival records. Modern historians are amazed at Bede's attention to supporting notes, as well as his lively style, which is unusual for any period. Still, and this point is to be remembered when considering most of the reference works of the Middle Ages, Bede's primary mission was to justify, support, and strengthen the role of Christianity. Everything else was extraneous, which explains his lack of attention to numerous major historical events.

After Bede, most chronologies were simply absorbed into almanacs. The remainder of the Middle Ages offered little by way of improvement or addition. Chronology and almanac became one and the same, that is, until the appearance of the new science of "*chronologia*," a humanist term coined in the sixteenth century.

The remarkable scholar Joseph Scaliger (1540–1609) was the founder of the *chronologia* school and made the greatest contribution to the scientific study of chronology in the Renaissance. A Dutch historian and philologist, Scaliger published his *Opus de Emendatione Tempore* (*Study on the Improvement of Time*) in 1583 and compared computations of time by various civilizations. He corrected the classical time tables and offered the world the first true chronology based on science rather than on myth. In 1509 he published a second major work on the same subject, *Thesaurus Temporum* (*The Thesaurus of Time*), which revised and edited the earlier work of Eusebius. After Scaliger, and to this day, separate historical chronologies became basic reference works in many homes and in all libraries.

Chronicles and Annals

A second cousin of the chronology, chronicles are defined as an historical account of facts or events that are arranged in order of time, usually continuous and detailed without analysis. Formulated in the Middle Ages, the chronicle was a record of what an individual saw and heard, usually at the time of the event. The chronicles usually were in Latin and concerned individuals and events drawn both from life and from manuscripts in the monastic libraries. And, while background material was often evident, including the Creation, the focus was on immediacy and generally all facts were included without much attention to importance.

A cousin of the chronicle is the "annal." Today an annal is synonymous with history and the Romans, and more particularly Tacitus (c. 55–117), who used the descriptor as synonymous with both chronicle and history. Prior to Tacitus, the soldier-poet Quintus Ennius (239–169 B.C.) coined the term annals in an epic poem *Annales*. His *Annals* begins with the flight from Troy and seventeen books later celebrates the Roman Istrian campaign. Little of the work is extant, but it differed radically from later chronicles in that it was more a poetic epic celebrating the development of Rome than a true history. Still, it rivaled the most distinguished of the Hellenic epics and its loss is truly a great disaster for an appreciation of Latin literature.

Among the earliest advocates of the annal was St. Jerome (c. 347–420), who advised the importance of a universal history for supporting Christian philosophy. He made the important point that it was not enough to simply list dates and events, but they had to be given some meaning by a narrative drawing from reliable sources, even if those happened to be pagan. Following the advice of Jerome, scholars and monks of the Middle Ages scrupulously kept annals. These tended to concentrate on an area familiar to the given writer and, for that reason, are relatively accurate. By the eighth century most annals were called chronicles, primarily because the chronicle tended to be more autobiographical than the annal and because the Christians wished to separate their work from the Roman annals.

Paul the Deacon (c. 720–799) was considered one of the best educated men of the eighth century. Conversant in Greek and Latin, he was the master of several other languages and cultures as well. He was in Monte Cassino from 773 to about 783, and left to become a member of Charlemagne's group of scholars at Aachen. A few years later he returned to Monte Cassino where he wrote numerous books. Among his earliest, best-known chronicles is the *History of the Lombards* (c. 774–785), a compelling narrative of his nation's past, chronologically vague but generally accurate.

Among the earliest of the chronicles, the *Anglo-Saxon Chronicle* is the source of the primary data for literature and history from about 871 to the middle of the twelfth century. It is said to have been started by King Alfred (871–899) in the ninth century, and begins at the beginning, with "five thousand two hundred years had passed from the beginning of the world to this year." Similar brief entries follow until the scribes come to their own period of history where their entries then become longer and are somewhat more than simply recording the births and deaths of kings (as well as battles, eclipses, etc.). The passage on William the Conqueror, for example, is a tribute by someone who must have known the king well and was as free with complaints as compliments, e.g., "Into avarice did William fall, and loved greediness above all." As the work grew, the quantity and quality recorded varied. It was completed in the year 1134, and until that time was written in Old English prose. Seven versions and a fragment are extant.[86] Building on these early efforts, Asser (d. 908) published a Latin biography of King Alfred and a chronicle of events between 849 and 887.[87]

Inaccurate and exaggerated as they may be, chronicles often are of help to historians and demographers. For example, "an entire genre of medieval literature is given over to the praise (*laudatio*) of cities, and even a moderately enthusiastic *laudatio* will boast about the number of churches, monasteries, hospitals, or schools; the goods imported; food consumed; taxes raised, and moneys spent. The chronicler Giovanni Villani included in his narrative a lengthy description, overflowing with numbers, of Florence in about 1338, and his figures have withstood repeated critical assaults."[88]

Chronicles, "*romans d'antiquité*" (verse romances), and "*chansons de geste*" (discussions of epic battles) describe items found in medieval encyclopedias. They are of interest to the world of reference in that much of the material in these forms note the "wonders of the palpable world. They celebrate the marvels of nature and manufacture: amazing creatures of land and sea, artificial constructions of the architect, goldsmith and weaver."[89]

One of the most famous chronicles of the Middle Ages was the *Historia Regum Britanniae* (1135–1138), compiled by a canon resident at Oxford, Geoffrey of Monmouth (c. 1100–1155). This history of Britain begins with the so-called foundation of the country by the Trojan Brutus and moves up to the late seventh century and the reign of King Arthur. More than two hundred manuscript copies of his work testify to its popularity and importance. While some of his *Historia* has a resemblance to fact, much of it is sheer myth. Geoffrey created characters whom Shakespeare, among many others, made even more famous, e.g., Lear, Cymbeline, and King Arthur. Still, King Arthur (who takes up almost a fifth of the history) assured the *Historia* a place for the ages. Geoffrey's *Historia* in turn set the stage for Wace's *Roman de Brut* and a vast amount of ensuing literature concerning the Arthurian legend.[90] Sir Thomas Malory (d. c. 1471) finished the standard version of Arthur while in jail. His *Le Morte D'Arthur* was published by William Caxton in 1485 and from that edition has come most of the modern adaptations of the Arthurian legend in prose and poetry.

One of the earliest chronicles that afforded numerous answers to medieval reference queries was *Le Roman de Troie* (c. 1160). Supposedly an eyewitness account of the Trojan war, it was written in verse form by Benoit de Sainte-Maure (fl. twelfth century). He was in the process of writing the *Chronique des Duc de Normandie* (c. 1175) when he died. The Norman history is relatively accurate.[91]

The *Deeds of Frederick Barbarossa* (*Gestat Friderici I imperatoris*; c. 1158) stands out as one of the few Medieval histories for which the author sought the facts and only the facts. There is much penetrating analysis of government, and its author Otto of Freising (c. 1114–1158) was a close friend of the German emperor, Frederick Barbarossa.

Chatty chronicles, as much fiction as fact, became the popular reference works of the thirteenth and fourteenth centuries. Most of these were written in the vernacular and copied and recopied. The subject matter inevitably was a blend of biography and history. The chronicles usually focused on a given set of events at a given period. An example is the reminiscences of Jean Joinville (b. 1225) about King Louis IX during the crusade of 1248. His *The History* (1305–1306) is a personal account. After it was written, the manuscript disappeared. In 1547, it was discovered and printed; it went into many editions.

Matthew Paris (d. 1259) is another member of the chronicle group, and famous for his account of events in Europe between 1235 and 1259. These are set out in his *Chronica Majora* (*Major Chronicles;* c. 1260), which contains not only his observations from the monastery in St. Albans, England but also excerpts from the works of others of the period. Fortunately he knew all of the leading figures of the day, including Henry III, and from them drew material for his massive work.

The best-known chronicler of the group, Jean Froissart (b. 1333), wrote a chronicle (c. 1400) that is the most detailed and most reliable in its coverage of events in the fourteenth century. Its primary focus is the Hundred Years War, and, as Froissart was friends with most of the principals in the struggle from 1325 to 1400, he offers accurate, firsthand reporting not only on battles, but on personalities, weddings, and courtly relationships. Today his chronicle is as valuable for the information it gives about chivalry and courtly ideas as history. As such, it is an encyclopedia of the period. The later Middle Ages French chronicles more closely tied to biography, concentrate on the words and actions of certain leading men of the period. Some aristocratic chronicles were written by the protagonists themselves. The *Conquete de Constantinople* of Geoffroi de Villehardouin describes the Fourth Crusade (1202–1204), in which he played an important part. Chronicles of this type remained popular until the end of the Middle Ages.

Throughout the Middle Ages, many smaller states and towns produced their own chronicles, but these tend to be even less factual and more involved with myth. At the same time, they reflect ideas of local identity and culture that are valuable to the modern historian.

One of the last chroniclers, as contrasted with the growing number of historians, was John Stow (1525–1605), a professional tailor and an amateur antiquarian. He began compiling chronicles and summarized his predecessors in his *Chronicles of England* (1580). In 1598, he gained lasting fame with his *A Survey of London,* written in the form of walks around the London wards and containing graphic word pictures of life at the time. It includes, too, information on the past history of London. Between 1577 and 1578, another chronicler, Rapheal Holinshed (c. 1580), published his *Chronicles*—essentially a history of Britain up to 1575. It proved a valuable biographical source book for dramatists, including Shakespeare; Marlowe, in turn, turned to it for information on Edward II.

While chronologies carried on as a reference form after the Renaissance, the familiar chronicle all but disappeared. In its place appeared the history, the expanded encyclopedia, and numerous other reference works that were not as grand in scope, but were considerably more reliable in detail. Today, the chronicle and the annal are of historical interest, and sometimes used in titles of books, if not always in correct form. Other than retrospectively, however, they are of little interest to the current reference scene.

In a fitting close, consider that even a straightforward chronology can be the focus of argument. Many disagree as to precisely when the next century makes its appearance. Skirmishes, primarily since the seventeenth century, have arisen among scholars, eccentrics, and mathematicians. "The twentieth century, which began January 1, 1901, will end on December 31, 2000 . . . As many entries in this list will indicate, plans to celebrate the opening of the twenty-first century and the third millennium at midnight on December 31, 1999, have become so widespread that anyone who tries to call attention to the error is disparaged as a pedant and ignored."[92]

Books of Days

Combining both chronologies and chronicles, usually in a shorthand form, the typical book of days is a popular work in many libraries and homes. It had its beginnings in the eighteenth century as a reference work.[93] Under each day of the year there is a wide variety of fact and fancy. Poetry and statistics and past activities of the weather may be given as background to holidays. Many are illustrated with quaint woodcuts. In order to appeal to the widest audience, the books of days tended to be general in content. There were exceptions, such as Sidney Lear's *For Days and Years* (London, 1878), which was concerned with "short reading and hymn for every day in the church's year." Throughout the nineteenth century (and to this day) such guides for religious observance remained popular.

The Directory for the Year of Our Lord, 1708 (actually 1707) contains the familiar listing of religious holidays, holy days, saints days, etc. But in addition the compiler includes "a particular account of all the victories obtained over the French, by the confederates, since beginning of the reign of Queen Ann." By the next edition, in 1709, he added "a perpetual almanack in the middle, with the rates of the water-men, coach men and car men."[94]

In the early nineteenth century a typical example of a book of day is William Hone's *Every-Day Book* (London: William Tegg, 1827). The book is applicable for almost any year in that there is little or no specific forecasting, as in almanacs. Rather, for example, for October 1 there is a short piece on "lawless court," followed by two pages describing the fourteenth century "order of fools." A stage accident of 1736 (October 1, of course) is reported as well as an essay on "mountebanks" and a single line indicating average high and low temperature for the day. Next comes October 2, and so on. The year before a similar, quite independent, 856-page volume was published.

Robert Chambers (1802–1871), cofounder of *Chamber's Encyclopedia,* published numerous other reference works from his Edinburgh firm. Among these, and still a basic reference aid, was the first carefully planned book of days: *The Book of Days,* "a miscellany of popular antiquities in connection with the calendar, including anecdote, biography, and history, curiosities of literature and oddities of human life and character."[95] First published in 1862, it set the format for many such reference works to come. Both American and English publishers picked up the pattern. *Red Letter Days,* a memorial and birthday book. (New York, 1879), was a revision of an equivalent English title published the nine years before. By 1894 a New York publisher had gained a large audience for his *Thoughts for the Occasion*—a "patriotic and secular, a repository of historical data and facts, golden thoughts and words of wisdom." The editor, Joseph Anderson, had struck on the idea of wedding both the secular and the religious in his close to six-hundred-page guide. From the mid-nineteenth century to the close of the First World War, some seven to eight hundred such books had been published in America and England.

Notes for Chapter 4

1. "A Romance of Almanacs." *Chamber's Journal,* January 12, 1884, 23.

2. The descriptor "almanac" appears first in medieval Latin. It was used under different names well before its surfacing at the end of the thirteenth century. In fact, most European and Middle Eastern languages have words for almanac, and many of these precede its first recorded use. Almanac (spelled, too, as almanack) seems to have its origins in "almanakh" (an Arabic descriptor), which the Arabs took from the Greek "almenichiakon," or calendar. Eusebius in his *Praeparation Evangelica* (c. 312) quotes Porphyrius (c. A.D. 232–305) as using "almenichika" as an Egyptian work for listing names and cures for diseases in astrological works. In Latin it was first used in the thirteenth century, if not earlier, according to the *Oxford English Dictionary,* which states that the earliest notices are 1267, Roger Bacon and 1345, Giovanni Vallani (Oxford English Dictionary vol. 1, 244. In 1508, Wynkyn de Worde printed *An Almanacke.* Some eighty years later

Shakespeare in *Midsummer's Night Dream* (iii. i, 54): "A calendar, a calendar: looke in the Almanack, finde out the Moonshine," i.e., find out when there will be a full moon. The moonlight, of course, was needed to illuminate the production of Paramus and Thisby.

3. The almanac as a partial diary became popular in the mid-sixteenth and seventeenth century when English almanacs often included a blank page facing each month's calendar. Often these pages were used to keep data on money transactions and came to be known as "blanks" to distinguish them from the standard almanac. "One of the reasons for both the popularity and the survival of almanacs was their suitability as diaries. Many surviving copies contain memoranda, accounts or farming notes." Bernard Cap, *English Almanacs, 1500–1800* (Ithaca, N.Y.: Cornell University Press, 1979), 61.

4. James D. Hart, *The Popular Book* (Berkeley: University of California Press, 1963), 42. While Hart is speaking of seventeenth century America, the same situation was true in England as well as in Europe.

5. Capp, English Almanacs, 1500–1800, 23. By 1775 in America, *Poor Richard Improved* sold some ten thousand copies a year, while Ames's more popular compilations circulated an average of sixty thousand copies annually between 1725 and 1764. The almanac fulfilled many of the purposes of today's tabloid newspaper or popular magazine. Also, it had the added feature of being a handy reference work, with information about sunrise and sunset, weather predictions, tides, tables of distances, recipes, lists of public officials, and numerous other facts, and all in an average of twelve pages. Despite their popularity, or because of it, "of the million of almanacs printed (in England between 1500–1800) only a few thousand copies survive . . . The majority perished when the year ended." (Capp, *English Almanacs 1500–1800,* 66).

6. A typical illustration is described by J.T. Buckingham in his *Personal Memoirs* (Boston, 1852), 20. "The title page had on it a large picture of a female, representing America, in a recumbent position, held down by men representing members of the British ministry, while Lord North was pouring Tea down her throat from an immense teapot." It hardly took an ability to read to understand that title page. Almanac publishers began to print portraits of themselves in English almanacs by the mid-seventeenth century. William Lilly, whose almanac circulated in the thousands for forty years was "probably the best known of anyone in England after the King." (Capp, *English Almanacs 1500–1800,* 23).

7. Joao Lisboa, "Popular Knowledge in the 18th Century Almanacs," *Histor of European Ideas,* vol. 11, 512.

8. Capp, *English Almanacs 1500–1800,* 20.

9. Capp, *English Almanacs 1500–1800,* 24.

10. Esther Jerabek, "Almanacs as Historical Sources," *Minnesota History,* (December 1934), 444–49.

11. In the British Library this is the earliest extant almanac. It is recorded on papyrus. Twenty-five of the probable thirty-eight to forty columns are preserved. Aside from the good and bad days, there are bits of information on when to avoid animals and how to escape the evil eye. Throughout Egypt, there are signs of almanacs at least in terms of calendars and astrology, e.g., at the Temple of Denderah (c. A.D. 40) one finds the annual journey of the sun charted, as well as the signs of the zodiac.

12. For a detailed discussion of the evolution of the Christian, Jewish, and Islamic calendars, see *Dictionary of the Middle Ages,* 1983, vol. 3, 17–31.

13. Ibid. vol. 1, 607. The Renaissance continued the tradition, but the unresolved problem was whether astrology was true or false. Not until the eighteenth century was astrology associated with pure superstition, although even to this day it has many advocates. Satires against almanacs and their claims as astrological aids for predictions go back to the Romans, but by the sixteenth century in England there was a mild wave of protest by theologians who saw in the almanacs a method of producing distrust in God. Capp, *English Almanacs 1500–1800,* 31–33.

14. The names of these signs may be translated as Hired Man (corresponding to Aries), the Bull of Heaven (Taurus), the Great Twins (Gemini), the Crab (Cancer), the Lion (Leo), the Barley Stalk (Virgo), the Balance (Libra), the Scorpion (Scorpio), Pabilsag—a god—(Sagittarius), the Goatfish (Capricorn), the Giant (Aquarius), and the Tails (Pisces). It is evident that our modern Latin names, derived from the star catalog in Ptolemy's *Almagest,* are mostly direct translations of the Babylonian names. F.R. Stephenson, "The Babylonians Saw That Comet, Too," *Natural History* (December 1985), 16. The article discusses in detail the diaries and later almanacs that recorded the Hally comet two millennia before Halley.

15. Petrus de Dacia in about A.D. 1300 appears to be the first to have used the "man of signs" (*homo signorum*) in an almanac. This astrological device shows a man with a open chest and stomach, surrounded by the twelve basic signs of the zodiac, each one of which thought to rule a different part of the body. In thirteen books, the *Almagest* was Ptolemy's major work. It is considered a model of astronomy for the time and dominated astronomy for more than a thousand years.

16. "Ephemerides," the plural of "ephemeris," is employed still as an umbrella decriptor for both almanacs and calendars. The relation to "ephemeral" is obvious.

17. The 1457 almanac was compiled by a Viennese mathematician, George von Purbach. It was, however, of limited use to laypersons. It was Purbach's pupil, Müller, who set the pattern for the content, shape, and style of the fifteenth to seventeenth century almanac.

18. The title page includes red and black ornaments. The twenty-four page quarto contains a calendar with eclipses and the motion of the planets.

In 1475, *Regiomontanus's* almanac, or *Ephemerides,* was published. Nearly eight hundred and fifty pages, it was more properly an astronomical aid than an almanac. According to legend Christopher Columbus was able to use the *Ephemerides* to calculate longitude. It also contained predictions for eclipses. Using the time of the eclipse at Nuremburg, the navigator could chart his longitude.

19. "Kalendars and Old Almanacs," *The British Quarterly Review,* 28 (1858) 338.

20. Ibid.

21. Cap, *English Almanacs 1500–1800,* 61.

22. Leslie Shepard, *The History of Street Literature* (Newton Abbot: David & Charles, 1973), 14. Whereas almanacs were considered street literature in most of Europe, not so in sixteenth century France where here they were astrological works, published in expensive quarto volumes for use by scholars. By the end of the century they had become, with the rest of Europe, cheap and mass produced. See also Victor E. Neuberg, *Popular Literature: A History and Guide.* Harmondsworth: Penguin, 1977).

23. Pamphlets, with an emphasis on text, tended to be the format of almanacs for the middle classes. Others, for the poor and near-illiterate, usually took the form of chapbooks, i.e., "chap books" with eight to thirty-two uncut pages, often with more illustrations than words.

24. Capp, *English Almanacs 1500–1800,* 205.

25. The *Kalendar* was translated from a French almanac by a Scotsman who had a poor command of both French and English. The result was a disaster, which was not made right until Wynken de Worde's revised edition in 1508. Once the almanac, with its perpetual calendar, was established, it won instant success and was published with variations for the next two hundred years.

26. Capp, *English Almanacs 1500–1800,* 86.

27. "English Almanacs Under James I," *Retrospective Review* (August 1854), 370.

28. Capp, *English Almanacs 1500–1800,* 33.

29. "A Romance of Alamancs," 23. Friday usually was a black day no matter what country. "There are even yet people who have a mysterious dislike to it, who never heard of the thirteen reasons duly set forth in these old almanacs, such as the killing of Abel, the slaughter of the Innocents, the beheading of John the Baptist etc." Ibid.

30. Joseph Goldberg, "The Eighteenth Century Philadelphia Almanac and its English Counterpart" (Ph.D. diss. University of Maryland, 1962), Goldberg, in his first chapter, explains the importance of Nostradamus to early almanac makers. As a predictor of future events—usually disasters—Nostradamus gained fame as an almanac compiler in St. Remy, France. Beginning in 1559 he issued regular, cryptic, and political predictions. In 1543, Copernicus in his *De Revolutionubus Orbium* struck the death

blow to astrology as a serious science, although it continued on as a major part of almanacs well into the twentieth century.

31. Chester Greenough, "New England Almanacs, 1766–1775," *Proceedings of the American Antiquarian Society,* 45 (October 1935), 290.

32. "English Almanacs Under James I," 368.

33. Capp, *English Almanacs 1500–1800,* 57.

34. Calvin Israel, "The Baroque Tendency in Early American Literature: The Achievement of Thomas Shepard II in his 1656 Almanac," *American Poetry* (spring 1988). Israel reprints much of the "splendidly composed baroque poems," which appeared only once in the almanac. The poet went on to become an American Puritan minister.

35. Lisboa, 511.

36. Merle Curti, *The Growth of American Thought,* 2d ed. (New York: 1951), 34.

37. Cornelius Walford, "Sham Almanacks and Prognostications," *Booklore* 2, (1885) 137–38. The most famous English almanac publisher of the seventeenth century, John Patridge, was a shoemaker by trade. He compiled his first work in 1681.

38. Capp, *English Almanacs 1500–1800,* 52.

39. The expiration of the Printing Act in 1695 spelled an end to the Stationer's power and the licensing system. Almanacs, as other works, could be published without external controls.

40. Cyprian Blagden, "Thomas Carnan and the Almanack Monopoly" *Studies in Bibliography,* vol. 14 (Charlottesville, Va.: University Press of Virginia, 1961), 26. Blagdan cites a 1750 diary example that had, in addition to the blank pages (for accounts, notes, etc.), lists of holidays, a directory of public offices, a table of monetary values, a list of Peers, an account of main roads, and other miscellaneous information.

41. W.T. Berry, ed., *Annals of Printing* (Toronto: University of Toronto Press, 1966), 124. No copy of what was probably a pamphlet of eight leaves, i.e., sixteen pages is extant. Daye allegedly printed an annual almanac from 1639–1646, but no copies are extant.

42. Robert K. Dodge, *Early American Almanac Humor* (Bowling Green, Ohio. Bowling Green State University Popular Press, 1987), 1. This 165-page collection of almanac humor is divided into eight chapters from "The Yankee" to "Soldiers and Sailors" with excerpts from American almanacs from 1776 to 1800.

43. Josephine Piercy, *Studies in Literary Types in Seventeenth Century America* (New Haven, Conn.: Yale University Press, 1939), 32. Piercy believes that the "standard of the almanac in America of the seventeenth century was higher than that of its model in England."

44. Dodge, *Early American Almanac Humor,* 594. Almanac publishing was highly competitive in eighteenth and nineteenth century America. "Ben Franklin had to compete with seven other almanacs when he started

Poor Richard. And Ames . . . was selling 50,000–60,000 copies a year of his Astronomical Diary." Marion Stowell, *American Almanacs and Feuds,* vol. 9, *Early American Literature,* (1975) 276. The article traces the major battles for sales during the Colonial years in America.

45. The title of the first almanac on December 28, 1732 was explained by Franklin, i.e., "Richard Saunders, Philomath." In his preface Franklin/Saunders pleads he is poor and published the almanac to make money. By 1740 the sales were so impressive (close to 10,000 annually) that in the 1739 issue Franklin explained "When I first began to publish, the printer made a fair Agreement with me for my copies, by virtue of which he runs away with the greatest part of the profit."

46. From Franklin's *Autobiography,* quoted in Marion Stowell, *Early American Almanacs* (New York: Burt Franklin, 1977), 80. See, too, C. William Miller, "Franklin's Poor Richard Almanacs: Their Printing and Publication" vol. 14, *Studies in Bibliography* (Charlottesville, Va.: University Press of Virgina, 1961), 46.

47. The collection was reprinted at least seventy-five times in English, but enjoyed international fame in that it was issued in sixty French and fifteen German editions, as well as at least a dozen other translations. *Poor Richard* was compiled and edited by Franklin for the first twenty-five editions to 1758. It continued, though, into the nineteenth century. Almanacs were neither sold nor produced equally throughout America. "In the same period in which the Virginia Almanac was printed in press runs of 5,000 copies (and even this figure is much larger than that of the average press run), New Englanders were buying 60,000 copies of a single almanac and supporting several others." Michael Warner, *The Letters of the Republic* (Cambridge, Harvard University Press, 1990), 23.

48. William Pencak, "Politics and ideology in Poor Richard's Almanac," working paper *Institute of Early American History and Culture,* 1991, 1.

49. Sidwell, 543. Colonial newspapers played a much larger role. Probably more was done to foment the Revolution by conversation and oral exchanges, both formal and informal, than by any form of print.

50. Chester Greenough, "New England Almanacs, 1766–1775," 315–16.

51. Allan R. Raymond, "To Reach Men's Minds: Almanacs and the American Revolution, 1760–1777," *New England Quarterly,* 51 (1978): 373. See, too, Daniel Boorstin, *The Americans, The Colonial Experience* (New York: Vintage Books, 1964), 160; and Clinton Rossiter, *The First American Revolution* (New York: Harvest Books, 1956), 207.

52. Capp, *English Almanacs 1500–1800,* 238.

53. *The Companion to the Almanac* (London: Charles Knight, 1828), 3, 6.

54. Capp, *English Almanacs 1500–1800,* 265–66.

55. Ibid., 269.

56. Ibid.

57. Herman Melville appears to have used *The American Almanac* (1845–1846) and its calendar pages as an important key to the novel *Mardi* (1849). See an explanation of how an almanac helped Melville chart the course of his third novel: Maxine Moore, *That Lonely Game: Melville, Mardi and the Almanac* (Columbia, Mo: University of Missouri Press, 1975.

58. "A Romance of Almanacs," 25.

59. Ibid., 23.

60. Martha Vicinus, *The Industrial Muse* (London: Croom Helm, 1974), 197. Comic almanacs in America were popular, and the best-known nineteenth century examples included a series on David Crockett. Comic items were also a regular part of standard almanacs.

61. George Littlefield, "Notes on the Calendar and the Almanac," *Proceedings of the American Antiquarian Society* (October 1914): 61.

62. Ibid, April, 1914, p. 64.

63. The problem is that numerous titles are not really almanacs in the historical sense of the word, but are simply slotted into this subject heading because it is convenient. *The Facts on File Yearbook,* for example, is many things but not an almanac either by use or by definition.

64. The brief statement, including a record of various ownerships is given on the verso of the title page in each issue of *The World Almanac.* It is now (1996) published by a division of Scripps Howard. Although suspended for a decade in the 1870s, *The World Almanac* celebrated its first century in 1969 with a reprint of the original 1869 publication, i.e., *The World Almanac for 1868.* For a detailed history of *The World Almanac* as well as views on the genre in general, see Margaret Morrison, "All Things for All People: *The World Almanac*," in *Distinguished Classics of Reference Publishing,* ed. James Rettig, (Phoenix, Ariz.: Oryx Press, 1992).

65. David Jafee, "The Village Enlightenment in New England, 1760–1820," *The William and Mary Quarterly* (July 1990) 332. The article supports and documents the notion of numerous Americans of the period that "self improvement and book learning were pillars of faith in a republican society" (p. 335).

66. Marvin Grosswirth, "Tired of the Weather Bureau? Try Old Farmer's Almanac," *Science Digest,* September 1976, pp. 63–68. The author discusses the state of weather predictions and the almanac in some detail. For a history of the almanac, see Robb Sagendorph, *America and Her Almanacs* (Boston: Little, Brown, 1970). The author was the owner and publisher of the *Farmer's.*

67. John Walsh and David Allen, "Testing the Farmer's Almanac," *Weatherwise,* October 1981, 212. The authors note that the almanac's "forecasting methodology is not documented with the utmost professional rigor."

68. Ibid., 213.

69. Nancy Bubel, "All About Almanacs," *Country Journal,* January

1987, 26. The author used *The Old Farmer's Almanac* for the mid-Atlantic area in November and December of 1984. "In my area . . . the predictions of mild weather during those months was right on the money."

70. Donald Jackson, "The Confessions of an Almanacophiliac," *Smithsonian,* July 1986, 160.

71. Arno Borst, *The Ordering of Time* (Chicago: University of Chicago Press, 1993), 105. The author gives a brief, readable history of time. See, too, Alan Samuel, *Greek and Roman Chronology: Calendars and Years in Classical Antiquity* (Munich: Beck, 1972), which is a standard German title (translated) of ancient calendars and chronologies. See, too, almost any general encyclopedias for a survey of the calendar, e.g., *Encyclopaedia Britannica* vol. 15, (Chicago: Britannica, 1993), 417–34.

72. Bernard Grun, *Timetable of History,* 3d ed. (New York: Simon & Schuster, 1991).

73. *The Annual of Opera,* 1597–1940 (New York: Rowman, 1984); Mortimer Adler and Charles Van Doren, *The Annual of America* (Chicago: Encyclopaedia Britannica, 1976).

74. *Dictionary of the Middle Ages,* vol. 3, 22.

75. These have been found in Scandinavia and England, and several are on display at the History of Science Museum, Oxford University. For a description of an unusual form, a fifteenth century ring almanac, see Saul Moskowitz, "An Almanac Ring from the Middle Ages," *Sky & Telescope,* February 1978, 124–25.

76. William Hone, *The Every-Day Book or the Guide to the Year,* vol. 2 (London: William Tegg (1827), vii. King Athelsant's "psalter" of c. A.D. 703 was a stick with marks that allowed the user, by facing the sun, to ascertain the day of the week. Lunar tables were part of this early stick almanac.

77. Moskowitz, "Almanac Ring from the Middle Ages."

78. Gregory solved the difficulty of the cumulated days. "He ruled that the days should be omitted in 1582 and that thereafter the Gregorian . . . system of leap years should be implemented. It was a reform fairly quickly adopted outside the areas of Russian and Greek Orthodoxy, not without some popular resentment against what was seen as a filching of ten days from a man's life." John Hale, *The Civilization of Europe in the Renaissance* (New York: Atheneum, 1994), 569.

Religion played a major role in reckoning time and this is not to overlook the Jewish and Islamic calendars of the Middle Ages. Generally they agreed with the earlier reckonings and the Julian calendar, but in specifics, such as the definition of the year, they differed, as they do to this day.

79. The medieval *Book of Hours* is a compendium of prayers and devotions. It received its name from the Hours of the Virgin, i.e., texts to be recited and sung at each of the eight periods of the liturgical day. Firmly established in Europe by the eleventh century, the *Hours of the Virgin* first were

part of the *Psalter*. By the later Middle Ages the composite *Psalter Hours* (with added supplementary texts) became known simply as the *Book of Hours*. There are hundreds of monographs about the *Book of Hours*, including numerous reproductions of famous copies, such as the *Tres Riches Heures* of the duke of Berry. John Harthan's *The Book of Hours* (New York: Thomas Crowell, 1977) is an excellent survey.

80. Robert G. Calkins, *Illuminated Books of the Middle Ages* (Ithaca, N.Y.: Cornell University Press, 1983), 245–46. Calendars were common, too, in other religious books, such as missals and breviaries as well as missals and Gospels. For a discussion of these, with particular emphasis on illumination, see various chapters in Calkins. Psalters are found as early as the ninth century, e.g. one of the most famous is the *Utrecht Psalter*, c. 850.

81. Elizabeth Eisenstein, *The Printing Revolution in Early Modern Europe* (Cambridge: Cambridge University Press, 1983), 29.

82. S.H. Steinberg, *Five Hundred Years of Printing* (New York: Criterion Books, 1959), 167.

83. Much has been written on chronology and related matters from calendars to time charts, e.g., see "Chronology, I: Egypt—to the end of the Twentieth Dynasty" in *The Cambridge Ancient History*, 3d ed. (Cambridge: Cambridge University Press, 1981), 173–93.

84. The archive was discovered at Mari on the middle course of the Euphrates, near the southern border of modern Syria. Mari, today called Tell Hariri, was a major station in the trade route of the second millennium B.C. to Sumeria. The archive in the Mari palace, discovered in the early 1930s, contains more than 20 thousand tablets, revealing the city's history prior to its destruction in about 760 B.C.

85. While there is no author, tradition holds that the Chronicles were written by Ezra and completed by others. Although it may have begun as early as 200 B.C. the completed work was not finished until about the first or, at the latest the second half of the fourth century A.D. See "1 and 2 Chronicles" in Robert Alter and Frank Kermode, *The Literary Guide to the Bible* (Cambridge, Mass.: Belknap Press, 1987), 365–74.

86. All of these versions derive from a single chronicle written by an unknown individual at Winchester in about A.D. 900. At the same time, an effort was made to keep the chronicle up-to-date, and through the middle of the twelfth century, each generation added new material. Growing as the chronicles did from previous manuscripts, it is not surprising that many of them represent the work of several writers. "Thus the Latin chronicle of Florence of Worcester (d. 1148) was continued by John of Worcester until 1141, then by Henry of Huntingdon until 1152 and thereafter by the monks of Bury St. Edmunds." *The Cambridge Guide to Literature in English* (Cambridge: Cambridge University Press, 1993), 177.

87. Asser De rebus gestis Aelfredi Magni (887) is the earliest biography of a secular figure written in England. The only extant edition is one of 1574. Parts were incorporated into later chronicles.

88. *Dictionary of the Middle Ages,* vol. 4, 137.

89. Peter France, ed., *The New Oxford Companion to Literature in French* (Oxford: Clarendon Press, 1995), 714. Specifically the "*chanson de geste*" was any of several French epic biographical poems of the eleventh to twelfth centuries. In writing about an individual, the chanson considered both real and legendary events and history were of interest to the focus of the work. The most famous is the "*La Chanson du Roland*" which at the end of the eleventh century tells the story of conflict that preserves the defeat of Charlemagne in the Pyrenees in 778.

90. Geoffrey derived much of his history from Bede and Gildas's *Conquestu Britanniae* (c. 540). Wace (fl. twelfth century) adopted the *Historia* in his *Roman de Brut* (1155). He is the poet who introduced the Round Table into the Arthurian myth.

91. Widely read, Benoit's history of Troy served as material for Boccaccio's and Chaucer's versions of the Troilus and Criseyde legend. Benoit, in turn, had drawn upon the reputed author of a lost pre-Homeric account of the Trojan War, Dares of Phrygia, as well as drawing upon Dictys Cretensis of Crete. The Norman history is an account of Anglo-Norman history to Henry I (1069–1135), the youngest son of William the Conqueror and king of England (1100–1135).

92. Ruth Freitag, *The Battle of the Centuries* (Washington, D.C.: Library of Congress, 1995), vii–viii. This volume is a chronological, annotated listing of major times in the discussion of when a century begins/ends, most of which are at the Library of Congress.

93. The earliest book of days is related to the development of the calendar and also is an integral part of an almanac. A book of hours, such as the *The Hours of Jeanne d'Evreaux* (1325–1328), contained calendars with occupations of the month on one page and zodiac signs on the other. Still, by the eighteenth century, the book of days was something quite different and divorced from religion.

5

Ready Reference Books:
Handbooks and Manuals

A booke of his owne making in his owne toong, which in the English speach
he [King Alfred] called a handbooke, in Greeke calle it Enchiridion, in Latin
a manuell.[1]

The ready reference book goes under many descriptors, but the most
common, the best known to the public and reference libraries are the familiar: manual, handbook, annual, and yearbook. Here one finds, too, directories, collections of quotations, etc. Ready reference works are compiled
and edited for the fast fact, and many are simply called fact books. When
did the Vikings discover Iceland? What's the address of the CIA in Washington, D.C.? When did St. Patrick live? What's the best car for my needs?
There are millions of questions from as many people as there are questions
that can be answered in a ready reference book.

In his overview of major reference works, James Rettig includes thirty-
one titles. Of these, one-third can be termed fact books, or ready reference
works. Among these, in no order but alphabetical: *Baedeker Guidebooks*
(handbook); *Bartlett's Familiar Quotations* (handbook); *Brewer's Dictionary
of Phrase and Fable* (fact book); *The Chicago Manual of Style* (grammar);
Emily Post's Etiquette (manual); *Encyclopedia of Associations* (directory);
Guinness Book of Records (handbook); *Moody's* (handbook and directory);
Robert's Rules of Order (manual); and the *Statesman's Year-Book*.[2] Representative of types, these are found in most libraries along with hundreds of
other similar titles. And as with fact/ready reference works, the distinctions
between, say, manual and handbook or yearbook are not always that clear
or even really necessary to clarify.

Pertaining to the hand, "manual" is associated with tasks performed by
hand (i.e., manual labor), exercise (manual drill) and in reference work: "a
book . . . of the nature of a manual; intended to be kept at hand for reference."[3] As a "small book for handy use" it primarily serves to instruct, to
help the user carry out some task. In the fifteenth century it could be a "Ritual Romanum" for priests, that is to say, "a book containing the forms to be
observed in the administration of the sacraments, etc."[4] By the next century
the manual was associated with a treatise on the art of counting on the

hands the dates of holy feasts. Gradually it became more and more associated with methods of operating and working.

"Manual" often is in the title of a modern reference book, the virtual synonym for handbook, which term comes from the late Latin to signify a book that could be carried in the hand or conveniently handled. Until the nineteenth century manual was the preferred descriptor. Then the German "*handbuch*" became popular, particularly as the term was associated with the tourist handbook, such as the popular nineteenth century Murray's *A Hand Book for Travellers on the Continent.* Actually, there is a fine difference not always observed by those passing out descriptive titles of reference books. Technically the handbook today means a work limited to a particular field or subject, i.e., a compendium of facts, data for use in a particular profession, study, etc. A manual may be the same, of course, although always in terms of explaining what to do.

A third synonym is the "vade-mecum" (from the Latin, "go with me"). This is the familiar book of facts used for ready reference and may be a handbook, a manual, or combination of both plus a treatise on a given subject. This Latin descriptor for a book that could be carried about for quick facts became common in the seventeenth century and was used until well into the nineteenth century when it was more or less replaced by handbook and/or manual. Today, vade-mecum is synonymous for books of rules, ideas, and thoughts that may direct a person's actions, as for example, "His vade-mecum was his heart and his conscience."[5]

The *Subject Guide to Books in Print 1995–96* has no entry for manuals, but does include over a dozen items under "Handbooks, vade-mecums, etc." Titles indicate the difficulty of categorization, of dividing off neatly almanacs, manuals, and handbooks. For example, under "handbooks" one finds the *Random House Handbook* as well as *The Club Treasurer's Handbook.* Also there is listed *The Pocket Almanac of Essential Facts and Facts That Matter.*

Early Manuals and Handbooks

In prealphabetic Greece the closest thing to a manual was on shipbuilding in Homer. Shipbuilders as well as other craftspeople, of course, hardly needed manuals. They learned their trade, as painters of vases, from working experts. Even in the Greek and Roman literate cultures, a published description of various processes was unusual.

Several of the earliest handbooks were concerned with passing on mathematical knowledge. For example, Archimedes (c. 287–212 B.C.) is famous for his handbook or treatise *Verba Filiorum,* which introduced into the West two of the classic Greek geometrical problems—the finding of two mean proportional between two given lines and the trisection of an angle.

The majority of surviving Greek and Latin handbooks and manuals are concerned with agriculture. The subject was of particular interest for readers in that it not only included the obvious suggestions for crops, but, more important, used agriculture as a springboard for a discussion of the good life. One of the oldest is Cato (234–149 B.C.); the censor's *De Agriculture* was written about 160 B.C. It describes old customs and superstitions and also serves as a practical handbook based on Cato's own experiences as a large-scale farmer. Varro's (116–27 B.C.) handbook on agriculture (*De re Rustica*) or *Treatise on Agriculture* in three books has reached us complete. The husbandry manuals consistently celebrate the position of the house father within the sociopolitical order. Varro states that, equipped with the knowledge of husbandry, the farmer should aim at two goals, profit and pleasure. By the first century A.D. Columella carried the same notions forward, tending to fill his *De Re Rustica* (c. A.D. 60) with anecdotes and stories rather than specific directions. Again, the handbook is more a philosophical treatise than a how-to approach. Even when Frontinus (A.D. 35–103) describes aqueducts in his *De Aquis Urbis Romae* (*Concerning the Waters of the City of Rome*), he tends to be more involved with stories than with directions.

Next to agriculture, rhetorical handbooks and manuals were among the earliest to be found in Greece and Rome. The most famous is by Cicero (106–43 B.C.). His *De Inventione* (c. 70 B.C.) is filled with appropriate arguments for public life and was supported in 55 B.C. by his three books of *De Oratore* in which he outlines the educational needs of an orator, which, naturally, includes free use of rhetorical handbooks. Similar manuals followed, such as Julius Victor's *Ars Rhetorica* (fourth century A.D.), closely based on the first century work by Quintilian, *Institutio oratoria.*

Scholars often make the point that handbooks and manuals, otherwise quickly dated, are invaluable historical sources for numerous subjects. "I would like to suggest that the study of these technical Latin manuals may help clarify our understanding of both earlier and later conceptions of rhetoric."[6]

From the Middle Ages to the Renaissance

The handbook tradition, with its collection of formulas but without much attention to demonstration, continued vigorously in the Middle Ages. There were few manuals, at least as we know them today. Typical of the scattering of such works was Chaucer's (1342–1400) *Treatise on the Astrolabe,* which he adopted from an Arab work of the eighth century. It was not until the advent of printing that manuals became truly descriptive of processes and of specific value to would-be experts.

The early Christian and Middle Ages reference works concentrated on matters of interest to monastic and later university communities. For example, handbooks against heresy had a widespread circulation in Europe from the fourth to the late sixth centuries. "All of them come under the general heading of useful works of reference containing concise explanations of heretical positions, refutations of such positions in brief and systematic form, or careful formulations of orthodoxy on difficult points."[7] While many of these were anonymous, several were by well known writers such as St. Augustine (354–430); his handbook *De Haeresibus,* (c. 428–9) outlined "an exposition of all the heresies since the coming of Christ."[8]

With the establishment of confession of sins to a priest, which apparently originated in sixth-century Ireland, handbooks or manuals (the two descriptors were used synonymously) became common. They were called "penitentials" and were devised to aid the priest. Penitentials were widespread during the Middle Ages. For example, the *Handlyng Synne* was inspired by the requirements laid down by the Fourth Lateran Council (1215–1216) that every Catholic must confess and be absolved at least once a year. The manual was used by the clergy to instruct their congregations about the sacraments and the vices and virtues. "The promulgation led to the creation of manuals in Latin for use by confessors and preachers, and eventually to vernacular tretieses to enable devout laypeople to example their own consciences.[9] Named after their reputed authors or after the manuscripts in which they are found, the penitentials date back to 549 with the *Penitential of Finnian.* By 591 the *Penitential of Columbanus* was available on the Continent, and it had a wide influence on the contents of later European penitentials.[10] Contents varied, but most had a schedule of tariffs that provided a suitable penance depending on the sin and the penitent's age, gender, and health.

Today the study of sermons and penitentials supply numerous details about life during the Middle Ages. "The handbooks offer a wealth of information about the nature of early medieval society dealing not only as might be anticipated with failings in religious obligations, sexual misdemeanors, capital crimes and other secular offenses such as theft, but also illustrating contemporary attitudes to the family, habits in marriage (and divorce), the treatment of illness, the status of slaves, or issues relating to unclean food or to public health."[11]

Another West European handbook for the clergy was the *Artes Praedicandi,* or a guide to rules and formal instructions in preaching. By the thirteenth century there was widespread availability of preaching handbooks and collections of model sermons. "Handbooks of themes, distinctions, authorities, concordances and examples undoubtedly formed a useful reference library for the preacher."[12]

Considering the central role of the church in preserving culture in the Middle Ages, the development of sermon literature is of some interest.

Manuals and collections of sermons were for many communities basic reference works. St. Augustine was the author or one of the earliest manuals on preaching in a chapter in his *De Doctrina Christiana*. Until the thirteenth century the primary audience for preaching was the monastic community itself. By the latter part of the twelfth century, sermons became more popular, more directed to a lay audience.

As religious conflict and reform swept across Europe, the sermon became a great communication vehicle. In an effort to upgrade the quality of preaching, particularly among those who did not attend university or were far removed from ideas, there was a great number of preaching manuals and collections of model sermons. While specific content varied, all gave models as well as basic techniques of preaching and composition. Most included quotations, stories, and the like to be incorporated into a sermon.

There had been collections of sermons prior to c. 1200, but they now grew in importance as major reference sources. Collections inevitably featured exemplar drawn from lives of saints, the Bible, classical literature, profane history, and moral and didactic texts, such as Alfonsi's *Disciplina Clericalis*. Jacques de Vitry (c. 1160–1240), one of the major scholars of the period, compiled at least four collections of model sermons and made systematic and extensive use of Christian and pagan quotations. His work was the model for hundreds of manuals to follow. He, as well as such near contemporaries as John of Abbeville and Guibert of Tournai, furnished similar manuals. By and large, most sermons were collected from the twelfth to fifteenth century by anonymous scribes who simply copied down the words of the various preachers. Manuals and handbooks—as well as their numerous cousins—were an invaluable source of information and guidance for the clergy throughout the Dark and Middle Ages. "One of the most durable medieval metaphors for the priest was the mute dog: a priest without his books—his gospels, his homilies, his penitential—was like a dog without a bark."[13]

Although closely associated with clerics, there was a group of Medieval handbooks and manuals that served laypersons as well. Iconographic manuals, which provided illustrations and descriptions of suitable images for given places and situations, derive from a long tradition of descriptions of art works used to disseminate compositions or full programs. "In 403, for instance, Paulinus of Nola . . . (described) mosaics in the churches at Nola and Fundi . . . And from the early fifth century until the end of the Middle Ages titulo (descriptive captions) circulated as guides."[14] Medieval artists relied heavily on the iconographic manual. One of the earliest, the *Mappae clavicular,* appears in the Reichenau monastery inventory of 821. Eraclius's *De Coloribus et Artibus Romanorum* dates from the late eleventh or early twelfth century. *De diversis artibus* by Theophilus (c. 1100–1150) offers advice for glass, painting, and metal techniques. "It is only from the postmedieval period . . . that a comprehensive painter's manual survives, the well-known *Hermeneia of Dionysios of Fourna,* written between 1730 and 1734 on Mt. Athos."[15]

The Renaissance

During the height of the Renaissance, in the fifteenth and sixteenth centuries, the majority of handbooks and manuals continued to be in Latin, primarily for the upper classes and of limited use among laypersons.[16] Only gradually did the advantages of profits of printing popular titles strike the publisher/printer. English language nonclerical handbooks could be numbered on two hands before 1600, and there were no more than two or three dozen manuals. Conversely, Latin and some European vernacular titles numbered in the hundreds, although, again, they were not as widespread as almanacs, commonplace books, and other types of reference works.

The handbook or manual in English, rather than in Latin, was a constant source of debate. Roger Ascham (1515–1568) has the distinction of being the author of the first manual on archery in English. The scholar published his *Toxophilus* (*Lover of the Bow*) in a dialogue form in 1545. More important, perhaps, was his insistence on the book being in English rather than in Latin. In his introduction he state he was writing "Englishe matter in the English tongue for Englishe men." At the same time, a second manual of his, published in 1570, two years after his death, was a guide to the mastering of Latin for laypeople. True to his insistence on the use of English, a good deal of the book deals with education.

Even scientific handbooks were not seen by sixteenth century publishers as particularly profitable. English printers "catered to the demands of the public, publishing educational texts, religious controversies, the Bible . . . Publications of the latest continental developments in medicine, botany and precision instruments waited."[17]

Medical manuals to assist laypersons in maintaining good health and sometimes short-circuiting less-than-well-trained doctors began to appear by the mid-sixteenth century. A typical example was Andrew Borde's *Breuyary of Health* where he treats each then-common disease with a brief description and a prescribed remedy or two. The most famous of the limited number of such guides in English was Thomas Elyot's *Castel of Health,* published in the first half of the sixteenth century. Although the knight was not trained in medicine, he had enough knowledge of it to write an easy-to-follow guide with instructions on how to maintain health. In many ways, Elyot was among the first authors to stress the ready reference book for laypersons and to encourage the useful in handbooks and manuals. Not incidentally he is famous, too, for his *Governour,* a combined treatise in English on education and etiquette for gentlemen's sons.

The rhetoric handbook, as from Greek times and throughout the Middle Ages, continued to be popular in the Renaissance.[18] A richness of style in speech and writing was appreciated. What today would be considered excessive was celebrated, particularly from the sixteenth through the eighteenth century. The baroque style in art and architecture, with complex richness of form and design, developed parallel with the dazzling patterns of writing and speech. And the rhetorical handbook, as well as the manuals on letter writing was the expanded thesaurus of words, phrases, quotations, etc. from which the individual drew to show a much-heralded copious style.[19]

Agricultural manuals became increasingly popular in Europe from the early sixteenth century. Most of these were in the vernacular as were translations of the aforementioned earlier agricultural treatises by Cato and Varro. The numerous sixteenth century translators and editors of the ancient works were often gentlemen farmers. They were faced with the same problems as the readers of the translated manuals—how to manage estates. Gradually the envisioned audience changed from the lord to the ordinary rural farm owners. And with that came manuals that stressed not only management but also cultivation. Publishers and authors, particularly among Lutherans, "did not want only to raise the self-esteem of the tillers of the soil, but also to change the public image of them . . . (Manuals) tried to convince the cultural despisers of the dirt farmer that he had his technical terminology as any other profession, and the exercise of his craft as well as the construction of labor saving devices required ingenuity and intelligence."[20]

First published in 1557, Tusser's *A Hundreth Good Pointes of Husbandrie* was a best-seller for almost a century. The collection of doggerel and miscellaneous practical and moral advice was edited for the literate layperson, not the lord of a manor. McRae demonstrates how "representation of the agrarian economy (in England) and social order can be traced through the pages of contemporary husbandry manuals . . . from the publication of Fitzherbert's *Book of Husbandrye* in 1523" through much of the sixteenth century. Fitzherbert's manual, which ran into nineteen editions (1523–1598), stressed the practical and new approaches to agriculture. The purpose of the manual is summarized with the compiler's exhortation that the work is for "a younge gentylman that entendeth to thryve . . . I advyse hym to get a copy of this present booke and to rede it frome the begynnynge to the endynge."[21] The text was primarily for manorial lords, as were the majority of such manuals during the seventeenth century in England.[22]

Hobbies, pastimes, and interests were the focus of numerous English handbooks that were written and edited primarily for the upper classes. Among the more famous was the *Boke of St. Albans* (1486), which contains the earliest example of color printing in England and discusses hunting, fishing, hawking, and heraldry. The audience for books on out-of-door sports was much larger than a few noblemen. Izaak Walton (1593–1683) recognized this and penned the best book on fishing ever written, the *Compleat Angler: or The Contemplative Man's Recreation*. Published in 1653, it remains in print and is a classic, not only as a handbook for fishing, but as a champion of the simple virtues. Toward the close of the seventeenth century (1694), one Richard Franck (c. 1624–1708) published his *Northern*

Memoirs to which he added *The Contemplative & Practical Angler.* This followed the much better-known and original manual on fishing by Walton. Sir Walter Scott (1771–1832) borrowed from both for his late novel *Redgauntlet* (1824), but, more important, he edited Franck and republished the fishing manual, with the memoirs, in 1821. The editing was superficial, as Scott admitted, because he was doing the work to assist a young friend. Incidentally, Franck gained a certain fame for being the only other critic besides Byron to condemn Walton's classic.

Among the earliest building manuals in English is the 1540 title printed in London called *The Boke for to Lerne a Man to be Wyse in Buyldyng of his Howse.* The same type of advice is found here as in modern manuals. Practical hints on everything from laying bricks to framing and joining are given in detail.

Emblem Books

Emblem books, where epigrams, maxims, adages, proverbs, and pictures are united, developed in the sixteenth century. They were another form of the manual. Allegory dates to Homer and Hesiod and was a favored aid to Greek philosophers and grammarians. Allegory, or to speak figuratively, soon was broadened to include symbolic representation or emblems. The Romans used allegory extensively for abstractions, e.g., Quintilian in the first century A.D. perfected the system of metaphors and multiple meanings. Augustine, who contrasted Rome with the City of God (c. A.D. 413) demonstrated the use of allegory by Christians as did the Medieval poem, "Romance of the Rose," and later Dante. These and numerous other writers before the sixteenth century, established the base for the emblem book.[23] A quotation or epigram was accompanied by devices or emblems that represented the idea of the literary thought. All emblem books consisted of a picture of an object or objects with some words that expressed the meaning of the figure. The dove, for example, equals purity. Aldus Manutius made his printer's device famous by combining an anchor and dolphin to express the principle of "hasten slowly." Printers' marks became some of the best-known emblems. A quote on folly, pride, luxury, love, fortune, life, death etch was accompanied by a device that represented folly, pride, luxury, etc. Thanks to these emblem books historians of iconography are now able in good part to identify the significance, say, of a sleeping dog in a work of art. Anyone who is convergent with software realizes the importance of emblems or icons. There is little basic difference in principle between the modern computer aid and the Renaissance books.

Originally the emblem books were published as guides to craftsmen, from painters to goldsmiths, who might want a device or emblem for their work. The combination of the epigram and the picture was drawn from

Greek and Latin allegory. By the late Renaissance the emblematic designs appeared in almost any art form from stained glass windows to tapestry and needlework.

An Italian lawyer, Andre Alciati, became synonymous with the printed emblem book that he compiled in 1531. It went through more than two hundred editions and influenced Geoffrey Whitney's *Choice of Emblems* (1585), the pioneering work in English. Whitney's work was published by the Platin press, and the Netherlands became the center of the vogue which lasted well into the seventeenth century.[24]

Secret Manuals

Manuals and handbooks of magic and mystery date back to the Mesopotamians and Egyptians. In a sense, *The Book of the Dead* is a handbook, and the epic of *Gilgamesh* suggests numerous magical processes in an effort to defeat death. Ritual magic, along with the necessary handbooks, is a study in itself, but the utilitarian ends of many magic recipes (from medicine to agriculture) encouraged such titles. These can be found through Greek and Roman literature as well as a part of the development of Christianity.

A group of Medieval manuals and handbooks were widely copied, yet considered secret. They were circulated extensively among those familiar with Latin and encouraged the idea that the world was full of marvels and secrets open only to the select few. Such works were well known to astrologers and to alchemists, as well as to those involved with black magic.

An example was *Secretum secretorum* (*Secret of Secrets*), which apparently derived from a tenth century Arab compilation. Today, the more than six hundred extant copies indicate that it circulated widely, at least among scholars. The handbook was a type of encyclopedia that covered numerous topics from crafts and politics to medicine.[25] The *Secreta Alberti* (*Secrets of Albert*) was a later compilation that covered secrets to be found in the careful analysis of animals, plants, and other natural items. The handbook included some two hundred formulas and recipes. An idea of why it was looked to for black magic may be gained by listing a few of its subjects, each of which offered a method of response: "To know whether your wife is chaste. . . To divine the future. To start a fire (using a lens). To make an incombustible garment (using asbestos). To make a sleeping man tell you what he had done. . . To make men seem headless. . . To make a lamp that makes any man hold it fart until he sets it down."[26]

The advent of printing dispelled some of the mystery of these books, many of which were given wider circulation in translated, printed editions. The suggested "Secrets Revealed" content for a handbook or manual, particularly in the sixteenth and early seventeenth centuries, became a sure key to a best-seller. The ready reference works may have revealed mysteries and secrets, but, more important, they gave useful, quite workable formulas for everything from removing stains and other household hints to curing diseases and making perfumes and cosmetics. A whole group of "professors of secrets" developed, particularly in Germany and Italy, who were on the fringes of the university and made a living translating and publishing the Latin Medieval secret books.

In exploring the history of the secret books, William Eamon goes a step further and claims they set the stage for the seventeenth century scientific revolution. The handbooks of secrets, he asserts, wed secrets, learning, scientists, doctors, and craftspeople in one common interest. The notion of experiment, scientific reasoning, and related matters were fostered by the reference works, out of which came the Royal Society in the mid-seventeenth century. Furthermore, thanks to people like Francis Bacon (1561–1626), the whole notion of a select group having access to scientific secrets (i.e., secret manuals) was questionable. The Royal Society made all its proceedings public.[27] Popular knowledge of the science was probably greater in the late Tudor and the Stuart periods than ever before or since.

Agriculture and Other Subject Manuals

With some 90 percent of the eighteenth century American and English population living on farms, often on the edge of the frontier, the most popular type of book—aside from the inevitable Bible—was the agriculture handbook or manual. This had been so since the early sixteenth century, but, as printing spread, the agricultural reference work became even more popular than it had been earlier or, for that matter, during the reign of Rome. Traveling peddlers might appear with such favors as *The Farmer's Companion* or Jared Eliot's *Essay Upon Field-Husbandry.*

In urban centers, particularly where educational institutions flourished, the manual or handbook concentrated on what Norbert Elias called "the civilizing process." Here guides to rhetoric and medicine as well as manuals of writing and everything in between flourished. The popularity of handbooks on medicine, agriculture, and related practical matters indicated to publishers the profitability of more works of this type in the vernacular. Between 1600 and 1800, the guides numbered more than five hundred. Many of these were reprinted and put out in new editions.

Handbook scope broadened. Now one could find handbooks on every subject from the military and mathematics to business and music. A study of the rise of the mercantile and middle classes in England and America shows a definite correlation between that growth and interest in ready reference books. The increased volume of fact and related books in the nineteenth and early twentieth century can be explained in a similar way: People who had hopes of rising into the middle classes felt compelled to master facts. One book of etiquette puts it this way, "Facts are invaluable in starting a conversation, facts for instance connected with mutual friends . . . and facts of mutual interest, public events of importance, or things appertaining to the moment."[28] Here and there in the vast parade of manuals on behavior, one finds surprises. There are, for example, numerous religious guides such as *A Manual of Godly Prayer* (1625) or *A Manual of Doctrine* (1742), but few overt sex guides until well into the twentieth century. At least one exception to this trend was a 1697 London guide "sold by Robert Barnham at the Goat in Little Britain" for six pence. The title is self explanatory, *A Manual for Husbands & Wives. Being Rules for Procreation: With a New Method for Begetting Children with Handsome Faces. Containing Full Instructions for the Wedding Night.*

An indication of the range of nineteenth century subject matter is evident in a few titles taken at random: *Accounting Handbook* (1818), *Handbook for the Public Galleries of Art* (1842), *The Handbook of Gardening* (1837), *The Handbook of a Man of Fashion* (1845), *The Traveller's Handbook* (1845), *A Handbook of Uterine Therapeutics* (1864), and *Appleton's Handbook of American Travel* (1871).

Manuals that taught the art of writing and penmanship (as contrasted with the ancient manuals on rhetoric) date primarily from the sixteenth century and are modeled after the work of the Roman scribe Giovanbattista Palatino whose *Compendio* . . . (1566) followed the even more popular . . . *Arto delo Excellente Scrivener* (1539) by the Venetian master Tagliente. Many of these writing and penmanship manuals were found in England and used by both the individual reader and by teachers, but few were published in England or America. "The beautiful writing books of the sixteenth and seventeenth centuries have been catalogued and studied by a long line of scholars. . . Jonathan Goldberg has written a Derridean account of some of these manuals. . . Many early manuals survived in very few examples, suggesting that they were copied and recopied until they were destroyed. . . On the other hand, many of the extant manuals bear no sign of use, implying that they were not employed to teach fine handwriting but were admired in their own right and so carefully preserved."[29]

The earliest extant Medieval handbooks on military technology date to the fourteenth century. Prior to then, the military was mentioned in various works, but rarely the focus of a particular handbook. An early example of the military manual is the c. 1335 treatise by a French physician on siege engines. A great number of military manuals began to appear in the fifteenth century. They literally breached a tradition by putting as much emphasis on illustrations as on text. Konrad Kyeser's *Bellifortis* (c. 1405), for example, features numerous types of artillery, firearms, and siege engines. The Medieval phase of the military manual ended with the advent of printing and the publication of such works as Roberto Valturio's *De Re Militari* (1472). Although new, the work borrowed liberally from Kyeser's illustrations. By the mid-sixteenth century the military handbook was almost as common as the almanac. "A series of technical handbooks known as the *Kunstbuchlein* was printed in many editions beginning in 1531–1532."[30]

Practical manuals for the drill and training of soldiers began to appear in the mid-sixteenth century and in some quantity from 1600. Still, "There is little evidence that men were prepared by formal weapons-instruction and drill, let alone by maneuvers, for combat."[31] By 1616 Ben Jonson, who had served with the army briefly, satirized in his *The Devil is an Ass* the whole notion that military maneuvers and fighting could be learned from manuals. "This scorn was only part of a wider and traditional bias against the idea that soldiering could be learned" from manuals."[32] The military manual from then to now continues to be a major source of interest, particularly for historians who turn to such works as *Manual Exercise and Evolution of the Cavalry; as Practiced in the late American Army* (1806) for invaluable source material.

Yearbooks and Annuals

The annual (or year-book) gained popularity in the eighteenth century. It is a collection of data pertaining to the past year's events. In a broader sense the annual can be a collection of almost anything from stories to accounts of meetings.[33]

Yearbooks in early English are associated with the law. Students took notes in court of actual legal arguments. As the "Year Book" the notes and reports were widely copied and circulation from about 1290. By the sixteenth century they were formalized and printed. *The Year Book* became the base of case law, the typical form of English common law. With Henry VIII (1491–1547) *The Yearbook* became a formal part of English law.

Numerous early annuals, such as the 1639 *Annual Report of the Official Boards of Sudbury, Massachusetts* were little more than minutes of meetings and actions of a government body. This practice has continued through to the present, and there are many titles, such as, the *Year Book of The Young Women's Christian Association of Albany* (1889). By 1694 Jacob Tonson had published in London a nearly two-hundred-and-forty-page annual that was little more than a collection of poetry, i.e., *The Annual Miscellany* for the year 1694 being the fourth part of miscellany poems. Then, too, almanacs might be termed annuals as well. For example, there was *An Episcopal Almanace* for the year 1674, which was treated as an annual in that the "almanac" was published for a half dozen years after the first issue. A similar approach is found in the subtitle of a New Hampshire publication, *Leavitt's Farmer's Almanac . . . and Miscellaneous Yearbook* (1797).[34]

One of the earliest eighteenth century annuals, and a model for many years to come, was Edmund Burke's *The Annual Register.* This compilation of world affairs for the previous year was published first in 1758 and by 1789 the title was expanded to include "or general repository of history, politics and literature for the year." Burke, the British statesman whose name failed to appear on the title page, retained editorship of the volume for the next thirty years. The "record of world events" is still being published by Longman.

With the close of the nineteenth century, the annual or yearbook as known today had taken form. *The Year-Book of the Scientific* or *The Year-Book of Pineapple Industry* are representative early twentieth century titles of works that carried on for decades.

Steele, as early as 1710, indicated that some annuals were a source of entertainment as much as information.[35] Few annuals or yearbooks of this type were published beyond the first edition. Catalogs are filled with such titles. *The Romance of Modern Travel: A Yearbook of Adventure* was issued in London only once in 1849, although the editor had hopes it would continue.

Keepsakes

One type of entertainment annual, for the most part limited to the Victorians, was the so-called keepsake. As the name implies these were annual collections of verse, prose, quotations, and almost anything else to set off the numerous illustrations. The gifts by the mid-1830s had developed into a minor mania. They were associated more with poor literature and sentimental illustrations than quality reference works. Thanks to the advent of steel engravings, c. 1823, which could be used for massive press runs, there were hundreds of different keepsakes published primarily from about the mid-1820s until the turn of the century.

The Keepsake (1829–1857) was the best known of the series—an English annual that boasted some outstanding illustrations, including a few from Turner. Americans soon recognized the profitability of such works, particularly as they tended to be awarded as prizes at graduation from grade and high school, as well as for birthdays and other occasions. The annuals continued to be published in America well after they went out of fashion in England during the 1850s.

Table Books

In the late eighteenth and nineteenth century, a famous type of fact book was the "table book," which began in the latter part of the sixteenth century. It was a blank notebook that one might use to gather material for a commonplace book.[36] By the nineteenth century, it had evolved for specialists into a synonym for a handbook of mathematical formulas or other tables. Most people, though, thought it was literally a "table" book—what today we would call a "coffee table book." It was more for ornament than for reading. Contents of the typical 1850s table book would range from plates of personalities and places to facts, fiction, etc. *Hone's Table Book* (1866) is representative of the nineteenth century type. In the introduction the compiler explains his collection of facts, to be consulted daily, come from his own readings of "out-of-the-way and in-the-way books" as well as from "gossip." The object of the text and numerous illustrations is to "blend information with amusement, and utility with diversion."[37] Table books served numerous purposes, not the least of which was "innocent entertainment." At the same time, the volume was an aid "to the cultivation of literature and of science; to minister to refined tastes, and foster larger intellectual sympathies." *Anecdotes Literary and Scientific* opens with alphabetical content pages that charts the course from "Anatomists and Anatomy" on page 1 to "Madman's Art" on p. 364. As the compiler admits "the contents . . . have been culled from many sources, and embrace a great diversity of subjects."[38]

Comparatively, today's one-volume encyclopedia, which is a close equivalent to the fact book, admits to no borrowing, but rather draws its data from editors, researchers and consultants who, apparently, gather original data and not from other facts books and encyclopedias. The purpose of consulting such a reference work is no longer fun, at least according to the modern publishers who don't seem to equate fun with facts. In reality, of course, nothing has changed since the first Roman turned to a fact book, but today the key word is power, not fun. It is the quest for power, e.g., *The Concise Columbia Encyclopedia* claims that to search for answers to questions is "to gain knowledge, to advance a step further each time on the road to power or wisdom."[39] This is supported by Francis Bacon's quote, "Knowledge itself is power." The *Webster's New World Encyclopedia,* "the new standard in single-volume encyclopedias," is more circumspect, giving no indication of where the information has been gathered from. It is left to the reader to decide the purpose of the work, although the jacket blurb claims it is useful if "you're looking for a handy source for your high schooler's class assignments, a reference to give depth and background to the daily news, or a fact-checker for your business or home office."[40]

Etiquette Manuals

After the often wild, unrestrained behavior of the Middle Ages, the so-called civilizing of the West began in narrow court circles in the sixteenth century. This is the period when manuals of behavior and etiquette gained a wider influence. A short treatise in 1530 by Erasmus, *De Civilitate Morum Puerilium* (*On Civility in Children*), established the base for etiquette books.[41] It was reprinted more than thirty times from 1530 to 1536 and in all had more than one hundred and thirty editions, thirteen of them in the late eighteenth century.

What is the Erasmus sixteen-page manual about? Elias explains: "Erasmus's book is about something very simple: the behavior of people in society—above all, but not solely, outward bodily propriety." By observing what Erasmus advises the prince's son not to do, one gets a fair notion of, for example, a typical dining room scene in an upper-class setting. He says it is bad form to be the first to dip into the dish of meat when it is put on the table. "Do not poke around in the dish." Also, one should wash one's hands before the meal, before diving into the meat. But even Erasmus's notions of good manners would be subject to change. For example, he advises against removing chewed food and putting it back on the plate. It's best "if you cannot swallow a piece of food, to turn round discreetly and throw it somewhere." Also, "do not be afraid of vomiting if you must," although away from the table.[42]

The popularity of Erasmus's work inspired others to go into more details. One of the most popular works was by Della Casas (1503–1556). He wrote the *Galateo*[43] between 1551 and 1555, and, by the early seventeenth century, translation had carried the guide throughout Europe. The first English translation was in 1576. One of the earliest English guides to etiquette is found in the *Boke of St. Albans* (1479). Although known today for its information on hawking and fishing, a latter section includes hints on good manners to set apart a gentleman or gentlewoman from both the raucous nobility and the ignorant underclasses. Thus, the idea was born among printers that etiquette would produce sales for the growing middle classes and those in the lower classes striving to elevate their status.

By the seventeenth century, there were scores of manuals on gentility, manners, and conduct. Manners and formal instructions for all, from youths to servants, were covered. The etiquette books used various titles and were described as "courtesy" books (or "curtoisie") in the fifteenth century. The most famous of these in England was John Russell's *Boke of Nurture,* which outlined traditional codes of conduct for the benefit of school children. (They often were called "babee books" or manuals specifically for the instruction of children and youths.) Although the guides were intended for the improvement of children, they also were aimed at the atrocious manners of their fathers and mothers. Texts, usually based on Medieval French works, drew from courtesy books that outlined conduct of civilly in the closed circles of knights and lords.

The seventeenth century saw, too, the rapid development of the importance of friendship as an essential social relationship. Closely tied to this, etiquette seemed particularly important to master. Almost without exception the etiquette books of the period stress the importance of good conversation, both by men and by women. Recommendations are specific and detailed. One French manual (*La Civilite Nouvelle* of 1671) considers the basic rules of conversation. Never bring up frivolous matters. Don't talk about melancholy things such as "sores, infirmaries, prisons, trails, war and death." And do not recount dreams. The French manual was translated into English.

Richard Brathwaite's manual, *English Gentleman and English Gentlewoman* (1630) points up the difference between the French and English. In England the *honnete homme* has numerous virtues other than class—he or she can be well mannered only if are virtuous. Modesty, compassion, and work assure the *honnete homme's* position in society. All of these qualities, and particularly the notion of work for gentlemen, are the antithesis of the French model.

The etiquette manuals offer a natural target for satire, and an early, successful broadside was fired at them in the mid-eighteenth century. In a literary counterpoint, Jane Collier addresses "the art of ingeniously tormenting." The second edition of her 234-page manual, published in 1757, offers husbands, wives and friends "some general instructions for plaguing all your acquaintance. . ." Here and there the author does suggest what one might anticipate in "polite" society.[44]

The desire for practical books extended to America. The founders of the new colonies needed printed guides to instruct them in the amenities appropriate to men but recently come to worldly success. Among the eighteenth century books dedicated to this end was *The Academy of Compliments,* which contained letter models, speech formulae, a glossary of difficult words, and even an anthology of songs. Other colonials preferred such works as Robert Cleaver's *Godly Form of Household Government* or Gouge's *Domestic Duties.*[45]

A basic quest of the nineteenth century manual was to help the reader gain and follow the proper rules of "respectability." The passion of respectability reached its zenith between 1840 and 1885, although it was a phenomenon that became apparent in the latter years of the eighteenth century and early nineteenth century. The cult was worldwide. The triumph of this new ideal can be ascribed to two major causes. The first was the rapid expansion of the middle and lower-middle classes. The second was the religious revival inaugurated by Methodist John Wesley (1703–1791). The doctrine of respectability and evangelism arose as a defense mechanism against the newly rich and, not incidentally, as a bastion of the sense of shame about body functions, including sex. The reading habits of several generations were formed by this goal of respectability and piety. The manuals of deportment multiplied and all stressed the new line. Regardless of the psychological and social overtones, the pious bourgeois sensibility was heightened by other factors, including fears of anarchy.

The Victorians' rules of right conduct were found in countless manuals. The more successful included Martin Tupper's *Proverbial Philosophy* (1838), which sold more than 200 thousand copies in thirty years. In America the editor of *Godey's Lady's Book* (one of America's most popular nineteenth century magazines) published *Manner or Happy Homes and Good Society* in 1866, and this was followed by numerous similar titles. By the turn of the twentieth century, both in England and America, the ever-increasing popular magazine had assumed much of the role of the etiquette manual. There were now weekly and monthly dispatches on good manners—a feature in today's magazines, as well.[46]

After the First World War, a new set of social values became evident that was to be found in the etiquette books, particularly in the most famous American title of all—Emily Post's *Etiquette, The Blue Book of Social Usage*. Published to this day, it was first issued in 1922. It has sold millions of copies and made the name "Emily Post" a synonym for etiquette.[47]

Developments in the Twentieth Century

Manuals, handbooks, and related ready reference works assumed major importance shortly after the middle of the nineteenth century. From 1850 to about 1914 there were more than ten thousand handbooks and manuals published; and for the most of the remainder of the current century the number jumped to over 160,000 in English. Whether it be the *Handbook of Aging* or *Manual for Writers of Term Papers,* the goal is to cover all major points of a subject to assist the individual reader in quest for particular facts or methodologies. And, not incidentally, the purpose of the increased publication was to increase publisher profits.

The publishing of ready reference works in the twentieth century follows patterns established earlier. Content and style were modified to meet the needs of the time. Little really changed in respect to audience or purpose. What did change drastically was the number of the titles, an increase made possible as much by social and economic developments as technological advances. By the 1980s, the computer had revolutionized the publication of ready reference works. First, it made possible the economical printing of fewer copies of a reference title as well as the abandonment of print for electronic formats. Most publishers combined the best of the two processes. An example is the ubiquitous directory, an almost ideal type of reference work for the computer. Established as a database, CD-ROM to online can be updated, revised, and edited every day or every year, or however often it may be needed. It may be consulted online or in print form with ease. It is among the first ready reference works to be a common online title, but it certainly is not the only one. In a short time, one imagines, almost all frequently consulted titles of this type will be available in electronic form.

A relative idea of the rapid prolification of ready reference books will be found in the brief history of directories. For the period 1820–1890, there are more than six thousand titles with the word "directory" in them compared to about sixteen hundred for the period 1800–1820. The numbers continued to grow with each decade. And the wide use of the computer and databases, as well as the evident need for such titles, explains why today there are more than fourteen thousand directories.[48]

"Directory", "manual" and "handbook" were synonymous throughout most of the Middle Ages and into the eighteenth century. Many considered a directory another type of guide, usually in association with religion. There were numerous Medieval directories of religious worship that often were little more than handbooks of prayer, e.g., *A Breefe Directory* (1576), which was published in London and contained "certayne sweete prayers." In 1585, Robert Parsons wrote *A Christian Directorie* for the purpose of "guiding men." *A Directorie for the Public Worship of God* appeared in 1645, and a *Directory for the Due Improvement of the Approaching Fast* was published in London in 1756. The directory is still in use today in this religious sense as a list of directions, rules, regulations, and prayers. The term might be employed, too, as a listing of holy days, such as *A Directory for the Year of Our Lord, 1708* with a list of saint's days, among other items. It was used in between a hundred and sixty and two hundred titles of books between 1650 and the middle of the eighteenth century. Prior to then, it was used only in a handful of printed works, usually for purpose of describing religious titles.

Directory became common, as employed today, in the mid-eighteenth century, e.g., the *Directory, of List of Principal Traders in London* (1732). Earlier examples existed but were infrequent and associated with religious lists. Actually, as early as 1677, the term was employed to indicate the rise of the most familiar of its uses from the eighteenth through the nineteenth century, as a city directory: *The London Directory of 1677,* published by Chatto and Windus that same year.

There were earlier English city directories such as the *Norwich Directory* of 1640, but until the nineteenth century the city directory was relatively rare, both in England and America. In view of small urban populations and the existence of closely knitted peer groups among other things, the need seemed not to exist. As the populations grew more heterogeneous and, more to the point, as publishers saw the possibility of profit, the city directory became the major type of its form through most of the nineteenth century.

There was a New York City guide by 1791, and from then to this day every city of more than twenty- or fifty thousand people could boast a directory. The early ones tended to be the work of local printers, but by the end of the century they were taken over by national publishers such as R.R. Polk. The first directories used a simple title such as *Directory for the City of Hartford for the Year of 1799,* but by the mid-nineteenth century it was common to use more elaborate titles, such as a *Sacramento Directory for 1887* containing "*Names, Places of Business, and Residences of All the Adult Population of the City, including Names of Merchants, Manufacturers, Business and Professional Men, Book-keepers, Clerks, Salesmen, Laborers, etc.*"

Guides to everything from the best restaurants and places to live to birds are part of today's fact-finding battalion. Many, by now, are well known. Roger Tory Peterson's *A Field Guide to Birds,* which has sold 5.2 million copies since 1934, is a favorite among both amateurs and experts. In 1983 the world celebrated the centennial of another famous guide, Daniel Beard's *The American Boy's Handy Book,* which was first published in 1882 as a series in the old *St. Nicholas* magazine. It would be many more years before Beard founded the American Boy Scouts (1910), and much of scouting was based on his *Handy Book* advice.

One of the few fact books to survive the nineteenth century and become a twentieth century guide is *Brewer's Dictionary of Phrase and Fable.* The fourteenth edition was published by Harper Collins in 1989, more than a century after the first edition of 1870. A student of the book asks, "Why has a work that was so much a product of its age survived?" and then replies that it, as several other early examples, still is a delight to browse and, more important, continues to serve as a practical ready reference source for out-of-the-way facts.[49]

Today's popular fact book tends to be subject specific and usually constructed around a lighthearted listing. Most of the scores of examples give away their content in the title. For example, *The Best and Worst of Everything* is a 340-page collection of the "best and worst people, places, and things in the U.S." Everything from actors to restaurants are noted and listed in the ten highest and ten lowest categories. *The 100% American* is a compendium of fifteen hundred "surprising, sometimes alarming, often hilarious facts about Americans . . . culled from hundreds of surveys, polls, census and government reports." Note that the better of the modern fact books carefully indicate sources, something rarely done in earlier works. The just plain *Factfinder* is more general in content, moves from the universe to entertainment in thirteen areas. Illustrations and charts set off the data for kids more used to television than books.

On ready reference works, from medical handbooks to lawn care, there is no end. The number grows with each passing publishing year. Some fear this development in that reliance of readers on quite simplified rules of conduct to rules of football may be less than stimulating to the imagination. The real problem of clarity, accuracy, and authority is overcome somewhat, if only for librarians, by excellent book reviews in the library literature.[50] Too many ready reference works have become sources of amusement and rapid answers to sometimes dense problems. Still, the form has never enjoyed a more prosperous time than the end of this century. And, there is every promise it will continue well after 2001.

Because it is impossible in a book of this type or size to do full justice to manuals and handbooks, much less other types of ready reference aids, we will consider in depth at last one important manual—the letter manual, whose history is, in a sense, the history of all ready references that have been of daily assistance to the public.

Letter Manuals

Letter-writing has been well called "The Gentlest Art," but it is an art that baffles contemplation in its scope, since the subject of a good letter may be anything on earth. . . In letters both contents and style may be almost anything.[51]

Few reference works are as personal as the commonplace book, but the letter is an exception. It played, and continues to play an important role in one-to-one reference situations where one expert is advising another or giving information to a layperson. While current letter manuals are of importance, they rarely take up much space in a reference section. This was not always the case, and historically they are a major consideration.

Communication in letter form is as old as the written word, and in Mesopotamia and Egypt a letter served as much as an official document as a personal source of contact. Numerous examples are found in cuneiform and Egyptian demonic writing. *Alexander the Great* (356–323 B.C.) is a typical example of how letters were employed for official purposes. Extant letters show that professional letter writers, or scribes, used the form as an administrative tool to tie together Alexander's vast empire.

Aside from the personal letter from and to people of no historical or literary importance, the genre takes numerous informational forms. Private correspondence between people of historical importance was avidly collected and published from the sixteenth century to the present.[52] Letter manuals, from the same period, taught people how to write both the familiar and the formal letter. There was even the epistolary novel.[53]

Until the early twentieth century, letter manuals were an integral part of education courses and reference in both Europe and America. The letters included, in the models highlighted, the correct form for everything from business to social situations. Primarily the letter manual was a guide for those who wanted to write eloquent, polite, and effective letters on all sorts of subjects, but who lacked the skill to express themselves adequately.

The concept of one-to-one virtually instant letters via e-mail seems new, but it is not. Until the post was well established, it was usual for someone within reach of another party to send a letter by private messenger. Messenger services were extensive throughout Europe and in early America. On foot or on horse the messenger might reach his destination faster than today's post. Usually the letters arrived, if not seconds after written, at least within hours after being penned. A perfect example with the built-in indication of the time span involved is Richard Steele's note to his wife from a coffeehouse on 7 May 1707: "Dear Prue. I am just drinking a Pint of Wine and will come home forthwith. I am with Mr. Elliot settling things. Yrs Ever Ever Richard Steele."[54]

There are numerous problems with published letters employed for reference purposes. One critic cites the difficulty: "To what extent can we consider a work edited for publication as the creation of the individual listed as its author? To what extent is our reading of a letter influenced by the certainty that it is an authentic record of its author's private thoughts and opinions, intended only for its original recipient?"[55] Another problem is that most letters are ephemeral, and while they may serve as building blocks in literature or science, in and of themselves they may not be of that much value. Even the delights and horrors of e-mail and related digital forms does little to really change the essential nature of the letter. "Letters are usually intended for a single recipient, or at most a small group of recipients. . . Letters rejoice in—and celebrate—the ephemeral."[56] Still, it is important to understand the place of the letter, as a major form of communication, in the history of reference and research.

Greek-Roman Letters

The letter or "epistole" (from *epistellein,* sent to) date from the earliest Greeks, from Homer to the Hellenistic, Graeco-Roman period. The majority tended to be short notes, often of an official, administrative nature. Beginning primarily with Plato the letter was used as method of expounding an idea, which might mean philosophical position (Aristotle), a treatise on literary criticism (Horace), or a wide range of other subjects.

The Greek philosophers were fond of using the letter form for philosophical arguments, e.g., Plato, Aristotle, Demosthenes, and Epicurus are only a few those who used their own or the work of others. It became evident that the writer of the letters probably had public consumption in mind rather than, or in addition to, direct correspondence with an individual. Along with the notion of a collection of letters came the next step—the preparation of the letters into such a form as to be an argument, or exhortation for a particular point of view. In fact, the collected letters became valuable reference works in special subject fields.[57] For example, there are quantities of extant Greek letters, but the majority were written to illustrate lessons in rhetoric. As such, the organized letters are a form of manual rather than personal communication. They are closer to proper speech, i.e., rhetoric, than the friend-to-friend written word.

The Athenian orator Isocrates (436–338 B.C.) may have been the first to use an open letter to shape public opinion. (To that point all extant letters were official, personal, or otherwise confined to a one-to-one form of communication.) In 346, he published his treatise *Phillippus* and thereafter wrote letters to prominent individuals begging them to take the lead in a war against Persia.

Early Letter Manuals

Letter manuals appear first among the Greeks, although probably they existed much earlier in Mesopotamia and Babylon. The manual continues to be a basic reference form to this day. The Greeks, as those before, and certainly after, discussed the specific formal structure of various types of communication. Representative letters were offered, as well as basic forms from contracts, surveys, and wills that might be a specific part of the traditional business letter. Model letters, complete with directions, rules, and specifics as to style, length, etc. were being circulated in late Greek antiquity. Examples are found in Greek comedies. The letter manual took a more serious turn with the Romans and collections of letters were usual. These were employed primarily as guides for official letters, but with a strong dash of artistic prose.

Artemon (fl. 2d century B.C.) apparently edited Aristotle's letters (no longer extant) and in the process gave advice on proper letter-writing. Several other experts had opinions, but Demetrius (c. 200 B.C.) was the most influential. In his treatise on style, he went into considerable detail as to suitable topics and approaches to letters. Also, he appears to be the first to publish a manual (*Epistolary types*) as did Proclus (c. A.D. 410–485). Numerous guidebooks and manuals on letters were published over this period of some 500 to 600 years, but "all in all the guidebooks do not seem to have had much direct influence. Even though they may not have been followed . . . they indicate that letter theorists were very much aware of the range of letter types."[58]

Letter-writing appears to be one area of literature where the Romans owed little to the Greeks and, in fact, themselves developed the personal letter to a fine art. "We have in Greek absolutely no such letters. . . There is very little likelihood that the Greeks of the great times wrote many matterful letters at all. They lived in small communities, where they saw each other daily and almost hourly; they took little interest in the affairs of other communities."[59] Conversely the Romans needed the letter to communicate with each other over most of Europe and a good part of Asia Minor.

In the Roman world, Cicero (106–43 B.C.) helps the modern reader recapture the past better than any other letter writer, if only because of the volume of his work and, that it was not destroyed. There are more than nine hundred extant letters from 58 to 43 B.C. Some are private, but the majority clearly were written for wider circulation. His most famous letters are those to his friend Atticus, to whom Cicero wrote "Whoever reads the eleven books of the correspondence hardly feels the need of an organized history of the time." Other notable, although in no way as comprehensive, letter writers must include Seneca (4 B.C.–A.D. 65) *Moral Letters* and the *Letters of Pliny the Younger* (A.D. 61–112), which demonstrate what should be a cultured man's interests and values.

Postal Service

In Rome there was an impressive interest in letter-writing, for, as one critic observes, "as Rome became the hub of the Mediterranean world written communication gained in importance. . . Men of wealth . . . had among their slaves couriers who could cover fifty Roman miles a day, and the companies of farmers had their own postal service . . . Augustus . . . instituted a system of post couriers along the main routes of the Empire."[60]

Prior to the Romans there were some attempts at mail service that went beyond a mile or two and was overseen by the government. The Persians were the first to develop a public mail service, probably based on an earlier Assyrian system, and, by the time of the Ptolemies (c. 300 B.C.), the Romans had adopted and maintained a public post. The speed and efficiency of the Roman post was not to be rivaled until the nineteenth century. As letters might be freely intercepted and later used against the writer, there were two approaches to safeguard privacy. The first, and most prevalent was to write in vague, superficial and sometime even coded forms. The second, used extensively by government officials, was to trust the message either in writing or in oral form to a special messenger.

With the fall of Rome some remnants of the "curus publicus" hobbled along. The continued decay of the roads and the unwillingness of communities to take up the expense of postal service caused it to disappear gradually until it was completely destroyed by the tenth century. By 987 there seems to be no traces of the once proud mail service.

With the growth of trade in the late Middle Ages private postal delivery began again. Post services often were provided by the universities as well as by international trading companies. Government postal service was primarily for diplomatic use, but by the mid-sixteenth century was broadened in some countries to include personal letters.

The pace of postal progress followed the economic and educational explosion throughout the latter eighteenth century and well into the twentieth century. Improved roads followed by steam powered railroads boosted the popularity of the post as did a penny stamp for letters in the mid-nineteenth century. In 1878, the Universal Postal Union was established to provide uniform framework of rules and procedures for exchange of mails throughout the world.

Christian Manuals

The earliest Christian letters are an important part of the New Testament, e.g., Paul's letters of around the middle of the first century. The Pastoral Letters, in the general style of Paul, are found throughout the Bible. In fact, letters are one of the more important literary modes in early Christianity from the third century through the Middle Ages. One basic reason for reliance on the form is suggested: "What better way to stress continuity with Paul than to form one's material into letters."[61] The letter form was used informally, but primarily by the Church to publish official documents and administrative decisions.

The educated Christians wrote letters, not only as a means of private communication, but also as a vehicle for philosophical exposition and the treatment of other intellectual subjects, as is evident, for example, in the letters of Cicero, Seneca, and Fronto. "On the whole, early Christian letters combined the familiarity of the private letter, the authority and community address of the official letter, and the expository and didactic functions of the philosophical letter. . . The persistence of Christian epistolography through the first five centuries attests to the usefulness of this genre to the ancient church, for it was well suited communication between widespread congregations and a valuable instrument for teaching.[62] Departing from the plain language of the Greeks and Romans, the Christians adopted a more artificial approach. Finally, letters and other forms of communication were "incomprehensible to all but scholars. A writer who hoped for a wider public and who had to deal with voluminous material could not employ this medium but was obligated to avail himself of a "sermo simplex" approaching ordinary speech."[63]

In the fourth century the letter reappears as a literary form. Symmachus (A.D. 340–402), the greatest orator of the period was representative of the last of the pagan writers. His letters, written to leading persons of his time, are collected in ten books. Ausonius (d.c. A.D. 395) appears as the first of the Christian writers who uses letters in his poetry. During the next centuries prior to the Carolingian Renaissance, there were numerous letter writers, such as, Ambrose (A.D. 339–397), Jerome (A.D. 348–420), and Cassiodorus (A.D. 490–583).

Letters in the Middle Ages

The development of a new society outside of the monastic communities and the rise of towns and universities required more and more written communication, usually by letter. Letters were highly formalized. By the eleventh century epistolary style was given a new name, "*dictamen*" from the old traditional "*dictare*," to dictate. From the time of Augustine the term came to mean "to write, to compose," particularly for works of poetry—hence the German "*dichten*" and "*dichter.*" The "*ars dictaminis*" became a major study of episto-lary composition. Textbooks, usually of rhetoric, offered models and examples. Also, there were formularies or books of form letters called "*dictamina.*" These covered all situations and persons of all classes and ranks. "The manuals and treatises on epistolary "dictamen," many of them anonymous, number several hundred and are found in a few thousand manuscripts. This vast body of dic-taminal material represents a major achievement of medieval civilization . . . extending from the twelfth century to the Renaissance."[64]

The letter manuals of the Middle Ages were usually of two sections. The first gave detailed explanations of how to compose the so-called five-part let-ter. The second was a section of examples. This combination of theory and models was one of the most popular reference works of the time. The ap-plication of rhetoric to letter-writing appears first in about 1087 when a monk wrote a treatise on the subject. He touched on all aspects from the proper form of greeting (depending on the rank of the individual being ad-dressed) to the patterns of the letter itself. The formulas, by Alberic of Monte Cassino, were used throughout the next five hundred years in nu-merous less scholarly manuals and handbooks. The five-part letter was firmly set by 1135 and consisted of the form of address, the narration or heart of the letter (two parts), the method of presenting requests for favors, and the conclusion or final part of the letter. Social status was all. The space given to discussion of the status of addressee and sender often took up a third or more of the manual. For example, Lawrence of Aquileia's *Practica Sive Usus Dictaminis* (c. 1300) devotes numerous pages to the proper seven social levels from the highest (pope) to the lowest (heretic).

Several professions became involved in letters. There was the dictator, usually a professional secretary who might be labeled as a notary, chancel-lor, teacher, or all of these. The major *dictatores* compiled manuals. Among the first extant example is *Adalbert of Samaria's Praecepta Dictaminum,* written about 1115 at Bologna. By the end of the century the modest man-ual developed into major reference works with epistolary models. These were studied in law schools as well as in classes of rhetoric. *Dictamen* man-uals spread throughout Europe. In 1321 Giovanni diBonaadrea's *Brevis In-troductio ad Dictamen* was both a manual and an adopted textbook in most schools. Taught with grammar and Latin, letter-writing became part of what today would be termed a standard business course for notaries and government officials.

By the early Renaissance the study of *dictamen* dwindled and disap-peared. No one is quite sure why, but as one scholar puts it: "Contributing factors are known [for its decline]. By its inflexible procedures, insistence on elegant style, and demand for brevity, dictamen . . . thwarted any cre-ative activity in the writing of personal letters . . . The use of . . . vernacu-lar languages . . . in the fourteenth and fifteenth centuries, for model letters and parts of the letter . . . was followed by vernacular manuals."[65]

Renaissance

By the Renaissance there were more than three hundred separate manuals or treatises dealing with this approach to letter-writing. Almost without exception each work ended with an appendix of model letters. The reader could master the form of the letter, then turn to several hundred examples that might be changed slightly for his or her purposes. Out of the letter manuals, and often by the same author, developed the *ars notaria* (the art of notary forms). Many letter manuals included legal forms that were separated for use by notaries and included such things as model leases, contracts, and other legal documents. Eventually the two forms split and what was once in one letter-writing manual was now in two or three other manuals dealing with notary and legal material.

The growing interest in scholarship during the Renaissance saw the circle of scholars and ideas widen. As the postal service improved, personal correspondence became increasingly important. Letters were used widely by reference book compilers, e.g. when they "broadcast an appeal for information they could be reasonably confident that it would arrive. Ortelius printed a message to his readers asking for fresh information and promising to mention their contributions by name. . . Over 3,000 letters to and from Erasmus have survived. . . Such juggernaut correspondence tapped into the less capacious ones that linked orthodox scholars."[66]

The Renaissance and the focus on the individual brought an increased interest in reliable personal letters and models. Vernacular letter-writing models were spread quickly with the advent of printing. The model based on simpler classical letter forms was adopted and readers were encouraged to treat letter-writing as an art rather than as a fixed form with specific, narrow rules. Antonius Sorg was among the first to take advantage of the development and, in 1483, he published at Augsburg the first of five editions of a German-language guide to letters, which included much of a personal nature. This was followed by several examples in other parts of Europe, but it was not until almost a hundred years later that an English title of the same type appeared. Published in London, William Fulwood's *The Enimie of Idleness* (Henry Bynneman for Leonard Maylard, 1568) was the first of what would be hundreds of letter-writing manuals in English. That much of it simply was copied from a French manual of the same type seemed of little interest to the English compiler or publisher. The manual outlined the basics of how to begin and end a formal letter and gave samples of form letters, either anonymous or by famous people.[67] Another type of manual consisted of simply reprinting model letters. The first appeared in English in 1576 as *A Panoplie of Epistles,* compiled by Abraham Fleming and printed in London. The fat quarto of close to four hundred and fifty pages was made up of model letters from fifty-seven authors, primarily translated from the Latin classical writers.

By 1586, manuals began to appear in London that were no longer translations or copies of French work, but rather were written specifically for the English audience. One of the first and most popular (and reprinted well into the seventeenth century) was Angel Day's *The English Secretorie* (London, 1586), with more than a hundred practical model letters under thirty-two subject headings. The miscellaneous approach had wide appeal, particularly as it represented a partial escape from classical models.

The early genius of the English-language manual was Nicholas Breton (c. 1555–1626). A graduate of Oxford who settled in London, he began writing poetry in the 1570s. While contemporaries ranked his poetry highly, it has lost much of its fame. What remains is a curious group of some sixty miscellaneous works, from satire to moral and pious pamphlets. One of the more successful was his *Poste with a Packet of Madde Letters* (1602), in which his imagination in composing lively, fascinating models swamped the drab examples found in earlier manuals. "Breton's sparkling and spirited letters were written with freshness and gusto. No attention was paid to rhetoric, nor to the rigid groupings of the formularies. The 153 models include family letters, friendly letters, love letters, letters on university life, courtship, consolation, etc. and completely reflect the varied social science of the early seventeenth century. Some are witty, some are scurrilous and many are diverting."[68] The manual, with minor revisions, was published for close to a century.

Eighteenth Century

The consensus is that the eighteenth century was the century of the letter. "Everybody wrote letters: and a surprising number of people wrote letters well. . . The rise of the novel in this century is hardly more remarkable than the way in which that novel almost wedded itself . . . to the letter form."[69]

Letters took many forms. And the forms and the involvement reflect larger issues. For example, women's letters became popular, primarily because "newly educated women could easily learn to write letters, and, as epistolary theory became more adapted to worldly culture, women's letters began to be considered the best models of the genre. . . Epistolarly writing by women was . . . rarely signed, and was often in fact produced by male writers. . . By the eighteenth century the practice of male authors appropriating the female voice . . . had became popular."[70] Examples of the epistolary novelist using women narrators include Pierre Laclos and *Les Liaisons Dangereuses* (1782) and Jean Jacques Rousseau with his *La Nouvelle Heloise* (1761). The epistolary novel disappeared for the most part in the nineteenth century, reappearing only from time to time, as, for example, in John Barth's *Letters* (1979).

Samuel Richardson (1689–1761) is best known for his epistolary novels, *Pamela* (1740, 1741), and *Clarissa* (1747–1748). All his major works are in letter form. Richardson was widely read, equally respected. Little wonder he placed letter-writing above most forms of communication, including personal conversation. With a letter the writer did not fear interruption or distraction. The loss of self to the pen and the chance for undisguised self-expression "foster the pleasures of getting outside of one's self."[71]

Urged on by his publisher, Richardson completed a practical letter manual in 1741, *Letters Written to and for Particular Friends on the most important occasions directing not only the requisite style and forms to be observed by writing familiar letters; but how to think and act justly and prudently in the common concerns of human life. Containing one hundred and seventy three letters. None of which were ever before published.* It is worth reading the whole, lengthily title as it summarizes scope, purpose and audience for manuals throughout the century.

Richardson's manual was published the same year as *Pamela* and proved to be an immediate success. Unlike others including Breton, he was more involved with the imitation than with the form. Instead of stressing rules of rhetoric, he stressed the need to focus on individual details and characterization. Much of this lesson appears time and time again in his novels. The letters were widely copied and, without acknowledgment, became part of manuals published from 1741 to the mid-1920s.

How much does Richardson's *Letters Written to and for Particular Friends* owe to predecessors? No one is certain, but it is unlikely he copied anyone. Conversely his publisher may have been urged on by the success of the *Young Secretary's Guide,* which first appeared in London in 1687. Giving specific directions for the business letter, as well as forms for bills, contracts, wills, etc., the guide went through numerous editions, including an American version in 1728.[72] The first part of the guide is devoted to model letters. This format is employed right up to the present day.

In "The Contents of the Letters" Richardson penned models that move from "a widow-mother, in answer to her son's complaining of hardship in his apprenticeship" to "a young lady cautioning her against keeping company with a gentleman of bad character." It should be stressed that the focus here, as on numerous eighteenth century books of this type, was as much on morals as on form. The purpose, according to Richardson, is "to inculcate the principles of virtue and benevolence; to describe properly, and recommend strongly, the social and relative duties; and to place them in such practical lights, that the letters may serve for rules to think and act by, as well as forms to write after."[73]

Eighteenth century letters, too, served as public battle grounds. A good deal of political controversy took the form of published letters. Also, from time to time the published letter served as a form of communication of new ideas, e.g., Arbuthnot's *Essay on the Usefulness of Mathematical Learning*

(1701). Beside this, the actual correspondence of the famous were collected, published, and studied, much as they are today.

From the Letter to Magazines

The letter hardly lost prestige in the nineteenth century, particularly the first half, although it receded as a major form of literature. The century saw some of the world's greatest letter writers, such as Sydney Smith and Charles Dickens, but correspondence—understood as an art form in the eighteenth century—became considerably more relaxed and "natural." At the same time, by the beginning of the twentieth century, the letter as a formal method of communicating ideas and acting as a reference source was by-passed by published books. The modern letter, to be sure, remains an important source of reference data.

Since the first letter was carved on an Egyptian monument or formed on wet clay by a Babylonian, there have been those convinced the letter is no longer a major form of communication. As a literary device it reached its peak in eighteenth century Europe, and began to decline when modern technology offered other avenues of communication. The "other avenues"—the telephone, the tape recorder, e-mail—have been a problem for librarians who have attempted to keep letters in their archives, usually in letter books. Publishers, too, have deplored the lack of letters to chart the course of an important life, and with the computer many foresee the time when messages, when letters will disappear unless maintained in permanent formats. Still, the fear of the disappearing letter is not new, and certainly will be of interest to the post office, which has more business in the mid-1990s than ever before. Warnings have been sounded for centuries and, as late as 1922, the critic and literary historian George Saintsbury (1845–1933) wrote: "On letter writing . . . there are current many clichés. The most familiar . . . for a good many years past has been that the penny post has killed it."[74] Saintsbury, of course, was fearful that free use of the mails by everyone would/had cheapened the importance of letters. The argument is heard today about e-mail.

By the twentieth century the form was taken over as much by etiquette books and basic grammars as by specific letter-writing manuals. Today any-one seeking help with a letter may find models in almost all etiquette books, as well as in guides for secretaries, basic grammar manuals, etc. Separate manuals for letter-writers continue, but are fewer in number than in past centuries.

As a form of reference communication, the letter continues to this day to be important. Still, it has problems and these were realized as early as the sixteenth century. Something else was needed. "In an age when knowledge itself was becoming nationalized, the letters in Latin that [scholars] exchanged were no longer enough to circulate information on the new works that were appearing throughout Europe. Thus in France, Colbert encouraged the founding (1665) of the *Journals des savants,* the first periodical that reviewed books. . . There were soon a number of similar periodicals—Bayle's *Nouvelles de la Republique des letters* . . . Jean LeClerk's *Bibliotheque universelle et historique,* or the *Acta eruditorum of Leibniz.*"[75] The magazine's development is considered in another lchapter.

Notes for Chapter 5

1. John Foxe (1516–1587), *Acts and Monuments,* popularly known as *Foxe's Book of Martyrs,* 1563, quoted in *The Oxford English Dictionary,* vol. 5, 60.

2. Rettig, *Distinguished Classics of Reference Publishing* consists of informative, delightful essays by as many people as there are reference works discussed.

3. *Oxford English Dictionary,* vol. 6, 141.

4. Ibid.

5. "Vade-mecum" in the sense of being a compilation of material about a particular point of view is illustrated in Gotthold Lessing's biting satire, *Vade Mecum fur den Herrn Samuel Gotthold Lange* (1754). The German philosopher destroyed the pretension of Lange as a translator and literary scholar. Vade-mecum can be, too, a collection or anthology, e.g., Baron von Münchhausen's famous tall stories in his 1781–1783 *Vademecum fur lustige Leute.*

6. Michael Leff, "The Material of the Art in the Latin Handbooks of the Fourth Century A.D.," in *Rhetoric Revalued,* ed. Brian Vickers (Binghamton, N.Y.: Medieval and Renaissance Texts, 1982), 76. For a discussion of two other early handbooks, see this same article. The Romans' simple shorthand title for handbook or manual was "*ars,*" from the Greek "skill," "way" or "method"; but translated as "art of" in a handbook on such subjects as rhetoric in *Ars Arengandi* and love in Ovid's *Ars Amatoria.* As long as Latin dominated, from the Romans through the fourteenth and into the sixteenth century, "*ars*" was a familiar way of identifying a handbook or manual.

7. Judith McClure, "Handbooks Against Heresy in the West; From the Late Fourth to the Late Sixth Centuries," *Journal of Theological Studies* 30 (1979): 180.

8. Ibid., 191.

9. *Dictionary of the Middle Ages,* vol. 8, 316. See, too, Joan Blythe, "The Influence of Latin Manuals on Medieval Allegory," *Romania* 95 (1974): 258–83. The author demonstrates how allegorical presentations in Medieval

poetry often were drawn from handbooks and manuals and, more particularly, in her article William Peraldus's *Summa de Vitiis et Virtutibus* (c. 1260).

10. For a discussion of the Medieval penitential, see *Dictionary of the Middle Ages,* 487–93, as well as the lengthy bibliography. For a detailed study, see John McNeill and Helena Gamer, *Medieval Handbooks of Penance* (New York: Columbia University Press, 1990) and Allen J. Frantzen, *The Literature of Penance in Anglo Saxon England* (New Brunswick, N.J.: Rutgers University Press, 1983. Frantzen points out that the handbooks are highly controversial and rarely translated in full because the "penitential . . . discuss sexual offenses. Sometimes these passages have been translated." But often they are deleted or left in the Latin.

11. Sara Foot (Book review), *History of European Ideas,* Vol. 17, No. 5, 1993, p. 680.

12. *Dictionary of the Middle Ages,* vol. 10, 79.

13. Frantzen, *The Literature of Penance in Anglo-Saxon England,* 151.

14. *Dictionary of the Middle Ages,* vol. 8, 91.

15. By the sixteenth century the terms "handbook" and "manual" were more associated with nationality than necessarily the form. The English and Germans preferred the descriptor "handbook," while other European countries used "manual." By the nineteenth century this division no longer is as apparent.

16. This is a rough estimate based on a check of holdings in OCLC member libraries as well as (RLIN). The handbook and manual were scarce because, as in previous centuries, craftspeople transmitted by word of mouth the how-to aspects of their trades and professions. Sr. Marina Gibbons, "Instructive Communication: English Renaissance Handbooks 1477–1550" (Ph.D. diss., St. Louis University, 1966). This is one of the few overviews of handbooks in a historical context. See "A classified check list of manuals of information . . . in England between 1477 and 1550," pp. 305–344 for not only a list of the manuals, but an extensive bibliography.

17. Gibbons, "Instructive Communication," 108.

18. See chapter 6 in this text on Dictionaries, Grammar, and Rhetoric for more on rhetorical handbooks, etc.

19. Gibbons, "Instructive Communication," 105. Erasmus quotes the Greeks and Romans to show they faced the same dilemma, e.g., "Quintilian notes too effusive and redundant copies in Stesichorus; but he mentions it in such a way as to confess that the fault should not be entirely avoided" (p. 14).

20. Manfred Fleischer, "The First German Agricultural Manuals," *Agricultural History* 55 (1981): 21. The author gives detailed information on two German handbooks as well as fascinating background information on the role they played in the Reformation.

21. Andrew McRae, "Husbandry Manuals and the Language of Agrarian Improvement," in *Culture and Cultivation in Early Modern England,* eds.

Michael Leslie and Timothy Raylor, Leicester: Leicester University Press, 1992, 36.

22. Ibid.

23. For a detailed definition of proverbs, adages, etc., see the first section of Adages, e.g. *Collected Works of Erasmus,* vol. 31, (Toronto: University of Toronto Press, 1982), 5–28.

24. Whitney freely admits he drew the emblems primarily from the existing titles, including Alciato and four others. Some 202 of Whitney's 248 emblems are from these sources. Among the best of the numerous studies of emblem books are Elizabeth Freeman, *The English Emblem Book* (London: Chatto and Windus, 1948) and Mario Praz, *Studies in Seventeenth Century Imagery* 2 vols. (London: Warburg, 1939).

25. *The Secretum Secretorum* has fourteen known separate English prose versions, partial or complete, translated between 1400 and 1702. The contents were added to and other materials were deleted from, depending on the translation and the country of origin. See *Dictionary of the Middle Ages,* vol. 11, 135.

26. This is attributed to Albertus Magnus (1200–1289) a Dominican scholar who later was sainted. It survives today in dozens of manuscript and printed forms and is filled with recipes that originally were written out to help in the study of natural science. In time they became famous as black magic texts. "Unusual natural effects (lenses, prisons, asbestos wicks and cloths . . .) are mixed with physiological and psychological effects (hallucinatory smokes, itching powders) with stage magic." Ibid., vol. 8, 35.

27. William Eamon, *Science and the Secrets of Nature* (Princeton, N.J.: Princeton University Press, 1994). In this scholarly study of the books of secrets and magic, Eamon makes the point that even with the urge to make secrets public, others were retained, e.g., the formula for gunpowder and many of Robert Boyles's chemical experiments. Today, the secrets of atomic energy, for one, are not readily available. There are several large library holdings of magic and related titles as well as private collectors of such manuals. See Eamon's bibliography.

28. *Society Small Talk* (London: Frederick Warne, 1879), 48.

29. H.R. Woudhuysen, "Sale of Books," *Times Literary Supplement,* 29 October 1993, p. 14.

30. *Dictionary of the Middle Ages,* vol. 11, 649. Before the Medieval period, there were numerous manuals and handbooks on warfare, most of which have been lost. Among these were a handbook on catapults (c. 240 B.C.), the artillery manual of Philo of Byzantium, and the tenth book of Vitruvius's *De Architectura* describing military devices.

31. J.R. Hale, *War and Society in Renaissance Europe 1450–1620.* (Leicester: Leicester University Press, 1985), 144.

32. Ibid., 145.

33. The encyclopedia yearbook—a feature of all major publishers of the

sets—is among the best known of its type. Unfortunately, few have any direct correlation with the contents of the main encyclopedia set. They are useful primarily as a summary of the year's past events and for special features, such as the *Britannica's* section on countries of the world.

34. Once an annual or yearbook begins, the assumption is it will be published once a year from then to eternity. As such, librarians treat it as a serial. The obvious confusion is that almanacs and many other ready reference aids are published once a year, usually at the same approximate date, but are referred to as almanacs, directories, handbooks, etc. and not as yearbooks or annuals. This is the stuff that makes cataloging an art.

35. *Tatler,* no. 261, 1710.

36. See chapter 3 of this text on commonplace books.

37. William Hone, *The Table Book, of Daily Recreation and Information: Concerning Remarkable Men, Manners, Times, Seasons, Solemnities, Merry Makings, Antiquities and Novelties, Forming Complete History of the Year, With One Hundred and Sixteen Engravings* (London: William Tegg, 1866), 2.

38. William Keddie, *Anecdotes Literary and Scientific* (New York: George Routledge & Sons, 1859), iv.

39. *The Concise Columbia Encyclopedia,* 2d ed. (New York: Columbia University Press, 1989), v. Apparently, knowing answers to such questions as "What is the population of Tokyo?" or "What sea does the Danube flow into?" will give the reader a passport to "the road to power or wisdom."

40. *Webster's New World Encyclopedia* (New York: Prentice Hall, 1992).

41. There were guides to manners before Erasmus, but they had a limited circulation due as much to the lack of a printing as to the lack of interest by the public. Hugh of St. Victor, for example, in his *De Institutione Novitiarum* (c. A.D. 1135) is concerned with some aspects of good behavior. And there were several other similar titles including, if only by implication, guides to the manners of knights and lords. And out of this need developed numerous manuals, among the earliest and best known being Castglione's *Il Cortegiano* of 1528, followed by Guazzo's *La Civil Conversatione* of 1574.

42. Norbert Elias, *The Civilizing Process: The History of Manners* (New York: Urizen Books, 1978), 55–58. This volume is by far the best history of early etiquette manuals as well as of manners.

43. Giovanni Della Casa. *A Renaissance Courtesy-Book* (1576, reprinted, Boston: Merrymount Press, 1914).

44. Jane Collier, *An Essay on the Art of Ingeniously Tormenting: With Proper Rules for the Exercise of That Pleasant Art,* London, 1757.

45. James D. Hart, *The Popular Book* (Berkeley: University of California Press, 1963), 14.

46. Andrew St. George, *The Descent of Manners* (London: Chatto and Windus, 1993). This work is a superior history of Victorian manners and etiquette manuals.

47. Richard Grefrath, "Code of Courtesy from the Roaring Twenties: Emily Post's Etiquette," in *Distinguished Classics of Reference Publishing,* Rettig, 98–112. This lively, brief history concludes with a useful bibliography. For coverage of American titles, particularly in the nineteenth and first half of the twentieth century, see Arthur Schlesinger, *Learning How to Behave* (New York: Cooper Square Publishing, 1968). Another history is Esther Aresty's *The Best Behavior* (New York: Simon and Schuster, 1970).

48. *Directories in Print* (Detroit, Mich.: Gale, 1993). This directory is an "annotated annual guide to 14,000 directories published worldwide. This is only one of several directories such as *British Directories, Guide to American Educational Directories, Directory of Scientific Directories,* etc. While certain directories, such as *The Encyclopedia of Associations,* are featured in newspapers and magazines, and new directories are routinely reviewed in the library press, there is little about the general form in the literature. Here and there one finds only hints of what might be possible, e.g., David Linton, "Mitchell's, May's and Sell's Newspaper Directories of the Victorian Era," *Journal of Newspaper and Periodical History* (spring), 1987, 20–29.

49. Charles Bunge, "An 'Alms-Basket' of 'bric-a-brac' *in* Rettig, *Distinguished Classics of Reference Publishing,* 28. Another version of the classic is *Brewer's Politics: A Phrase and Fable Dictionary.* (London: Cassell, 1993). This is a cousin to the more famous Brewer and, as the title suggests centers in on politics, and particularly British politics.

50. Today, the primary frustration with manuals, whether they be for the operation of computers and VCRs or instructions on lawn mowers and the meaning of life, is their density of prose. See "All You Have to Do Is . . ." *National Review,* September 4, 1981, p. 1041, for a typical response to this situation.

51. Peter Wayne, *The Personal Art an Anthology of English Letters* (London: Longmans, Green, 1949), viii–ix.

52. Kenneth Randall, *History Comes to Life Collecting Historical Letters and Documents* (Norman: University of Oklahoma Press, 1995). This thorough survey of not only letters, but also many other handwritten documents covers from the Greek and Roman times to the present.

53. The epistolary novel—a novel consisting wholly or almost completely of letters—was a popular form begun in France in the mid-seventeenth century. The most prolific period for the genre was from about 1750 to the 1820s both in France and in England. In France among the more famous titles: *Rousseau's La Nouvelle Heloise* (1761) and *Les Liaisons Dangereuses* (1782). The genre declined and virtually disappeared in the nineteenth century. The epistolary novel has its roots in Greece in the fourth century B.C. when students wrote fictitious letters as a practice in rhetoric. Late Hellenistic and early Roman extant letters often reflect the style and the spirit of some famous orator or philosopher whom the student was copying. The real beginnings of the letter as a form of fiction is in the work

of Alciphron, whose letters of an Aelian farmer of around A.D. 200 are copied from classical literature, but are primarily fiction.

54. Rae Blanchard, *The Correspondence of Richard Steele* (Oxford: Oxford University Press, 1941), 201.

55. France, *New Oxford Companion to Literature in French,* 457.

56. Felix Pryor, *The Faber Book of Letters* (London: Faber and Faber, 1988), xii.

57. Hellanicus (c. 400 B.C.), the prolific Greek writer, attributes the personal letter form (as contrasted with the century old government-business letter) to Atossa, the Persian queen and mother of Xerxes (480–465 B.C.). An even cursory glance at some much earlier Egyptian letters will show that Atossa's invention of the personal letter is more myth than fact. See Miriam Lichtheim, *Ancient Egyptian Literature,* vol. 1, (Berkeley: University of California Press, 1973.

Greek letters traditionally are divided into six classes, which to this day are a useful categorization: private letters; official letters; literary letters; letters employed as a medium for the exposition of ideas; spurious letters, usually attributed to famous people; and imaginative or epistolary novel type of letters. See "Letters, Greek" in *The Oxford Classical Dictionary* 2d ed. Oxford: Clarendon Press, 1970, 598. See, too, the adjoining "Letters, Latin."

58. William G. Doty, *Letters in Primitive Christianity* (Philadelphia: Fortress Press, 1973), 11. Nevertheless, letters followed a distinctive form and "probably the most striking feature of someone who has read through Hellenistic letters in Greek and in Latin from about the fourth century B.C.E. to the fourth century C.E. is the fact they are so amazingly stereotyped and bound to tradition . . . phrases of concern for the other's health, greetings, and mention of . . . praying for him, appear again and again in phrases which change so slowly that the history of the letter can actually be charted by these minute and gradual modifications. . . The end result . . . is a mass produced print of stereotyped phrases, rigid external structure, of brevity and of a detached impersonality matched only by our own most formal [letters]" (pp. 12–13).

59. George Saintsbury, *A Letter Book* (London: G. Bell and Sons, 1922), 11.

60. *The Oxford Classical Dictionary,* 599.

61. Doty, *Letters in Primitive Christianity,* 65. See Alfred Barnett, *Paul Becomes a Literary Influence* (Chicago: University of Chicago Press, 1941). There is a vast literature on the *Pauline Letters* and related letters. See, for example, Michael Goulder's "The Pauline Epistles" in *The Literary Guide to the Bible* Robert Alter and Frank Kermode (Cambrdige: Harvard University Press, 1987), 479–502. See, too, related comments on letters in the same volume.

62. Harry Gamble, *Books and Readers in the Early Church* (New Haven, Conn.: Yale University Press, 1995), 36–37.

63. E.R. Curtius, *European Literature and the Latin Middle Ages* (New York: Pantheon Books, 1953), 149.

64. *Dictionary of the Middle Ages,* vol. 4, 173. "More than 300 separate treatises of the ars dictaminis have survived in manuscript form. All were written in Latin. The most famous authors were Italian . . . There were virtually no English authors . . . [The letter-writing manual] deserves further study, because it illuminates some fundamental medieval ideas about both the nature of language and the complexities of social relationships in a feudal society" (vol. 10, 358–59).

65. Ibid., vol. 4, 176.

66. Hale, *Civilization of Europe in the Renaissance,* 290.

67. Prior to the publication in English, there were several manuals in Latin as well as in Italian and Greek that were little more than compilations of such masters as Cicero and Aretino. By the sixteenth century French manuals became popular throughout Europe. The French were copied and translated until the early eighteenth century, and, although by then their influence had waned, certain writers (such as Jean-Louise de Balzac and Jean Puget de la Serre) strongly influenced English letter-writing manuals as late as the mid-nineteenth century.

68. Harry B. Weiss, *American Letter-Writers 1698–1943* (New York: The New York Public Library, 1945), 6.

69. Saintsbury, *A Letter Book,* 21. Samuel Richardson, Jonathan Swift, Lady Mary Wortley-Montagu, Earl of Chesterfield, Horace Walpole, and Tobias Smollett, are but a few of the outstanding letter-writers of the century.

70. Elizabeth Goldsmith, ed., *Writing the Female Voice Essays on Epistolary Literature* (Boston: Northeastern University Press, 1989), vii. As the notes accompanying each of the essays will indicate, the study of women and letter-writing has become particularly popular in the past twenty or thirty years. There are scores of books on the subject and related matters of women's studies.

71. James Carson, "Narrative Cross-Dressing and the Critique of Authorship in the Novels of Richardson," in *Writing the Female Voice* edited by Goldsmith, 98.

72. The subtitle of the guide is instructive of the typical reference work of the day, and certainly of letter-writing manuals. The anonymous author (called "John Hill, Gent." by the publisher) describes in great detail the content: "A speedy help to learning in two parts: I. containing the true method of writing letters upon any subject, whether concerning business or otherwise, fitted to all capacities, in the most smooth and obliging style, with about 200 examples never before published: as also instructions how properly to entitle, subscribe, or direct a letter to any person of what quality soever: together with full directions for true pointing, and many other notable things, II. containing an exact collection of acquaintances, bills, bonds,

wills, indentures, deeds of gift, letters of attorney, assignments, releases, warrants of attorney, bills of sale, counter securities, with notes of directions, relating to what is most difficult to be understood in the most legal sense, form, and manner: to which are added the names of men and women, cities, counties, sums of money, days, months, years of date, trade, &c. in Latin, as they ought to be placed in any Latin obligation: with an interest table." John Hill, *Young Secretary's Guide*

73. Samuel Richardson, *Familiar Letters on Important Occasions* (1741; reprint, New York: Dodd, Mead, 1928), xxvii. Earlier manuals were addressed almost entirely to men, but by the eighteenth century publishers became aware of the interest of women in letters. After all, Richardson's popular novels were based on letters to and from women. Standard manuals soon began to include women's letters, but Richardson was among the first.

74. Saintsbury, *A Letter Book,* 1.

75. Henri-Jean Martin, *The History and Power of Writing* (Chicago: University of Chicago Press, 1994), 301.

6

Dictionaries, Grammar, and Rhetoric

English speakers have adopted two great icons of culture: The Bible and the dictionary. As the Bible is the sacred Book, so the dictionary becomes the secular Book, the source of authority, the model of behavior, and the symbol of unity in language.[1]

A dictionary, sometimes combined with encyclopedic information, constitutes the oldest source of reference for laypersons and to this day is the cornerstone of the most meager home library. As basic tools of communication, dictionaries serve all literate people. The art of lexicography began with compilation of word lists in Sumerian and Akkadian cultures around 3000 B.C. As the skills were refined, lexicographers developed glossaries and then dictionaries. The early cuneiform inscribed clay tablets were "initially unilingual and copied in all areas where cuneiform script was used until the end of the third millennium B.C."[2] Mesopotamian lexicographical evidence is imposing "not only in size (it runs into tens of thousands of entries), but because of the diversity . . . with thematic lists of professions . . . and various human activities, lists of compound words, synonyms and antonyms, and a collection of simple signs and compound logograms of the cuneiform script."[3]

Language origins and history provide a subject for vast speculation. Here concern is limited to a few of Indo-European languages from the Greek (which originated c. 1600 B.C.) to Latin (from about 600 B.C.) to modern Romance and English languages. Even with these necessary limitations the area is large and much discussed by scholars and laypersons.[4]

Dictionary Development

The descriptor "dictionary" appeared first in 1225 in the title of a work by John Garland, an English scholar.[5] Pierre Bersuire employed a dictionary as a "phrase book" in a Bible commentary in 1340. The commentary contained a list of 3,000 words used in the Bible, hence "dictionarium." The term was used first in English in 1538 when Thomas Elyot used it in the title of his wordbook. As with most reference works, there is a borderline region of description and definition for dictionaries. "Is a geographical index setting out place-names with their Latin equivalents a dictionary or a gazetteer? The answer I think is both. . . I counted in a few weeks over a hundred distinct kinds of dictionary titles. . . All of this is merely another way of saying that dictionaries cannot be identified merely by reading lists of titles."[6] Among dictionaries with deceptive titles are cornucopia, catholicon, guide, and word finder.

The dictionary, as the encyclopedia, follows ancient precedent. Inclusion of proper names, historical tables, geographical data, mythological background, etc., probably goes back to the earliest concept of a dictionary. Encyclopedias also included one or more word lists. The first English dictionary-encyclopedia is from the aforementioned Elyot. His Latin-English dictionary of 1538 included numerous biographical sketches as well as historical and literary subjects. Revising Elyot's *Bibliotheca Eliotae* in 1559, Thomas Cooper moved the extra material to a section at the end of the dictionary. Thus began the struggle for arrangement. It continues to this day, with publishers either using an alphabetical approach or setting off the extra material in various subsections. Alphabetical order, a component of the modern dictionary was not common until the invention of printing in the mid-fifteenth century. Order tended to be in terms of themes, topics, classes, etc. This procedure is prevalent today in the modern traveler's small phrase book or pictorial wordbooks. Numerous theories explain why it took so many centuries for alphabetical order to become standard. Perhaps in dealing with well-defined topics, as found in concurrent encyclopedias of the time, scholars were too accustomed to the topical approach to consider alphabetization practical. Alphabetical order in many reference books did not become that usual or popular until well into the seventeenth century.[7]

There are several forms of dictionaries, and the lines are not always clear between the types. They usually are divided into general-purpose and special, limited-usage dictionaries. General-purpose dictionaries range in size from the "unabridged" (with some 472 thousand entries) to the more common "desk" or "college" editions (with some hundred and fifty thousand to a hundred and eighty thousand entries). While the smaller dictionary goes back to the eighteenth century, it was perfected and marketed first on a large scale in the United States.

Beyond the general dictionary is the special, technical, scholarly, or otherwise limited-usage type. Less grand and more limited in scope are hundreds of titles in English that include crossword puzzle aids and dictionaries of slang, engineering, religion, and clichés. The most frequently used are the bilingual dictionaries that are divided between English and another language. The earliest in English was published in 1547 as a guide for the Welsh to English.

The primary purposes of a dictionary, in any language, is to offer a working word list of the spoken and written language.[8] Depending on the purpose and scope of the work, technical, obsolete, or archaic words may be included or excluded. Once the list is determined, then the procedure is to turn to succinct definitions, usually in order of current rather than historical usage. The proper use of a word is normally indicated by such labels as "dialect" and "slang." Here dictionaries are divided. The majority report descriptively what is spoken and written without more than casual comment about proper usage. Prescriptive dictionaries clearly state the appropriate usage of the word. Spelling, pronunciation, and etymology follow, although the latter usually is only brief, if not completely missing in smaller dictionaries. Illustrative quotations, which may be no more than made-up sentences in minor dictionaries to show the word's use, or elaborate quotes drawn from literature and the current press are a necessary consideration.

Burgess points out another use of the dictionary, and one not unfamiliar to librarians. "William Pitt the Elder is said to have read through [Bailey's 1721 dictionary of about 40,000 words] twice, as if it were a novel. This is a legitimate way to approaching a dictionary, if it is not too bulky, it makes a suitable bed companion for insomniacs."[9]

In determining the arrangement, scope, and purpose of a dictionary, a lexicographer asks the question, "What is it that the ordinary educated public wants from a dictionary. . . . The answer . . . may be disheartening to lexicographers, for users are apparently not much concerned about the things to which lexicographers devote their attention." According to several studies, "Americans seldom consult (a dictionary) for anything except meanings and spellings."[10] Word origin, grammatical explanations, fine discrimination between near synonyms, and even pronunciation are of limited interest to the average layperson. The failure to find a word means for most people that the word is not acceptable, i.e., the entry of a word is perceived as a seal of approval.

Early Word Lists

The earliest extant Sumerian and Akkadian word lists (c. 3000 B.C.) appear to be sections of grammars employed in the *eduba* (schools). Often, too, the lists are bilingual indicating the degree of cultural and economic traffic between various parts of Mesopotamia. Aside from the exercises and grammars, word lists were used in government and religion. Usually they listed only the difficult words found in documents. Similar aids were used later by the Hittites, Babylonians, and other Middle Eastern civilizations that came and went over the centuries.[11]

Greek lexicography, from which the Western tradition arises, probably developed without benefit of reference to Mesopotamia or Egypt. The first extant Greek word lists are current from the time of Democritus

(b. about 460 B.C.). The Greeks "glossa" or "glossary" meant any list of words belonging to a dialect, literary or vernacular, of another region or period, i.e., unfamiliar and/or difficult words.[12] In whole or in part, numerous glossaries and word lists have survived. They show the importance "of such aids to reading in an age when the literary and spoken languages diverged considerably. Some of these are mere jejune lists; others are works of scholarship in which entries are supported by quotations."[13] The value of the word lists, particularly before printing, is threefold: "(a) their interpretations sometimes contain or provide evidence for Late Latin or Early Romance words; (b) they sometimes contain latent evidence for readings in the text of an author; (c) occasionally they transmit some fragment of ancient learning."[14]

The first comprehensive dictionary, based on the previous word lists, was the Aristophanes of Byzantium (258–180 B.C.). As the leader of scholars at the Alexandria Library and a well-known philologist, Aristophanes's work is all but lost. Fragments indicate that what was probably called *Lexeis* consisted of different sections of lists, definitions, and explanations as to usage, drawn from all fields of literature—prose and poetry. A second Alexandrian grammarian, Pamphilus (c. A.D. 55) produced what today one might term an unabridged dictionary. It also seems to have been made up of numerous previous word collections. Only a bit of the summary of the original ninety-five books exists, although a twice-removed version made in the fifth or sixth century by Hesychius of Alexandria is extant.[15]

The beginning of the Latin dictionary is found in the fifth century B.C. when Verrius Flaccus, a freed slave and the most erudite of the Augustan scholars, compiled his *Libri de Significatu Verborum.* Here he quoted freely from earlier authors and arranged the work in alphabetical order.[16] Dedicated to Cicero, Varro's *De Lingua Latinia* (c. 43 B.C.) is one of the first Latin grammars with etymology. Collison claims "he [Varro] is the first classical scholar to have dealt with language in a comprehensive fashion" and goes on to assert that much of this work, although only fragments exist, would have constituted the first Latin dictionary.[17]

The decline of scholarship, which followed the fall of Greece, was assuaged somewhat by the interest of Rome in preserving the best of classical Greek. A desire to write in the classical Greek style created a need for dictionaries that was met by scholars from the time of Hadrian (A.D. 117–138) to Commodus (A.D. 180–192). The dictionaries, of which only fragments remain, reminded Romans of the Athenian writers. It became customary among the cultured to use quotations and Attic Greek in correspondence and writings much as was done by English speakers with French from the eighteenth through the early twentieth century. Commonplace books primarily filled this need, but now and then a definition or translation was needed that might be found only in the bilingual dictionary.

Medieval Dictionaries

The first step in the development of the Medieval dictionary was defining difficult words and/or giving synonyms that made the word(s) or phrases in a single manuscript understandable to the average reader.[18] The written-in explanations could be in Latin (usually the original language of the manuscript) or in the vernacular, or both. Given several manuscripts with such lists, one might arrange them in alphabetical order in a separate work. The combined word lists would then help in the study of other texts. An outstanding example of this is found in the eighth century *Corpus Glossary*. The work consists of difficult Latin words followed by easier Latin synonyms or Anglo-Saxon equivalents.[19] Monastery teachers were the first to compile glossaries in the early Medieval communities.[20] The process was simply to copy, usually in alphabetical order, marginal and interlinear notes found in the monastery's own collection of manuscripts. Usually these were from Roman, but rarely Greek, literature and the Bible and commentaries. The local glossary might be widely copied and was added to by other monastic communities and again copied. The larger derivative compilations were drawn upon for both encyclopedic and later dictionary publications.

As all of the glossaries and lexicons had to be copied by hand, there was much space for error when duplicate copies were ordered. In a letter to a scribe, a compiler of the ninth century wrote, "I charge you particularly to give the greatest care to correcting your copies, so that they merit being called perfect."[21] At best, the average scribe was less than an excellent copyist. As one critic put it, "Anyone who has learnt to paint a parchment and to hold a pen in his hand is deemed fit to be a scribe, but be totally ignorant, incapable of mental effort, and lacking in technical know-how."[22] Depending on the skills of the scribes, it might take a week or a month or more to copy such a work. Delays were frequent, often due to other work of the monks. Glossaries were seen as useful, but not as priority items.

Word lists produced at Charlemagne's court were much the same as in the late Roman period. "The number . . . is very large and they differ greatly in size, age, and value; for it would be a grave error to suppose that all these word lists, compiled between the sixth or seventh and the tenth centuries were, so to speak, original works."[23]

Oversimplified, but close to truth, is the assumption that Latin and Romance languages coexisted as spoken languages from about the second century B.C., but had become mutually unintelligible by the ninth. At any rate, bilingual lists seems to have been common by the ninth century.[24] Latin was the universal language of educated individuals during the Middle Ages and until the general printing of books in the vernacular in the late fifteenth and sixteenth centuries. It was the language of the literate, primarily because they were taught Latin and it was used in theological works, including the Bible, grammars (such as the ubiquitous Donatus), encyclopedias, dictionaries, and other reference works. Latin was a practical way of overcoming the difficulty of mastering the scores of European dialects and languages. One might, for example, speak German or Old English or French and, if educated, read Latin. It was the first language of government and scholarship, and the second of the small educated group who made up society. At the same time there sprang up lexicons, such as the Latin-English glossary compiled by Ælfric of Enysham (c. 955–1010) about the end of the tenth century, which indicates students with little or no Latin background had to master Latin as a second language. His dictionary or grammar or vocabularium, as he called it, was in eighteen parts, not alphabetically by words but instead by such subjects as God and diseases, beasts and trees, and metals and "general terms."

Other than among scholars, Latin was unusual. "In England and Germany at any rate, daily speech bore no resemblance to Latin. It is difficult to see how under the circumstances the use of the vernacular in the early stages (of education) could ever have been avoided."[25] The trainee scribe in a monastic community was expected to gain a proficiency in a dead language, i.e. Latin. Without the intervention of a native speaker, Latin was taught (as Sumerian) by universal rules that were fine enough for translations, but lacked any sense of a living language.

Often forgotten in the history of dictionaries is the puzzle of pronunciation. No one knows precisely how Classical, let alone pre-Classical Greek was pronounced, nor does anyone know precisely how Medieval Latin was pronounced. Therefore, beyond that are the cultural implications of words, much of which is lost. "Can any dictionary ever give us a clear sense of a dead word in a dead language as the full experiential sense men possess of their own living words? Of course not. . . Even a vast computerized dictionary . . . (cannot) recreate consciousness . . . as far as the edges of imagination, fantasy, emotion . . . It takes some amount of linguistic skill, imagination, and a critical sense to use a dictionary as well."[26]

Dictionaries and Encyclopedias

The combination of encyclopedic type information with the dictionary became popular for numerous reasons, although a major one was the scarcity of books. It seemed wiser and easier—particularly when books had to be copied by hand—to put as much information between one set of covers as possible. The first encyclopedia compilers included word lists and glossaries. As the focus shifted to the dictionary, the compilers included encyclopedic data. There are close to a hundred Medieval hand-produced books extant that boast such a combination. One thing these books generally had in common was the dictionary compilers tendency to plagiarize encyclopedic information from earlier works.

An early example of the dictionary-encyclopedia can be found in Papias of Lombard's *Elementarium Erudimentum Doctrine*, (c. 1053). The *Elementarium* was partly a dictionary containing alphabetically arranged definitions, and etymologies for many words. It also was an encyclopedia, in that many entries . . . went beyond a simple definition of the term. "Moreover, it contains many geographical, geological, medical, botanical, historical, theological, and even mythological names of terms, for which encyclopedic information is provided. In addition (it) is partly a grammar."[27]

Another aspect of the combining of various types of reference works was the practice of bringing together into one book several dictionaries as well as miscellaneous information in order to offer a practical guide for students, teachers, and travelers. An example is the lexicon compiled by Photius (c. 810–891), who twice held the patriarchal throne at Constantinople and was an adviser to the emperor. His lexicon was composed of definitions and brief quotations of classical texts, many of which are no longer extant and known only through Photius's lexicon. Photius traveled widely and, before taking one journey, compiled a list of books with critical summaries, which he considered of value to his brother.[28]

The first major dictionary of the Middle Ages was the *Suda* in the tenth century. The compiler is not known, although for a long time *Suda* was thought to be his name rather than the title of the reference work. The *Suda* included much encyclopedic information, such as biographical and Biblical data, as well as about thirty thousand headings, words and phrases. The alphabetically arranged words were drawn from a hodge-podge of collections. Today its value is primarily as a source of otherwise lost ancient and Byzantine works.[29]

The *Suda* is a landmark because up to that time most lexical efforts were simply compilations of different glosses and the *Suda* integrated the glosses into one alphabetical order. At the same time, "for each term a synonym or a translation was provided, in much the same form that the vocabularies appended to language textbooks appear today."[30] Also, the compiler provided examples of usage and meaning drawn primarily from literature. Thus the transition from glossary to dictionary was made.

Glossaries

The glossators gained attention primarily in the field of law. From the sixty to the twelfth century, most Western law was based on the Roman model and was incorporated into the seven liberal arts—or, more particularly, rhetoric and dialectic. In time, though, even the *Justinian Code* (533–553) became corrupted and confused, as much from failure to copy it correctly as from interpretation. With the twelfth century the decline of canon law had reached such a point that the glossators increased in number and gradually established a common base of interpretation that became the law of European countries. By the mid-thirteenth century the *Glossa Ordinaria* was published and became the basic text for all teaching law. Paradoxically, it became more important, more official than the then legal texts it was supposed to explain and illuminate. Out of this developed a whole group of postglossators or commentators who explain Roman law from about 1250 until the early sixteenth century.

The glossaries (variously called postils, commentaries, interlinear notes, etc.) became separate, distinct books when early fifteenth century printers sought out marketable reference works. Eventually various new forms appeared. Manuscript interlinear notes and glosses in the Bible might take up more space than the Bible text itself. Printers turned these notes into several different titles—glossaries, books of homilies, i.e., inspirational addresses for ministers. A 1566 reference work of this type published in London was called *A New Postil Conteinyng Most Godly and Learned Sermons Upon All the Sunday Gospelles*. The form, at least as a formal published work, gradually disappeared in the seventeenth and eighteenth century.

Today, though, much the same reference work appears as a "commentary." Here there are detailed notes or glosses on the text of a well-known, usually much-assigned, classroom work. For example, G.S. Kirk, ed. *The Iliad: A Commentary*. Cambridge: Cambridge University Press 1985. This particular title covers Homer through books 1–4. Other commentaries take the reader through the whole of the *Odyssey*. Here, as in similar reference works, the analysis is line by line of the text, and the whole is in the best tradition of the medieval glossaries and interlineary notes.

Dictionary Combinations

The *Catholicon* of Giovanni Balbi of Genoa, published c. 1286, was a combination grammar, encyclopedia, and dictionary that drew many of the words from Papias and Huguccio's labors of some hundred years before.[31] The *Catholicon* (with the brief dictionary following the grammar) became a standard reference work in the churches of France as well as in numerous monasteries and universities. (In 1460 it was printed, probably by Gutenberg.)

By about the late tenth and early eleventh century compilers sought a wider audience. This explains the sudden addition of prefaces in which the purpose, scope etc. of the dictionary is outlined. They were no less derivative in content than their informal predecessors, but they presented themselves quite differently. A typical book for wide distribution, the bilingual school text, acted as a dictionary with from as few as two hundred words to as many as three thousand. Texts had one or more elements in common: (a) an alphabetical dictionary, usually of verbs; (b) a dictionary by topics; (c) scenes from everyday life in which the words are illustrated "and finally, (d) one many have some texts for reading practice, such as some Aesop fables, extracts from a mythological handbook. . . ."[32]

Latin to the Vernaculary Dictionary

Words lists and glossaries aside, the first true English dictionary was not published until the early seventeenth century. This late development was as true for most of Europe as it was for England. Until the wider spread of literacy, the growth of nationalism, and the use of the vernacular in print, the majority of people who could read and write turned to Latin with its well-established word lists and dictionaries. The use of Latin, its gradual decline, and the development of the vernacular dictionary can be illustrated briefly in the English experience. With the mass exit of the Romans from Britain in 410, the Germanic Anglo-Saxons crossed to Britain. During the first two hundred years of their occupation there is little contemporary linguistic evidence, except they virtually eliminated the earlier Celtic languages. The Germanic tongue gradually evolved into what is now known as Old English. By around 700, Bede and Alcuin, as well as other scholars, made Northumbria a major cultural center,[33] where texts consistently began to be written in Old English rather than Latin exclusively.

After Alfred, who ruled from 871 to 899, until the Norman Conquest in 1066, the most noteworthy contributor to the development of an English dictionary was Ælfric (c. 955–1010). A prolific writer, he is best known for his *Lives of the Saints*. He also wrote a grammar for his students studying Latin and translated it into Old English. Although students and scholars drew on Latin grammars, it was Ælfric who compiled the first bilingual work expressly for readers and writers in the vernacular and Latin, which included a word list, one of the earliest of its kind in English. The words were arranged in about a dozen broad categories like God and angels, trades, animals, and parts of the city. "Ælfric's schema is representative of his time. The Schoolmen were well disposed to the idea of classifying . . . in a thematic net. Ælfric's is the tradition of the vocabularium, the (usually bilingual) word list by means of which the young cleric could acquire Latin, his passport to religious and cultural elevation."[34] The English-Latin dictionary had about twelve thousand English entries with Latin equivalents. This type of dictionary persisted throughout the sixteenth and seventeenth centuries. The first English difficult-word dictionaries derived their word lists primarily from Latin-English, rather than English-Latin dictionaries. This resulted in the wholesale anglicization of Latin words and phrases.[35]

The emergence of nationalism and printing (c. 1455) as well as urban centers accounts in no small way for the quickened interest in national languages. A larger English-speaking reading public, made possible by the advent of printing and the expansion of commerce, guaranteed an interest in early English word lists. These bilingual lists primarily were concerned with difficult words, that is to say words borrowed from Latin, French, and other languages that might appear in a student's book.

True, Latin remained the scholar's key to success until well into the eighteenth century, but printing made possible literature in the vernacular for the average, literate person. Also, as business began more and more to cross frontiers of languages, the necessity for knowing several languages became apparent. Coupled with the need for accurate translations from the Latin, Greek, and, for that matter, from one European tongue into another, the stage was set for vernacular dictionaries.

In 1480, William Caxton (c. 1422–1491) was the first to print a French-English word list in parallel columns of twenty-six leaves. By 1496, Richard Pyson had published the first Latin-English list compiled by John Standbridge.

Other lists were used primarily to teach grammar to children. As early as 1499, Pyson published the *Storehouse for Children*. Some fifty years later, in 1556, there appeared *A Short Dictionarie for Young Beginners*. It gained a wide circulation not only for use with children, but for adults mastering the language.

John Palsgrave's (d. 1534) *Lesclaircissement de la Langue Francoyse* (1530) was the first English-French dictionary to help English language students understand written French. A combination of dictionary and grammar, it was a typical sixteenth century bilingual publication and one of the first grammars of the French language, primarily made up of tables of nouns, verbs, etc. with French equivalents. Palsgrave took seven years to compile his work, and there were some peculiarities. Numerous English words are without the French equivalent. "Perhaps he started from an already established word-list, an English Latin list for example, and tried to find French equivalents."[36] Where he did not (find the equivalents), he simply left the French out. The word order, too, was typical for the period. Palsgrave lists words alphabetically, but in various sections he lists by parts of speech, e.g., nouns and adjectives. The user was expected to know the parts of speech in order to find specific words.

Elizabethans, intent on what one critic called a "more refined and elegant speech," sought new words. Also new words were needed to make adequate translations, particularly from the Latin, and to find labels in the vernacular for technological developments. The problem for the modern lexicographer is simply put: When exactly does the Latin (or French or German) word become English? The *Oxford English Dictionary* offers dates for most, if not all, of the so-called loan words, which became part of the English language.[37]

Combining an effort to lower the price of books and at the same time print familiar works that had an assured market, it is not surprising that among the early text books Donatus was favored.[38] Close behind in popularity was the aforementioned *Catholicon.* Several dictionary-encyclopedias, such as Varro's *De Lingua Latina,* then about fifteen hundred years old, were printed and kept in print for centuries. The rash of printed, late fifteenth century dictionaries reached a monumental climax with Robert Estienne's *Thesaurus Linguae Latine* of 1531. The father of Henri Estienne II who gained fame for his Greek dictionary, Robert (1503–1559) had become head of the firm in 1526, and the Latin dictionary guaranteed his success. By 1539, Francis I made him King's printer, and in 1541 he was commissioned to supply the King's library with books printed in Greek type by the equally famous Claude Garamond.

Sometimes major claims are made as to the influence of dictionaries (and related works, such as encyclopedias) on Renaissance literature and art. Arguments vary, but the stress is on the intermediate role of reference works. Their classical references strongly influenced the writer and painter and Renaissance creativity. Often the encyclopedia would serve as both an interpreter and a source of, say, mythology to be used by the creative Renaissance individual. Dictionaries, particularly in the vernacular, and often with encyclopedic information included, served an equal purpose. As preservers of the classics in a digest form, the reference works were handy tools for creative writers and artists.

Guillaume Budé (1467–1540) standing between Petrarch and the scholars of the late sixteenth century, sought tirelessly for information about Greek and Latin. He published numerous books, but his *Commentarii Linguae Graecae* (*Commentaries on the Greek Language*) (1529) was among the first special or subject dictionaries. It included a compilation of Greek legal terms. The work itself was "a hotch-potch of notes interspersed with short essays, some of which run to over a thousand words. The stylists and wits condemned it, and the treasures of shrewd observations that lighten its pages have not been sufficient to save it from oblivion."[39] Also, Budé is famous among librarians as the first librarian for what was to become the Bibliotheque Nationale.

Lexicographical activity, if only slightly, turned from Latin and Greek to the production of vernacular dictionaries in the sixteenth century. Lay readers, government officials, and merchants were the natural purchasers of the printed works. By 1571, the earliest list of German words was published, and in 1573 Dutch was given a major part in the French-Latin-Dutch dictionary of Christophe Plantin (1514–1589). Three years later the famous Dutch printer and publisher issued the first Flemish dictionary. A comprehensive dictionary of Italian came out in 1575, and in 1584 a French-Italian dictionary was published. By the end of the sixteenth century lexicography was firmly established and the grip Latin held over Europe was relaxed "to the extent that Erasmus himself felt it necessary to provide a guide to its correct use and pronunciation, while the French courts of justice no longer considered its use essential."[40]

By the fifteenth century Greek virtually had disappeared, but the Renaissance focused on the need for Greek and with this came a series of dictionaries. There were close to fifty Greek-Latin works printed in the fifteenth and sixteenth centuries, and while most of them are of little or no interest today, there are some exceptions. The first major one was the *Thesaurus Graecae Linguae,* edited and published by Henri Estienne in 1572. "With little help . . . he succeeded in published a huge dictionary replete with citations from the authors, with the senses within the entry well ordered and documented by suitable contexts . . . and covering nearly all the classical Greek authors known at the time." Dedicated to heads of state, including Queen Elizabeth I of England, as well as to leading universities by implication, the dictionary proved a financial disaster. Estienne spent the last twenty years of his life seeking funds throughout Europe. On one of his travels he died in a public hospital in Lyons (1598), befriended by no one.[41] The massive five-volume work was plagiarized in 1579. The stolen edition enjoyed great success because it was shorter than the original, less costly, and for the first time in a large dictionary, primarily, in alphabetical order. "This case probably is the first in history where the public's preference for the alphabetical sequence of entries was strongly manifested."[42] Published by Joseph Scapula, the dictionary was republished, with modifications, well into the nineteenth century.

Europeans delighted in compiling dictionaries of hitherto unknown languages, which they came across in their exploration and travels. Many were used to translate the Bible into the language of the "natives" of Persia, the Americas, and elsewhere particularly in the later seventeenth and early eighteenth centuries. Roger Williams (c. 1600–1683) was the first among Americans to consider the native Indian languages of some importance. His book, *A Key into the Language of America,* published in London in 1643, was the earliest of what would be scores of such works in the centuries to come.

First English Dictionaries

The development of the English dictionary follows three primary formats. The first dictionary, of 1604, had some 2,560 entries and established the compact dictionary as the norm from then until today's inexpensive paperback. The second type was encyclopedic, which became folio size in the late seventeenth century, although even then it had no more than about seventeen thousand words, padded out with other information. The third type was the scholarly dictionary—the initial work of Samuel Johnson in 1755. His was the grandparent of the *Oxford English Dictionary* and today's unabridged works.

Reading, writing, and, for that matter, speaking Latin was so common in England and Europe that literate individuals saw little need for an English dictionary with definitions in English. Writers in English introduced new words based on Latin or from any language they happened to know. If spoken English did not have the necessary word, they simply imported it from France or from the Latin. The problem, for not only students but readers of English, became apparent. How was one to understand a word in Latin, French, German, or whatever language introduced by the writer into a text as English. It was one thing to understand the spoken language, and quite another to grasp the sometimes willful introduction of new words in writing.

The dilemma of the ordinary, baffled reader was resolved in part by Robert Cawdrey, who in 1604 published what has come to be considered as the first English dictionary.[43] His *A Table Alphabetical* offered succinct, often amusing, often wrong definitions of "hard words" from the Latin, French, Greek, Hebrew, etc. likely to be found in books published in English. A reader, who was a contemporary of Shakespeare, would find only 2,560 entries. Comparatively, the average English-Latin dictionary of the period had eight times as many, or twenty thousand items. If a step backward in coverage, the dictionary was a great step forward in that it was the first to explain the meaning of English words in English.

Today's typical college or desk dictionary has about a hundred and fifty thousand to a hundred and seventy-five thousand words. If the first 1604 dictionary listed under three thousand words, and even two hundred years later the number was well under a hundred thousand, this does not mean more words were known to early English writers and speakers. Cawdrey published his work some twelve years before the death of Shakespeare, who by then had used some thirty thousand different English words in his plays. It simply never struck the early compilers that they should attempt to record all words—a notion which held until the late nineteenth century and the dawn of the *Oxford English Dictionary.*[44]

In his instructions to the users of the text, which he hoped would be teachers and pupils throughout England, Cawdrey stressed the need to know the alphabet or "the order of the Letters as they stand, perfectly without booke." He was fond of using "k" to indicate "a kind of." For example, Bay "k" tree; Beagle, "k" hound; or Citron, "k" fruite. This was a handy way of disposing of a definition. The dictionary was limited primarily to definitions, and there was no indication of pronunciation and little assistance with spelling. Etymologies were somewhat limited. "G" or "gr" stood for Greek and another symbol indicated the derivation was from the French. Definitions were succinct such as "Magitian (g) one using witchcraft";

"Abash, blush" or "Abbridge, short"; "Hempisphere, halfe the compasse of heaven, that we see; Bashfull, blush, or shamefast." Cawdrey's definitions were little more than synonyms. For example, in Cawdrey "Prompt" was followed by synonyms "read, quicke"; and "Magnitude" was followed by simply "greatness." Many of these were taken from Latin-English dictionaries. Creative plagiarism is the key to the earliest English dictionaries. Perhaps inadequate and even careless, the dictionary caught on with users and went through four editions by 1617.

From 1604, with the first purely English dictionary, to Johnson's 1755 landmark, there were dozens of major dictionaries published. And there are many more lesser works, as well.[45] In 1616, John Bullokar, an English doctor, published the second English dictionary, *An English Expositor.* In it there were more words than in Cawdrey's first dictionary and the definitions were a bit more precise. Still, it was a crude effort. In his note to "the courteous reader," Bullokar explains "that in my younger years it hath cost me some observation, reading, study, and charge," of Latin, Greek and other languages to master "the signification of . . . words."[46] The work gained popularity and was printed eleven times by 1731.

Henry Cockeram's *English Dictionaire* (1623) claimed several distinctions. His was one of the first efforts to distinguish acceptable from unacceptable words.[47] He managed this by dividing his work in three parts. "The choicest words . . . now in use" came first, followed by a shorter section of "vulgar words . . . I have also inserted (as occasion served) even the mockewords which are ridiculously used in our language." Definitions, as the custom, were brief and often humorous, e.g., "Phylologie. Love of much babbling." The third book was a mishmash of miscellaneous topics, "a recital of several persons, Gods and Goddesses, Giants and Devils, Monsters and Serpents. . ." Primarily there were lists of names, notes on birds and herbs, and miscellaneous lore. This was the earliest encyclopedic feature in an English dictionary. The work went through twelve editions, the last coming out in 1670.

The encyclopedic additions to Cockeram's dictionary were in accord with the times. The audience for such reference works fully expected more than words and definitions. "Almost every dictionary compiler in England . . . expressly aimed to make his text useful to students of literature, especially poetry. . . (Such) aims are expressed on title pages or in prefaces."[48] To this end the compilers included Latin and English phrases, and encyclopedic data such as fables, proverbs, etc. often as not from Erasmus's *Adagia.* Representative native proverbs frequently were included. There were masses of fascinating misinformation, e.g., a hippopotamus may be made tame by "drynkyng the juyce of barley."

Despite faults of fancy, the bilingual dictionaries drew upon the great classical writers for illustrations of meaning and usage. In so doing, the authors became better known to students. A good example of a dictionary compiled for the use of the more sophisticated reader is found in Thomas Blount's *Glossographia* (1656): "or a dictionary interpreting all such hard words . . . as are now used in our refined English tongue." A barrister of the Inner Temple, Blount (1618–1679) compiled several other works, but none so famous as his glossary. He drew words primarily from his own reading, and, because the words had given him trouble, he would proudly show sources where he found their meaning. Despite competition from earlier works, the *Glossographia* went through five editions, and for each, including the last in 1681, Blount added words. "What Blount writes about strange words found in his reading and others heard among London trades-man reveals a sensitive ear and an awareness of words."[49] While Blount "borrowed" an amazing number of words from previous English and bilingual dictionaries, he had almost as many original definitions: "Tomboy, (a girle or wench that leaps up and down like a boy) comes from the Saxon tumbe, to dance. . . ." "Hony-Moon, applied to those married persons that love well at first and decline in affection afterwards—it is hony now, but it will change as the moon." The examples illustrate Blount's interest in etymology. He was the first English lexicographer to attempt any serious effort to trace the history of words and cite the authorities upon which he based his conclusions.

Edward Phillips, a nephew of Milton, plagiarized much of Blount in his widely popular *The New World of English Words* (1658). The work included among its eleven thousand or so entries what Phillips "borrowed" from a 1554 Latin-English dictionary. In the important English dictionaries published before 1700 there was a gradual shift from the "hard words" to terms in technical, professional related fields. A perfect example was Phillips's dictionary, in which he included chemistry terms from Robert Boyle and fishing expressions from Isaak Walton. No matter where Phillips got his material, the new dictionary proved popular and went to a fourth edition in 1678 with an addition of somewhat more than two thousand words.

Phillips's work dominated the English dictionary scene until the appearance of John Kersey at the turn of the eighteenth century. One of the first professional lexicographers, Kersey brought out his *A New English Dictionary* in 1702 with twenty-eight thousand words. While little is known about the compiler, the dictionary itself occupied much the same position in England as Webster in America does today. Kersey was the place the average person turned for not only accurate definitions, but spelling. This latter feature was borrowed from earlier spelling books and used to ensure the work's great success. Essentially, though, "the importance of this work . . . lies in its introduction into the English dictionary of the bulk of the English language—that is, of the essential words of daily speech, writing and reading."[50] In his *The Art of Reading and Writing English* (1720), Isaac Watt expressed a common opinion, "The best dictionary that I know . . . is entitled *A New English Dictionary.*"[51]

Helping the reader out with words and grammatical aids was well and good, but it wasn't until the early eighteenth century that it struck anyone that there might be a need for a simple direct approach that would list all of the then-known English words. The recognition of such a need was the genius of Nathaniel Bailey and his *Universal Etymological Dictionary* (1721).[52] Bailey's combined interest in etymology and definition made his work a great success. It went through twenty-four editions by 1782. Dr. Samuel Johnson used the 1731 edition as an aid for his compilation of his great dictionary. Bailey, who had read widely and was anxious to make it apparent, fondly included Latin, Greek, and Hebrew proverbs and bits of wisdom to counterpoint the English phrase that might illustrate how a word was employed. For example, he used "An old dog will learn no tricks," immediately followed in Latin by "The old parrot pays no attention to the strokes of correction." A Greek proverb, also in Greek, followed.

While there were several halfhearted efforts before the eighteenth century to consider etymology, it was not until Bailey's dictionary that a systematic approach was evident. The principles of tracing, say, the word "clergy" from the Greek, Latin, and French to the English, are explained in the preface. From Bailey to the present "the more serious English dictionaries commonly included etymologies (in their titles too, in many cases) and the quick reference books did not."[53] The major step on the road to scientific English language lexicography was taken in the eighteenth century. Intense scholarly activity coupled with the need to publish accurate bilingual works for the growing merchant class fueled the interest. Correct pronunciation was vital as was a proper understanding of foreign words.

From Cawdrey to Bailey little thought was given for the need for pronunciation. True, such information could be found in grammars and spelling books, but not in dictionaries until Bailey included a bit of help in his work. He simply showed an accent on the syllable that received the main stress. Details were lacking. On the title page of his *Dictionarium Britannicum* (1730), Bailey boasts that he offers "both the orthography and orthoepia of the English tongue."

It wasn't until Thomas Sheridan's *A General Dictionary of the English Language* in 1780 that pronunciation was indicated, much as it is today, by the use of both stress and sound, often through respelling the entry word. The most successful and most often reprinted pronunciation dictionary was John Walker's *Critical Pronouncing Dictionary* of 1791. He had a key to his system on every page and put most of focus on pronunciation. Walker gave definite advice on approved and disapproved pronunciation, such as it was better to say "interesting" rather than "intristing." Walker's pronunciation system was widely copied, and well known into the twentieth century. There was warfare between Sheridan's and Walker's two dictionaries until Walker won on a technicality. Because Sheridan was Irish many readers believed he could not speak authoritatively for pronunciation of English. This cut into Sheridan's sales, Walker forged ahead as the guide throughout the British Isles, and in much of early America. Walker's pronunciation guide became as famous and as popular as Johnson's dictionary; as late as 1904 a revised edition of his work appeared.[54]

Dependence on grammar books rather than dictionaries for grammatical information was the norm until the 1735 when Tomas Dyche published his *A New General English Dictionary* with a smattering of grammatical hints. Individual words, as in all dictionaries today, were labeled as a part of speech, i.e., nouns, verbs, adjectives, and particles, but the usual eight parts were reduced to four. Dyche simply would indicate a verb with a (V) or a noun (or substantive) with an (S). In the tradition of previous compilers, Dyche was a schoolteacher who had published several highly successful grammars where he stressed popular pronunciation. This became known among teachers as the "Dyche system."

Proper Usage

It would take at least another hundred years before there was a market for a dictionary that would give the uninitiated the necessary hints about "correct" English. Reading Dryden, Pope, and Addison would serve as examples; but a direct reference work was needed. People wished to acquire a mastery of English equivalent to the respected authors, comparable to speech found in high society. Out of this need would grow many grammars, spellers, and miscellaneous works, but the real solution came with the dictionary, which encouraged proper English as well as discouraged what was considered unacceptable usage of words.

Lexicographers today generally argue that their primary role is to record, not to dictate the language. There is hardly consensus, particularly in many European countries where, as early as 1634, the French established the Academie Française with duties to "fix" the French language, among other things. Efforts to bar unacceptable words and phrases continues right up until the early 1990s. For example, on March 14, 1994 the French Culture Ministry drafted a law that certain English words could not be employed. The proposed law had to be passed by the National Assembly, and it would determine what could be used in radio and television broadcasting, advertising, etc. Among English words to be banned and replaced with French expressions were air bag, best-seller, brunch, talk show and data bank. A new Paris tabloid sniffed that all proposals designed to legislate on the use of language give off a stale smell. The stale smell reaches back to the seventeenth century and the French Academy. Other European countries organized academies as well, but in England the effort to regulate by law failed. Later, Americans would put their trust in dictionaries to indicate proper speech.[55]

Average people, and certainly creative writers, have had little patience with those who dictate what words to use or ignore. "Writers like Chaucer, Shakespeare and Milton had no access to . . . dictionaries. Spelling did not much worry them . . . Milton spelled in his own creative manner . . . As for meaning, an empirical consensus prevailed . . . If Shakespeare required a word and had not met it in civilized discourse, he unhesitatingly made it up."[56]

In England, the desire to codify and prescribe was expressed by Lord Chesterfield in 1754, the year before Johnson's dictionary was published. "The dictionary would in Chesterfield's view not only settle spelling and meanings, but would also serve to help the linguistically insecure in their choice of words."[57] To a certain extent Johnson did indicate proper usage, as dictionaries do to this day, but came nowhere close to the rules established by various European academies. Generally, the practice from the eighteenth century to the present in English and American dictionaries has moved from the authoritarian to the authoritative. One group believed the prescriptive role of a dictionary should dominate. Another school believed it more important to describe the language as it was used (with gracious notes as to general acceptance or rejection of some words and usage). The controversy reached a climax with the 1962 publication of *Webster's Third New International Dictionary* (1961). The editors decided to turn from prescriptive to descriptive entries—a custom soon to be followed by the majority of desk and college works. Today's dictionaries are authoritative in that, depending upon the publisher, they indicate a word is or is not "proper" English. They usually note exceptions about the same word or phrase. Few simply state the word is unacceptable.[58]

Thanks in part to Noah Webster's insistence on lexicographical authority in his dictionary, many Americans, even to this day, believe the dictionary is a source of language standards. Students, at least until the advent of the prescriptive track taken by the 1961 *Webster's Third New International Dictionary,* were lead to believe the dictionary was a lawgiver. Today the need for guidance remains, but few dictionaries claim such a role. An exception is the *American Heritage Dictionary of the English Language,* which gives usage advice via its own Usage Panel of experts. Many feel this is more an advertising gimmick than anything near the prescriptive policy of earlier dictionaries.[59]

Today's dictionary indicates what some or the majority of people use in written and spoken English. One may agree or disagree about it being aesthetically pleasing or proper. The individual writer or speaker is permitted small eccentricities, "but in the main, we must cling to what the dictionaries say. They speak not with the authority of their editors, but with that of the language community. My idiolect, or personal manner of using English, must finally bend to the consensus of the tribe."[60] Returning, however, to the eighteenth century, it was Dr. Samuel Johnson who established rules for good and bad usage of words in English. After publication in 1755 his dictionary became the authoritative place to turn, both for laypersons and for law courts.

Johnson's Dictionary

It had taken forty French academicians some fifty-five years to produce a dictionary for the Academy.[61] Dr. Samuel Johnson believed he could do the same for English by himself and in three years.[62] Underwritten by a syndicate of booksellers, the dictionary was to take eight years.[63] Although he did much of the work, Johnson had a small staff who soon ate up the advance.[64] Johnson labored on, and in 1750, the publisher began issuing the massive two-volume work in parts. It was completed in 1755.

The completed dictionary defined some forty thousand words and employed more than a hundred and fourteen thousand quotations drawn from Johnson's wide reading back to the Elizabethan period.[65] Johnson was the first effective English lexicographer. He was specific and detailed. He drew examples from only about a hundred years (1560–1660) and explained why certain types of words were excluded, including highly technical terms. He made no excuse for leaving out slang, as well as, for the most part, dialect.[66] Above all, he excluded proper names, a practice not followed by Webster and other American lexicographers.

Johnson established the first precision definitions as he did the arrangement of the definitions chronologically (still followed by Merriam-Webster) to indicate the semantic development of the word. His prejudices are by now clichés, e.g., he defined "Oats—A grain, which in England is generally given to horses, but in Scotland supports the people."[67] He made some errors, such as giving "leeward" and "windward" the same meaning. He offered no excuses and explained to a lady that the problem was, "Ignorance, madam, pure ignorance."

Johnson's dictionary "set a new standard for subsequent dictionary-makers in most departments of their trade, and in many ways it also elevated English lexicography to the status of an art."[68] But there were drawbacks for publishers. Given the best, few people wanted to purchase another dictionary. Johnson's work held a virtual monopoly until Noah Webster's major *American Dictionary of the English Language* in 1828.[69] Johnson's greatest assets to publishers was his name. A good century after his death Dent published (1891) a dictionary with his name in the title.

After Johnson

Despite Johnson's gigantic step forward, numerous individuals and publishers did contribute to the refinement of dictionaries in the eighteenth and nineteenth centuries. Among the English were William Kenrick's work of 1773 that established rules for syllabification and pronunciation that could be understood by layreaders. John Ash's *New and Complete Dictionary of The*

English Language (1775) established the use of brief, yet accurate etymologies in a popular reference work.

A major work after Johnson, John Horne Tooke's (1736–1812) *Diversions of Purley* began publication in 1786, and the second volume came out in 1805. Here the focus was on etymology, but as Anthony Burgess observes, "This was a dangerous book that went in for philosophical conjecture about the origin of words and was quite capable of deriving 'hash' from the Perian 'ash' meaning stew."[70] A liberal, who supported the American Revolutionary War, and went to jail for his trouble, Tooke believed in the evolution of language and was in strong opposition to the Johnson school.

Charles Richardson, whose dictionary became a part of the less than successful *Encyclopaedia Metropolitana* (1817–1845), published it separately between 1835 and 1837 as the *New English Dictionary.* It put almost total emphasis on illustrative quotations, drawn particularly from early English literature. Although much flawed, the focus offered suggestions for the later compilers of the *Oxford English Dictionary.*

Hyde Clarke was among the first to offer more than a hundred thousand words in his *New and Comprehensive Dictionary,* 1855. John Ogilvie began *The Imperial Dictionary* in 1850. It became extremely popular and was updated in 1882. The work's success was due to at least three points. First, it came at a time when publishers realized there was a large, new literate public for dictionaries. Second, it was encyclopedic in size and scope, offering black-and-white illustrations. Third, the definitions were solid, if not imaginative, and there was a new emphasis on science and technology.

Toward the end of the century William Whitney revised Ogilvie's *The Imperial* and turned it into virtually a new American work. This became what even today is considered a triumph— *The Century Dictionary.* While it focused almost as much on encyclopedic material as words, the twenty-four parts (issued between 1889–1891) often are compared to the *Oxford English Dictionary.* Still, the *Century* was not primarily a historical work and the fine quotations are not used exclusively to support etymology. The reputation came as much from its size and handsome illustrations and typography, as its purpose. "In all ways, *The Century* is a tastefully elegant dictionary, typical of its times in assuming with quiet confidence that all essential knowledge can be encompassed within the covers of one work."[71]

Oxford English Dictionary

The Oxford English Dictionary[72] is without question the most important scholarly work of English lexicography. It promises to hold that position into the twenty-first century. Much has been written about the beginnings of the multivolume work, and today as it embraces the new technologies from CD-ROMs to online services, is equally of interest. Directed origi-nally to a scholarly audience, the *New English Dictionary,* known today as the *Oxford English Dictionary* or *OED,* sought to represent the entire Eng-lish language from A.D. 1150 to the present. The dictionary offers the ety-mology of every word, current or obsolete, as well as definitions and pro-nunciation based on millions of supporting quotations.

The *OED* as an idea began with the founding of the Philological Society in London in 1842.[73] The members involved themselves in collecting both current and obsolete words with supportive quotations to trace the history of the word and sometimes its numerous meanings. Particular emphasis was placed on stripping the dictionary of heretofore encyclopedic and tangential information and concentrating on material relevant only to lexicography. Numerous strong-willed individuals, such as Frederick Furnivall and Arch-bishop Richard Trench, pushed the project forward until by 1879 an agree-ment was signed with Oxford University Press to publish the dictionary. The editor by this time was the now famous James Murray, a Scot who had been drawn to the project through his study of Scottish dialect. The first volume was published in 1884, but it was not until 1928 that the great work was finished. (A 13th supplementary volume was issued in 1933.) Murray was by then dead, but coeditors, such as William Craigie and C.T. Onions, saw the first edition to its completion.

The Oxford English Dictionary was a remarkable engineering feat, but un-like works of Brunel, it was seen from the start as something that could never be finished. "A dictionary is obsolete as soon as it appears, in the sense it cannot keep up with the influx of new words into the language. It requires periodical supplementation. . . . Thanks to the computer, it has been pos-sible with immense speed to incorporate these many additions into the ex-isting body of the original work."[74] In the second edition of the *OED,* in the early 1990s, an effort was made to correct the understandable short-comings of the first edition. Among the corrections were a less Anglocen-tric focus, with words and support from other English-speaking countries; corrections and modifications to better indicate first usages; and the inclu-sion of slang.

Early American Dictionaries

In 1744, John Adams called for an American Society of Language to reg-ulate American English. He added that "to this day there is no grammar nor dictionary extant of the English language which has the least public au-thority."[75] If no more came of the call for an American academy than it had in England, at least foresight lead Adams to predict the future international role of English. It "is destined to be in the next and succeeding centuries more generally the language of the world than Latin was in the last or French in the present age."[76]

By 1751, Benjamin Franklin urged every American family to have at least one dictionary. The next logical stage, particularly after Independence, was to call for American dictionaries modeled after the familiar English pattern. The final step, taken by Noah Webster, was to publish a dictionary exclusively for Americans.

Before the American Revolution educated settlers used British dictionaries. Samuel Johnson's work of 1755 was as popular in America as in England. Variations of it taken over by American publishers were found in America well up until the Civil War. The first dictionary to be published in America, although of English origin, was the *Royal Standard English Dictionary* (1777) issued by Isaiah Thomas of Worcester in 1788.[77] The first dictionary to be written and published in America, suitably enough, was the work of Samuel Johnson, Jr., no relation to the English Johnson.

A School Dictionary by Samuel Johnson, Jr. (1767–1836) was printed and sold in New Haven in 1798. The 198 pages listed 4,100 words with some quaint definitions such as: "lout, to bow awkwardly" or "nustle, to fondle, to cherish." Other definitions, taken from English dictionaries, were somewhat better. Possibly encouraged by modest sales, Johnson teamed up with Reverend John Elliott to bring out the second American dictionary, *A Selected, Pronouncing and Accented Dictionary* two years later in 1800. This had more than double the number of words of the earlier effort. Today it is remembered as the first dictionary to suggest how to pronounce American as contrasted with the English of England.[78] Little is known of Johnson other than he was a Yale graduate and a teacher who died after this single claim to fame in 1836.

Caleb Alex Ander's *Columbian Dictionary* of 1800 was the first to boast of an emphasis on American words. The title page proclaimed "many new words, peculiar to the United States." Four other dictionaries appeared before Webster's *Compendious* of 1806. All had one thing in common. They included numerous Americanisms including Indian terms (wampum, tomahawk) and particular national nouns, such as dime and minuteman. Aside from that, they hold little interest and made no contribution to the history of the form.

Webster's Dictionary

Early American lexicography was less than impressive, and it would take Noah Webster (1758–1843) to revolutionize and establish the pattern for an American dictionary. Webster's very name is synonymous with "dictionary," yet few people today have any idea about him or his struggle to domesticate the American language. "A man of severe mien and stubborn industry, Webster divided his allegiance between conservatism and audacity. Long after the fashion changed, he went about in black knee breeches and black silk stockings. . . . When he considered the English language and American education, he felt it his mission to improve the one and correct the other."[79] After graduating from Yale in 1778, Webster studied law and took up teaching to make a living. He found there were no texts to teach students how to spell. At age twenty-four he began working on a response to the lack of material. A year later, in 1783, he had a grammar published in Hartford. By 1804, Webster had modified this beginning work and issued *The American Spelling Book.* This was to teach a popularity not achieved by any other book in America except the Bible.[80]

An American polymath, Webster became friends with George Washington and other American leaders. He gave gratuitous advice to them all and, although he had never studied medicine, he did not hesitate to publish a two-volume text on diseases. Unable to get out of debt, he moved from New Haven to Amherst in 1812 in order to save money. He began work on a dictionary that he offered on a subscription basis for ten dollars. This failed. He borrowed money from his daughter to do research in Europe on a dictionary. He completed the seventy-thousand word work at Cambridge, England. At an age when most men retire or, more likely, had died, Webster published his two-volume quarto, *An American Dictionary of the English Language.* This was 1828 and Webster was 70 years old.

Webster realized what both the British and Americans would know later, as expressed by playwright George Bernard Shaw, "Britain and America are two countries divided by a common tongue." This holds true for specific words. Today an English "biscuit" is an American "cookie"; an English "vest" is American "undershirt." In England a "lift," a U.S. "elevator." Pronunciations differ. "Watch out for 'riders' when they are talking about 'writers' and be prepared for a 'waiter' to turn into a 'wader' without warning. So writers ride and waiters wade, which isn't surprising when a 'dot' is a 'dart' and a 'pot' is a 'part.'"[81] For their part the English pronounce schedule as "shedule" and lieutenant is "leftenant."

In the nineteenth century, many words were indigenous to America or did not have the same meaning here as in England. For example, Creek (a small estuary in England) was synonymous with a small stream; Clapboard (used in making barrels) was a siding in America; and phrases such as Stump orators, and Friends meeting were peculiar to this country. Among his numerous Americanisms were several borrowed from the Indians: caribou, moccasin, squash, tomahawk, and wigwam. More often, Webster simply used existing English words with American meanings: congressional, gubernatorial, and log house.

A democratic social structure in America had the effect of eradicating differences of dialect and produced at a minimum sectional uniformity. Dialect uniformity struck foreign visitors as remarkable because it so differed from, say, England where Thomas Sheridan observed that in London "two different modes of pronunciation prevail, . . . One is current in the city, and is called cockney; the other at the court-end, and is called polite pronunciation."[82]

The attitude of the English was that most Americans were peasants in manner and in speech. Americans were set on destroying English with barbarizing language "as when they progress a bill, jeopardize a ship, guess a probability, proceed by grades, hold a caucus. . . ."[83]

As numerous admiring critics have pointed out, Webster's dictionary was a mixed work. Its strengths were Webster's careful definitions and genius at finding American words. On the other hand, many definitions and words were narrowly focused on New England. Also, lacking American literary works from which to draw quotations and trace etymology Webster tended to rely almost entirely on the Bible for supporting quotations.

Webster was determined to change the spelling of many American words. He had a specific method, but only a few of the changes he initiated in his dictionary caught on with the Americans. Some examples of Webster's spelling preferences include music (musick); theater (theatre); honor (honour); and defense (defence). At the same time he had a rather eccentric view of spelling and numerous words were not adopted, i.e. wimmen (women) or ake (ache). Slang was excluded as was any term with sexual overtones. Until well after the Second World War, American lexicographers of popular dictionaries kept the bias in place.

Despite Webster's well-written definitions, his first dictionary was not a success. Many reasons are given, from the high price for his work, to his efforts to reform spelling. Also, his etymologies did not please scholars. The true reason was the *Dictionary* had limited sales because it was in competition with Dr. Johnson's better-known effort. Many think Webster would have disappeared from the American scene except for the publicity efforts of his publisher who backed a second edition in 1841, two years before Webster's death. The well-advertised second edition saved the *Dictionary* from oblivion, but its continued success was a stroke of luck. After Webster's death George and Charles Merriam purchased the right to the dictionary from his family. The brothers, printers and booksellers in Springfield, Massachusetts, initiated two unique policies for dictionary publishers. First, they decided to publish only dictionaries. Second, they struck on a continuous revision plan whereby the main dictionary and its abridgments were updated at regular intervals. The brothers had a natural sense of salesmanship and early learned the wisdom of linking Noah Webster's name with their own, i.e., Merriam-Webster. Henceforth until today the name of "Webster" is synonymous with dictionary.[84]

In 1847, with new owners, the dictionary underwent a serious review by a professionally trained lexicographer, Chauncey Goodrich. The vocabulary was increased, and the etymologies were vastly improved. In fact, his modifications were the base, the beginning of today's Webster's dictionaries, which became leaders in the United States and much of the world.

Noah Porter succeeded Goodrich as editor, and Karl Mahn was employed to change and update Webster's etymologies. The 1864 edition was so far removed from Webster's initial work as to be entirely new. It was revised several times until 1890 when Merriam bought the first *Webster's International Dictionary*. It is ironic that the now-accepted dictionary worldwide was to drop "America" from the title. In 1909 another edition became *Webster's New International Dictionary*. The second edition appeared in 1934, and the controversial third edition (in use to the end of the present century and beyond) was published in 1961.

The shift in the editorial policy of the *Third New International* from permissive to descriptive entries caused a storm of protest. The use of supporting quotes from popular writers and movie stars did not help. The statement about "ain't" was the center of the protest. It is "used orally in most parts of the U.S. by many cultivated speakers."[85]

Beyond Webster

Other than from Dr. Johnson's dictionary, Webster (and later owners) had little competition. Early on Joseph Worchester was an exception with his *Comprehensive Pronouncing and Explanatory Dictionary of the English Language* (1830). Webster accused Worchester, who had once worked for him, of plagiarism. A relationship between the two works is obvious, but as Landau observes "Anyone who had read . . . (the) history of lexicography is by now aware of how much each lexicographer owes to his predecessors. This is as true of Webster as of Worchester."[86] Younger than and as hard a worker as Webster, Worchester published numerous dictionaries and was favored, generally, by the middle and upper classes in America. He held closer to British standards of spelling and pronunciation than Webster did. These standards appealed to educated people in urban centers while Webster's work found favor in rural, frontier sections.

In 1860, the indomitable Worchester brought out the highly acclaimed *A Dictionary of the English Language,* which shifted the balance away from Merriam, but only temporarily. G. & C. Merriam, as aggressive as they were direct, carried the battle to the state legislatures where they "influenced" lawmakers to support the Merriam-Webster dictionary. Four years later Merriam published the first unabridged dictionary. This was the final shot in the battle and by the 1870s Worchester and his dictionaries had faded into history, with Merriam the clear victor.

Isaac K. Funk, whose name was associated with Funk & Wagnalls for more than a century, issued his first dictionary in 1893. Until well toward the end of the twentieth century, the name Funk & Wagnalls was associated with dictionaries as much as Webster was. The *Standard Dictionary of the English Language* differed from Webster and others in that definitions were given in order of importance and use rather than in historical order, which was only one of several popular and widely imitated innovations. Another more questionable feature was the inclusion of encyclopedic information, with proper names and long informational entries for many words.[87] By the 1930s, after numerous different size and type of dictionaries, the *New Standard* had become the only real rival to Webster as an unabridged work. It had 458 thousand entires. Unfortunately, the firm failed to revise the work thoroughly and by the 1960s, the volume was still drawing upon the only major revision in 1913. This failure eventually destroyed the series.[88]

Modern Dictionaries

Webster set the pattern, modified to be sure by those who took over his work; but today's dictionary is not that much different from the nineteenth century titles. Even a cursory look at Kister's 1992 comparative guide to dictionaries will indicate both the number of dictionaries available today and the numerous publishers who make them possible. While Merriam-Webster's unabridged work goes unchallenged as the largest of the group, Kister reviews 300 English language dictionaries "of which 132 are for adults, ranging from the largest works . . . to very small pocket dictionaries that contain only a few thousand words."[89] Another 168 entries focus on dictionaries for young people.

While the late eighteenth and nineteenth century had forms of abridged dictionaries, it was not until the 1930s in the United States that the now popular desk or college dictionary became popular. Pioneered by Edward Thorndike, the dictionary with one-hundred and fifty thousand to one-hundred and eighty thousand words was soon taken on by all major publishers such as Clarence Barnhard's *American College Dictionary* (1947) and the best-selling tenth edition of G&C Merriam.

In the 1930s, Thorndike also pioneered the children's dictionary. His series of Thorndike-Century titles was based on the simple principle of including only those words likely to be found by the average child in reading matter. For example, in 1944 Thorndike compiled *The Teacher's Word Book of 30,000 Words*. The number of words was dictated by his research, both as a lexicographer and psychologist, into the frequency of their occurrence in a large group of books, newspapers, magazines, etc. suitable for younger readers. Today a whole range of dictionaries is available for elementary through high school. Arguments about limiting vocabulary by age or by reading matter. Saul Landau says, "It is not self evident that a dictionary or any other book for children should avoid using words that challenge the reader to add a new word to his vocabulary."[90]

Today's dictionary show two major lines of change and development. The most obvious is the new technology that allows one to search a dictionary online or on CD-ROM, e.g., the second edition of the *Oxford English Dictionary* as well as countless desk and college dictionaries available as separates or parts of computer software. This permits everything from comparing etymologies to automatically correcting spelling errors.[91] The more expensive dictionaries, such as the 1993 enlarged *American Heritage Dictionary,* reflects a second line emphasizes combining a dictionary with an encyclopedia. Here everything from locations of universities and colleges to maps and historical documents may be located. The public has the freedom of selecting only one basic reference work while the publisher has the advantage of charging more. This carries on a tradition of many centuries and today is just as debatable as the first time the combination was made. As noted, American publishers tend to stress the encyclopedic aspects of the dictionary and, thanks to the advent of CD-ROMs and multimedia information sources, these aspects are more likely to grow than to diminish.

The Random House *Dictionary of the English Language* raised outside matter to about 20 percent of the entire work. A great success, this helped to make it the first dictionary in the twentieth century to make the bestseller list. When Webster's was purchased by the Britannica, encyclopedic material, deleted much earlier, returned, in the popular college editions, if not in the unabridged work. The result of the inclusion of such things as manuals of style, atlases, historical events, biographical data, etc. in a dictionary is twofold. First, it increases the price of the volume and, second, as most people keep a dictionary for generations, the basic information soon is dated. The latter problem may be solved with frequent publication of CD-ROMs and/or online access to the dictionary-encyclopedia, but this remains for the future to determine.

Looking back over the three-to-four-thousand years of dictionary history, it is remarkable how little the basic form has changed. The first Sumerian dictionary and today's modern American one are both, tributes to literacy and the delights of the spoken and written word. There is little more to say, other than to ask the perennial reference desk question, "Just how many words are there in the English language?" Estimates vary, particularly if neologisms, slang, scientific vocabulary, etc. are included. Webster's *Third New International Dictionary* contains some four hundred and fifty thousand words, but if all the English vocabulary from the beginning was included, the estimate would be from 5.5 to 6 million words.

After centuries, how many words are really used by the average individual? No one knows, but in general the figure ranges from under a thousand to an average of about thirty thousand. Shakespeare employed a maximum of thirty thousand words, and "even our most prolific and admired writers seldom exhibit more . . . in a lifetime of writing."[92] Of course, words known but not used far exceed the thirty thousand employed in writing. Still, the thirty thousand represents less than ten percent of extant English words, but they "account for more than 90 percent of the words appearing on any page of literature we care to examine . . . 10 percent of the vocabulary of English covers 90 percent of the text of all volumes of literature in our libraries."[93] The exception is technical writing. These tend to be words used once or twice and lost in the ocean of technological change.

Fortunately for dictionary publishers, from the beginning to this day, language is in constant flux and change, if only in subtle definitions, and the changes are enough to guarantee a new edition next week. Of dictionaries, someone once said, there is no end. Whether you agree or not, of new editions of dictionaries there never will be an end.

Grammar

> "The liberal arts are to be the foundation for the enduring worth of any culture . . . antiquity is held up as an example for its commitment to the preservation of great texts rather than to embalming the bodies of its great men—its commitment to a heritage of books, not of relics."[94]

Closely associated with dictionaries, grammar[95] was a major consideration of teachers from the earliest Greeks. As one of the three parts of the trivium (grammar, dialectic, and rhetoric), grammar was considered the most important. As a result, there developed early major reference works (handbooks and manuals) and textbooks focused entirely on the subject. Until the nineteenth century it was difficult to separate the two, and for the most part a person with a query about grammar would turn to a school text.

Grammar is the heart of even the earliest educational efforts, hence "grammar schools" even to this day. Thanks to the alphabet, it is relatively easy to master the basics of handwriting and phonology, i.e., the ability to translate letters into sounds and sounds into letters. Minimal grammar books seem to be the first textbooks in the third and second centuries B.C. in Greece and later in Rome. Unfortunately, except for fragments, most of these have been lost.

The first extant grammar was developed by Dionysius Thrax (c. 170–90 B.C.) in the second century B.C. Based on work by Stoics, which are lost or obscure, the grammar discussed the eight parts or structure of words. The headings are indicative of content: meaning of words, pronunciation, language, difficult words. Usually examples are given for each of the discussions. To this point Greek grammar was primarily prescriptive with no attention to syntax. Still, "it had an immediate vogue which lasted until the Renaissance, and its authority was continued in the catechisms derived from it which then took its place. Latin grammar early fell under its influence . . . and through Latin most of the modern grammars of Europe are indebted to it . . . An immense corpus of commentary grew up in Hellenistic, Roman and Byzantine times around Dionysius' brief text."[96]

Quintus Ennius (239–169 B.C.) was among the first Romans to attempt to adapt Latin to Greek literary models. "He also encouraged by example the use of regular grammatical forms and normative ideals tending to elegance and economy. The movement was . . . perfected by Cicero . . permitting Latin authors more easily to render Greek works on law and philosophy."[97] Unfortunately only a shadow of his works survived time.

Systematic syntax made little progress until the appearance of Apollonius Dyscolus (second century A.D.). Like Dionysius, he was from Alexandria, but aside from that little is known of his background. He published some twenty books, of which *Syntax* is the most famous. Here he set down the rules for articles, pronounces, verbs, propositions and adverbs. Marked by a constant quest for universal principles, *Syntax* was to strongly influence grammarians through the Middle Ages.

Following in the grammatical footsteps of his father Apollonius Dyscolus, Aelius Herodianus concentrated on the accentuation of words. An immense work of twenty volumes, which now exists only in citations, contained rules of accentuation and was widely used in rhetoric. This and other works of Herodianus do survive, but, again, only in quotations and citations. Considered with his father as one of the great grammarian of history, he was influential throughout the Middle Ages.

Greek grammar dominated the eastern Mediterranean from the earliest Roman conquests through much of the later Byzantine empire. Literary Greek, at least, became the tongue of the educated. Latin only prevailed among the Roman military. In Italy itself, Greek and Latin were the marks of an educated person, but from about the third century A.D. Greek gradually faded away, and by 384 even the Roman liturgy was Latinized.

The difference between pagan and Christian traditions is found in work by St. Jerome (c. 340–420). He was familiar with the Greek and Latin classics and recommended the study of profane literature to learn how to defend the Gospels. From the beginning of the Middle Ages until the Renaissance, Jerome was the representative of humanism in the Church. The argument—the tension throughout the Middle Ages—was that one could be both a Christian as a citizen and a pagan as a master of rhetoric, dialectic, and grammar.

Donatus and Priscian

Latin grammar was codified by two major figures, both of whom loom large throughout the Middle Ages and whose books were found in almost all libraries. They are Donatus and Priscian.

Strongly influenced by the Greeks, the Romans shaped Latin grammar not as much on the work of the two Alexandrians—Apollonius and Dionysius—as on that of the scholars at Pergamum. The Romans devised the school grammar book, usually in three distinct parts: the arts of grammar, the parts of speech, and oration. Despite the wide educational interest in the subject, there are no extant scholarly Latin grammars.

Based on his own experience as Roman grammar school teacher, Aelius Donatus (fl. mid-fourth century) published a short school grammar, and although original, it—now lost—was primarily a summary of what had gone before. Later he issued two grammars, *Ars Major* and *Ars Minor,* combined and refined as *Ars Grammatica,* a school text. In modern print it would be no longer than fifty pages, and was an ideal textbook, as well as handy reference work.[98] In time the author's name was synonymous with grammar and grammar lesson. Donatus's influence seems to have been everywhere in the Middle Ages. Isidore of Seville, as described in the earlier section on encyclopedias, devotes his first book in his *Etymologies* to grammar in the style of Donatus.[99]

One of the most important teachers of the Middle Ages, Priscian (fl. early sixth century) was born in Constantinople and later taught there. Priscian is sometimes compared to Janus—looking backward to antiquity and forward to the Middle Ages. His eighteen-volume grammar (*Institutiones Grammaticae*) was the definitive Latin grammar of the time. He wrote the work at the urging of Latin scholars in Rome who feared the language was being corrupted by the Ostrogoths and other invaders. Specifically Julian, a Roman patrician, called for a basic grammar based on tradition and Greek authorities. Priscian met the challenge and drew upon Apollonius Dyscolus. The first sixteen books are concerned with part of speech, while the last two consider syntax. Most of his examples are drawn from standard Latin authors such as Cicero and Virgil.[100] Thanks to the content and the examples, the grammar became vastly popular throughout the Middle Ages.[101]

While Donatus was short and to the point, Priscian's *Institutiones Grammaticae* was a major reference work. As a reference grammar, it was the source of most grammatical teaching and scholarship throughout the Middle Ages. Again, its popularity may be measured by the great number extant manuscripts of the grammar. Also, numerous commentaries were compiled.

Medieval students of Latin were taught how to both read and speak the language of Rome, even if they were hundreds or thousands of miles distant from Italy and more familiar with their own vernacular. Donatus was the basic text, the basic handbook each student had to master. From Donatus the student proceeded to the two-volume Priscian, which not only provided additional rules of grammar, but copious quotations from classical authors. Too long for a textbook or even a teacher's handbook, Priscian was quickly abridged and summarized and comments freely written on finer points likely to be considered in a classroom.[102]

In the Latin universities grammar was a required, basic subject for everyone.[103] As the population of the universities increased, so did the need for advanced grammar texts in addition to the standard Donatus and Priscian. Two additional grammars appear in the thirteenth century: *Graecismus* by Berhard of Bethume (d. 1212) and *Doctrinale* by Alexander of Villedieu (d. 1240). Both works became basic in universities and so remained until the Renaissance humanists in the sixteenth century convicted them of lacking any classical merit and drove them out. The *Doctrinale* was entirely in verse, possibly to ease the difficulty of memorization of rules. While Villedieu's work was looked down upon by the theoretical grammarians, who rapidly distanced themselves from the popular grammars, it was widely read and used.

The great forward step in grammar was taken by Hugh of St. Victor (c. 1096–1141) and his encyclopedia *Didascalion.* Here, as noted earlier in the chapter on encyclopedias, he elaborated the hierarchical system of the seven liberal arts. "He did not merely develop the existing tradition which made the trivium preparatory to the Quadrivium on utilitarian grounds or on the excuse that the study of sounds was in essence ancillary to the study of things. He completely transformed men's thinking about the subject by postulating that the aim of the disciplines must be to cover the whole of experience."[104]

By the early Middle Ages every school was, theoretically, to teach the trivium (grammar, dialectic, and rhetoric), with the quadrivium taught only to outstanding students. In reality, for lack of teachers as much as students, many schools taught only grammar. Hence the term "grammar school" meant, by the early Middle Ages, not an age group, but a school with one basic course.

During the twelfth century the study of grammar was pushed aside by an increasing interest in dialectic. Even those who concentrated on grammar, fine tuned it with dialectic and ignored, they finally deleted, grammars with quotations from Greek and Latin authors, particularly those who did not fit into a given scholar's dialectic pattern. Northern Europe favored the new school that took the title of Scholastic theology, while in the south the grammars and the Latin and Greek authors were maintained and proved instrumental in the humanistic trend of the Renaissance.

The Scholastics, who feared that the classics would somehow prove a danger to young Christian students, abandoned the quotations (from Homer to Cicero and Terence) that Priscian used to illustrate his grammar. The Scholastic grammarians simply made up their own sentences and examples without regard to classical literature. As a result universities tended to divide into two camps—one that sided with the new approach and the other that built grammatical teaching around classical literature. The hostility was used as a theme in the famous satirical-allegorical poem *La Bataille des Sept Arts* (1236) by Henri d'Andeli.

After the twelfth century, a growing tertiary literature provided access to primary sources and secondary commentaries that hence brought more focus onto reference. Most of the tools associated with a modern reference service were modified in the Middle Ages. The encyclopedic tradition was fixed. Digests were equally popular forms. Indexing and annotated bibliographies blended with digests. By the thirteenth century, the construction of tertiary reference works to order the classics and produce a synthesis began to be a regular occupation of librarians and junior scholars.

Renaissance to Modern Times

Anyone involved with grammar compilation and publication at the time of the Renaissance inherited two things: the manuals of Donatus and Priscian and the importance of Latin. The task of the sixteenth century grammarians was to show how Latin and its two heralds could be applied to English. While the Renaissance failed to produce a Donatus, it did turn to serious study of the vernaculars. Grammars underwent a revolution. No longer tied exclusively to Latin and to a lesser extent Greek, they explored the new recognized, vernacular languages of Europe.

Gradually English gained not only popularity, but esteem and, by the time Chapman made his famous translation of Homer in 1611, he would proclaim in a note to the reader that no language surpassed the vernacular English for elegance. While this was naturally a part of patriotism, and claimed by most European nations for their own speech, it represented some truth. This was the age of Shakespeare's best years (1589–1610) as well as other masters of the language.[105]

From the Renaissance to the mid, twentieth century, despite advances and new fields of focus, grammar remained primarily modeled after the Latin grammar of Priscian. Each country adopted its own grammar texts, often based on Priscian, for use in elementary and secondary schools. In 1567 William Lily's *A Shorte Introduction of Grammar* was published. It became vastly popular and soon was simply called "Lily's grammar." The first high master of the St. Paul's school in London, Lily wrote a Latin grammar in English in 1510 for his students. It became the official grammar of England and held that position for over three centuries. There were worthy rivals, but Lily's grammar had the advantage of being the only authorized work of its kind.[106]

By the sixteenth century the grammar of the schools had limited connections with the studies pursued by scholars. Furthermore "for most people prescriptive grammar has become synonymous with 'grammar', and the prevailing view held by educated people regards grammar as an item of folk knowledge open to speculation by all, and in no wise a formal science requiring adequate preparation such as is assumed for chemistry."[107] Both in England and in America dictionaries and grammar manuals established laws of usage. It was a given that there were universal, prescriptive rules for grammar, both written and spoken.

Several grammars were published in America between 1765 and the nineteenth century, but the first one of any significance was Noah Webster's *A Plain and Comprehensive Grammar* (Hartford, 1784). In his *Philosophical and Practical Grammar* (1807), Webster challenged the century-old concept. Grammar was an art, but more important, a science. There were laws of grammar that required a prescriptive, not a descriptive, approach to the subject. Not all agreed, but generally this attitude won the high ground and prevailed until the mid-twentieth century.

In the mid-nineteenth century, a popular grammar directed to the average layperson was published. It was Henry Alford's *The Queen's English: Stray Notes on Speaking and Spelling*. At about the same time in America, Richard White's *Words and Their Uses, Past and Present* was published.[108] Both titles concentrated on weeding out bad grammar and particularly solecisms. Both titles were later quoted by Henry Fowler.

Asked what is the most influential grammar of the mid and late twentieth century, most scholars would immediately reply Henry Fowler's *A Dictionary of Modern English Usage*.[109] First issued in 1926 and revised by Sir Ernest Gowers in 1965, this is the standard other grammars follow. The publisher, Oxford University Press, reports it continues to sell five thousand to ten thousand copies each year. Fowler deals extensively with grammar and syntax, analyzes how words should be used, identifies clichés and common errors, and settles almost any question that might arise concerning the English language. The dictionary and the Gowers revision have a special flavor treasured by all readers. Fowler commented on practically everything that interested him, and the hundreds of general articles can be savored for their literary quality as well as to their instructional value.

American grammars of the early part of the twentieth century were little more than reprints of late nineteenth century works, particularly William Cobbett's *Grammar of the English Language*. This and others stressed correct usage with rules and exercises. In 1919, Henry Mencken's first edition of the much revised *The American Language* appeared. Now a standard reference book in many libraries and homes, this work described the American language as it was written and spoken, not necessarily as dictated by grammars. An exception to Mencken's blast was George Curme's *A Grammar of the English Language*. Called "the most substantial American grammar of the twentieth century,"[110] Curme's detailed treatment is another basic reference work in use to this day.

E.B. White and William Strunk's *Elements of Style* (New York: Macmillan) is one of the few books on grammar and writing that can be read for pleasure. *The Elements of Style,* first published in 1959, but now in a paperback edition, is a concise guide for those who want the right rules while learning the skill of writing with simplicity and grace. The work is by now a fabled reference guide, distinguished as much for its ease of use as for its good sense. As a staff member of the *New Yorker* magazine, E. B. White practiced what he preached, giving the impression that anyone could learn to write as well as he by following the rules in his manual. Although that claim may not be quite right, the well-organized guide does make it possible for the user to find an answer to almost any puzzle of proper usage.

Webster's Dictionary of English Usage (Springfield, MA: Merriam-Webster, 1995), constantly updated and an example of a current reference work for those seeking grammar help, will answer vexing problems of usage, particularly when employed with Fowler. Arranged alphabetically from "a, an" to "zoom" it is extremely easy to use. The editors tend to follow the prescriptive school, as does the publisher, but there is a discussion of different points of view. See, for example, the ubiquitous "ain't" and the ten columns of discourse with scores of illustrative quotes devoted to it. (There are twenty thousand quotations used throughout to emphasize this or that point of usage.)

William and Mary Morris's *Harper Dictionary of Contemporary Usage* (2nd ed. New York: Harper & Row, 1985) is one of a dozen or more reliable current grammars widely used by laypersons. In alphabetical order, from the proper use of abbreviations, to "you know" in speech, the guide represents the work of some one hundred and sixty-five experts who comment on various aspects of speech. Where there is contention, and this often is the case (e.g., "hopefully"), a usage panel is polled and asked "would you accept?." Percentages of yes and no answers are given. For example, in speech, 58 percent of the experts oppose the use of "hopefully," while in writing the no votes rise to 76 percent.

The constant need for current, reliable grammars is explained by a lexicographer. He notes that from generation to generation certain grammar problems present themselves. In an informal poll in 1989, he found that points of usage that worried people were between you and I (and similar pronominal construction), different from/to/than, lay/lie, may/might, shall/will, and split infinitives. These points of usage had been in dispute since at least the time of Henry Alford's *The Queen's English* (1864). No one was particularly impressed or showed that their worry was therefore in any way diminished.

Rhetoric

The second member of the trivium, rhetoric, means simply "the craft of speech." It is the art of prepared and delivered discourse and was a major part of the curriculum from the time of the Greeks and Romans, through the Middle Ages, and into the early part of the Renaissance. It remained a basic study until the early or mid-nineteenth century. Then it lost favor because it was too closely associated with the artificial, rather than with the supposedly sincere work of midcentury writers and speakers. Only after the Second World War did rhetoric regain more than historical interest for scholars. Now, modern rhetoricians are interested in the study of language and linguistics, rather than simply the aspects of good speaking, and rhetoric has been resurrected with emphasis no longer on the speaker, but on the reader. Today it is a major study in at least the larger universities.

Many disciplines have and do borrow from the twenty-five-hundred-year history of rhetoric. Letter writing at one time fell within the teaching of rhetoric, and today the modern literary critic borrows from rhetoric. Classical rhetoricians used the metaphor, the dialectic, and so does the average formulator of literary studies. As the art of persuasive writing and speaking, rhetoric is a field of study that continues to strongly influence reference publishing, at least at the popular, nonscholarly, level. It is the subject of a vast number of guides, manuals, and handbooks for laypeople on how to win an argument and sway an audience by the proper use of words and gestures. This wide use of how-to books has given rhetoric a pejorative meaning. "It's just rhetoric" is a cliché for criticizing a speech or written work, i.e., rhetoric is equated with insincere or grandiloquent language.[111]

The Greeks considered rhetoric a gift of the Gods, and in Homer eloquence of speech is a major accomplishment.[112] Homer often is cited as the father of rhetoric because about one-half of the *Iliad* and two-thirds of the *Odyssey* consist of speeches, often quite long. During the growth and development of democracy, which afforded the widest field for political and legal oratory, rhetoric became a formal part of Greek education. It gained momentum with the development of democracies in Syracuse and Athens where politicians and representatives of viewpoints had to express themselves in a public forum. Inevitably, handbooks appeared and taught the finer points of rhetoric, which at this point in about the fifth century B.C., became the art of forensic speaking.

Two Sicilians stressed the need to exaggerate or underplay, as the case required, in trying to persuade people to a point of view. According to legend, the first teacher of rhetoric is Corax (fl. 5th century B.C.) who issued a handbook, now lost, on the use of rhetoric in speech. In the same time of Corax, Tisias was teaching in Syracuse and published a handbook on the same subject which also was lost. Nothing more is known of the two, other than Plato, in the *Phaedrus* (267 fl.), indicates that Tisias was a pioneer in the subject. Understandably, early rhetoric teachers in Athens tended to be members of the school of Sophists, i.e., educators who stressed the importance of winning arguments.[113] Rhetoric became so valued that traveling philosophers, i.e., the Sophists, charged money for instruction in the subject.

Gorgias (c. 483–376 B.C.), a leading Sophist considered persuasion more effective than rational thought, published works on rhetoric and had a strong influence on sophistry and on the whole of rhetoric. He is quoted possibly more than anyone else in later manuals and handbooks on rhetoric. Gorgias's primary contribution was his emphasis on style and delivery. A contemporary, Thrasymachus (c. 430–400 B.C.) played an important role in the development of Greek oratory. He wrote an involved handbook that stressed the need to master elocution and the rhythms of style.

In about 420 B.C., the Sicilian Gorgias appeared in Athens and rhetoric changed. "Eloquence" becomes the key descriptor for him, the master of rhetoric. Despite Plato's rejection of rhetoric—as well as poetry—it was too well-entrenched to be scuttled by a single philosopher. Aristotle, the pupil of Plato and teacher of Alexander the Great, restored rhetoric and poetry in numerous works, particularly in his *Poetics.* With this history, the audience was established for reference works in rhetoric. About 340 B.C. the first of a long line of manuals and handbooks was published, primarily for use of students and teachers, but probably widely read by literate laypersons.

There were many Greek orators. How many were influenced by actual courses, or handbooks, in rhetoric is questionable. What is more certain is that the average Athenian did need some rhetorical training for success in almost any type of enterprise. Unfortunately, all of the manuals that might have been used have disappeared. The only exception is the *Rhetorica ad Alexandrum,* the single surviving pre-Aristotelian rhetorical manual. This may have been written by Anaximenes in c. 350 B.C. Much of the material is pedestrian and far from original and possibly explains the almost immediate success of Isocrates (c. 436–338 B.C.) the author of the Greek system of education and the first great teacher of rhetoric. A pupil of Gorgias and Theramenes, he turned to speech writing for others in around the 390s B.C. The next logical step was to teach rhetoric, and in 380 he published the *Panegyricus,* which in its argument for Greek unity set out the basics of rhetorical practice. The two dozen or so extant orations of Isocrates represent Attic oration at its best. These speeches were studied for generations and were often employed as models in various handbooks and manuals.

Just as letter books focus on samples of letters for all occasions so does the modern speech book often use similar models. Who began this trend? The first record of model speeches and exercises is the *Tetralogies of Antiphon* (c. 480–411 B.C.), which set the pattern for centuries to come, and later gained much use in schools of law. Typically each book, or set of exercises, contains four samples: the opening speech of the prosecutor; the response by the defendant; the prosecutor's reply to the response; and, finally, the defendant's conclusion. Antiphon, the Athenian orator, usually employed imaginary situations (often murders), but a few probably were based on real events. "He established a standard form of structure [for the handbook or manual]—an introduction, describing the circumstances of the case; a narration of the facts; arguments and proofs, sometimes interspersed with evidence; lastly, a peroration."[114]

With the second century A.D., Greek teachers of rhetoric appeared in growing numbers in Rome. Here, though, the move was from philosophy and theory to the practical needs of the Rome. Gradually, as the Empire spread, the artistic and literary Greek rhetorical style returned. The oldest Latin manual is the *Rhetorica ad Herennium* (c. 85 B.C.) whose author is unknown. Cicero's *De Inventione,* which seems to have borrowed from this earlier work, added little to the art. In fact, both works, as others from the time of Cicero (106–43 B.C.), were little more than repetitions of earlier Greek titles.

Roman to Medieval Rhetoric

Rhetoric and oratory in Rome grew up with the Empire and, while it was much influenced by the Greeks, it developed its own style. By 92 B.C. there were a number of Latin rhetoric handbooks available, of which two were outstanding. The *Rhetorica ad Herennium* (c. 86–82 B.C.) by an anonymous author who wrote as clearly as he employed suitable examples of students.[115] Cicero's (106–43 B.C.) *De Inventione* (c. 80 B.C.) while not a complete rhetorical manual, came close. He wrote related works such as *De Oratore* (55 B.C.) and the *Orator* (c. 46 B.C.). The primary goal of all these works was to teach the reader how to sway an audience by speech. Cicero lay out a systematic plan, evident in all of his seven books on the subject. His *Topica* was to have a great influence during the Middle Ages, as it was to influence Boethius and his study of the subject.

Cicero in his *De Inventione* set out five parts of rhetoric: the discovery of valid arguments; proper arrangement of the arguments; the proper language to employ; the use of memory; and the methods of delivery (i.e. pronunciation). To this day many of these steps are employed in both serious and modern how-to-do-it manuals.[116] While rhetoric gave way to the practical aspects of oratory, prominent scholars and writers of the Empire such as Cornelius Celsus incorporated rhetoric as a major theme of his encyclopedia (c. 14–37 A.D.).

Quintillian in his *Institutio Oratoria* (*"The training of an orator"*) (c. 96 A.D.) wrote the most influential textbook, manual and handbook of the history of rhetoric. Although about oratory, most of the materials, examples, rules etc. were based on the long history of rhetoric. Covering the training of an orator, from a child to a man. The 12 books discuss every aspect of this subject.[117]

With the fall of the Republic and the rise of the Augustus, rhetoric, as in Greece before it, lost. If opponents to the Emperor were not encouraged to speak against him, at least rhetoric's finer points could be taught in school. Eventually the teaching took on a new dimension. It became tied closely to poetry and literature. With that rhetoric regained lost ground.[118]

While Cicero and Quintillian influenced scholars during the Middle Ages, it is difficult to separate their thoughts from more basic handbooks and manuals. The wide-spread grammars of Donatus and Priscian incorporated some of the material in Cicero, for example, but Donatus probably had a stronger influence on the average student than the Roman orator. Even where it was not known or admitted, most schools of the Middle Ages followed the Roman pattern, not only in rhetoric, but in grammar and the dialectic.

With Christianity rhetoric continued to flourish, but more as oratory than a scholarly study. Also by the second century it helped to support a new emphasis on extravagant eulogy. Marcus Fronto (c. 100–166) was not only the foremost Roman orator of the time but the teacher of the future Emperor Marcus Aurelius with whom he later carried on an extensive correspondence. The letters show a master of eulogy, and reflect the importance of this is rhetoric to come.

St. Augustine (354–430) in his *Christian Doctrine* (396–426) established the use of rhetoric and the need for verbal effectiveness to support and spread the Christian doctrine. St. Augustine freely admitted rhetoric and truth, so beloved of the Greeks, had separated company. In fact, rhetoric was primarily associated with sophistry oratory which was "empty eloquence," and often used to make a bad argument. The "good" Christian, then, might be defeated in oration by the evil sophist. The solution—master rhetoric and use it for a Christian purpose.

Cassiodorus, (c. 487–583) as the encyclopedia compilers before him, chose rhetoric as one of the subjects in his *Institutiones;* and it became a standard course in the education of monks. He, too, helped to canonize the seven liberal arts. He pointed out that rhetoric helped the Christian speak well, while grammar was the source of liberal studies and the dialect helped separate out truth from the false. Cassiodorus used the four arts of the quadrivium (mathematics, astronomy, geometry and music) as sciences and part of the educational program.

Hrabanus Maurus (780–856), a pupil of Alcuin, was the next significant figure in the development (or the loss) of rhetoric. In his *De institutione clericorum* (On the education of the clergy, 819) Maurus stressed the importance of mastering rhetoric in order to convert the pagans to Christianity. A major Medieval application of rhetoric was the teaching of "Ars praedicandi" (The art of preaching). While St. Augustine gave his approval to this form of study, it is hardly a medieval or Christian invention. Its roots lie in Hebrew liturgies which were adopted by the Christians. The Judaic discussion of a given text at the weekly synagogue service became part of the Christian preaching method. While early Christian writers were not specific on the problems of preaching, particularly to the less educated, less expert congregation, St. Augustine's *Christian Doctrine* devotes several books to the question. "Augustine's strong defense of rhetoric was an extremely important factor in convincing Christians of his time that it was critical to employ the human art of rhetoric; many of his contemporaries, disgusted with pagan literature and drama, argued that more things Roman should be rejected . . . Augstine's defense of rhetoric was a turning point in this debate. Why, he asks, should Christians be so foolish as to let only evil men learn how to use rhetoric well?"[119]

Although St. Augustine established the basic principles of preaching, it was not until some 600 years later that the first manual appeared on the subject. The relative late appearance of such a reference work is easy to explain. Christian preachers, given the approval of St. Augustine, simply adopted Latin, and to a lesser extent Greek examples of rhetorical works. The need for separate manuals came only when a more sophisticated approach to Scripture and to preaching seemed necessary.

The now medieval art of preaching resulted in over 300 treatises from 1200 to about 1500. While each differed in particulars, they all followed a specific pattern: a theme, with quotations; explain the quotation and theme; divide into parts and then develop each part. Beyond that the basic format of the medieval thematic sermon remained a constant for many centuries, and is even in use to this day.

In addition to the manuals on preaching, a whole group of other reference works developed around those aids. There were concordances to Scripture sermon outlines and collections of complete sermons; collections of useful quotations and stories to be used to elaborate themes.

Rhetoric Divided

Two medieval rhetorical genres evolved in response to needs. The first, letter writing, was obvious. (See a discussion of this in the section of letters). The second, "ars poetria" (verse writing) appeared in the 1170s and may not seem so obvious as a work of reference. Not so for Medieval students who had at their call some half dozen Latin reference works by 1280 which championed the place of verse in the study of rhetoric and grammar. In one sense the student was studying what today would be called a literature course, but here the almost entire focus was on Latin Poets, and particularly Virgil and Horace. Geoffrey of Vinsauf's *Poetria noval* (New poetics, 1208–1213), for example, gives detailed instructions on how to plan a poem, putting words in proper order, and then how to deliver the poem orally.[120] The mechanical approach appealed to scholars, and the manual was one of the most popular. There are at least 100 extant copies. On the other hand this type of a-b-c approach to poetry begs for parody, which Chaucer, among others, did in his "Nun's Priest Tale."

Although extremely popular while it lasted, the poetry writing courses and manuals seem to have died out by the middle of the thirteenth century. The last major work was Everard the German's *Laborintus* (c. 1275). His preface was filled with woes familiar to teachers as much today as during the Middle Ages. Everard complains that students no longer could count, more or less read. They were less than interested in poetry, and downright surly. Matters were made worse, perhaps, by the relative lack of interest in Everard's guide. Teachers, students and laypersons, such as they were, preferred Geoffrey's *Poetria,* which was used until well into the sixteenth century. If poetry manuals disappeared in the Middle Ages, they were resurrected in the eighteenth century and, of course, are about as basic to a reference collection about writing today as when first introduced some 800 years ago.

Just as today many deplore the television set and the computer as undermining reading and education, so did teachers of rhetoric frown on the printing press (c. 1450). They were correct in that the widespread use of print played down the need for rhetorical training. Both as an educational device and as a philosophical theory rhetoric all but disappeared by the seventeenth and eighteenth centuries—at least in terms of scholars.

Prominent humanist teachers of rhetoric, who claimed familiarity with the Greek and Latin classics, by the mid fifteenth century could justify rhetoric as a path to speaking well, and living virtuously. The emphasis on virtue shaded all education, at least for the time. Pupils should be experts in rhetorical analysis and have a broad understanding of the classics. While agreement was general on this point, there was wide variation on particulars, and on which guides, i.e. which manuals and handbooks to follow. Here it was much an evaluation of the truth of the writings as their logical arguments and conclusions. And on this there was mixed opinion. "Renaissance scholars built around their texts a vast wedding cake of interpretation, mingling ancient, medieval, and modern ingredients in the hope of disguising the awkward pagan features and apparent errors of the texts."[121]

The single best guide to the rationale for the rhetorical handbooks is Erasmus' *De Copia* (*De duplici copia verborum ac rerum* or *On Copia of Words and Ideas of 1512*). In the second half, which essentially is a handbook to how one should be employed, Erasmus offers 150 variations on a single sentence. "Your letter has delighted me very much." He demonstrates how the highly desired copious style, by judicious use of synonyms, antonyms, quotes, excerpts, etc. may twist and turn to say the same thing in hundreds of ways. He classifies these under such numerous headings with the frequent use of descriptors such as "amplification of speech", "varying", "description", "enriching", and "multiplication". With that, he over and over again calls for style, discrimination and precision in the employment of "riches piled up."

Genius that he was, Erasmus saw the obvious dangers in having such a great store of examples for speech or writing. Much of the opening of *De copia,* using Quintillian and Virgil for example, stresses the need to balance between the concise (i.e. the fewest words) and copia (i.e. a profusion of words). The problem, as Erasmus recognized, is that the average person has difficulty striking an even balance. Most, particularly in the sixteenth to eighteenth century, erred on the side of the verbose.

English language versions of Erasmus' handbook on rhetoric soon followed. Two of the more popular were Richard Sherry's *A Treatise on Schemes and Tropes* (1550) and about one hundred years later in 1654 Thomas Blount's *The Academie of Eloquence.* Both illustrated the value of using tropes (i.e words to mean something different from their ordinary definition) and schemes (i.e. a figure consisting of arrangement of words in artificial order).

The so called "Ramist system" in the sixteenth century stressed elocution and pronunciation as the only two offices proper to the by now much devalued study of rhetoric. Named after a professor of philosophy, Peter Ramus (1515–1572), the system was established in a book inspired by Ramus, *La Rhetorique Française* (1555). Style, and more particularly figures of speech, became the primary educational function of rhetoric. While Ramus really had little to say about proper gestures, pronunciation, this was picked up by Francis Bacon (1561–1626), Lord Chancellor of England in 1618, and a superior lawyer. The physical, nonverbal aspects of rhetoric fascinated Bacon who, in turn, set off a series of studies from his time to this day on the subject.

Rhetoric to Modern Times

The New Philosophers of the eighteenth century,[122] who rejected the external senses as relevant to mastering knowledge, tended understandably to be hostile to the rhetoric of oratory. Masters of the art responded in several ways, but most solved the problem of conflict by ignoring the philosophers and returning to the training of skilled speakers. Claude Buffier (1661–1737), for example, published a popular treatise on memory, eloquence and even grammar, as well as a dozen or more other reference works. While he, and others drew upon the classics and a few Medieval thinkers, they tended to explore at greater length the importance of eloquence in speech.

With gradual power given to the House of Commons, the English quickly continued on their path of using rhetoric in politics and particularly to master the skills of argumentation. If by the mid eighteenth century a university degree was not needed, but skill in oratory was required, it is not surprising the amount of stress put on the matter as a practical way of manipulating and getting ahead in the world. Lord Chesterfield (1664–1773) in one of his famous letters to his son stressed the importance of mastering speech and eloquence— "manner is all, in everything; it is by manner only that you can please, and consequently rise."[123]

While Chesterfield hardly was representative of the average English person, at least his advice was followed by enough people to warrant publication of many manuals on elocution, that is the proper way of speaking, pronunciation and gesture. *The Art of Speaking in Public* (London: 1727) was an English version of a French manual in which the author promises to teach "the graces of action and the attracting charms of eloquence." In other words, with different emphasis, the manual is similar to the works of Cicero, Quintillian et al through the Middle Ages. The primary difference here and in manuals to follow is the focus on the language of the body.

In discussing nineteenth century rhetoric, Conley observes that "there are at least four strands . . . a powerful continuing presence of Classical influence, the ongoing interest in thearts of election, the belles letters tradition, and an emerging scientific perspective on communication."[124] Meeting the need of this combination of interests were such English speech manuals as Thomas Ewing's *Principles of Elocution* (1815), which was reprinted 36 times up to 1861 and Richard Whatley's *Elements of Rhetoric* (1846). The latter, in four parts, stresses the methods of contrasting an argument (with particular emphasis on the power of syllogisms), the power of emotions, the necessity for style (i.e. elegance was stressed), and on the actual delivery, or elocution. Most manuals of the nineteenth and early twentieth century followed this general pattern with a particular focus on the pragmatic.

Americans tended to employ the English manuals, and Whatley's work was widely used in the United States. In fact the basic ideas in Whatley were picked up by other American authors and, to this day, were stressed as important to mastering rhetoric, or, more precisely, public speaking. It is from Whatley and his numerous imitators over the past century and a half that basic principles of speaking were established. This may sound familiar. First, the reader should pick a subject. Next the proposition is to be clearly stated. The speaker should then outline the proposed speech. The talk should be written out, using simple, direct language and drawing upon words and styles of approved authors. Beyond that the reader is told how to deliver the talk.

Early colleges in the United States, (17th–18th century) from Harvard to Princeton, stressed the training of ministers. A good number of courses were concerned with rhetoric and many of the European manuals were employed. However, most emphasis was placed on classical writers. Paralleling oratory was a focus on delivery and elocution, tailored for ministers. With the end of the Civil War and more secularized colleges, as well as the development of land grant institutions, the focus changed to using rhetoric in business, i.e. required courses in writing and speech.

Down to the Revolution of 1830, Europe was convinced that rhetoric was important, primarily as a method of civilizing students. Isaac D'Israeli, the father of the English prime minister published a series of manuals called *Curiositities of Literature and Ameties of Literature* (1791–1793) which celebrated the joys of rhetoric and poetry.

The teaching of rhetoric took another path when there arose a great interest in teaching reading aloud, (i.e. in this century, called "oral interpretation"). As might be expected, the primary beneficiaries of this movement were would be actors. Others found that handbooks and manuals on this aspect of rhetoric was useful in other professions from politics to the law. Still, ministers were the great advocates of elocution and numerous manuals on the subject were published in the eighteenth and nineteenth centuries for their particular use.

By the close of the nineteenth century rhetoric as a method of oral composition and delivery had fallen into discredit. The once proud discipline was by then, as often now, associated in most people's mind with florid delivery and purple prose. The negative views continued until the mid 1940s when it was rescued by American universities where faculty tied rhetoric to the new study of communication. For the most part speech classes, in the older sense of rhetoric and dialectic, were split off as separate studies. After World War II the theories of rhetoric were applied to the film, television, newspaper and any form of communication. The focus on training students how to communicate took place in a separate communications department, or more likely be part of an English and speech department.[125] Rhetoric, although under different names, was back!

Notes for Chapter 6

1. John Algeo, "Dictionaries as Seen by the Educated Public in Great Britain and the USA," in *Worterbucher (Dictionaries)* vol. 1 (New York: Walter de Gruyter, 1989), 29. Algeo points out that a 1970s Gallup survey showed more than 90 percent of the persons questioned had at least one dictionary—considerably more than the 70 percent who had cookbooks.

2. Mary Snell-Hornby, "The Bilingual Dictionary," in *The History of Lexicography* R.R. Hartmann (Philadelphia: John Benjamins, 1986), 209.

3. Ibid. Sumerian was probably a dead language when the earliest bilingual lists were compiled. Much like Latin or Greek, it was used by the Mesopotamians as the accepted language of scholarship. The term "word list" and "*lexeme*" indicate words of a language arranged in some systematic order, not always alphabetically, and often without definitions, pronunciation keys, etc. Consequently, "word list" is a term used to avoid the indication of the completeness of a dictionary or lexicon.

4. James Hulbert, *Dictionaries: British and American,* rev. ed. (London: Andre Deutsch, 1968). This is a short, popular approach to lexicography, while Robert Collison's *History of Foreign Language Dictionaries,* London: Andre Deutsch, 1982 casts a much wider net and offers an excellent survey. The most extensive coverage is found in the three-volume *Worterbucher,* which is an international encyclopedia of lexicography with scores of scholarly contributors.

5. John of Garland used this term to identify a list of Latin words a student should master. Arrangement was by subject, common enough until the sixteenth century. Only a few words are given English equivalents.

6. Theodore Besterman, "On a Bibliography of Dictionaries" *Proceedings of the British Society for International Bibliography* (October 1942): 64–65.

7. While the single alphabetized list was the norm in the earliest English dictionary, there were some pleasant separations. A 1623 dictionary included three alphabetical lists consisting of (a) encyclopaedic matters, (b) "choice" words used in polite society, and (c) a list of common words with more acceptable synonyms. For a clever, clear, and informative discussion of alphabetical order and the dictionary, see "The Problem of Alphabetical Order" in *Eric Partridge in His Own Words,* ed. David Crystal (New York: Macmillan, 1980), 64–78.

8. Any dictionary must explain the meaning and use of the "word," with linguistics playing a major role. The basic word unit composed of phonetic form and semantic content is a "lexeme," and an understanding of the variables in a "lexeme", is a valuable contribution of linguistics. See R.R. Hartmann, *Lexicography: Principles and Practice* (New York: Academic Press, 1983).

9. Anthony Burgess, *A Mouthful of Air* (New York: William Morrow, 1993), 333. This is an old story and framed in many ways, e.g., "A salute to the Irishman in the fable, who bought a dictionary to read. He found the story hard to follow, but at least every word was explained as you went along." Claude Rawson, "Samuel Johnson Goes Abroad," *New York Review of Books,* 20 August 1991, 17.

10. Algeo, "Dictionaries as Seen by Educated Public," 31–32. Also, the author points out that "users tend to assume that order represents preference"—a dangerous assumption for the Merriam Webster dictionaries where preference of order is given to historical development of the word. Nor are usage labels—scarce as they may be—of much use in that few Americans understand their meaning, Colloquial, for example, is "a label that is almost universally misunderstood."

11. See *Worterbucher,* 1682–86, for examples of bilingual Sumerian and Akkadian lexicography. Deciphered in the middle of the nineteenth century, cuneiform script opened the way to modern Sumerian, Akkadian, etc. Two outstanding examples of bilingual dictionaries of ancient Middle Eastern languages are *The Sumerian Dictionary of the University Museum of the*

University of Pennsylvania (Philadelphia: University of Pennsylvania Museum, v.d.) and *Chicago Assyrian Dictionary* (Chicago: University of Chicago, v.d.). For a discussion of the Sumerian dictionary, see review in *Journal of Near Eastern Studies,* 1987, 55–59.

12. See Rudolph Pfeiffer, *History of Classical Scholarship* (Oxford: Clarendon Press, 1968), 42+, for a discussion of Democritus (who was a coeval of Socrates). The first glossaries were definition and interpretation of Homer and Hesiod. By the Medieval period the interlinear of marginal interpretations of difficult or obsolete words were a part of most manuscripts, and these later were collected into separate glossaries.

Today, a glossary usually means a collection of specialized terms with their meanings. More often than not, a lengthy glossary, which may be multilingual, is labelled as a dictionary of, say, slang, medicine, law, or whatever; whereas a brief explanation may take the form of a footnote.

13. *Oxford Classical Dictionary,* 469.

14. Ibid. The comparative philologist who "will find much to interest him in classical Latin words that have changed—(and) mark an instructive stage in the transition from Latin to the Romance languages." The early Medieval glossaries "play a by no means negligible part in the history of language." M.L. Laistner, *Thoughts and Letters in Western Europe,* rev. ed. (Ithaca N.Y.: Cornell University Press, 1957), 224.

15. For a discussion of his work in lexicography, see Pfeiffer, *History of Classical Scholarship,* 1974.

16. Some trace of this lost work can be found in Paul the Deacon's *De Verborum Significatu* published in the mid-eighth century.

17. Collison, *Encyclopedias: Their History through the Ages,* 30.

18. Little is known about lexicography in the early Christian centuries, at least when divided off from the Roman works. Fragments and references to Christian-oriented glossaries and word lists are not unusual, but none seems to have had much influence on the main stream of dictionary history. For a detailed discussion of the grammars and the teaching of grammar, see Stanley E. Bonner, *Education in Ancient Rome* (Berkeley: University of California Press, 1977), and particularly chapters 14 and 15.

19. Collison, *Encyclopedias: Their History through the Ages,* 24–40, offers a detailed listing of extant examples of early Christian compilers of glossaries, word lists, etc.

20. Titled by their opening words, *Abstrusa* and *Abolita,* the two oldest of all the Latin glossaries, were compiled no later than the early seventh and eight century respectively. The first is made up almost entirely of glosses on Virgil, including some from the Bible. The latter also used marginalia to Virgil as well as from plays of Terence.

21. St. Anselm, quoted in Collison, *Encyclopedias: Their History through the Ages,* 46.

22. Ibid, 47.

23. M.L. Laistner, *Thought and Letters in Western Europe,* 222.

24. See Brian Stock, *The Implications of Literacy,* 1983. The most impressive of the early sixth century bilingual word lists, the *Philoxenus Glossary,* served to assist Italians living in southern Italy who spoke Greek but had to know Latin. Little of the work remains as such, but it was drawn upon heavily for later bilingual Greek-Latin efforts.

25. Bolgar, *The Classical Heritage,* 407–8.

26. Donald Howard, "Lexicography and the Silence of the Past," in *New Aspects of Lexicography,* ed. Howard Weinbrot (Carbondale: Southern Illinois University Press, 1972), 15.

27. *Dictionary of the Middle Ages,* vol. 9, 391.

28. The compilation, known as the *Bibliotheca* (alternatively *Muriobiblos*), is a fascinating production, in which Photius shows himself to be the inventor of the book review. In 280 sections which vary in length from a single sentence to several pages, Photius summarizes and comments on a wide selection of pagan and Christian texts." Reynolds and Wilson, *Scribes and Scholars,* 55.

29. Ibid. vol. 11, 501. "Suda" means bulwark.

30. Collison, *Encyclopedias: Their History through the Ages,* 51.

31. The dictionary (c. 1175) of Huguccio of Pisa was borrowed from extensively by Osbern of Gloucester (c. 1123–1200) to compile his *Liber Derivationum* (c. 1150), which proved extremely popular and was a standard reference work, on its own, until well into the fifteenth century. It is found in more than two hundred manuscripts. Osbern's dictionary is among the first to stress the importance of etymology.

32. A.C. Dionisotti, "From Ausonius's Schoolday. . ." *The Journal of Roman Studies* 72 (1982): 86, 87.

33. *The Lindisfarne Gospels* (c. 600–700) were copied in the eighth century and a product of Northumbria. The main text is in Latin with an interlinear Anglo-Saxon translation, or gloss.

34. Tom McArthur, "Thematic Lexicography," in Hartmann, *The History of Lexicography op. cit.,* 163. Ælfric was one of the finest Anglo-Saxon stylists of the late tenth and early eleventh century. In 1005 he became abbot of a community in Eynsham, outside of Oxford. He had the distinction of producing the first Latin grammar in English for the novices who had never studied Latin.

35. *Worterbucher,* 1946. The difficult words were derived from the primary sources for vocabulary, i.e., the Latin-English dictionaries of the Middle Ages and the Renaissance. By the late seventeenth century, there was more extensive borrowing from literary works and from learned journals, particularly for technical words. Also, the much admired dictionaries of the French Academy and the Italian Academy were raided for English dictionaries.

36. Douglas Kibbee, "The Humanist Period in Renaissance Bilingual

Lexicography" in Hartmann, *The History of Lexicography,* 140. For a detailed discussion of the early English bilingual word lists and dictionaries, see the first chapter of Tetsuro Hayashi, *The Theory of English Lexicography, 1530–1791* (Amsterdam: John Benjamins, 1978). The first two books of Palsgrave's grammar were published by Pynson, the third by Haukyns, his assistant, after the death of Pynson. Little is known of the compiler, but the work is not only a landmark in grammar, but an important example of early English printing.

37. For a discussion of the loan words process, see Jurgen Schaffer, "Elizabethan Rhetorical Terminology," *Dictionaries, Journal of the Dictionary Society of America,* no. 3 (1980–81) 7–17.

38. The grammarians forged the most influential word lists, primarily in connection with their grammars. And of this group, the best known and most influential was Aelius Donatus (fl. fourth century). The Donatus grammar became so widespread, so famous that well into the Renaissance Donatus was a synonym for grammar. Almost as famous, Priscian, a teacher of Latin from Byzantium in the sixth century, often used Greek myth and history as examples in his various grammatical lexica.

39. Bolgar, *The Classical Heritage,* 377. The leading classical scholar in France, Budé was divided by his family and administrative duties and diplomacy, but he managed to produce one of the masterpieces of the century.

40. Collison, *Encyclopedias: Their History through the Ages,* 72.

41. *Worterbucher,* 1698. The term "thesaurus" was introduced by the Estiennes, and it is because of these dictionaries that the word generically acquired the meaning "nearly exhaustive philological dictionary," as one of its senses. Reedited in another arrangement with supplementary material, the dictionary was republished twice in the nineteenth century and "will probably preserve Henricus's name for eternity." Pfeiffer, *History of Classical Scholarship,* 110.

42. Pfeiffer, *History of Classical Scholarship,* 110.

43. Some argue that Richard Huloet's English-Latin dictionary of 1552 was the first English dictionary because it contained brief English definitions. Another candidate is Richard Mulcaster's *Elementarie* (1582), but his listed only eight thousand English words without definitions. Interestingly enough, the compiler claimed his word list, which followed grammatical rules, included "all the words which we use in our English tung." There is evidence that Cawdrey drew most of his information from previously published works, and particularly, (1) Edmund Coote's *The English Schoolmaster* of 1596, made up of grammar, vocabulary, catechism, and prayers. His vocabulary was made up of English difficult words with simple definitions; (2) a Latin-English dictionary compiled by Thomas Thomas in 1588, who furnished Cawdrey with many definitions; and (3) a famous Medieval medical book, translated anonymously from Latin into English in 1599.

44. Some indication of English vocabulary, as differentiated from the

wide-spread use of Latin and later French among scholars, may be seen in the size of the early English dictionaries. Cawdrey's first effort of 1604 had some 2,560 entries and a folio, fifth edition of a dictionary at the end of the seventeenth century raised the number to about seventeen thousand. A 1721 dictionary had forty thousand entries, a normal number until Dr. Johnson's 1755 edition of with fifty-five thousand.

45. For a discussion of some of the lesser known figures in the history of early English dictionaries, see M.S. Hetherington, "Old English Lexicography . . . 1550–1659," in *Papers on Lexicography in Honor of Warren N. Cordell* edited by J.E. Congleton (Terre Haute: Indiana State University, 1979), 141–150.

46. "Curiously enough, both Robert Cawdrey and John Bullokar addressed the dedicatory epistles to ladies of high rank . . . the tradition of compiling dictionaries of difficult words for the benefit of the female sex and 'unskilled' persons has been maintained by most of the lexicographers far into the 18th century" Hayashi, *The Theory of English Lexicography,* 41.

47. As earlier lexicographers, Cockeram selected his words from any printed sources. One of these was Thomas Dekker's *A Strange Horse Race* (1613). "As Cockeram went through Dekker's pamphlet, he marked words that he thought would be likely entries for his Dictionaire." At the same time he drew upon other dictionaries such as Bullokar's *English Expositor* for definition of Dekker's words. James A. Riddell, "Some Additional Sources for Early English Dictionaries," *Huntington Library Quarterly* 46 (1983) 228.

48. D.T. Starnes, "Literary Features of Renaissance Dictionaries," *Studies in Philology* 37 (1940): 27, 29.

49. DeWitt Starnes and Gertrude Noyes, *The English Dictionary From Cawdrey to Johnson, 1604–1755.* (Chapel Hill: University of North Carolina Press, 1946), 38. This volume is by far the best general history for the period. The two authors offer invaluable clues to where each compiler collected words by simply comparing an "original" work with earlier dictionaries. The amount of overlap and downright plagiarism is impressive.

50. Ibid., 70.

51. Ibid., 75.

52. Thirteen years after Bailey's death, the largest and best edition of his work was published. Under the editorship of Joseph Scott the 1755 dictionary "was designed as a bookseller's measure to hold the market against that redoubtable newcomer in lexicography, Samuel Johnson." Starnes and Noyes, *The English Dictionary from Cawdrey to Johnson,* 179. This concluding chapter in their history gives a detailed description of the edition.

53. *Worterbucher,* 1948.

54. Hulbert, *Dictionaries: British and American,* (23) observes that "In truth the speech of a cultivated English man or woman of the eighteenth century would sound provincial, even rude to us. . . Pronunciation noticeable

in some well known surnames (today) such as Taillefer (Tolliver) and Beauchamp (Beecham) was common enough in many words in ordinary usage."

55. "Bar English?" *New York Times,* 15 March 1994, p. 1+. The article points out that several efforts by the French in the past twenty years to bar English, to legislate proper usage, have failed. The Academie no longer (if ever) has any real power.

56. Burgess, *A Mouthful of Air,* 332.

57. N.E. Osselton, "On the History of Dictionaries," in *Lexicography: Principles and Practices,* R.R. Hartmann, 19. Chesterfield looked to the English Royal Society for support, but found little assistance. The Royal Society (founded in 1662) was somewhat equivalent to the other European academies, but never enjoyed the interest in words found in France. Various efforts were made by such writers as John Dryden and Alexander Pope to establish the Society as a language watchdog, but their efforts failed.

58. The older academic tradition of prescriptive notes was scuttled in a paper read before the Philological Society of London in 1857. A dictionary is an inventory of language, reflective of the changing culture. It is descriptive. Dictionaries must give all the words of the language, good or bad, and record instances of their first use. This constituted one of the most sustained pieces of dictionary criticism in the nineteenth century. It "was to act as a catalyst for work on the OED, which has indeed remained largely true to the ideals" outlined in the paper, "The History of Academic Dictionary Criticism. . ." in *Worterbucher,* vol. 1, 226.

59. The comments of panel experts goes back to the turn of the century and is a useful method of checking language. Still, "a comparison of usage notes in two editions of the *American Heritage Dictionary* and of the composition of the Usage Panels for those editions leads to the conclusion that the Panel has not in fact been used significantly as a basis for usage guidance." Algeo, "Dictionaries as seen by Educated Public," 31.

60. Burgess, *A Mouthful of Air,* 349.

61. Published in 1694, the massive *Dictionnaire de la langue française* is still influential. Five years after the Academy was founded, work began on the dictionary.

62. Allen Reddick's *The Making of Johnson's Dictionary, 1746–1773* (Cambridge: Cambridge University Press, 1990) is only one of dozens of works concerned with the famous dictionary. See Reddick's bibliography.

63. A document as fascinating as the dictionary itself, *The Plan of a Dictionary of the English Language* was published by Johnson in 1747. An Anglican and a Tory, Johnson believed and practiced the modified prescriptive approach, which he made clear in his call for subscribers.

64. Johnson worked with at least six assistants, five of them Scots. They were employed primarily as secretaries, copiers, and all-around workers to assist the primary compiler.

65. The process by which Johnson assembled and employed the quotations is the topic of numerous articles. See, for example, *Worterbuch,* 1949. "One third of all Johnson's quotations come from just four writers. Shakespeare (15%), Dryden (11%), Milton (5%), and Addison (5%). If one then adds in Bacon, Pope, and the Bible, this covers 50% of all his illustrations of English usage." Osselton, "*On the History of Dictionaries,*" 19.

66. Slang made an early entry into English dictionaries. One 1676 compiler (Elisha Cole, *English Dictionary*) explained these words were necessary to know "to save your Throat from being cut, or, at least your Pocket from being pick'd." *Worterbuch,* 1946.

67. Less well-known descriptions run from "Frigorifick, causing cold. A word used in Science" with an example from Quincy; and "Gossip, a tippling companion," as well as "Job (a low word now much in use, of which I cannot tell the etymology) 1. Petty, piddling work." Johnson was berated for his sometimes circular definitions. The classic example: "long, not short" and "short, not long."

68. *Worterbuch,* 1954.

69. Johnson's dictionary went through countless editions and reprints in quarto, octavo, and even pocket-size abridgments. It enjoyed the greatest circulation of any dictionary until that time—some six thousand copies of the folio were printed by 1778; and forty thousand copies of the octavo edition were published to 1786.

70. Burgess, *A Mouthful of Air,* 336.

71. *Worterbuch,* 1992. The *Century* proved to be an invaluable dictionary-encyclopedia that was revised and enlarged to twelve volumes in 1911. It was America's closest competitor to the *Oxford English Dictionary,* although its two hundred and fifty thousand quotations fell somewhat short of the *OED's* 2.5 million quotes. Still, the work contained more than five hundred and thirty thousand definitions as well as much encyclopedic information, particularly of a scientific and technical nature. Long out of print, it is found in many research libraries and remains useful.

72. There are scores of books and articles on the *OED.* Donna L. Berg, *A Guide to the Oxford English Dictionary* (Oxford: Oxford University Press, 1933) is an analysis of what constitutes the compilation of the *OED* including how main entries are determined and the operation of cross-references. Along the entertaining way, the author gives some information on the history of the set, right up to 1993. See, too, K.M. Murray, *Caught in the Web of Words* (New Haven, Conn.: Yale University Press, 1977) for a biography of James Murray, who edited the set. See bibliographies in both works. A less-than-flattering analysis of the work is offered in John Willinsky, *Empire of Words* (Princeton, N.J.: Princeton University Press, 1994).

73. One of the founding members was Henry Sweet who gained fame as the phonetician Henry Higgins in *Pygmalion,* later *My Fair Lady.* In

1879, he signed the contract with what is now Oxford University Press for publication of the dictionary.

74. Burgess, *A Mouthful of Air,* 343. The Grimm brothers, Jakob (1785–1863) and Wilhelm (1786–1859) launched the massive equivalent to the *OED* with their *Deutsches Worterbuch* in 1818. After wars and generations of effort the dictionary was completed in 1960, or 142 years after it began.

75. Ronald Wells, *Dictionaries and the Authoritarian Tradition* (The Hague: Mouton, 1973), 50.

76. Ibid.

77. The interrelationships of British and American publishers continue to this day and there is much exchange and interaction, e.g., the *American Heritage Dictionary* was the subtext for the British *Reader's Digest Great Illustrated Dictionary* and Longman in England and Merriam in America frequently exchanged works.

78. With the second edition Johnson increased the words to more than ten thousand. Larger, but little better than the first dictionary, the compilers bragged that, at least, it deleted words "highly offensive to the modest ear." Not quite. The French *foutra,* described in a modern French-English dictionary as "indecent" and abbreviated as "f. . .," was included for the first and last time in a grade-school dictionary.

79. Israel Shenker, *Harmless Drudges. Wizards of Language—Ancient, Medieval and Modern* (Bronxville, N.Y.: Barnhart Books, 1979), 125–26.

80. His "blue-backed" speller went through numerous editions until Webster's death in 1843. It became one of the most popular schoolbooks ever published, with estimates that it sold more than 100 million copies by the early twentieth century. Despite the sales, Webster was a miserable businessman who went on frequent author tours where he regularly insulted the audience. Arriving at Philadelphia, he was given a congenial welcome only to respond, "You may congratulate Philadelphia on the occasion of my presence here."

81. Deborah Devonshire, "Diary," *Spectator,* 12 February 1994, p. 7. For an extensive list of "modern varieties of English: British and American, see Morton Benson et al., eds., *Lexicographic Description of English* (Amsterdam: John Benjamins, 1986), 13–174.

82. Quoted in A. Delebridge, "On National Variants," in *The History of Lexicography,* Hartmannm, 23.

83. *Quarterly Review* (1814): 528–29.

84. The Merriam brothers did not secure the copyright to "Webster," and the descriptor may be used on any dictionary today. The only way to differentiate the original Webster from others is that the Springfield company does copyright "Merriam" usually found on the cover, title page, and verso as "A Merriam-Webster." See Robert Leavitt, *Noah's Ark* (Springfield, Mass.: G&C Merriam Company, 1947). The study was written to mark the

hundredth anniversary (1947) of the first Webster dictionary under the imprint of G&C Merriam.

85. For a collection of comments about the new descriptive policy, see James H. Sledd, *Dictionaries and That Dictionary* (Chicago: Scott, Foresman, 1962).

86. Sidney Landau, *Dictionaries* (New York: Charles Scribner's, 1984), 15. A former Funk & Wagnalls editor and experienced lexicographer, Landau equally is a witty, informative writer. His guide to dictionaries is one of the best.

In retrospect, lexicographers agree that "when we examine the evidence that the characteristic shape of the American dictionary of the English language as it developed in the nineteenth century owes at least as much to Joseph Worcester as to Noah Webster . . . Worcester's neatness, precision, caution, moderation, and elegance, together with his handling of synonym and of such things as divided usage and idiomatic phrases, clearly influence" Webster dictionaries. Joseph Friend, *The Development of American Lexicography: 1789–1864.* (The Hague: Mouton, 1967), 102–3.

87. Between Samuel Johnson and the *Oxford English Dictionary,* English lexicographers have tended to avoid reliance on encyclopedic information in dictionaries. Today "American dictionaries contain much more outside matter than the dictionaries" of other countries. In Webster's first effort there were numerous appendices. His rival, Joseph Worcester, followed the same procedure. "This was truly populist lexicography aimed at informing the common reader who often only had two books at his disposal: a Bible and a dictionary." Margaret Cop, "Linguistic and Encyclopedic Information Not Included in the Dictionary Articles," in *Worterbucher,* vol. 1, 761.

88. Funk (1839–1912) was a Lutheran pastor and a supporter of the Prohibition party. He founded the firm with Adam Wagnalls (1843–1912). The unabridged work is out of print, having been withdrawn in the late 1970s. Desk and college dictionaries with the Funk & Wagnalls name appear occasionally and are distributed by other publishers. All of these works are dated. A floppy-disk edition was published in 1988, but it, too, is dated.

89. Kenneth Kister, *Kister's Best Dictionaries for Adults & Young People, A Comparative Guide* (Phoenix, Ariz.: Oryx Press, 1992), xvii. By and large, the best critical discussion of these and 300 other dictionaries are to be found in this Kister's basic guide. Thomas Kabdebo lists more than forty-five hundred titles by subject in his *Dictionary of Dictionaries* (London: Bowker-Saur, 1992).

The number of English-language dictionaries today is impressive. And technical, special, scholarly, and other than general titles and the number climbs rapidly. A search of OCLC, RLIN, or other networks will show close to fourteen thousand English-language dictionaries available, although many, to be sure, are now out of print.

Subject dictionaries, or glossaries as they were known, vastly outnumber the general form. Political language, for example, is the target for numerous satirical dictionaries. Examples from the early 1990s include Henry Beard, *The Official Politically Correct Dictionary;* Edward Herman, *Beyond Hypocrisy;* and Norman Solomon, *The Power of Babble.* Before them one finds a long line of examples extending back to the early nineteenth century includes Ambrose Bierce and his *The Devil's Dictionary,* Mark Twain, H.L. Mencken, James Thurber, George Orwell, and Russell Baker.

90. Landau, *Dictionaries,* 15.

91. The first general dictionary compiled with the aid of a computer was the 1965 edition of the *Random House Dictionary of the English Language.* After that the computer became as common as the pen or typewriter in compilations. "Computers have been used extensively in all phases of the preparation and composition of the more than one hundred dictionaries and other reference books edited, written, or compiled by me or under my direction since." Letter to the editor by Laurence Urdang, editor of the 1965 Random House edition, in *The Times Literary Supplement,* 7 January 1994, p. 13.

92. D.R. Tallentire, "The Mathematics of Style," *The Times Literary Supplement,* 13 August 1971, p. 973.

93. Ibid.

94. Lisa Jardine, *Erasmus Man of Letters* (Princeton, N.J.: Princeton University Press, 1993), 63. Jardine is paraphrasing Erasmus.

95. Grammar (from the Greek *gramma,* letter) was the art of proper reading and writing, which was the primary concern of grammar lessons for the Greeks and Romans. Only later did it become broader in scope. Linguists generally agree that languages as diverse as English and Armenian descend from Proto-Indo-European, spoken some five to six thousand years ago. The genealogical chart, which developed from the basic tongue, can be divided some 34 million ways, but a simple schematic tree form normally is in 10 parts and shows how the descendants of the original Indo—Europeans might have spread across Europe and Asia. Little is known about Egyptian or Mesopotamian grammar, primarily because the West showed no interest in the subject other than when studying the various area languages. On the other hand, India and Sanskrit tradition has had a major impact on tracing the history of the European languages.

96. *The Oxford Classical Dictionary,* p. 352.

97. Loeb Classical Library Volume, vol. 1, *Remains of Old Latin* (Cambridge: Harvard University Press, 1935), xvii.

98. The popularity of Donatus is testified to by the number of copies found in Medieval libraries. Few reference works were found so often in so many libraries.

99. Donatus became famous equally for his commentary on Terence and Virgil. The latter is missing, but Servius quoted so much of it that the so-called *Servius Danielis* is virtually the whole of the Virgil commentary.

100. Priscian cited numerous lesser-known writers as well. As a result, many Greek and Latin authors are known today only through quotations and examples in his grammar. In fact, numerous Medieval authors who cited classical works probably knew them only through Priscian and not through direct reading of the classics he cited.

101. Between the thirteenth and fourteenth centuries, the favored grammars (Donatus and Priscian aside) were known as *modistae.* For example, a common title was *De Modis Significandi Tractatus* (*Treatise Concerning the Modes of Signifying*). While each title varied, there was a common goal to include grammar in the account of universal knowledge. The authors made the case that grammar was a separate discipline that was to be valued for the light it would shed on metaphysics, logic, etc. Grammar was a speculum, or mirror, that reflected the underlying fundamentals of language and knowledge. Highly theoretical and speculative, these grammars had little influence on the mainstream, although they became part of the university curriculum. At any rate, they rarely achieved the place of reference works.

102. Bolgar, *The Classical Heritage,* 232.

103. In a few monastic communities, the vernacular was considered and one of the oldest vernacular grammars is the Irish *The Scholar's Primer,* probably compiled in the eighth century. The first extant Latin grammar written in the vernacular was the work of Ælfric (c. 1000), abbot of Eynsham, and was designed for English schools. It was written in Old English. R.B. Robins, "The Evolution of English Grammar Books Since the Renaissance," in *The English Reference Grammar,* ed. Graham Leitner, (Tübingen: Max Niemeyer, 1986), 282. Since the sixteenth century, the writing of English grammars has enjoyed a long tradition.

104. Greek continued to be the dominant language in the Byzantine Empire. As the Empire became smaller and then expanded, it was found that Greek was a rapidly disappearing language. Teachers were forced to compile Greek grammars, usually with examples from the Bible and classical Greek authors. In fact, almost all of the Byzantine grammars were elementary textbooks, often based on the style of Apollonious Dyskolos (Dyscolus). During the early Renaissance, these grammars became somewhat popular in Europe when scholars rediscovered Greek.

105. *Encyclopaedia Britannica,* vol. 23 (Chicago: Britannica, 1993), 42.

106. In 1906, *The King's English* appeared, the first joint effort of Henry and Francis Fowler. After the death of Francis, Henry Fowler compiled *A Dictionary of Modern English Usage* (1926), which under various editors has become one of the standard reference grammars of the day.

107. Emma Vorlat, *The Development of English Grammatical Theory 1586–1737* (Leuven, Belgium: Leuven University Press, 1975). This detailed history considers Lily as well as his numerous rivals and grammatical developments over the period covered.

108. Henry Alford, *The Queen's English: Stray Notes on Speaking and*

Spelling (London: Strahan, 1864) and Richard White, *Words and Their Uses, Past and Present* (Houghton, Mifflin, 1871).

109. John Algeo, "American English Grammars in the Twentieth Century," 119. A more modern English approach, which transcends national boundaries, is Randolph Quirk, *A Comprehensive Grammar of the English Language* (London: Longman, 1985).

110. Robert Burchfield, "The Fowler Brothers and the Tradition of Usage Handbooks," in *The English Reference Grammar,* ed. Leitner. The early twentieth century grammars were published as follows: William Corbett, *Grammar of the English Language* (New York: Appleton, 1818); Henry Mencken, *The American Language* (New York: Knopf, 1919); George Curme, *A Grammar of the English Language,* 2 vols. (Boston: Heath, 1931, 1938).

111. A "rhetorical question," for example, is a query for effect with no answer expected, favored by orators and politicians. In an average book of synonyms, or thesaurus, rhetoric is equated with such words as bombast, windy, florid, flowery, overblown, pompous, glib, exaggerated, etc. Contrasted words also tell much about a notion, and the current contrasts of rhetoric are plain, unadorned, literal, homely, etc.

112. Thomas Conley, *Rhetoric in the European Tradition* (London: Longman, 1990. Republished in 1995 by the University of Chicago Press). This volume is the outstanding history of the subject in English and is indicative of the new appreciation of rhetoric as the foundation stone for such modern studies as semiotics and poststructuralism.

113. The Sophists became extremely powerful in the educational system of early Athens; today the term "sophist" refers to specious argument because of the bad mess they received from Plato and other contemporary philosophers.

114. *The Oxford Classical Dictionary,* 74.

115. This is so similar in style and tone to Cicero, that for 1500 years it was thought Cicero wrote the work. Later evidence proves this is not the case.

116. The influence of Cicero's *De inventione* and *Rhetorica ad Herennium* in the Middle Ages can be judged by the fact there are over 600 separate, extant commentaries on these works. Even here, though, there are visible influences of dialectic and grammar, particularly after the twelfth century.

117. As Quintillian discusses everything from memory to gesture and dress, the book proved of great use to future actors. Rules for delivery appear as late as the seventeenth century, and taken almost directly from Quintillian, in John Bulwer's *Chironomia and Chirologia* (1644). While the book enjoyed only a limited audience in his time and through the Middle Ages, it became popular in the Renaissance as an educational guide. Interestingly enough, the Roman stopped short of deploring the use of rhetoric

to avoid the truth as well as censoring those who employed the art with less than integrity. The paradox was ducked, although the implication was certain—truth and eloquence did not necessarily join as brothers.

118. Plato wanted to banish all mimetic poetry, i.e. poetry which in tragedy, comedy and epic reproduces emotions—including evil and the base. In Plato's *Republic* the only poetry allowed, because it will not adversely effect readers/listeners, are hymns to the gods and songs in praise of the good person.

119. *Dictionary of the Middle Ages. op. cit.* Vol. 10, 361–362.

120. Today Geoffrey's book is useful in that he has numerous verse examples, some of which are no longer extant other than in his manual. The good to excellent literary examples, of course, accounts in no small way for its popularity during the Middle Ages.

121. Anthony Grafton. *Defenders of the Text.* Cambridge, MA: Harvard University Press, 1991, p. 31. A major argument was whether to go to the classics. For example, should Christian morals be read into pagan texts? Should fifteenth and sixteenth century attitudes towards freedom, government and education be laid over the interpretation of the Greeks? Also, there was the question of the proper canon. Which of classical writers were important, less important etc. If all of this sounds a familiar modern struggle in philosophy and literature departments, Grafton is aware of the similarity. "We too seek both to interpret texts historically and to make them accessible as classics in the present. What felt and unfelt contradictions will our readers—if we find any—perceive in our humanism?" (p. 46)

122. The primary voices of the New Philosophy were Descarte, Hobbes and Locke as well as such writers as Jonathan Swift.

123. Letter 247, March, 1751.

124. Conley, *op. cit.,* p. 236.

125. The study of language is at the heart of today's university rhetoric courses, e.g. I.A. Richards' *The Meaning of Meaning* (1923); Kenneth Burke's *Rhetoric of Motive* (1950) are two classics in the field and used still in numerous universities.

7

Maps and Travel Guides

Maps become a source to reveal the philosophical, political, or religious outlook of a period, or what is sometimes called the spirit of the age. . . . The essence of iconographical analysis is that it seeks to uncover different layers of meaning within the image . . . Maps, once we learn how to read them, can become uniquely rewarding texts."[1]

Maps, and from day to day point of use, atlases, have played an important part in reference services. Today almost all computer programs, from CD-ROMs to Internet, include various types of maps sites. Even automobiles now have miniature television guides which lead the driver from street X to street Y, or from city to city. In a library, maps may be treated separately from atlases or become part of the larger geography unit in the reference section. Derived from the Greek words "geo" and "graphien," i.e. "the earth" and "to write," geography is the study of the earth's surface. It is a discipline as well known to the grade school student as the the cartographer.[2]

A combination of graphics and reference points, a map is so familiar as to hardly need definition,[3] but they may be divided in several ways: (1) *Atlases,* a collection of maps in one or more volumes and so called as Atlas was the god who held up the pillars of the universe and his name was given the form by Mercator's early collection of maps in the mid sixteenth century. (2) *Chart,* a map usually designed for navigation by sea or by space flight. This type of map appeared first in the early thirteenth century. (3) *Thematic* maps are designed to show a certain subject from population to climate. A related version is the historical map which traces the routes of armies and the changes in borders from the beginning of recorded time to the present.

Historically there have been several basic types of maps. The first, a limited area map, was usually based on the first hand observation, exploration and careful measurement. This served needs of locals to accurately understand a small area. A more ambitious cousin to this type was the navigational chart of seafarers. The continent or world map might be based as much on guess and mythology as on scientific theory. Only by the end of the nineteenth century could it be claimed that the globe was accurately mapped,[4] although even to this day that world map is being refined and added to by satellite observations tied to computers.

The author or authors of maps are sometimes difficult to isolate. Most maps are a product of numerous people. A surveyor, an engraver, an editor, a draftsman, a cartographer . . . all, or one may be the author of the finished map. Sometimes, but not often, the individuals are identified separately. Usually it is indicated as the work of a single publisher.

Most early maps, i.e. from the Greek until the sixteenth century, are lost.[5] Any generalizations based on the few surviving examples is perilous, and at best only indicative of probable trends in cartography. Even with the beginning of the age of discovery in the fifteenth century, only a few charts and maps survive. This is striking as many more must have been employed, if only by seamen. Columbus, for example, used at least four maps in his voyage to America, but only one is extant—a rough sketch of a coast. Furthermore, "many libraries and collections were not in the habit of preserving obsolete maps . . . (which) were considered to be ephemeral."[6] This attitude continued well past the Renaissance and explains why even "the large and beautiful maps of the sixteenth and seventeenth centuries are now so rare."[7] Only after Richard Gough published his *British Topography* (1780), followed by similar books in the next 50 years, was interest aroused in the collecting of maps and atlases.

Unlike most reference works, maps and atlases are promising decorations which often tempt thieves. The most valuable, with some notable exceptions, are maps published from the mid to late sixteenth century through the mid nineteenth century, and of these the work of the Dutch mapmakers, from about 1570 to 1670, are the most treasured. Collecting is made easier because antique maps are well documented. There are numerous reference works which list mapmakers, their works and their value.[8]

Early Maps

The earliest extant examples of cartography are found in the Babylonian clay tablet maps of about 2300 B.C. Actually, the making of maps probably goes back much further, and rough maps may have been a part of the equipment of early hunters and farmers from 9,000 or 3,000 B.C., if not earlier. No examples of this period survived, although markings on cave walls, which may be dated as early as 20,000 to 14,000 B.C., possibly represent game trails of animals and early peoples.

Still, the earliest specimen of maps are the Babylonian tablets. They are matched by map drawings and paintings of a similar characteristic found in Egyptian tombs. Both in Mesopotamia and Egypt the primary concern was the agriculture. Mapping land features included fertile areas to roads and locations of religious structures. Interestingly enough, the Middle Easterners were concerned only with immediate areas, and there is little evidence of mapping on a larger scale. The only exception seems to be a Babylonian tablet (c. 1,000 B.C.) which shows the known earth as a disk, surrounded by water with, as might be imagined, Babylonia in the center.

Egyptian inscriptions, such as one dated c. 1493 B.C. indicates maps were widely used for military campaigns and exploration. Herodotus claims the Egyptian campaigns of about 1400 B.C. were mapped in detail. The Egyptians were skilled in geometry and astronomy, which indicates they were probably masters at cartography, particularly land surveying.[9]

Greeks to Ptolemy

The Greeks, particularly when they took to the seas, relied on maps, none of which have survived.[10] On the coast of Turkey there appears to have been a Greek map center as early as the sixth century B.C. Herodotus about a century later often mentions maps and charts in his history, and in Aristophanes (c. 448–380 B.C.) play *The Clouds* (423 B.C.) the characters point to a map of the world with Athens in a prominent place. One to two hundred years later Greek literature is dotted with references not only to maps, but to globes, although, again, none is extant.

The first cosmographer to develop a theory of the earth and how it relates to the greater universe was the Greek astronomer and geographer Anaximander (fl. sixth century B.C.).[11] He made a map of the world, which apparently was used for centuries, but no copies have survived.

Pythagoras (c. 580–500 B.C.) is credited with being the first Greek to describe the world as spherical. The theory was accepted throughout classical history.[12] The Greeks envisioned two polar zones, as well as arbitrary subdivisions by other zones which confused geographers until well after the age of discovery beginning in the fifteenth century. Alexandria by 200 B.C. was the home of numerous scholars who charted geographical paths followed until well into the Renaissance. Among the primary figures: A student of Aristotle, Dicaerchus (c. 326–296 B.C.) was the first to establish the parallel of latitude and longitude. He was equally an early biographer (particularly of Homer and the Greek dramatists), a philosopher and an historian who made the first attempt at an early history of culture. The boundaries of Dicaerchus description were Gibraltar and the Himalayas with an assumed ocean in the eastern part of the world. Despite this early development, it was not until the first part of the sixteenth century that Portuguese cartographer constructed navigational maps which took into consideration the earth's curvature and convergence of meridians. Only from about 1500 did latitude graduation appear, with longitude graduation about 20 to 30 years later.

Eratosthenes (276–194 B.C.) determined the circumference of the earth, and his result (approximately 25,000 geographical miles) was close to accurate. Unfortunately he was overruled by the findings of Posidonius (130–50 B.C.) who came in with a figure much smaller than the actual circumference.

Hipparchus (fl. about 140 B.C.) divided the earth into 360 degrees and lined the globe surface with parallels of latitudes and meridians of longitude. In addition he invented and improved on the astrolabe which gave early navigators a relatively accurate way of shooting the sun and determining their position. (The instrument was used until the days of Drake.)[13]

Herodotus (c. 484–425 B.C.) had little but scorn for map makers. "I cannot help laughing at the absurdity of all the map-makers—there are plenty of them—who show ocean running like a river round a perfectly circular earth, with Asia and Europe of the same size. He then proceeds to describe "the size and shape of these two (Asia and Europe) continents."[14]

Compared with Greece, Rome did little to improve geographical thought and cartography. Tied to the practical and the pragmatic, the Romans turned away from the Greek philosophical and scientific wanderings about the globe. Romans tended to concentrate on getting from point A to point B in their expanding empire. The result was maps which showed roads and sea routes, primarily of the Mediterranean areas and of Europe.[15] City and town plans, as well as surveyor's maps equally were common.

The only outstanding Roman geographer was, in fact, a Greek—Strabo (64 B.C.–20 A.D.). Most knowledge about Roman and Greek geographers comes from Strabo. About 20 B.C. he published *Geography* which is an account of early writers on the subject.[16] His combination political encyclopedia and gazette stressed facts useful to a military commander or a province governor. He seems to have had little immediate impact. His name is not found in Roman literature and appears again only when rediscovered in the Renaissance.[17]

Marinus of Tyre (fl. early second century A.D.) established a pattern of interest in explorers and their voyages. He is among the first in Alexandria to interview mariners in order to learn practical knowledge about navigation from East Africa to the Indian Ocean. Marinus, at least today, is best remembered for the accident of having Ptolemy as a student.

Ptolemy (c. 90–168 A.D.) was the Greco-Egyptian mathematician who proved to be the last great astronomer before the Renaissance, and Copernicus (1473–1543). He is a key figure in the development of maps. His eight volume *Geography* remained useful until well into the sixteenth century. The first volume offers a general discussion of principles of map and globe construction. In the next six volumes there are over 8,000 place names with their approximate latitudes and longitudes. Most of these were obtained from older, now lost maps, and are relatively accurate. In the eighth, and most important of the volumes, Ptolemy gives specific instructions on the mathematics and other principles of drawing maps as well as other aspects of then known cartography.[18] Unfortunately, all of the Alexandrian scientists maps were lost, and the earliest extant examples are from the fifteenth century. Europe had to wait until the time of Columbus and daGama for the *Geography* to reach Western universities.

Ptolemy is noteworthy for eliminating myth and speculation. Even Plato's lost Atlantis—somewhere in the Western Ocean—is deleted. "For all his intellectual honesty Ptolemy paid the penalty for his errors and his fame, and the explorers of the Renaissance too often had to unlearn what he had taught them and then learn all over again, the hard way."[19] The numerous inaccuracies, such as showing Europe and Asia covering one half the globe, was confusing to early explorers. Columbus, for example, some 13 centuries later, confused the shape and size of the world, as well as distances, by putting too much trust in Ptolemy's work.

The Islamic geographer Edrisi (1100–1166 A.D.) is typical of the scholarly Moors and it was he who updated Ptolemy. Interestingly enough Ptolemy's astronomical treatises, known to the Arabs as the *Almagest* (the greatest) was translated from the Arabic earlier.[20] By the mid-thirteenth century it became a practical handbook of seamanship under the name of *Sphaera Mundi*. "It grew to be one of the best known and most useful books of all time; many manuscript copies have survived, while upwards to thirty incunabula editions testify to its popularity in the Columbia period."[21]

Medieval Maps

With the fall of Rome, the Church put Biblical interpretation ahead of cartography. This resulted in the theory of a flat earth with the Garden of Eden and Paradise just out of reach of humans. In the sixth century Christians formulated a map based almost entirely on the Bible. Here the earth is flat and follows the pattern of the by then familiar T-and-O maps which show the earth as a disk (O) and then subdivide it into contents with bars (T). Usually it was limited to the Mediterranean, the Nile, and bits of Russia and Europe. The primary exponent of these views was a monk who should have known better. This Christian cosmographer was Cosmas Indicopleustes (i.e. Indian traveler, fl. 540 A.D.) whose map of the world includes Paradise set off from men by an impassable Ocean Stream.[22] (Others who drew similar maps placed Paradise in the visible world, but surrounded by impenetrable barriers.) Cosmas traveled extensively in the Middle East, but seems to have drawn most of his material for his *Christian Topography* from native scriptural interpretation rather than from earlier Greek and Roman scientists. Despite the name of "Indian traveler," and despite his claims to have visited India, this is highly unlikely. He did know Ethiopia and Persia, as well as the lands around the Red Sea, but not much further east. The result is his book has an astonishing mass of misinformation of men and beasts, as well as places. "Geography in the hands of literate Christians was the most wonderful of medieval sciences, excessively rich in meaning but far poorer than pagan geography in empirical mathematical data."[23]

Isidore of Seville's (c. 560–636) section in his encyclopedia on geography was quoted and paraphrased throughout the Middle Ages. Most commentaries, including poems and treatises on geography, depended upon Isidore. Other sources were from parts of larger works by the Venerable Bede (c. 673–735) (*Ecclesiastica History*); and Orosius (fl. 414–417) (*Liber Glossarum*). Much of this copying, was due to the lack of travel or any trade in Europe. The average scholar's notion of geography was what was found in earlier books. Science had little to do with maps, and often a Christian cosmographer overlooked or ignored earlier findings.[24]

Despite numerous references to maps, only a handful have survived before the eleventh century. Of these the so called "Albi map" (preserved in Albi, France) was drawn about 750 A.D. and is the earliest extant map of western Europe. Nothing is known of its origin, but it gives a fair idea of how Europeans saw their home in the mid-eighth century. About the end of the seventh century a map drawn at Ravenna shows the earth as far east as India; and by the eighth century maps extended eastward to Ceylon. In the ninth century maps of western Europe were broadly accurate, but failed miserably in details. With the advent of the sea charts, the Church began to update its cartography and by the fourteenth century a movement was underway to bring the Church in line with current scientific findings.

While a handful of early Christian maps are available, no trace remains of secular cartography much before the thirteenth century. Charlemagne (724–814) apparently had numerous maps, but these were destroyed or disappeared.[25]

Two thirteenth century scholars, Albertus Magnus (c. 1200–1280) and Roger Bacon (1214–1294) postulated several minor, wrong geographical theories, but between Bacon's death and the early fifteenth century there were no impressive geographical studies. This is amazing in that it was the period of the major medieval journeys, including the Polos and their successors. Cardinal Pierre d'Ailly (1350–1420) shattered the silent lack of interest with his *Imago Mundi* a major world geography and his *Cosmographiae Tractatus Duo*. Primarily drawn from other earlier writers, both of his works offered little new material, but the compilations did strongly influence Columbus who apparently kept the *Imago Mundi* as bedside reading.

Sea Charts

Scandinavian exploration and raids began by the beginning of the eighth century. By the middle of the next century Vikings had settled in Ireland,

Spain and many sections of Europe. While they left no maps or guidebooks, the Viking were pioneers in geographical discovery as well as primary players in the better known role of raiders and colonizers in much of Europe. The Viking sagas, reliable in detail or not, at least indicate the westward voyages across the North Atlantic from Greenland to the coast of North America.[26]

In 1187 there is the first record of a magnetic compass in Europe, and with that the navigators were given an opportunity to map, if not the world, the major known sea routes.[27] By the Eighth Crusade (1270) there is at least one reference to a sea chart, and a few years later (c. 1275) the first extant Medieval chart was saved for history. This is known as the "Carta Pisana" (found in Pisa) which is a hand drawn map of the entire Mediterranean Sea.[28] Updated, revised and improved by seamen and pilots who moved about the Mediterranean, the charts gradually became more precise and reliable for navigation. The essential problem was that each map was hand drawn and methods of rapid, accurate reproduction were not available until well after the invention of printing and wide use of engraving in the fifteenth century.[29]

Unquestionably, the actual experience of seamen was the single greatest influence on the late Medieval and early Renaissance maps.[30] There was a burgeoning of data as the explorers pushed beyond Europe and the Mediterranean. By the mid-fourteenth century there was a growing interest in Africa, particularly by missionaries. Marco Polo sparked trade with the Far East and China after the description of his travels. The so called "age of discovery" was at hand and the horizons of geographical knowledge were expanded dramatically in the Renaissance.

Until the middle of the thirteenth century no European had traveled much beyond Baghdad, and it wasn't until 1234 that a Franciscan monk, sent by the Pope, was the first European to explore the Mongol Empire in Central Asia and China. Kubla Khan removed the capital to Peking and by about 1256 he welcomed the brothers Polo. By 1292 and their return to Venice, other travelers and merchants followed routes from the Near East to the Chinese capital. Although virtually unknown to each other until the thirteenth century, Europe and China (as well as India) had been trading for centuries before through Near Eastern ports. The conquests of Gengis Khan from Mongolia to the Danube in 1241 changed all of that. After the mid thirteenth century the Golden Horde withdrew and in their wake merchants began to foster trade with China and India. Knowledge of the Great Khan and his court was brought back first by Franciscan friars, sent on a diplomatic mission by the Pope. After his travels from 1245 through 1247, the friar was followed by other priests. The exploration culminated with Marco Polo's travels from Venice to the court of Kublai Khan from 1271 to 1275. Polo and his party stayed in China for 17 years and he explored most of the area from Tibet to Burma. After his return in 1295 he served with a

Venetian force, was captured by Genoan troops and while in a Genoa prison he dictated his Description of the World (later known as *Travels of Marco Polo*) to an imaginative writer.[31] Thanks to the book's exaggerated description of wealth in China and other Asian realms, individuals and governments sought routes to China, and even Columbus, several centuries later studied the *Travels* for sea route possibilities.

Neither Polo nor the ghost writer of the *Travels* drew any maps, but cartographers used the *Travels* to devise new maps Polo described. An outstanding example of this is the so called *Catalan Atlas,* assembled in 1375, which shows Polo's route across Asia with numerous figures and animals.[32] By late thirteenth and early fourteenth century, the Great Silk Road was crossed and criss-crossed by European merchants. In 1378–1370 the Tartars were driven out of China and replaced by the Mings who, once again, closed the country to foreigners. "The direct trade came to an end by the middle of the fourteenth century and the great black curtain rolled down again, cutting all Europe and Asia and confining Europeans once again to the termini of the trade routes."[33]

Neither a cartographer or explorer, Henry the Navigator (1394–1460) of Portugal launched the era of seagoing European exploration by financially supporting the work of others. The Prince of Portugal established a type of geographer's think tank which supported exploration and mapmakers. He directly and indirectly set explorers to Africa and set in motion the travels of Vasco daGama (1460–1524) around Africa to India. This voyage overturned the idea of Ptolemy that the Indian Ocean was similar to the Mediterranean. By 1508 a published map showed an accurate picture of southern Africa and the Indian Ocean as charted by daGama. The cartographers of the early Renaissance applied portolian principles to coast lines revealed by the great discoverer. The first extant example is a chart, dated 1448 which shows the African coast and ports from England southward.

The only early surviving printed chart for use by navigators was published in 1539. The woodcut chart of the eastern Mediterranean was compiled in Venice from reports of pilots and navigators.

Another type of manual was the so called "sea book." This offered navigators sailing directions, specific routes, and descriptions of countries, seaports and areas. Most, from the second half of the fifteenth century, were illustrated, usually with rough maps. However it was not until 1544 that a sea book appears with both charts and coastal views. After the mid-sixteenth century the manual always included one or more illustrated sea charts. "The process led by an easy transition to the first printed sea-atlas . . . by Plantin in 1584–1585. . . . [printing] marked an epoch in nautical cartography. Not only did it eliminate, or at least reduce, the risk of copyists' errors in the charts; it also introduced a wide range of representational symbols, in forms still used today . . . soundings, reefs and hazards, leading lines, navigational marks, anchorages."[34]

Renaissance Maps & Atlases

The geographical Renaissance may be dated approximately from 1410 when a manuscript Latin version of Ptolemy's *Geography* became available in the West. Jacobus Angelus in 1406–1410 reintroduced Europe to Ptolemy. "Its discovery must have created a stir then that the discovery of a missing play by Shakespeare would now . . . Ptolemy's fundamental principle of geography was the accurate fixing of positions by latitude and longitude."[35] The majority of extant map incunabula constitutes various edition of the Ptolemaic atlas, beginning with a 1477 Bologna edition. Although probably no more than 500 copies were made of any edition of Ptolemy in the fifteenth century, he strongly influenced geographical ideas and cartographic advancement. The ancient work became the prototype for maps of the world, as well of individual countries and Europe for most of the century, and well into the sixteenth century as well.

The convergence of Renaissance classical discoveries, improvements in the sciences, newer and better constructed ships, as well as subtle navigational instruments resulted in the continuous improvement in maps—particularly to meet the needs of the great voyages of discovery during the fifteenth and sixteenth centuries. By 1512 the traditional publication of Ptolemy's *Geographica* treatise saw numerous additions, including more than 20 modern, engraved maps of Europe. The maps were corrected and revised with each new discovery, each new voyage. They became increasingly accurate, increasingly representative of the true world.

Before the Renaissance the map was more symbolic than real, more an idealized version of the world as seen from the Mediterranean (Ptolemy) or from the pulpit (the T-O Christian maps). The printing press allowed comparisons of maps throughout Europe. Editing and corrections paralleled advances in astronomy and mathematics. The result was a succession of maps between the late fifteenth and early seventeenth century which put Europe, Africa, India and much of the rest of the world in correct focus.

Printing and sophisticated engraving tools and methods made it possible by the sixteenth century to publish maps which were not only more accurate, but considerably more esthetic than anything heretofore available. Moving gradually from woodcuts to copper engravings, cartographers were able to produce very fine impressions. The process was employed until well into the twentieth century when photolithography and later computer printouts made even more precise maps possible. Still, nothing surpasses the sheer beauty of the sixteenth and seventeenth century maps and atlases.

By the sixteenth century cartography was almost a science, and certainly popular among laypersons who collected world maps as well as ordered surveys of the local terrain. In 1513 appeared the first cousin to the printed atlas, a collection of maps based on Ptolemy. In 1579 Christopher Saxon completed the first national compilation of regional maps which were widely used and copied. If Europe was more or less mapped by the close of the sixteenth century, the remainder of the world was in constant flux between new exploration and new approaches to cartography.

Independent publishers and cartographers suddenly appeared in quantity, particularly among the Mediterranean cities. Primarily involved with nautical charts, they set the pattern for such things as graduation in longitude (c. 1520). Thanks to Venice being the center of trade map publishing cartography was highly developed. It reached its zenith in the works of Giacomo Gastaldi (c. 1500–1565). He made over 200 maps which circulated throughout Europe. He appears to have had a strong influence on the two Dutch cartographers, Ortelius and Mercator. In the world of reference his major claim to fame is that in 1548 he produced the first world atlas in pocket size format.

Gradually geographical manuals and textbooks, called *Cosmographiae* began to appear. This featured geographical and related information on history and the natural sciences. Most included elaborate maps and illustrations. The genre pattern was set first by Peter Apian (1495–1552) who in 1524 issued the best known of the Cosmographiae title *Cosmographicus Liber.* The professor of mathematics in Vienna had the advantage of owning his own printing press and publishing his own texts. His 1534 title gained immediate popularity and went to over 15 editions. For many decades the book, updated with triangulation surveying methods in 1533, was the standard handbook for geographers as well as surveyors.

Sebastian Munster (c. 1448–1552) was another popular publisher of geographic manuals. His *Cosmography,* first published in 1544, was among the largest and most elaborate. It equally was among the more authoritative, probably because first and foremost the German was a scholar who was as interested in translations as in geography and mapmaking. (He published the first German Bible translated from the Hebrew). Because they were recognized as being so accurate, at least for the time, Munster's maps were reprinted, and copied throughout Europe. They strongly influenced the standard decorating scheme of maps and atlases. Munster filled all the blank spaces in each separate map of a continent with design from shipwrecks to kings and mystical races, including one eyed and one legged persons.

The Americas

Maps followed the explorers, and for every great voyage of discovery there came massive changes in the local and world maps. One example is the name of America and the voyages of Columbus. Christopher Columbus (1451–1506) greatly misjudged distances and locations, and was probably years behind the Vikings in the discovery of America. When he did make a landfall here he thought he was in the Indies, a short distance from China and Japan. Despite four voyages he never gave up the idea of the Indies. Unfortunately the only surviving map is one he sketched of the northwestern coast of what is now Haiti and the Dominican Republic.

Amerigo Vespucci's (1454–1512) name was fixed to North and South America by Martin Waldeseemuller (1470–1518). Vespucci was a Florentine sent by the Spanish crown in 1497 to what is now Haiti (i.e. Hispaniola) to investigate Columbus. After other exploration trips Vespucci circulated a letter about this travels called "The New World" in which he pointed out that Columbus had found new lands, not the Indies. In 1507 Waldseemuller published his *Introduction to Cosmography* in which he proposed the new land be named after Vespucci, i.e. America (a Latin form of Amerigo).[36] Peter Martyr printed the first accurate map of both the Americas in 1534. The so called *Ramusio Map* experimented with the problem of projecting a sphere on a flat plane by using a cylindrical equidistant projection.

In 1511 Waldeseemuller produced a map of Europe, the first which was relatively accurate and free of Christian map maker tradition as well as corrective of the Ptolemaic influence. This was issued and reissued and culminated by mid-century in the work of Mercator.

The Map as Art: Ortelius and Mercator

In describing the world map of Pierre Descelier (1550) a critic indicates what makes many maps so captivating, so much a work of art: "The map glows with colour: coats of arms, wind-roses, ships, trees, habitations, animals imaginary or half-understood, all wonders of delicate complexity. The numerous human figures are the same mixture of legend and unreliable reports as the beasts. Here are Amazons (in Russia) and pygmies fighting cranes (in Canada)."[37]

In the sixteenth century Dutch mapmakers, and particularly Abraham Ortelius (1527–1598) and Gerard Mercator (1512–1594), dominated map publishing. They had few rivals in Europe. The Dutch not only published what are now considered works of art, but, more important, scientifically accurate maps and charts based on contemporary voyages and scientific discoveries.

Belgian born Gerard Mercator (1512–1594) in 1569 produced the milestone in the history of cartography, the world map with the projection which bears his name. The great world chart of 18 sheets is one of the world's most famous maps. Mercator not only composed the works, but also engraved them. The projection did many things, but primarily allowed "straight" sailing on a uniform compass course. If the parallels of latitude were farther and farther apart as the poles were approached, if Greenland became the size of South America, Mercator's projection—faults and all—was a scientific distortion which revolutionized cartography.[38] Mercator, who is probably the only well known cartographer in the world, founded a family publishing empire. Under the protection of a nobleman, he avoided further religious persecution (he had been jailed as a heretic in 1544). With his death the business went to his son Rumold, and then on to nephews who sold the firm in 1606. Using the Mercator copper plates the partners who bought out the family, continued to issue maps for decades.

Atlas and Globe

An atlas is defined simply as a bound collection of maps, usually with an index of place names. Depending on how elaborate the publication, various amounts of related geographical materials from photographs and charts to encyclopedic texts will be included. The expansion of geographical skills and knowledge during the sixteenth century resulted in the rapid growth of wall maps of the world (few of which are extant) and more important the development of the atlas, usually constructed from collections of sheet maps.[39]

Martin Behaim (c. 1436–1507) of Nuremberg is credited with the construction of the first known extant terrestrial globe in 1492, and this was the beginning of a minor industry from that time onward. Behaim's globe was constructed from a wooden sphere to which was pasted painted parchment map sections in six colors by another artist. Featuring over 1,000 place names, it was completed in 1492 about the time Columbus set sail. The globe particularly is of interest because it shows the world Columbus must have envisioned before his voyage . . . including the contemporary view that the Atlantic separated the west coast of Europe from the eastern side of Asia.

Ptolemy was put to rest in the mid-sixteenth century by one of the world's most famous cartographers, Abraham Ortelius. In 1570 his history making *Theatrum Orbis Terrarum* (Theatre of the world) appeared in Antwerp. In Latin and a half dozen European languages it went through 40 editions before it ceased being the primary atlas of the period in about 1624. In the first edition there were 53 maps, and in the last 166. The period of cartographic incunabula, characterized by a slavish following of old doctrines and strongly influenced by Ptolemy, was closed. The new period trusted the knowledge of the earth to first hand exploration and scientific investigation rather than to the ancient classics.

As a trained engraver Ortelius derived his authority from others, but his distinctive artistic style marked maps from that point forward. Ortelius gained additional fame when appointed geographer to King Philip II of

Spain in 1575. He is particularly remembered by librarians for his pioneering work in the collecting and selling of maps and atlases. Ortelius can be said to be the first to show a considered interest in the collection and the preservation of maps. He lived in various places throughout Europe and at each place he purchased and sold maps.

The first time anyone used the term "atlas" in the title of a collection of maps was in 1585 when Mercator published his *Atlas sive Cosmographicae.* He followed the lead of Lafreri [see footnotes #39] and prefaced his collection with an engraving of Atlas holding up the world. Mercator's atlas was built around the modern notion of the form. He not only wished to include maps, but a good deal of text. The publication came out in parts, with the first section appearing in 1585, the second in 1589, and four months after Mercator's death, the complete work in 1595. The atlas became a best seller of sorts, and other mapmakers, in and out of Holland, recognized the importance of the atlas form.

Before the growth of nationalism, the sixteenth century cartographers demonstrated a remarkable objectivity. "Neither atlases or maps showed a Europe biased towards the West. Devoid of indications of national frontiers until late in the [sixteenth century], they were not devised to be read politically. And the busily even spread of town names did not suggest that western had any greater weight of economic vitality than eastern Europe."[40]

The atlas as a form captured the interest and imagination of people, and it became the dominant layperson's cartographic format. Some describe the seventeenth century as the age of atlases, primarily because not only were there numerous new works, but publishers had learned from Ortelius and Mercator how engraved plates might be used over and over again for various editions—thus improving profits, if not always the reliability of the atlas. Jodocus Hondius, for example, purchased the plates of the Mercator atlas and until 1637 published 40 different editions. While he did add descriptive texts, the maps themselves were little changed from the original 1595 work. (Ortelius' *Theatrum* continued to be printed until 1612, but then disappeared.)

A serious rival to the Mercator-Hondius atlas appeared in the person of Willem Blaeu (1571–1638). After studying astronomy, Blaeu took up the construction of scientific instruments in Amsterdam. From this he was led to an interest in maps, and in 1604 published the first of a series of maps of individual countries. He became famous for a world map which was published in 20 sheets and formed a map eight feet across. (Only one example is extant). He turned to atlases and in 1608 published the first atlas for seamen, updating this in 1623.[41] By 1630, using plates from the Hondius family, he issued his first general atlas. This was the beginning of what was to become the *Atlas Major* or *Grand Atlas* of 600 maps in 11 to 12 folio volumes—a work carried on by Blaeu's and his family and published in several languages between 1662 and 1663.

Not only was the Blaeu atlas one of a kind, but it became one of the most expensive books of any type published in the seventeenth century. Today individual maps from the volumes are sold at high prices because the Blaeu effort represents the height of the decorated map/atlas.[42] Each map was colored by hand and the margins had massive decorations from figures of the gods to natural history and astronomical signs. Then as now they are considered as much works of arts as accurate maps. And they were accurate in that the Blaeu atlas represented almost everything known about the world in the seventeenth century, including a relatively true depiction of China. Given the success of the atlas, a great number of other publishers entered the field. The engraved maps of this period, although rarely up to the quality or interest of Ortelius-Mercator-Blaeu continue to fascinate collectors and often make up a fascinating part of a library's rare book collections.

Until the mid eighteenth century printed atlases were too bulky, and much too expensive for the average person. An ingenious French geographer, Bruze de la Martiniere, published the answer in a pocket atlas of France in 1734. Thereafter, relatively inexpensive pocket atlases were common, often being little more than reductions of the larger, more ornamental titles.

John Ogilby (1600–1676) spent most of his life as a publisher of Greek classics, but in his late 60's he turned to map and atlas publishing. By 1675 he produced the first road map in the forms of strips (similar to the American Automobile Association's trip guides) on separate pages. The route could be followed, in the same scale, from strip to strip.

Eighteenth Century Cartography

Two major developments occurred in cartography during the eighteenth century—(1) careful attention to the scientific, accurate construction of maps; and, (2) a virtual end to the decorated map. By the close of the century, the traditional monsters, compass points, mermaids and the like had disappeared in the interests of scientific cartography.

Emphasis on accurate maps was the major change. Up until the advent of the highly trained cartographer, maps had been based as much on anecdotes of travelers as accurate soundings of sea pilots. Governments and companies now saw the need for reliable maps, particularly as better charting equipment was available from chronometers to accurate surveying tools.[43] One of the earliest recognitions of this major new turn in map production took place with the systematic mapping of countries anxious to establish definitive borders. Beyond that the same cartographers were sent out to construct maps of territories and newly explored areas. Wars or peace often turned on the skills of the cartographers, not to mention the political-land aspirations of the governments. Out of this developed today's ordnance surveys and government agencies such as the U.S. Geological Survey.[44]

England, during the eighteenth century, dominated the seas and much of the globe. The private and public sectors were willing to spend money on charting navigational routes as well as major world points where the English might trade or conquer. England became the dominant cartographic center, and it is no accident that the prime meridian for longitude reference now passes through Greenwich.

Nautical or often called "Admiralty Maps" were the great contribution of the eighteenth century. Commissioned by Northern Europeans in quest of trade, they were particularly accurate in matters nautical as well as in describing immediate surroundings of a particular port of anchorage. *The Atlantic Neptune* (London: 1774–1784) is an example of this type of collection, the six volume of charts offer detailed descriptions of most of the Atlantic coasts trade routes and centers.

In the late seventeenth and to the nineteenth century one family made great strides in measuring and surveying, which in turn facilitated more accurate reliable maps. The four generations of the Cassinis began with Jean (1625–1712) who was born in Italy but became a citizen of France. It ended with Jacques Cassini (1748–1845) who finished the first national French atlas in 1791, only to see it delayed because of the French Revolution. Finally, the *Topographic . . . Atlas of France* was published 1793 by the French Academy of Sciences. It set the pattern for all national atlases to follow, from surveys in India to the United States.

Mapping America

Native Americans seem to have drawn maps long before Europeans. Evidence of geographic knowledge comes from the Indians who proved to be experienced guides. Most European maps of America in the seventeenth and part of the eighteenth century are derived from information given by native Americans. The Jamestown, Virginia, colony was the subject of a rough map in 1608, and the first engraved map of Virginia was printed in Europe in 1612. It was not until 1677 that the first map printed in America appeared in a book concerned with the Indian wars. John Foster, a Boston painter, illustrated his book with a crude woodcut map. This covered parts of New England. Foster rightfully claimed it was the "first that was ever here cut." By 1700 there were maps of Philadelphia, and surveys (including those of George Washington) were common in the colonies. Benjamin Franklin published a map of Maryland-Pennsylvania boundaries in 1733.

After the Revolutionary War, the new government of the United States passed the Land Ordinance of 1785 which authorized a series of surveys and maps to chart the new country. The first survey began in southeastern Ohio in 1785 and by 1857 had reached west to Kansas. An American silversmith, Abel Buell (1742–1822) in 1784 announced a complete map of the United States. He had published "the first ever compiled, engraved and finished by one man, and an American."[45] Other, even better maps of the Colonies had been published abroad, but Buell's effort, a year after the establishment of the United States as a nation, was indeed the first from North America. Matthew Carey (1760–1839), by far the most famous Philadelphia publisher after Franklin, published the first American atlas in 1795.[46] *The American Atlas* contained both the old and the new, i.e. older plates of European and world countries were imported by Carey from England, and the new plates of the United States were engraved in America.

William Clark (1770–1838) of the (Meriwether) Lewis and Clark expedition has the added distinction of being the first to draw a map of western North America. Published in 1814, and based upon his travels with Lewis from St. Louis to the Pacific Ocean, the map is one of the most influential in American history before the Civil War. It served as a guide for thousands of trappers and pioneers in the westward migration, particularly across the Rocky Mountains and into Oregon.

The first, and really thorough atlas which stressed the United States, was published in 1832 by Henry Tanner. His *New American Atlas* was the best in American cartography of the time, particularly as it began to include part of the country heretofore virtually unmapped between the Mississippi River and the Pacific Ocean.

Nineteenth and Twentieth Century Maps & Atlases

The primary focus on early maps has meant that "the study of mapmaking since the eighteenth century has been comparatively neglected."[47] This particularly is true of thematic cartography which developed in the mid nineteenth century, and which is concerned with economic, social and physical phenomena. Given this broad definition, thematic maps virtually are unlimited in scope and purpose. There are almost as many potential maps, say, entries in a general encyclopedia. This particularly is true today. The sophistication of thematic maps knows few limits. A particular shading may show educational levels in this or that place or projections may demonstrate economic developments in, say, northern Europe.

Thematic maps had to wait upon statistics and concern for scientific and social systems of measurement—both of which gradually developed and then blossomed after 1840. Until then thematic maps had more or less been limited to secondary positions in scholarly journals, of which before 1780 there were scarcely a handful. In the nineteenth century and after the first World War the number of scientific and scholarly journals became a flood. Many of them called for charts and thematic maps to illustrate an article.

The culmination of the scientific-cartographic thematic atlas came in 1845 with the publication of the first volume of the *Physical Atlas*. Originally an idea of Alexander von Humboldt (1769–1859) the atlas covered hydrology, enthnography, meteorology, and related subjects with extensive explanations and notes to the maps. This was "a monumental achievement, bringing together an enormous amount of information about the physical geography of the earth and encompassing many more subjects than had been treated in the numerous smaller atlases."[48]

Humboldt was the outstanding fixture in maps and exploration of the nineteenth century. The German aristocrat made numerous contributions to cartography and geography, particularly after travels in Latin America (1799–1804). Humboldt was a pioneer in the reliable, easy to understand theme map. For example, types of plants were illustrated in relationship to various places and altitudes. He was convinced masses of information could be presented in a similar fashion. Also, he developed the isothermic map, the same basic type of weather map found in most atlases to this day. "Humboldt thus laid the groundwork for modern geography, with its emphasis on direct field observation and accurate measurements as the basis for generalizations. Innovations in the nineteenth century also played important roles . . . the rise of geographic societies and organized government surveys of natural conditions and resources . . . Geography as an academic discipline . . . became well established in Germany in the 1870s."[49]

The scientific mark of approval formally was given geography with the founding of The Royal Geographical Society in London in 1830. The Society functioned first to support exploration (e.g. David Livingstone, Ernest Shakleton, Robert Scott et al) and today encourages wider study of geography in schools. Some 40 years later the U.S. Geological Survey was established by Congress to publish topographic and geological data. Today the USGS produces and publishes maps from those out of the National Mapping Program to more modest local maps based on its own surveys. (Numerous other government agencies are involved in maps, including the CIA, the National Oceanic and Atmospheric Administration etc.)

In 1675 Great Britain's Royal Observatory was given a home at Greenwich, now a London borough. Around 1800 it was suggested nations adopt a single prime meridian so that maps of the world would have a single frame of reference. It took almost a century, but in 1884 Greenwich was chosen at the starting point in the measurement of longitude. (Almost from the beginning of maps latitude was fixed at the equator, i.e. between the poles). With longitude being measured east and west of Greenwich, the world was divided into 24 time zones, with, again, Greenwich at the center of the first of the time zones.

Following this spirit of cooperation between nations, in 1891 it was first suggested that every part of the world should be mapped on the same scale and with the same projection. By 1913 agreement was reached on standards for an international map of the world. Among other points, 15.78 miles on the ground would be one inch on the map. By the mid 1990s only a portion of the international map had been completed. Furthermore, it may never be finished in that changes of projections and, more important, the reliance on satellite mapping has made the notion all but obsolete, at least for many professional geographers.

The first atlas published west of the Mississippi appeared in 1877 when Rand McNally of Chicago published their *Business Atlas*—known today as the *Commercial Atlas and Marketing Guide.* By the mid 1890s Rand McNally had over 30 atlases available and positioned itself as the leading atlas publisher not only in the West, but in the whole of the United States and much of the world.

Improved printing techniques and mass production radically changed the appearance of maps by the mid nineteenth century. The decorative maps disappeared in favor of more functional, less expensive works. Between railroads and fast boats, the prospects of travel changed, too, and with that the needs were more explicit for maps of particular areas drawn to precise scale and for special needs.

At the end of the nineteenth century, geography and cartography were well established and subjects of research and scientific investigation in all western countries. By the end of World War I geography had become well established in the United States. The creation in 1903 of a department of geography at the University of Chicago was the beginning of American academic recognition in the United States of the subject.

Until the first World War less than 10 percent of the globe was completely mapped. During the second World War the air forces of the various countries began major programs of aerial photography which, in turn, was employed for construction of accurate maps. Major areas of the unmapped earth were covered during the years of war and the various editions (and names) of the *World Aeronautical Chart* provided major information for map makers.[50]

Although Europe and North America were well mapped by the beginning of World War II, much of the remainder of the globe was less than reliable on maps. For example, when the Germans invaded Russia in the early 1940s there were no accurate maps available of the country they were to try to take. Military needs and after the war, the requirements of new governments and, more important, business, resulted in a massive attack on the globe which means that today most, although not even now, all of the world is fairly well available on accurate maps and globes.

After World War II international ties among geographers and cartographers were more evident, particularly because of the founding of the International

Geographical Union with close to 100 member countries. Attention turned from purely parochial matters to more abstract notions of physical and human systems—which, in a simpler form, are now standard material in even the most inexpensive atlas. For example, there usually are sections on such things as the plus or minus of human actions on environment, acid rain, pollution, population growth, resource use in various area of the world etc. When one turns from maps and atlases to the larger field of geography all of these and other considerations are divided and subdivided into geographic areas of study such as human geography, physical geography and regional geography. Suffice to conclude that each specialization has its own reference works from maps to manuals and encyclopedias.

In the early 1990s the University of Chicago published a book on "How to lie with maps."[51] Historically the monograph traces both intentional and unintentional fibs, e.g. Mercator projections were (are) sometimes employed to make enemy territory look much larger than reality. Something is left to the knowledge of the viewer as when the U.S. Geological Survey map of Maryland showed a peak without indication it is the location of Camp David. Then there are highway maps familiar to everyone which make interstates look quite simple from road to road when they either don't exist or are complex.

A major interpretative question to be asked of any map is its relationship to other maps. There are different approaches to such comparisons, but the basic ones include the comparative study topographical features from highways to coastlines; the study of place names; and the comparison of maps printed from the same printing surface (carto-bibliography). One or all of these methods offers a way of identifying provenance and developments of maps.[52]

Age of Computers

An early 1995 struggle between Canada and Spain over fishing rights off the 200 mile international boundary demonstrated the powers of computer based maps. The Spanish made their arguments based on printed maps. The Canadians, who won the dispute, employed computer derived maps which showed the fluctuating, underwater ecosystem of the fish in what is known as the Grand Banks.

Cartography, refined during the Enlightenment, is now in turmoil. "A craft that once languished . . . has become a mainstay in innumerable disciplines, all of the seeking to visualize, or map, their data . . . The old craftsmen worked with paper, ink and a list of coordinates; the new breed has massively parallel computers crunching ever-expanding loads of information."[53]

Computer software, from the simple road map to the complex guides to the heavens, had reduced many individual maps and atlases to a series of key stroke. The map library of the future will be software and its manipulation. All of this now comes under the general heading of GIS, Geographic Information Systems.

The first map generated by a computer was published in 1950. The black and white weather map was the forerunner of a revolution. A century or so ago it might take decades to prepare and print a new map. Today it can be done in days or even a few minutes. Computers are used for every step of cartography from the actual surveying and distant measurements to physically producing the map(s). Digital data eventually will replace most printed maps, from individual maps in automobiles to maps of the world and the universe. Given a database anyone with a computer can today produce maps whose quality and accuracy are far superior to those of only a few generations ago.

Since the early 1970s satellite maps have become relatively common and by the mid 1990s a French satellite could detect ground objects only 33 feet wide. The computer generated maps are used in scores of ways, including as an aid to cartographers working on new methods of engraving and printing individual maps and atlases. At a more sophisticated level the data can trace everything from the earth's magnetic field to specific, heretofore unmeasured contours as well as indications of natural resources from oil to timber. Perhaps the highly technical aspects of cartography will infiltrate the average classroom and home. It may be almost to late. "American people are cartographically illiterate. Half the school children . . . could not point to France on a map of Europe . . . and some cannot even tell north from south."[54]

Take heart, though, libraries not only offer masses of atlases, maps, thematic maps, computer maps and works on geography, but guidance in their use. Today the most important map, at least for the puzzled layperson, may be the map of the library—and where to find help.

Travel Guides

Because many people of diverse nations and countries delight and take pleasure, as I have done in times past, in seeing the world and the various things therein, and also because many wish to know without going there, and others wish to see, go, and travel, I have begun this little book.[55]

Travel books and, more specifically travel guides, are among the earliest literary forms, and reference sources found in every civilization. The guides tell people what to see, where to stay, and, often, what to avoid. Based on the reliable notion that most men and women enjoy adventure, or at a minimum reading about it, the travel book is as old as civilization: "Soon after the Fall, human beings took their first journey—in this case into exile from Paradise."[56] Travel had begun.

Marco Polo in the thirteenth century probably was the first great travel writer. He was followed by hundreds of others, including Casanova in the eighteenth century and D.H. Lawrence in modern times. Among the thousands of travel guides there is nothing to compare with these gems of travel literature.[57] The reason is obvious. The guide, to succeed, had to be accurate and reflect needs of contemporaries. Conversely, literary accounts of travel could be as fanciful or as accurate as the narrator chose.

> [Literary travel accounts are] "only those books written by travelers who employed a narrative organization. For this reason, travel guides clearly do not form a subclass of travel literature . . . [A guide] is simply a compilation of information that would be of assistance to travelers . . . [They are] aimed only at a specialized audience looking for practical help while traveling."[58]

In a study of nineteenth century guidebooks, which he avidly collects, the novelist Alan Sillitoe indicates the value of these titles. They suggest an oblique view of cultural trends and biases.[59] A close reading indicates, for example, that the typical nineteenth century Baedeker or Murray guide were concerned about pointing out to women where they would/would not be welcome and/or in danger. In one of Murray's red books it is noted that "The line of demarcation between the baths [in Venice] of the two sexes is not sufficiently observed to make the bathing pleasant for English ladies." And it is added that in Pompey the more explicit statues are locked away, including a statuette of Priapus.

Englishmen were advised to leave servants at home as local servants could deal more effectively with the native hotel keepers. Just as today's guides warn against the purchase and use of drugs abroad, so Murray warned his readers to control their tempers and avoid fights. Foreigners had heavy fines and imprisonment for the pugnacious.

If attitudes vary, monuments and landmarks rarely do, or at least that much. As a result, "one of the pleasures in reading old travel books is to discover how little the best things in life have changed . . . Henry VI's statue has been standing in the center of Eton's School Yard for a long as anyone can remember, and Bath looked to travelers in the 1780s the pleasantest town in England as it does to us."[60]

From the late seventeenth to the early twentieth century, the nonfiction travel account was second only to fiction in popularity. "There are no books which I more delight in than in travels" wrote Joseph Addison in a 1710 issue of the *Tatler*. In the late nineteenth century William Morris observed of all books, travel accounts "are more cherished."[61] This notion gradually changed. One will find in the *Cambridge History of English Literature* the comment that "no one expects literature in a book of travel."[62]

Many literary eighteenth and nineteenth century travel accounts mixed fiction with fact, personal observations with readings from other books. An excellent example of this type is Daniel Defoe's *Tour Through the Whole Island of Great Britain* (1724–1727) which is a factual itinerary mixed with fiction.

A correspondent for a popular English journal observed midway through the nineteenth century that travel literature had changed dramatically from earlier decades, earlier centuries. It was considerably less literate, and nothing could compare, for example, with either Laurence Sterne's *A Sentimental Journal* (1768) or Henry Fielding's *The Journal of a Voyage to Lisbon* (1755). Furthermore numerous nineteenth century travel accounts returned to those "legends of lying travelers." There was little information, in other words, to be had from literary travel accounts. One had to turn to more reliable travel guides.

Many literary travel accounts gave sometimes less than accurate background information. By the early nineteenth century the literary travel book usually consisted of chatty and sometimes trivial gossip about a place and its people. The travel guide, often confused with its cousin, depended more on research and "on-the-ground" studies of conditions. Above all, the guide avoided the personal feelings, the sometimes overpowering sentimentality of the typical imaginative travel work of the period. "In the opening decades of the nineteenth century, two kinds of accounts achieved prominence: the purely entertaining travel book and the instructive travel guide. . . Pleasure clearly becomes divorced from instruction."[63] As Batten points out, during most of the eighteenth century and well into modern times it is difficult to tell a guide from a book about travel when only the title is considered. For example a 1768 title, *Gentleman's Guide in His Tour Through France* might or might not be a guide or a book about travel. It is the former. Today catalogers have much the same problem, at least this side of well established guides such as Fodor, Michelin, etc.

Here the discussion is primarily limited to guidebooks, not travel books. "The difference between a travel book and a guide has sometimes been likened to the distinction between the description of a meal and its recipe in a cookery book."[64] Travel books are included for the earlier centuries primarily because they were *the* guides, although fairly personal and subjective. Only with the nineteenth century was the travel guide developed in terms of today's modern titles.

Early Guides: Greek-Roman

In Mesopotamia, Gilgamesh was among the earlier recorded early epic heroes and travelers. The first version of his adventure was written in about 1800 B.C. Herodotus (484–425 B.C.) reported on Egyptian pilgrimages taken as much for pleasure as for religious reasons. Tourists were visiting 1,000 to 1,500 year old pyramids and leaving their signatures, messages and graffiti on the monuments. Some five to six hundred years later Homer composed the *Iliad* and the *Odyssey* which, in a sense, celebrated travel. By 875 B.C. the Assyrians had cavalry and travel mobility. Darius the Great (521–486 B.C.) built roads and provided transportation which knit together his Persian Empire from Egypt to Iran.

In about 500 B.C. Hecataeus drew a map of the world and became one of the world's earliest cartographers. To illustrate his map he wrote a "journey-round-the-world" which was another first in that it was one of the earliest travel books. Actually, the focus was on a description of peoples and places he encountered on a voyage of the Mediterranean and Black Sea, with some diversion to Persia and India. While the map is lost, there are fragments of the travel book which Herodotus apparently made use of, but never cited. Herodotus is the first example of pure travel literature, although a mixture of history, mythology and opinion as well. His adventures of exploration in Persia, Asia Minor, Mesopotamia, Babylon and probably Egypt can be claimed to be both the beginning of Western history writing as well as the first work of travel.

The author of the first travel romance, i.e. a cross between pure fiction and fact, turned to India and Persia for his explorations. This was Ctesias (b 416 B.C.), a Greek doctor at the Persian court and the author of another early travel and history book on Assyria-Babylonia. The material was gathered from official records, but Cltesias used his imagination in order to contradict and refute Herodotus' version of the same civilizations. Ctesias was heavily influenced by Herodotus, although he failed to admit as much and said his stories came from witnesses other than Herodotus. Except for fragments, the work has disappeared. More of a travel work than a history, Ctesias account of India, based on reports of visitors, was the earliest record until Alexander's invasion. It, too, is of questionable authority.[65]

Travel to view games at Olympia and similar centers, the need to consult oracles at Delphi and, most important, trade around the Mediterranean explains the focus of travel guides of the Greek-Roman period. Travel only for pleasure was uncommon because of the discomforts as well as numerous hazards. The person who traveled widely to see and to learn was rare, even considered not quite respectable. Why would a person at peace with himself and his surroundings wish to go abroad, or so was the reasoning of those who discouraged travel.

With the conquest of Greece by Rome, power shifted to Italy and by the first century A.D. merchants were traveling the length and width of Europe as well as to ports in northern Africa and the Near East. Pilgrims traveled for ritual health hopes to various Mediterranean temples, and thereby set the precedent for Christian pilgrims in the Medieval period. Others moved about for pleasure, curiosity and often to view or participate in athletic events. The rich traditionally left Rome for their annual rounds of out-of-town villas and others simply traveled for sightseeing.

Pliny (23–74 A.D.) included in his *Natural History* important data on his travels and countries including Germany from which Tacitus drew much information. Unfortunately of this and other works only the *Natural History* survives. Arrian (b. 180 A.D.) is best known for his work describing the campaigns of Alexander the Great, but in the final eighth book he goes into great details about Indian customs and the countryside. He was a peculiar combination of Greek historian, philosopher, governor and army officer. Today it is his descriptive historical and travel writing that has earned him a place as one of the earliest travel writers.

Actual travel guidebooks must have been used by these early travelers, but none is extant. There are infrequent references to such guides in classical and Roman literature, although here the guides seem to have been limited to describing single places and single, often fantastic people. Toward the end of the fourth century B.C. Diodorus apparently wrote a guide to the towns and sights of Attica, but, again, no copy exists. Heliodorus (fl. 2nd century B.C.) apparently wrote a guide to the Acropolis in Athens and one Polemo of Illium, a contemporary of Heliodorus, wrote a dozen books for tourists which described major points of interest from Delphi to Troy.

The available guides to individual places and monuments had numerous drawbacks which made them less than popular or universal: (1) They tended to be inaccurate and often out-of-date as well as based as much upon second or third hand observation as the imagination of the author. (2) In either rolls or late codex form they were too bulky for carrying about. (3) Most important, books, in any form, were expensive, and certainly not to be risked on a hazardous trip. As a result travelers tended to read the guides before they embarked rather than take them along as on-the-spot aids.

By about 160 A.D. tourism in the Roman empire had reached a level of popularity which prompted Pausanias (fl. 150 A.D.) to publish the first true guidebook, i.e. *Guidebook of Greece* or *Description of Greece* between about 160 and 180 A.D. It is the only guidebook to have survived from ancient times.[66] The ten books or sections give the history of an area, town or city as well as the topography. While descriptions of scenery are uncommon, Pausanias describes religious and historical monuments and remains. His real strength was his ability to describe artistic signs and monuments.

If guidebooks were lacking, there was no shortage of guides. They were everywhere. "They were not only at the great tourist sites, such as Athens or Troy, but even in small towns that boasted few attractions . . . A satirist has a character in one of his pieces utter the fervent prayer: 'Zeus, protect me from hour guides at Olympia, and you Athena, from yours at Athens.' The ancient guide shared with modern descendants the inability to stop, once he was launched on his patter."[67]

Reinforcing the Greek and Roman knowledge of travel and geography was a large body of myth and fable and fiction about wealth, natural wonders, and magic. Some stories can be traced back to Homer, others to

Ctesias who lived for seventeen years at the Persian Court (c. 400 B.C.). Pliny passed many myths along, primarily from Ctesias. By about 200 A.D. Gaius Solinus had written a book of fantastic wonders which enjoyed universal popularity. Solinus was the earliest known Roman plagiarist. He lifted, almost verbatim, parts of Pliny's *Natural History* and writings of others for his *Collectanea Rerum Memorabilium* (Collection of Memorable Things). This a group of stories, history, myths, customs and views on what was then known of the geographical world. Solinus did make some additions to Pliny, such as a description of the British Isle and the myth about the lack of snakes in Ireland. Republished in the sixth century as *Polyhistor* (Many stories) it had a lasting affect on mapmakers who turned to it for odd items to fill in their maps. Giant ants, dog-headed people, and similar monsters from the then unknown parts of the world, described by Solinus and friends, served to decorate early maps. Historians point out that the notion of monsters in unknown lands tended to prejudice early explorers. They tended to treat all native residents as savages.

Fiction to Fact

Before the Renaissance, books of travel, from *Gilgamesh* to the *Exodus,* from Homer and Herodotus to Virgil and Horace were works of great charm, often of inspiration but of limited reliability for the traveler seeking a guide. Only with the Age of Discovery, when a given amount of verification became possible, did travel information seem to move from essentially the stuff of novels to a reliable, practical use.

Based as much on borrowing from other works, as the imagination of the compiler and writer, the early travel books struck an uneasy balance between travel accounts and the pleasures of fiction. Eventually—by the end of the nineteenth century—the tension between fact and imagination resolved itself in a separation of the scientific (i.e. the factual description of an area) and the novelistic. Travelers reports shifted from the popular press to inclusion in the Royal Society's *Philosophical Transactions.* And the novel took over from Mandeville and others who had written fiction as much as travel literature. A third branch developed, and this was the travel guide which was of interest to laypersons and represented useful facts rather than fiction or scientific findings.

The early Christian historian Orosius (fl. 378–420) completed the first Christian saga, *History Against the Pagans,* in 418 A.D. In addition to demonstrating how the Romans suffered because of lack of faith in God, the Spaniard drew heavily on calamities from Livy, Justin and Tacitus. Along the way are sometimes fantastic descriptions of the world which influenced later cartographers and travel writers. The eleventh century manuscript in the British Library, *The Wonders of the East,* is in the tradition of both Orosius and Pliny. *The Wonders* is divided into short chapters on plants, animals, bits of zoology, botany and other materials normally associated with a short encyclopedia. There is even a section on cooking. It is difficult to slot *Wonders* into any single category, but it seems to be a significant forerunner of the Medieval series of wonder books about the world.[68]

Facts were scarce in early travel literature. And as the form became a self contained genre, it became more personal, more impressionistic. "Its interest had come to lie largely in the sensibility of the particular writer, less and less in the capacity or obligation to inform."[69]

An excellent example of the combination of fiction and travel is found in the lasting myth of Prester John. Prester (i.e. priest or presbyter) John came to be part of the geographical mythology in about 1145 when there is a record of how a certain John, both king and priest, who lived somewhere beyond Persia had waged war against the Medes and Persians in an effort to aid Jerusalem.[70] About 1170 the myth became "fact" when a mysterious, faked letter was received from this king of India confirming his vast wealth and power in unparalleled Christian Utopia.[71] With that the quest for the realm began and continued on until well into the eighteenth century. Prester John gradually moved from India, when cartographers were unable to find his kingdom, to Central Asia and from there, in the late fourteenth century to Africa, and more precisely to the true Christian kingdom of Ethiopia. By the end of the fifteenth century a book was printed in Florence which was a poem celebrating the life of Prester John, "lord of India and Ethiopia." The myth was so persuasive that Prester John's kingdom, no matter where it shifted, continued to be noted on maps until the beginning of the eighteenth century.

Medieval travel books served two audiences. The first, and by far the largest, was the group of readers who had to stay home, but sought an imaginative tour of places and events far away. During the Middle Ages this often was the Holy Land, followed by China, the world in general, and the New World. Hence the three most famous and popular works for stay-at-home travelers during the Middle Ages and early Renaissance was Marco Polo's (c. 1254–1324) *Description of the World,* Jean Mandeville's (1300–1372), *Travels* and Christopher Columbus' (1451–1506) *Journal.* The three shared another peculiar trait—all are second hand accounts. Marco Polo dictated his adventures to his cell mate, a Frenchman; Mandeville plagiarized most of his material; and the journal of Columbus was edited, abridged and partly summarized by a Spaniard. Polo was the first of the group (i.e. c. 1295), followed by Mandeville (c. 1357) and then by Columbus who at least had the experience of discovery to vouch for the accuracy of his letters and journals. Of the three Mandeville was the more widely read, primarily because there were so many copies published after the development of printing.

Mandeville's *Travels* was one of the most popular, if not the most popular books of the Middle Ages. The book's popularity is due to Mandeville's highly imaginative descriptions of people and places both in Europe and in the Near East. Into this he weaved well known descriptions of legendary monsters and creatures who occupied the same territory as objective scientific fact. "It is a fitting culmination to a tradition reaching back to the Odyssey."[72] By the time of Mandeville, pilgrimages to the Holy Land had dropped off sharply, and the Crusades were over. Readers were ready for less familiar travel literature, and Mandeville's hoax met that need in what today may be recognized more as fiction than true travel literature. The author borrowed extensively from various other travel works, including a detailed set of itineraries of travels to the Holy Land from about 1250 to 1351. Ironically, biographical data about one of the most famous travel writers of all times is unknown.[73]

Medieval Pilgrimage Guides

The beginnings of Christianity, the fall of Rome, the disappearance of pagan antiquity did not diminish interest in travel works. "From Herodotus to Pliny to Solinus to Isidore of Seville to Vincent of Beauvais to Sebastian Munster: each link of the chain binding the oriental lore of antiquity with that of the Renaissance is securely fastened to the next."[74]

Pilgrimages originate in Christianity where the contempt for the world inspired ascetics to a life of aimless wandering. More important the rise of cult relics (bodies and bits of bodies of saints) which were intercessory support at the least and would work miracles of healing at the most, caused pilgrims to direct their travels to the place of the relic(s). By the Renaissance there were major shrines throughout Europe and the Near East. Another reason for travel was the desire to do penance, and a compulsory pilgrimage to a shrine was common punishment for grave sins. Finally, some thought the chances for salvation higher if they made a pilgrimage. While pilgrimages began early in the fourth to seventh centuries, and were particularly favored by the Irish, they reached their height of popularity in the eleventh to thirteenth centuries. In order to merit the most often taken pilgrimages were to Jerusalem, Rome, and Galicia (in southeast Poland). The medieval period was the great age of pilgrimages from points in Europe to Rome and from Rome to the Holy Land. The Crusades increased the volume of travel as well as the beginnings of trade and business throughout Europe and much of the Near East and Mediterranean.

"The world maps of the Middle Ages drew heavily upon theory and imagination, but another tradition of mapmaking was at work . . . Among these were road maps, or itineraries, descended from the highway maps made by the Romans. The medieval version of the road map was the pilgrim's guidebook."[75] Pilgrims guidebooks were written from the fourth century on. Many included maps which give detailed accounts of distances. Markers include inns, churches, mountain passes and other natural and manmade monuments.

Pilgrimages to Jerusalem began as early as the fourth century, but in the early years of Christianity most of the travel was to shrines in Western Europe, and more particularly Rome. From the latter came early guidebooks which listed churches and relics. One of the earliest extant guides dates from the ninth century and gives itineraries which allow a pilgrim to visit all of the churches and outstanding reliquaries in Rome. While the pilgrims were drawn from all classes, the Irish and Anglo-Saxon monks appear to have been the most numerous travelers.

By the twelfth century there were numerous pilgrim's guides which tended to promote a given shrine such as *Tours* or *Canterbury.* In addition forts across Europe were described in order to enable the traveler to find the maximum safety with the minimum amount of travel. In fact many of the medieval guides were little more than itineraries.[76]

One of the earliest examples of Christian pilgrimage travel literatures is the *Itinerarium Egeria.* As the title suggests this is an account of a trip by a nun, Egeria, of her journey to Egypt, Palestine and parts of Asia Minor. Egeria probably was Spanish and made the journey c. 386–400 A.D., although some believe it was 381–384 A.D. The Abbess set out from what is now southern France on a pilgrimage to the Holy Land. The early part of the travel book is lost, for it opens with her ascending Mt. Sinai and moves through the Near East. Much is sketchy, but apparently she was on her journeys for some four years, often staying in monastic communities. The journal has proven valuable for its observations, not so much of points of travel, but on the descriptions of churches, and monasteries, particularly around Jerusalem.[77] Pilgrims by the eleventh century had as many motives for travel as they differed in class, education and wealth. Still, it was not until the end of the fourteenth century that the trips became more than difficult tasks, took on, indeed, a certain amount of pleasure. The primary example of pilgrims in quest of enjoyment as well as religion is, of course, Chaucer's pilgrims.[78]

In 1250 Matthew Paris (fl. 1200s) prepared a map of a Britain which gave specific directions to English pilgrims on how to reach Dover. Beyond that other maps were necessary to chart the sea voyage and the way to Rome and beyond. Paris, a Benedictine monk at St. Albanys by 1217 is best known for his histories, but equally is regarded as the first major British cartographer. His colorful map of 1250 is only relatively accurate, but at least shows major landmarks, including castles and churches. A series of strip road maps carried the pilgrim from Dover and shore sea crossings, and landmarks between London and Jerusalem.

The first "modern" travel guides as we know them today appeared in the fourteenth century. The particular focus was on the Holy Land and places to see, places to stay, people and things to avoid. The early 1350s guidebooks "are the sadly degenerated offspring of Egeria's (work) . . . Almost all the places described are places where some scriptural joy (or, by this time, apocryphal) event took place."[79] Drawn from numerous sources, the guides included the standard information on absolutions and indulgences as well as sometimes lengthy anecdotes. They were read as much for assistance as for information about a place many readers would never visit. Better ones included eyewitness accounts, often plagiarized from earlier works, including Egeria.

Guidebooks for pilgrims became relatively common, but only after the development and spread of printing. For example, *Information for Pilgrims unto the Holy Land,* was printed by Wynkyn deWord in 1498 and was widely distributed in England and throughout much of Europe. Pilgrimages came under attack during most of the fifteenth century by those who saw little point in outward forms of religion, including pious travel. The volume took a precipitous decline at about the time of the deWord publication.

Renaissance Travel

With the beginning of the Renaissance few knew anything about Asia and Africa and nothing about the existence of North America. Thanks to voyages and exploration the curtain on the world outside of Europe and the Near East was gradually raised. By the end of the Renaissance printed books had opened the word to anyone who was able or cared to read. The voyages of Bartholomeu Dias (1457–1500) and Vasco daGama (1460–1524) in the sixteenth century gradually demythologized the world. The geographical writings of the fifteenth and sixteenth centuries, and particularly the great prose epics of Richard Hakluyt's (1533–1616) *Principal Navigations,* not only expanded knowledge of cartographers and geographers, but inspired a mass of reference literature as well as belles letters and drama.[80]

Renaissance travel literature [outside of Spain and Portugal] developed primarily in Italy and Germany, but the only real rival of the Spanish and Portuguese were the English who by the middle of the sixteenth century began the development to perfection of a special variety of travel literature—the accounts of voyages and travels. Printed accounts of the great voyages of discovery launched modern travel writing on its course. The voyages not only offered various entertainment, but, for the most part, accurate rather than imaginative accounts of the geography, customs, culture and fauna and flora of other sections of the world. There were several early sixteenth century attempts at such collections, but the first real effort to bring exploration to the attention of average readers was in 1553 when a young Cambridge graduate, Richard Eden, translated and published in English a part of Sebastian Musnter's *Cosmographia* which dealt with the voyages of Columbus, Magellan and others. Eden made several other translations of voyages and was in the process of work on *Decades* when he died in 1576. Once the course was set for geographical literature in English, others followed, leading to Richard Hakluyt.

Hakluyt was the most famous collector of voyages in England. The interest of the British cleric was aroused when he saw certain books of cosmography and maps and talked about voyages with English explorers. He carried on a wide correspondence with sea-captains as well as map makers from Ortelius to Mercator. His first collection, *Divers Voyages Touching the Discovery of America,* was published in 1582. His major contribution, *The Principal navigations, Voyages and Discoveries of the English Nation* was published in 1589, and enlarged to three volumes in 1598–1600. With his death the work of collection continued under the leadership of Samuel Purchas and later became part of the mission of the Hakluyt Society, which to this day republishes records of early voyages and travels.[81]

With the publication of Sir Walter Raleigh's account of Virginia (1596), preceded by Robert Harcourt's narrative, *A Briefe and True Report of the New Found Land of Virginia* (1588), a massive number of published travel accounts traced settlements and exploration in North America, including Captain John Smith's *A Description of New England* (1616).[82]

The voyage and exploration collections fitted in nicely with the seventeenth century mania for collecting "curiosities." The collections allowed the reader to view the curiosities, the differences between various parts of the globe, and were particularly appealing for their exotic lure.[83] A mark of the full blown eighteenth century Grand Tour was the return to England of the tourist with antiquities and art treasures. As an imperial power, England soon built up a private collection which was eventually to be the source of the National Gallery and other institutions throughout Great Britain.

The Grand Tour: 17th–18th Centuries

The English and Irish loved to travel and were among the most enthusiastic of the medieval pilgrims. After the Reformation, after the English could no longer continue Catholic worship, they invented the institution of educational travel during the sixteenth and seventeenth centuries. By the eighteenth century this was known as the "Grand Tour," and was much a part of the upper class way of life.

The phrase "Grand Tour" does not appear in print until a travel guide by Richard Lassel was published in 1679, i.e. his *An Italian Voyage.* The Tour had been a part of the education of a select few for at least a century. Francis Bacon (1561–1626) in an essay on "Travel" stressed the need to venture to Europe to meet important scholars, and leaders. Thus a major purpose of the Grand Tour was established early. It was needed to lay a ground work for a career in diplomacy or the arts. As a kind of finishing school, the Tour lasted from one to four or even five years. A few scholars, but primarily well off noblemen made the Tour.

> The Grand Tour symbolized "a particular feature of English aristocratic culture which no other national aristocracy could . . . boast. . . . The oafish and ignorant young English squire, setting forth two centuries ago . . . knew that he had at least twelve months in which to wear off his rough edges . . . Slowness [of travel] produced one rather unfortunate consequence. Traveling was so leisurely that few travelers could cover the ground completely."[84]

Along with the Tour came guidebooks. Among the early justification for the Tour was Andrew Boorde's *Introduction of Knowledge* (c. 1548) which set the pattern. An ex-monk, Boorde (c. 1490–1549) was widely traveled, and drew upon his life for the material for his guidebook. Descriptions are given of countries and places as well as verse portraits of various national types, from the point of view of the English. Also, there are common phrases appended to each description of an individual country. Usually these were in French and English. (Latin, even by the sixteenth century was becoming less and less the international language, particularly of non-scholars.) Specific advice came with James Howell's *Instructions for Foreign Travel* (1642). Howell (1594–1666) was a much traveled diplomat, who as a Royalist, was imprisoned shortly after the publication of his guide. At the Restoration he was made the court's official histographer. He later went on to write guides to Scotland and to London.

Although from time to time challenged,[85] Boorde and Howell are considered the fathers of the travel guide genre in English. From these works developed offshoots such as traveler word guides and gratuitous bits of advice for all situations. Among the latter, and found paraphrased in many guides during the seventeenth and early eighteenth century: "Never journey without something to eat in your pocket, if only to throw to dogs when attacked by them." "Keep your distance from [sailors] . . . they are covered with vermin." "In an inn-bedroom which contains big pictures, look behind the latter to see they do not conceal a secret door, or a window." "Women should not travel at all and married men not much."[86]

One of the earliest guides and/or account of the Grand Tour was Thomas Coryate's *Coryate's Crudities* (1611). He explained in great detail what to find in the various European countries outside of England. The descriptions range from forks in Italy to significant points of interest.[87] Coryate, as other travel manuals and handbooks featured sections on proper conduct among foreigners. *A Letter of Advice,* published in 1670 advised young people to avoid seductive sin while abroad.[88] Another theme consisted of warning English travelers not to adopt either foreign customs or dress. At no cost should one alienate fellow English travelers by accepting foreign manners. Popular literature and drama by the seventeenth century used the image of the traveler who took on European ways as an object of amusement and scorn.

> "Detractors of educational travel, [in the sixteenth and seventeenth centuries] convinced of the extraordinary dangers English travelers faced abroad, completely denied the usefulness of sending young men to tour the Continent to complete their education . . . Despite the threatening scenarios described by some critics, wide spread evil or sinister Irishmen returning from abroad did not precipitate the emergence nor support the subsequent popularity—of these negative images."[89]

While today's travel guide focuses almost entirely on practical advice—from where to sleep to what to see—the Grand Tour guides were of a different sort. Rather than offer facts, most stressed advice on how the traveler could improve his education and what social errors to avoid. "Authors generally gave their readers a summary of the best countries and cities to visit and the best qualities to observe, always remembering to fear God . . . and advice that would keep him from corruption."[90]

Illustration

In 1764 George Reeves introduced maps to English guide books with the publication of his *New History of London.* Wood and steel engravings allowed accurate representations of large areas as well as small sections of city streets. Following a tradition of several centuries for popular literature, many of the publishers simply kept using the same engravings edition after edition, even after streets had changed. The English publishers tended to use representative illustrations for churches, well known buildings and even personalities. The same woodcut might be employed to illustrate a dozen or more different, say, parks. [Among European publishers only Karl Baedeker in the nineteenth century had the good sense to keep his illustrations current and useful, to provide up-to-date maps, and to eschew all advertising.]

By the 1870s photographs were sparingly introduced, but by the turn of the twentieth century photos were common and considerably more current than the old engravings. Improved printing methods encouraged better, accurate illustrations in guides, and while the early nineteenth century works were fortunate to include only a handful of maps, by the end of the century almost all guides featured both local and regional maps. In addition, there often were photographs of important sights, and particularly churches and cathedrals.

Nineteenth Century Tours

The decline of the leisurely classes, the rise of the middle classes with limited time and limited funds worked a major change in the purpose and scope of travel guides. No longer were they written for someone with unlimited money and equally unlimited time. Now they were for busy people who had budgets to follow and, more important, lacked the education to know X or Y painting from another, let alone a good hotel.

Travel in the nineteenth century was open to almost anyone with a bit of money and a sense of adventure.[91] The great nineteenth century wave of technology brought travel to the upper middle class family for the first time. Railways linked seaports with cities and the cities built the ships which carried people around the globe. Tourist hotels were established throughout Europe in the early part of the nineteenth century. With the new wealth of the English tradespeople and bourgeoisie travel books and guides appeared in greater numbers and the suggestions of what to see, what to do more pragmatic, less esthetic and learned.

The Rev. William Gilpin set the pattern for late eighteenth and early nineteenth century guide books. His *Observations on the River Wye* of 1770 was aimed at training the reader to see major sights. And he accomplished this by pointing out what was to be visited and how it was to be viewed. While by 1815 Gilpin's picturesque way of looking at landscapes had been the object of scorn (e.g. Jane Austen's *Northanger Abbey,* for one), his approach to perception of best and better was the stuff of all guidebooks to follow.

Gradually mass tourism developed. This gathered speed in tandem with fast railroads and ships. By the 1850s London to Rome took only four and a half days by train, and by 1900 it was cut in half. The Orient Express cut a three months journey in the 1700s to 60 hours. At the same time the length of the visit went from one to three years to two to three months.

George Bradshaw founded the railway timetable in 1839, and along with his publisher William Adams, had a virtual monopoly on the English guide. A full, first edition was published by Adams in 1847 for the Continent, and by 1851 he had published a guide to London and its environs. These all went through several editions, even after the death of Bradshaw (1853). With the death of Adams the guides were discontinued, but only for a brief time, and were put on a regular schedule to be published until the early 1960s.

Most English had a restricted knowledge of languages, so the guides encouraged they hire a courier. "The question is whether one should be engaged from the Italian Couriers' Club in Golden Square, where it was possible to make some enquiries about his antecedents, or picked up haphazard on the way through Paris. . . . The courier was to make all bargains and pay all bills, so as to save the family unbecoming cares and mean anxieties."[92]

The nineteenth century witnessed the nouveaux riches on the move,

"Whole families of vulgarians spawned by the Industrial Revolution, hell bent on adding culture to wealth . . . Guide books grew out of a real need. Someone had to tell all those tourists where to stay and what to see. Already the demarcation line between travel and tourism was clear. Travelers want to find their own way, preferably in areas where they are unlikely to meet a compatriot for six months."[93]

Guide Features

Travel writing, as well as guides for the nineteenth and early twentieth century followed two or three chronological periods. The first, from the late eighteenth century to the 1820s primarily involved travel accounts by individuals. Usually they were young men motivated by self education, and often in the more serious pattern of the former Grand Tour. The few guides of the period catered to this group. By the middle of the century, relatively rapid transportation and improved economic conditions opened travel to women, to families and to the ubiquitous groups accompanied by trained guides.

The third period, from the 1850s and 1860s until World War I saw the continuous, some would say relentless development of the tourist industry. And along with that came the scores of travel guides which pointed out places to see, places to avoid and places to look for good meals and lodging. Travelers obvious motives were self-improvement, status, adventure, and escape.

Thomas Martyn's *The Gentleman's Guide to His Tour Through Italy* (1787) is an example of the late Grand Tour genre guidebook. The book gave careful instructions concerning what places to avoid, what pictures to examine, and what natural scenery to enjoy. Thirty years later Marianna Starke's *Information and Directions for Travellers on the Continent* (1820) showed the change which had taken place in the type of individual likely to consult a guide. Now it was the practical traveler, and more particularly the woman who might want to know how safe a particular hotel might be or the merits of transportation in France.

Authors, compilers and even editors of most of the nineteenth century early guides remained anonymous, often disguised by a byline such as "A traveler" or "A Lady" or "A Gentleman." Usually the descriptor was accurate, e.g. Harriet Martineau (1802–1876) the sister of the well known minister, published her travels, mid century, and in some cases even earlier.

The most famous nineteenth century author of a guide was William Wordsworth (1770–1850) who wrote *A Guide Through The District of the Lakes* (1835). Originally this was to be an introduction to another author's guide, but Wordsworth expanded it for later publication. Wordsworth also wrote *The River Duddon: A Series of Sonnets* (1820) and a volume of poems, *Memorials of a Tour on the Continent* (1822), both of which were based on his travels.

The Great Exhibition of all Nations, held in London in 1851, was not only symbolic of the Industrial Age, but a gold mine for guidebook publishers. It typifies an historical approach. Gather more than a few thousand people together in one place over a period of time and they will need assistance to evaluate not only what to see, but where to stay and where to dine. At least 44 guides were published in London in 1851, and an additional 16 to 20 in foreign languages. "Though the sheer number of so called new guides was impressive, the quality was, as usual, poor. Those publishers who felt unable to compile their own guides from existing guides, or even to rewrite the appropriate sections from the *British Almanac and Companion* combined with the official catalogue of the Exhibition, called in a variety of journalistic hacks and literary word spinners . . . Even the smallest of guides appear to have included a map, and most managed a picture of the Crystal Palace."[94]

Other guidebook publishers had learned the value of stressing what Renaissance cosmographers and world travelers knew well—emphasize the exotic of foreign lands. "Those with leisure, sophistication and social advantages can afford the luxury of turning away from . . . complexity to some ideal of the simple life, the noble savage, or the 'Paradise isle of modern' travel guides."[95]

The accuracy of many guides, particularly near the close of the nineteenth century, were called into question when it became apparent that the publisher was using them to promote other of his activities. For example, a guide might say the center of interest in a given town was the circulating library, failing to note the library was owned by the publisher. Then, again, the publisher might be on the payroll of a hotel, group of restaurants, a railroad etc. In keeping with trends in popular magazines and newspapers, the publishers of guide books welcomed advertising, even when the ads might be in conflict with recommendations in the guide. By 1894, for example, one famous series turned over 100 of the 350 or so pages to ads, usually of hotels and shops.

Others might take a moral stance, as for example, against atheist or Catholic memorials.[96] In most cases, though, the lack of accuracy was due to the carelessness of the compiler and publisher. The son of the man who published guides, for example, found numerous "errors in the German part" of their guidebook. A dutiful son, he added that he "had taken great pains, ever since I first went abroad, to collect information to improve it."[97]

Major Guide Publishers

One of the earliest publishers of guidebooks in England, or for that matter in Europe, was the firm of John Murray (1778–1843). The guides in distinctive red covers soon became known simply as "the Red Books." Murray explained how early in the century he had set out to tour Europe, only to find there was a lack of English language books he could consult. He began to issue a series of handbooks in 1820. The dozen or so *Hand-Book for Travellers* covered Russia to Asia Minor and all of Europe.[98]

The works sold well, but Murray had the problem which to this day bother compilers and publishers, i.e. the guides "dealt rather drastically with places and hotels, and shrill complaints often reached [the publisher]. Unlike some of his competitors, Murray apparently considered the reader of more importance than the feelings (or the bribes) of hotel keepers. Murray responded to one complaint with "It is preposterous to think that *Handbooks* should not have the power of praising or condemning hotels." Another difficulty, solved only in the years of rapid printing and computers after the 1980s, was that the books were too often out-of-date. The "new editions were brought out at too long intervals, and travelers found—occasionally— that the hotels which [were] recommended had disappeared."[99]

Richard Ford (1796–1858) was one of the more popular author's of Murray's *Hand-Books for Travellers*. His *Spanish Handbook* took him five years to write. Actually it proved more of a traditional travel books than a guide, but in the first three months of publication sold close to 1500 copies—an astonishing number for the period. (The most successful of the works was the guide to Switzerland, but even at eighteen different editions between 1838 and 1891 it sold only 45,000 copies). Another favorite was John Mason Neale (1818–1866) who was more concerned with theology than travel, but between writing hymns and church history, he completed Murray's *Hand-Book for Travellers in Portugal* (1855). John Murray III wrote several of the handbooks including the guide to Holland (1836), Southern Germany (1837) and France (1843). In 1850 he suggested that Anthony Trollope write a guide to Ireland, but this was never completed or published.

The Red Books achieved immortality in a rhymed tribute which appeared in *Punch.* A few verses:

"The wind and tide have brought us fast,
The Custom-house is well-nigh past.
Alas! that this should be the last;
        My Murray.

"So well thou'st played the hand-books' part
For inns a hint, for routes a chart,
That every line I've got by heart.
        My Murray.

"Once I could scarce walk up the Strand;
What Jungfrau now could us withstand,

When we are walking hand in hand,
             My Murray?

"But oh! too well some folk I know,
Who friends on dusty shelves do throw,
With us it never shall be so.
             My Murray."[100]

While Murray dominated the nineteenth century English travel guide, he did have some competitors among whom was the Edinburgh firm of Adam & Charles Black. The publisher began with an 1839 guide to Edinburgh and by the late 1870s had issued over a dozen handbooks, primarily, although not exclusively, to England, Scotland, Wales and Ireland.

Karl Baedeker (1801–1859) was the founder of the most famous of German, or for that matter European guidebook publishers. In his early guides he freely admitted his debt to John Murray for the idea of such works. In fact, as he said, much of the material in the first books was drawn directly from Murray's Red Books. In 1829 he brought out his first guide, but it wasn't until the second that the Leipzig publisher evolved a basic system for the series. He stressed practical information for middle class travelers who were seeking the best in reliable hotels. Paralleling this was basic information on sights. His "star" system indicated the best and better hotels and things to see. From time to time the publisher made unexpected, usually incognito trips to update and modify his star system.

The guides averaged between 500 and 700 pages, were bound in red with gold lettering and usually included maps and plans to cities and institutions, particularly churches and museums. Information on transportation, hotels, passports and the like was given in full. Many of the guides are collectors items, and as one observer noted: "Making allowances for changes wrought by God and man, the guide remains as accurate as compendium . . . as has ever been written."[101]

While Baedeker began with a guide to the Rhine, by the time of his death the series covered almost all of Europe. In 1846 Baedeker published a French edition, followed by an English translations in 1861. Among the earliest guides to America was the Baedeker 1893: *The United States—With Excursions to Mexico, Cuba, Puerto Rico and Alaska.* By 1909, the guide was in its fourth edition and in the hands of many of the 40,000 European annual visitors. Under his sons, and particularly the innovative Fritz (1844–1925) the publisher gained in fame. In spite of two World Wars the firm remains in business and is held in high esteem throughout the world.

The content of the early Baedeker's was similar to that found in other guidebooks "personal opinions, poetical extracts, and verbose descriptions."[102] Gradually Baedeker began to realize the real selling point would be a book which appealed to the middle class tourist and would point out good, but inexpensive places to stay and eat. "With teutonic thoroughness, Baedeker provided . . . detailed maps and plans, a large type face to indicate the relative importance of the places mentioned; and lastly, the celebrated use of asterisks as marks of personal recommendation . . . It was not the first time that a system of recommendation had been used . . . But the idea of a personal choice for the culturally ignorant . . . was completely new."[103]

Today the Baedeker guides normally are divided into sections from the first which gives background and practical information on weather, visas, currency etc. to the major section which concentrates on the cities and towns of interest to a tourist in a given country or geographical area.[104] Selected hotels and restaurants are listed in another, usually concluding section. The 1996 *Books In Print* lists about 50 Baedeker's (published in the United States by Prentice Hall/Simon & Schuster) covering both cities and countries.

Thomas Cook (1808–1892) was the leading advocate of organized mass tourism. He began what turned into the world's largest tour company in 1841. As a booksalesman and Baptist preacher he organized a train to carry people to a temperance meeting. Two years later he offered tours to over 3,000 school children to places in England. By 1846 he had published his first travel guide, a *Handbook of the Trip to Liverpool.* In the 1850s he offered tours abroad, from America to the Paris Exhibition of 1855. In the 1870s Mark Twain declared "Cook has made travel easy and a pleasure. He will sell you a ticket to any place on the globe."[105] By the 1880s Thomas Cook & Son was as well known as the British Empire itself, and just as much as part of that world organization.

Thomas Cook & Sons had effected a revolution in tourism. "No longer the preserve of peripatetic aristocrats and eccentrics, tourism was now an industry . . . In Europe Cook's organized tourism extended the privileges of the upper classes to the bourgeois . . . [Cook also] reinforces rigidly hierarchic distinctions between white ruling classes and coloured subject peoples."[106]

Moving naturally from the manufacture of tires for automobiles, the French firm, Michelin began to issue maps and guidebooks for motorists. The first Red Guide was published in 1900. It stressed where to find a reliable garage as well as sites of interest in French towns. Even with the first guide there were a mass of symbols—for everything from amenities such as quiet hotels to restaurants. The symbols became identified closely with the guides.[107] Until 1957 the guide was limited to France, but with the explosion in tourism by the early 1960s there were guides for most European countries as well as leading American sights. (Paralleling the Red Guides are the Green titles which are limited to describing the rating museums, and other points of interest in a city of region.) All of the books have excellent maps, but in addition Michelin publishes separate maps for motorists and tourists.

By the end of the nineteenth century and through all of the coming century, the specialized guidebooks proved almost as popular as the basic works from Baedeker, Murray et al. One particular type was the "social" guide, usually to a large city which pointed out the "best" places to stay in order to be considered a member of "good" society. Charles Pascoe's *London of Today*, for example, noted in the 1892 edition that "There are degrees of Society with the capital S . . . but money you must be provided with, and that too, in an agreeable measure if you wish to get into Society."[108]

Travel in the Twentieth Century

In the twentieth century, and particularly after the second World War, relatively inexpensive airfares made travel a part of daily living. As travel within a country became easier, so did world travel. By the mid 1960s the "leisure industries" had developed to a point where almost any middle class American and European could move over the face of the globe. Linked with rising affluence and more vacation time, this second half of the twentieth century brought about the phenomenon of "the barbarians in our age of leisure."[109]

A rough comparison of the interest in nineteenth century travel and by implication travel guides may be had by checking the number of periodical articles on the subject of travel published between 1800 and the mid 1960s. From 1802 to 1881 *Poole's Index to Periodical Literature* cites about 100 articles from primarily popular magazines. The *Nineteenth Century Readers' Guide,* covering 1890 to 1899 lists about 30 items, while by the late 1930s and early 1930s the same *Guide* has, for only three years, as many titles as published from 1802 to 1981.[110] By the mid 1960s the number has doubled again, which is hardly a surprise to anyone who has examined travel books and guides in any medium sized to large book store.[111]

The basic pattern for the modern English language travel guide was established in 1918 with the publication of the first "Blue Guide." Edited by L. Russell Muirhead the Guide established the combination of accommodation-history-food-amusements-church services-passport and visa requirements, and other items of interest to tourists in an easy to follow, usually small fat blue covered volume. Road routes as well as major and minor forms of transportation are included along with road atlases and up to 40 or more city street maps. Usually a single book is given over to a country or smaller group of countries in a given geographical area. Single volumes, too, are devoted to large cities and historical interest, e.g. *Blue Guide: Boston & Cambridge.* Known for accuracy the guides—proved a favorite of the British War Office in the second World War. They used them for the maps and the specific data on small bits of territory. The 1996 *Books in Print* lists dozens of the works *from Blue Guide: Barcelona to Blue Guides: Southern Italy.* Today they are published in the United States by Norton.

The Blue Books are the English substitute for Baedeker. The guides after the second World War stress roads and routes tourists should follow. "With this format, points of interest are conveniently grouped together in a sequence of routes, with accompanying descriptions that are intended to serve as a constant companion to the motorists, though they will equally serve the selective visitor who plans to do the country in a few weeks."[112]

American Guidebooks

Travel books and guides seem to parallel even the earliest American settlements. John Smith (1580–1631) related his adventures, and almost from that point forward every ship to America brought a visiting traveler. Most of the early books concentrated on personal experiences and "descriptions" of various areas. After the Revolutionary War, "the travel literature about America became more exciting. Now there was a new focal point of interest in the great experiment in federalism . . . Between 1800 and 1860 travelers circulated constantly on the 'grand tour' which was from New York to Boston and back, to Philadelphia, Baltimore, and Washington, then south. . ."[113] Often, too, a tour would go further West to the Ohio and Mississippi valleys. After the Civil War, the railroad allowed a different, wider route, and a growing number of travelers followed the trek westward from the Great Plains to California and the Oregon country.

As in Europe, the nineteenth century produced an impressive number of American travel guides and accounts of travel. Most of the travel was from Europe to every corner of America, and, before the Civil War, particularly to the Southern States. After the War, interest moved more and more to the West. By the 1880s all of the United States, including the major cities, had travel guides.

One of the most influential travel books of the nineteenth century motivated young Americans to hike through Europe rather than follow a Cook's tour. The youthful account by Bayard Taylor (1825–1878), *Views Afoot* was first published in 1846 and went through numerous editions until World War I. Thousands followed the journalist—diplomat's future advice. The leisurely travel account set the stage for the more formal travel guides, as well as hundreds of titles similar to Taylor.

The glory time of the Anglo-American travel book was roughly from 1810 to 1890. The books prepared tourists to receive impressions so that "the proper conditions and the proper exposure might create permanent images in their minds."[114]

Europe had been so much a part of the ideal life of the American thinking man and woman that its transition from the world of speculation to that of fact could never be experienced with equanimity. "Americans in England wrote home about and speculated in diaries and published accounts about numerous things, but among these inevitably were notes on the English road system. Good roads, rare enough to America, ensured that travel need no longer be difficult."[115]

George Putman was among the first American publishers of guides with *The Tourist in Europe* (1838). John Sherburne's *The Tourist Guide* (1847) proved equally popular as did Roswell Park's *Handbook for American Travellers in Europe* of 1853. All of this was simply a preamble to what was to come, with the boom in travel in the last decades of the nineteenth century, there was a flood of similar guides. "Boston newsman Curtis Guild produced *Over the Oceans* in 1871, *Abroad Again* in 1877, and *Britons and Muscovies* in 1888. William Hemstreet came out with *The Economical European Tourist* in 1875 . . . Most prolific of them all, with seven different guides for different parts of the world, was Thomas Knox, who began with a basic *How to Travel* in 1881. Other such books are Morris Phillip's *Abroad and at Home* in 1893; Moses Sweetser's *Europe for $2 a Day* in 1875."[116]

Rand McNally entered the map-atlas publishing business with a travel guide: *Western Railway Guide—The Traveller's Hand Book to All Western Railway and Steamship Lines* (Chicago, 1871). With that the company began a lucrative list of guides which became standard for many travelers in any of the states or territories as well as many places in Europe. The company's first maps appeared in the 1872 edition of the *Guide*. "Rand McNally developed the wax engraving method of mapmaking, producing broad changes in American map techniques.[117]

With the end of the first World War the wealthy American tourists and bohemians began to arrive in Europe. They had replaced the now bankrupt aristocracy and the nouveaux riches no longer felt inferior. If France was the American intellectual's first choice, other Americans discovered the delights of England as well as the Italian Riveria.

"The Second World War marked a watershed. Before it, in the twenties and thirties, organized tourism was chiefly a matter of trains, boats or coaches. Post 1945, such travel was increasingly by aeroplane, thus allowing tourists to go to newer mass destinations from Spain to India and Australia."[118] Each decade since the 1940s has seen a massive increase in the number of people going abroad by plane. The Europeans and Asians "invade" the United States and the Americans compete with the Japanese in European travel.

Today each travel guide has a distinctive focus, or at least those guides which manage more than one edition. For example, the Eugene Fodor guides, published since the 1960s, are particularly strong on background essays by individual experts. They cover everything from restaurants to historical sites. The Temple Fielding books, which began publication about the same time as the Fodor titles stress the cost of everything and the comments are as sharp as they often are perceptive about food, places and lodgings. Fodor is directed to the seasoned, usually better off traveler, while Fielding is the ideal aid for the beginner with less money.

In a real sense the existence, the publishing of travel guides is a mark of democracy. No totalitarian states offers their citizen's free exit, more or less guides to other lands. The basic convention of travel guides, almost from the beginning, was much the same. All assumed the reader was free.

Notes for Chapter 7

1. J.B. Harley. "Text and Contexts in the Interpretation of Early Maps," p. 11, 13. In David Buisseret, ed. *From Sea Charts to Satellite Images.* Chicago: University of Chicago Press, 1990.

2. "Cartography" today means almost any process involved with the construction of a map. In a narrower sense, cartography means the actual drawing of the map. Only at the close of the nineteenth century did cartography become a true science, and today, helped by computers and satellites it is growing even more sophisticated.

3. *Map* can be defined as "a graphic representation of all or part of the earth's surface; sometimes this definition may be much more restrictive, taking in such elements as scale or orientation." The map is part of the study of *Geography,* i.e. "the science of describing the earth's surface, formerly used in contrast to choreography (the mapping of an area of regional size)." Buisseret, *op. cit.* pp. 317–318. Some notion of the number of maps may be gained from the Library of Congress Collection. In 1992 the Library had 53,000 atlases and 4 million maps as well as 300 globes and an uncounted amount of software.

4. As late as the 1850s Europeans had only a sketchy notion of Africa and a cartographer (William Cooley) could claim there were no mountains in Africa. He was discredited only with the discoveries by Europeans of Mount Kenya and Mount Kilimanjaro.

5. While the history is limited to Europe and North America, it should not be forgotten that maps developed in Asia, Arab countries and China as well. There are, for example, Arab world maps from 1154 and the oldest Chinese map is from about 1137. Later Christian missionaries and explorers used these, and maps developed in other sections of the globe, to piece together considerably more accurate world maps then had been available to Europe. See the chapters "Islamic cartography" and "World maps of the later Middle Ages" in Bagrow, (footnote 6) for an overview of early contributions outside of Europe. For cartography of non-Western societies see the ongoing series of histories published by the University of Chicago *The History*

of Cartography, Vol. 2—*Book One: Cartography in the traditional Islamic and South Asian Societies* (1992); Vol. 2—*Book Two: Cartography in the traditional East and Southeast Asian Societies* (1995); Vol. 2—*Book Three Cartography in the traditional African, American, Arctic, Australian and Pacific Societies* (Scheduled for 1997). Edited by J.B. Harley (deceased) and David Woodward, the first volume in the series appeared in 1987: *Cartography in prehistoric, ancient and medieval Europe and the Mediterranean.* For a summary, at least of the early 1980s, see George Ritzlin, "Reference Books for the History of Cartography," *AB,* March 18, 1985.

6. Leo Bagrow. *History of Cartography.* Rev. by R.A. Skelton. London: C.A. Watts, 1964 p. 19.

7. Ibid, 20.

8. See, Raymond Lister's *Antique Maps.* Hampden, CT: Archon, 1970; and Arthur Robinson *The Look of Maps.* Madison: University of Wisconsin Press, 1986. Joel Makower ed. *The Map Catalog,* 3rd ed. New York: Viking, 1992. See, too, several journals including the British quarterly *The Map Collector.*

9. The oldest extant Egyptian map is the "Turin Papyrus" (so called as it is preserved in the Turin museum). This is from around 1300 B.C. and appears to show roads in what is now part of the Sudan.

10. While the early Egyptians unquestionably had sea charts of at least the eastern part of the Mediterranean, none exist. It was for Homer and the legend of the Argonauts to establish interest by Greeks in understanding the world around them.

11. Cosmography, i.e. a description with words and maps of not only the earth, but the universe which is governed by cosmic principles and speculation. Today's cosmographer turns to science, but until the middle of the Renaissance, much of the speculation was drawn from religion, early travel accounts, and imaginative speculation.

12. Only the early Medieval Christians returned to the more ancient notion of a flat earth. The view was hardly shared by Christian scholars.

13. See, Bagrow, *op. cit.,* pp. 32–37 for a brief discussion of Greek cartography. Other histories, and there are many, detail this period of maps.

14. Herodotus *The Histories.* New York: Penguin Books, 1983, p. 282 (4/36).

15. Historians record that Augustus had a map made in the first century A.D. which showed all 50,000 miles of roads in the Roman Empire as well as major points of interest. No copies exist. A Roman road map (known as the Peutinger Table) of the third or fourth century A.D. [of which there are no extant copies, and even its origin is in question,] was copied from an original by a monk in 1265 A.D. and this was acquired in 1508 by a scholar named Peutinger. The far from accurate copy at least indicates the scope of the map. "It is a long narrow strip of parchment, more than 21 feet long, 1 foot wide, in twelve sections, and was intended to serve as a portable road

guide . . . It extends from Britain to the Gange . . . but most of Britain, all Spain, and west Mauretania are missing." *The Oxford Classical Dictionary.* 2nd ed. New York: Oxford University Press, 1970, p. 808. See Bagrow, *op. cit.* pp. 37–38 for a history of the map and its probable origins.

16. Seventeen books of Strabo's survive. Only one *Geography* (the second) is concerned precisely with mathematics and cartography. He was among the first to offer a philosophy of geography, and while more interesting and valuable for his contributions to history, he remains a key figure in the early developments of geography.

17. Refugees from Constantinople and other Byzantine points fled to Italy and brought with them many manuscripts including the *Geography* which was translated into Latin in the early fifteenth century. Also, sections of the manuscript were saved by the Arabs. Combined, the work was printed at Bologna in 1477 and by the seventeenth century some 21 Latin or Italian editions had been published thus making it the key work in the early development of cartography in Europe.

18. Ptolemy left no maps, but from his 8,000 places and their coordinates, the Renaissance cartographer was able to construct a world map.

19. Penrose, *op. cit.,* p. 6.

20. As an astronomer Ptolemy excelled himself and made possible close map construction and reading. His *Almaqest* (also preserved by the Arabs), catalogued over 1,000 stars, in close to 50 constellations. In this he surpassed even the Babylonians and Egyptians who from c. 2500 B.C. had been studying the heavens. Not incidentally, Ptolemy had difficulty trying to explain the role of the planets, a problem only solved by Copernicus in 1543.

21. Penrose, *op. cit.,* p. 8. The Moslem scholars of the early Middle Ages preserved the Greek-Roman culture, including the sciences and much geographical knowledge. The twelfth and thirteenth century universities of the West looked to the Moslems for the "lost" classical knowledge, including the work of Ptolemy.

22. The major scholars of the Dark Ages and early Middle Ages, such as St. Augustine and the Venerable Bede upheld the Greek idea of a spherical earth. Unbending bigotry among later Christians accounted for the flat earth notion. By the thirteenth century the theory of the spherical earth came to be accepted by all except the most reactionary of the Christians. "Beatus" maps, more about Christian dogma than original points on the earth, were based on the Bible and included such features as Paradise and the Garden of Eden.

23. Campbell, *op. cit.,* p. 54.

24. Traditional concepts, varied wildly concerning the exact shape of the sphere. "Abelard, for example, tried . . . to reconcile a spherical earth with a disk surrounded by the ocean . . . Whatever its merits, Abelard's floating earth, when applied to cartography, justified placing north at the top."

Dictionary of the Middle Ages. New York: Charles Scribner's Sons, 1985, vol. 5, p. 396.

25. See Bagrow, *op. cit.,* p. 45 for a "chronological table of medieval world maps."

26. Apparently a clever forgery, the so called Finland map at Yale, appears to chart discoveries in North America in the mid fifteenth century before the voyage of Columbus. Some scholars still argue that while the map may be a fake, the voyages themselves, the places recorded on the map probably are valid. A few believe, in fact, the map will prove to be valid.

27. Who invented the compass and where is as much a mystery as the place and name of the person who invented the wheel. While a form of the compass probably was in use from the earliest navigational adventures, its only written record appears in China in about 1,000 A.D. and in Europe some 100 years later. At any rate, since the thirteenth century there is considerable material about the variations, types and uses of the compass in Europe and most parts of the world.

28. Such charts are called "portolans," i.e. portolano or pilot guide. Generally they chart sailing courses, point out ports of entry, various anchorages and other features useful for sailors and traders of the Medieval period. The place(s) of origin of the portolan chart is not known. Some speculate the Norse were the first to make such charts, while others believe the Arabs responsible for the discovery. Probably the charts developed in various places at various times as needed. The related Greek (i.e. handbook) *Peripulus of the Erythraean Sea* is an extant sailing manual from the period of Pliny which covers the familiar ports on the Indian Ocean and mentions, for the first time, China. It, as other earlier periplus, did not contain maps, but did have explicit sailing directions.

29. While primarily of the Mediterranean and Black Sea, the numerous extant examples of these charts from time to time include further points from the coast of Africa to the Atlantic. Although each was hand drawn they followed definite patterns, e.g. the majority include the compass magnetic rose which shows the distances and directions from different compass readings (i.e. roses) on the map.

30. Petrus Vesconte at Genoa in 1311 issued the first sea chart based on scientific cartographic principles. Vesconte produced a group of maps, as well as atlases, which he dated. He also made available (c. 1312) a world map.

31. For a discussion of Polo's adventures from the point of view of cartographers see Newton, *op. cit.,* Chapter 7 "The opening of the land routes to Cathay," and chapters in Campbell, *op. cit. The Travels of Marco Polo* was one of the most popular books of the Middle Ages. It is represented today by close to 140 manuscript copies, and numerous incunabula.

32. A survivor of the Middle Ages, and among the finest maps of the period *Catalan Atlas* is on 12 sheets. Published in 1375, (before the term

"atlas" had come into use), in Catalonia, the individual hand drawn maps are the work of cartographer Abraham Cresques. Despite elaborate decoration it is one of the more accurate maps of the period.

33. Mercator, *op. cit.,* p. 152.

34. Bagrow, *op. cit.,* pp. 120–121.

35. Penrose, *op. cit.,* p. 9.

36. Over 1,000 copies of Waldseemuller's *Universalie Cosmographia,* showing an abbreviated form of what was then known of North America, and the name "America" used for the first time on a world map, was published in 1507. Folded out it was an enormous map of 4 × 8 feet. The 12 sheets, printed from woodblocks, were folded. Only one copy is extant. The name was quickly adopted by others and was in general use by the middle of the sixteenth century.

37. Randolph Stow, "The World was All Before Them" *The Times Literary Supplement,* August 4, 1995, p. 16.

38. The problem, as any school child soon learns, is that the Mercator projection forces exaggerated sizes, i.e. Greenland in the upper latitude appears much larger than reality. And while Mercator designed his map for seamen, it gained more fame as a wall chart in nearly every schoolroom from the seventeenth century to the present. Projections are an effort to overcome map distortion caused by showing a natural round surface on a flat surface. A drawn chart or a computer printout suffer the same problem, although the smaller the surface portrayed, the less the distortion. World maps are the worst, city maps the best. Projections are a study in themselves, but primarily may be divided into a half dozen or more categories from the Mercator projection, which is cylindrical, to the modern elliptical, or Robinson projection.

39. Before the first real atlas, i.e. a collection of individual maps and published as such, there were several forerunners to the form: *The Catalan Atlas* (so called because it was prepared in Catalonia) appeared in 1375 but is not a true atlas in that it is a single map on folded multiple sheets. Ptolemy's *Geographia,* particularly in Renaissance and later editions, served as a type of atlas, but this was not its principle purpose. Waldseemuller published an edition of Ptolemy in Strassburg in 1513. In so doing created the cousin of the first modern atlas. While there is some question as to whether Waldseemuller actually produced the maps, generally he is given credit for the work. The atlas format derives from a custom, originated by Antonio Lafreri in about 1556. The Roman publisher brought together as many as 160 separate maps in one volume. He used the figure of Atlas, but failed to call his collection an "atlas" in the 1556 edition or in other collections published until 1575.

40. John Hale. *The Civilization of Europe in the Renaissance.* New York: Atheneum, 1994, p. 20.

41. Robert Dudley (1574–1679), explorer, courtier and cartographer

was the first to publish a detailed sea atlas (*The Mysteries of The Sea,* 1646–1647). It included 145 charts which employed the new Mercator projections. Although published in Florence and in Italian, it also is the first atlas compiled by an Englishman.

42. The maps/atlas become increasingly valuable when in 1672 most of the engraving were destroyed in a fire. The few remaining plates were purchased by other mapmakers and used for a century or more to follow.

43. John Harrison (1693–1776) solved the problem of reading longitude at sea by his invention of a marine chronometer in 1765. The benefits of the much valued, much sought after instrument were immediately evident. Captain James Cook, for one, used it on his second and third Pacific voyages. More important to cartographers it now permitted the accurate location of island and coastlines which could be plotted scientifically on charts. See Dava Sobel's *Longitude, the true story of a lone genius who solved the greatest scientific problem of his time.* New York: Walker & Co. 1995. This brilliant history made the best seller list, an unheard of event for such a book.

44. All major countries have agencies and bureaus responsible for mapping, e.g. the United States Geological Survey, the British Ordinance Survey, the French Institute Geographica National etc. Each, in turn, issues maps many of which are found in major reference collections throughout the world.

45. Actually Lewis Evans (fl. mid 1700s), who worked for Benjamin Franklin after coming to the Americas from Wales, published an earlier map, but only of the Northeastern colonies in 1752. This was followed by "the middle British colonies" in 1755. Data was gathered from travelers and was quite accurate. Apparently both maps were used heavily by British troops during the revolution. The first atlas devoted entirely to the Americas was Cornelius Van Wytfliet's Description is *Ptolemaicae Augmentum* (Louvain, 1597). For a detailed description of this atlas see Donald Gallup "The First Separately Published atlas entirely devoted to the Americas. . ." *Papers of the Bibliographical Society of America,* Vol. 76, No. 1, 1982, pp. 63–73. See, too: James Wheat and Christian Brun *Maps and Charts Published in America Before 1800: A Bibliography.* New Haven, CT: Yale University Press, 1969.

46. Some claim the American atlas was the *American Pilot,* which appeared three years before Carey's title. The claim, however, is based on an atlas of coastal charts and not a world atlas.

47. Arthur H. Robinson. *Early Thematic Mapping.* Chicago: The University of Chicago, 1982, p. 1X. This is the basic book on the subject of thematic mapping, and the seven chapters cover maps to the early twentieth century.

48. Ibid, 66.

49. *The New Encyclopaedia Britannica, op. cit.,* Vol. 19, p. 878.

50. On a more modest scale, aerial maps have been available since the mid-nineteenth century, although it was not until World War I that special cameras allowed precise pictures of locations. The United States' satellite to study the earth from outer space was launched in 1972, followed by countless others from then to the present.

51. Mark Monmonier. *How to Lie With Maps.* Chicago: University of Chicago Press, 1991. See, too: Dennis Wood *The Power of Maps.* New York: Guilford Press, 1992 which reminds readers of the political function of maps—a function which often encourages lies.

52. David Buissert and Christopher Baruth, "Aerial Imagery" in Buissert, *op. cit.,* pp. 283–309. This is an excellent explanation of the subject with numerous examples.

53. Jack Hitt, "Atlas Shrugged . . . a new science of mapmaking." *Lingua Franca,* July/August, 1995, p. 25.

54. "The First Family of American Maps," *The New York Times,* November 15, 1991, p. xx15.

55. Gilles Le Bouvier. *Le Livre de la Descriptions des Pays.* (Mid 15th Century) quoted in *Dictionary of the Middle Ages.* New York: Charles Scribner's Sons, 1989, vol. 12, p. 162.

56. Mary B. Campbell. *The Witness and the Other World.* Ithaca: Cornell University Press, 1988, p. 1.

57. A bibliography published in Paris in 1959 (*Avecles Guides Bleus.* Hachette) includes some 4,000 titles in print. Not all are strictly guidebooks, but it gives some indication of the popularity of the genre. Today in America there are from 2,00 to 3,000 travel and guidebooks in print. See, too: Edward Cox *A Reference to the Literature of Travel,* Seattle: University of Washington, 1938, 3 volumes; and Sarah Anderson *Anderson's Travel Companion* Aldershot, England: Scolar Press, 1995. Anderson annotates over 12,000 travel titles both fiction and nonfiction.

58. Charles L. Batten. *Pleasurable Instruction: form and convention in eighteenth century travel literature.* Berkeley: University of California Press, 1978, p. 2.

59. Alan Sillitoe. *Leading the Blind: A Century of Guide Book Travel 1815–1914.* London: Macmillan, 1995. See, too: Elizabeth Bohls *Women Travel Writers and the Language of Aesthetics 1716–1818.* Cambridge: Cambridge University Press, 1996.

60. Nigel Nicolson, "Enlightened Travels," *The Spectator,* September 16, 1995, p. 56.

61. *Cambridge History of English Literature.* New York: Macmillan, 1943, p. 265.

62. Batten, *op. cit.,* p. 29–30.

63. "Recent Travels," *Fraser's Magazine,* No. 50, 1854, p. 245.

64. John Vaughan. *The English Guide Book.* Newton Abbot: David & Charles, 1974, p. 63.

65. Alexander romances fed early travel accounts, and Alexander is the great hero of early European travel literature. He often appears as a central figure in secular travel books where he kills monsters or observers, and describes them from a distance. See Campbell, *op. cit.,* pp. 68–72.

66. Nothing is known of Pausanias other than what may be deduced from his book.

67. Lionel Casson. *Travel in the Ancient World.* Baltimore, MD: Johns Hopkins University Press, 1994, p. 265.

68. For a detailed discussion of this celebrated manuscript, see Campbell, *op. cit.,* Chapter 2, "The Fabulous East Wonder Books and Grotesque Facts."

69. Ibid, p. 167, which goes on: "Travel literature was involved in the development . . . of the modern novel, the renewal of heroic romance, and the foundations of scientific geography. That such various discourses are so mutually entangled in the corpus of . . . travel literature is a fact of real importance to the histories of all of them, but perhaps most of all to the history of literature." See, too: Philip Gove. *The Imaginary Voyage in Prose Fiction.* London: Holland Press, 1961. The first part is a discussion of the form, which the author believes is so close a cousin to the novel to sometimes make it indistinguishable from fiction. The second part is an "annotated check list of two hundred and fifteen imaginary voyages from 1700 to 1800." The vast majority are in English, French and German. The most famous entries include *Robinson Crusoe* and *Gulliver's Travels* along with less well known fiction.

70. The legend of Prester John appears in manuscript form only in the twelfth century, but it probably predates this in oral form by many centuries. In a manuscript chronicle of circa 1158 there is reference to a "Johannes Presbyter" who lead a victory over the Persians. This same Prester John was a fabulously rich king, as well as a priest, who reigned over most of India. (Oral accounts seem to have placed him in what is now Ethiopia, and the "India" was considerably more than modern India, and may have included other lands as well.) Almost equaling Prester John is power was the myth of the lost continent of Atlantis, started by Plato, and the El Dorado where there were rivers of gold.

71. Arthur Newton. *Travel and Travellers of the Middle Ages.* London: Routledge & Kegan Paul, 1926. The forged letter from Prester John explained how he ruled three Indias. (Quoted in full in Newton, pp. 174–178.)

72. Campbell, *op. cit.,* p. 18.

73. Mandeville created a character, one Jehan d'Outremuse of Liege. The stories in the book were gathered from various sources including authentic narratives as well as pure fiction. The result is hopelessly muddled and inconsistent with any clear system of either travel writing or geography. While today the true and false are easily separated, the average reader totally confused the two. For an extensive discussion of Mandeville, see Newton, *op. cit.,* Chapter 8, "Travellers' tales. . . ."

74. Campbell, *op. cit.,* p. 13.

75. Rebecca Stefoff. *The Young Oxford Companion to Maps and Mapmaking.* New York: Oxford University Press, 1995, p. 30.

76. The irony of travel during the Middle Ages is that this was the period when there were laws against serfs leaving the land and the highest religious orders stressed monks remaining in one place. In addition, for much of the early Middle Ages travel was downright unsafe and transportation was as poor as it was irregular.

77. Campbell points out that while Egeria was the first Christian to render an account of a journey to the Near East, she was hardly the first to write about its places. "In his Vita Constantini, Eusebius Pamphili (250–340) . . . had written extensively about the churches erected in and around the Holy Land." Campbell *op. cit.,* p. 18.

78. Written between 1380 and 1400, the *Canterbury Tales* follow what is probably the earliest Middle Age-Renaissance record of travel for pleasure. This is Petrarch's description of his ascent of Mt. Ventoux in 1336.

79. Campbell, *op. cit.,* pg. 127, 128.

80. The historical-geographical narrative began in Portugal. Gomes de Azurara (d. 1474) left an account of tropical Africa. Other Henrician voyages were related by Portuguese travelers and diplomats, terminating with Juan de Barros (1496–1570) who set to work in 1540 to tell the story of his country's empire. The result was a massive four volume *Decades* covering the period from 1420 to 1538.

81. Samuel Purchas (1575–1626) was a cleric assistant to Hakluyt and compiled the Hakluyt Posthumous in 1625. Coverage is of the Mediterranean, the East and the West Indies as well as Florida.

82. For a detailed discussion of primarily travel literature in the fifteenth and early sixteenth century see Chapter 17 "The Geographical Literature of the Renaissance." in Boies Penrose *Travel and Discovery in the Renaissance 1420–1620.* Cambridge, MA: Harvard University Press, 1952.

83. Stephen Bann *Under the Sign.* Ann Arbor: University of Michigan Press, 1995. This is a detailed study of the phenomenon of the "cabinet of curiosities" which developed in the early seventeenth century. Many of these collections are the cores of numerous modern museums.

84. R. S. Lambert, ed. *Grand Tour.* New York: E.P. Dutton, 1937, p. 11, 12.

85. E. S. Bates. *Touring in 1600.* Boston: Houghton Mifflin, 1912, p. 43–43.

86. Ibid, p. 59.

87. A Byzantine princess brought the fork to Europe (i.e. Venice) originally, but Coryate is credited with its introduction into England.

88. Anon. *A Letter of Advice to a young gentleman leaving the university concerning his behavior and conversation in the world.* Dublin, 1670.

89. Sara Warneke. *Images of the Educational Traveller in Early Modern England.* New York: E.J. Brill, 1995, p. 295.

90. Ibid, p. 6.

91. Upperclass young men from other countries followed a similar pattern of travel, although not as extensively as the English. Outside of England, the usual approach was to appoint a youth to a diplomatic journey and/or post. Women rarely traveled abroad before the nineteenth century. A minority did follow men on the Grand Tour, but they were unusual. After the end of pilgrimage, women found it difficult to travel abroad except as the wives, daughters, sisters or servants of male travelers.

92. Lambert, *op. cit.,* p. 164.

93. "Been There, Seen That, Got the T-Shirt," *Guardian Weekly,* September 17, 1995, p. 28.

94. David Webb "For Inns a Hint, for Routes a Chart: The Nineteenth-century London Guidebooks." *London Journal,* Vol. 6, No. 2, 1980, p. 210–211.

95. Louis Turner and John Ash. *The Golden Hoardes.* London: Constable, 1975, p. 19.

96. The other side of all this was that guides began to be issued in which the thrills and sins of the town might be savored. Harris', for example, *List of Covent Garden Ladies,* is self explanatory and ran through numerous editions in the 1780s. By the mid-1850s the warnings seemed to have been deleted.

97. Vaughan, *op. cit.,* p. 44.

98. By 1900 Murray had published, and most were still in print, over 60 volumes. John Murray, and later his son and grandson, was among the most famous publishers in Europe. Among the early authors, although certainly not of guide books, were Jane Austen and Byron. Murray published, too, a group of popular magazines.

99. George Paston. *John Murray.* London: John Murray, 1932, p. 164–165.

100. Ibid.

101. Trevor Christie, "Baedeker Had a Guidebook for It," *Saturday Review,* January 6, 1963, p. 30.

102. Webb, *op. cit.,* p. 212.

103. Ibid.

104. Some early readers, as today, are disturbed by the asterisks and other marks of good, best and better. Baedeker was accused of being a "kultur-diktator." Such markings offer a one-sided view of anywhere, but between tradition and sales there is no question they are the primary reason many people purchase the guides.

105. Quoted in Turner, *op. cit.,* p. 55. See his Chapter 3 for the biography and history of Thomas Cook.

106. Ibid.

107. Andrea Michelin (1853–1931) began the guides, and it was he and his staff which devised the rating of restaurants with the occasional note that a visit was worth a special trip. Not a few disappointed cooks have been known to commit suicide on the basis of a poor showing in the Michelin red guide, i.e. less than the wished for 3 star rating. No one has died over failure to appear in the Michelin green guides which rank important places and sights.

108. Webb, *op. cit.,* p. 213, quoting C.E. Pascoe *London of Today* (1892 ed.), p. 112.

109. Turner, *op. cit.,* p. 12.

110. *Poole's Index to Periodical Literature, 1802–1881.* Gloucester, MA: Peter Smith, 1963 (a reprint of the original); *Nineteenth Century Readers' Guide to Periodical Literature 1890–1899.* New York: H.W. Wilson Company, 1944; *Readers' Guide to Periodical Literature.* Wilson, various dates.

111. With the advent of mass tourism came popular photography. Susan Sontag observes that photography develops in tandem with one of the most characteristic of modern activities: tourism. The tourist's job is to take pictures and the good guidebooks explain what is to be photographed. See: Susan Sontag. *On Photography.* New York: Farrar, Straus & Giroux, 1978.

112. J.A. Neal. *Reference Guide for Travellers.* New York: R.R. Bowker, 1969, p. 128. Although dated, this is a useful bibliography, with descriptions of each guide series, of major and many minor guides in print in 1969.

113. Thomas Clark, "Travel Literature" in McDermott, John *Research Opportunities in American Cultural History.* Lexington, KY: University of Kentucky Press, 1961, p. 53–54.

114. Christopher Mulvey Anglo. *American Landscapes, a study of nineteenth century Anglo-American travel literature.* New York: Cambridge University Press, 1983, p. 254.

115. Ibid, p. 30.

116. Allison Lockwood. *Passionate Pilgrims: The American Traveler in Great Britain, 1800–1914.* New York: Corwall Books, 1981, p. 294. In William Hemstreets *The Economical European Tourist,* (New York: S.W. Green, 1875) the author pointed out that by the 1870s one could travel for three months in Europe for $433—somewhat more than the $2 a day plan, but still reasonable.

117. John Tebbel. *A History of Book Publishing in the United States,* Vol. 2. New York: R.R. Bowker, 1975. Rand McNally now publishes (since 1948) the *Mobil Travel Guides.*

118. Turner, *op. cit.,* p. 93.

8

Biography

"The art of biography
Is different from geography.
Geography is about maps,
But biography is about chaps."[1]

Biography, "the written history of a person's life," as well as autobiography, "the biography of oneself narrated by oneself"[2] is one of those reference works which serves to both inform and entertain. Librarians find the biography section may be as inviting as fiction. One reason is not hard to discover, for as author Bernard Malamud pointed out: "There is no life that can be recaptured wholly; as it was. Which is to say that all biography is ultimately fiction."[3] At the same time the librarian will often turn to biographical reference works (which includes everything from indexes and bibliographies to diaries, chronicles, journals, letters and history) to answer both ready reference and in depth research queries. The ubiquitous, universal use of biography in reference is explained in part by Thomas Carlyle who, in a famous quotation, observed: "The history of the world is but the biography of great men."[4]

The Oxford English Dictionary notes that the descriptor biography "and its numerous connections (biography, biographee, biographer, biographic, biographical etc.) are recent. No compounds of the group existed in Old Greek."[5] Still versions of the word, e.g. "writing of lives" were used in Greek and Latin before any words of the O.E.D. group appeared in English. "Biographist" was used by Fuller, 1662; biography by Dryden, 1683, biographer by Addison 1715 . . . all the others are later. The term "autobiography" does not appear in English until the eighteenth century. Conversely, autobiography, no matter what it was called, has been about since the Greeks and Romans.

In describing attitudes toward biography, Leon Edel, the biographer of Henry James, demonstrates the wide differences in opinion of the art, e.g. George Eliot: "a disease of English literature," W.H. Auden: "always superfluous and usually in bad taste." On the other hand James called biography "one of the greatest observed adventures of mankind."[6] Martin Amis described the 1993 biography of Philip Larkin as the product of "a lowly trade." And Edmund White in *The New York Times Book Review* claims biography as a form has become "the revenge of little people on big people." Or as James Atlas puts it: "The biographer's real intent is to enact revenge: The writer, like the murderer needs a motive."[7]

Author Joyce Carol Oates makes the point that the use of psychoanalytic methods to find the hidden personal myth about a subject is dangerous because the author "will quite naturally project his own personal myths onto the subject." Unless founded on meticulous research and facts, a biography which seeks to find the subject's inwardness may end up "reductive, arbitrary, vulgar, and confusing—the subject will be a massive Rorschach of the biographer's own personal myth."[8]

Granted all of these comments are pointed to individual biographers and biographies, but much the same can be said of numerous reference works, or at least those where there is more than a minimum of information. Even the directory type "Who's Who" can be subject to many of the enumerated problems, and particularly the sin of the subject projecting a "personal myth."

It was not until well into this century that biography would become a trustworthy reference aid. Earlier biographies, whether dictionaries or individual stories, tended to reflect what the biographer wished to emphasize. Little importance was placed on facts for the sake of facts.

> "From its inception, biography was marked by its . . . tendencies to exaggerate a person's achievements and virtues . . . Heroes were created by using historical detail as a backdrop to display nobility of character . . . Equally important for the uniqueness of biography . . . was its propagandistic, often polemical, mood."[9]

Before the mid twentieth century biographers prided themselves on shaping a life story to make a point. St. Jerome, (347–420), for example, added fancy and fact together to draw up a biography of 135 Christian writers (c. 392). The idea was to demonstrate the intellectual powers of early Christians. Another example is the by now famous life of St. Anthony of Egypt by St. Athanasius (fl. fourth century) which claimed feats for Anthony somewhat beyond current notions of truth. Victorians thought it bad manners to display less than admiration for an individual.

Less than reliable biography, from the first to yesterday's publication have several usually obvious faults: a) celebration of the person rather than a candid appraisal; b) mixing in suppositions and downright fiction about the person; c) reliance on the individual to represent a given idea, theme, historical moment etc.; d) the undue intrusion of the biographer's ideas, personality and psychological biases.

Reference Biographical Works

Aside from individual biographies, the earliest form of reference works in this field were biographical dictionaries. These are collections of individual biographies of a few lines to many pages. In the sense that they grouped biographies of major figures together in one work, the early publications of *Suetonius* (c. 69–140 A.D.) and *Plutarch,* (c. 46–120 A.D.) as well as the medieval *Lives of the Saints,* might be termed the first biographical dictionaries. Robert Slocum makes a fine distinction between the various titles: None of the early efforts "is a biographical dictionary; they are collected biographies whose chief aim is didactic—biographical information is subordinate."[10] This nice division is not always that apparent, and even Solcum admits cracks in his distinction between "didactic" and using titles for biographical information.

Today's reference biographical sources differ from standard biographies in other major ways: (1) The data tends to be concise and focuses on the individual, the particulars of his or her life. Historical interpretation, grand themes, imaginative conclusions about a person's life are avoided. The only signs of interpretation is the necessary element of selection of data. (2) The facts normally are strung out in chronological order. Generally it is an outline of events rather than, as in extensive biographies, the subtle aspects of a person's personality. (3) The focus is objective. Enthusiasm or disgust for an individual usually is avoided. (4) As the emphasis is on facts and truth, plain information is quite enough. Imaginative writing about the unfolding of a life is not usual. (5) Various forms of autobiography, other than the "Who's Who" directories were the subject fills in his or her own history, are uncommon in reference work. The reference librarian may use bibliographies, indexes and other sources to help someone find autobiographical material in letters, diaries, journals, memoirs and formal, individual published autobiographies.

Simple listings of biographical sources is a normal aspect of the genre in the age of computers. For example, *Biographical Books,* compiled in 1981, is no more than a printout of *Books in Print* biographical entries from 1950 to 1980. The 45,000 entries are arranged alphabetically, but there is a vocation index as well as other entry points. Biographical dictionaries and collective biographies are included.[11]

Reference and book length studies normally are based on either: a) first-hand knowledge of the subject, often supplied by the individual in a filled out questionnaire; or b) research to trace the biographical activity of a dead individual. In some rare cases it is a combination of both methods of gathering data. (2) Both forms try to avoid distortion or falsification. The exception may be the conscious or unconscious inclusion or exclusion of matters which will foster inference and conjecture. Which is to say, even the briefest "Who's Who" or the multivolume biography can never be completely objective. Reference and more literary, interpretive biography part company at several points. The most obvious is that reference titles avoid both fictionalized biography or fiction presented as biography.

Biography is divided generally into three or four historical periods. First, the Greco-Roman tradition as typified by Plurarch's *Parallel Lives.* Here ethics and morals are the goal of biography. Hagiography is the focus of Medieval biography, e.g. Einhard's *Life of Charlemagne*. The third stage, from the Renaissance through the eighteenth century, gradually recognized the importance of the individual. Here, of course, Boswell's *Life of Johnson* is the prime example. The fourth and present period is not only involved with the historical life, but the complex psychological problems involved with the recreation of a life in a biography. Now the emphasis is learning the "truth" about an individual and, equally, the meaning of that life.

Biography Beginnings

Egyptian and Mesopotamian inscriptions saluting the dead, as well as now lost funeral orations, represent the earliest forms of biography. As these were meant as tributes, the pattern was early established of biography being synonymous with the laudatory and exemplary characteristics of the deceased. The flattering, uncritical remarks gained favor throughout the early history of the form and, in fact, it was not until Lytton Strachey's by now famous *Eminent Victorians* (1918) that the art of the critical, debunking biography became the norm.

There is no agreement on the earliest known biographers, although generally the credit is given to two or three: Xanthus of Lydia (c. 450 B.C.) who wrote a book on Empedocles, the Greek philosopher-scientist; Skylax of Caryanda (c. 480 B.C.) may have written a biography of Heraclides the philosopher. The Greek poet Ion of Chios (c. 490–421 B.C.) is considered by many to be the father of biography. He had brief sketches of contemporaries Pericles, Cimon, Sophocles and others in his memoirs. Plato's (427–347 B.C.) life of Socrates in *The Apology* and the *Phaedo* was to be matched only some 400 years later by the life of Jesus, or more specifically the four lives in *The New Testament*.

The sketch or brief life dates back, at least in the West, to Plutarch's (46–120) *Parallel Lives of the Noble Grecians and Romans* (c. 105–115) and Suetonius' (c. 69–140) *Lives of the Caesars* (c. 130 A.D.). Today the closest thing to these short lives will be found in newspapers and magazines where there is a mingling of imaginative character evaluation and chronological facts about an individual. A typical modern example is the "profile" in almost any issue of *The New Yorker,* at least prior to the current editor Tina Howe.

Suetonius followed the Plutarchian pattern, although he tended to be more critical of the individual emperors. The moral evaluation shaded the biography, but here and there the individual comes through—particularly in Suetonius' notion that physical characteristics were points of revelation about character. "Bright eyes," for example, were equated with boldness while pale skin, such as Caligula's, meant cowardliness. In a very real way

Suetonius set the pattern for centuries to come—biography was not so much a portrait of an individual as the molding of the person to fit a preconceived model.

The "apothegm" which flourished in classical literature was rediscovered in the Renaissance. Defined as an aphorism or a brief narrative, usually of an anecdotal nature, the apothegm celebrated the deeds and sayings of the classical greats from Socrates to Alexander the Great. Also, the sayings might show the wisdom and wit of lesser known people. The sayings all shared one thing in common—a method of instruction, usually in a painless fashion. While few Greek apothegms survive, the Romans used them extensively. Some surface in literature of the Middle Ages, but only incidentally.

The Greco-Roman tradition, and particularly Plutarch, established patterns of biographical "research." Plutarch "assembled his materials—ancient lore, old wives' tales, stories of splendors and glories, miseries and defeates— traveling the length of the Mediterranean in his historical quest . . . (He was) an historian who sought the meaning of great lives as a form of moral philosophy."[12] Plutarch saw only minor differences between history and biography, particularly in terms of research. Biographers did differ from historians in that they concentrated on moral illustrations of what a man should or should not do in society. History concentrated on action. In either case it was customary to make little distinction between facts, fiction, myth and epic poetry. Plutarch's "Life of Solon," for example, is as much fiction as fact. "Solon's biography is not so much an account of his life as it is of what people . . . believed to be the significance of his life."[13]

While not a separate discipline or study until the eighteenth century, biography was implanted in history from almost the beginning as it was in "lives" which were published separately or as part of a history, e.g. *Lives of the Saints* (throughout the Dark and Middle Ages) and the biographical piece on the Emperor Tiberius in Tacitus' *Annals* (c. 56 A.D.). Today there are numerous combinations from the traditional cultural historian who relies on individual biographies to the psychoanalyst who combines history and biography. "Nobody nowadays is likely to doubt that biography is some kind of history."[14]

Basics about daily lives of the Greek philosophers, the Roman emperors, the lives of Biblical figures, were not considered in early biographies. "Neglect of the domestic being did not mean lack of knowledge about it, and about its maturing, . . . it meant that the authors of early lives had a different sense of their mission than do modern authors."[15] The turn came in the fifth century B.C. when the individual became unique. The change widened history to include the life of the self rather than simply the public life or the life which reflected the public interests. Still, biography tended to be more impersonal, more symbolic than individual.[16]

The modern writer conceives of the individual forming and being formed over a long period of time by history. "We tend to emphasize the self as a creature of history and history as a human creation."[17] Biography is history in a new form, and the subject reflects a historical period and attitude. "This person, we say to ourselves as we encounter Franklin arriving in Philadelphia, has lived history."[18] Then, too, another common theme of modern biography is "the responsibility of having to comprehend the very motives of his subject."[19]

Late Antique and Medieval Developments

Throughout most of the Dark and Middle Ages, the biographers followed the patterns established by the Greeks and Romans. A new dimension was to employ biographical polemics for conversion of pagans to Christianity. This lead to a standard idealization of the Christian hero. The majority of subjects, from clerics and popes to writers and philosophers were held up as "divine sages" or vehicles for the word of Christianity and more particularly the persuasion from disbelief to conviction. "Biographers saw their subjects "through prisms of divine sonship or godlikeness . . . The ideal facets of his life might be emphasized."[20] Then as now readers turned to the biographies to find out details about another individual, and, equally in many cases, to help explain problems of contemporary life. If one grants this is at least partially correct, then it can be seen why the Christian biographers put so much focus on imaginative writing to convince readers of the delights and rewards of their religion as demonstrated in the lives of exemplary individuals.

During the Dark and Middle Ages the lives of the saints was a standard biographical source. The hagiographic biography of saints and venerable personalities were circulated in manuscripts as early as 400 A.D. in Gaul. As collections of short biographies these may be termed among the earliest of the biographical dictionaries, although it may be stretching the definition of such reference titles. Be that as it may they continued in number and popularity for over 1,000 more years and even to this day are a source of lively, if not always accurate data.

The lives varied in form, length and literary appeal, but all shared several common elements: (1) Most were based on exotic and apocryphal figures. (2) All were panegyric and often more fiction than reality.[21] (3) Early lives were primarily in Latin, but by the twelfth and thirteenth centuries the vernacular for the obvious purpose of reaching more people. (4) There were both individual lives, such as the Life of St. Thomas Becket by Guernes de Pont-Sainte-Maxence (c. 1174) and collective works such as Jacobus da Voragine's *Legenda aurea*.[22]

The various *Lives of the Saints* gained immediate success in manuscript form and were often recopied as well as printed from the fifteenth century on. Their primary gift was the realization that even though helped by God, saints were individuals. "The self, simple but willful, began to assert its centrality in Western thought . . . (through) the biographical consequences of the Christian concentration upon self."[23]

Although more concerned with Christianity and doctrine than with individuals, St. Jerome (347–420) established the medieval form for biography in c. 395 with his *De viris illustribus,* (concerning famous men) a series of individual lives beginning with the Christian fathers and ending with Jerome himself. Some consider this little more than a bibliography, rather than a biographical collection. It serves both purposes in that it sketches lives and gives notable books by and about the person listed. The biographical and the logical combination was favored among many early Christian intellectuals, including Isidore of Seville.[24]

Frequently cited as the author of the first autobiography (*Confessions*) St. Augustine (354–430) set the stage for the genre in that most of the work celebrates his own conquest of himself and the world. Virtue, in his case, was God given.

With the exception of St. Jerome and St. Augustine after the fall of Rome and well into the late Middle Ages there was little contribution to biography. The church and society buried the individual in the needs of religion and, later, the feudal state. What biography there was concentrated on hagiography, which sometimes contained anecdotal material, but for the most part has little to do with an individual protagonist. History, such as Bede's *Ecclesiastical History of the English People* (c. 730) interwove a few biographical sketches and portraits. Still, there were a few pleasant exceptions such as the life of Charlemagne by Einhard.

Einhard (c. 770–840) was as well known for his education as for his diminutive size. Recommended to Charlemagne's court, the child of a noble family came to the famous palace school at Aachen in the early 790s. Alcuin was in charge, but when Alcuin retired to Tours, Einhard seems to have succeeded him, an expected move as Einhard by then was a personal tutor to Charlemagne. After the ruler's death, Einhard wrote the *Vita Caroli Magni* (c. 830–833).[25] His life of Charlemagne exerted a major influence on biographical writing throughout the Middle Ages. More than 80 manuscript copies are extant. While the account has several factual errors, it is unique in that it is the only manuscript by a man who knew Charlemagne well, and because it is written with so much verve and style it proved to be one of the most popular books of the Medieval period. Invaluable as a relatively accurate history, it includes descriptions of old German narratives, the codification of German tribal laws and details of numerous military campaigns.

The first English biography of a layperson, rather than a saint was Bishop Asser (d. c. 908) *Life of Alfred the Great.* . . . This is a chronicle of English events between 849 and 887. While most is history, the personal touches about Alfred indicate Bishop Asser knew him well.

The "gesta" or notable deeds of action and adventure were closely linked to biography, although as in the lives of the saints, more fiction than truth. By and large the most famous collection is the *Gesta Romanorum* of anecdotes and tales about heroes. Compiled in the early fourteenth century, it proved a source of inspiration to many English writers from Chaucer and John Gower to Shakespeare, and established the legends of numerous characters who would appear in English literature from Pericles to Apollonius of Tyre. Although based on a Latin collection, the authorship of *Romanorum* is not known.

The Renaissance to Dr. Johnson

The Renaissance was almost as disappointing as the Middle Ages for biography.[26] Here and there a work appeared, such as the incomplete Thomas More's *History of Richard III* (c. 1513). The remaining period of the Renaissance was relatively barren, again because many educated writers and readers thought it ill advised to frame history in the words of, or through the eyes of an individual, no matter how famous. Scholars continued to divide history and biography with the latter receiving less than favorable comparison, or, at best, being a literary curiosity.

Two sixteenth century biographies—William Roper (1496–1578) *Life of More,* and George Cavendish (1500–1561) *Life of Wolsey*—were two manuscript biographies which had a limited influence on the history of biography, but set the stage for "character sketches" which were a combination of historical fact and fiction. The first English professional biographer is a title given to Izaak Walton (1593–1683) for his five lives of prominent Englishmen: John Donne, 1640, George Herbert, 1670; Henry Wotton, 1651; Richard Hooker, 1665 and Robert Sanderson 1678. These are quite as marvelous as his treatise on angling. In his history of biography, Harold Nicolson claims Walton was England's first "deliberate biographer." His was "certainly the most important biographical work in English literature prior to Johnson."[27]

The single greatest biography effort of the seventeenth century was by John Aubrey (1626–1698). *Brief Lives* is reminiscent of today's short biographical entries, say, in *The New York Times.* They are considerably more imaginative, above all more involving. A leader in the intellectual circles of the day, Aubrey was a friend of Thomas Hobbes (1588–1679) of whom he penned a brief sketch and, in fact, was friends with many of the people he profiled. The work is noteworthy on numerous counts, but it is among the first to break from hero worship and to paint a reliable, usually accurate personal portrait. His great sense of style and wit anticipates the modern biography. Aubrey can be read today with as much enjoyment as when it was first written.[28]

After a century of hardly any noteworthy biographical effort, the eighteenth century discovered Dr. Johnson's (1709–1784) *Life of Savage* (1744), unquestionably "our first masterpiece in biography."[29] By 1777–1780 Johnson had completed his memorable *Lives of the Poets,* and by 1791 James Boswell (1740–1795) had published his *Life of Samuel Johnson,* which the author himself termed "the most entertaining book that ever appeared." It also established the pattern for scholarly biography, "and a method of biography which is essentially national and essentially suited to the British temperament."[30] Much has been written about this landmark work. Its importance to the eventual development of reference work in biography was its focus on the realities of one man's life rather than reworking a stereotype. Unfortunately, biography as a method of propaganda for this or that point of view hardly disappeared with either Boswell or Johnson—but they at least showed the way. More important, Boswell's work was a true classic. Over time it gave biography the credibility it so sadly lacked.

The lives of the daring fascinated early eighteenth century readers, and collections concerning criminals in particular sold well. An early example was the *History of the Lives of the Most Noted Highwaymen, footpads, housebreakers, shoplifters, etc.* (1714) by Captain Alexander Smith. Between 1722 and 1725 Daniel Defoe wrote several biographies of criminals, and Henry Fielding published (1743) *Jonathan Wild,* and his adventures in the underworld. The interest peaked with the publication of *The Newgate Calendar* in 1774. Running to five volumes this covered crime and prominent English criminals from 1700 to 1770.[31]

Nineteenth to Twentieth Centuries

The pioneering study, *Eminent Victorians* (1918) by Lytton Strachey, tore down the Victorian biographical superstructure and put in its place the "scientific" or "intellectual" objective biographical approach.

If the nineteenth century opened with the insights of Thomas Carlyle (1795–1881) about "famous men" it ended and plunged into the twentieth century with Sigmund Freud's (1856–1939) concepts of the individual. Until then John Locke (1632–1704) and the German philosophers dominated the shaping of biography. Will and spirit were all. With Freud a new factor entered and the great age "of professionalism was upon us . . . and with its arrival somebody was sure to make private lives professional matters even if Freud did not."[32] Specialists in biography took over the genre, e.g. the pioneers.

One reason that biography was a late development was the lack of intimacy in literature until the late eighteenth and early nineteenth centuries. Intimacy, according to Hannah Arendt, "is a realm opposed to the 'social' and the antithesis between the intimate and the social replace an older one between the private and the public."[33] Gradually the shift from the public to the private life lead to today's version of biography. In the quest to discover a person's "true identity," to measure success the modern biographer turns to psychology, in depth research and analysis of the person's place in the time of his or her most noteworthy contributions. Still, in terms of focus today's popular biography is much the same as the eighteenth and nineteenth centuries—a mixture of the literary, the journalistic, the sensational, the mixed truths and fiction, the historical, the psychological and, well, most about any combination which will sell.[34]

Twentieth century works stress factual truth, and have an added dimension of psychoanalysis. The nineteenth century saw the return of earnest hagiography, better described as "Victorian biography" which, to say the least, was inimical to trustworthy, relatively objective biography. Biographies written during the nineteenth century "stressed emotions, feelings, and entire human character . . . but they were too partial and limited; as a result, these truths, when you read them, seem to be creating a mythical hero more than a true man. This is why they chose their characters only amongst geniuses. With the twentieth century came the time of synthesizes, due to the progress of psychological sciences."[35]

Development of Biographical Reference Sources

Taken in its broadest sense the biographical dictionary, a term which can be applied in a limited way before the nineteenth century, showed some strength in the period between 1500 and 1800. Among the more important of the few biographical dictionaries published in the sixteenth century was, Giorgio Vasari's (1511–1574) *Lives of the Painters* (1550) and the biobiographical aspects of Konrad Gesner's *Bibliotheca Universalis* (1543) which is discussed in another chapter.[36] André Thevet (1516–1592) was a cosmologist for the French kings of the period and probably a master liar in that his famous tale of travel in Brazil (1557) was made up from other accounts as was his patchwork *Lives of the Greeks and Romans* (1584). In all his writings he drew charges of plagiarism as well as gullibility on the part of his readers.

With the seventeenth century a better case may be made for at least the beginnings of biography as a reference work. Still, even then the primary focus was as much on history as on entertainment, and the facts were liberally ignored. Of the close to 65 dictionaries published in the seventeenth century the most widely known, and probably used were Thomas Fuller (1660–1661) *The History of the Worthies of England* (1662);[37] and Louis Moreri (1643–1680) *Le Grand Dictionnaire Historique* (1674) which was more involved with encyclopedic type entries than biography, but useful for biographies.[38] The work went to 20 editions, the last being published in 1759.

The most famous compiler was Pierre Bayle (1648–1706), the pre-Enlightenment philosopher and Huguenot who was forced to live in Rotterdam where he taught and lived until his death. In Holland Bayle became a well known writer. In 1684 he began editing one of the first international scholarly journals. By 1697 his biographical work began to be published, i.e. the *Dictionaire Historique et Critique*.[39] Here he employed biography for didactic purposes and used important figures to illustrate his ideas of religious and philosophical importance. The form was to deliver fairly objective treatment of the personalities, from antiquity to the seventeenth century, and then elaborate on their lives and ideas in enormous columns of notes.

The biographical dictionary took form in the eighteenth century, and while no more than two dozen were published, they established the pattern. Representative samples would include the one volume *New and General Biographical Dictionary,* published in London in 1761. It was the first major English biographical dictionary. It's only competitor was the 1747–1766 London issue in seven volumes of *Biographia Britannica.* This achieved great success and was published and several editions, culminating with Alexander Chalmers edited edition of 1812–1817. The *Allgemeines Gelehrten—Lexicon, darinne die gelehrten alle stande dowohl mann* (. . . Leipzig: Gleditsch, 1750–1751) was 4 volumes edited by Christian Jöcher (1694–1758). It continued to 1897. The *Lexicon* is useful to this day, although compiled in the mid-eighteenth century. As one of the earliest biographical dictionaries, its particular strength is the focus on Medieval personalities and the numerous bibliographies.

Nineteenth Century

Following the by now well known pattern of the spread of printed materials, the rise of literacy and the increased economic ability of the middle classes to purchase reading matter, nineteenth century biographical works reflected all these social and the political changes. Towards the end of the century and the beginning of the next, the spread of public libraries and the suggestion of systematic reference services to come resulted in an increased number of biographical reference aids. These developed into the collected lives of everyone from saints and rulers to thieves and explorers. The biographical dictionary became more refined.

Among the earliest moves to produce a truly international biographical reference work occurred in 1811–1828. The French bookseller and publisher

Louis-Gabriel Michaud produced the first edition of his *Biographie Universelle*.[40] The initial 52 volumes was supplemented by his son, Joseph Michaud. After Joseph's death the work of 45 volumes was completed by Ernest Desplaces, and it is this second edition which remains the basic French biographical dictionary up to the publication of the *Dictionnaire de Biographie Francaise*.[41] Over 300 famous and relatively famous writers contributed to the initial set and second edition, and to this day it is a useful source of data, particularly as the articles tend to be long, detailed and accompanied by useful bibliographical information. The "catch" as in so many early dictionaries is that the initial editor had strong royalist and Catholic biases (somewhat corrected in the second edition). As long as the editors and writers focused on French personalities the work was of a high standard, but, as with so many other titles of this type, as soon as they wandered over the French border to other times and places the errors of fact became numerous.

Countless other nineteenth century international biographical dictionaries appeared about the same time as Michaud. One English work actually began publishing earlier, although later editions were patterned after Michaud. John Aikin's *General Biography*, in 10 volumes, began to appear in London in 1799.[42] It proved a financial winner and was soon revised and updated by Alexander Chalmers as *The General Biographical Dictionary*, published in 32 volumes between 1812 and 1817.[43] Chalmers, who apparently borrowed as freely from Michaud as others of the period, did do a complete revision of the earlier Aikin effort, e.g. "Of the lives retained from the last edition . . . there are very few which are not, either in whole or in part, rewritten, or to which it has not been found necessary to make very important additions."[44] Similar sentences would come down from Chalmers to the present as a justification for, once again, publishing a revised work.

Chalmers faced up to the problems of selection, for which a "superior degree of judgment is expected." Essentially he relied upon published works of a similar nature, "particularly on the Continent" and from time to time noted for whence he had drawn his information.[45] But "references to a variety of books, pamphlets, and records" were skipped. Despite careful editing, the compiler admitted that from time to time there are "almost unavoidable errors" such as repeating the same biographical data under two different names of the same individual.[46]

The sometimes deplorable lack of accuracy, bordering on the amusing, in early biographical dictionaries is due to three common factors: (1) Most of the people working on these guides had limited education, and few had any training in the rigors of research. (2) Most compilers drew upon previously published works, truth, fiction and all, without double checking the data. (3) There was a conscientious effort to: a) maintain heroes among the dead and b) allow the living to adjust their own sketches to make them appear as heroic as possible. It is, for example, almost impossible to find an unkind word, a critical remark in any of the popular nineteenth century biographical dictionaries.[47] An exception, to be sure, are the popular presentations of the lives of criminals and similar appealing, highly anti-social individuals. Note, though, that this all follows pretty much the standards established for individual biographies and the compilers of reference works were simply following, certainly not leading, the market and the supposed needs of readers.

American Sets

There were certain fundamental similarities between biographical dictionaries of various countries, but American works reflected definite biases. Populists, fundamentally Christian, and convinced of the superiority of everything and everyone American, the compilers and editors harvested what they believed. The majority of entries, no matter what length or on whom they focused, indicated the convictions of the people who decided whom to accept and whom to reject and how to shape the lives for the readers—readers whom they rightfully imagined were much like themselves. Understandably then the emphasis on occupations was heavily weighed in the favor of clerics, followed closely behind by "acceptable" authors, educators, musicians (including church musicians), composers and physicians. Scientists and businesspeople, so important today, were virtually passed over; although by the turn of the century "men of commerce" began to assume an important place in the reference works.

This essential parochial view of leaders was common to most American published biographical reference works until after the second World War. Then, assuming an international leadership role, as well as giving Americans more exposure to people throughout the world, reference publishers and compilers of biographical works became more objective, certainly more tolerant of differences between individuals. The result was much modified biographical sources, culminating in online and CD-ROM updates of everything from essay length biographies to short directory entries.

Drawing for initial ideas, but neither content or style from the English biographical dictionaries, a group of enterprising American publishers set the pattern for nineteenth century works celebrating prominent Americans. The scope, broad and generous in whom was included, usually was indicated in a subtitle *Contemporary American Biography* (New York: Atlantic, 1895) in its initial volume explained the biographical sketches were "representative of modern thought and progress, of the pulpit, the press, the bench and the bar, of legislation, invention, and the great industrial interests of the country." It is not difficult to draw a broad profile of gradually changing American notions of personal importance and virtue in most of the nineteenth and early twentieth centuries by studying these very subtitles.

After several rivals failed, Thomas Rogers (1781–1832) brought out one of the earliest American biographical reference works: *A New American Biographical Dictionary*. Published first in the early 1820s, by the fourth edition (Philadelphia: Bradford 1829) Rogers had constructed a descriptive subtitle which more or less reflected early attitudes about the great and near great in the United States. The editor explained his 400 page biographical reference work was limited to "departed heroes, sages and statesmen of America. Confined exclusively to those who have signalized themselves in either capacity, in the Revolutionary War which obtained the independence of their country." The War of 1812 did not count.

Well up to the Civil War, the focus was on men, with a nod to a few women, who had been major figures in historical sense. Abner Jones (1807–1852) in 1855 edited *The American Portrait Gallery* (New York: Emerson, 1855) and followed this tradition. The subtitle: "Portraits and brief notices of the principal actors in American history. From Christopher Columbus down to the present time." Line drawings allowed by the mid-nineteenth century the addition of pictures of subjects in the biographical guides. This addition soon became a major attraction.[48] A more ambitious effort appeared in four volumes in 1853–1854. This was John Livingston's *Portraits of Eminent Americans* (New York: Cornish, Lamport). It was originally issued as a serial, each part coming out monthly with its own cover title—*American Portrait Gallery*.

By the 1850s, too, the advantage of more short biographies, rather than longer, sometimes one to two page entries, was noticed. Attention shifted to occupations such as authors, and gradually business people, although most of the dictionaries continued to depend heavily on military men, now with the addition of Civil War commanders. (Here, they were almost exclusively from the North.)

A study of the compilers and editors of representative American nineteenth century biographical reference works reflects their contents. For example: Samuel Allibone (1816–1889) *A Critical Dictionary of English Literature and British and American Authors*.[49] Allibone was librarian of the then newly endowed Lenox Library (i.e. New York City Library), and "devoted to literary pursuits." He earned a good living as a director of an insurance company. Beyond that he married a wealthy woman and apparently had leisure for his interest in literature and, as reflected in his biographical sketches, theology and, more particularly, Sunday schools. In 1854, after years of diligent work, the first volume of his still useful *Critical Dictionary* was published. Eventually three volumes, and later with supplements by other compilers, the five volume set included close to 47,000 authors. In the preface to the supplement, Allibone who was equally a popular historian, claims "history and biography have ceased to be pompous and ponderous . . . In short (biography) . . . has lost the old class distinctions and become democratic."[50] For purposes of reference, Allibone saw the benefit of close indexing and there were 40 classified indexes of subjects. Not only an expert on Sunday schools and biography, Allibone took great delight in lecturing on books and libraries. A contemporary described him in words he often used for favorite writers in his own compilation: Allibone was note-worthy for "his gracious manner, the invincible sweetness of his temper, his charm as a companion, his skill as a raconteur, his quips and jests and daily whimsies."[51]

Allibone, and his successor, were among the first to appreciate the popularity of a reference work for the average person possibly struggling to educate him or herself, as well as for children. The result are short, yet relatively accurate entries which focus more on "modern" life rather than antiquity. "Brief" somehow is equated with popular and the editor makes a point of explaining: "Longer notices . . . often merely have presented the same facts in an expanded form." Here and there critical estimates are given "in the form of extracts" from other biographical sources.[52] Most of the material was gathered from other biographical works, dutifully credited in the introduction of the supplementary volume. Also, data was taken from "miscellaneous reading," "published biographies or autobiographies," and "several hundred English and a few American authors have, in response to applications, furnished the material required."[53]

While the American counterpart of the *Dictionary of National Biography* did not take shape until the 1920s, there were numerous similar efforts, some minor, others of major importance during the nineteenth century. The more outstanding examples of the early efforts to document American lives include about a half dozen titles, many of which, despite sometimes less than accurate information, are employed today for historical research.

One of these works, from which Allibone freely admitted he drew material, was compiled by Samuel Drake (1828–1885) *Dictionary of American Biography.*[54] Born into a family of antiquarian bookpeople—his father ran a bookstore in Boston—Drake spent the Civil War selling books in Kansas. By 1871 he was back in Boston where in 1872 he published his *Dictionary.* The reference work was typical of the period in that the scope had been enlarged to include almost anyone of importance. The subtitle reads: ". . . including men of the time, containing nearly ten thousand notices of persons of both sexes, of native and foreign birth, who have been remarkable, or prominently connected with the arts, sciences, literature, politics, or history, of the American continent. Giving also the pronunciation of many of the foreign and peculiar American names, a key to the assumed names of writers, and a supplement." The "Key to assumed names of writers" was an early effort at a systematic dictionary of antonyms and pseudonyms.

According to Drake, he had spent some 20 years collecting the biographies, often from other works. In the preface he expressed the typical problem of someone trying to expand a standard work. There was a need for "correct proportions" and this meant trying to balance a mass of material from New England and New York with lesser known personalities from other parts of the United States. The work proved a financial success. Drake apparently spent the remainder of his life operating a stationery store in Boston and editing various titles of which the best known is Schoolcraft's *Indian Tribes of the United States* (1884).[55]

The first major American effort to rival the British *Dictionary of National Biography* began publication in 1888 as *Appleton's Cyclopaedia of American Biography*. "It is proposed to provide a Cyclopaedia of Biography for the New World worth to rank with . . . the great French *Dictionaries of Universal Biography*, and the . . . *National Biography of Great Britain*."[56] The short and numerous essay length articles include some 15,000 individuals, as compared with about the same number for the DAB and DNB. Several important differences are obvious: a) prominent living Americans were included, and b) "America" was broadened to include Canada and much of South America, as well as some 1,000 "of foreign birth who . . . are closely identified with American history."[57] Put together by the editors, with the assistance of a staff of writers and "the most competent students of special periods and departments of history," the idea was to "render the *Cyclopaedia* educational as well as entertaining and instructive." Each of the volumes was illustrated with "at least ten fine steel portraits" and "between one and two thousand smaller vignette portraits . . . accompanied by facsimile autographs and also several hundred views of birthplaces, residences, monuments and tombs."[58]

James Grant Wilson (1832–1914) was editor of *Appleton's*. A native of Scotland who settled in Poughkeepsie, New York as a bookseller, Wilson was a publisher of religious magazines in Chicago by 1857. At age 30 he received a commission as a major in the Illinois Cavalry, and was one of the few publishers of biographical dictionaries to take an active part in the Civil War. After the War he settled in New York City and launched a new career writing biographies, primarily for newspapers. From that developed *Appleton's* which he edited jointly with a John Fiske.[59]

Evert Duyckinck (1816–1878) edited the *National Portrait Gallery of Eminent Americans*.[60] The son of a New York City publisher, Duyckinck was one of the few nineteenth century compilers to have a college degree, graduating from Columbia College in 1835. Thanks to a wealthy family, he was able to travel in Europe for a year and returned to New York where he married and wrote literary articles, as well as edited several literary magazines . . . all of which seemed to have made a good reputation. Duyckinck became an expert on both Thackeray and Washington Irving, but in order to make money he turned to reference book editing. His first successful text was the *Cyclopedia of American Literature* (2 vols., 1855), one of the earliest American biographical dictionaries devoted to American writers. A supplement was published in 1865, and the *National Portrait Gallery*, followed in 1861–1862. He gathered a personal library of over 17,000 books which he left to the New York Public Library.[61]

By the mid nineteenth century the pattern of collective biography was a combination of history and art. Inevitably the essay length sketches included, as in the *National Portrait Gallery of Eminent Americans,* "original full length paintings" of the subjects.[62] The focus, too, was on morality. "The key to history . . . the lives of the men of America are the proper studies for the youth of America. It is particularly so with the men of the Revolutionary era."[63] As with other reference works of this type the purpose was to inform and improve the moral outlook of the reader, for "after all allowances are made, it still holds good that the Representative Men of America are of high moral excellence."[64] The four to six page entries open with a sketch of Benjamin Franklin and move on to such figures as John Paul Jones and Daniel Boone.

With the industrialization of America and the advent of a national railroad system, biography now interpreted "prominent" as those who achieved success in industrial and commercial fields. For example, the suitably titled *Twentieth Century Biographical Dictionary of Notable Americans* had as a subtitle: "brief biographies of authors, administrators, clergymen, commanders, editors, engineers, jurists, merchants, officials, philanthropists, scientists, statesmen and other who are making American history.[65] The key phrase "who are making." The biographies many of which occupied about a single page, featured line drawings of the subject with their signatures dutifully below.

The change in subject matter, focus and emphasis in collective biography is no better illustrated than in the ongoing *National Cyclopaedia of American Biography* which began publication in 1892 and continues to this day.[66] Entries, of both living and dead prominent Americans, are written primarily by the publisher's staff which employs questionnaires submitted by the subject (or, if deceased, the family) for background information.

In the initial volume the publisher attempted to explain why his work differed from others. A wider net was cast to include many of the new professions "who contribute so much to the material and physical welfare of the country.[67] This included everyone from engineers and architects to business personalities. There was a great focus on "numerous families which have ancient lineage and records . . . the genealogy and history of this families (is) recorded and perpetuated."[68] The "chief personalities" were to include entries of young people who seemed to be making a mark, although not yet officially recognized.

Most entries are essay length. The entries of several pages often are accompanied by an illustration, facsimile signature and on occasional a sketch of the person's home. Groupings of biographies are by profession and by family, thus making alphabetical order impossible, particularly as this was an ongoing project. The solution—an index which "in these days . . . is becoming more and more acknowledged by scholars and literary workers."[69] In each volume there was a full, analytical index, covering all the preceding volumes. *The Cyclopaedia* was published by James Terry White (1845–1920). In his own biographical reference work White is covered in a column and one-half—the usual length for all but the most famous of entries. The notice explains he was orphaned early in life, managed a high school education and moved to California in 1862 where by 1865 he was hired by Bancroft, the most famous of Western book publishers. Less than a decade on he established his own publishing firm, James T. White, which primarily acted as a West coast representative for the publishers of the *Cyclopaedia*. By 1886 he had moved to New York, and five years later brought out the first volume of *Cyclopaedia*. As a publisher he developed a platoon of editors and writers and soon turned the still published set into "the largest compilation of its kind in the United States," a position it held until well into the 1920s. By the turn of the century he was a published poet with a wide audience because of "many quotable lines reflecting memorable spiritual experiences common to every one."[70]

Dictionary of National Biography[71]

The popular, apparently profitable biographical dictionaries, both here and in Europe, culminated in the nineteenth century with the introduction of the biographical dictionary to end all dictionaries—the *Dictionary of National Biography*. Still, once the pattern was established there were many national copies, including the United States. Today the sometimes massive sets are as much a fixture of Western nations as their flags, encyclopedias and national libraries.[72]

Somewhere between the idealistic Victorian biography and the modern psychological study, the now famous *Dictionary of National Biography* recorded for all time the lives of the men and women who structured Britain and the Empire. Inspired by earlier European models, and especially the French *Biographie universelle,* the DNB was unique in many ways. It served as a model for similar national biographies to come, and to this day is considered the most important reference work for English biography. In the brief description of the work, the *Guide to Reference Books* summarizes its content: "Containing signed articles by specialists, and excellent bibliographies; important names are treated at great length, minor names more briefly, and all are generally reliable and scholarly. Scope includes all noteworthy inhabitants of the British Isles and the Colonies, exclusive of living persons; also noteworthy Americans of the colonial period."[73]

DNB editor Leslie Stephen (1832–1904) shaped the entries in opposition to the focus made famous by Thomas Carlyle (1795–1881).[74] The contemporary of Stephen saw the hero as the essential ingredient of biography and from his life of Cromwell to Frederick the Great, as well as *The French*

Revolution, he shaped biography in an image as a visible power. Stephen had other ideas. In a departure from the labored, detailed historical lives, Stephen was for the strategies of character and experience rather than the biographies of ideas. His view, of course, found an exponent in "that intuitive chronicler of sensibility, Lytton Strachey . . . (and) the particular point of view . . . that a man's interior life, no less than his actions, illuminates his character . . . with Stratchey biography appropriates the whole range of human experience."[75] Stephen was convinced "the full blaze of modern biography has left not even the minutest detail untouched."[76]

The author of a work on English philosophy as well as a manual for Alpine climbing, Stephen also was editor of the middlebrow literary *Cornhill Magazine.* When the magazine failed to show a profit, its owner removed Stephen and charged him with editing the DNB. Launched in 1882, the collective biography was under the complete charge and the biographical formula of the then 50 year old Stephen. "In late life Stephen described the function of the DNB as primarily that of codification . . . Doing well by the second rate people was the main job . . . There had to be a plan . . . for separating the sheep from the goats. To use his metaphor, the DNB had to be a causeway through the morass of antiquarian accumulation."[77]

The purpose of the *DNB* was to celebrate the nation's history through the exemplary lives of its citizens. And while the editors attempted to avoid the myths and fiction of earlier biography, there is no question the completed set was a tribute to Victorian values. These values were reflected not only in the essays, but in the exclusion of most women whom Stephen considered unworthy of inclusion. Other missing figures include clerics (whom Stephen disliked), and trade unionists.[78] There were rigid rules for inclusion. First, and typically from that time to this, the person had to be dead. Second, the work was to reflect national growth not only through the lives of the great but by an examination of what Stephen called "second-rate people; the people whose lives have to be reconstructed from obituary notices, or from references in memoirs and collections of letters."[79] Third, the biographies were to stress importance of fact and primary sources. "The writers were instructed to be in sympathy with their subjects but to keep eulogy within bounds."[80]

In shaping the lesser important biographies, Stephen set the pattern for editors to come. He had several rules, still applicable to the genre: (1) The first rule was condensation, the virtue to which all others (had to be) sacrificed. (2) The biographer should distance himself from the subject, being as objective as possible. (3) At the same time the entry should be personable and reflect the character of the subject. As (2) and (3) are almost impossible to reconcile, the *Dictionary* as all such works since represents a compromise between fact and interpretation.

Stephen's successor, Sidney Lee, followed the pattern set by the first editor, but "was also a Victorian prude who enjoyed expressing his prudery and tended to complain about his biographies' morals rather than ignore them."[81] He, for example, disapproved of Laurence Sterne and said as much making very little of the English author's genius.

A common feature of ongoing sets of biographical reference, such as the DNB, is the constant attention to changes in social and political notions of what is and is not important in determining entrance into the sacred biographical pages. With one editorial eye on the biases of early editors, such as Sidney Lee, and on the newly famous, from motion picture celebrities to politicians, the current compilers must add, delete and adjust to suit a modern audience's needs. Victorians celebrated male intellectuals and empire builders. The 37,000 names in the original set and supplements are predominantly male, and only 3 percent of the entries are female, although Queen Victoria 98,000 word entry is the longest in the dictionary. About 12,000 new names are expected to be added in the overall revision of the set, which is to be completed in the early part of the next century—and of these the new editor, Colin Matthews, promises many will be prominent women. Among the early additions—all Victorians—are Frances Anne Vane-Tempest, Lady Londerry, a magnate who ran coal and iron industries after her husband's death; Catherine "Skittles" Walters, a courtesan who offered her services to the most prominent politicians of the day; and Ellen Chapman, a lion tamer.[82]

Twentieth Century . . . and Beyond

With the twentieth century three major changes took place in biographical reference works. First, most became universal in nature, not limited to a single country or time period, they include major figures everywhere and in every period of history. Second, men no longer enjoyed exclusive space, and women and minorities began to be appreciated, particularly after the 1970s. Third, and possibly most important to both publishers and to reference workers, the dictionaries subdivided into subject interests from architecture to physics. Almost from the beginning of such subject oriented works, authors dominated the field. Little has changed, and today the majority of subject biographical works are devoted to writers. The next large group cover composers and musicians. Commerce, the primary focus from the 1870s to the 1940s, is now way down the reference list.

The twentieth century witnessed development of by now five familiar types of biographical reference, which originated in the nineteenth century, but did not reach reference status until modern times.[83] First, was the national biography (as for example the *Dictionary of National Biography*) to celebrate the great of a nation and in so doing the country and its achievements. Second, was the universal biography (as for example Chalmer's

General Biographical Dictionary); which was an effort to take in all important figures of all times and places. Third, was the by now familiar subject biography which concentrates on people who excel or simply take part in a given occupation or profession. Of primary interest to the public then, as now, was the collection of author biographies such as the well known *Contemporary Authors*. Fourth was the growth of the familiar *Who's Who* which lists living, "important" people usually of a single nation, section of a nation, or, by the twentieth century, leaders in professions and occupations.

A fifth major development was the index to biographical sources which today represents the basic key for librarians to biographical sources. One of the earliest biographic indexes was the work of Lawrence Phillips.[84] His 1871 dictionary was among several which predated the more exhaustive indexes of the twentieth century. Still, the principle was the same. Phillips listed over 100,000 names and after each indicated where information on the person could be found. The information was mined from 40 biographical collections and related titles.

Somewhat related to the index format, the "best" biographical sources was another early favorite. Among the best of these is Eduard Oettinger's *Bibliographie Biographique* first published 1854.[85] The 26,000 entries were expanded in future editions, and the work was translated, with additions, for publication in America in 1889. The compiler arranged alphabetically the subjects, with dates and brief descriptors and their claim to fame, and then, in chronological order, books and other published works about each of them.

Following an old pattern, but this time with the aid of a computer, the *Biography and Genealogy Master Index,* indexes the contents of over 700 biographical dictionaries (in over 1900 editions) and related works.[86] Updated each year, the result is an index to some 10 million citations, and while many names are repeated in various sources, the end result is an avenue of approach to almost every famous person from the beginning of time to the present.

Building both upon previous sets and the earnest new approach to biography which stressed facts and character rather than rumor and opinion, the *Dictionary of American Biography* was published between 1928 and 1937.[87] The 20 volumes, and subsequent supplements, were based on principles set down by the *Dictionary of National Biography,* and included only dead individuals who contributed to American life. The signed articles set a standard for detachment, although many capture the flavor of the writer and the sometimes combative style of the person being described. With each supplement additions are made, and inaccuracies in previous articles corrected. The result is an ongoing work which includes sketches of close to 20,000 individuals.

While the biographical dictionary, and particularly the one devoted to occupations, professions and subjects dominates the reference field, an equally used form is the directory type, or "who's who." Published originally in London by Baily Brothers in 1849, *Who's Who* was primarily a brief listing of nobility, with a nod to members of Parliament and important officials.[88] The names, with a description, were listed under subject headings. In 1896 Adam Black took over the work and changed its focus so it included brief biographical sketches, in alphabetical order, of "all the most prominent people in the Kingdom, whether their prominences is inherited, or depending upon office, or the result of ability which singles them out for their fellows in occupations open to every educated man and woman."[89] A parallel work was *Men of The Times* (London: 1852–1887). Published by David Bogue, various editions of this appeared in New York as well as London. By the thirteenth edition, 1891 the title was changed to *Men and Women of the Times* to take into account the growing number of entries for women. When Black became the owner of *Who's Who* he purchased *Men and Women of the Time* and incorporated it into *Who's Who* in 1901.

Autobiography and Related Forms

There are other facets in the development of biography which are outside the study of reference works. Still, a contender for notice is autobiography. In a sense most of today's biographical dictionaries and directories are a form of autobiography. The 75,000 to 85,000 entries in a typical *Who's Who in America,* for example, are primarily a collection of autobiographical sketches. Individuals fill out questionnaires, and statements about everything from hobbies to political convictions, and in that way offer a capsule autobiography which is incorporated into the reference work.

The English term, "autobiography," made its appearance only near the end of the eighteenth century, first, apparently in Italian and German literature of the sixteenth century then later in English.[90] The *OED* observed autobiography's first use in English was in a Robert Southey's article in 1809.

The first example of autobiography tied to history is from England in the fifteenth century. Titled simply *Her Book,* this recounts the travels of one Margery Kempe through the late Medieval world. *Her Book* was published and disappeared, except for a pamphlet of prayers taken from the work and published in 1501. "Margery Kempe, the sobbing mystic or hysteric, of Lynn in Norfolk, dictated an account of her bustling, far faring life, which, however concerned about religious experience, racially reveals her somewhat abrasive personality and the impact she made upon her fellows."[91] This biased summary is accurate enough, but fails to take into account the exemplary text which offers the picture of an individual, subversive woman of the early fifteenth century. Some, in fact contend the work is really fiction, although accurate enough in its narrative explanation of life.[92]

Benvenuto Cellini, (1500–1571) the first authentic author of an autobiography (1558–1562), explains in his opening words that such a work is the duty of anyone who has "performed anything noble or praiseworthy," to records the events of their own lives. In England the autobiography, (although under other descriptors) became a popular form in the sixteenth and seventeenth centuries, particularly among ministers and explorers. After a detailed study of English autobiographies, William Matthews reported: "Few autobiographies put into their books very much of that private, intimate knowledge of themselves that only they can have . . . They fit themselves into patterns of behavior . . . suggested by . . . their period."[93] As another wag puts it, an autobiography allows its author to write about everything except him or herself.

> "In the epoch of the Enlightenment, when the importance of autobiography was recognized, it was still believed that man's nature was fixed and identical everywhere and at all times . . . In the nineteenth century that belief was destroyed by the historical consciousness (with the recognition . . . of the infinite natural multiplicity of an individual life."[94]

Autobiography and memoir are synonyms, but with a subtle difference. The former emphasizes the personality, the latter focuses on social and historical elements of a life. Some biographies touch both areas, e.g. *The Education of Henry Adams* (1918) Henry Adams (1838–1918) left out valuable things about himself in his autobiography only to include sections on theories of history. Which makes the point that most of the great autobiographies are incomplete: "Cellini, Franklin, Jonathan Edwards, Mark Twain and Henry James, or else they are imperfect, like Adams."[95]

Diary, journal, and memoirs are often confused. Journals tend to be autobiographical. Williams defines a diary as "a day-by-day record of what interested the diarist, each day's record being self-contained and written shortly after the events occurred."[96] A journal is somewhat the same, but differs in two important respects: a) It tends to be more autobiographical, while at the same time, b) It tends to reflect a particular aspect of the journal writer's life. Williams offers one sure litmus test: Journals, memoirs, autobiography, etc. are written with readers in mind, with publication as the eventual goal. Many diaries may have the same goal, but in general are more private and restricted to the eyes of the person keeping the diary.

For every published autobiography, memoir or diary there are innumerable manuscript versions in the libraries of historical institutions, private organizations, universities etc. Most of these are omitted from standard listings and bibliographies, although usually can be located through the various guides to manuscript collections, e.g. see *Guide to Reference Books* (Chicago: American Library Association, various editions/dates).

Genealogy is a major aspect of biographical reference service, but equally is highly specialized. At the same time, most biographical reference titles are of some help in genealogy so an understanding of basics is necessary before launching even the most basic genealogical search. For a "selected list of books" on genealogy see P. William Filby *American & British Genealogy & Heraldry* (Chicago: American Library Association, 1970).

Anonyms and pseudonyms puzzled readers from the earliest time that an individual name became important. And to aid the reader, there were early dictionaries such as Adrien Baillet (1649–1706) *Auteurs Deguisez* (Paris: Dezallier, 1690). Even earlier Friedrich Geissler (1636–1679) offered help to Latin readers with his *De Nominum Mutatione* (Lipsiae: 1669). The early eighteenth century saw a dozen or more similar titles published.

Conclusion

The late Nicolas Slonimsky wrote a type of manual for would be biographical dictionary compilers. In his preface to the sixth edition of *Baker's Biographical Dictionary of Musicians,* he explains the joys and agonies of preparing a biographical reference source. "I will go mad if I have to continue this for a long time," and "Another music editor . . . deliberately rented a room on the ground floor lest he should be tempted to jump out the window in despair over the contents of the book."[97]

Cruising through one of the most literate and informative prefaces in the history of reference works, one finds such rules of the game as: (1) "There should be no . . . spirit of acceptance for the purple prose that some editors indulged in while describing the life and works of admired persons." (p. xvii) (2) Beware of diaries, letters and autobiographies as material for the biographical dictionary. "The desire to recreate one's life according to one's fancy is universal, and artists are particularly apt to imagine, and at time consciously to contrive, the tales of might-have-been." (p. xviii) (3) "How much of a personal life ought to be reported in a dignified biographical dictionary?" The editor takes several paragraphs to answer that important question. (pp. xxiii–xxiv) (4) "It is amazing that grown men and women would deliberately falsify their vital statistics, particularly their dates of birth, in order to appear younger in a reference work." (p. xxv)

On and on it goes. Anyone remotely interested in the bibliographical dictionary is strongly urged to read the preface in whole. Born in St. Petersburgh in 1900 at least according to the entry in his own dictionary, Slonimsky died in 1996. "Disdaining the inexorable statistics of the actuarial tables," he continued editing the dictionary almost until his death.

Notes for Chapter 8

1. *The Oxford Dictionary of Quotations* 4th ed. New York: Oxford University Press, 1994, p. 64. From the writer Edmund Bentley and his *Biography for Beginners*, 1905. Today it might be more "correct" to add women, but would it rhyme?

2. *Webster's Third New International Dictionary*, Springfield, MA: Merriam-Webster, 1961.

3. Bernard Malmud. *Dubin's Lives* (1979). Quoted in *Bartlett's Familiar Quotations*. 16th ed. Boston: Little Brown, 1992, p. 736.

4. In *On Heroes and Hero Worship*, 1841. Quoted in *Bartlett's Familiar Quotations*. 16th ed. Boston: Little Brown, 1992, p. 412. Today "men" would be followed by "and women." Emerson picked up the same notion with his "There is properly no history; only biography." *Ibid.*, p. 431. If further explanation is necessary, the *The New Encyclopaedia Britannica* (Chicago: Britannica. 1993, vol. 2, p. 222) elaborates: "Biography can be seen as a branch of history, because it depends on a selective ordering and interpretation of materials, written and oral . . . It can also be seen as a branch of imaginative literature in that it seeks to convey a sense of the individuality and significance of the subject through creative sympathetic insight."

5. *The Oxford English Dictionary.* Oxford: Clarendon Press, 1970, vol. 1, p. 870. "Biography and autobiography are so conspicuously present in the high finance world of modern American publishing that high minded opponents of the industry's practices find it easy to think of the genres as split . . . between serious books and promotional students." Reed Whittemore *Whole Lives: Shapers of Modern Biography.* Baltimore: Johns Hopkins University Press, 1989.

6. Leon Edel. "The Art of Biography." *New Republic*, February 10, 1979, p. 25.

7. James Atlas, "The Biographer and The Murderer," *The New York Times Magazine*, December 12, 1993, p. 77.

8. Joyce Carol Oates, "The Biographer's Pitfalls" (Letter), *New Republic*, March 3, 1979, p. 30.

9. Patricia Cox. *Biography in Late Antiquity.* Berkeley: University of California Press, 1983, p. 15–16. General biography, and particularly popular biographies, are probably no more reliable today than they were in the time of the Greeks. But the distinction has to be made between popular and reference. Today's biographical reference aids are quite trustworthy, although far from perfect. The reference form of biography reflects the needs of users, not the needs of the biographer, subject or publisher.

10. Robert Slocum. *Biographical Dictionaries and Related Works.* Detroit: Gale, 1967, p. xv. *Supplement*, 1972. As the subtitle indicates, this contains more than dictionaries, although they make up the largest single category.

The subtitle is clear as to scope: "an international bibliography of collective biographies, biobibliographies, collections of epitaphs, selected genealogical works, dictionaries of anonyms and pseudonyms, historical and specialized dictionaries, biographical materials in government manuals, bibliographies of biography, biographical indexes, and selected portrait catalogs." Between initial volume and the supplement, Slocum listed 8,271 entries in his *Biographical Dictionaries.* Arranged by subject (i.e. biography by vocation) and by national or area biography (Africa to what was Yugoslavia), there is an introductory section on bibliographies. Detailed author, title and subject indexes pull the whole together.

11. *Biographical Books, 1950–1980.* New York: R. R. Bowker, 1981. A selective guide to the same titles, as well as others published prior to 1950 will be found in Margaret Nicholsen's *People in Books,* New York: R. R. Bowker, 1969, 1977. See, too: *The American Biographical Archive.* New York: Bowker-Saur, 1986+ is a microfiche of "almost 400 of the most important English language biographical reference works in the United States and Canada originally published between the eighteenth and the early twentieth centuries." This does not include the *Dictionary of American Biography.* A companion volume: *British Biographical Archive,* by the same publisher, consists of 310 "of the most important English language biographical reference works originally published between 1601 and 1929." Also available on microfiche.

12. Glen Bowerstock, "Suetonius" *in* J.D. Browning, ed. *Biography in the Eighteenth Century,* New York: Garland, 1980, p. 28. "As a result of the famous and often reprinted translations of Plutarch by Amyot, North, and Dryden, Plutarch's name had become [in the eighteenth century] almost synonymous with the genre of biography . . . Plutarch is like the Bible: you can find an appropriate quotation in support of whatever you are doing." Ibid.

13. Mary Lefkowitz, "Patterns of Fiction in Ancient Biography," *American Scholar Spring,* 1983, p. 209.

14. Arnold Momigliano, *The Development of Greek Biography.* Cambridge: Harvard University Press, 1993, p. 6. This is the basic book on the subject, covering, as it does, biography from the fifth century to the first century B.C. The author is as brilliant as he is dependable.

15. Whittemore, *op. cit.,* p. 6.

16. Just as Hartmann Schedel's 1493 *Nuremberg Chronicles* considered the woodcut of a city or of an individual suitable enough to illustrate many cities, many individual portraits, so did earlier biographers show more concern with concepts, stereotypes than with individuals. These writers were involved with the *notion* of saints, kings, poets and soldiers rather than specific morning to night activities of a particular person. Along the way, of course, there are differentiations made between X and Y, but in the end it is a biography of an ideal rather than a richer or hungry man or woman.

17. Alfred Kazin, "Writing About Oneself," *Commentary*, April, 1979, p. 67.

18. Ibid, p. 69.

19. James Atlas, "Literary Biography," *American Scholar*, Summer, 1976, p. 448.

20. Cox, *op. cit.*, p. 134.

21. Whittemore, *op. cit.*, p. 55. In 1563 came Foxes's *Acts and Monuments* that bloodsoaked martyrology which enjoyed universal popularity, and which with its vivid zest for torture pandered to the growing taste for realism.

22. Ibid, p. 55.

23. Ibid.

24. St. Jerome's "old age was spent in a cloister near Bethlehem, busy with his translating, with his book of biographical sketches after the manner of Suetonius . . ." R. R. Bolgar. *The Classical Tradition.* Cambridge: Cambridge University Press, 1977, p. 51.

25. Einhart was influenced strongly by Suetonius' *Lives of Caesars,* and even some of the words used were borrowed without apology from the Roman biographer. Still the portrait of Charlemagne essentially is accurate.

26. Petrarch in 1337 began a literary work concerning the men and heroes from the earliest times. He never completed his study, although between he published a collection of lives of Romans. This set the pattern for a series of such works, such as Boccaccio's *De casibus virorum illustrium* (1356, 1374).

27. Harold Nicholson. *The Development of English Biography.* New York: Harcourt, Brace, 1928, p. 66, p. 69.

28. See Anthony Powell *John Aubrey and His Friends,* 1963 as well as the English author's edition of the best selection from the *Lives* (1949). Aubrey's work was in manuscript form and not published until the nineteenth century. The history of the biography is discussed by Powell.

29. Nicholson, *op. cit.*, p. 76.

30. Ibid, p. 109.

31. In 1824 the lawyers Andrew Knapp and William Baldwin published a second series in four volumes and a six volume work in 1826. The last Newgate Calendar appeared in 1886.

32. "Your Intimacy." *The Times Literary Supplement,* July 7, 1995, p. 36. Arendt believes Rousseau invented intimacy, or was the first theorist of it.

33. Some would argue that it was more than chance that the modern novel, as a genre, was born at the same time as biography. Both forms, after all, concern people who, in one case may or may not have existed, and in the other, did actually exist.

34. Jean-Mitchell Raynaud, "What's What in Biography" *in* James Walter, ed. *Reading Life Histories.* Canberra: Australian National University Press, 1981, p. 90.

35. Whittemore, *op. cit.*, p. 117.

36. With the sixteenth century the biographical dictionary as a reference work became somewhat more important, and Slocum lists 16 such titles for that period. Gradually, they grew in number and by the seventeenth century the figure quadrupled to 64.

37. Thomas Fuller was a prolific author and a gatherer of facts in commonplace books. His *History of the Worthies of England* was the first attempt at a dictionary of national biography.

38. Louis Moréri *Le grande dictionnaire historique.* Lyon: 1674. An abbreviated edition in English was published by Jeremy Collier in 1694 an in 1701 as *The Great Historical, geographical and poetical dictionary.* The initial French one volume work was expanded to 10 volumes and published in Paris in 1759.

39. Pierre Bayle, *Dictionnaire Historique et Critique.* Paris: 1697, 2 vols. This was updated, revised and issued as 16 volumes in Paris in 1820. Meanwhile, an English version was issued in London from 1734–41. The 10 volumes was updated by Peter Bernard, Thomas Birch and others, and included particularly persons "of Great Britian and Ireland, distinguished by their rank, actions, learning and other accomplishments."

40. *Biographie Universelle (Michaud) Ancienne et Moderne.* Paris: 1811–1862, 85 vols. Joseph Michaud died in 1858 and the initial 52 volumes were added to by his successor Ernest Desplaces. A new edition was published by Madame Desplaces in Paris between 1843 and 1865. This was 45 volumes. Today the set is of interest in the history of copyright, e.g. in 1852 the publisher charged Didot Freres, another Paris publisher with plagiarism. Many articles from Michaud were simply lifted and included in Didot's *Nouvelle Biographies.* In 1855 Mme. Desplaces won her suit and Didot was forbidden to continue copying from his rival. *Nouvelle Biographie Universelle Ancienne et Moderne.* (Paris: Firmin Didot Freres, 1852). This title, after the law suit with Michaud was changed to *Nouvelle Biographie Generale depuis les temps les plus recules jusqu'a nos jours.* Paris: Didot, 1853–1966. 46 volumes. Edited by M. le Dr. Hoefer, this set, minus the pirated material, has numerous more names than its rival and is useful today for minor characters (particularly in the first one half of the alphabet).

41. *Dictionnaire de Biographie Francaise sous le direction de J. Balteau, M. Barroux et M. Prevosts avec le concours de nombreux collaborateurs.* Paris: Letouzey et ane, 1933 to date.

42. John Aikin (1747–1822). *General Biography: or Lives critical and historical, of the most eminent persons of all ages, countries, conditions, and professions, arranged according to the alphabetical order.* Chiefly composed by John Aiken and William Enfield. London: Robinson, 1799–1815. 10 vols.

43. *The General Biographical Dictionary, containing an historical and critical account of the lives and writings of the most eminent persons in every nation, particularly the British and Irish; from the earliest accounts to the present time.* New ed., rev. and enl. London: Nichols, 1812–1817, 32 vols. Edited

by Alexander Chalmers (1759–1834). According to his own dictionary, Chalmers was "a British editor and critic, born at Aberdeen in 1759. About 1778 he came to London, where he wrote for literary periodicals, and edited the *Spectator, Tatler* and various other works. His edition of *Shakespeare* (1809) is commended.

44. Ibid, p. vi.

45. Ibid, p. vii. Elsewhere (p. x) Chalmers complains that foreign sources are sometimes questionable because most "have been made by Catholics."

46. Ibid, p. viii.

47. All of his favoritism towards the biographies is understandable when one realizes that until the early twentieth century, and certainly from the beginnings of biography among the ancient Greeks, that panegyrical treatment was the accepted approach. Biography might be a subdivision of history, but it has its own characteristics and damaging veracity was not one of them.

48. *The Illustrated American Biography* (New York: Emerson, 1853).

49. *A Critical Dictionary of English Literature and British and American Authors, living and decreased from the earliest accounts to the latter half of the nineteenth, century. Containing over forty-six thousand articles (authors) with forty indexes of subjects.* Philadelphia: Lippincott, 1854–1871, 3 vols. In 1891 John Kirk edited a supplement "containing over thirty-seven thousand articles (authors) and enumerating over ninety-three thousand titles."

50. Ibid., p. viii.

51. *DAB, Dictionary of American Biography,* New York: Charles Scribner's Sons, 1974, vol. 1, p. 218 and *The National Cyclopaedia of American Biography,* New York: James T. White, 1892, vol. 6, p. 227.

52. *A Critical, op. cit.*

53. Ibid. Published before international copyright was recognized in the United States and domestic copyright more a law than actually enforced (at least for large sections of a book or article), the editor was quick to admit that use has been made of entries in the first 25 volumes of the still to be completed *Dictionary of National Biography.* Also "Several works, chiefly English, devoted to local, professional or other special subjects, have proved extremely valuable." (p. iv)

54. *Dictionary of American Biography.* Boston: Houghton, 1872. This was published in another edition in 1879.

55. *DAB, op. cit.,* vol. 3, p. 430; *National Cyclopaedia of American Biography,* vol. 4, p. 103.

56. *Appleton's Cyclopaedia of American Biography.* Ed. by James Grant Wilson and John Fiske. New York: D. Appleton, 1887–1900, 7 vols., p. 1. Charles Dick and James Homans revised this work and it was published as *The Cyclopaedia of American Biography.* New York: Press Association Compilers, 1915–1931. 12 vols.

57. Ibid, p. 2.

58. Ibid.

59. *DAB, op. cit.* vol. 10, p. 333–334.

60. *National Portrait Gallery of Eminent Americans.* Ed. by Evert A. Duyckinck. New York: Johnson, Fry, 1862, 2 vols. There continued to be versions of this throughout American history, e.g. James Herring. *The national portrait gallery of distinguished Americans.* Philadelphia: Rice, Rutter, 1868, 3 vols.

61. *DAB, op. cit.,* vol. 3, p. 561–562; *National Cyclopaedia, op. cit.* vol. 1, p. 431.

62. *National, op. cit.,* p. v.

63. Ibid., p. vi.

64. Ibid.

65. *The Twentieth Century Biographical Dictionary of Notable Americans.* Ed. by Rossiter Johnson and John Howard Brown. Boston: The Biographical Society, 1904, 10 vols. This began as: *The Cyclopaedia of American Biographies.* Boston: Cyclopaedia Publishing Company, 1897–1903, 7 vols. In 1904 the title was changed to *Twentieth Century . . .* and issued as 10 volumes.

66. *The National Cyclopaedia of American Biography.* New York: James T. White, 1892 to date. Irregular. In 1984 the publisher, now in Clifton, NJ, issued a 576 page index to the entire set to date.

67. Ibid, vol. 1, p. 1.

68. Ibid.

69. Ibid, p. 2.

70. *National Cyclopaedia,* vol. 19, p. 404.

71. *Dictionary of National Biography.* London: Oxford University Press, 1885–1901. 66 vols. Supplements 1912 to date. Reissued 1908–1909 in 22 vols. On January, 1885 the first volume of the *DNB* appeared, and for the next 16 years a new volume appeared each quarter until the 66 volumes was complete in 1901. Today supplements are issued every four or five years, much more frequently than in the early decades. An out-of-phase supplemental volume was published in 1993 with the subtitle Missing Persons—which included 1086 new entries "overlooked" by previous editors.

72. By the nineteenth century, the national biographical dictionary was a fixture in most Western European countries, e.g. 23 volumes in Sweden (1835–1857); 24 volumes in the Netherlands (1852–1878); and Germany 45 volumes between 1875 and 1900. France as an equally ambitious publisher and the *Biographie universelle* in 40 volumes came out between 1843 and 1863. Most of these were made possible by heavy government subsidies. Britain's failure earlier to produce a similar work was due to lack of financial support, either public or private, until the first volume of the monumental *DNB* in 1885.

73. *Guide to Reference Books.* 10th ed. Chicago: American Library Association, 1986. p. AJ 144.

74. The three responsible for the first edition of the *DNB* included the father of Virginia Woolf, Leslie Stephen; George M. Smith (1824–1901) head of an English publishing firm which issued the works of William Thackeray, Charlotte Bronte and Mrs. Gaskell among others; and Sidney Lee (1859–1926) as an assistant editor under Stephen. Smith's firm underwrote the cost of the set. In *Whole Lives op. cit.* (pp. 65–79) Whittemore compares Stephen's daughter, Virginia's, approach to biography in essay and in fiction with that of her father. "She went back to her father's handling of the genre as a rebel looks for targets." (p. 66)

75. Ibid, p. 57–58.

76. Ibid. The longer biographies of well known figures were so famous as to be included in numerous sources. The real problem was picking and choosing in the second rate ranks.

77. Ibid.

78. Stephen's strong moral convictions meant he failed to emphasize or often get to the inner lives of his subject. Whittemore *op. cit.* (p. 61) illustrates this failing in his biographies of Locke and Hobbes.

79. Johannah Sherrer. "The Most Amusing Book in the Language: The Dictionary of National Biography" in James Rettig, ed. *Distinguished Classics of Reference Publishing,* Phoenix, AZ: Oryx Press, 1992, p. 57–58.

80. Ibid.

81. Whittemore, *op. cit.,* p. 60. While the primary role of Stephen and Lee was editorial, both contributed entries. Close to 400 were the work of the primary editor, while Lee was responsible for 820 articles. More than one-half the original set was written by 34 regular contributors.

82. "History Wakes Up to its Courtesans and Heroines," *The Sunday Times* (London), April 23, 1995, p. 5. Women, generally excluded from the national biographies, now take their place in revisions, annuals etc. to these sets. There always was an interest in including women, although as today, primarily in separate works. Among earliest examples: 1766 *The Female Worthies; or memoirs of the most illustrious ladies of all ages and nations . . .* London: (Crowder, 1766. 2 vols.) 1848–1850: *The Women of the American Revolution.* (New York: Baker & Scribner. 3 vols.) Edited by Elizabeth Ellet (1818–1877). Republished in two volumes in 1900 by G.W. Jacos, of Philadelphia/1893: *A Woman of the Century; fourteen hundred-seventy biographical sketches accompanied by portraits of leading American women in all walks of life.* (Buffalo: Moulton, 812 pp.) Edited by Elizabeth Frances Willard (1839–1898).

83. Categorization of biography depends on whom is doing the categorization, but most agree, from A.J. Walford to Robert B. Slocum that the five divisions listed here are at least a broad enough net to include all types. Slocum, for example, in his *Biographical Dictionaries* uses: 1) Universal biography; 2) National or area biography; 3) Biography by vocation. The "who's who" and indexes are included among the three sections.

84. *Dictionary of Biographical References* ed. by Lawrence Barnett Phillips. Philadelphia & London, 1871. The third edition, edited by Frank Weitenkampf appeared in 1889. And this included references to the full 40 titles, published both in England and America. See, too: Joseph Haydn (1786–1856) *Universal index of biography.* London: Moxon, 1870.

85. Eduard Oettinger. *Bibliographie biographique ou dictionnaire de 26,000 ouvrages, tant anciens que modernes* . . . Bruxelles: Stienon, 1854. 2 vols. The second volume is a listing of general, national and local and subject biographical dictionaries.

86. *Biography and Genealogy Master Index.* Detroit: Gale Research Company, 1975 to date, annual. (1975–1977: called *Biographical Dictionaries Master Index*) Available, too, online and on CD-ROM. For each entry, there is date of birth (and death), and the names and dates of the biographical sources where the person is listed. It can be confusing as no effort is made to correct spelling of names, various order of names etc. *Biography Index* (New York: The H. W. Wilson Company, 1946 to date, quarterly) is useful, too, in that in indexes biographical material in over 3,000 periodicals. As early as 1885, an Italian publisher issued a similar work, indexed 225 to 400 periodicals for biographies. This was *Catalogo Metodico* . . . Rome, 1885. Versions of it still are published.

Indexes to obituaries began as early as the 1880s, but the first recorded effort (William Musgrave's *An Obituary of the Nobility* . . . 1882) got no further than the first volume (A to B) in an effort to cover obituaries published prior to 1800. The Harleian Society picked up the effort and completed it in 1901. The result is an index of 90,000 names "with reference to the books where the persons are mentioned." Technically interest in the dead goes back to the earliest biographers, and by the eighteenth century there was a concerted effort to record inscriptions: *Monumenta Anglicana: being inscriptions on the monuments of eminent persons deceased in or since 1600* (to the end of 1718) London: Gowyer, 1717–1719. 5 vols. Edited by John LeNeve (1679–1741).

87. *Dictionary of American Biography.* New York: Scribner, 1928–1937, 20 vols. Reissued as a 10 volume set in 1974 with nine supplements to 1994.

88. *Who's Who.* London: Black, 1849 to date, annual. The American *Who's Who in America* (Chicago: Marquis, 1899–annual) was a direct copy of the initial English work, although focusing on Americans. At the same time some non-Americans are included if they have a strong influence on American life.

89. Ibid, p. vi.

90. Germs of hints of autobiography can be traced back to the earliest Mesopotamian and Egyptian writers, but usually within a broader context than the individual. For the best discussion of these years before the formal acceptance of autobiography as a genre, see George Misch *A History of Au-*

tobiography in Antiquity, Cambridge, MA: Harvard University Press, 1951. Prior to the use of "autobiography" the typical descriptor was "memoir." "The word of French origin corresponds to the Latin "commentarii" which in turn served as a reproduction of a Greek concept (hypomnemata). "This concept includes a definite type of writings irrespective of their content—those only sketched or written without care." Misch, *op. cit.,* p. 6. Other similar descriptive titles, before the adoption of autobiography as a descriptor, include "confessions," "life stories," etc.

91. *Encyclopaedia Britannica, op. cit.,* vol. 23, p. 190. The title: *The Book of Margery Kempe (1432–1436).* The manuscript was not published until 1936.

92. Lynn Staely. *Margery Kempe's Dissenting Fictions.* University Park: Pennsylvania State University Press, 1995.

93. William Matthews. *British Autobiographies; an annotated bibliography of British autobiographies published or written before 1951.* Berkeley: University of California Press, 1955, p. viii. (Arranged alphabetically by author with subject indexes: professions, places, reminiscences, wars, general topics etc.)

94. Misch, *op. cit.,* p. 5.

95. Peter Shaw, "The Uses of Autobiography," *American Scholar,* Winter, 1968, p. 178.

96. William Matthews. *American Diaries.* Berkeley: University of California Press, 1945, p. ix. See, too: Laura Arksey. *American Diaries;* an annotated bibliography of published American diaries and journals. Detroit: Gale, 1987. 2 vols. The first volume covers titles from 1492 to 1844 and the second moves from 1845 to 1980. Diaries are in chronological and alphabetical order. This is an updated, revision and much better approach than the earlier: William Matthews. *American Diaries.* Berkeley: University of California Press, 1945. This covers titles from 1629 to 1861. Another related title is the same author's *Canadian Diaries and Autobiographies.* Berkeley: University of California Press, 1950.

Biography has a long and distinguished place in reference. At the same time, it was not until the late eighteenth and nineteenth centuries that biographies were published as distinctive reference books. Until then they usually were single titles give over to an equally singular individual.

97. Nicolas Slonimsky, ed. *Baker's Biographical Dictionary of Musicians.* 8th ed. New York: Schirmer Books, 1992, p. xv. The preface to the sixth edition is preceded by an equally amusing and graceful preface to the eighth edition. Both are worth reading. Need it be added that *Baker's Dictionary* is the basic work of its type and found in most libraries.

9

Bibliography, Serials, and Indexes

> Through [bibliography] we are able to grasp how the learned and perhaps the not-so-learned worked, what books they used, what gave them their opinions on this matter or that; and thus we can follow some of the ramifications in the development of their ideas . . . Preacher, lawyer, courtier, physician, writer—all made use at first or second hand of these books of reference, just as standard for them as the *Encyclopaedia Britannica* . . . is standard for us today."[1]

Today a "bibliography" usually is understood to mean a list of books, databases, recordings or any other form of communication. It is where the curious turn to find the publisher, price, author or whatever bit of information is wanted about an item. Those researching a topic, be it simple or complicated, turn to bibliographies for what has been, or is going to be published on the subject. Typical examples range from the ubiquitous *Books in Print* to the more esoteric, more limited *Guide to Historical Literature.* There are several thousand bibliographies available in libraries, and hundreds are published each year.[2] "Systematic" or "enumerative" bibliography is, as the terms imply, the logical arrangement and listing of books with consistent basic information about each title such as author, title, publisher, date of publication, etc. The result is a listing to be used for everything from establishing whether or not a book is available to be purchased, to the year it was published, to the name of the publisher etc.

Bibliographies, in the sense of a descriptive list of books or other communication media, are a relatively new reference work. Whereas the average person identifies bibliography with a systematic, enumerative list, as do most librarians, it has, and has had many more meanings.[3] The historical understanding of the term is important in that it is a method of tracing the process itself. The word appears as early as the fifth century BC, in the work of Greek comic poets, but it had the more limited meaning of "writing or copying books."[4] Not even Dr. Samuel Johnson in his definitive dictionary of 1755 bothered to list bibliography, although Diderot's *Encyclopedia* of 1777–1779 at least mentioned several scholars who were bibliographers. Only with the massive publishing and distribution of books in the mid nineteenth and twentieth centuries did bibliography take its place as the ubiquitous reference work it is today.

Enumerative bibliography has served two purposes, other than simply listing books. The most dominant during the first century or so of printing, was to select and choose books aimed at supporting a point of view, and here one thinks of bibliographies composed by early dedicated Catholics and Protestants. The second, and one which came into favor in the nineteenth century and the development of self education, is similar to the first, but is composed of the "best" of books for personal education, regardless of points of view. A subsection of the second motive is the scholarly subject list for a narrow group of users interested in all and/or the best in a given subject area.

Analytical Bibliography

A close relative of enumerative bibliography, "analytical," "descriptive," "historical" or "critical" bibliography is concerned with the study and the physical and intellectual aspects of the book. This type(s) of bibliography literally describes the book in modest to finite ways, depending on the purpose of the bibliography. Essentially the bibliographer is interested in sorting out the first edition, the first impressions etc. in order to establish, if possible, the primary text as the author intended. Questions of interest usually include: (1) How to describe the book in a specific, uniform way. (2) How much, or how little detail to record. (3) How much to record about the production and publication of the specific title. Other social-political issues involved with the title often are considered as well. There are bibliographies of bindings, graphics, printer's, ornaments, advertising and subscription lists, etc.

Descriptive bibliographies are responsible for excellent modern author bibliographies, bibliographies of presses and publishers, as well as bibliographies of libraries. Possibly the ultimate example of descriptive bibliography is *The Printing and Proof-Reading of the First Folio of Shakespeare* (Oxford, 1963), in which a collator was employed by the author.[6] The work, show the textual difference in printings or issues which are not usually described.

The dean of American bibliography, Fredson Bowers, once exclaimed that "A true bibliography is primarily an analytical bibliography,"[7] and thus dismissed enumerative bibliography. But few bibliographers, today at least, would agree. Properly constructed enumerative bibliographies, particularly in a day of computers, are more used, more valuable to the majority than the laborious analytical type which provide essential data for textual studies, but are of limited, use. Which is to say both, or all types of bibliography have their place in today's world of reference. In terms of daily use by the majority of people, though, enumerative bibliography is vastly more familiar.[8]

Beginnings of Bibliography

Bibliography, as noted, is a comparatively recent reference tool. There is little sight of it until the seventeenth–eighteenth centuries. At the same time, from the Romans through the Middle Ages to the Renaissance, aspects of bibliography appear. Catalogs aside, such as employed at the library in Alexandria and probably in numerous private collections, the consensus is that the first shadow of a genuine bibliography is Galen's *De libris propriis liber* (*A book about my own books*). The former gladiator-physician, who lived from about 129 to 199 A.D., gained fame as the court physician in the Rome of Marcus Aurelius. Considered a fine teacher, he published numerous books on medical theory and practice, and is remembered today for his knowledge of anatomy and physiology. He was second only to Aristotle in influencing science during the Middle Ages and early Renaissance, and considerably more current than the Greek philosopher. Galen's second century bibliography was an effort to list his library which he classified. Some 500 titles are under such broad headings as anatomical works, Hippocratic writings, grammar and rhetoric etc.

The majority of early manuscript and print bibliographies, roughly from the fifth through the fifteenth century, were far less systematic. The lists of the works of theologians are faulty and incomplete, if not downright inaccurate. The primary purpose was to spread the faith, to spread propaganda. Each bibliographer slavishly copied the work of his predecessors, errors and all. (The circle was finally broken by Tritheim with his impressive listing of 1494.)[9]

St. Jerome (c. 340–420), a student of the most famous grammar teacher of his age, Donatus, turned to bibliography as a part of biography. Actually, there is an argument whether he actually did compile a biography, but be as that may his *De viris illustribus* (Concerning famous men, 393) consisted of short notes on 135 Christian writers. According to Besterman, and many others, the book was really a type of bibliography in that "the main emphasis lies on the writings of the subjects, rather than on their lives."[10] In all of the early Catholic bibliographies the common purpose was to provide ammunition for dogma. "At the beginning of his work, St. Jerome declares his intention of showing the enemies of the church how many good writers she had already produced."[11]

The by now familiar bibliography at the end of a book appeared first in Venerable Bede's (c. 673–735) *Ecclesiastical History of the English People* (731). Some 40 works Bede considered of importance to his history are listed in a rough classified fashion as "Notitia de se ipso et de libris suis." These include his and other works. They are the earliest bibliography at the end of a history, or for that matter, any form of book.

Bibliography in the Middle Ages

In most of the surviving documents of the Middle Ages the closest claim to the present meaning of bibliography is found in numerous lists or inventories of books made by private collectors as well as by monastic and cathedral schools. Most are incomplete even in the listing or description of a specific title.

Employing the metaphor of an elaborate garden, Richard Fournival of Amiens, nicely categorized knowledge by garden plots. He then moved his plots into his library where the analogy crystallized into a catalog and floor plan for his books. According to Reynolds and Wilson his *Biblionomia* (c. 1250) is not "the imaginary projection of a bibliophile, but the actual catalogue of Fournival's own carefully collected library. It must have contained about 300 volumes and in size and range could challenge the monastic and cathedral libraries of his day."[12]

Near the close of the thirteenth century, the Franciscans (probably at Oxford) compiled the *Registrum Angliae de libris doctorum et auctorum veterum.* This is a list of works, by about 100 authors, found in cathedral and monastic libraries in England and southern Scotland. A systematic method was employed for the listings. The author, then his titles, and names of the libraries where the works were found. The most popular author was St. Jerome. His *Epistolae* was found in 39 libraries.

John Boston of Bury (fl. c. 1410) is the father of the idea of a union catalog. His *Catalogus & scriptorum ecclesiae,* unlike other listings from the seventeenth century to the early fifteenth century, recorded titles in not one or two, but 195 English monasteries. Arranged alphabetically by authors, each entry includes the special interests of the 700 or so authors. Where John found a book in a monastery he recorded it after the author's name with an identification number peculiar to the individual library. Unfortunately, author names are listed without titles. Authors and titles appear, but without any reference to a library. Apparently John copied other sources and was not too methodical about what he found where. "Nevertheless, he clearly is entitled to all the credit of having initiated a type of catalogue."[13]

The shortage of books during the early Middle Ages—an average monastery would have no more than 10 to 50 individual title, accounts for limited interest in bibliography systematic lists appeared only when: (1) There was a booktrade where knowledge of both new and older titles was imperative for business; and (2) There was active production of both new and older titles, i.e. for the most part after the wide spread of printing in the late fifteenth and early sixteenth centuries. Until formal bibliography appeared individuals, from scholars to publishers, depended primarily upon a network of informants and communication by travelers, augmented by book fairs.

By the late Middle Ages the book trade gradually developed in the university communities. In order to insure accurate, copied texts the universities established rules for the stationarii (booksellers) including notification to the public of what was available. Publishers provides a list of books, but as distribution was limited, as were potential customers, the lists were limited in both terms of distribution and size.[14]

Richard deBury (1286–1345), the bishop of Durham, was among the first book collectors of the late Middle Ages. He is best known as the author of the famous *Philobiblon* (The Love of Books) which is a treatise published on the joy of collecting published in 1344, and printed in 1473. As an English ambassador in Europe he had the opportunity to examine and buy manuscripts from both private and clerical sources. Also he had books copied for him, largely from deteriorated exemplars. In 1313 he met a fellow collector at Avignon. This was Francesco Petrarch, (1304–1374) considered to be the father of the Renaissance. United by a love of books, if not theology, the two collectors recognized how each could help in the rebirth of knowledge. The younger Petrarch enlisted not only the help of deBury, but friends through Europe in the endless quest for books.[15]

Petrarch's and deBury's humanist culture, with reliance on discovering older books, developed a third bookseller's market, outside of the traditional academic and ecclesiastic markets. Individuals now became involved with collection, with building personal libraries. They sought out books across Europe and became an important source of income for a growing number of equally independent booksellers. "Ideal" libraries, neither too small or too large were the focus of lists, or bibliographies to be used by collectors and booksellers. The lists rarely numbered more than 100 to 200 titles.[16] An example: Angelo Decembrio's *Politia literaria* (c. 1450). The work was among the first bibliographic humanistic texts. The listed books are described in conversations among scholars who are instructed on how to select and arrange the titles.[17]

Advent of Printing and Bibliography

With the advent of printing, with the ability in one day to publish more copies of a work than could be hand copied in a year, there arose a need to get adequate information of books available to a wider public than the university or monastic community. "New tools for providing information came into being: prospectuses, handbills, and bulletins of works published or in preparation gradually were transformed into true catalogs."[18] In Germany, the fatherland of the booktrade, the beginnings of bibliography may be found in "the hand lists, or posters, announcing one or more books, similar to those employed earlier by copyists, that were fastened to the doorposts of churches . . . In universities towns these lists were attached to the doors of the university."[19] One of the earliest is the 1469 list by Johann Mentel of Strassburg. By the sixteenth century these modest broadsides had developed into printer/publisher catalogs which were distributed at book fairs.

A few publishers listed their books e.g. Swenyheym and Pannartz's *Registrum librorum impressorum* Rome, 1470. More substantial catalogs came later from Estienne, Aldus, Plantin and major publishers throughout Europe. For example, Aldus's 1498 *Libri graeci impressi,* was a single sheet of classical titles. By 1513 the list had grown to five pages. Aldus unwittingly may be the first publisher to issue a publisher's catalog with information on not only books published, but information about those to be issued. While not considered standard bibliographies, these early publisher catalogs at least served a major purpose. They let the public know what books were available, if only from one printer.[20]

The first substantial bibliography, after the invention of printing, followed the pattern established by St. Jerome, Isidore of Seville and other early scholars. The focus was on authors acceptable to the Church. In 1494, at Basel, the Abbot of Sponheim, Johann Tritheim (1452–1516) published his *Liber de scriptoribus ecclesiasticis* (Books about ecclesiastical writers). The volume ran to over 300 pages and included information on over 1,000 authors, most of whom were associated with the Church. The bibliography was a combination of biographical data and a listing of the particular author's work. The "bio-bibliography" or author catalog was a familiar format, but Tritheim harnessed the printing press to expand it considerably. The bibliography contained representative samples of Europe's monasteries and printer-publishers. After each author's biographical sketch, Tritheim included in chronological order the author's basic writings. In all around 7,000 books are listed. An alphabetical index of authors was added. "The contrast between the feeble theological bibliographies of the manuscript age and this first attempt in the printing era is very striking."[21]

Tritheim established, too, the bibliography as a standard reference work. If he was not the first to compile a bibliography, he was the first to recognize its potential importance as well as the first to stress an alphabetical index of main chronological listings. Tritheim gained his training in the Benedictine monastery of Sponheim. A brilliant scholar, he became the head of the monastery in 1483. He was 21 years old and had just finished his 15 month novitiate. One of his earliest efforts was to reorganize and catalog the monastic library. He became, too, an avid collector; and the initial 48 volumes in the library was built to over 2,000 books and manuscripts under his supervision. As he became more and more involved with bibliography, he was called upon by other monastic communities for assistance, and from this, possibly rose the idea for the compilation of his then massive listing of ecclesiastical writers.

Tritheim compiled other bibliographies: *Catalogus illustrium viorum*

Germaniae (Mainz, 1495)—a list of over 2,000 works by over 300 writers arranged in chronological order, again with an alphabetical index. In 1492 he finished the *De origine, progressu et laudibus Ordinis Carmelitarum*, which lists work of 75 Carmelite Order writers. Published in Mainz in 1494 this really was little more than excerpts from his original *Liber de scriptoribus.*

Not far behind the more ambitious bibliographies were the bibliographies of individual authors, often compiled by themselves. Erasmus was among the first writers to construct his own autobibliography, *Catalogus omnium Erasmi Roterodami lucubrationum* (Basel, 1523). A year later he revised the listing which was in narrative, chronological form. A table indicated the classification of his works as he would have them arranged in a complete edition. In this matter he closely followed the pattern of Galen, some 1300 years before. In 1544 Jerome Cardan (1501–1576) listed his writings, *De libris propriis* at the end of his edition of his *De sapientia.* Each work is numbered in the margin. What is remarkable about the bibliography is that it was published when Cardan was only 43, and long before he had published his more important works—works which were never included as there was no update of the original bibliography. Cardan, astrologer, mathematician and physician, gained fame as the first person to describe accurately typhus fever and as the author of an equally famous work on algebra, *Ars magna.*

Until well into the sixteenth century the majority of public, private and institutional libraries had relatively small collections, developed, for the most part from earlier monastic and lay holdings. As there were no more than a few hundred books, the problems of bibliography were negligible, as, of course, were any difficulties of arrangement and classification. Catalogs were hardly needed, either. The few books were easily found as they were shelved according to subjects. Theology usually came first, with medicine and law following and so on. Books tended to be arranged by size rather than by author.

It was a century where bibliography was the extension of humanism. Bibliographers were interested primarily in authors and their texts, not in the books themselves. "The author continued to receive the interest of the compilers, but gradually the time came when the author was sacrificed to the complete and technical description of the book . . . But a long period was required for this transformation."[22]

Bibliography in the Sixteenth Century

During most of the sixteenth century European scholars turned their efforts to understanding, and listing, authors of antiquity and modern men of learning. Thanks to the Reformation and the development of sophisticated scientific groups, as well as freedom of travel, there developed a new interest in current matters. Along with this involvement came subject bibliographies covering every interest from medicine and law to traditional theology and education.

Among, the earliest printed subject bibliographies was the first medical bibliography *De medicine claris scriptoribus* (Lyons, 1506). Compiled by Symphorien Champier (1472–1533) it is an overview of medical writing from the Greeks to the sixteenth century. Ancient, philosophical, ecclesiastical medical writers are in the first three parts followed by a longer division of Italian medical authors and concluding with English, German, Spanish and French writers. The lists are spasmodic, not well organized and really trustworthy only in the overview of writers who were near contemporaries of Champier. In quest of books on civil and canon law Giovanni Nevizzno of Asti (d. 1540) visited libraries in major Italian towns and cities as well as Lyons. After the laborious travel he produced a bibliography of 40 pages with a listing of a thousand printed books. Enlarged and edited it was reprinted many times.

And so the pattern was set for subject bibliographies throughout the sixteenth and seventeenth centuries. Normally they were arranged chronologically and built around the writings of primary figures in each field, whether it be zoology (Gesner's *Histotis animalium* Zurich, 1551–1558) or agronomy (Joachim Camerarius', *Catalogus authorum . . .* Nuremberg, 1577).

From the beginning, bibliographers fared badly with writers. Champier, who was the first Frenchman to follow bibliography as one of several careers, was the butt of jokes by Rabelais. In 1533, Pantagruel goes to Paris and Champier is the not too thinly disguised compiler of a bibliography of an imaginative library. Real or imaginary, the attitude about bibliographers has changed little. Most are considered nitpickers, and particularly those concerned with analytical and textual bibliography. Many spend what to other seems like arid lives compiling and analyzing the works of others. Be that as it may, bibliographers and bibliographies are the foundation upon which the modern library is built . . . or at least organized. Anyone who has surfed on the internet, for example, will appreciate the necessity of order and consistent enumeration.

The sixteenth century saw the first outlines of national bibliographies focused on the study of national literatures and biographical data about the writers. Usually under the term "bibliotheca" (selected list of books), this type of bibliography gained wide attention and was popular to the early part of the nineteenth century. While these tended to concentrate on authors rather than fencing in all of the nation's published books, at least the early national bibliographies prototypes were moving in the direction of today's works.

Although he had numerous precursors, and certainly numerous contenders for the title of "first bibliographer" Conrad Gesner (1516–1565) is considered the founder of the art. He was the first systematic bibliographer to describe books and to establish a workable classification system for more than a handful of titles. He was the first to dream of universal bibliography, of capturing in one place *all* the books ever published—a formidable notion that only today is being realized. Along the way the Zurich scientist gained a wide reputation for his mastery of botany, medicine and natural history. Unfortunately, he was struck down by the plague before he realized his full capacities as a scientific writer and bibliographer.

In 1545 his famous *Bibliotheca universalis* (Universal bibliography) was published. In a folio volume of some 1300 pages Gesner listed over 12,000 Hebrew, Greek and Latin titles known to him, primarily first hand, from various library investigations. The libraries he used were in Italy, as well as in German speaking areas, and included the private collections of scholars such as Erasmus. Alphabetical by the name of authors, the bibliography is prefixed with a summary list of the writers in alphabetical order. Gesner's subtitle to his *Bibliotheca* of 1545 serves to remind modern readers that little changes: "A work . . . not only necessary for the building of library collections, but more useful for the better ordering of studies for all students of art or science." To this day bibliographies serve the same purpose.

From the standpoint of arrangement, Gesner followed a plan much copied and still used to this day. The first part of *Bibliotheca* was arranged alphabetically by author, and not, as in many previous bibliographies, chronologically. There is an index, too, of authors by surname. The second part, *Pandectae* (Zurich, 1548) rearranged the first part by subject. Argument arises as to the wisdom of the subject divisions, but the overall plan for the bibliography fulfills the need not only to include data, but to offer a method of quick retrieval. Gesner may or may not have had a logical plan for the subject arrangement. Besterman points out: "It would be difficult to find much to say in defense of this scheme."[23] At the same time Besterman admits that Gesner had nothing really to go on in that before him there was no logical classification of books and certainly little or none during his lifetime. Most libraries simply arranged their limited number of titles by broader subjects from theology and philosophy to mathematics and law.

Not only did Gesner list titles, but he often annotated them, including digests of their contents and often extracts from their texts. His curiosity carried him beyond his initial bibliography. Between editing several classics he prepared several subject bibliographies. His classic on animals (*Historiae animalium*), appeared in 1551. Here he listed over 251 writers whose works he had drawn on for his treatise. Then, in 1552, he prepared another bibliography of botanical writers for Hieronymus Bock's herbarium. A surgical bibliography was compared in 1555, a bibliography on *Dioscorides commentators* in 1561, and for his famous edition of Galen (1562–1561) he compiled a then definitive list of Galen's works and commentators.

Gesner both felt that there was a need for a guide to available books available and to books which might not be available much longer due to natural destruction as well as the dangers of war, and particularly from the threatened invasion of Europe by the Turks. In another step, Gesner called for the establishment of public libraries, "to preserve books for a long time . . . printed books are soon dispersed and can no more be found. Those worn by private parties usually disappear after a short period of time through lack of proper care." His establishment of bibliography to serve readers and satisfy needs for information, seemed to him the only valid reason for his work. In this Gesner was centuries ahead of his times, particularly in his desire to make books available to everyone who needed them in libraries. Unlike earlier bibliographies, Gesner wanted to give a broader dimension to his work . . . He wanted to help insure the transmission of the cultural documentation of the past to succeeding generations. More important, as he said himself, he prepared the bibliography not only for scholars, but for everyone, including those with little education who have a desire to learn. Gesner published several other editions, (1545–1549) and by his death the work in total covered more than 15,000 books by about 3,000 writers.

Gesner's advanced ideas of public education and public libraries, the Catholic church saw as a threat. Consequently, Gesner was included in the *Index* among authors who were considered heretical. Paradoxically, the Church employed Gesner's bibliography to help in deciding what to include in the *Index*. Church censors found grouped together (in Gesner's *Pandectae*), the works they wished to place in the *Index*.[24]

Gesner's work had been the final expression of an age in which culture knew no boundaries, when the nations of the continent and the British Isles were linked together. The universality of his *Bibliotheca universalis* was defined not only by the encyclopedic idea of humanistic culture, but also by means of an international language.

With the decrease in the use of Latin and the increase in the vernacular, emphasis shifted from the international to the national, and the first bibliographies to focus on particular countries originated in England. John Bale (1495–1563) published the first English national bibliography. In 1548: *Illustrium majoris Britanniae scriptorum . . . summarium* (Summary of the writings of the most eminent Britons).[25] Order by authors in chronological sequence, was preceded by a listing of the authors alphabetically. A new edition (1557) and a supplementary volume (1559) with an index concluded the effort which listed about 1400 English authors. Bale added to earlier efforts by visiting libraries, bookstores and binderies where he found fragments and whole works of many of the writers he listed.

By 1553 as the Protestant archbishop of Dublin, Bale gained little favor among Catholics. He was a constant reformer of the Church. The pressure grew on him so that by the end of his career he had to flee to England where he was given a post at Canterbury. Altogether remarkable, he is known today as much for his plays as for his bibliographic works. He wrote several anti-Catholic plays between 1537 and Cromwell's fall in 1540. Although highly biased, particularly against Roman Catholic authors, Bale did manage a given amount of objectivity which even to this day makes his bibliography of value to historians.

An Italian national bibliography of sorts appeared in 1550–1551, and a more impressive French title in 1584, but it was not until Andrew Maunsell's *The Catalogue of English Printed Bookes* (1595) that national bibliography reached maturity and sophistication. It would be a model for similar works to come for many decades, even centuries.

A former draper, Maunsell is recognized today as the first professional bibliographer in England, and the second in the history of bibliography. He is preceded only by Gesner. Turning from his London business to bookselling, Maunsell became obsessed with the idea of preserving from oblivion all of the books published in England. He was anxious to use English and not Latin, to eliminate manuscripts in favor of only printed books, and made an effort to edit the copy for clarity and precision.

Besterman observes that Maunsell was "the first bibliographer inspired by modern bibliographical ideals."[26] Maunsell developed a systematic method of describing listed books and to categorize titles by subjects in a logical method. This was a true national bibliography in that Maunsell attempted to list everything, not just "best" or books for sale by booksellers. Full bibliographic information is given, often for the first time. The author's name,[27] translator (where relevant), full title, publisher, date of publication, format and other by now standard bibliographic descriptive measures are given for virtually each of the close to 3,000 items. The first part, covering religion and theology, includes some 2,500 titles; as compared with barely over 300 for sciences.

No better summary of the purpose and the goal of bibliography will be found than in this first national English bibliography compiled by Maunsell. He explains a bibliography is needed because: "many excellent Bookes (are) written, and Printed in our own tongue; and that many of them after twenty or fortie years Printing, are so dispersed out of Booke-sellers hands, that they are not only scarce to be found, but almost quite forgotten." Also, the Catalogue will "be delightsome to all English men that be learned, or desirous of learning: for hereby they may know even in their studies, what Bookes are eyther by our own Countrymen written, or translated out of any other language."[28]

Maunsell set a pattern which was supported by increasingly careful attention to records of what was published.[29] National bibliography became common in Europe. And following Maunsell, Louis Jacob founded a journal devoted to listing new French books beginning in 1643. By the end of the sixteenth century bibliographies became more common, more and more a part of the development of printing and publishing. Also by then the basic principles of bibliographic description and organization were established.

The first trade bibliographies (i.e. collections of titles from catalogues issued by individual publishers) appeared in the mid sixteenth century, but failed to make much of an impression. "The first cumulation of the semi-annual German [book] fair catalogs . . . was made by Nicolaus Basse and covered the period from 1564 . . . to 1592 . . . Useful as these compilations were . . . they did not establish a tradition to be continued."[30]

Seventeenth Century Bibliography

Despite differences in focus, the bibliographic work of the seventeenth century closely resembled the process of earlier centuries. The bibliographers tended to be avid readers with a desire to capture all the information then available for a given subject area, or, in some cases, for the purposes of a universal or national bibliography. Most, no matter what their goal, were selective. They included only what was of interest to them. "If the sixteenth century had rediscovered antiquity, the seventeenth rediscovered the Middle Ages . . . (i.e.) the task of dealing with medieval documents and papers."[31] The clergy began producing bibliographies (covering every conceivable topic of theological interest) of manuscripts from the forgotten monastic libraries. Bibliographers depended on the contents of libraries and from the very first the bibliography rarely was any better than what was found in those libraries. Gesner, for example, based his sixteenth century work on what he found in major city and monastic libraries. As libraries developed in the seventeenth century so did the base for more and more bibliographies.

At the same time, scientific bibliography gained in importance. While the historians studied literary medieval texts, the scientists turned to facts. Out of this came the founding of the Academie des Sciences and the *Journal des scavans* in 1665,[32] *The Philosophical Transactions* of the Royal Society a year later in London and similar journals throughout Europe. The journals functioned as bibliographies, alerting services and points of contact for discussion.

In his *De dignitate et augmentis scientiarum* (Worth and growth of sciences) of 1605 Francis Bacon (1561–1626) organized a pattern for a history of learning, i.e. *Historia litteraria*.[33] The book was a vast influence throughout Europe and inspired Gabriel Naudé's (1600–1653) numerous writings, including his *Advis pour dresser une bibliotheque* (Advice concerning the erecting of a library) published in 1627. He ends this work by calling for a wider study of the history of books and literature, which is to say a history of learning as envisioned in part by Bacon.[34] The ideal library was based on three models which Naudé greatly admired: Oxford's Bodley

Library (1602), the Ambrosian Library in Milan (1609), the Augustinians' public library in Rome (1605).

While Besterman and other historians of bibliography question the honored role of Gabriel Naudé as a distinguished master of the profession, generally he is considered by the less informed, or perhaps the less willing to split definition hairs, as an early advocate of bibliography. Be that as it may, few would deny he helped to popularize the descriptor, e.g. his 1633 Venice publication, *Bibliographia politica.* By the mid seventeenth century the concept of bibliography as knowledge and literary history was linked as "Bibliotheca" i.e. a library or collection of books. Bibliography was the keystone to a library. This concept lead to the notion of bibliography (and a library) as being the essential path to knowledge. By acquiring an understanding of books one crossed the first necessary border to research. This, in turn, opened the gates of the eighteenth century Enlightenment, and the by now well known cliché that the knowledge of books is the better part of learning.

After Bacon and Naudé came the men who were professionally involved with publishing, with book collecting and with, to be sure, bibliography. These individuals were well known in their own time, but today forgotten. At the same time their work helped shape the nature of bibliography, not only for the seventeenth century, but for all time. A few of the more prominent bibliographers and their contributions which were typical of the time would include: An avid book collector, (1) Joannes Hallervord (1644–1676) published a supplement to Gesner, and in so doing established the custom of adding the printer and publisher of each title, as well as citations to previous bibliographies. (2) The historian and geographer Andre du Chesne (1584–1640) issued numerous bibliographies, and he only failed to include pagination in the otherwise complete bibliographical data. (3) The Austrian travel writer Martin Zeiller (1589–1661) turned his command of all the period's travel books into what many people believe is the first travel bibliography, i.e. *Fidus Achates of 1651.* (4) Edward Phillips (1630–1696), while best known for the biography of his uncle, John Milton (1694) also composed a bibliography of the most eminent poets of all ages, *Theatrum poetrarum* (London, 1675). When Naudé and other seventeenth century bibliographers addressed themselves to "best books," the lists were limited, usually to 300 to 500 writers and then only their "notable" books were selected. Several chapters usually were given over to bibliographers[35] and bibliography, but the remaining sections would move in a predictable fashion from theology, law and medicine to outstanding Greek and Latin authors.

Heinrich Vogler's *Introductio universalies* (Helmstedt, 1670) explains how to learn about the best books (read book dealer catalogs). The main part of the treatise "covers particular lists of authors and writing, collections of authors of individual disciplines, nations, and order, and of female authors; and the biographical and pictorial works that go with them." Vogler, too, discussed library catalogs and reference works. Always objective, he did not actually list the "best" and "better" titles, but outlined the steps to achieve such knowledge. In a sense it was the first modern textbook in bibliography, and it went through three editions, the last being published in 1720. Vogler was among the first to be faced with a true information explosion, caused in no small part by the printing press and, equally important, improved methods of transportation and merchandising which made books available throughout the whole of Europe. The need became more and more apparent that someone, or some technique had to be developed to ascertain what was worth reading in general and in particular.

Adrien Baillet's (1649–1706) conviction was that "one would go further in the arts and the sciences if one had sure knowledge of the books which must be read and of those which should be omitted."[36] In his *Jugemens des scavans* (Paris 1686) he lays down rules for selection of books and a classification system and used its principles. The professor was persuaded of uselessness of many books and he held "that the first duty of a librarian was to designate those which were required reading. It was this which made him undertake the *Jugemens* which was . . . a simple compilation of the major best-known works with some reflections on others . . . The first volume was intended to train the reader, and was made up of general information about books and the first printers . . . The last five volumes (of 9) . . . dealt with books on the art of poetry since the Renaissance."[37]

Bibliography in the Eighteenth Century

By the close of the seventeenth century, bibliography's primary concern was with authors, literary history and with "best" lists under the name of *Historia litteraria*. "The Bibliothecae (booklists) were considered both contributions to the history of learning and aids for learning about books."[38] The interest paralleled the rapid development of both personal and institutional libraries, as well as the related antiquarian book trade. The relatively new business drew to it bibliographers who developed a thorough way of describing books in their catalogs. In Paris, later of Holland, Prosper Marchand (1675–1756) developed a book trade classification system including a systematic method of compiling bibliographies. Marchand was followed by Gabrield Martin (1679–1761) who modified the classification system and issued numerous catalogs.

Johann Fabricius (1668–1736) bridged the seventeenth and eighteenth centuries and contributed greatly to the substance and history of bibliography. His *Bibliotheca graeca* (Hamburg, 1705) was a careful, pattern setting work which listed each author with a detailed listing of his works. Versions of the given work, in manuscript and printed form, were noted. He was "one of those erudite men who carried specialist bibliography to its highest level of achievement in the eighteenth century."[39]

Whereas bio-bibliography dominated the earlier centuries, by the eighteenth century there was a shift to enumerative bibliography, to classification, to descriptive bibliography.[40] The eighteenth century became the spring board for treating bibliography as the history of books, as today's critical, analytical bibliography. Avid book collectors throughout Europe organized, analyzed and cataloged rich collections. A single example is Jean Baptiste Osmont's "*Dictionnaire typographique, historique et critique des livres rarees . . .*" (1768).

Armand Camus (1740–1804) is representative of the new bibliographer. Both before and after the French Revolution he set the pattern for the organization of libraries. His "*Lettres sure la profession d'avocat . . .*" published first in 1773 underwent numerous editions and the bibliographic section became a model of its type.

The development of book collecting, which ran parallel with developments into the history of printing and textual bibliography, saw several innovative bibliographies in the eighteenth century.[41] Joseph Ame was the first English bibliographer to describe and estimate the value of English books. His *Typographical Antiquities* (London, 1749) included items from the origins of printing to 1600. In 1785–1790 another amateur, William Herbert enlarged the Ames bibliography. His specialty was typography and in England this developed into the bibliographic discipline of "typographical bibliography," or today's "historical bibliography." Private owner catalogs were valuable as subject bibliographies. For example, *La biblioteca aprosiana* (Bologna, 1673) is the inventory of a private library which highlighted Italian vernacular literature. (The sometimes haphazard arrangement of such lists is obvious in this work where titles are arranged according to names of donors.) By the eighteenth and nineteenth centuries the private catalogs were largely a gentleman's whim. For example, the Crevenna catalogue of 1775–1776 was a gentleman's library of standards works, including more than a thousand incunabula titles. From the gentleman's library lists developed more ambitious works by wealthy bibliophiles. The pattern was established by Thomas Dibdin with his *Bibliotheca Spenceriana* (1814–1815; and supplements from 1822 to 1823). Often not only was a book listed but the history of a particular copy or series of copies was given in great detail.

Thomas Horne wrote the standard early nineteenth century title on bibliography, *Introduction to the Study of Bibliography* (London, 1814). A senior librarian at the then British Museum, Horne was interested in both the history of books and the system of classification adopted for arranging a library, Horne both lead and followed. He led in his approach to classification, but followed tradition in his interest in rare books. In this respect his work is an effort to list the basic titles of value to the antiquarian bookperson, as well, of course, the librarian. Here he was in step with the more famous Dibdin. Together, Dibdin and Horne established the idea, at least in England, that bibliography consisted primarily of the knowledge and the description of rare books.

The first comprehensive large library catalogs were published near the turn of the seventeenth century in the Netherlands. The Bodleian catalog at Oxford was issued in 1605, followed by a more ambitious effort in 1620 and a supplement in 1635.[42] For a century or more there were such catalogs, but a surprisingly great number of otherwise advanced institutions failed to do little more than list titles available.

Between 1740 and 1880 there was a renewed interest in library catalogs, and American efforts appear with the Harvard catalog of 1790 and the Library Company of Philadelphia's catalog in 1807. The first complete catalog of the British Museum was the 8 volumes *Libri impressorum . . .* (1813–1819). The great institutional catalogs with which the public is familiar today only began with the British Museum catalogue of 1841 and the updated, totally revised Bodleian catalogue of 1843–1851. Finally, in 1881 the British Museum *Catalogue of Printed Books* began to appear and has been updated ever since. By 1898 the Bibliotheque Nationale was begun as was the Library of Congress catalog.

By the end of the eighteenth century, bibliography took on still another meaning which differed from the previous century. What had been a focus on the history of the book and literary history gradually shifted to a simple list of books and descriptive cataloging of titles. The shift was a movement away from the scholarly to the active role of bibliography in bookselling. Bibliography was now an aid for sales, of both new and older books.[43]

Nineteenth Century Explosion of Bibliographies

Bibliographies increased dramatically in the nineteenth century. The reason is obvious. There was an explosion of the number of books, journals, newspapers and other forms of communication. In addition to the traditional explanation there were secondary, yet important other reasons for the increase in the form: (1) An increase in the number of universities, teachers and researchers. (2) An emphasis on education outside of theology, and (3) An equal focus on the education of the great middle classes and those who aspired to such status. All of this was made possible, in no small part, by the same technology that created faster and more efficient methods of printing and the ability to carry printed material from one end of the country to the other.

In the judgment of the French bibliographer Malclés, the period from

1790 to 1810, "launched a previously non-existent theory of bibliography."[44] Much of this was brought about by the confiscation of books by the government after the Revolution of 1789.[45] Central libraries were needed to house the titles as were experts to protect, catalog and arrange the books. The experts turned bibliography at this point to mean "everything which dealt with books."[46] By 1810 the demands of publishers and booksellers for order and identification of titles created the professional bibliographer. Along with the need to find individual titles in the new flood of books came scientific and technological changes and a proliferation of journals. Libraries, too, took giant strides to house and classify the printed matter. As Malclés puts it, up to the early nineteenth century the primary purpose of bibliography had "been to save the texts of the past from loss or oblivion. From now on, it should disseminate the current advances of learning. To fill this role, current bibliography, national as well as specialized, was first added to, and soon succeeded, the retrospective bibliographies which had reigned for centuries."[47]

The Parisian bookseller, Jacques-Charles Brunet (1780–1867) "brought universal selective bibliography to its highest degree of perfection. . . . In 1810, Brunet published the first edition of his *Manuel du libraire et de l'amateur de livres.* He was to spend fifty years in perfecting it up to the fifth and last edition in 1860.[48] Originally the "Manuel" was a three volume author listing of rare books, with notes on their singularity from illustrations and binding to typography. The last volume was a classified index. The final 1860 fifth edition, in six volumes, contained over 40,000 titles. In an appreciative note, Malclé observes that Brunet "was wise enough not to make his work simply a dry list . . . his long discussions, his strokes of humor and character . . . seeded it with movement and life. The technical and literary details are all there, together with original observations, personal remarks, and occasional unforeseen sallies."[49]

The *Manuel du libraire* affirmed the present day role of bibliography in library systems. For well over 100 years it was frequently updated and became the "bible" of booksellers and not a few librarians. It established itself as the standard French bibliographical dictionary. Brunet focused on definitions and explanations. He wanted to make "known valuable books, to give an idea of their value . . . and everything related to the physical aspects of a book." By the third edition he had listed, too, over 30,000 editions of rare books. He had a methodical index which allowed the reader to find individual titles and variants. So, the bibliography was not only instructive, but it equally was a source of information on prices as well as well chosen recommendations as to the best books for "instructive and pleasurable reading." Bibliomania reached new heights in the nineteenth century. Among the addicts was Charles Nodier (1780–1844). The poet, historian and novelist also was a librarian with eccentric ideas and equally eccentric bibliographies, e.g. *Bibliographie des fous, De quelques ouvrages excentriques*

(1834–1835). In the library he directed, Nodier held meetings with who were to become France's leading authors, Victor Hugo to Sainte-Beauve. His interest in books was infectious and it was only one step to an informal book club.[50] More important, for history, at least, he championed the Romantic movement.

Still, those "who gathered the knowledge of all that concerned books and libraries under the designation bibliography were only a minority composed mostly of antiquarian book dealers, bibliophiles, and librarians."[51] The majority simply thought of bibliography as the knowledge and description of books for purposes of organization.

A major development in English national bibliography was the appearance in 1773 of the first *London Catalogue of Books.* This began as a retrospective list of available titles in London, and served this role until well into the nineteenth century. While the listing was useful, it had a major fault—the publishing date for each title was missing. Arrangements varied, but by the early nineteenth century it primarily was alphabetical by either author or title.

A rival to the *London Catalogue* appeared in 1853. Published by Sampson Low, *The British Catalogue of Books* was soon merged with its rival. *The English Catalogue,* as it came to be known, covered published in Great Britain and Ireland, and included a variety of publications from books to pamphlets. Low hardly had the field to himself, for by 1858 Joseph Whitaker began *The Bookseller,* which listed all titles issued in the United Kingdom, "and the chief works published abroad" during the previous year. In 1874 Whitaker brought out the first number of *The Reference Catalogue of Current Literature,* a collection of publishers' catalogs issued every three to four years. It soon developed into an alphabetical listing, and by 1913 it claimed to have over 200,000 entries of books in print. In 1924 Whitaker's *Cumulative Book List* first appeared, a British equivalent of the American *Cumulative Book Index (CBI).*

In the United States the Federal Act for Copyright (1790) was an early effort to bring order out of chaos in publishing. From 1790 to 1800, only about 600 titles were recorded, although later bibliographies indicates close to 17,000 titles were published for the same period. Pushed as much by the vision of profit as by the need to control the rapid development of publishing, bibliography in the United States was a major consideration by the period after the Civil War. As early as 1847 there was a compilation of publishers catalogs, as well as an early version of today's *Publishers Weekly* which began formal publication in 1872, under the guidance of Frederick Leypold.

Leypold (1835–1884) began publishing weekly bibliographies in 1868, and by 1869 had published the first volume of the *American Catalogue of Books for 1869* a compilation of publisher's catalogs which was the forerunner of the *Publishers' Trade List Annual* (1873). In 1910 the *American*

Catalogue disappeared, as much from lack of support as competition from The H. W. Wilson Company's *Cumulative Book Index*. The *CBI* had been established in 1898 and marked the beginning of one of the world's leading commercial bibliographer and index publishers. Oriented to the book trade and libraries, the CBI provides an author, title, subject guide to current books. With *Publishers Weekly* (1872) and the *Cumulative Book Index* (1898) the United States entered the era of true national bibliographies.

By the late nineteenth century, W.S. Sonnenschein turned away from scholars to the lay public and published in 1887 *The Best Books. A reader's guide*. After 1887 numerous editions were issued until the work culminated in the six volume guide in 1935. Here one found over 100,000 titles, although almost all of them were in English. This was the forerunner of a massive number of "best" guides for laypeople, of which today's example is the equally six volume *The Reader's Adviser* (New York: R.R. Bowker, 1988), which by the mid 1990s had gone through 14 editions.

Universal Bibliography

The growth, indeed the information explosion after the mid-nineteenth century propelled bibliography into a place of reference importance. Simple listings of books were no longer sufficient. Now a national bibliography included not only books, but newspapers, government publications, dissertations, maps, music and other communication forms.

Paralleling the interest in national bibliography was the knowledge that an international or universal bibliography was a useful, indeed an essential tool for research. In the United States Charles Jewett in 1850 called for "that cherished dream of scholars, a universal catalogue."[52] In England there was a request for the British Museum to prepare an index to the catalogs of all the libraries in the world. "In 1872 Henry Stevens, an American bookseller living in London, proposed the creation of a universal catalog . . . He wished to create a register of every book, big and little, that is published."[53]

What had primarily been conjecture and conversation, turned into reality in the 1890s—universal bibliography became a distinct possibility. There was now in place numerous national bibliographies to feed into the larger effort and there was a recognition of the practical value of such a work. What was envisioned by 1893 was an international bureau of bibliography directed and supported by the nations of the world. Two Belgium lawyers, Paul Otlet (1868–1944) and Henri Lafountaine (1853–1943) organized the International Institute of Bibliography in Brussels in 1895. Intended to be the editorial center of universal bibliography it was madeup of scores of scientific associates, government organizations and anyone interested in putting everything on cards which had been printed since

Gutenberg's first work. By 1900 there were some 17 million cards organized along the lines of Melvil Dewey's system, but under the Universal Decial Classification title. By 1908 Otlet had floated the notion of a international central library, with support of some 200 organizations. By 1910 he had held the first meeting of the World Congress on Bibliography. Despite his energy and intellectual achievements Otlet could not find the funding ultimately to carry on the project.[54]

Twentieth Century Bibliography

With the twentieth century bibliography underwent numerous changes. In the United States, for example: 1) National and international bibliographies flourished, as well as expanded trade bibliographies.[55] 2) Subject bibliographies became more and more numerous, paralleling increased amounts of information as well as increased numbers of formats from videos to CD-ROMs. a) In an effort to control specific pieces of information in narrow subject, primarily scientific fields, "documentation" centers were established in the 1930s and through most of the 1960s. Here documentation was an umbrella descriptor of all information, from periodical articles to unpublished reports, available in a subject field.

(3) The traditional, individual bibliographer (usually supported by his own funds) tended to disappear. "At the dawn of the twentieth century, bibliography as a profession had attained its majority and won its freedom. It had defined the goals, discovered its rules, and forged its methods."[56]

a) Bibliographies were taken over by private publishers, such as R.R. Bowker and The H.W. Wilson Company; as well as by national libraries and individuals supported via a university or foundation.

b) An enormous bibliographic apparatus throughout the world brought together individual bibliographies, both general and specialized, which, together, gave a collective picture of what was available.

c) Estimates are that individual titles of books (not copies) published throughout the world in the past decade (c. 1985–1995) and more than twice the total production from the beginning of printing (c. 1455) to about the middle of the nineteenth century. Today, about 650,000 to 700,000 new titles are published each year in the world.

(4) Bibliographies with periodicals, pamphlets, reports, etc. as well as books became more common. At the same time judicious selection rather than being all inclusive became the usual formula.

(5) The traditional "best" book bibliography continued, although for the most part limited to specific subject areas and/or forms from reference works and magazines to recordings.

By the close of the nineteenth century still another distinction was made—this time between bibliography, which had been closely associated with libraries, and with a relatively new descriptor "library science." As one authority put it: "Bibliography is the science of books . . . library science deals with the classification and the description of the external characteristics of books."[57] James Duff Brown broke with English tradition and stressed library science and classification. In fact, to this day his name is associated with his *Manual of Library Classification* (London, 1898) and his *Manual of Library Economy* (1903) as guides to students. In 1906 the Islington librarian published *A Manual of Practical Bibliography* which completed the frontal attack on bibliography launched in his previous two books. Brown urged librarians to move away from antiquarian books. He poked fun at traditional bibliographers who spent their time describing one of a copy books. As contrasted with systematic, enumerative bibliography, the more esoteric analytical, historical and textual bibliography had decreased in volume of publication, if not in importance. Analytical, descriptive bibliography had become increasingly more sophisticated and cast a wider net to include not only the book, but other formats as well as the place of the book in the wider context of a whole society or social group. Brown called for the "scientific bibliographer" concerned with accurately listing books. He stressed the need for accurate information on pagination, title pages, and material familiar to anyone searching bibliographies today. And another important contribution was to make bibliography a part of library science rather than using bibliography as an umbrella term for all types of library work.[58]

Arundell Esdaile followed Duff Brown with his by now standard *A Student's Manual of Bibliography*, 5th rev. ed. by Roy Stokes (Metuchen, N.J.: Scarecrow, 1981). Published first in 1931 it has undergone several revisions and remains a basic title in the field. The manual gives a brief history of book production from the earliest period in the Near East to the modern computer age. This, however, is more a background than an in depth study, and most of the *Manual* is concerned with the pragmatic aspects of describing the book. Esdaile combines interests of the antiquarian book bibliographer and the modern enumerative bibliographer, but focused on historical bibliography, i.e. "biology."

Louise-Noelle Malclés (known simply as Malclés) wrote the first general history of bibliography (*La Bibliographie,* 1956). The former Sorbonne librarian and teacher blessed the modern definition of enumerative bibliography as a knowledge of titles only, not necessarily a complete knowledge of books. She carried the term a step further and defined "bibliographer" as someone who not only knows titles of books, but is familiar with the subject area in total and is, in fact, the ideal reference librarian. Usually this is a bibliographer working in a special subject area.

In an effort to bring all data of a narrow subject area into focus, "documentation" centers were established from the 1930s through the 1960s.

Here most of the focus was on technological and scientific subjects which required current data drawn as much from unpublished reports and scholarly journals as from books. Organizations and societies developed in support to channel talent into the documentation centers which, by the 1950s included the social sciences and humanities as well as the sciences. The end result is that today each major discipline has its own current bibliographic/documentation centers, and many support numerous bibliographies—as often in the form of abstracting and indexing services as retrospective titles.

The advent of computers, networks, catalog databases and related technologies revolutionized bibliography. Now it is possible in a central point to prepare cataloging information which may be used throughout the nation, indeed throughout the world. At the same time the bibliography grows in size as each library, and particularly national libraries, add their holdings to the easily accessed databases. Today, for example, OCLC, built upon the holdings of the Library of Congress plus its thousands of members results in a bibliography of over 30 million items. Combined with national catalogs from England, France, Germany and so on, and one may literally achieve close to universal bibliography. Obviously not everything is included, but by now one can be relatively certain that a thorough computer assisted bibliographic search will turn up, or at a minimum point to, all the data necessary for most purposes, for most retrospective research.

Indexes

An important, major cousin of bibliography, the index is considered an all powerful search tool which augments book bibliographies. As descriptors, "index" and "bibliography" were synonyms until the sixteenth century, when the former took on an identity all its own. By the early sixteenth century "index" was synonymous with a table of contents prefixed to a book, a brief list or summary of the matters treated in an argument; also a preface, prologue. This definition soon was bypassed for the term's current meaning. The index is, this side of encyclopedias and dictionaries, about as well known as any other form of bibliography or reference work. Today it is defined as "a usu. alphabetical list that includes all or nearly all items (as topics, names of people and places) considered of special pertinence and fully or partially covered or merely mentioned in a printed or written work (as a book, catalog or dissertation) that gives with each item the place (as by page number) where it may be found in the work, and that is usu. put at or near the end of the work."[59] More simply, the index helps to locate what is needed. Often, too, it is embellished with cross references, subheadings, and other finding aids. The *Oxford*

English Dictionary defines "index" in its current use as "to enter (a word, name etc. in an index) and gives a 1761 example of its use, i.e. "Every material Fact or Circumstance in this Description is indexed under its proper head." The earliest use of the descriptor, but not as employed today, was as a synonym for "the fore-finger: so called because used in pointing." A 1398 example is given.[60] In a broader historical sense "index" goes back to the Egyptians. The term was used for the little slip attached to papyrus scrolls on which the title of the work was written—and sometimes the name of the author.[61] By the end of the Roman Republic the term also came to mean, understandably, title of the book. In the first century "index" was extended to include not only the title, but table of contents or a list of chapters.

Index, as a metaphor, was used first by Christopher Marlowe (*Hero & Leander* ii. 129; 1598). "As an index to a book so to his mind was young Leander's look." Shakespeare in 1609 established the plural of index (i.e. indexes rather than the Latin indices): "And in such indexes, although small pricks/To their subsequent volumes, there is seen/The baby figure of the giant mass/Of things to come at large." (*Troilus and Cressida* Act 1, Sc. 33; c. 1602).

Concordances

The first modern indexes were conceived as a method of analyzing the contents of the Bible. The goal was to make specific lines and paragraphs of the Bible available to the "common reader" who had access to relatively inexpensive printed editions. These became known as "concordances," i.e. the alphabetical arrangement "of the principal words contained in a book, with citations to the passages in which they occur."[62] And the first pioneer of Bible indexes, or more specifically concordances, was Alexander Cruden. In 1737 he published the complete *Concordance to the Bible.* Cruden's *Concordance* was by no means the first good index, but there is no doubt that his example provided a useful stimulant to the achievement of high standards by other contemporary indexers. In fact, the eighteenth century was the first great age of the index.

Until the age of the computer in the late twentieth century, many analytical bibliographers turned over a good part of their day to compiling concordances to show where all the more important words appear in a given text. Emphasis shifted gradually from the Bible to the classics, and then to modern writers. Just, for example, as there is a concordance to the work of Shakespeare, so is there another to the complete poems and plays of T.S. Eliot. This latter, published by Faber of London in 1996 is typical of the genre. The compiler, John Dawson, explains he began the work in 1972.

Today one would use a computer, and, in fact, computers have more or less replaced the printed concordance. One simply puts in the whole text, say of Eliot, and then searches the text word by word—thus eliminating the need for a separate index or concordance.

And the point of all this today? There are many reasons for concordances—in print, or as a computer software program. It enables a careful scholar to say whether X or Y poem or passage is truly by, say Shakespeare, based on where and how many words etc. appear in the poem or passage. A concordance is a type of fingerprint which is peculiar only to a single author. Given that print and one may determine the validity of questionable works. Also, there is the sheer fun of it all. What, for example, are the nine most frequently used words by the late T.S. Eliot? "The nine words turn out to be, in descending order of frequency, 'know, think, time, like, see, say, want, good, man.' Here, statistically established beyond question at last, are Eliot's great interests. It will be a revelation for all who mistrust more humdrum forms of reading."[63]

Modern Index

Modern indexes which give exact locations of names, subjects, and keywords, came about only with printing. Prior to that no two manuscripts, were exactly alike, particularly as to page numbers. An index was impossible to compile for more than one copy. Inventories or catalogs, which were construed as indexes, were common enough in the Middle Ages, and even before that in the Middle Eastern libraries. Books and book catalogs boasted rough indexes. Chapter headings might be so full as to constitute an index or overview of content. Still, the necessity of detailed book indexes, more or less indexes to other materials, was not really apparent until the sixteenth century.

Indexing, in the sense in which it is understood today, is an advanced art, and its principles were not very easily grasped at first. Our present term "index" is an abridged form of the earlier "index locorum" (index of places) or "index locurum communium" (index of commonplaces) which one meets with in early printed books. The elements into which an index breaks down a book are, basically "places" in the text and simultaneously topics or "places" (topoi, loci) in the mind."[64]

Author Roy Porter bemoans the problem of compiling an index: "It's a game which, try as he might, the scholar can't win. He can hear his cost-conscious publisher demanding prune, prune! (won't just a name index do?) . . . Yet there can be something equally frustrating about finding the other extreme, the index of the over elaborate variety which, like an Elizabethan codpiece, promises more than it can perform."[65] Indexing is only for those "who really like an orderly approach to life." Despite that, an indexer can have a considerable amount of pressure, particularly when deadlines for book and periodical indexes must be met. "But the craft has its pleasures, too." One indexer, for example, "likes the intellectual challenge it provides."[66]

Early Index Cousins

Aside from the *Index Librorum prohibitorum*[67] the term "index" was not widely used until the first half of the nineteenth century. Index, throughout its history, has been called many things, some true synonyms, but most only related in the sense that the term simply a method of summarizing content. Favored terms include: summary, syllabus, inventory, catalogue, table, calendar, register and many more.

The earliest known catalog, bibliography, or some might say an index was Callimachus's guide to the contents of the Alexandria Library in the third century B.C. Still, this is a matter of interpretation. It fits in that every index is a bibliography, but not every bibliography an index. The fine definition would have pleased Callimachus, a careful man.

Summaries or "tituli" developed from early abstracts which summarized content. These were employed primarily in government before the Christian era and there are records of abstracts of contracts as early as the third century B.C. The concept carried over into the "tituli" and more precisely into notes, or summaries found often in the margins of manuscripts. The marginal summaries were codified in later works and served as an index of sorts. Similar summaries were employed by many of the early writers, including reference works such as Pliny's *Natural History.*

Lacking proper indexes or concordances, copies of the Bible had the individual books prefaced by summaries (tituli or capita). These were in use as early as the second century A.D. to help find material, particularly as the chapter and verse arrangement of the modern Bible had not been as yet fixed.

Arrangement of subject terms in alphabetical order was practical only after the general adoption of the codex (c. fourth and fifth century A.D.). An example of this is the eighth century subject index to the Bible by John of Damascus. He boasted that it was now easier to find things in that he had compiled "tituli" in alphabetical order. Still, despite this advance, it was hardly popular. There is a consensus that alphabetical indexing was not used again until well into the fourteenth century, and then only when needed by scholars and students at the universities. The earliest of the fourteenth century indexes were modest, even superficial. A greater step forward was the systematic use of numbered chapter headings.

Book Indexes

In his analysis of the *Nuremburg Chronicle* (1493) Witty gives an example of typical individual book indexing in the early years of printing. "Most of the index entries (the index is in the front) were taken verbatim from the text and sometimes not entered under what would seem the proper keyword; e.g. the statement about the invention of printing in Germany is entered under *Ars imprimendi libros* with no entry at all under any form of (printing) . . . Alphabetization . . . is rough—not ordinarily past the first syllable."[68]

Prior to the eighteenth century, indexes, such as they were, represented the work of the author of the book being analyzed. By early 1700 London's Grub Street was not only the home of hack writers but of underpaid indexers. By 1762 Oliver Goldsmith in his *Citizen of the World* dismissed indexers as pretentious, generally ignorant and fair targets for mockery. He describes an "author" as someone who "writes indexes to perfection."

The lack of adequate book indexing drove Thomas Jefferson to index his own works. Exactly how many books he analyzed is unknown because many of his personal titles were lost in a fire. Of the surviving books, three have short indexes, of which two are inscribed on the end pages and the third is a separate sheet bound with the book. In his personal papers will be found an extensive although incomplete index to Benjamin Barton's *Elements of Botany* (Philadelphia, 1803). The index was probably made during Jefferson's second term as President. He favored it because of his fondness for American science in general and botany in particular. He had 36 volumes about botany in his library—but none had an index. Why, then, did Jefferson bother to index this book? He was an inveterate indexer, and as the subject interested him, it was a delight to turn to Barton. Also, he was compulsive to a point where "he carried a notebook with him constantly and recorded in it every cent he received or spent . . . for more than sixty years."[69]

Today most book indexes are arranged alphabetically, although the arrangement can differ from chronological to numerical. In the early indexes little or no attention was given to alphabetical order. The entries might be placed under the major letters of the alphabet, but after that the entries would be in haphazard order. While printers and publishers did attempt to be consistent, there was no really accepted arrangement until Diderot's *Encyclopedia* set the pattern in the mid eighteenth century. Entries followed a strict alphabetical order—an order which until this day dictates most arrangement.

Book indexing improved, too, during the nineteenth century. Indexes were necessary for multiple volumes in a reference work such as the 22 volume, seventh edition *Encyclopaedia Britannica,* (Edinburgh, 1827–1842). "The index was an astonishing achievement of detail and conciseness, as well as a masterpiece of clarity and layout."[70]

Turning to the five volume index to the Yale edition of *Horace Walpole's Correspondence* (i.e. vols. 44–48, *Complete Index*. New Haven, CT: Yale University Press, 1983) a critic observes this may be the last "such compendious guide for which the compilers did all their work by hand and mind, the last such big index innocent of the microsecond-fast electronic fingers, files and fitness of the processor."[71]

Periodical and Newspaper Indexes

Indexes to material other than in books developed, naturally enough, parallel with the growth of magazines, journals and newspapers. At the same time, the considered, thorough periodical index came well after the first journals and magazines. To understand the need for indexes, it is necessary to first consider, if only briefly, the history of serials.

Magazines and journals, as well as newspapers serve most reference librarians as sources of relatively current information. They are the raison d'être for indexes from *The Reader's Guide to Periodical Literature* to *Science Citation Index*. For research, particularly from the nineteenth century, the magazine and newspaper are invaluable. This may change with the rapid developments in digital forms of communication. The printed magazine or newspaper may be replaced by a similar digital cousin on command at a computer terminal.

Prior to the mid-fifteenth century, the only means of rapid communication was oral, i.e. two scholars or laypersons discussion a problem face to face; or, more likely, by letter.[72] Primarily, though, the handwritten book, diligently copied and passed from scholar to scholar; monastery to monastery, university to university was the primary form of communication—rapid or otherwise.

The printing press (c. 1455) made possible the efficient duplication necessary for the circulation of newspapers and magazines. Still, it was not until 150 years after the invention of printing that the first newspaper was pulled from a press, and another 50 years (1665) that the first journal appeared. In the interim between Gutenberg's discovery and the early newspapers and journals there were other forms of printed communication which served, if only in part, the role of the still to be born journal.

Pamphlet

The brief booklet, known today as a pamphlet (i.e. no less than five pages, no more than 48) preceded both magazines and newspapers as a method of carrying propaganda to a large audience. Among the earliest

English language pamphlets is one which celebrates an English victory. Dated September, 1513 the 12 page report documents the battle of Flooden Field. Published by a London printer it came out only nine days after the battle.[73] Wars proved a favorite subject of such newsbooks or pamphlets, e.g. another early one is the account published in 1548 concerning action in the Anglo-Scottish wars. There are countless examples of these sixteenth century English titles, although none would qualify precisely as a newsbook or newspaper in that none shared the characteristic of the serial, i.e. intended to be published on a regular schedule from the time of the first issue until eternity (which in reality might be no more than a few months).

The French referred to printed pamphlets as "canards" because they tended to be as slight in content as ephemeral in lasting power. These were used as much for advertising as for official government and church pronouncements. Often in a briefer form, as handbills, they were employed to list books available from booksellers and printers.

Rapid reproduction made pamphlets extremely cheap and easy to publish. A century by century survey of such material tells the historian much about the true interests of the day. Content was as varied as readers. "The bishop's most recent pastoral letter would be affixed to the church doors . . . Mathematicians posted challenges to their colleagues at the gates of the colleges . . . Streets were lined with death notices, notaries' announcements of sales, announcements of the decrees of the Parliament and edicts of the king, and notices of spectacles."[74]

Widely used throughout Europe, pamphlets gained popularity in the wake of the Reformation. Both sides employed them to sway opinion for or against the Pope. They flourished in England, Germany and France from 1523 until 1589 when the religious pamphlets were outlawed in many parts of Western Europe. Numerous other pamphlets were controversial, often banned by the authorities. As a result printer, author and distributor (who could be one and the same) tended to leave his/their names off the publication. At the same time the noncontroversial works, which tended to be more fiction than nonfiction, praised heroism, marvelous events, and generally had the flavor of a modern *Enquirer* or similar gossip tabloid. Thanks to their low cost, pamphlets became vehicles for popular reading—from fiction and autobiography to travel accounts and social propaganda. Leading sixteenth and seventeenth century authors who turned to pamphlets include Thomas Dekker (1570–1632) the English playwright; Robert Greene (1558–1592) who specialized in autobiographical pamphlets and descriptions of London crime; Thomas Nashe (1567–1601) worked with Greene, published various anti-Puritan pamphlets and gained lasting fame as the author of *The Unfortunate Traveller* (1594). Under the Puritans and particularly during the English Civil War the pamphlet as propaganda flourished once again, but gradually lost its influence with the Restoration in 1660. By then the newspaper and the early journals were taking over the primary role of the pamphlet as a news source.

With the Restoration (1660) the printers and publishers in England began to realize the audience for reading matter gradually was changing. "The scholar ceased to be the main representation of the literate and literary public: the man of the world . . . became the client to whose taste the discerning publisher adapted himself. The politician, business man, or man about town . . . had neither the leisure nor the inclination to obtain the latest intelligence from books; he preferred the newsheet which, being really only a sheet, showed him more or less at a glance the news."[75]

With the close of the seventeenth century, the pamphlet languished only to be revised as political weapons both in England and in the British North American colonies. Certainly the best known American pamphlet is Thomas Paine's "Common Sense" (1776) and, later, the various units of what was to become *The Federalist Papers*. Pamphlets of a similar nature were found in France before the Revolution. During the nineteenth century the English pamphlet became famous for pleading political causes. By the end of the first World War the pamphlet had changed course and then, as today, is primarily used as a format for brief bits of information, e.g. from the government to learned societies to business.

Newsletters

Personal and official letters date back to the earliest civilizations, and whether written on clay tablets, papyrus, wax, or bark were of the same stuff as today's letters. The more functional newsletter, particularly for commerce, trade and business, made its earliest appearance in Rome and was used throughout the Medieval period. Most of these were informal. The formal newsletter, with a fairly consistent purpose and format, if not frequency of publication appeared during the sixteenth and seventeenth centuries. Handwritten "news-letters," which might be copied many times over for wider distribution, circulated between the primary headquarters of a business and its agents throughout a given country or most of the world. These probably were employed from the beginning of trade, but became famous in the sixteenth century when the German firm of Fugger turned them into a definitive form of communication. The German merchant and banking dynasty (which dominated European business from the fifteenth to seventeenth centuries) perfected the newsletter. They circulated it not only among the firm employees but to clients who looked to the letters much as today's investors put faith in financial newsletters and guides. Printers soon realized the value of the essentially private Fugger communications and by the middle of the sixteenth century were reprinting them in whole or in part.

While the newsletter continued and an informal source of specific information, and flourishes to this day, particularly in financial circles, it gave way to the newsbook and news sheet broadside in the seventeenth century.

Coranto and Newsbook

The general newsletter gradually became known as a coranto. A coranto consisted of a single leaf with the text in two columns on both sides. [The term "coranto" comes from the French "courante," running or dance. In turn this came to mean anything done swiftly and currently. News printed quickly took the form of a courante, couranto or corant.] It flourished throughout Europe during the first part of the sixteenth century, but generally became an obsolete term by the seventeenth century.

The first extant coranto is the Strasbourg *Relation,* published in 1609. (An earlier version was probably published in the Netherlands in 1605, but no copies are extant). As the title indicates, the *Relation* was as much a pamphlet as a coranto. In any case, the corantos appeared throughout Europe and particularly were favored in the Netherlands.

On December 2, 1620 Petrus Keerius of Amsterdam published the earliest known extant coranto in the English language. It was in the form of a small folio broadside and printed on both sides in two columns. Apparently there was only one of these and it was not until almost a year later (September 24, 1621) that the first coranto of a series was issued in London.[76] This was titled: *Corante, or news from Italy, Germany, Hungarie, Spain and France.* The subtitle indicated it was translated from a Dutch copy printed at Frankfort.

The newsbook was another early version of today's newspaper. Usually it was quorto size with from sixteen to twenty-four pages.[77] It contained anything and everything which might be of interest to potential readers, but the early seventeenth century issue concentrated on events and personalities (as often fictitious as fact) in Europe rather than in England. Nathaniel Butter, considered by many as the father of English journalism, published the first coranto on September 24, 1621. He began a more systematic approach in 1662 with the weekly issue of newsbooks. Some 50 were published to October 2, 1623. Butter took on several partners during this period. Although the initial newsbook collapsed, Butter continued on with similar titles until 1632 when the government forbid further printing of the newsbooks. The censorship dated from October 17, 1632 to December 20, 1638, when Butter and his partner were given the official word to continue with newsbooks. Butter died in February 1664, and according to one source he "died very poor."

By the time of the English Civil War and the execution of Charles I in 1649 the newsbook was history and its next manifestation would be as the familiar newspaper.

Newspapers

While the noun "newspaper" was not used until 1670, the first newspaper in English appeared as the *Weekley Newes,* in 1622. The numbered series was edited by Butter. Censorship virtually halted the development of newspapers from about 1632 to 1642, but by the time of the English Civil Wars (1642–1651) there were over 300 news publications, many of which today might be termed newspapers.[78] Newspapers flourished in London, and despite restrictions spread to the provinces by 1690. The "gazette", a term derived from the Italian coin "gazeta", charges for reading the news to the public in the sixteenth century, became by the seventeenth century a clue that the paper was approved by the government, e.g. *LaGazette*, approved in France by Richelieu and English papers under the censorious Licensing Act of 1662-1694. Thanks to a better postal system, early in the eighteenth century, it was possible to sell a London newspaper throughout the whole of England. In 1702 appeared the first single sheet daily newspaper, *The Daily Courant.* It published until 1713, and drew most of its news by translating material from European courantos. The triweekly *Review,* edited by Daniel Defoe from 1704 to 1713 was the first English paper to stress local news and political controversy.

London rivals soon appeared, each stressing in the title the frequency of the paper: *The Daily Post* (1719) the *Daily Journal* (1720) and *The Daily Advertiser* (1730). Until it ceased publication in 1807 the *Advertiser* assumed the role of a national newspaper and was similar to today's *New York Times* or the London *Times* or *Telegraph.* Stressing both English and news of the Continent, the *Advertiser* put equal emphasis on business news and a mass of advertisements, primarily from booksellers and publishers. It was the ideal voice of the upper and middle class Englishperson of the eighteenth century. By the close of the century *The Times* (1788 to date) and *The Observer* (1791 to date) had begun publication. The shape of English journalism could now be traced in the history of these early nineteenth century newspapers.

A London printer, Benjamin Harris published the first newspaper in America. His *Public Occurrences* was issued in 1690, but was stopped after the first issue by the Massachusetts governor. The paper offended the political opinions of the colonial officials, who finally solved their problem by sponsoring their own newspaper, the *Boston Newsletter* in 1704. Actually this was little more than a place to publish government documents. Benjamin Franklin's brother took over the paper in 1719 and switched it over to an independent newspaper called the *New England Courant* in 1721. After the Revolution independent newspaper spread throughout the United States, encouraged by the First Amendment to the Constitution which guaranteed "the freedom of speech or of the press."

Early Magazines and Journals

Drawing upon the news approach of the early newspaper and its numerous antecedents, from pamphlets to newsletters, the first magazine had another audience in mind—the scholar. By the mid-seventeenth century the newspaper was well established in Europe and England, and its primary appeal was to the average, literate citizen. Not so the early magazines, or more properly journals. They sprang from the needs of scholars for information about their subject matter in particular and news books in general.

The earliest journals were directed almost exclusively at the scholars. Philosophy and academic subjects dominated the pages of the first such journal, Johann Rists' *Monatgesprache* from Germany in 1663. French and English versions, as those from other parts of Europe followed the same pattern. Bridging the communication of two individual and a group of people with similar interests, the scholarly journal helped to turn associations of two or three to communal ones of thousands.

In 1665 appeared the first of a series of learned journals: (1) *Journal des Scavans,* later called *Journal des Savants,* started in Paris; (2) *Philosophical Transactions,* was the first publication of the Royal Society in London. Similar journals were published in Italy, Germany and throughout Europe from 1668 to the close of the century.

Unlike today's scholarly journals, the early titles put considerable emphasis on abridgment of books as well as synthesizing information. This approach had its critics who pointed out that the seventeenth century *Reader's Digest* approach to science and literary scholarship could only lead to superficiality. "Many love and seek out these Abridgments . . . because they are appropriate to their laziness, because they want to skim over the surface of things, and because they consider themselves skillful when they know the general definitions, and terms of the arts. But judicious persons believe rightly that it is better to be entirely ignorant of things than to know them badly."[79] Why read an entire book or paper when a summary could be found in a journal? The argument is a familiar one, and leveled at early encyclopedias as well as numerous other types of reference books which served to summarize rather than offer the content of a library.

Pierre Bayle (1647–1706) and his *Nouvelles de la Republique des Lettres* (1684) established the much copied pattern of a literary journal. Published in Holland, where there was comparative freedom of the press, particularly for the numerous Huguenots who had fled from France, the *Nouvelles* was a lively success. As all such journals to come it was published in the vernacular, focused primarily on lengthy book reviews, and carried news about authors, ideas and institutions. Then as today, the disseminating of information consisted of such things as letters to the editor, what had been and what was going to be published, who was working on what project (often accompanied by extracts) and the like. Within the early part of the eighteenth century the journals had fairly well replaced the regular news-letters which sometimes circulated between scholars who were friends with similar interests.

The "review" which began slowly in the eighteenth century, and became an extremely popular type of magazine in the nineteenth and early twentieth centuries, owed its success to what the editors and writers considered definitive judgmental reviews of books. The middle classes, and particularly those emerging in England, looked to the reviews for what to read, what to praise, what to damn and what to ignore. Both English and foreign publishers were considered in the lengthy reviews, which often had massive extracts to give the reader not only an idea of content, but of style.

The argument that people who read the journals never turned to the original books reviewed, abridged or otherwise discussed was admitted as true. Still, the objections were more noisy than heard, and by the early part of the eighteenth century the proliferation of journals swamped the critics. While the one-to-one conversation about ideas and people continued by letter and face to face, the journal offered more choices, broader fields to consider. What had been limited to specialists and scholars now was open to the literate public.

The first popular or at least semi-popular magazines adopted the tone of the newspapers and newsletters. *The Mercure de France,* which began with another name in 1672 focused on entertaining and agreeable news about individuals, as well as the traditional news notes and book reviews. The earliest English counterparts to the *Mercure* were the *Athenian Mercury* (1691) and *The Gentleman's Journal* (1692).[80]

Eighteenth and Nineteenth Centuries

By the eighteenth century the learned journal was as much a part of the cultural scene as the more relaxed, certainly better read *The Spectator* (daily from 1711 to 1712) under the direction of Richard Steele and Joseph Addison. Magazine publishers early learned there were different levels of interest and of audience appeal. John Dunton, for example, published the first magazine devoted entirely to the interests of women in 1693—the *Ladies' Mercury.* Steele and Addison, as well as Daniel Defoe and his *The Review* (1704–1713) looked to the short witty essay to draw better educated, certainly better informed readers, both men and women. *The Tatler,* a triweekly written by Steele from 1709 to 1711, carried news and comments as found in today's literary review.[81] Steele and Addison seemed to have learned from the success of the first truly popular magazine, the *Mercure de France* which was filled with anecdotes, verse, and bits of gossip about the court and officials. They were followed by several similar publications including the *Penny Weekly* in London, the *Athenian Gazette* or the *Athenian Mercury* which was published from 1690–1697. Another shorter lived success was Ned Ward's *The London Spy* (1698–1700) which reported on London events.

By and large the first true effort to reach a mass market was Edward Cave's *The Gentleman' Magazine* (1731–1907).[82] The first real general periodical in England, it was read throughout Europe and in most of the North American colonies. By the nineteenth century competition by scores of other titles diminished its popularity and readership, but it continued into the twentieth century. One reason for the almost immediate success of *The Gentleman's Magazine* was its extensive use of woodcut and copper-engraving illustrations. A Belgium publisher was the first to use an illustration in a newsheet (1620), and he was followed by others in Europe and England. Still, illustrations until *The Gentleman's Magazine* were exceptional. It really was not until the first part of the nineteenth century that illustrated newspapers and magazines, particularly those directed at a large audience, became the rule rather than the exception.

In 1741 Andrew Bradford's *American Magazine* appeared, the first in the British Colonies. Three days later Benjamin Franklin issued his *General Magazine*. The two Philadelphia publications did not last more than a few months, and such was to be the case with at least 100 more titles until the turn of the nineteenth century. Colonists and later citizens of the United States who were able to read comfortably tended to subscribe to better known, certainly better written and edited British magazines.

A pioneer in mass audience magazines, Charles Knight introduced his London weekly *Penny Magazine* in 1832. This opened the eyes of other businesspeople who soon began publication of inexpensive, easy to read magazines. The last quarter of the century, both in England and the United States magazine publishing boomed.

Early popular periodicals had offered much more than entertainment or information. Turning to a magazine, readers joined the "commonwealth of letters" which offered them rapid improvement and qualified them for positions of importance. "A magazine may be compared to the sun; for as that luminary exhales the water of the ocean . . . so this miscellany draws forth the drops of human genius."[83] Self education was to be found in the periodical pages as was the fallout of self importance and self assurance. Too much of the latter could be dangerous. In an early issue of Yale's *The Literary Cabinet* (1806) the editor made it clear he "wanted a way to promote writing without distinguishing persons, and thought . . . He had found the solution in the magazine, with its diffuse composition and circulation."[84]

There are thousands of books and articles on the history of journalism and reading in the nineteenth and early twentieth century, both in Europe and in America, and while there are numerous points of view there is a broad consensus about several aspects of the periodical revolution: (1) Technology, from fast printing presses to railroads criss crossing the landscape, set the stage for a wide distribution of reading material. (2) The same technology brought about the industrial revolution with development of urban centers and better paid middle class which could afford equally better education and purchase of reading matter. (3) Advertising in the latter part of the nineteenth century allowed publishers to ask only a token sum for their publications. Subscriptions were a minor part of the profit. A large circulation, guaranteed by low prices, brought in advertising income and high profits. The evidence on who was reading what is sketchy and controversial. Still, there were more readers with more money able to buy periodicals.[85]

This side of profit, early newspapers spread through the United States and democratic sections of Europe for one major reason—to insure a literate, well informed electorate. Literacy, learning and knowledge were and are essential to the preservation of a democracy.[86] The obsession with an informed electorate continues to this day, although now it tends to be away from print to television and other digital formatted information.

Until the mid-nineteenth century, the book dominated popular reading. It continued to be important, but in terms of numbers of readers the newspaper and the magazine won the field, and would keep it to this day. The trend began in the eighteenth century. By 1820 the combined annual circulation of London newspapers, for example, was close to 30 million, or almost four times the circulation of papers 60 years before. Similar rates of growth were found throughout Europe and the United States.

Thanks to technological advances, which by 1814 pushed production of *The Times* of London up to 50,000 copies per hour, the circulation of newspapers increased dramatically throughout the nineteenth and early twentieth centuries. The expansion of circulation meant room for more and more newspapers serving various segments of the public, and by the Crimean War (1861–1865) the reporter and correspondent had become important elements of modern journalism. By the 1900s, large city newspapers had circulations close to one million and newspapers publishing, now augmented by advertising, had become a major business. Between 1880 and 1900 the number of American newspapers more than doubled (from 850 to over 2,000). The tabloid newspaper with additions of cartoons and gossip columns as well as massive numbers of photographs became part of the world scene by the end of the first World War.

The real impetus to the mass circulation of periodicals was the discovery of advertising. Instead of simply making money from subscribers, it was found that as much, and in most cases more money could be earned by selling advertising in magazines, and, at the same time, newspapers. The discovery that was to make Madison Avenue famous was devised between three Americans: Samuel McLure who began *McLure's Magazine* in 1893; Frank Munsey and *Munsey's Magazine* (1889–1929); and first and foremost Cyrus Curtis who achieved astronomical advertising revenues for his *Saturday Evening Post* and his *Ladies Home Journal.*

Shortly after the second World War, the American popular magazine lost ground, as did newspapers, to television. The response was twofold: first, general magazines more or less disappeared; second, the specific subject magazine (from sports and women's interests to automobiles and investment) took command of the newsstands. At the same time the explosion in university education and the number of teachers spelled the beginning of a tremendous growth in scholarly magazines covering every subject possible. Coupled with rapid advances in technology and a popular interest in finance, the specialized, sometimes highly esoteric journal gained a place in homes and libraries not enjoyed since the eighteenth century.

A measure of the explosion in periodical literature since World War II is simply to compare the number of indexes available in 1940 with the number held in libraries (whether in print, online, on CD-ROM or whatever) in the mid 1990s. Whereas before 1940 major and general indexes might be no more than 100 or so, and certainly no more than that purchased by libraries, today there are well over 5,000 indexing and abstracting services world wide. They are marshaled to index the some 170,000 or more periodicals, including newspapers, which now are found in every corner of the globe.

Index Development

The sometimes desperate need to know what was going on explains in no small part why the first seventeenth century scholarly journals devoted large sections to notes and specific references to publications of interest to readers. The bibliographic sections increased both in size and importance as the amount of information gathered momentum. By the eighteenth century the early general journals began the continuing process of splintering into even more refined, more specific publications—again with their own bibliographic sections.[87] Indexes, particularly to the individual journals, paralleled the growth in bibliographic enterprise.

Much as there is an ongoing rivalry in today's periodicals between the advertising department and the editorial staff, so much the same type of argument arose between the writers and the indexers. Both wanted, required more and more space in journals.[88] One had to go, and naturally enough this was the lesser read indexes. Squeezed out of the average journal, the bibliographer took the next natural step which was to develop independent indexing services. There are early examples of collective periodical indexes: a) *Beughenm's Apparatus ad historiam litterariam* (Amsterdam 1689–1681) covered some nine journals in it journal section; and by 1790–92 the *Repertorium uber die allgemeinen deutschen Journale* . . . included the first systematic arranged bibliography of periodical contents. John Edmands in 1847 issued a pamphlet *Subjects for Debate, with Reference To Authorities* which was a highly selective subject index to periodicals. The pamphlet proved such a success that William Poole persuaded the publisher George Putnam to issue *An Alphabetical Index to Subjects Treated in the Reviews and Other Periodicals* . . . in 1848. This included indexing of some 39 titles from their inception to down to 1848. It was expanded by Poole in 1853.

The first general periodical index was published by the London firm of Sampson Low in 1859: *Index to Current Literature.* The quarterly, which ceased publication in 1861, indexed some 26 American and British publications, *plus* "and to every book in the English language . . . in serial publications."

Researchers and educators in the late nineteenth century wanted tools which would help them on a day to day basis in their profession. Also, they needed some control over the proliferation of specialized journals. The subject index was a natural result. Sponsorship tended to be limited to those who used the indexes, i.e. universities and scientific groups. *Index Medicus* (New York, 1879) was among the first new type of bibliography index. It was followed by the *Engineering Index* (1884). And in London the first *Science Abstracts* was published in 1898.[90]

Modern Indexing

At the opening of the twentieth century there were four major American general periodical indexes: *Poole's Index to Periodical Literature* (232 periodicals published from 1802–1881); William Fletcher and Richard Bowker's *Annual Literary Index,* which included both periodicals and a limited number of books; a German index (1896) which was the early acorn for the massive and current *Internationale Bibliographie der Zeitschriften literatur,* and the *Cumulative Index to a Selected List of Periodicals,* a Cleveland Public Library effort which began in 1896. (By 1903 it was merged with the *Readers' Guide*). In 1901 the bookseller H. W. Wilson launched the *Readers' Guide to Periodical Literature* followed thereafter by a wide group of subject indexes.

A monthly index to the periodical literature of the United States and Great Britain was part of the *American Bookseller* by 1880 and disappeared in 1881. The first successful effort was published as the *Cooperative Index to Periodicals 1883–1891* in 9 volumes by Leypold and the American Library Association between 1884 and 1892. The monthly publications was at first part of the *Library Journal,* and appeared separately in 1884 with entries for 85 periodicals.

In 1905 R.R. Bowker began publication of the *Library Index to Periodicals and Current Events,* which cumulated into the *Annual Library Index.* By 1908 over 123 periodicals were indexed. In 1911 Wilson merged *Bowker's Annual Library Index* with the *Guide.* With that there came a number of rivals, but none was to succeed; and the *Readers' Guide* dominated popular indexing well into the age of computerized indexes in the 1980s.[90]

With the advent of H.W. Wilson's *Readers' Guide to Periodical Literature,* indexing became a systematic science, a reliable guide, for the first time, to periodical literature. Nothing like it had ever been seen before. There was a high standard of consistency in the subject headings, as well as numerous cross references.

Computer Indexes

The computer, or more precisely computer software programs, revolutionized the compilation of all types of indexes. If nothing else, it assured for the most part a continuity of form, a uniformity of references. Whereas today almost all indexes are computerized, it is well to remember the pioneers. They are numerous, but three outstanding examples would include:

1) Hans Peter Luhn. He appeared on the information scene as an engineer for IBM and his 80 plus inventions not only shaped computer programming, but new developments in indexing. In 1958 he offered KWIC (key words in context) as well as KWOC (key words out of context). The former simply takes key words from the title and arranges them in alphabetical order for indexing purposes; the latter is a method of "salting" words in the title where there are not enough to indicate the contents of the article. While much of this has been enveloped by computer programs today, the principles remain in such indexes as "Article First" of OCLC.

2) ERIC Educational Research Information Center index was conceived by Allen Kent and others in the mid-1960s. Many people were involved with the concept which resulted in the education index. ERIC was the first computer based system in other than a science. Essentially the system is made up of 16 to 22 decentralized subject clearinghouses which acquire, analyze and abstract documents for ERIC's index, *Resources in Education.* (It includes, too, journal articles in its companion, *Current Index to Journals in Education.*) As a government sponsored index it is made available at a relatively low cost online and on CD-ROMs by various organizations. The importance of ERIC in the history of modern indexing is that it afforded individuals the government funding to proceed with a now much copied system.

3) Eugene Garfield. A chemist by education, and strongly influenced by the writings of H.G. Wells Garfield struck on the idea of indexing by developing Luhn's KWIC principle and from this developed the citation index in 1961. He organized his own publishing firm and began with the *Science Citation Index,* which essentially is to index the writings by experts in a given area. He later developed similar indexes in the social sciences and humanities.

Despite efforts of bibliographers, from those at the Library of Congress to others in indexing companies, there is no consensus about many matters from the spelling of a foreign name (i.e. Lyof Tolstoy or Leo Tolstoy) or a married name (i.e. Hester Thrale or her second married name, Hester Piozzi). There are rules, established for the most part by the Library of Congress, but they will be ignored or may differ from publisher to publisher, country to country. "It is reasonable to suggest that . . . (bibliographer and indexers) undertake dates, name spellings cross-reference arrangements, indexing policies generally, and come up with standard procedures."[91] That hopeful wish was uttered some 30 years ago. It still is to be realized, although matters have improved considerably.

A more fascinating question is the fate of indexing. Given periodicals online in full text, for example, is an index necessary? Most general and specialized users would say "yes"; so the real question is an index economically feasible when one may through searching key words and phrases find what is needed. Granted it may not be as exact, granted it may take longer, but it does save money. These are only a few of the questions which the indexer, the publisher, the reader has to face as the index moves into the next century. No one really knows the answer(s), but they will evolve just as the bibliography, the periodical, the index evolved.

Notes for Chapter 9

1. J.M. Spargo, "Some reference books of the sixteenth and seventeenth centuries: a find list." *Papers of the Bibliographic Society of America,* Vol. 31, 1937, p. 135.

2. Usually the bibliography is organized and governed in terms of scope and purpose such as works about railroads, books published in the United States, titles written by X author etc. Today the term is inclusive of all communication media—from books and films to CD-ROMs and manuscripts. Here and throughout this chapter the term "book" is used in a generic way to indicate all the various forms of communication considered in a bibliography. And, of course, up until the end of World War I bibliography primarily was concerned only with books, as well as in a more limited sense with other printed material, particularly periodicals.

3. The meaning of "bibliography" differs from country to country from bibliographier to bibliographer. It has gone so far that a German bibliogra-

pher, Rudolf Blum, wrote a complete book on "clarifying the successive meaning of the term . . . through the centuries." (p. 7) But even here he limited his focus to bibliography in the sense of a "list of publications belonging to a certain category, compiled in order to announce their appearance and describe them." (p. 8) He left analytical and textual bibliography, among other of its forms, to another text, as well he might. Rudolf Blum *Bibliographia: An Inquiry into its Definition and Designation.* Chicago: American Library Association, 1980. (Originally published in German in 1969).

4. Historically, the term did not come into limited use until well into the eighteenth century, and did not become popular until the twentieth century. At the same time, from the earliest publishing there have been lists of books (i.e. papyrus rolls, cuneiform tablets etc.) which today would qualify as bibliographies but then simply were described as lists, catalogs and the like.

5. In the twentieth century the emergence of scientific critical, analytical or textual bibliography (each has a slightly different meaning) was brought about by such specialists in England as Alfred Pollard, Ronald McKerrow and Walter Greg. Greg was more theoretical than the others and stressed the important of bibliography as a guide to the correct literary text transmitted over a period of time. In this he equated critical bibliography with textual criticism—a definition not all accept. Arguments raged over the purpose of analytical or descriptive bibliography. "Purists" such as Fredson Bowers thought the purpose was to present all the evidence about a book which can be determined. Others argued that the object was to assist in the history of the book and assist collectors as much as textual bibliographiers who might use the work of Bowers et company. Nevertheless, the various types of bibliography (other than systematic, enumerative bibliography) may be placed under the broad umbrella of the history of the transmission of literature, broadly divided into the history of physical book and the history of the text.

6. The focus on Shakespeare texts at the turn of the twentieth century changed the direction of bibliography. As one authority explains: "Editors had previously tended to assume that all the early texts of Shakespeare had equal authority and that it was perfectly proper to select readings which, in their view, improved the text . . . The earlier editors were handicapped, in addition, by their ignorance of printing and book production . . . and by a lack of understanding of the nature of the texts they were dealing with." Experts such as A.W. Pollard, R.B. McKerrow and W.W. Greg changed all of this. The three developed what today is known as "critical or analytical bibliography"—a system based primarily on close investigation of the physical features of the book. The conclusions often gave evidence which was beyond the usual literary opinion. "Bibliography: in *The New Encyclopaedia Britannica.* Chicago: Britannica, 1993, vol. 20, p. 581.

7. Fredson Bowers, *Principles of Bibliographical Description* (Princeton, NJ: Princeton University Press, 1949, p. 34.

8. "Looking to the future, it seems that a general advance [in descriptive/analytical bibliography] will be slow . . . The relatively easy access to imprint information which computer databases give cannot conceal that bibliographical analysis of prolific book producers is laborious and time consuming." T.H. Howard-Hill, "Enumerative and descriptive bibliography," in *Book Encompassed,* Cambridge: Cambridge University Press, 1994, p. 128.

9. As Middle Age manuscripts lacked title pages, description centered on the understood title. Unfortunately, the title might vary from manuscript to manuscript of the same work; and, as a consequence, the only true method of identification was the incipit, or the first words of the text.

10. Theodore Besterman, *The Beginnings of Systematic Bibliography* New York: Burt Franklin, 1968. (Originally published in London in 1940, the Franklin work is a reprint of the 1940 book), p. 4.

11. Luigi Balsamo, *Bibliography, History of a Tradition.* Berkeley, CA: Bernard M. Rosenthal, Inc., 1990. (Originally published in Italy, 1984), p. 8.

12. L.D. Reynolds and N.G. Wilson, *Scribes & Scholars* 2nd ed. Oxford: Oxford University Press, 1974, p. 102–103. The books were given to the Sorbonne in 1272, but are now lost.

13. Besterman, *op. cit.* p. 6.

14. For the most part, book production was tied to monastic communities and later to scribes in and around university communities. This tended to be parochial in the extreme and there was little circulation outside of the university communities of these titles.

15. As there was little interest in other than "accepted" titles by the Church, monastic bookcases often held small boxes and hampers filled with unread, unexamined manuscripts of many centuries old. These were to be the base for Petrarch's scouting mission across Europe in search for lost or much adulterated manuscript exemplars.

16. Vespasiano da Bisticci, a Florentine bookseller who was an expert on locating exemplars, built a library for Cosimo de'Medici of 200 volumes by putting 45 copyists to work producing the complete library in a little under two years.

17. Actually, Decembrio wrote down the instructions of Guarino Veronese whose voice is the major one in the work and who established the new cultural canon. Interestingly enough he excluded popular works by such as Petrarch, Dante and Boccaccio. They were fine for diversion, but not for scholars.

18. Balsamo, *op. cit.,* p. 22.

19. A. Growoll. *Three Centuries of English Booktrade Bibliography.* London: Holland Press, 1964 (first published, 1903), p. 1.

20. There is some disagreement whether these early lists and catalogs

really were bibliographies, e.g. "The history of bibliography should not be confused with that of the catalogs of the first booksellers and collectors or with library catalogs . . . (They are) not related to bibliography in spirit or in methods of compilation." The author admits the catalogs served "as a springboard for bibliography." Louise Noelle Malclés. *Bibliography.* Metuchen, NJ: Scarecrow Press, 1973. (Trns: Theodore Hines), p. 13.

21. Besterman, *op. cit.,* p. 8.

22. Malclés, *op. cit.,* pp. 28–29.

23. Besterman, *op. cit.,* p. 16.

24. Considered dangerous to the faith, this was a list of books forbidden by the Roman Catholic Church. Compiled by official censors, the list was formulated in a decree of Pope Gelasius I about 496 when he listed both recommended as well as books to be banned. It was not until 1559 that the first formal list was compiled in which "index" was used for the first time. It was published by the Sacred Congregation of the Roman Inquisition, and went through 20 editions before it was abolished in June, 1966.

25. John Leland (c. 1506–1552) preceded Bale *Index librorum prohitorum* (Index of forbidden books). His work, though, remained in manuscript form and had little direct effect on the development of national bibliography. Leland's *Commentarii de scriptoribus* was probably completed a month before Gesner's work, i.e. c. 1545, but was not published until 1709. Today Leland is remembered more for being the librarian of Henry VIII and searching the monasteries for useful books and manuscripts. The purpose was to gather material for a work on the "history and antiquities of this nation." Leland went mad in 1547, but a version of his work (*The Laborious Journal and Search of John Leland*) was completed by his friend and fellow bibliographer, John Bale (1549).

26. Besterman, *op. cit.,* p. 28.

27. Maunsell was the first bibliographer to put the surname before the given name in an index of authors. Add to this several other major additions: a) anonymous works were listed by title and by subject; b) full typographical and format notes were not original, but they followed the pattern established by Gesner.

28. Andrew Maunsell's dedication of his *Catalogue of English Printed Books* (1595) quoted in Besterman, *op. cit.,* pp. 28–29.

29. The registrars of the Company of Stationers of London, (1554–1841), for example, contained entries of publications issued by members as a confirmation of copyright. While the registers hardly included all publishing (university publications were exempt) they do offer a historical national bibliography jumping off place.

30. Archer Taylor. *Book Catalogues.* 2nd ed. Winchester: St. Paul's Bibliographies, 1986, pp. 88–89.

31. Malclés, *op. cit.,* p. 31.

32. In the first issue of the first scholarly journal, *Le Journal des Sçavans*

(January 6, 1665), the editor explained one purpose of the publication was to annotated and briefly report on new books. Privacy was given to new titles which reported on equally new scientific findings. While published in France, the *Journal* had a much wider influence in that the lists of books often were copied and republished in other journals throughout Europe. The *Journal* listing included about 44 percent foreign titles in the early years, but by the mid-eighteenth century the rapid growth of the French book trade, the decline in the importance of Latin, cut the total to less than 20 percent. National bibliography, in a sense, had taken over even the international journals.

33. As employed by Bacon and his successors, "historia" not only meant history, but knowledge. Literary history was considerably more than the study of authors and their writings. It encompassed the whole of litterae or learning and knowledge. "The *Historia litteraria* was therefore by no means merely an antiquarian subject, but had a practical purpose: it served as an introduction to the scholarly world and a source of information about . . . the arts and sciences." Blum, *op. cit.,* p. 41.

34. Naude's *Advis pour dresser une bibliotheque,* went through numerous editions and was translated into Latin and English as well as, later, many European languages. His handbook listed desirable titles, but was a bibliography only in an incidental fashion. He was more concerned with the elements of a good library which consisted of: (1) The best editions of all principal authors. The stress was on "all" in that anyone who contributed to knowledge should be included whether or not one agreed with the conclusions of the author. (2) The collection eventually should be made available to the public, for collecting books only for themselves, only for an individual, was wrong. Private philanthropy was a necessary part of being a humanist.

35. The first compiler of a bibliography of bibliographies was a Jodocus a Dudinck, a native of the Low Countries who had the misfortune to author a book whose only copy or copies has been lost. There is no sign of the 1643 work, although it is listed in several bibliographies. Given that Philippe Labbé (1607–1670) may stake the claim to be first of the bibliographers of bibliographies with his *Bibliotheca bibliothecarum* (1671).

36. Balsamo, *op. cit.,* p. 73.

37. Malclés,*op. cit.,* p. 38.

38. Blum, *op. cit.,* p. 68.

39. Balsamo, *op. cit.,* p. 113.

40. G. Thomas Tanselle, "The descriptive bibliography of eighteenth century books," in *Eighteenth Century English Books.* Chicago: American Library Association, 1976.

41. Ibid.

42. In 1627 the Bodleian Library published a compilation of titles in the *Index librorum prohibitorum.*

43. The distinctions were not that clearcut. See, for example, the

explanation of the evolution of the meaning of bibliography in the late seventeenth and eighteenth century in Balsamo, *op. cit.,* pp. 136–142.

44. Malclés, *op. cit.,* p. 72.

45. Confiscation of books, from church to aristocrats, was a common feature of the French Revolution. After millions of books flooded into government depots someone realized they had to be checked and distributed. A special bibliographic bureau was established in Paris to meet the problem, and the first suggestion was a catalog, an enumerative bibliography, of all the books collected. By the nineteenth century, a good decade after the project began it faded away. The books were dispersed gradually to libraries and booksellers as well, in some cases, to their original owners.

46. Malclés, *op. cit.,* p. 76.

47. Ibid., p. 84.

48. Ibid., p. 98.

49. Ibid., p. 99.

50. Bibliographical societies, by tradition if not definition, are primarily interested in collecting rare books. And to this end spend time on the art of analytical, historical and textual bibliography. The Grolier Club, founded in 1884, is the oldest bibliographical society in the United States. Outside of New York, the Bibliographical Society of America (1899) is the most famous followed by the Bibliographical Society of the University of Virgina (1947). The Bibliographic Society, established in London in 1892, has a membership of from 1,500 to 2,000 members (from libraries to booksellers). It promotes bibliographical research and scholarship through publication of monographs on manuscripts, printed books, printing and publishing history from the Middle Ages to the twentieth century. It supported the publication of both the first and second edition of *A Short—Title Catalogue of Books . . . 1475–1640* (London, 1926, 1992). This is a complete list of every book published in Britain, or in the English language, from Caxton, in the fifteenth century, to 1640.

51. LeRoy Linder, *The Rise of Current Complete National Bibliography,* New York: Scarecrow Press, 1959, p. 106.

52. Ibid.

53. Ibid.

54. "Otlet's failure would seem to have been due more to a lack of conviction on the part of his contemporaries of the necessity of the work which was Otlet's dream than to the inadequacy of material means." Malclés, *op. cit.,* p. 124.

55. See Malclés, *op. cit.,* p. 105, for a chronological listing of the "first current national bibliographies founded in the nineteenth century."

56. Ibid., p. 107.

57. Blum, *op. cit.,* p. 143 (quoting Charles Langlois, 1896).

58. In America a work by Reuben A. Guild was similar in approach and message to that of Brown. Guild's *The Librarian's Manual* (New York,

1858). He used the term "library economy" to describe topics now of interest to catalogers and technical services. He stressed the need of enumerative bibliography, although with due respect to historical bibliography.

59. *Webster's Third New International Dictionary.* Springfield, MA: Merriam-Webster Inc., 1961, p. 1148. The best general books on indexes published in the mid 1990s are: Hans H. Wellisch *Indexing from A to Z.* 2nd ed. New York: H.W. Wilson Company, 1996; and Edward T. Cremmins, *The Art of Abstracting.* 2nd ed. Arlington, VA: Information Resources Press, 1994, and Brian O'Connor *Explorations in Indexing and Abstracting.* Englewood, CO: Libraries Unlimited, 1996.

60. *The Oxford English Dictionary.* Oxford: Oxford University Press, 1933, vol. 15, p. 204. By the early eighteenth century, printers used the term "index" in the conventional way as well as the descriptor of a piece of type shaped like a pointing finger. The forefinger pointed out something of interest.

61. The title tags which were placed at the end of parchment rolls to identify them may be called "indices," and in a sense these tags represent the earliest consistent, if extremely simple and basic, indexes. They were used from the earliest papyrus rolls, (i.e. c. 2,000 B.C.). Parallel with this basic index were the clay envelopes which encased cuneiform tablets used as a writing surface throughout the Middle East (c. 2,500 B.C.+).

62. Robert Collison, *Indexes and Indexing,* 3rd ed. London: Benn, 1969. "A little history," p. 16. See, too: "Concordances and cocordancing—a short history," *English Today,* July, 1992, pp. 29–32. Note that much of this short article comes from Chris Trebble and Glynn Jones *Concordances in the Classroom.* London: Longman, 1990.

63. "NB" *The Times Literary Supplement,* February 23, 1996, p. 16.

64. Walter J. Ong, *Interface of the World.* Ithaca: Cornell University Press, 1977, p. 166.

65. Roy Porter, "Lies, damned lies, and scholarship," *History Today,* September, 1985, p. 7.

66. "The best part of every book comes last." *New York Times Book Review,* March 10, 1991, p. 23.

67. *Index librorum prohibitorum* ("Index of forbidden books").

68. Francis Witty, "The Beginning of Indexing and Abstracting," *The Indexer,* October, 1973, p. 197.

69. Jack McLaughlin, "The Organized President," *American Heritage,* July/August, 1991, p. 88.

70. Collison, *op. cit.,* p. 19.

71. Joseph Reed, "The Index to End All Indexes" *Papers of the Bibliographical Society of America,* No. 4, 1984.

72. Some claim a Roman publication devoted to government business was a forerunner of the magazine/newspaper, but this is questionable. The *Acta Diurna* (i.e. Daily events) appeared in 59 B.C.

73. More specifically these accounts would be called "Relations," i.e. nonperiodical pamphlets published in England which usually gave accounts of battle. Bibliographers refer to these also as: Discourses or Narration.

74. Henri-Jean Martin. *The History and Power of Writing.* Chicago: University of Chicago Press 1994, p. 296. As Martin observes the spark of revolt could be made by postings on city walls. Little has changed, e.g. the attention of the modern Chinese government, for example, to censoring posters as well as concern about newspapers and other printed materials.

75. S.H. Steinberg. *Five Hundred Years of Printing.* New York: Criterion Books, 1959, p. 175.

76. The coranto, published until May or June of 1622, was probably edited by Nathaniel Butter (the father of English journalism). At any rate, Butter did sign the first newsbook published in England on October 15, 1622. This developed from the early Coranto. A Thomas Archer (fl. 1603–1634) who is mentioned in correspondence, apparently published the first London coranto in 1621. There is no extant copy of this work by the bookseller.

77. Newsbooks are variously identified and called correctly or not: *Diurnall* or *Mercurius,* as well as sometimes simply a *Pamphlet, Coranto* or *Broadside.* There are specific differences between all of these forms, although when news is the primary content they do share a more or less—usually less schedule of continuous publication.

78. The Star Chamber decree against newsbooks and newsletters of any type was put into force by Charles I on October, 1632. Miffed at criticism of his foreign policy, Charles maintained the censorship until 1638. In celebration of the lifting Butter and his partner Nicholas Bourne brought out a 96 page issue of their vastly expanded coranto and newsbook.

79. Anne Goldgar. *Impolite Learning.* New Haven, CT: Yale University Press 1995, p. 55. Goldgar is quoting Adrien Baillet, an early eighteenth century French scholar.

80. *Gazette,* a common name for many early newspapers, comes from the Italian coin, "gazeta." (The small part of a penny.) This was the charge for reading news about the Turkish wars which was posted in Venetian communities in the 1560s. *Mercury* is a more obvious choice in a title as Mercury, of course, was the messenger of the gods. Other even more obvious ties to news and popular in newspaper titles: *Herald, Express, Times* etc.

81. There are no more famous periodicals than *The Tatler* (1709–1711) and *The Spectator* (1711–1714) in Eighteenth century England. The format, the content, the matter of editing contributed not only to their success, but set the pattern for subsequent magazines to come until the early part of the Industrial Revolution.

82. Cave was the first to use the term "magazine." In this case because his title contained a monthly collection of essays, articles, opinions and the like gathered from other sources, much in the style of the modern *Reader's*

Digest. In 1738 Dr. Samuel Johnson joined Cave and the material in the magazine turned to original contributions, and particularly political comments as well as parliamentary reports.

In view of some argument over the definition of magazine, there is debate as to the publisher of the truly first such medium. Generally, though, the German *Edifying Monthly Discussions,* published from 1663 to 1668 is given that distinct honor. Published by a theologian as well as a poet, the journals stressed scholarly materials.

83. Michael Warner. *The Letters of the Republic.* Cambridge, MA: Harvard University Press, 1990, p. 140. The author is quoting Hugh Brackenridge and his *United States Magazine* of 1778.

84. Ibid, p. 141.

85. Carl Kaestle. *Literacy in the United States.* New Haven, CT: Yale University Press, 1991.

86. The notion of a newspaper-periodical reading general public did not gain general approval until the nineteenth century. Parliament, in 1712 passed the Stamp Act which taxed every newspaper sold, as well as magazines. Although the Act was repealed in 1766, the protest throughout the American colonies against the Act contributed in no small part to the struggle for independence a decade later.

87. The sections were called often "collectenea." Here one found notices about articles in other journals, notes on books, news notes, correspondence, etc. By the dawn of the nineteenth century many of these developed into extensive bibliographic sections and became "bibliography," or a similar term. Other titles: "Index analytique," "Current periodical literature" or "Zeitschriftenshau." By the twentieth century almost every major learned journal had such a section with relatively timely notes on the periodical literature of the subject matter of interest to readers. By 1906 these notes in the "library work" of *Library Journal* were to lay the foundation for what later was to become *Library Literature* (1921 to date).

88. The first two scholarly journals, *Journal des sçavans* and *Philosophical Transactions* had current indexes. By the end of the eighteenth century the pattern of individual periodical indexes took a leap forward with cumulative indexes.

89. By the nineteenth century the need for indexing became increasingly evident. For example, in England a law was proposed, but never passed, which would make an index a necessary requirement for copyright.

90. Despite the pressure to publish indexes to the growing number of periodicals, the British did nothing until W.T. Stead edited his *Annual Index* in 1890. The index included the major British titles and entries which were arranged alphabetically by subject, or author or catchword in the title. Later editions were simply called *Index to the Periodicals* until it was discontinued in 1902. The British thereafter tended to depend, as the Americans on the *Readers' Guide* for an index to general periodicals.

91. "Trade Winds" *Saturday Review,* April 29, 1967, p. 10. Lack of standardization is evident in other aspects of an article or book: "My bete noire is the fact that each publishing house and every scholarly journal nurtures its own particular house-style for citations. Every time a typescript migrates from one journal to the next looking for a good home, there's the immense fag of changing single quotes into double quotes, Roman numeral into Arabic, capitals into lower case (and in this process, how many real errors creep in?) . . . It is a piece of conspicuous time-consumption, a left-over from the days when scholars were meant to be leisured and the more dry-as-dust the better. New brooms please! Roy Porter, "Lies, demand lies, and scholarship," *History Today,* September, 1985, p. 7.

10

Government Documents

Who, or why, or which, or what is the Akond of Swat?[1]

In Edward Lear's nonsense verse the Akon of Swat might well be a stand in for the government document which covers all the "w's" of information. And can be, sometimes just as silly. Along with the development of government, the government document or publication is one of the oldest marks of civilization. Almost from the first settlement there was a need for documents to support the laws, directives and daily business of government. Inevitably documents touch on the who, what, why, which and even where of information. Literally everything is available in a government document. One has to look.

There almost are as many definitions of a government document—often in legal jargon covering numerous pages—as there are governments and forms of government. The best definition, certainly one of the more concise was issued by the Unesco Convention Concerning the Exchange of Official Publications and Government Documents between States in 1958. A government publication is one executed by the order and the expense of any national governmental authority. The descriptor "national" can be inflated to "international" or "world" or deflated to "state," "province," "local" etc. Unesco then names the type of documents it considers, at least at the national level, as official: "Parliamentary documents, reports and journals and other legislative papers; administrative publications and reports from central, federal and regional governmental bodies; national bibliographies, State handbooks, bodies of law, decisions of the Courts of Justice; and other publications as may be agreed."[2] Essentially, the three large divisions, particularly of federal and local documents, are judicial, executive (presidential, prime minister etc.), and congressional, parliamentary etc. There are countless variations on these headings, divisions, particularly in terms of 5,000 years of history, but most documents fit, if not always well, into one of the three sections.[3] Until the reformation most countries or areas had a fourth division—the church. The religious leader issued what, for most intents and purposes, had the same authority as the official government order or decree. Often the theological-lay power was one and the same, e.g. in much of ancient Egypt and Mesopotamia.[4]

A sense of order, relatively cheap labor, and inexpensive writing materials resulted in a mass of public documents pouring out of the Middle East prior to the conquest of Alexander. Greece, too, was involved with recording matters of state, and the Romans found reliable records necessary to govern much of Europe. With the fall of Rome, throughout the Middle Ages, and much of the period thereafter, public records and archives, were never treated with care. In fact, except for some isolated cases, the government document as something worth keeping and distributing was recognized only in the past 150 to 200 years. Generally the document was considered ephemeral and even the concept of saving more important titles (i.e. creating an archive rather than an undifferentiated mass depository) was rarely considered.

No matter by whom prepared or for what purpose, government documents the world around tend to share certain basic principles. (1) Readability and style are of minimum interest. (2) This side of a totalitarian state, the document tends to be a reliable source of information as contrasted, often, with reports taken by reporters from the document. (3) Organization is logical, yet not often easy to follow by nonexperts. (4) There is no competition. Lacking competition, it is fruitless to evaluate a government document the way one might a standard reference work. The government simple says: "take it or leave it." (5) Most important, documents over every interest from how to change a diaper to volumes of hearings on the implications of the information age.[5]

There is a major distinction between government and private publications. The government printer is just that, and makes no decision as to what should be or not published. The government printing office simply publishes what it is ordered to publish by the government and its numerous offices and agencies. In the United States, as in other Western countries, much subsidiary publishing is done by the various departments and agencies themselves.

Government Patterns

Government documents developed from the orderly administration of government in areas of justice, finance and taxation, foreign affairs, internal affairs and so forth. Each service, each administrative body had its own officers and simple to complex administrative structure. Each had a hierarchy of information which recorded administrative details in order of importance.

The earliest settlers (c. 3,000 B.C.) tended to follow a definite pattern of government. First there were village leaders who gradually increased power and territory to become monarchs. Paralleling this change was increasingly elaborate religions and powerful religious leaders. The political-theological power was supported by the army as well as by specialists in technical areas. Requirements for literacy, for documents, encouraged the organization of bureaucracy and officials charged with record keeping. The latter varied from civilization to civilization, but generally were scribes with special training in not only writing, but forms and procedures. This pattern was followed in Egypt and throughout Mesopotamia for well over 3,000 years, and became increasingly refined under the Greeks, Romans and during the European Middle Ages. The broad zones of government necessitated measures to insure laws and pragmatic records for everything from taxes to engineering projects.

Here and there in the river of history were major bleeps in the flow, in the pattern of government. Greece, for example, questioned the rule of the few in favor of rule by the qualified citizens. The foundation, particularly in Athens, was shaky as it was in early Republican Rome, but both systems worked well enough for a surprising number of years, i.e. roughly from 500 B.C. to the time of Augustus and the first century A.D. Gradually Rome gave way to instability and failure as the government moved east to Constantinople and by the fifth century had collapsed in Europe. Latin Christendom more or less ruled until Charlemagne, who in 800 A.D., reestablished some semblance of government. Between then and the Renaissance it was a tug of power war between the papacy and the growing strength of nationalism, monarchs and trade.

With the fall of Rome the tidy method of government document publication, the well understood laws, simply disappeared to be replaced by an ever changing, ever shifting mass of documents affirming and then canceling regulations which governed everything from trade and government to church and the military. Common law, or the mutual understanding of the importance of custom (supported or not by published laws and documents) saved European society before it reemerged in a more orderly fashion around 1400. By then most of the national governments, under monarchies, were strong enough to command respect within their territories and equally aware of the need for centralized bureaucracies, laws and the government document to spread and explain order.

Once territorial boundaries were established, once the majority of people within those lines shared a common language and culture considerably more parochial than the spiritual boundaries, for example, of the Holy Roman Empire of the Middle Ages, then one had the national state. The nationalistic movement took centuries to succeed, but was aided in no small way by government documents, which asserted laws and rules of conduct for the state's citizens, and the printing press (c. 1455) which allowed the rapid dissemination of those same documents. Not only did printing increase literacy, but more important, it increased the importance of the individual. A new force was soon at work—the people, or at least people lead by intellectuals questioned the absolute power of monarchs and church.

The Reformation many believe would not have succeeded without the printing press and the ability to spread quickly documents and propaganda for the Protestants. Gradually, too, the rise of parliaments, particularly in England reintroduced after some 1400 years the idea of a republic form of government. And with the English Civil War, the French and American Revolutions, a radically new period of government had emerged. Democracy slowly evolved throughout much of the West and with it the ever increasing need for documents to help rule and explain.

Today the nation-state remains the norm, and the documents it issues while different in substance from country to country, are similar in form and in purpose. Whether or not the claims of individual nations are incompatible with the future remains to be seen, but for now, at least, the government document is a universal source of information.

Egypt and Mesopotamia

Egypt, Sumeria, Babylonia, Persia and the whole of the Middle East developed sophisticated bureaucratic systems from almost their inception to their demise. These in turn, built remarkable runs of government records.[6] Libraries were constructed primarily to house the archives and secretaries and scribes served both as recorders, authors and publishers. Much of this system was passed on to the rest of the Mediterranean and from there to Rome and throughout Europe.

Dating from about 3,000 B.C. cuneiform inscribed clay tablets from Mesopotamia are the oldest extant form of writing. Egyptians, about the same time, employed hieroglyphics inscribed on stone monuments and tombs. In all probability writing may have been introduced at least a thousand or more years earlier, the ancient writing which has come down to a modern age is from the Tigris-Euphrates and the Nile areas. Almost without exception the ancient Sumerian, and later Babylonian, Hittite and Assyrian clay tablets were concerned with government, i.e. were, in fact, government documents. Legal codes, proclamations, annals of ruling houses and similar information was not limited to clay tablets, but, if of enough importance, were inscribed on stella, cliff faces and anywhere else where they might be seen and read.

There are now some 600,000 clay tablets from the Mesopotamia region extant, most of which are government documents. They are matched in number only by business records which, as often part of the ruling houses' activities, might be considered official documents as well. Here and there one finds a snatch of a personal correspondence, versions of the epic Gilgamesh etc. but this seems more an accident than a concerted effort at preservation. Probably there were more scribal, informal communications than government documents. Unfortunately these have totally disappeared giving an over proportionate importance to government proclamations, laws etc. Distinct legal codes which might be termed reference works developed relatively late. The kings, priests and other rules carried out the judicial function in Egypt and the Middle East from the earliest beginnings of civilization but codes only gradually developed. The majority have been lost. Certainly the most famous among those saved is the king of Babylonia's 3,600 lines of cuneiform carved on a diorite column, The Code of Hammurabi (c. 1792–1750 B.C.).

A highly centralized government with records kept at the royal court, Egypt inevitably had an excessive number of documents. On papyrus they consisted primarily of land and tax records. The material was organized and catalogued in a central office under the control of the vizier, who for some 3,000 years occupied a position equivalent to the Superintendent of Documents in the United States. The duties of the vizier are well documented for the Fifth Dynasty (2750–2625 B.C.) and there is evidence these duties remained the same until the fall of Egypt and the rise of Rome. Essentially the vizier was in charge of four departments: (1) Royal writings, or laws; (2) Sealed Writings, or registration documents of property, contracts etc.; (3) Archival writings; and (4) Taxation records.

Excellent as the Egyptian record administration proved, time proved more persistent. The fragile papyrus, unless sealed by the sands or a tomb, simply disintegrated and the best of records disappeared. Fortunately for historians, the more durable clay tablets of the Mesopotamian area defined time, if not the vagaries of destruction by men.

In Egypt there are considerably more extant religious records than documents of either government or commerce. Preserved in tomb art, the writing came down through the centuries as it was inscribed in stone. Mortuary texts are found, too, on coffins which survived in the tombs. What tomb writing is preserved on papyrus rolls tends to be as much concerned with stories, poetry and epic myths than with governmental activities.

Greece

There are few documents from the Mycenae-Mionoan civilizations, and with their downfall in about 1200 B.C. the Greek Dark ages closed over a civilization which would not appear again until the appearance of city states bordering on the Aegean Sea in about 800 to 600 B.C. The city-states (polis) gave rise to a democratic form of government foreign to earlier Mediterranean's civilizations. From the early polis to the end of the Hellenistic age, Greece, or more precisely the individual city states, developed political and social administrations which, in turn, produced public documents. The scribes and secretaries had the responsibility of registering and maintaining documents. Greece, and particularly Athens, during the classical period (c. 500–350 B.C.) spent much time and effort in preserving documents. "Decrees of the assembly decision of the council, financial records, and a large volume of other material were accordingly put before the eyes of the public—either painted on walls, written on whitewashed wooden boards, or carved on stone steles. A remarkable amount of the latter form of publication has survived."[7]

Papyrus was the primary form for the records, but for mass distribution wooden boards were often employed. The permanent laws and regulations were on a stele. Aside from methods of inscription, archives were maintained by the individual city states. The best known is that of the Metroon in Athens (from the name of the Mother of the Gods) built about 500 B.C. as a temple. It was to contain laws and decrees, records of government meetings, budget and contract matters, records of laws and trials and equally by then accepted documents of government. "Whatever the mode of storage and arrangement, reference service seems to have been efficient . . . Although we are not certain if Aristotle used them . . . we know that the Macedonian Krateros obtained from them the material for his collection of decrees of the Council. . . Preservations must have been satisfactory. . . During the third century A.D. the Roman Favorinus consulted Meletos' affidavit . . . in the archive."[8]

In the classical world of Greece there was a prejudice against complex legal codes. The assumption was that any free, literate citizen should be able to not only understand the law, but be able to handle his own transactions. Where there was a written law, it tended to follow the earliest extant example (c. 650 B.C.) which establishes certain basic principles. Few laws were written down, and those that were have disappeared. "Athens is the only classical Greek city from which we have enough information to give us a reasonably full account of its legal structure. . . Only a few texts of laws have survived. . . Drakon is said to have drawn up the Athenians' first written code."[9] By the fourth century B.C. the Athenian law was the most advanced and elaborate of any people, and the bits of surviving code are a tribute to democratic justice.

Rome

In the third and second centuries B.C. Roman power spread throughout Italy and much of the Mediterranean. In using the military to preserve the frontiers, the Romans equally were involved with maintenance of law and order which, in turn, meant a well developed bureaucracy. The Republican form of government spread the need for documents, and even with the fall of the Republic (c. 31 B.C.) and a restructuring of the state and the empire, the methods of publishing documents remained a constant. With the decline of the Empire and the rise of Constantine in 324 A.D. the urgency of maintaining archives fell off. Fortunately, both the Roman Catholic church and the Eastern Orthodox church developed archives and document publishing similar to the Roman model.

The Tabularium in Rome's Forum was the official state archive. Erected in 79 B.C. it typifies the order the Romans sought to bring to documents and to archives. Cheap, readily at hand and used almost from the beginning of the Roman rise to power, wood tablets were preferred for most of the documents. As a result, few have survived, although they are numerous enough when the Romans almost reluctantly turned to papyrus in the early part of the first century A.D.

Records of the Senate and other governing bodies were carefully maintained as were the censor office records—which consisted primarily of census data, although the censor had other duties as well. As the Empire expanded so did the need for housing records and they soon were found in other parts of Rome other than in the Tabularium, as well as throughout the Roman empire. State archives were administered by a large bureaucracy under the charge of the quaestors—the low, but beginning rung in the rise to power for civil service officers. They, in turn, had scores, of subordinates. The governing system for archives was as detailed as it was complicated and thorough. Under the rule of the emperors, beginning with Augustus, secret archives arose—and disappeared down through the centuries. These, in turn, had their own methods of organization, their own purposes which today are all but lost.

Julius Caesar is said to be the father of the notion of combining a newspaper with a government document. Under his orders an *Acta Diurna* (daily events) was issued from 59 B.C. as a way to promulgate official pronouncements and report on government activity. The sheets were posted in prominent places in Rome and throughout the Empire. Gradually, in order to get more people to read the sheet, the *Diurna* enlarged its scope to include such matters as gladiatorial contents results; births, marriages and deaths of notable Romans; reports on trials, executions; and, from time to time, news from the astrologers. Still, its primary role was official and not a medium for popular news and gossip. The daily hand written sheet was copied and recopied and posted throughout Rome and most major parts of the Empire.

The Roman Empire was the first to develop a detailed law code, and equally the first to define the role of paid legal advisors. "The development of Roman Law is one of the most significant, original, and enduring achievements of the human spirit. The Roman achievement lies both in the creation of legal rules . . . and in isolating the idea of law from other concepts such as morality, religion, or economic welfare."[10] Codification of

Roman law began as early as the fifth century B.C. with the "twelve tablets," drawn up to insure the rule of the patricians in Rome. These were incorporated into the next important document, the *Tripertita* of 198 B.C. which included additional laws and commentaries. The emperor Hadrian (117–138 A.D.) charged jurists with consolidating and establishing laws as written codes. The tradition culminated in the Byzantine-Roman emperor Justinian (527–565) and his codification of Roman law. A century had past since anyone had attempted such a task, and Justinian's plan was even more ambitious. Justinian appointed the jurist Tribonian to be in charge of completely recodification of the Roman law. He was to compile an entirely new code which removed repetition and contradictions. Under Tribonian, it took only 18 months to publish the Code (April 8, 529). Incidentally it was the last major legal work published in Latin. The *Corpus Juris Civilis* demanded modification and additions,[11] and from the seventh to twelfth centuries was adopted, by most of Europe.

Medieval Documents

Along with the widespread use of the Roman code, came a natural development in reference—the publication of handbooks and manuals which described and elaborated upon the legal codes. These appear from about the tenth century. The practical handbooks, which went through numerous editions, served to rearrange the laws in such a way that they could be consulted and understood with a minimum of difficulty. Paralleling the handbooks was the growth of the legal profession, and most particularly legal scribes and notaries who provided authentication and places to store and maintain legal documents. By the twelfth century law became a major study in the then relatively new universities across Europe and university teachers of law took over the drafting and explaining of Roman law.

Lack of literacy and a deep cultural decline in Europe from the fall of Rome to the early part of the eleventh century explains the virtual lack of archives, other than legal records, for the period. What nonlegal documents existed came from the members of the church. From the early popes—Innocent I (401–17) and Bonface I (418–22)—the Vatican made an effort to preserve its papers, its archives, its official documents. The archives were regularly examined by those within and outside the Vatican. "People all over Europe, over a long period of time, turned to the papal archives for documents that could be used in local situations."[12] The surviving documents from the archives "display vividly the wide range of activities and interests of the papel administration."[13]

Papal letters and bureaucratic rules and regulations were the two primary types of documents. Registers of the letters and documents are missing, but indications are they began in the late fourth or early fifth century. Before the thirteenth century there is no partial or complete surviving register in original form, and only sometimes inexact copies exist. Lacking original copies of papal documents before the ninth century, it is difficult to draw convincing conclusions either about form or content. Most authorities agree that these theological documents were based on Roman models and were issued from official record offices, i.e. chanceries. By the ninth century the monastic library, as well as the Vatican librarian took over many of the chancery duties, but by the Renaissance the chancery office had been reinstated.

Outside of the Vatican, clerics generally were charged with the maintenance of lay government documents. The choice was not so much a matter of religion as the necessity to hire someone who was literate, i.e. a cleric.

Medieval government administrative records offer "great value in objectivity and accuracy [because] the clerks who copied them did not seek to influence later opinions, and they usually recorded what they saw."[14] These normally are divided into two broad categories: surveys and serial documents. The former are inventories of estates and manors, the earliest dating from the Carolingian Empire in the eighth century. An example of a survey, and one of the most exhaustive for the period, is the work of Irminon, Abbot of St. Germain-des-Pres near Paris. He investigated and recorded statistics on more than 4,700 households in 25 manors. "This one document has profoundly shaped our conception of human settlement and of the manorial economy in early medieval Europe."[15] Similar to the modern census, the fiscal survey originated later in the eleventh century. The best example of this effort to count heads and wealth is the *English Domesday Book*. (This is given the title because its entries, as Last Day judgments, could not be altered). The 1086 survey includes most of the Norman realm in England, although London is missing. A comparable survey was not undertaken again until 1377.

The manorial and fiscal surveys were augmented by court records, or more broadly serial records which provide observations over a limited range of activities. For example, baptismal records, wills, and manorial court decisions are termed serial records, i.e. they record names, events etc. over a long period of time. Many began in the Carolinigian period and were carried through the Renaissance. Careful study shows the reconstruction of daily life patterns over a number of centuries.[16]

A major source of government documents is found in Medieval histories. Compilers, unlike their cousins in the Greco-Roman period, had no compulsion about literally lifting documents and incorporating them into their work. For example, in the last part of the twelfth century legal and administrative English records were incorporated into texts and histories. Matthew Paris (d. 1259) for one was given access to documents by King Henry III, and left behind a large group of transcripts of road and ecclesiastic documents.

Developed from the Roman and later the Byzantine models, early European administrative structures centered around royal courts and were as elaborate or as simple as the complexity and size of the court. With the end of the feudal system, the development of stronger national governments (c. 1200–1250 A.D.) major government bodies gradually emerged in Europe and by about 1350 A.D. in England. The primary division were justice, treasury and ruling councils.

Medieval and early Renaissance government documents before the advent of printing became an increasingly familiar form. There were so many business and government controversies, all requiring laws, decisions and opinions, that the documents simply poured out of virtually every urban center across the whole of Europe. Church publications, too, added to the flood.

Renaissance

With the Renaissance came a revived interest in Greek and Latin, as well as a concern about what was chronologically accurate. A professor at Padua, Ermolao Barbaro, was a careful student of Aristotelian texts and made an effort to correctly assemble contemporary Greek commentaries on the philosopher and his ideas. He also sought to show how Aristotle gradually broke away from the influence of Plato, and in this he was aided by his friend Politian, who lectured at Florence. The ordering of texts by Politian was highly influential in his collation of the first printed version of the *Justinian Code* (1490). This, in turn, was followed by commentaries on the *Code,* out of which developed a school of scholars. By the sixteenth century, these same men had laid the foundation for the history of laws and of institutions.

Chancery offices, roughly equivalent to scriptoriums in the Middle Ages, and our modern government document printing offices, generally were in charge of the drafting and distribution of government publications. The Romans began the practice of entrusting this work to specialists, and with changes in government throughout the Middle Ages, the formula was more or less maintained. For example, well into the twelfth century every court had a chancery office (sometimes called capella, or chapel) where clerics prepared the necessary documents. By the thirteenth century there usually was a Bishop or Cardinal named to what today would be the post of the Superintendent of Documents. He was called the chancellor, and exerted considerable power. With the Renaissance the offices of chancery changed, particularly as the paperwork due to printing having increased a hundredfold. Various countries adopted various alternatives. England is typical. Here, particularly after Henry VIII, power shifted from the papal dominated chancellor to the king's secretaries who were put in charge of state records.[17]

By the twelfth century the Records were divided by place of their keeping. The Treasury contained records of the Courts of Justice as well as documents of concern to the King. From the thirteenth century the term "Treasury" was employed to indicate a repository not only of plate and jewels, but of government documents. Chancery records were kept there until they were housed in the neighborhood of Chancery Lane in the fourteenth century. The first efficient organization of the papers was made by Walter Stapleton in 1323. The Bishop of Exeter as well as the Treasurer of England he gained questionable fame by being mobbed and beheaded in 1326 after being mistaken for an army officer. *Stapleton's Calendar* brought some order to the growing number of documents, but it was not until 1377 when a Rolls House was created to house the papers. Primarily the records were kept in the Tower of London, and by the sixteenth century William Lambarde was the first of a number of dedicated Keeper of the Tower Records who managed to keep most of the papers from the destruction of Civil War and the carelessness of numerous bureaucrats after the Restoration.

"The story of the housing of the [English] Public Records is one which has given rise to few reflections,"[18] particularly before the conclusion of the eighteenth century. And where there are early histories of government documents, they tend to be less than precise, less than definite. The result is much conjecture. In England, for example, the *Domesday* survey or census is well known, but what happened before William The Conqueror ordered official records of this type be kept. There are meager official records, of course, prior to William, but apparently no consistent effort was made to preserve them, more or less record their content.

State papers, and particularly earlier versions of decrees, laws, diplomatic and ministerial documents, were better preserved than the legal documents. With Henry VIII and the importance of the Secretary of State's office, the preservation of modern series of state papers began to be given attention. By 1578 the State Paper Office was established and thereafter, with varying results, efforts were made to recover state papers which otherwise would have fallen into private hands.

In 1561 Francois Baudouin, a French legal historian observed that law books were the stuff of history. From this new idea developed a whole on-going investigation of the law and institutions in terms of historical impact and importance. Much of this is of concern to reference librarians concerned not only with today's laws, but with the development of those laws over decades or millennium.

The combination of scholars involved with historical development and others concerned with immediate problems of documentation, government and law would presuppose a renewed interest in government itself, as well as documents. Yes, and no. Yes, in that forms of government became a central focus of scholars, as well as politicians who arose to challenge a central monarchy, at least in England. No, in that the documents themselves were of little real concern to anyone, at least those this side of necessary operative titles—from current laws to tax bills and the like. The result was the virtual destruction of most government documents until well into the nineteenth century.

Inevitably, no matter where they were stored or how recorded, the government and government documents burst their housing. They were either destroyed at that point or "sold for glue by the soldiers and workmen employed to remove them."[19] In 1619 Francis Bacon pleaded to establish a general records office. It went nowhere.

English Documents

As various forms of government developed, so did the approach to issuing documents. Here only two examples, England and America, are given. Still these are representative of much of the West during the period from the Renaissance until about the first World War, 1914.

While there are notations about official papers and books from as early as the reigns of Edward I and Edward II (1239–1337), little attention was paid to such matter. As Edwards observes: "As late as Henry VIII (1491–1547), the lists of books are mixed up with lists of beds and tables. And even in the reign of Elizabeth (1533–1603), the office of 'keepers of the books' is conjoined with that of 'distillers of odoriferous herbs'; the worthy pluralist having, it may be noted, a better salary as a performer, than as a librarian."[20] It was not until the appointment of Richard Bentley as keeper of the Royal Library in 1694 that any interest was shown to content, organization and use of the holdings. Bentley (1662–1742) was a scholar, a dull individual, but under his jurisdiction at least attention was paid to the need to keep the Library current. This was achieved by securing copyright copies from the Stationary Company.

The State of Paper Office had been unofficially a storage place for official documents for many decades. The papers were described as "those that have been kept at Whitehall of long time; and those that were brought [from other places]."[21] Housed in a single room, the Office by 1618 was in need of more space. A year later a fire at Whitehall destroyed much of the buildings, but not the papers which escaped. After the restoration the Office improved its quarters, but by the turn of the century (1706) a Select Committee of the Lords called for sweeping changes in acquisitions and cataloging as well as housing. And while more space was found, nothing else was achieved. Another query in 1800 found the Office had about 3500 volumes and a vast mass of unbound and unsorted papers, some of which dated back to 1246. By mid nineteenth century more order was apparent when the Office became part of the Public or General Record Office. When King George II presented the collection to the British Museum in 1757 there were about 10,000 printed volumes and some 2,000 manuscripts. Among the latter were many documents.[22]

In 1772 the report of a Committee of the House of Commons led to establishing a copying department to avoid "the practice of removing records to the private residence of the officials, which had been usual since the thirteenth century."[23] Still, it was not until 1838 that the Public Record Office Act was passed "to establish one Record Office and a better custody, and to allow the free use of the said Records."

Among those "said records" were the important reports on the daily activities of Parliament. "The history of the reporting of Parliamentary debates is a long and complicated one.[24] Primarily it was a matter of what was to be public record and what was to be kept within the walls of Parliament. Early members vehemently opposed recording of their arguments. Understandably so because often the King upon reading the notes would subject members to fines and often imprisonment. Regular printing of parliamentary proceedings began in 1680, but it was not until the eighteenth century that any particular care was given to either the documents or determining what was or was not to be published. In 1803 T.C. Hansard appeared and, ever since then the so called Hansard Debates have recorded parliamentary action.[25]

A prerequisite of a successful government documents program is a central point of printing and distribution, i.e. a government printing office. This was not easily achieved in many European countries as much because of the profit to be made by private bids as by the reluctance of the bureaucracy to move against traditional practices. Until the mid eighteenth century the publication of English government documents was primarily a matter of letting contracts to private printers and publishers. Gradually this changed, as much due to the new volume of documents as the need to weed out corrupt business practices. In 1786 Her Majesty's Stationery Office was created. Her/His Majesty's Stationery Office was established as a procurement agency for paper and office supplies, not for publishing. The Office remained opposed to being the government printer. It was considered less expensive to have documents printed privately. Largely as a counterbalance to rising contract prices for printing, the Stationery Office in 1914 was ordered to print at least some documents. From then on the Stationery's printing office grew, but to this day much of the printing is done still by private contractors. At the same time the HMSO put more emphasis on sales of government documents and books by establishing book stores throughout England.

U.S. Documents[26]

Although the United States began official business as a nation in 1776 little attention was turned to preserving government documents. Printing was another matter. Why? It was lucrative. Until 1818 the European procedure was followed by Congress. Publication of official documents was left to bid. The lowest bidder (although more often the bidder with the most political ability) was given the contract for that year's work. Private printing proved less than satisfactory and the need for a central national printing office was evident. Nevertheless from the establishment of such an office in 1860 to almost the turn of the century, the public printer was either elected, selected or named to suit the political party in power.[27] Even with centralized publication in 1895, the then established Government Printing Office used questionable procedures to contract printing until almost the close of the second World War. Today the printing is truly centralized, but from time to time the challenge is made that printing should return to private bidders.

Some notion of the importance of government documents to officials can be judged from the fact that it was well over a 100 years after the founding of the country that any effort was made to systematically index and classify documents. In 1895 the first concerted effort to index government documents took place with the passage of the Printing Act. The act provided the Superintendent of Documents should prepare a monthly catalog and index of public documents.[28] John G. Ames, Chief of the Documents Division of the Department of the Interior, constantly worried about the time lag between when a document was published and when it was made available in libraries. Usually they were distributed so slowly as to be, as he termed it, "ancient history" in terms of reference use. It was he who worked towards the centralization of printing and distribution and saw through the Printing Act of 1895 which speeded up distribution.

Soon after 1895, and by 1903, the United States Superintendent of Documents adopted a classification system for government publications. For the past century the system has been used as a model throughout the world, including the United Nations. The reason for the success of the Superintendent of Documents Classification System is that it provides an easy method of shelving material and, given the proper indexes, a fast method of retrieving documents. With the adoption of digital storage, the same system is applicable.[29]

The 1895 Printing Act proved important as a bibliographic support. It encouraged and financed three basic bibliographies: (1) The biennial *Document Catalog* which alphabetically, by author (i.e. usually issuing agency) of the published documents. (2) *The Document Index* (1895–1933) which indexed all Congressional documents. This was replaced by another index. (3) *The Monthly Catalog* (1895 to date) which remains the basic listing of issued documents. A retrospective aid, *The Checklist of United States Public Documents, 1789–1909* was first compiled by John G. Ames in 1893, and then greatly expanded for the third edition in 1909.[30]

In terms of the American experience, the 38 volume *American State Papers* (1832–1861) which covered activities from 1789 to 1833 were the earliest effort to compile a reference work suitable to find specific documents. The first true bibliographic aid was A.W. Greely's *Public Documents of the First Fourteen Congresses, 1789–1817* (1900). A Congressional Medal of Honor winner, and a veteran of 47 years in the army, he joined the army at age 16 in 1861 and did not retire as a Major General until 1908. Greeley studied early American government publications between Polar expeditions, for which he won the Medal. Greeley's listing of some 5,000 titles is only partial for the period, but is reliable and used to this day.

If Congress was indifferent to indexing and organization, they were at least anxious to make documents available to the public. Convinced government documents, if only in part, were a key to democratic process Congress in 1857 passed the Depository Library Act which makes documents available in libraries throughout the nation. Today the larger research library takes all documents, but the majority are selective depositories in that they pick and choose what is needed. Eventually, with all government documents freely available in full text online and/or on CD-ROM, it is conceivable that every library in the country will be a depository library in the sense anything since, say, the mid 1990s will be available to a citizen at a computer terminal.[31]

Conclusion

Today the majority of government documents, from the federal to the local level, are well organized and indexed. Most are easy to find. The major problem, aside from cost, is storage. Even this likely is to be solved by electronic systems. An interested researcher may sit down at a computer terminal and not only find citations to government documents, but, in an increasing number of situations, call up the texts of those documents.

Then, too, there is the internet and the world wide web which makes each Congressperson and individual in the executive and judiciary a type of "next door neighbor" with home pages, instant updates of data, and even friendly gossip.

There is no lack of documents, and, but for all the most secret, there is no lack of access. The difficulty today is pinpointing what is important, less important and pure garbage. That difficulty has yet to be solved—although a friendly reference librarian goes a long way towards the solution.

Notes for Chapter 10

1. Edward Lear. *The Akond of Swat,* 1855. Quoted in *The Oxford Dictionary of Quotations.* rev. ed. New York: Oxford University Press, 1992, p.

413. The fifth "w," where, is missing in Lear, but certainly not in the reach of government documents.

2. Ray Prytherch, ed. *Harrod's Librarian's Glossary* 8th ed. Aldershot: Gower House, 1995, p. 462. The best detailed discussion of the whole subject will be found in the standard guides to documents: Joe Morehead *Introduction to United States Public Documents,* 4th ed. (Littleton, CO: Libraries Unlimited, 1996.)

3. The descriptor "archives" is used in conjunction with government documents in that public records often are housed in a repository called an archive. The difficulty here is that "archive" may mean, too, a place where any group of original manuscripts, transactions or records are maintained—private or public or business or ?—and an archive is not necessarily a government documents depository.

Historians, who study all types of documents, not just government publications, use the term "diplomatics" (from the Greek diploma for doubled or folded) as a descriptor for the study of official documents, i.e. legal and administrative works, reports, official studies and surveys etc. For the most part diplomatics is concerned with the study of early and Medieval documents.

4. Until the sixteenth century and the advent of government documents and their regulation and distribution, normally a document meant it was either public (i.e. the products of rulers and theologians) or private which consisted of all other documents. From the Greeks to the Romans the two types of documents were normal, but after the collapse of the Carolingian empire (in the latter part of the ninth century) private documents gave way almost entirely to those of the church and of the ruling groups. This was the rule until the early Renaissance when business, as well as personal documents became, again, as important as government laws, edicts, degrees and similar publications.

5. James McCamy. *Government Publications for the Citizen.* New York: Columbia University Press, 1949, pp. 6–16.

6. While there were thousands, if not millions of public documents from the third millennium B.C. until the fall of Rome in the fifth century A.D. most have disappeared because of no care, but primarily as the majority were on papyri which was destroyed by the simple process of disintegration. Lack of interest in preservation, plus the ravages of time and natural and human disasters has resulted in only small traces of the vast hoard of Greek and Roman documents. Information is derived almost exclusively from literary sources, inscriptions and other second and third hand information. Conversely, excavations of well preserved clay cuneiform tablets in Mesopotamia has resulted in the direct study of the archives, or at least what is left of them. And as about nine-tenths of the tablets are documentary in nature, the researcher has a good idea of the content and care of such materials.

Under the Romans, Egypt has been described as the biggest business organization of the Ancient World with Alexandria as the heart of the system. If most of the ancient Egyptian documents were lost, the "modern" Egypt (c. 300–600 A.D.) preserved at least 100,000 papyri or fragments of letters, accounts, legal and government documents, and the like. These, of course, are only a small part of the daily activities of the document offices, but they suggest depository content and interest of the archivists. The vast quantity of records required fine administrative tuning and there were numerous offices and divisions such as the property record office and the regional-state archives.

7. Michael Grant and Rachel Kitzinger. *Civilization of the Ancient Mediterranean.* New York: Charles Scribner's Sons, 1988, vol. 1, pp. 635–636.

8. Ernest Posner, *Archives in the Ancient World.* Cambridge, MA: Harvard University Press, 1972, p. 113. See pp. 102–115 for an extensive study of the Metroon and its contents.

9. Ibid, vol. 1, pp. 594–595. For detailed discussion of Greek and Roman law see pp. 589–630. Athens established its first written law code in 621–620 B.C. Drakon drew up the law, and while little is known of the code, it was extremely harsh. Hence the derivation of "draconian."

10. Ibid, 607.

11. Shortly thereafter a second codification took place, this time the principle writings of all the ancient Roman jurists. The *Digest* (sometimes called the *Pandects*) condensed some 2,000 treaties into 50 books, and took three million "verses" (which constituted opinion and law) into 150,000. All of this was done in three years. "Finally in 533 there appeared the *Institute,* a hand book of extracts from the two main books designed for use in the imperial school." John Norwich, *Byzantium The Early Centuries,* New York: Viking, 1988, p. 532.

12. Rosamond McKitterick, ed. *The Uses of Literary in Early Medieval Europe.* Cambridge: Cambridge University Press, 1992, p. 91.

13. Ibid.

14. *Dictionary of the Middle Ages.* New York: Charles Scribner's Sons, 1984, vol. 4, p. 137.

15. Ibid. Described as "extents," the English surveys are a great resource for demographics and historians. The surveys diminished in number and importance after the thirteenth century as the serfs and manors were replaced.

16. The oldest surviving part of an original medieval document is a fragment from 788. Prior to this time some 2,500 letters are extant, but only as copies. Furthermore, no other archives are extant although there is evidence from the fourth to ninth centuries there were other major public repositories at such places as the Ravenna and in the Germanic kingdoms.

17. Differences between state papers and other documents are

explained—in great detail by Hubert Hall. *Studies in English Official Historical Documents.* New York: Burt Franklin, 1969. [Reprint. Originally published Cambridge University Press, 1908] in Chapter 2 "The Classification of Archives," pp. 53–74.

18. Ibid, 2.

19. Ibid, 25.

20. Edward Edwards. *Libraries and Founders of Libraries.* New York: Burt Franklin 1969. (Reprint of 1865 edition), p. 145.

21. Ibid, 181–182.

22. In 1753 the British government obtained the collection of Hans Sloane (1660–1753) and opened the British Museum. Gradually other book and manuscript collections were added, as well as copyright copies of all books entered at the Stationer's Company (for copyright fulfillment). In 1759 the library was opened to the public on the present site of the Museum—which was constructed between 1823 and 1852. Only in 1972 was the British Library separated from the British Museum, although until the 1990s its primary holdings were in the Museum building, among other places.

23. Hall, *op. cit.,* p. 26.

24. James Olle. *An Introduction to British Government Publications.* London: Association of Assistant Librarians, 1973. Following the traditional catch-up method, Parliament ordered in 1836 the compilation of a *Catalogue of Parliamentary Reports,* 1696–1834. The reports cover virtually every subject from prisons to the condition of East Indian affairs. *Hansard's Catalogue . . . 1696–1834* was published in 1953, and while far from perfect it at least is useful in locating some often hard to find documents. For a listing of other guides and current bibliographies, indexes etc. see the latest edition of *Walford's Guide to Reference Materials.*

25. P. and G. Ford *Luke Graves Hansard.* Oxford: Blackwell, 1962. This is a short biography and history. The authors, too, have edited several bibliographies which are of assistance in understanding British documents.

26. J.H. Powell. *The Books of a New Nation: United States Government Publications, 1774–1814.* Philadelphia: University of Pennsylvania Press, 1957. This is the best single source of historical information on American government documents to 1814 and includes much bibliographic information as well. See too: Anne Boyd, *United States Government Publications.* New York: The H.W. Wilson Co., 1949, chapter 1.

27. In 1818 a joint committee of Congress recommended establishing a national printing office. It was not until 1860 that enabling legislation for the office was passed.

28. LeRoy Merritt, *The United States Government as Publisher.* Chicago: University of Chicago Press, 1943. See Chapter 1 for a brief history of the United States Government Printing Office. In 1846 Congress created a Joint Committee on Printing but it was not until 1852 that a Superintendent

of Public Printing was approved for appointment, and another eight years before the government was authorized to purchase its own printing plant. By 1861 the first publications were coming from the Government Printing Office.

29. The classification systems are explained in two separate chapters by Doris Dale and the Superintendent of Documents in Bernard Fry and Peter Hernon, eds. *Government Publications: Key Papers,* New York: Pergamon Press, 1981.

30. Joe Morehead. *Introduction to United States Public Documents.* 4th ed. Littleton, CO: Libraries Unlimited, 1996. This is the basic guide and outlines the scores of other bibliographies and guides which fill out the period from the birth of the country until the early part of the twentieth century. Beyond that each chapter offers detailed current guides. See, too, the historical introductory section to: Everett Brown, *Manual of Government Publications.* New York: Appleton-Century-Crofts, 1950, pp. v–xii. James Child. *Government Document Bibliography* 3rd ed. Washington: Government Printing Office, 1942, pp. 6–25.

31. The Depository Library Program was established in the late 1850s, but its origin goes back several decades when Congress called for the printing of extra copies of official publications for free distribution to libraries. The Act has been expanded several times, (1962, 1974, 1977 etc.) to include new means of distribution, including electronic.

Epilogue

Computers and Reference Sources

"Historically, the computer can be conceived only as the product of two modern developments, the first culminating in the seventeenth century, the second in the nineteenth: the mechanization of our world-view and the industrialization of skilled manual work . . . The computer has become a historically important symbol of the late twentieth century, a symbol of a logical perspicacity in the midst of senseless information."[1]

Although this is a history of reference sources primarily to the end of World War II, an afterward is necessary concerning the development of computers and reference services. Computers are both the conclusion and the beginning of the next phase of the history of reference books. After the development of high speed presses and before the computer there were scores of technological advances which influenced the development of reference works. Still, it was the computer, some 50 years ago, which revolutionized both the storage and the retrieval data. Today basic searching of an index, for example, is done at a computer terminal as is the quest for a particular book from a library a block away or 6,000 miles distant. Add to this vast networks of information, CD-ROMs, rapid developments in storage of full texts and the history of the computer becomes a history—if only in the latter years—of reference sources.

The computer concept had its beginnings in basic, yet highly effective digital, and to a lesser extent analog, calculators. An abacus, the earliest calculating device probably was employed as early as 2500 B.C. by the Babylonians as an aid in commerce. It was somewhat similar to the still used Chinese or Japanese abacus with counters positioned to indicate number values from ones to hundreds, to thousands and so forth. Different types of abacus were employed by the Greeks, Romans and people throughout the Middle Ages in both Europe and Asia. While by the seventeenth century it had faded out in Europe it is used still in Asia.

In the slow movement towards the modern computer there are key names and dates: The Scottish mathematician, John Napier (1550–1617) discovered logarithms in 1614 and established the necessary base for computer calculation. Next the philosopher and French mathematician Blaise Pascal (1623–1692) devised a machine for addition and subtraction. Most of these early discoveries culminated in the twentieth century adding machine

which, in turn, was replaced by the electronic calculator. In a more fundamental way the early seventeenth century breakthroughs established the
ground on which theoretical scientists would construct the modern computer.

Building upon these and other discoveries, the English inventor Charles
Babbage (1792–1871) in 1812 announced the completion of his "analytical engine," considered by many to be the truly first step towards today's
modern computer. The analytical engine is considered the first direct computer firmly linked to modern machines. Most of the principles of today's
digital computer were formulated by Babbage. Lacking power (i.e. electric-
ity) for his machine, Babbage had to rely on complex gears and wheels to
make the calculations. "To imagine its scope, the construction of the machine was similar to trying to construct Big Ben out of watch innards."[2] In
addition, even the best craftsmen of the day could not construct the machine Babbage envisioned. Add to this the inventor's impatience and downright hostility to the average person, and the problems with finding funds
for the machine were multiplied. He failed to complete either of two machines upon which he worked, and spent the family fortune in the effort.
What he did achieve was to establish a set of concepts which a century later
would be turned towards construction of the modern computer.

George Boole (1815–1864) whose Boolean logic is known to any sophisticated user of an information database, was among a handful of experts
who improved the use of the punched card and helped to develop sophisticated methods of storing and searching data. Boole developed what is
known as Boolean algebra which uses the binary system of 1s and 0s as a
logical representation. Quite simply a "1" equals "yes" while a "0" equals
"no." Babbage saw this kind of equation could be used in a machine which
would flip switches to 1 or 0 to indicate yes or no.

By 1881 the U.S. Census Bureau was using punched cards to automate
census collection. Invented by Hermann Hollerith, the company which
manufactured the eighty column card became (in 1922) International Business Machines.

Alan Turing (1912–1954) was the first major twentieth century expert in
computers, and particularly their application to practical problems. He devised the "Turing machine" which performed computer functions. During
the second World War he served with the British Government Code and
Cypher School [GC&CS] at Bletchley. Here he helped with breaking the
German secret code with the use of his logic and, of course, his machine.[3]

By the early 1940s a team at Harvard, produced the first Mark I com-
puter which used electromagnetic circuits. In 1945 researchers at the
University of Pennsylvania produced the first totally electronic computer.
Generally this is considered the birthday of the modern computer. The
Hungarian-American mathematician John von Neumann (1903–1957)
used binary numbers and a memory system which to this day remain basic

to computer design.[4] The Pennsylvania computer, "called Eniac (electronic numerical integrator and computer) weighed 20 tons, occupied a whole room, "and resembled something from an early science fiction movie with its flashing pink lights, clicking switches and miles of cable. But it worked just in time to confirm the design calculations for the world's first atomic bomb in 1945."[5] Eniac employed the earlier findings of Babbage and company in that data was fed in by means of stacks of punched cards, and the machine then converted the number to a series of Is and Os sending the resultant stream of data through a series of switches called logical "and" and "or" elements. Today's personal computer, though many thousand times faster than the Eniac, and a fraction of its size, still uses the same principles and full room computer.[6]

Vannevar Bush (1890–1974) set out a plan in 1945 (*Science, and Endless Frontier* Washington, DC: Public Affairs Press) which established the outline of the then ideal information system—essentially a computer with a vast memory. The MIT engineering professor, and later head of the U.S. Office of Scientific Research and Development, "had significant influence on the government and its attitude toward resources for the Library of Congress and other large libraries, especially for obtaining the literature of other countries so that at least one copy would be available in the United States."[7]

Norbert Wiener (1894–1964), the father of cybernetics (i.e. the relationship between machines, organizations and humans in communication) was a child prodigy who received his Ph.D. Harvard degree at age 18 and gained fame as a mathematician at MIT. With the publication of his landmark book on cybernetics,[8] Wiener became world famous and continued important contributions to the theory of information.

The primary difficulty with early computers and reference services was "ease of use." The computer was based on the notion of experts, of "hackers," who thought everyone was as interested in mastering a program as themselves. On the contrary. Most people then, as today, only want an answer. An individual, for example, purchasing an automobile wants an automatic transmission not a kit that will tell them how to install the transmission.[9] One solution to the complex personal computer was made by Claude Shannon. A graduate student at MIT when Wiener was there. He moved to Bell Labs, where he was involved with communication systems. He argued computers would be programmed to work with symbols as well as numbers, and was an early pioneer of the computer which could play a game of chess.

With the close of World War II there was rapid progress with computer design. IBM made the computer a viable commercial product and from the early 1950s to about 1958 developed the so called first generation of computers. As late as 1954 *Scientific American* detailed the future of the computer in the office. Editors pointed out that they were impressive, but much too large for practical purposes. Transistors were introduced about 1958 to open the way for the second generation. Miniaturization began the third generation. Transistors were replaced in the early 1960s with planar integrated circuits. The fourth generation witnessed the development of the microcomputers in the 1970s. In 1971 the Intel 4004 was introduced. This was the first processor to be built on a tiny single silicon chip. Because it was no larger than a fingernail, it was dubbed a "microprocessor." The method has been in use ever since. From then to the present there was the rapid development of smaller and smaller personal computers, more and more sophisticated software, and national and international marketing of data processing, and networks.

The first digital databases appeared in the late 1960s and early 1970s. The majority of these online databases were a) numerical and b) indexes and bibliographies, as they remain today. All of the latter were word oriented. Beginning in the 1980s there was a rapid growth of CD-ROM image and audio databases. Other types of reference works, and particularly popular encyclopedias, found a new format in CD-ROMs. With the increased sale of multimedia capable personal computers, the CD-ROM/online figuration took over the popular imagination.

The fifth generation of computers opened formally in 1981 when a conference was held on the subject in Tokyo. This was to be the advance and practical use of an artificial intelligence computer, i.e. an AI. By the mid 1990s the project was doomed, although plans for AI continue to this day at a much less rapid pace.[10]

A University of California professor explains what the future is likely to hold for the computer: "Microprocessor performance will easily keep doubling every 18 months through the turn of the century. After that it is hard to bet against a curve that has outstripped all expectations . . . [but] one desktop computer in 2020 will be as powerful as all the computers in Silicon Valley today."[11]

Beyond and part of the computer revolution is the network—from the local area network to Internet. Working together, and with a subtle finding device (no matter whether it be Gopher or a ride on the World Wide Web), reference works from the far reaches of the globe are available at a computer terminal. Here one is more likely to request a document, a page, a paragraph about a given subject rather than from a specific form of reference books.

Currently, the race between CD-ROMs and online access to information is likely to conclude with online as a winner; particularly when it becomes more reasonable in price. Eventually CD-ROMs, or a type of memory system like it, will be relegated to popular entertainment; while online will be used almost exclusively for reference formats.[12]

One simple gauge of the influence of computers on reference services in particular, and libraries in general, is to examine the beginning dates of periodicals devoted almost exclusively to computers. There were several scholarly computer journals before the late 1970s, and particularly *Datamation*

(1957); but the majority of journals, and therefore the vast interest in the field did not really develop until the early to mid 1980s. Today there are several hundred journals covering all aspects of computers and information science, but among the earliest: *Online,* a standard title in the field began in 1977 followed by the same publisher's *Database* in 1988. Four years before, the first issue of the more general *American Society for Information Science Bulletin* began publishing. Popular computer magazines, such as *PC* (1982) and *Byte* (1975) and *MacWorld* (1985) followed the library lead.

Basic sections of the "information highway" were well in place by the 1990s. The revolutionary changes in the storage and retrieval of reference materials continues, and one suspects within a decade most printed reference works, (although certainly not most printed books and magazines) will be available to the user in front of a computer screen.[13]

Notes

1. Arno Borst. *The Ordering of Time.* Chicago: University of Chicago Press, 1993, p. 126–127. The founder of Microsoft, Bill Gates has a brief, history of the computer in his book *The Road Ahead* (New York: Viking, 1995). He traces the computer from Gutenburg in the fifteenth century to Alan Turing in the twentieth century. Much of the book is a fairy tale, but the historical data is accurate, and entertaining enough.

2. H.P. Newquist. *The Brain Makers.* Indianapolis: Sams Publishing, 1994, p. 32. After the death of Babbage, work was turned towards better calculating machines, and mass production. The Babbage notion of artificial intelligence had to wait until the second World War to be a viable project again.

In 1995 a section of the Babbage calculator was sold at auction for $282,000. *The New York Times,* October 9, 1995, p. D4.

3. Much has been written on Turing, but for a brief, fascinating account see Chapter 4 "The Nazi Codes, Computers, and Poisoned Apple" *in* Newquist *op. cit.*

4. "The electric light bulb, we all know was invented by Thomas Edison. The telephone by Alexander Graham Bell, and the computer? If you took a hundred people off the street and asked them who invented the computer, 99 would have no idea, and one would say VonNeumann." *The New York Times,* February 19, 1996, p. D3. John von Neumann made equally important contributions to quantum physics, logic and the theory of games and participated in the development of the hydrogen bomb. He proposed, too, the use of computer techniques to test the feasibility of dying the polar ice caps so as to decrease the amount of energy they would reflect. With this Iceland would be warmed enough to give it the climate of Hawaii.

Needless to add, the notion remains a theory only. Herman Goldstine. *The Computer from Pascal to von Neumann*. Princeton, NJ: Princeton University Press, 1972, pp. 167–183. This is a good overview of von Neumann's contribution. The book in total is a useful summary of the history of the computer up to the end of 1960s. Much of the information in the latter chapters is, of course, dated.

5. *The (London) Times,* June 9, 1995, p. 19. The quote is from an obituary of John Eckert (1919–1995) who with John Mauchly (died 1980) perfected the first electronic digital computer at the University of Pennsylvania.

6. Some idea of how the full room computer has been reduced to a desk top is found in Michael Malone's *The Microprocessor* (New York: Telos, 1995). The author points out that the first IBM Personal Computer chip in the late 1970s had 29,000 transistors and could carry out 330,000 instructions in a second. The new microprocessors, with Intel's Pentium chip has close to 6 million transistors and can carry out 300 million instructions a second.

7. Dorothy Lilley and Ronald Trice. *A History of Information Science 1945–1985*. New York: Academic Press, 1989, p. 12.

8. *Cybernetics: Or control and communication in the animal and the machine*. New York: Wiley, 1948. In this pioneering work Wiener not only had a best seller, but made the term "cybernetics" popular. The author worked to refine cybernetics and particularly its relationship to computers, for the remainder of his life.

9. John Cherry, "Human-Computer Dialogue" in *Encyclopedia of Library and Information Science*. New York: Marcel Dekker, 1985. Vol. 38/Supplement 3, pp. 205–225. This is a lengthily discussion of early efforts to bring the computer to the layperson.

10. Newquist, *op. cit.* The later part of this book is concerned with rise and fall of AI as a practical, money making proposition. It is an excellent overview of the topic in non-technical, easy to understand language.

11. David Patterson, "Microprocessors in 2020," *Scientific American,* September, 1995, p. 67. See too the section on "Information Technology." [The number celebrates the magazine's 150th anniversary issue.]

12. For a detailed account of the growth of CD-ROM and online searching and formats see the: "The State of Databases Today" by Martha Williams in each issue of the two volume *Gale Dictionary of Databases* (Detroit: Gale Research Inc.). In the January, 1996 issue there are listed 5,340 online databases and about 3,000 CD-ROMs.

13. Geoffrey Nunberg, ed. *The Future of the Book*. Berkeley: University of California, 1996. This is one of a score of books (naturally) which explore the future of the printed volume. The collection is split evenly between the prophets of a computer world and the conservatives of a continuing world of printed books. Take your choice.

Chronology of important dates in the history of reference sources along with dates of parallel, influential events

Learned aids—encyclopaedias, dictionaries, grammars—are used constantly, but with off hand ingratitude to their compilers.[1]

B.C. (Dates are approximate.)

2,500	Library at Nippur (Babylonia) organized. First library in Egypt.
2,000	Library at Tell el Amarna (Assyria) founded.
1792	*Code of Haamurabi*—one of earliest government documents distributed widely.
1304–1168	Egyptian almanac appears.
1200	*Gilgamesh* epic recorded.
1,000	Alphabet of 22 signs appears in Byblos.
900–800	Homer's *Iliad* and *Odyssey.*
650	Library at Nineveh (Government archives of Assyrian Ashurbanipal). Some prose found. Approximately 25,000 to 30,000 clay tablets.
652–660	Babylonian almanac appears.
485–424	Herodotus, "father of history."
470–399	Socrates
388	Plato (428–347) founded Academy with library.
335	Aristotle (384–322) founded library for scientific research.
320	Hellenistic education introduces concept of "enkyklios paideia" (i.e. a rounded education consisting of seven liberal arts.)
307	Alexandria Library—first major research library with probable reference services. Approximately 500,000 papyrus rolls or about 80,000 individual titles. In 47 partially destroyed by fire; 640 A.D. library scattered.
287–212	Archimedes introduces one of the first handbooks/manuals, his *Verba filiorum,* a mathematical work.
280–206	Chrysippus, father of the commonplace book.
195	Pergamum Library (Turkey) founded. Approximately 160,000 to 200,000 rolls. Virtually destroyed in 133 B.C.
70–19	Virgil
40	Public library planned by Caesar. After death libraries developed and probably spread through Empire—but considerably more limited than today's library.
58	M.T. Varro (116–27 B.C.) *Discipline*—an encyclopedia.
60 B.C.–100 A.D.	Numerous private Roman libraries noted in literature, e.g. Sammonicus with 60,000 rolls; Atticus with 20,000 rolls; others by Cicero, Lucullus et. al.

A.D.

23–79	Pliny the Elder compiles first encyclopedia in 37 volumes, *Historia naturalis* (*Natural History*).
85	Gospels completed.
90	Birth of Ptolemy (c. 90–168) key figure in cartography. Author of *Geography.*
100	Emperor Trajan establishes government documents library, i.e. public records office and general library: Bibliotheca Ulpia.
123–170	Aulus Gellius compiled *Attic Nights,* a Roman type of commonplace book.
129–189	Galen, father of first bibliography: *De libris propriis liber*—(A book about my own books).
160–180	Pausanias' *Guidebook of Greece.*
313	Christianity official Roman religion.
353	Constantine establishes research library in Constantinople; by c. 1200 estimated to have 3 million volumes. Largest library in the West or East.
354	Earliest extant calendar-almanac.
411	St. Augustine (354–430) *City of God.*
415	Clog/calendar almanacs appear and are used to sixteenth century.
476	End of the Western Roman Empire.
520	Priscian's *Institutiones grammaticae.*
530	St. Benedict founds Mt. Cassino monastery and system established for acquiring, copying and retaining books. By 800 about 220 monastic libraries. Estimated size of collections: Vivarium, 551: about 120 codexes; Reichenau, 724: about 415–1,000 volumes; St. Gall, 841: about 400 volumes; Cluny, 1100: about 570 volumes.
550	*Justinian's Code,* i.e. codification of Roman law.
560–636	Isidore of Seville (560–636) *Etymologiae* (Book of origins or etymologies) in 20 parts. Major medieval encyclopedia. Venerable Bede (672–735) introduces Christian calendar. Alcuin (735–804) takes over from Bede as England's most famous scholar and leaves York to aide Charlemagne's educational program.
800	Arab libraries founded and flourish from Cairo to Spain. Cairo collection (c. 1175) estimated to be 1.1 million volumes. Cordoba: 400,000 volumes with 44 volume catalog.
831	Einhard completes *Vita Caroli Magni.*
842	Hrabanus Maurus (776–856) *On the Nature of Things*—an encyclopedia.
850	The Patriarch of Constantinople (Photius, 810–891) completes a commonplace book, the *Bibliotheca.*
871	*Anglo Saxon Chronicle* begins.
959	*Suidas* (Fortress), a Greek lexicon completed.
1000	The major Old English poem Beowulf published.
1002	Aelfric (c. 955–1010) completes his grammar, *Vocabularium* at Eynsham, near Oxford.
1086	Government documents, Census—The English *Domesday Book.*
1120	Hugh of St. Victor (c. 1096–1141) *Didascalicon*—an encyclopedia.

1147	Geoffrey of Monmouth completes *Historia regum Britanniae* (History of England).
1200	Cathedral schools founded. Urban centers, build around bishops need which expanded to schools which expanded to universities: Durham c. 1200: 600 volumes; Canterbury c. 1300: 5,000 volumes; 1200.
1209	Growth of universities: Cambridge founded.
1240	Bartholomew Glanville, *On the Characteristics of Things;* or *Properties of Things*—encyclopedia.
1245–1260	Vincent de Beauvas (c. 1190–1264) publishes his *Speculum triplex* (Great Mirror) encyclopedia.
1266	Roger Bacon (1213–1292) *Opus majus* (Great work), encyclopedia.
1273	Thomas Acquinas (c. 1225–1274) *Summa Theologiae* the quintessential Roman Catholic encyclopedia.
1286	John Balbi's *Catholicon,* a treatise on Latin, published.
1295	*Travels of Marco Polo.*
1304–1374	Petrarch, Italian poet and father of the Renaissance.
1357	*Travels of Sir John Mandeville* completed.
1307–1321	Dante's *Divine Comedy.*
1387	Chaucer (1340–1400) completes *Canterbury Tales.*
1400	Jean Froissart (1337–1410) French *Chronicles.*
1416–1459	Poggio Bracciolini (1380–1459) discovers "lost" manuscripts. In 1416 found first complete text of Quintillian's *Institutio oratoria.*
1455	Johannes Gutenberg (c. 1400–1468) prints the first Latin Bible. Issues in gradually over 400 years, mass production.
1457	First printed almanac.
1470	First printed bibliography—catalog of Sweynheym and Pannartz lists of books printed from c. 1463–1470.
1475	Vatican library, languishing over many centuries, becomes a major concern with annual authorization of library funds; 1500 volumes, one of largest in Europe.
1486	*Booke of St. Albans,* manual on hunting, fishing etc.
1494	Johannes Tritheim publishes first substantial printed bibliography, book about ecclesiastical writers.
1497	First English almanac.
1500	Erasmus (1465–1536) completes commonplace, *Adagia,* followed by *Parabolae* (1513) and *Apopthegmatum* (1531).
1507	*Introduction to Cosmography* published with America appearing for first time.
1516	Erasmus completes *New Testament* with Greek and Latin texts.
1520	Beginning of Reformation in Germany.
1524	First published geographical manual.
1527	Castiglione (1478–1528) publishes one of the earliest etiquette books, *II Cortegiano* (The Courtier) on manners for the aristocrats.
1530	Erasmus publishes influential etiquette book, *On Civility* . . .
1535	Thomas Elyot Dictionary of Latin and English published.
1536–1550	Some 800 monastic libraries closed in England: 6,000 books dispersed.

1537	Augustinians in Mexico establish first library in the Americas.
1537	French establish "legal deposit" at Blois palace: by 1547 3,000 volumes, primarily manuscripts (only 200 printed books).
1545	Conrad Gesner (1516–1565) publishes his *Bibliotheca Universalis*.
1563	John Foxe's *Book of Martyrs*—first English edition.
1564–1616	William Shakespeare
1564	First bibliographies/catalogs issued at Frankfort Fairs.
1565	*Theatrum Humanae Vitae*, Theodor Zwinger's (1533–1588) commonplace published.
1569	First Mercator map published.
1570	Oretelius publishes first atlas, *Theatrum Orbis Terrarum*.
1571	*Bibliteca Laurenziana* (Florence).
1580	John Stow (1525–1605) complete his *Chronicles of England* (known as *Annals of England* in later editions).
1583	Joseph Scaliger (1540–1609) publishes his *Opus de emendatione tempore* (Study on the improvement of time), a study of calendars and chronology.
1595	Andrew Maunsell publishes *Catalogue of English Printed Books*. Lists only printed books.
1597	Thomas Bodley contributes book collection to Oxford. By 1605: 5,600 volumes; by 1620: 16,000 volumes.
1600	Shakespeare completes *Hamlet*.
1600	School libraries urged by Charle Hoole in his *A New Discovery of the Old Art of Teaching School*, published in London.
1604	Robert Cawdrey *Table Alphabetical of Hard Usual English Words*.
1605	Francis Bacon (1561–1626) *The Advancement of Learning*.
1620+	Francis Bacon, *Great Renewal*, encyclopedia.
1622	First issue of *Weekley Newes*, London.
1623	Francis Bacon, *Advancement of Learning*.
1627	Gabriel Naude *Instructions Concerning Erecting a Library*.
1630	Willem Blaeu publishes his *Atlas Major*, largest atlas to date.
1632	John Davies, *Welsh Dictionary*.
1633	Galileo forced to abjure theories of Copernicus.
1635	First inland postal service, between London and Edinburgh; five years later eight postal lines are running in England.
1637	Thomas Hobbes (1588–1679) publishes a *Briefe on the Art of Rhetorique*.
1638	Harvard Library founded; fire destroyed many books in 1764; but by 1790: 12,000 to 13,000 volumes; 1818: 28,000.
1639	First printing press in North America at Harvard.
1642	James Howell's *Instructions for Foreign Travel* published.
1644	John Milton (1608–1674) publishes *Areopagitica* on freedom of the press.
1650	World population estimated at 500 million; by 1850 it has doubled; and by 1960 over 2.6 billion.
1656	First subscription library in colonies founded in Boston. Lasting, first subscription library opens in Philadelphia by Franklin, 1731.
1657	*L'encyclopedie des beaux esprits*—believed to be first reference book with encyclopedie in title.

1657	Comenius (1592–1670) *Oribs sensualium pictur* ("The illustrated world of things we can feel") a cumilnation that is ancestor to a whole host of textbooks, encyclopedias, and dictionaries.
1658	William London's trade bibliography of books published in England: 3,000+ titles.
1659	William Somner: *Dictionarium Saxonico-Latino-Anglicum.*
1660	James Howell, *Lexicon Tetraglotten*—in English, Spanish, French.
1662	Thomas Fuller, *The Worthies of England*, published posthumously.
1665	*Journal des Scavans* appears, a weekly in French to list selectively books and some critical reviews.
1665	The first journal published in England—*Philosophical Transactions of the Royal Society* begins as voice of new science.
1665	First issue of the *London Gazette.*
1670	John Milton publishes his *The Historie of Britain.*
1670	John Ray publishes his *Collection of English Proverbs.*
1674	Louis Moreri (1643–1680) *Le grand dictionnaire historique.*
1693	Richard Bentley takes charge of Royal Library which is to become the British Library.
1699	James Kirkwood of Scotland proposes public libraries supported by taxes, but only for "approved" students, schoolmaster and ministers.
1700–1800	Estimated populations: France 18 to 26 million; England 5 to 9 million; American colonies 250,000 to 5 million. Cities in 1700; London largest with 674,000 (1990: 9 million); Paris, 600,000; (1990: 8 million); Vienna, Rome approximately 200,000. *Literacy:* average 5 percent of population.
1701	Yale library founded—by 1766, 4,000 volumes (largest in colonies).
1704	John Harris, *Lexicon Technicum,* encyclopedia.
1710	English copyright act which provides one copy of each book to be deposited at the Royal (later British) Library.
1711	Addison and Steele begin publishing *The Spectator.*
1718	One of the earliest circulating libraries, i.e. rents books, founded in England. By 1742, several thousand volumes advertised by major English circulating library.
1721	Daniel Jablonski (1660–1741) publishes the first short encyclopedia in Danzig, *Allgemeines Lexikon.*
1723	Harvard Library prints first catalog: 3,500 volumes listed; 1790 = 12,000 volumes; 1827 = 25,000 volumes; 1840 = 40,000 volumes; 1866 = 114,000 volumes (95,000 pamphlets); 1923 = 2.5 million.
1726	Publication of Jonathan Swift's *Gulliver's Travels.*
1728	Ephraim Chambers (1680–1740) publishes his two volume *Cyclopaedia, or an Universal Dictionary of Arts and Sciences.*
1731	Subscription library opened in Philadelphia by Benjamin Franklin.
1732	Benjamin Franklin publishes first issue of *Poor Richard's Almanack,* which is published to 1757.
1737	Alexander Cruden publishes his *Concordance* of the Holy Scripture. William Oldys publishes *The British Librarian.*
1742	Yale library has 2,500 volumes; 1870 = 55,000 volumes.
1742–1753	Charles Viner publishes the 23 volume *Legal Encyclopedia.*

1749	Henry Fielding's *The History of Tom Jones.*
1751–1772	Denis Diderot's (1713–1784) *Encyclopedie* published.
1755–1773	Samuel Johnson *Dictionary of the English Language* published.
1759	British Museum opened.
1761	*Old Moore's Almanac,* becomes a bestseller: 82,000 copies sold.
1762	Sorboone Library in Paris opens.
1763	First issue of *Almanach de Gotha.*
1768	First of 100 weekly issues of the *Encyclopaedia Britannica* published.
1771	First edition of the *Britannica* in 3 volumes.
1776–1783	American Revolution
1776	First volume of Edward Gibbon's (1737–1794) *Decline and Fall of the Roman Empire.*
1786	Government document—Her Majesty's Stationery Office founded.
1788	Hannah Moore's *Thoughts on the Importance of the Manners of the Great to General Society.*
1790's	English book clubs (i.e. subscription libraries) emerge; by 1821 over 500. Average collection 100 to 200 volumes. Social libraries (i.e. subscription libraries) emerge in the United States; by 1815 more than 450. Average collection 50 to 100 volumes. Largest to 10,000 volumes; with 25 to 50 with 3,000 volumes.
1791	James Boswell (1740–1795) *Life of Johnson.*
1792	First issue of *Farmer's Almanac.*
1795	First American atlas published by Matthew Carey.
1796	Brockhaus publishes first edition of *Konversations Lexikon* in Leipzig.
1800	Library of Congress founded, 1500 volumes by 1804; Jefferson's Library purchased 1813, 6,000 volumes; 1865, 1 million.
1803	*Hansard Debates*—records of parliament—begin publication.
1808	Goethe *Faust,* Part I, published.
1809	Washington Irving, *Rip Van Winkle.*
1813	Jane Austin, *Pride and Prejudice.*
1813	Congress agrees to furnish each state one copy each of its journals and documents—as well as to major colleges and historical libraries.
1817	Hegel publishes his *Encyclopedia of the Philosophical Sciences.*
1820	John Murray begins publishing travel guides, i.e. the *Red Books.*
1823	James Fenimore Cooper's first of the Leatherstocking novels published—*The Pioneers* (1826: *The Last of the Mohicans*).
1828	*American Dictionary of the English Language* published by Noah Webster (1758–1843).
1829	Karl Baedeker publishes his first travel guide.
1834	Robin Carver. *Book of Sports*—first book on baseball.
1837	First issue of England's weekly *Publisher's Catalogue* (*English Catalogue of Books*).
1844	Elizabeth Barrett Browning: *Poems.* Ralph Waldo Emerson: *Essays.*
1848	Karl Marx and Engels (*Communist Manifesto*).
1850	British Parliament pass Public Libraries Act for England and Wales.
1851	Herman Melville: *Moby Dick. The New York Times* begins publication.
1853	British Museum library reading room opened: rotunda with 20,000 reference books.

1854	George Boole publishes explanation of Boolean logic.
1860	Bibliotheque Nationale worlds largest library: 1 million volumes.
1860	Jacques Charles Brunet (1780–1867) completed his landmark *Manuel* begun fifty years before.
1861	American Civil War opens—ends in 1865. Mrs. Beeton (1836–1865) *Book of Household Management*.
1861	First publications of U.S. Government Printing Office.
1865	Lewis Carroll (1832–1898) *Alice's Adventures in Wonderland*.
1868	First issue of *Whitaker's Almanack*.
1868	First issue of *World Almanac* published.
1869	Frederick Leypold (1835–1884) first volume of *American Catalogue of Books* appears.
1872	*Publisher's Weekly* founded; 1876 *Library Journal* founded.
1875	3,000 public libraries reported in U.S. with average holdings: under 5,000 volumes; 17 over 50,000.
1876	Melvil Dewey publishes *Classification and Subject Index*—launching Dewey decimal system.
1876	Pierre Larouse publishes *Grand Dictionnaire*, French encyclopedia.
1877	Rand McNally publishes world's first *Business Atlas*.
1880	First electric lights.
1881	Henry James, *Portrait of a Lady*.
1884	*Oxford English Dictionary* begins publication; completed in 1928.
1889	Punch card system devised by H. Hollerith.
1891	Conan Doyle's *Adventures of Sherlock Holmes*.
1895	U.S. Printing Act passed, and *Monthly Catalog* begins publication.
1896	Nobel Prize initiated.
1898–1919	Carnegie donates funds for public libraries to some 1500 communities.
1900	Anton Chekhov *Uncle Vanya*.
1901	*Reader's Guide* launched as the first general index for laypeople.
1903	First airplane flight by Orville and Wilbur Wright.
1907	First issue of *Chemical Abstracts*, and the first modern abstracting service.
1907	First volume of *Cambridge History of English Literature*. Completed in 1927.
1908	Henry Ford produces the first Model T and assembly line production.
1914	World War I begins/ends in 1918.
1917	Sigmund Freud *Introduction to Psychoanalysis*.
1918	Airmail service on regular schedule between New York and Washington.
1918	The *Blue Guide* travel series first published.
1922	Emily Post's first edition of her *Etiquette*.
1924	E.M. Forster, *A Passage to India*. 2.5 million radios in American homes.
1933	Court rules James Joyce's *Ulysses* (1922) is legal in the U.S.
1939	World War II begins, ends in 1945.

National Libraries

Bibliotheque Nationale

1622 as Royal Library: 6,000 titles
1714: 70,00 volumes
1818: 1 million volumes
1908: 3 million volumes
1960: Over 6 million volumes, manuscripts etc.

British Museum Library (Now British Library)

1753 Hans Sloane leaves some 50,000 volumes and 2,000 manuscripts to yet to be built library.
1759 Library opens.
1960 Over 7 million volumes, manuscripts, etc.

Library of Congress

1800 Money appropriated for books.
1802 Congressional library opens. By 1814 about 3,000 volumes, primarily for legal reference.
1817 Jefferson library (some 5,700 volumes) purchased.
1850 Some 50,000 volumes, second only to Harvard in size.
1870 Registry of copyright placed under Library of Congress: 2 copies each printed work to the national library.
1875 300,000 volumes
1897 Moves into own building.
1960 13 million books, 18 million manuscripts, plus millions of other items.

---

[1]Jasper Griffin. "The Guidance That We Need," *The Times Literary Supplement,* April 14, 1995, p. 13.

Index

About the Author

William A. Katz is a professor at the School of Information Science and Policy, State University of New York at Albany. He received his Ph.D. from the University of Chicago and is now editor of *The Reference Librarian*, a quarterly devoted to issues in modern reference and information services, and *The Acquisitions Librarian*, concerned with collection development. He is the editor of *Magazines for Libraries* and has compiled a second edition of *The Columbia Granger's Guide to Poetry Anthologies* as well as the seventh edition of his *Introduction to Reference Work*. He is editor of a series on the history of the book for Scarecrow Press including his *A History of Book Illustration* and *Dahl's History of the Book*.